SMALL
BUSINESS

AN ENTREPRENEUR'S PLAN

Third Edition

Lee A. Eckert
Saddleback College

J. D. Ryan
Irvine Valley College

Robert J. Ray
Chapman College

The Dryden Press
HARCOURT BRACE COLLEGE PUBLISHERS

Fort Worth   Philadelphia   San Diego   New York   Orlando   Austin   San Antonio
Toronto   Montreal   London   Sydney   Tokyo

Editor in Chief	Robert A. Pawlik
Acquisitions Editor	Ruth Rominger
Developmental Editor	Bill Teague
Project Editor	Jon Gregory
Production Manager	Alison Howell
Book Designer	Sue Hart
Cover Illustration	Jane Burrell

Address for Editorial Correspondence
The Dryden Press, 301 Commerce Street, Suite 3700, Fort Worth, TX 76102

Address for Orders
The Dryden Press, 6277 Sea Harbor Drive, Orlando, FL 32887
1-800-782-4479, or 1-800-433-0001 (in Florida)

ISBN: 0-03-096585-3

Library of Congress Catalogue Number: 92-71877

Printed in the United States of America

4 5 6 7 8 9 0 1 2   0 8 5   9 8 7 6 5 4 3 2

The Dryden Press
Harcourt Brace

Preface

We were excited when The Dryden Press asked us to prepare a third edition of *Small Business: An Entrepreneur's Plan*. It validated the hard work we'd done putting the book together in the first place. It meant we were on the right track in entrepreneurial education. It meant we'd found our niche in the marketplace.

From the first—pulling together case studies and matching them with Action Steps and explanatory boxes and tables and side-bars—we wanted *Small Business: An Entrepreneur's Plan* to be helpful, informative, easy to read, accessible, interesting, and fun. Luckily, we found a publisher with the same goals. And the book was born.

Entrepreneurs are an adventurous lot. They chafe under authority. They love controlling their own destinies. They know that 60-hour weeks are normal. They know that working the hundred-hour week is entirely possible, especially at start-up time. So if you're an entrepreneur and you're not having fun, if you're not soaring with high glee, you won't last.

YOUR PERSONAL ROAD MAP

This book—with its 87 "action steps"—is your personal road map to success in small business. Beginning with Action Step 1, the book will guide you through the bustling marketplace—through trends, target customers, and promotion; through shopping malls, spreadsheets, and hushed, gray bank buildings; through independent businesses that are up for sale and through franchise opportunities—all the way to your own small business. Along the way you'll meet fascinating people, you'll have fantastic adventures, and you'll have some fun. Furthermore, by completing the action steps, you will be drawing a customized road map for small business

---

FUTURE FOCUS

A note to the recently displaced worker or the frustrated job seeker: We would like to have you consider self-employment as a career opportunity. Skim the "Future Focus" boxes at the beginning of each chapter for a quick peek at how you might quickly convert adversity to opportunity.

If you develop a sound, independent business, you will be in control of your own destiny and you can decide never to fire yourself.

The new frontier of the early 21st century will be discovered and mastered by entrepreneurs. This text will help you to focus on the future.

success: a complete Business Plan that clearly evaluates and illuminates your opportunity for entrepreneurial success.

On the Way

You will start your journey by taking a careful look at yourself and your skills. What work pleases you? How secure is your present job? How long does it take you to get organized? What internal drives make you an entrepreneur?

Next, you'll step back and look at the marketplace. What's hot? What's cooling down? Where are the long lines forming? What are people buying at the supermarket? How is it packaged? What distinguishes the up-and-comers from the down-and-outers?

Then you will brainstorm a business that will fit into an industry niche. You toss numbers around—to get a feel for how they turn into money—and you keep having fun.

Then it will be time to profile your target customer, assess the competition, figure out some clever promotional strategies, and scout locations. By that time you will be almost halfway through this book, and you will know where you're going and feel that you're in control of your own destiny.

That's when you can get serious. **Chapter 8** will help you to look ahead to the day you open the doors of your own business. It will help you anticipate trouble spots and problems that could slow you down, or even cripple your effort. **Chapter 9** continues this line of probing by helping you pull some numbers together. Using spreadsheets, you'll get the figures out of the shoebox and onto a computer so that you can really crunch them.

The Three Doorways

At this point you will have completed more than 40 action steps, and it'll be time to leave academia for a little while to see what's out there in the real world of small business. The easiest way to learn about the real world is to investigate some businesses that are on the market. One purpose of **Chapter 10**, "Buying a Business," is to bring you face to face with the first of three doorways to small business. (The other two—franchising and starting up a new business—are discussed later.)

In your investigations, find out why the sellers are selling. What are they asking? How much are they asking for the goodwill they've established? A business up for sale is like a laboratory in which you can investigate for free. We will remind you often to take along a notebook but to leave your emotions and your checkbook at home.

Before deciding among the three doorways, you will need to think about raising money, the best legal form for your business, building a winning team, and the contents of your entrepreneurial toolkit (**Chapters 11–14**). After pulling your toolkit together, you are ready to consider franchises and engineering your own start-up. If you are a neophyte entrepreneur just testing the waters of small business for the first time, you will certainly want to examine franchises—several of them—to see what they offer. **Chapter 15** will help you do this. For the first-time entrepreneur who is accustomed to the power, image, and "family" feeling of a large corporation, franchising can provide a helpful security blanket. On the other hand, if you are an entrepreneur with more experience, you should consider the option of Doorway Three: your own start-up, built from the stuff of your dreams and your personal strengths.

Your Complete Business Plan

By the time you reach **Chapter 16** you will have gathered enough material to write a complete Business Plan for showcasing your business to the world—that is, to bankers, vendors and lenders, venture capitalists, credit managers, key employees, your family, and your friends. Your finished plan will be a blueprint for your business. It will provide a walk-through of your industry, generate excitement in potential lenders, demonstrate your competence as a thoughtful planner, and underline the reasons customers are going to clamor for your product or service. Your plan will also serve you as a means of channeling your creative energies.

Let's think about that for a moment.

One reason you're reading this book is that you're creative. You like to build, to pull things together, to plant seeds and watch things grow, to develop projects, to produce. When your mind is cooking, you probably come up with more ideas than you can handle. *That* is when you need a plan. A plan will help you keep your entrepreneurial energies on track while the creative steam rises. Perhaps you've always dreamed of working for yourself—being your own boss. Well, you can have that dream if you're *prepared*.

FEATURES THAT WILL HELP

This book includes many features designed to help you on your journey.

Keeping Track of Your Slice of the Pie

Figures A, B, and C portray a complete Business Plan as a pie chart, with each slice of the "pie" representing a part of the plan. Each chapter of the book is designed to help you complete one or more of the parts of your Business Plan. You will notice that a pie illustration appears at the beginning of each chapter. Those pies show which part (or parts) of the plan is addressed by the action steps in each chapter. The pies will also help you to track your progress as an entrepreneur; when all the pieces of the pie are in place, your Business Plan will be completed and you'll be ready to open your doors.

A The product or service

B The market and the target customer

C The competition

D Marketing strategy

E Location

F Management

G Personnel

H Projected income statement
   (Profit and loss)

I Cash flow projection

J Projected balance sheet

Action Steps

Our roadmap to success in small business is composed of 87 action steps. Completing these steps should *quadruple* your chances of reaching your business goals. You see, the world of business is like a maze—a series of twisting corridors and paths—and the action steps are designed to thread you through the maze, from A to B, to C, and so on.

Each action step is an exercise that accompanies our explanation of a particular portion of the "maze." In fact, the steps grew naturally out of the material of this book. For example, in Chapter 1 we profile Nancy Tremaine, a literature major who became successful in small business because she dug into her skills repertoire to find out what she was good at. Nancy's case is tied to Action Step 8, "Inventory Your Personal Skills."

Model Action Steps

To help you visualize some of the action steps, we have reprinted model action steps at the ends of Chapters 1 through 8. These eight action steps were completed by a student named Pete Craigmoe. When he took our entrepreneurship course, Pete was working for the Santa Fe Railway and dreaming of taking early retirement so that he could work on his novel. Pete used the steps to focus on a small business that would create corporate newsletters. He now spends 30 percent of his time making money with desktop publishing and the other 70 percent writing his novel.

Opening Windows

In each chapter Figures and Tables are like windows that open up onto useful information and concepts. Examples include the best places to set up your booth at a trade show (Chapter 6), the U.S. Census's database of demographic information (Chapter 7), and a convenient four-part grid that allows you to identify the best candidates for balancing out your team (Chapter 13).

Staying on Track

Other features help you stay on track and focus on the task at hand. **Learning Objectives** at the beginning of each chapter identify the educational goals of the chapter. **Future Focus** boxes show how to see the bright side of future trends. **Marginal Definitions** help you build your business vocabulary. **Think Points for Success** push you to think further, deeper, and more successfully about what you have learned. **Key Points from Another View** come from articles in magazines like *Entrepreneur* and *Entrepreneurial Woman* to give you a new perspective on the issues raised in the chapter. If you need more information about the topics we discuss, the **References** section at the end of almost every chapter will direct you to it.

Built-in Study Guide

What good is a study guide that keeps getting misplaced? We put our Study Guide right in the same book, so you will always have it ready. Complete all or some of the exercises in the Study Guide as you feel necessary.

NEW TO THE THIRD EDITION

The third edition of *Small Business: An Entrepreneur's Plan* has required some heavy updating. The world's moving faster; we're keeping up. The tables carry fresh information. The boxes and sidebars bristle with new marketing data, new insights on customer behavior, products, competition, demographics, who's buying what and why. The end-of-chapter references—books, essays, articles—have been updated. If you have read *Megatrends,* futurist's John Naisbitt's eighties bestseller, you need to know about *Megatrends 2000,* which looks ahead, not only at Europe 1992, but also to the Pacific Rim in the 21st century.

In addition to the weighty information update, we've added a new chapter on how to write a mini-business plan. This chapter arose out of surveying our users—professors of business and entrepreneurship across the United States and Canada, where *Small Business: An Entrepreneur's Plan* goes forth in a special Canadian edition— who suggested that the full-blown plan, which takes a year out of your life, might not be suitable for fast-start service businesses like auto detailing and house cleaning.

Chapter 17 answers this concern. With quick footwork, an eager entrepreneur can pull together a **Fast-Start Mini-Business Plan** and get a business going in a couple of months, monitoring and refining your numbers as you go. The fast-start plan is perfect for part-timers (moonlighters, students still in school) who are testing the ebb and flow of the marketplace. Our students use it. We hope yours will too.

Other brand new features include the **Future Focus** boxes and **Key Points from Another View** identified above.

THIS BOOK IS FOR YOU

To Dreamers and Beginning Entrepreneurs

The book can be used on at least two levels. One level is fast-track. That's for the action-oriented entrepreneur who wants to get on with the start-up. The other level is slower, and it's for the creative dreamer who can afford to take the time to savor the atmosphere of the business arena.

As you're reading the book, keep pencil and paper close by so that you can jot down ideas. Get used to brainstorming. Also, it's not a bad idea to carry a cassette recorder in your car so that you can record ideas that occur to you while you're driving. The inspiration that you get from a freeway billboard four hundred miles from home might be the seed from which your winning business will grow.

Our point is that this is *your* book. Use it in whatever way suits your needs. Make notes in the margins; use a "highlighting" pen. Use the book as a handbook or as a textbook, or as both. It's designed for a wide range of creative, energetic people who want to own their own business, and someplace in that range of people is *you*. Good luck!

To Their Instructors and Mentors

As in previous editions, a generous Instructor's Manual is available, with lecture outlines, sample business plans, test items and more. Like this book, the Instructor's Manual is improved thanks to comments from you and your colleagues. Thanks again for selecting *Small Business: An Entrepreneur's Plan* for your students. And please keep writing. Hearing from you keeps us in touch with our customers.

ACKNOWLEDGMENTS

We couldn't have written this book without a lot of help from a lot of people. The book is built on a foundation of case studies, and the action steps are taken from real-life tactics in the marketplace. Many entrepreneurs have succeeded out there in the real world, and we've just tried to tell you how they have done it.

Our thanks go to:

Terri Baas, president of Candela Corporation

Greg Beck, president of the UCI/Orange County Venture Forum

Jeanette Cox of Mega Travel

Jim Fitzpatrick, publisher of *Entrepreneur* magazine

Check Goodson and Tom Herndon of Dana Niguel Bank

Cheryl Moore, president of "Something Moore"

Al Slattery, president of ASA/Advertising

Rosemary Utesch of Mega Travel
Steve Waddell of the U.S. Small Business Administration

We are grateful to Scott Isenberg and Bill Teague of The Dryden Press for their help in shaping this work into a book that we are proud of. We also thank the other members of our Dryden book team. They are Ruth Rominger, Lise Webb, Jon Gregory, Sue Hart, Alison Howell, Traci Keller, and Kathryn Stewart. Thanks go to Gail Hiduke for updating tables and references.

Last but not least, we thank Priscilla, Barbara, and Margo for their constant support and understanding.

Lee A. Eckert
J. D. Ryan
Robert J. Ray

Contents

Preface

1 Doorways to Small Business

2 The Big Picture: Charting Trends for Your Small Business

3 Power Marketing

7 **Location**
133

8 **Surprises You
Can't Afford**
163

9 **Numbers and
Shoebox
Accounting**
183

13 Building a Winning Team
265

14 The Entrepreneur's Toolkit
285

15 Buying a Franchise
297

16 Pulling the Plan Together
313

STUDY GUIDE

Contents

S M A L L
BUSINESS
AN ENTREPRENEUR'S PLAN

Third Edition

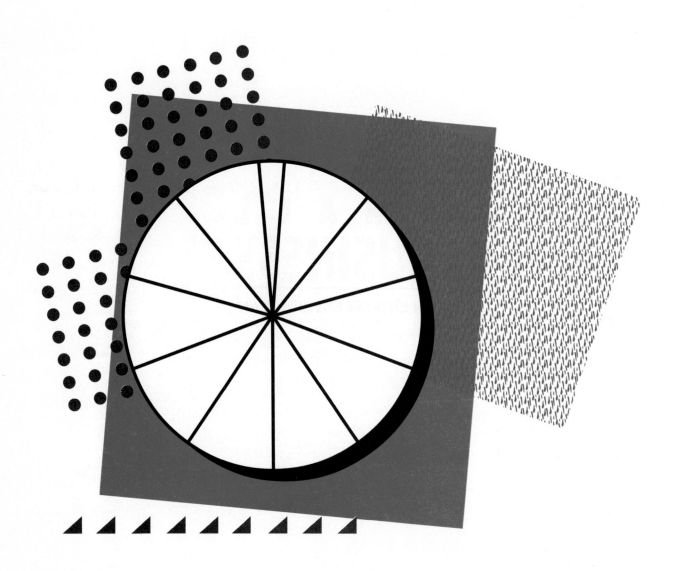

FIGURE 1.1
Before you begin to write your Business Plan, investigate the doorways to small business.

1 Doorways to ◢ ◢ ◢ ◢ ◢ ◢ ◢ Small Business— Your Great Adventure

Learning Objectives

- To understand where business is headed in the next 5–10 years.
- To learn how you can fit in, survive, and prosper in business.
- To brainstorm a clear picture of success in small business.
- To be able to identify successful and unsuccessful businesses in your community.
- To discover your personal strengths.
- To improve your information-gathering skills.
- To expand your knowledge of small business through interviewing small business owners.

FUTURE FOCUS

Take a quick look at your own unique talents that can catch an emerging opportunity. Take out a clean sheet of paper and list ten things that matter most to you. They could include financial security, making things, fixing things, changing things, helping others, having fun, making things grow.

This will give you a snapshot of your values. The best business for you is the one that includes what's most important to you and matches with emerging opportunities. Make your list and read on.

Business Plan
a blueprint for your business start-up or expansion

L ife is short, and you only go around once. So you want to make sure you're getting what you want, having fun, making money, and being the best person you can be.

How do you do that?

Some people do it by going into business for themselves. If *you* are thinking about owning your own business, this book is written for you.

Try this line of thought: What do you want to be doing in 1999? In 2005? What's the best course of action for you right now? What might be the best business for you? What are your strengths? This chapter will address these questions.

This is the age of the entrepreneur. There are almost 17 million small businesses out there. Each year, more than 650,000 new corporations are started. Most new jobs in the private sector are being created by firms with fewer than twenty employees. Yes, it's a great time for the entrepreneur. You could have the time of your life. Come along with us!

KNOCKING AT THE ENTREPRENEURIAL DOORS

There are three doorways to small business ownership (Figure 1.2). Doorway One is buying an ongoing business: you look around, find a business you like, and buy it. Sounds pretty easy, doesn't it? A business broker will make it sound even easier, so beware.

Doorway Two is buying a franchise: you find a logo you like, one with national visibility, and you buy it. In exchange for your money, the franchisor supplies you with inventory, advice, and a product or service that is well known in the marketplace. Sounds pretty easy, doesn't it? A slick franchisor will make it sound even easier.

Doorway Three, our favorite, is starting a new business—a business that is compatible with your interests and skills, one that is backed up by careful research that shows strong customer need. Entering the world of small business by *any* of these doorways demands a carefully designed **Business Plan**—words and numbers on paper that will guide you through the gaps, the competition, the bureaucracies, the products, the services. The 87 action steps presented in this book will show you exactly how to write a Business Plan and how to have fun as an entrepreneur!

What about These Three Doorways?

Sixty-seven percent of all entrepreneurs enter the world of small business by buying an existing business or a franchise operation. When these people have gained some experience and confidence, many of them decide to start a totally new business from scratch. However, few entrepreneurs are happy with just one business. They start up. They sell. They start up again. And they become experts at writing Business Plans.

No matter which doorway you choose, you're going to need a Business Plan. If you buy an ongoing business, you may inherit the seller's Business Plan. It's still smart to write one of your own, however. Ask the seller (again and again, if necessary) for the data you need for writing your own plan. That way, before you commit to purchase, you can check out those claims of huge potential profit and endless goodwill for yourself.

If you buy a franchise, you'll be buying a Business Plan from the franchisor. Until you see it, however, you won't know for certain if you'll need to prepare one of your

FIGURE 1.2   There are three doorways to owning a small business. Doorway One is buying an ongoing business. Doorway Two is buying a franchise. Doorway Three is starting up a brand-new business.

own as well. If you don't understand the franchisor's plan, by all means write your own. Writing a Business Plan is a lot cheaper than plunking money down on a franchise that may not work.

If you start your own business, a Business Plan is a must, an *absolute must*. That plan stands between you and failure.

What's Happened to the Forty-Hour Week, the Golden Parachute, and the Gold Watch?

Good question. Just how serious are you about entering the bustling arena of small business? Can't you get a job—executive recruiters call it a "position"—in "big business"? How much pressure is there on you to travel the entrepreneurial road through one of these small business doorways?

Let's say that you decide not to go into small business after all. Let's say you discover some things about yourself as you read this book, perhaps that you don't thrive on competition; that you think a 60-hour work week is madness; that you get edgy when you think about mortgaging your house for start-up money. And so you decide entrepreneurship is too much work for too little gain. You read the book—enough of it, anyway, to get the picture about entrepreneuring. You try some Action Steps—you find them stimulating, and fun, but they take time away from your weekend, the beach, the movies. You have this dream of wearing a suit to work and driving a snappy sports car. You see yourself working a 40-hour week and when Friday comes you hop into your snappy car and peel off for a great weekend and do not—repeat, not—take work home with you.

So you close the book on small business planning with a snap and snatch up the classifieds and start hunting for a *real job,* a job with a corporation, a job with a future. And in your mind is this scenario: "Okay, enough of entrepreneuring. It's too hard to pronounce. It's impossible to spell. I'm going to work for a big company, something visible, something with clout and prestige and a logo and great perks."

Good thinking, but is that scenario still realistic? Or is it a misty dream out of the distant 1960s?

What's Happening to Big Business?

Big business, once the backbone of America, is clearly in transition. During the 1980s, mergers flourished, firms downsized, and many firms ceased to exist. The world shrank and became an electronic global village.

> By 1990, 46 percent of the 1979 Fortune 500 were gone! New firms, such as Apple, Compaq, and MCI had taken their places in this elite group. Firms within entirely new industries reached the Fortune 500 in a very short time—growth in the 1980s was phenomenal.
>
> Only 11 percent of our work force is employed by Fortune 500 firms.
>
> Manufacturing that used to be done on U.S. soil is now being handled offshore.
>
> Technology allows Next Inc. to produce $1 billion worth of computers with five manual-assembly workers and fewer than 100 other employees.
>
> Foreign capital is pouring into the United States. Japan, Britain, and Germany continue to invest heavily in the United States. Our investments offshore continue to grow, with many multinational firms headquartered in the United states achieving over 50 percent of their sales overseas.
>
> Companies such as IBM and Apple are announcing strategic alliances. Outright mergers of major banks, airlines, and appliance, software and tire manufacturers continue at breakneck speed.

The world is changing, and you must assess the changes and act accordingly. You want to survive. You want to have fun. You want your life to have meaning. You want substance and honesty and security and success. So, in order to decide which road to take, do some research and keep your eyes open. You will come up with

BOX 1.1   Naisbitt's New Directions for the 1990s

In his best-selling book, *Megatrends,* John Naisbitt identified ten major trends for the 1980s. In his book *Megatrends 2000,* he looks at the trends affecting us in the 1990s and beyond. According to Naisbitt, we will be influenced by the following:

1. the booming global economy of the 1990s
2. a renaissance in the arts
3. the emergence of free-market socialism
4. global life-styles and cultural nationalism
5. the privatization of the welfare state
6. the rise of the Pacific Rim
7. the decade of women in leadership
8. the age of biology
9. the religious revival of the new millennium
10. the triumph of the individual

some insights on the direction of big business. To get you started, read the list of trends found by researcher and author John Naisbitt in Box 1.1.

The Direction of Big Business

In some respects, the direction of big business is obvious. In other respects, we can only speculate. Consider these things:

75 percent of employees work in the service sector. By the year 2000 it is estimated that only 4 percent of employees will be involved in manufacturing.

Retraining is in everyone's future. Futurists estimate that 18-year-olds today will have five to seven different careers—not jobs. Who will be responsible for this retraining? Big business? Colleges? Or new, innovative firms that respond to this need?

The Information Age is upon us, allowing firms located anywhere to operate as global firms responding to global customers.

Businesses must begin to respond to employee needs for day-care, elder care, and flexible work situations.

The U.S. work force is definitely in transition. According to the Hudson Institute, white American men will account for only 15 percent of growth in the work force through the year 2000. Our work places will be multicultural and multiracial. As we face a possible labor shortage, we will draw more on the elderly and the physically challenged.

THE AGE OF THE ENTREPRENEUR

The business world is changing faster and faster, so what do you do? Life is not what you thought it would be, so what do you do? The big firm you wanted to work for is now closed. The job you trained for is obsolete. What do you do?

entrepreneur
a visionary self-starter who loves the adventure of a new enterprise

Hang in there! You live in a great country. And that greatness is not a matter of size alone. Smaller companies, those with fewer than 500 employees, employ almost half the workers in the U.S. New start-ups create the new jobs. These jobs are created by an absolutely unique partnership—the marriage of money and work. The money comes from our unique system of venture-capital financing. The work comes from the driving force of the **entrepreneur.**

Pioneering is alive and well in America. In 1990, 625,000 new corporations were founded. If you add partnerships and sole proprietorships, experts estimate that 1.3 million new enterprises were added to the U.S. economy *each year.* In the last decade of the twentieth century, entrepreneurship should blossom and grow. The fields—biotechnology, semiconductors, computers, telecomputing—are ripe and ready for harvest, so plant early. The nineties will certainly be the Age of the Entrepreneur.

To hammer home our point, we want you to complete Action Step 1.

Do you really have job security? Are you sure? Scan the last three or four issues of *Business Week* or two to three weeks of the *Wall Street Journal.* Did you notice any companies announcing a layoff or plant closing? Did you read of a company president being fired? What would happen to your job if the head of your company died?

You may have had a good job for 20 years. You may belong to a union. But if the managers of your company are not doing a good job, you could be out of work tomorrow. Ask around. Talk to other workers in other jobs. Think about the deal the UAW made with GM.

How secure is a job in big business? Derek Campbell's experience is not uncommon.

ACTION STEP 1

Assess your job security.

On a sheet of paper write down your present job title, the firm or organization you work for, how long you've worked there, how many hours a week you work, and the three tasks that take up most of your time.

Are you on the phone a lot? Do you shuffle paper? Do you spend time in meetings? Does your job put you on the road more than once a week? How do the three tasks you listed square with your job title?

Now, rank your job security on a 1–10 scale. How easily could you be replaced? If you currently are not working, rank the job security of your mother or father, brother or sister, friend or relative.

"After 5 years of faithful service as a pilot, I was furloughed by the airline that employed me, so I had time to look around and think about my future. One of the books I read was *Megatrends.* It was like seeing a lighthouse beacon after a long, dark sea voyage."

When Derek Campbell got furloughed the third time from his pilot's job with a major airline, he was frustrated and angry at the world. He had done his work and loved flying the big planes, but the airline industry was in chaos. Size didn't make any difference. Even the giants were in trouble.

"Three furloughs and you're out," Derek said. "For me, that was the handwriting on the wall. I was fed up with working for someone else, tired of being a puppet on someone else's string. It was time to call a few tunes of my own."

Like a lot of entrepreneurs, Derek was a workaholic. His first move was to make a list of his past accomplishments, his strengths, his skills. He had a bachelor's degree in engineering, an MBA, and several years' experience as an instructor in the Marines. And he'd always been interested in computers.

Derek hired himself out as a computer consultant. His work was largely on the phone, making contacts, locating prospects. Then he'd go out for a location visit and size up the problems.

"Literally everyone on my list could have used some kind of computer," Derek recalls. "And that's what gave me the idea for a computer school. There was, on the one hand, a crying need for more efficiency. And on the other hand, there was a lot of fear and misunderstanding about computers in general and about small computers in particular."

So Derek kept his consulting business going while he organized a founder's team to help him brainstorm strategies for opening a computer school. It was an interesting mix of people: two lawyers, another ex-pilot, a banker, a marketeer from big business, a numbers wizard, an expert in corporate mergers.

Derek used his microcomputer to create a stunning eighty-five-page Business Plan. The plan helped him get a line of credit from a local bank for $40,000. And nine months after the idea had first hit him, Derek and his team began offering their first class, Computer Fundamentals.

"Planning makes all the difference," Derek says. "The minute we opened the doors, we had business. That told us we had targeted our industry, and our particular segment, accurately. Of course, if you don't stay in there punching, don't keep your image right out there, business tends to fall off. But gap-analysis helped us find our foothold in the marketplace—computer education—and it's paying off fast. We're in the information business to stay. We're not pushing hardware or software. We're here to teach people how to help themselves by learning the vast capabilities of the microcomputer."

Derek leans back, clasps his hands behind his head, smiles, and adds, "And the best part of all, it's great fun!"

Why did Derek Campbell succeed? He was successful because he:

1. was able to turn adversity into opportunity.
2. knew his strengths—engineering, teaching, computers.
3. saw a gap in the marketplace.
4. knew where to go for information to develop a Business Plan. (The plan proved on paper that his computer school would earn him a handsome return on his investment.)
5. was ready for self-employment.

Derek Campbell became a beneficiary of the Information Age.

Plotting Your Future

What Derek Campbell had to reckon with was change. Although change is occurring at a much faster rate than it was a generation ago, projecting future needs is easier than you might imagine. There are clues that point the way.

Two thinkers who can help guide you into the future are John Naisbitt (see Box 1.1) and Faith Popcorn, the founder of BrainReserve, a trend-analysis firm based in Manhattan. Box 1.2 summarizes some of the trends Faith Popcorn has noted. See also Box 1.3. The "future wheel" in Figure 1.3 illustrates an imaginary combination of Naisbitt's idea of "the electronic cottage" with Faith Popcorn's concept of "cocooning." We call this combination "the enchanted fortress."

Briefly, the "enchanted fortress" is where an imaginary family of the future lives, works, and plays. It is a world within a world. The family eats here, bathes, exercises, gets tanned, watches movies, does their banking electronically, and is protected from

BOX 1.2   Faith Popcorn's Predictions

Faith Popcorn is the founder of BrainReserve, a trend-analysis firm based in Manhattan. Her job is forecasting the tastes and whims of American shoppers for such clients as Campbell Soup Co., Eastman Kodak, and Pillsbury. Popcorn coined the term "cocooning" for the recent tendency for people to retreat to the safety of their homes. The trend is the result of our collective desire to insulate the home from impending danger.

There are some of BrainReserve's predictions for the 1990s:

demise of supermarkets

computerized ordering of clothes, restaurant food, groceries, and so on

continuing and expanding trend of "going home," cocooning

people will see the power of the individual and will take action on their own

we will be concerned not so much with weight but with fat content and our scales will be changed to reflect this concern; food manufacturers will continue to respond to this trend

as the baby boomers continue to age, they will do everything in their power to push back the aging process

---

BOX 1.3   The Cocooning of Magazine Readers

Top 10 Magazines in Circulation in 1990
1. *Modern Maturity*
2. *Reader's Digest*
3. *TV Guide*
4. *National Geographic*
5. *Better Homes and Gardens*
6. *Family Circle*
7. *Good Housekeeping*
8. *Ladies Home Journal*
9. *McCall's*
10. *Woman's Day*

Source: *Advertising Age,* August 20, 1990.

ACTION STEP 2

Look into your business future by drawing a future wheel.

Get a pencil and paper and spend ten minutes modifying our future wheel (Figure 1.3) into your own enchanted fortress. There is no such thing as a wrong idea or a wrong direction. Just close your eyes for a moment and allow your imagination to take over. See how many additional lines and balloons you can connect. This will also introduce you to brainstorming. You can predict the future as well as anyone else; all you need to do is mesh information with your imagination and go for it!

ACTION STEP 3

Brainstorm three new businesses capitalizing on the "cocooning" trend.

Open your eyes.

Get a pencil and paper. Write the word *cocoon* in the center of the page and draw a mind map using the trends that radiate out from it. Repeat the same mind-mapping process you used in Action Step 2. Allow yourself to get a little far out; release your creativity. Refer to Figures 1.3 and 2.4 for inspiration.

Mind mapping allows you to plot a chain of ideas graphically without losing your train of thought. If you are mind mapping with a group, use a large writing board or poster board to encourage participation.

intruders by an invisible wall. The enchanted fortress is a personal "warm fuzzy." It reunites the family after two decades of fragmentation.

There are only two problems with this fantasy life: how to afford it, and cabin fever. Both these problems are handled by leaving the enchanted fortress and returning to the world outside. How do you leave? Well, you go out through an escape tunnel to your car. And what is your car? It's a cocoon on wheels, packed with electronic gadgets, and designed to be as warm and fuzzy as your home.

Action Step 2 gives you the opportunity to stretch your imagination—to fantasize your own "enchanted fortress." After you've designed your dream home, go on to Action Step 3 and explore the small-business implications of "cocooning."

What Is a Small Business?

Businesses are classified by a coding system known as *Standard Industrial Classification Codes.* You've probably heard the abbreviation: SIC. (We deal with SIC codes in depth in the next chapter.) When a person goes to the SBA to borrow money, three criteria linked to the SIC codes are used to determine how small is small; that is, a *small* business is one that

1. does not dominate the industry,
2. has less than $10 million in annual sales, and
3. has fewer than 1,000 employees.

There are exceptions to each of these criteria.

For the purposes of this book, we define a small business as any venture with spirit, any business you want to start, any idea you want to chase into the marketplace. It may be part-time, something you do at home, something you try alone, something you need a team for.

If you prove it out on paper—in your Business Plan—first, there's a good chance you'll be successful. This means that if you are going to fail, you will fail only on paper. And if you *plan* to *win,* you probably will.

FIGURE 1.3 This future wheel portrays "the enchanted fortress"—a combination of "the electronic cottage" and a "cocoon." It was developed through brainstorming. Refer to it as you brainstorm in Action Step 3.

The Myth of Small Business Failure

It seems you can't talk to anyone on the street about small business without having the subject of failure come up. After all, the U.S. Small Business Administration tells us that 55 percent of all small businesses fail in their first five years. Actually, these SBA figures are misleading.

The SBA bases its conclusions on the U.S. Census of Business, which is taken in years that end in a 2 or a 7. This means that if you start a business in 1993 and you aren't *at the same address* when 1997 rolls around, your business is counted as a failure. Or, if you start out as a sole proprietor, then take on a partner and change your business name, and then merge with a corporation and move into the corporate GHQ, you will also go down on the charts as a failure.

ACTION STEP 4

Assess your interests and abilities.

Do you have what it takes to make it in small business? To find out, profile yourself as an entrepreneur. You won't be a perfect fit, because there is no such thing. Nonetheless, you will get much more out of this book if you will mentally immerse yourself in the role of the successful entrepreneur. Fantasize yourself in a new and exciting venture. Entrepreneurship isn't for everyone, and you will probably need some help along the way. Keep your mind open and your pencil sharp. The opportunities are unlimited.

This action step will help you to assess your abilities and interests and get your creative juices flowing. Complete as much as you can in the spaces provided, and feel free to write things in the margins. You will probably come back to this step several times.

How would your best friend describe you? _____

How would your worst enemy describe you? _____

How would you describe yourself?____

How much money do you need to survive for six months? _____
For twelve months? _____

How much money can you earn in your present position in three years? _____ Five years? _____ What is the maximum potential of your earning power? _____

Are you comfortable taking moderate risks? _____

Are you constantly looking for newer and better ways to do things? _____

What can you do better than most people? _____

Where do you live now? (Describe your home, residential area, geographical area, amenities, etc.) _____

In what way would you like to change any of the above? _____

Do you enjoy being in control? _____
How do you spend your leisure time? _____

Do you look forward more often than backward? _____
How important is winning to you?____

Who do you know whose strengths might complement some of your weaknesses? _____

Furthermore, if you latch onto a trendy fad, ride it for a year or 18 months, and then take your profits and go on vacation, you're also classified as a failure. This is how the SBA statistics report the business success of Mr. Dahl, the man who created the Pet Rock back in the seventies. He identified a fad and produced a product to take advantage of it. When the fad wound down, Mr. Dahl took his profits and left the marketplace. That's not failure. That's smart marketing!

If You Fail to Plan, You're Planning to Fail!

To get the maximum benefit from this book, you'll need to go beyond the classroom walls and experience the risks and joys of entrepreneurship. You'll also read a lot, of course, and you'll construct your own Business Plan.

The action steps will help you with your Plan. They'll also give you energy boosts that will help you maintain momentum. If you'd like to see some examples of how action steps have been handled by one student, turn to the appendixes at the end of some of the chapters of this book.

You've looked at job security, and you've tried a future wheel. Now do Action Step 4, a sort of a self-assessment guide to the world of entrepreneuring. It'll help you learn some things about yourself.

Then, we'd like you to meet Judd O'Herlihy.

At forty, Judd O'Herlihy was unhappy with his dead-end job as branch manager of a major electrical manufacturer. He was making good money, but that did not make his job more bearable. Judd needed change.

Seeking a fresh direction for his life, he registered for a career guidance class at a local community college. At the second session the instructor–counselor gave the class some aptitude tests. Then the instructor asked them to list every accomplishment in their entire lives that gave them a good feeling.

Judd hated writing, and he resisted the process at first. However, his list soon began shaping up:

1. ball monitor, third grade
2. 2nd prize, paper drive, fourth grade
3. pole vault, new high school record, age 16
4. organized Lion's Club pancake breakfast, 5,000 served, senior in high school

He was playing with the idea, making fun of it, when he remembered something else from his high school years. He'd bought old cars and fixed them up. The first car was an Alfa Romeo 916. He'd bought it for $800 and resold it, after the fix-up, for $1,500. Remembering the cars made him think of other accomplishments. He'd been an Eagle Scout, a decorated war hero, a carpenter and cabinetmaker, and a fair trumpet player. After he and his wife bought a house, he'd designed and contracted to build their swimming pool. After catching the spirit of the exercise, he filled up three pages. But only one thing on his list held his attention—building that swimming pool.

The instructor asked Judd to explain why this was so high on his list.

"Well," Judd said, thinking back. "We wanted a pool for the kids, so I asked several pool contractors for bids. I have five kids. I wanted a bigger-than-average pool so they wouldn't be fighting over territory. My specs were simple. I wanted a 40-foot pool, 30 feet wide, with 12 feet under the diving board. My pool didn't fit the specs of any of the contractors. They had standard plans, with only eight and a half feet under the diving board. One contractor even told me that to go deeper would violate the city code. So since their plans didn't fit my yard, and since they had knocked each other pretty hard trying to get my business, I lost confidence in the whole crowd. Only one contractor offered to do the pool. It would cost double, he said, and he was certain I wouldn't like it."

The instructor asked Judd what he did then.

"I was discouraged, but summer was coming and my kids kept pressing me. So I said, 'What's the big deal with a swimming pool? It's just a concrete hole in the ground attached to some plumbing.' So I looked in the yellow pages and located a civil engineer who considered himself a pool specialist who got turned on by out-of-the-ordinary designs. For less than $300, the engineer pulled all the permits and showed me how to find the best subcontractors.

"My friends and neighbors tried to dissuade me," Judd went on, "but I collected bids anyway. I got bids from diggers, steel riggers, electricians, tile people, gunnite and concrete contractors. When I tallied them up, I discovered I could get my pool—with the 12-foot depth I wanted—at about half the cost of the lowest bid from the big-time pool firms.

"So I built the pool myself. Along the way, every subcontractor showed me how to save money. I photographed the process and kept detailed notes. In less than a month, the pool was finished. It was perfect. The neighbors came around asking questions, and I helped them subcontract their pools. I even wrote a 16-page booklet, 'How to Contract Your Own Concrete Pool and Save 50%.' I advertised the booklet in the pool sections of some newspapers and sold 2,000 copies for $9.95 each. My cost, including mailing, was 96 cents. We got the pool we wanted, and the profit from the booklet paid for it twice."

"A great story, Mr. O'Herlihy!" said the instructor. "But tell me. If this was so rewarding, why didn't you go on building?"

"Too busy," Judd said.

"That's too bad," said the instructor. "With talent like *that,* you should *make* time."

Later that night when Judd was about to fall asleep, he was still glowing with the memory of his pool-building. He woke up his wife. "Honey!" he said. "Wake up. I'm going to build us a *house!*"

"Yes, dear," said Linda O'Herlihy. "Now go to sleep."

The memory of a single past accomplishment changed Judd's life. With new confidence, he quit his job and started building rental units. Today, Judd O'Herlihy has his own company and is financially independent. He'll never work for someone else again.

Action Step 5 focuses on some of your past accomplishments. The purpose of this is to give you confidence. After all, you've come *this* far, right?

Action Step 5 should trigger your imagination and give you confidence that will get you rolling. Small business is your dream, your venture. When you get going on it, you'll learn more about yourself than you'd learn through group therapy or from several years with a psychiatrist.

Joe Talmadge gained a lot of confidence when he inventoried his skills and interests. Although he'd once felt the thrill of bringing a new product into the marketplace, he was working for someone else and feeling frustrated. And frustration made Joe even more inventive.

The autumn that Bailey's Irish Cream® hit the marketplace, Joe Talmadge was working as a specialty liqueur marketing expert for a major distillery. The figures for that fall speak for themselves. The suppliers had 100,000 cases of Bailey's out in the marketplace and they thought it would last through Christmas, which was 2 months away. Market surprise. The Bailey's sold out in four days. And Joe Talmadge saw an opportunity: a gap in cream-based liqueurs.

In their kitchen at home, Joe and Ann Talmadge got creative with some old family recipes until they came up with a smooth taste. Joe wanted to position his product against Ireland, the home of Bailey's, so he found a family of wine makers in Italy. They'd been in business for 300 years, which gave Joe the depth of history he wanted, and they had a fantastic supply of old bottle molds embossed with their regal family logo. This was just the image Joe was after. Gambling a little, Joe named his liqueur "Creme de Napoli."

There were problems—manufacturing, distribution, the basic instability of cream, the Italian government and its endless red tape—but Joe persevered and selectively

ACTION STEP 5

Assess your accomplishments.

Begin by listing all the things in your life that have made you proud. What, for example, has given you the most satisfaction? What is your sweetest memory? How old were you? What were you doing at the time? Were you alone, or with someone? How did it feel to be victorious? How did it feel to be in control?

Then move to the present. Where are you now with your accomplishments? What have you done lately that you're proud of? What about the future? Where do you want to be in three years? In five years? In ten? In twenty?

Also, list things that you *don't* like to do or that you don't do *well.* All entrepreneurs have their weaknesses. What you want is a business that takes advantage of your strengths. If you can identify your likes and dislikes, then you can direct yourself toward things that you enjoy and avoid the things you hate. You may find some surprises when you review your lists.

spent money in his test market. It took several months, but he gradually expanded his market area, proving he had a winner. And 2 years after he and Ann had concocted the recipe for Creme de Napoli at their kitchen table, Joe Talmadge sold the product to a major international liquor maker.

How much did his product bring? Creme de Napoli sold for more than a million dollars. As part of the deal, Joe worked for the purchasers for 1 year at a very good salary.

But Joe is an entrepreneur; he loves risk and he likes being in control. Working for someone else frustrates him. Thus, 6 months after selling Creme de Napoli, he left the international liquor giant to start his own marketing-consulting business.

Joe understands the market and is good at helping businesses solve problems. He travels a lot and loves his work. And he is financially secure so that he doesn't have to work unless he chooses to.

When Joe thinks back, he remembers how it all started at the kitchen table, being creative, working with his wife, taste-testing, trying to come up with a product to position against Bailey's.

How can *you* operate like Joe Talmadge? First, you need to get organized. Action Step 6 will help you to do that.

Some people have the feeling that getting organized will stifle their creativity. Marci Reid was like that until she saw the value of her Adventure Notebook.

Marci Reid loved to travel, so when she graduated from high school, she got herself a job with a travel agency. For 14 months she worked as a secretary, learning the business. From her first week, Marci kept a diary form of notebook, listing what seemed to be important elements of the travel business.

Over the next dozen years Marci worked for three different travel agencies, and her diary/notebook grew. She spent 4 years in Europe—France, the Greek Islands, Spain—and when she returned home she knew it was time to strike out on her own. By then her diary/notebook filled four volumes.

"I know the travel business," Marci said to a friend. "All I need are a few more business skills. Then I can have my own agency."

Marci read and reread her notebooks. She spent time boiling down the information. Then she consulted with her family and with a friend she'd been considering for a partner. Everyone she talked to was excited. Marci's friend also was tired of working for other people and enthusiastically agreed to be her partner. So, for 3 months, the two friends hunted for a location for their new business. When they'd found three they thought would work, Marci enrolled in a course in entrepreneurship. She knew she needed help in refining her voluminous notes into a workable Business Plan.

"In the first class, it was made really clear that you've got to plan every move," said Marci. "I admit I fought the idea at first, mostly because I was so eager to get started, but also because I thought that too much planning would throttle my creativity. But then as I examined each step of building the Business Plan, the patterns began to appear and I saw how things would work out in the long run. Then I didn't feel cramped at all. My travel industry diary became my Adventure Notebook.

"It was high anxiety once we opened up for business. Our contractor was four months behind, so we had to rent temporary space almost ten miles away from our target customers. And since we couldn't get our location right away, our banker chopped our line of credit in half. Luckily, we had followed the advice of our instructors and we had a back-up bank. Then an airline strike forced us to stay up three nights rerouting customers. Without a plan, we'd have gone under.

"Adventures in Travel is three years old now, and my partner and I are thinking about another start-up. The other evening, I brought out my Adventure Notebook—the one I'd used to plan our travel agency—and read through it. I was amazed at its accuracy. I think that shows that you can do a lot in life if you get organized.

"On this next start-up, believe me, we'll do even more planning. You can dream yourself silly, but when you go into business for yourself, you need to put those dreams behind you and get down to the nitty-gritty—customers, sales, profit, winning."

ACTION STEP 6

Organize your information.

If you're the typical entrepreneur, you probably write 90% of your important data on the back of an envelope. That's fine, but now that you're doing this for real, get yourself an organizer, some kind of container (a shoebox, a briefcase, a folder) to put those envelopes in. Even better, compile an **Adventure Notebook**, something with pockets so that you can keep track of small items like ticket stubs.

Your Adventure Notebook should have:

a twelve-month calendar

an appointment calendar

a priority list of things you need to do

your name, company address, and phone number (at the front, in case you leave it somewhere)

an idea list

a "new eyes" list, for keeping track of successful and not-so-successful businesses you come across, plus notes about the reasons for their success or failure

list of possible team members (Who impresses you and why? What are their key attributes?)

list of possible "taxi squad" members—experts who serve as resource people when you need them, such as a lawyer, a CPA, some bankers, successful businesspeople, and so on.

Most people begin a new business with less planning than they give a family vacation. Marci's Adventure Notebook was the incubator for ideas that helped her prepare her Business Plan, which proved, on paper, that she could be successful. As Marci and her partner continue in business, they continue to update their plan. Now we'll show you how to select a business idea and how to start planning for its success.

Adventure Notebook
storage place for valuable business information

WHAT IS SUCCESS?

Success is how you define it.

Action Step 7 is optional, but it's fun. Thinking about success can be stimulating and enlightening. What makes a business successful? Unsuccessful? How do *you* measure success? How do your friends measure it?

You and your friends can only speculate about what businesses are doing well. Only a detailed examination of their books would give the whole picture, but we still urge you to exercise your marketplace intuition. Personal observation is a good way to become more aware of what is happening to small firms in your community. For example, next time you eat out, try this:

Estimate the number of customers in the restaurant.

Estimate the total number of customers the restaurant serves each day.

Estimate the average price per meal.

Multiply that average by the total number of daily customers.

Do this for other businesses you patronize as well. Pretty soon you'll begin to get the feel for which businesses are losing and which are winning. Observe small businesses with **new eyes,** and success factors will begin to emerge.

Success is a personal, subjective thing. Whereas income and return-on-investment are measurable, success wears many faces. You need to think about this as you start your adventure. This success checklist will help you. At the end of it, add other items that might signify success to you.

Do you measure success in dollars? How many?

_____ $50K a year?

_____ $100K?

_____ $250K?

_____ $1,000,000?

_____ return-on-investment? How much? _____

Or do you measure success in other ways?

_____ being able to enjoy a certain life-style

_____ friendly customers who appreciate the service

_____ power (You know how things should be done. When they're done your way, you feel terrific.)

_____ being able to live where you want

_____ providing employment for others

_____ being the best business in your area

_____ looking out the door and seeing long lines waiting for your service

_____ time to do what you enjoy doing

_____ teamwork (a smooth operation with lots of key employees reporting to you)

ACTION STEP 7

Survey your friends about success.

The next time you're at a party and there's a lull in the conversation, pass out paper and pencils and ask people to list three to five small businesses (IBM does not count!) they perceive as successful. Then ask them to list the signs of those firms' success and the reasons for their success.

Group the negative thinkers together in a Devil's Advocate Group and have them list unsuccessful businesses and point out the reasons those firms are losing out.

After the party look at the two lists together and attempt to come up with insights about the way *you* feel about success.

new eyes
observation with intuition

_____ fame (your face on TV, your name a household word)

_____ being in control (You like things done your way. You feel uncomfortable giving up control.)

Do you measure success by concrete achievements—like the car you drive or the location of your dream house?

_____ in the heart of a lavish up-scale residential area

_____ a penthouse atop a tall building, in the poshest metropolitan area

_____ anywhere that's safe

_____ a place where your kids can play

_____ a cozy cabin on a quiet lake

_____ a fancy, beautifully decorated city apartment

_____ a tropical island, isolated, quiet

_____ your name on a building

_____ hanging loose, doing what makes you happy

_____ _____

_____ _____

_____ _____

After you have thought about what success means to you, complete Action Step 8 to see how equipped you are to achieve it.

CONDUCTING RESEARCH

Research opens doors to the Information Society. There are three approaches to research. You'll need a combination of all three to make it big in small business.

Primary Research

Primary research is carried out by interacting with the world directly by talking to people—perhaps interviewing them. You might ask small business owners questions like: Where were you when the entrepreneurial bug bit? Whom do you bank with? How did you choose your lawyer? Your accountant? What would you do if you started up tomorrow, knowing what you know today? Customers can be asked questions like: Is there something we don't carry that you need? How else can we be of help to you? How did you learn about our business? Vendors and suppliers are asked questions like: What advertising works best in businesses like ours? What products are hot? What services are being offered?

Secondary Research

When you read, second-hand, what someone else has discovered, you're carrying out **secondary research**. You go to the library and look up "small business" in the Business Index. You locate and read magazine and newspaper articles that contain information you think will be helpful. Databases are also available.

Or you write to trade associations in your industry. You find data on sales that will help you project how much money you can make in small business. Good techniques here will save you lots of footwork.

ACTION STEP 8

Inventory your personal skills.

What's in your skills repertoire that could launch you into a hot growth industry?

Review your work on the previous action steps for clues to your personal strengths. Then list all the things that you can do and are good at. Use action verbs wherever possible in these lists—words such as sell, write, negotiate, soothe, counsel, synthesize, coordinate, build, fix, create, analyze, compile, teach, persuade, tend, plant, nurture, supervise, help out, copy, add and subtract, follow instructions, delegate, lead.

What kind of work do you do?

What kind of work do you enjoy?

What are your hobbies?

What really excites you?

Do you like to work alone?

Are you a self-starter?

If you were to ask three people who know you well to list your three major skills, what would they say?

Circle the action verbs in your lists. Make a list of your top five skills. While you're at it, list five skills that you do _not_ possess.

---

personal skills
your strengths, where you shine, the tools that will help you be successful in business

primary research
interacting with the world through interviews, observation, etc.

secondary research
reading about someone else's primary research

"New-Eyes" Research

New-eyes research provides a variety of fresh ways to look at a business. You play detective. You might become "mystery shopper" to check out your competition. You might sit in your car and take telephoto pictures of a business you're thinking about buying; when **target customers** appear, you photograph them so that you can profile them later. You may stand in a supermarket and, trying not to look nosy, observe what's in people's shopping carts. For example:

> Steak + Scotch + Cigarettes + Twelve-pack of 7-Up = Party time

> Cereal + Dog food + Diapers + Baby food = Family with children

Doing this allows you to develop a **psychographic profile** of your target customer. See Figure 1.4.

New-eyes research is fun. Combined with books, magazines, trade journals, publications like the *Wall Street Journal,* and talking to people, it will get you all the way to your Business Plan. And the Business Plan will either make you a success or show you that your idea isn't worth any more of your time.

It's time to start filling your Adventure Notebook. Action Step 9 will get you going.

How to Develop a Business's Profit Profile

When you're interviewing a business owner, attempt to develop the business's profit profile. Here's how you do it. In the course of your interview, find out a few key numbers. These include such figures as gross sales, cost of goods sold, rent, salaries (owner, management), and how much they spend on marketing (advertising, commissions, promotions, and so on). You can estimate the other expenses and come up with a range that will give you perspective when it comes time to work with your own numbers.

For example, let's take a business with $500,000 in sales. The cost of goods sold (C of GS) averages 53 percent. Rent is $2,000. Total salaries are 15 percent of gross sales. They spend 6 percent of their gross on marketing. Those are the only numbers you learned from your interview. Based on them, you can estimate benefits, including FICA costs, at 20 percent–30 percent of salaries, and other expenses (supplies, utilities, phone, accounting, legal, auto, entertainment, and so on) at 8 percent–12 percent. Combining what you were given with your estimates yields this profit profile:

	High Side	Low Side
Sales	$500,000	$500,000
C of GS (53%)	−265,000	−265,000
Gross Profit	235,000	235,000
Less: Marketing (6%)	30,000	30,000
Salaries (15%)	75,000	75,000
FICA/Benefits	15,000	22,500
Rent ($2,000/mo.)	24,000	24,000
Other Expenses	40,000	60,000
Net Profit	51,000	23,500

ACTION STEP 9

Investigate the marketplace for opportunities with "new eyes."

Interview at least three people who are self-employed. One of them should be in your own area of interest. (If you're a potential competitor, you may need to travel 50 miles or more to get real help.)

Successful entrepreneurs love to tell the story of how they made it. Being up front about what kind of information you want from these people and why you want it, make appointments with them at times and places convenient to *them*. You may be amazed at how much help you get.

Open-ended questions are best, because they leave room for embellishment. Here are some suggestions to start you off:

When did you decide to start your own business?

What was your first step?

Do you remember how you felt?

If you had it to do all over again, what would you do differently?

How large a part does creativity play in your particular business?

Are your rewards tangible or intangible?

What was your best advertisement or promotion?

What makes your business unique?

How important is price in your business? Would a price war increase your customer base?

Depending on how you hit it off, you might be able to think of these first interviewees as sources of marketplace experience. They may be able to help a lot when you start to assemble your "taxi squad"—your lawyer, accountant, banker, and so on.

It's helpful to take some notes during the interviews. If you want to use a cassette recorder, however, be sure to ask permission.

Don't worry about evaluation at this stage. The information will fall into patterns sooner than you think.

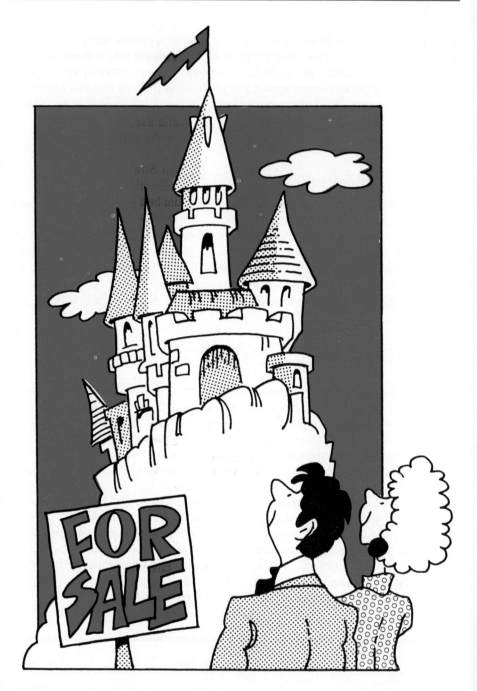

FIGURE 1.4 How would your target customer spend $100,000? Developing a psychographic profile of that person will give you clues.

On the high side, the profit profile is slightly better than 10 percent, or $51,000. On the low side, it's slightly below 5 percent, or $23,500. (That $23,500 is not as low as it looks; the owner has already taken out a salary and most likely auto and entertainment expenses.)

BLACK MONDAY

Back in 1929, October 29th was the important date. The stock market crashed and changed history. We thought that could never happen again. "Too many controls," we said. "Lots of government regulations and safeguards. Too many lessons learned."

Well, on October 19, 1987, the Dow Jones Industrial Average crashed over 500 points—the biggest point-drop in history—and investors lost billions of dollars. Since then, in spite of reports from the Securities and Exchange Commission and the Fed and a mountain of investment newsletters, we're *still* trying to figure out what happened.

A popular TV program for stock investors is "Wall Street Week." Each week a panel of guest experts discusses the market and the direction the market is going. And each week the experts disagree. Maybe that should be a clue. If the *experts* can't agree, what are *we* doing playing the game? As far as we are concerned, *playing* is the key word. We are strong believers in the old saying, "There ain't no free lunch." If you're going to invest in the stock market, you had better not only do your homework, you'd also better be sitting in front of your TV and PC with modem connected when the market is open. As we learned on October 19, 1987, the market moves at electronic speeds, and you must be prepared to move just as rapidly. October 20 was too late.

If you had money in the stock market, you know what happened to it. But what happened to the deal makers who were at the controls that fateful day? Well, money got tight and they left their jobs. And on March 14, 1988, a lead story in the *Wall Street Journal* reported on a dozen top executives from prestigious New York financial firms. Five of the dozen had taken the entrepreneurial route and formed their own businesses.

If you enjoy sitting in a dimly lit room watching numbers roll across a TV screen, and you like the 2001 feeling of sitting in front of a green screen and talking with HAL, well, investing in the market may be for you. But if you like to be in control, to be a mover and a shaker, to be one who makes things happen instead of having them happen to you, then invest in yourself, in your own business, in something that is fun and exciting. Put your dollars into something that can grow and expand as a direct result of your efforts. Many entrepreneurs find investors who believe in them and decide to share their dream. People like to be a part of something new and exciting.

Anyway, have fun, keep your new eyes peeled, and talk with customers, suppliers, and competitors. Don't be a ticker-tape watcher and develop ulcers because all you can do is watch.

Key Points from Another View
Part I:
BRACE YOURSELF FOR THE HIDDEN PERILS OF ENTREPRENEURSHIP

First-time business owners face a host of problems when they find themselves out on their own for the first time with a whole new set of challenges:

- Big changes have a psychological cost.
- A new entrepreneur can expect an avalanche of insecurities.

- Entrepreneurs must be able to cope with the bad things and turn them to their advantage.
- Responsibility to others compounds the stress of striking out on their own.
- During the first year, more than half of all small business owners work at least 60 hours a week; 25 percent work more than 70 hours.

Despite all the unexpected problems, start-ups can be made easier by keeping these things in mind:

1. Get advice—talk with other people who have gone through the experience.
2. Write a business plan—this helps you ward off self-doubt and fear of failure.
3. Know your strengths and weaknesses.
4. Assess your values—if you are clear about your goals, and about what you really value, you'll unconsciously push your business in that direction.
5. Stay detached—remember you are not your business.
6. Keep communication with your spouse and children open.
7. Try for emotional equilibrium—the highs and lows of entrepreneurship are exhausting. Be sure you're prepared for the roller coaster.
8. Remember to have fun—despite the perils of start-up, there is still plenty to enjoy.

From: "The Obstacle Course," by Kristin Von Kreisler Bomben, *Entrepreneur,* July 1990, 175–179.

Part II:
FATAL BUSINESS MISTAKES THAT YOU CAN AVOID

1. No Business Plan. All businesses are different, yet each one should answer the following questions:
   - How do you define your business, and what do you hope to accomplish in it?
   - Who is your competition?
   - What inventory is needed?
   - What do your profit and loss statement and your financial projections look like?

2. Inadequate Working Capital and Cash Flow. Ninety-five percent of small business start-ups don't break even in the first month. Most businesses need enough working capital for 12 months before they're in the black. Some take 18 months to 2 years to turn a profit.

3. Inadequate Financing. Problems with cash flow or working capital can be rectified if the company is adequately financed. If you don't have enough equity to start with, the business will fail.

4. Poor Management Skills. Many entrepreneurs think they can do everything themselves, and become trapped by their own deficiencies. The business people who succeed are usually the ones who have the good sense to ask for help.

5. Errors in Judgment. Entrepreneurs must cover all contingencies and have a strong fall-back position. The idea is not to go too far out on a limb that you expose yourself to error.

6. Lack of Knowledge, Skills, and Desire. Even if knowledge and skills are acquired, if the entrepreneur lacks the desire and motivation, the business is doomed to fail.

From: "Fatal Business Mistakes that You Can Avoid—Six Reasons Companies Fail," by Bob Weinstein, *Entrepreneur,* January 1990, 297–302.

SUMMARY

Ten years ago, the big story in the business world was the end of smokestack America and the rise of the Information Society. Today, we are living in the Information Age, and half of us are doing information jobs. By the early 1980s, less than four decades after the United States moved from an industrial economy to a service economy, the information industry was doing $800 billion a year—almost half of the gross national product. Changes are afoot for the entrepreneur: big business is still down-sizing; foreign investors are buying up chunks of America; Megatrends have become global; manufacturing has become more efficient, more robotic, and more quality-oriented. And still the smaller firms lead with innovation and the creation of jobs.

THINK POINTS FOR SUCCESS

◄ Change is accelerating everywhere, and that includes the world of business. Change creates problems. Entrepreneurs are problem solvers.

◄ The Information Society is no longer big news. It's here. To see what's next, scan the environment with new eyes. What does 2010 hold for you?

◄ To find your doorway into your own business, gather data and keep asking questions.

◄ Get reckless on paper before you get reckless in the marketplace. Brainstorm. Draw a future wheel. Confirm your venture with numbers and words before you enter the arena.

◄ Even though you may not be in business yet, you can intensify your focus by writing down your thoughts about the business you think you want to try. Stay flexible.

◄ Remember: We are entrepreneurs. Work is our fun. We never sleep.

REFERENCES

Bellman, Geoffrey. *The Consultant's Calling: Bringing Who You Are to What You Do.* San Francisco: Jossey-Bass, 1990.

Bolles, Richard. *The Three Boxes of Life: And How to Get Out of Them.* Berkeley, Calif.: Ten Speed Press, 1981.

Bolles, Richard. *What Color Is Your Parachute?* Berkeley, Calif.: Ten Speed Press, 1991. A fine book which allows one to assess strengths and dreams, revised periodically.

Brown, Buck. "Small Business: Business Failure Rates Aren't So Bad After All." *Wall Street Journal,* May 20, 1988. [Another myth dispelled. Common knowledge says four out of five start-ups fail during the first 5 years. Wrong, say two researchers from the SBA and Babson College in Massachusetts. For 8 years, the researchers tracked all companies formed between 1976 and 1978 who had ratings from Dun & Bradstreet. The findings: only three out of five failed during the first 6 years. Companies that added employees had a better chance of surviving. Only 49 percent of service companies added employees, compared to 69 percent in manufacturing.]

Brabec, Barbara. *Homemade Money: The Definitive Guide to Success in a Home Business,* third edition. Naperville, Ill.: Brabec Productions, 1989.

Buzan, Tony. *Use Both Sides of Your Brain.* New York: NAL-Dutton, 1991. [Teaches the fine art of mind mapping, which helps the fine art of brainstorming.]

ACTION STEP REVIEW

The keys to success in small business are planning and momentum. In this chapter, nine action steps help you focus on both.

1 Assess your job security. Do you have it? By looking at your current work situation, you can assess your motivation for the entrepreneurial plunge.

2 Brainstorm your way into your business future by using a "future wheel."

3 Brainstorm with the "cocooning" concept to generate ideas for new businesses.

4 Focus on your entrepreneurial qualities that are waiting to be used.

5 Look back on your past achievements.

6 Organize your information. If you fail to plan, you're planning to fail.

7 Survey your friends about success. How does the world measure success? What does success mean to you?

8 Assess your skills. What *can* you do, and what do you *like* to do?

9 Interview small business owners who are doing something like what you'd like to do with your own business.

Covey, Stephen. *The Seven Habits of Highly Effective People.* New York: Simon & Schuster, 1990.

Edwards, Betty. *Drawing on the Right Side of the Brain.* New York: St. Martin's Press, 1988.

Edwards, Sarah, and Paul Edwards. *Making It on Your Own.* Los Angeles: J. P. Tarcher, 1991.

Emmerling, John. *It Only Takes One: How to Create the Right Idea—and Then Make It Happen.* New York: Simon & Schuster, 1991.

Goldratt, Eliyahu, and Jeff Cox. *The Goal: A Process of Ongoing Improvement.* Croton-on-Hudson, NY: North River, 1987.

Hill, Napoleon. *Think and Grow Rich.* New York: Fawcett Crest, 1987.

Home-Based Business: The Basics of Doing Business from Your Home. Washington, D.C.: U.S. Small Business Administration, Office of Management Assistance. Small Business Management Training Instructor's Guide, No. 109, 1984. [Produced by the American Association of Community and Junior Colleges under contract to the SBA, Contract No. SBA 4873-MA 80.]

Keirsey, David, and Marilyn Bates. *Please Understand Me: Character and Temperament Types.* Del Mar, Calif.: Prometheus Nemesis Books, 1978. [Excellent, easy-to-use personality profiling system.]

Klein, Charna. *Consultant's Reference Guide.* Metuchen, N.J.: Scarecrow Press, 1989.

McCormack, Mark. *The 110% Solution.* New York: Villard Books, 1990.

Naisbitt, John. *Megatrends.* New York: Warner Books, 1988.

Naisbitt, John. *Megatrends 2000.* New York: Avon, 1991. [A must read for entrepreneurs.]

Naisbitt, John. *Reinventing the Corporation: Transforming Your Job and Your Company for the New Information Society.* New York: Warner Books, 1986.

Raphel, Murray. *Minding Your Own Business.* Raphel Marketing, 1989.

Rico, Gabriele. *Writing the Natural Way: Using Right-Brain Techniques to Release Your Expressive Powers.* Los Angeles: J. P. Tarcher, 1983. [Introduces a form of mind mapping called "clustering." Good stuff for the entrepreneur in a hurry.]

Ries, Al, and Jack Trout. *Positioning: The Battle for Your Mind.* New York: Warner Books, 1988. [Two NYC ad men offer advice on how you can position yourself in the minds of prospects and stay there.]

Schwartz, David. *The Magic of Thinking Big.* New York: Prentice Hall, 1990.

Staples, Walter Doyle. *Think Like a Winner!* Gretna, La.: Pelican Publishing, 1991.

Timmons, Jeffrey. *The Entrepreneurial Mind.* New Boston, N.H.: Brick House, 1989.

Tolchin, Martin, and Susan Tolchin. *Buying into America: How Foreign Money Is Changing the Face of Our Nation.* New York: Times Books, 1988.

Wayman, Lynn. *Starting and Managing a Business from Your Home.* Washington, D.C.: U.S. Small Business Administration, Starting and Managing Series,, Vol. 2, 1986.

Weaver, Paul H. *The Suicidal Corporation: How Big Business Has Failed America.* New York: Simon & Schuster, 1988.

White, Richard, *The Entrepreneur's Manual.* Radnor, Penn.: Chilton Book Co., 1977.

Wright, Richard W., and Gunther A. Pauli. *The Second Wave: Japan's Global Assault on Financial Services.* New York: St. Martin's Press, 1988.

position
establish your image in the eyes of the target customer

APPENDIX 1.1 · Model Action Step 8: Inventory Your Skills.

1. What kind of work do you do?
Writer—editor, primarily in journalism, secondarily in advertising. Also more than moderately skilled in brochure production.

2. What kind do you really enjoy?
Working as a writer and/or editor in a highly competitive atmosphere, where spot news is breaking or where there is plenty of action.

3. What are your hobbies?
Writing, editing, furniture building and refinishing. I spend all my weekends doing these things. Formerly was active in camping, astronomy, wildflower photography, shell collecting. Often I took up a hobby merely to become proficient as a writer in that area.

4. What really excites you?
The thrill of discovery during competitive research. Thoroughly trouncing the competition.

5. Do you like to work alone?
It's all right. I do a lot of it these days, although most of my career has involved working with others, usually as an editor/mentor.

6. Are you a self-starter?
Definitely. Always have been.

7. What would three people say about your three major skills?

1. He's a top-notch editor, with a special eye for tasteful, appealing layout in a publication. He knows how to work with top-drawer art directors and the finest printers. He knows a great deal about professional-quality desktop publishing.
2. He's a good writer on spot news, on people features, and in explaining complex things like science and chemistry for the lay reader. Because of his age, he is not a good advertising copywriter for the following VALS: Sustainers, Emulators, I-Am Mes, and probably is marginal with Experimental audiences. His greatest affinity is with these VALS audiences: Achievers, Belongers, Societally Conscious, and Integrated. (Note that the graphic arts industry today is probably dominated by people in the Experimentals and Achievers VALS life-styles.)
3. From lack of practice, he's long over the hill as a working photographer, but he is a good photo editor because of his lengthy experience and training as a photographer.

8. Boldface your skills in this list.
Sell, **write**, negotiate, soothe, counsel, **synthesize**, **coordinate**, create, **analyze**, compile, teach, persuade, tend, plant, **nurture**, **supervise**, help out, copy, add and subtract, follow instructions, delegate, lead.

Your top five skills:

1. Write
2. Nurture
3. Analyze/Synthesize
4. Create
5. Lead/Supervise/Delegate

Five that are impossible for you:

1. Personal selling on a sustained and effective basis.
2. Getting excited over bookkeeping: adding and subtracting. (My wife complements me here; she is outstanding in this field.)
3. Negotiating from a tough stance. I'm too much of a patsy. (But once again my wife has excellent skills in this area.)
4. Teaching large groups or persuading large audiences. I'm best with small groups of half a dozen. I was not effective over a period of time with a class of 30 students.
5. Tending, copying, or doing routine, repetitive work.

FIGURE 2.1
Chapter 2 will help you to prepare part A of your Business Plan, "The Product or Service."

2 The Big Picture— Charting Trends for Your Small Business

Learning Objectives

- To understand how to analyze the potential for small business success by applying the life-cycle yardstick to industries, products, services, and locations.
- To determine what business you're really in.
- To become excited about the techniques of brainstorming.
- To use diagrams and mind maps to explore market segmentation.
- To discover market signals that indicate trends and opportunities.
- To discover market forces that underlie the trends.
- To be able to deduce a person's life-style from the contents of his or her shopping cart.
- To select information sources that are efficient.
- To begin your search for the business that best fits your aptitudes.
- To increase your ability to read market signals that forecast future needs.

FUTURE FOCUS

For every business that has fallen on hard times, there are two that have the potential to exploit emerging new opportunities.

To discover those within your area of interest, observe media channels (The *Wall Street Journal,* trade journals, PBS's "Wall Street Week") and note which firms and industries investors are pursuing, and whose stocks are showing higher-than-average price earnings ratios. Watch the classified ads to see who is hiring and the business pages to see who is acquiring new space for expansion. In each business cycle, new ventures are emerging and growing.

segment
an identifiable slice of an industry

trends
pathways to your future

gap
an area of the market where needs are not being met

market research
collection and analysis of data pertinent to your current or potential market

A Business Plan begins with the "big picture"—the industry overview. Industries go through life cycles. Products and services within industries also progress through the process—birth, growth, maturity, and decline. The industry overview helps you gain perspective on your "niche" and helps the reader (lender or investor) understand why you have chosen to pursue this segment of the market.

WHY LOOK AT THE BIG PICTURE?

To be successful in small business you need to know two things: what business you are really in, and where your business is on the great life-cycle yardstick. Entrepreneurs tend to be in a big hurry. They want to push on, to get on with it, to throw open the doors to customers, and to read the bottom line, and that's not all bad. But before *you* charge into the arena, step back and examine what's going on in your industry **segment**. Where are the lines? The crowds? What are people buying? In what part of your community do you see "Going Out of Business" signs? Where are the start-ups? What's hot? What's cooling down? What business segments will still be thriving 5 years from now? If you opened the doors of your new business today, how long would it be before your product or service was no longer valuable?

So look before you leap. Brainstorm with your family and friends and interview your potential customers. Study the marketplace. Read industry journals. Use your new eyes. And use this chapter to help you define the **trends** and **gaps** in your industry—in other words, to see the big picture.

Recognizing Opportunities

What are the best business ventures to pursue today? Where can you find a business that will really pay off? One that will make you rich? One that will make you famous?

Only you can answer the question, because the best business for you is one that you enjoy. The best business for you uses those experiences, skills, and aptitudes that are unique to *you*. The early action steps in this book are designed to help you discover what is unique about you. Who are you? What are your skills? What turns you on? What do you already know that distinguishes you from other people?

As a consumer, you know, for example, that restaurants have a high failure rate. One week you're having dinner at The Hound and Glove; the next week it's locked up with a CLOSED sign on the door. You don't want that to happen to your business. That's why *you* do **market research**. That's why you're going to make sure your business serves a *need*. This means that you will automatically enter the marketplace from a position of strength.

Let's back up and get the big picture. Before the Industrial Revolution, most people were self-employed. Farmers and sheepherders were risk takers because they had to be; there were few other options. The family functioned as an entrepreneurial unit.

The growth of the megacorporations in the twentieth century should not be seen as a threat to the small entrepreneur, but as an opportunity. First, most large corporations are dependent on small business to produce support products and support services. Second, bigger isn't better, and many small businesses—even those whose markets are expanding rapidly—are barely noticed by the large corporations. And there lies the opportunity.

The exploding need for specialized products and services is mind boggling. You may see as much change in the next 10 years as your parents have seen in their lifetime, and change creates opportunities for fast and flexible firms. If you stay in touch with change and the exploding market niches that change creates, you will always see more opportunities than you can pursue. Action Step 10 will give you some perspective on change.

KNOW YOUR REAL BUSINESS

The Importance of Stepping Back

Watch a painter at work at an easel. She works close to the canvas, layering the paint with brush and spatula. But at regular intervals, the painter will step back for a long view of the work. Up close, the artist can see only brushstrokes and colors. From a few feet back, the entire painting can be seen. From a few more feet back, the landscape being painted becomes apparent.

What business is the painter in?

Watch a carpenter framing a new house. He works close to the wood, nailing with quick strokes of his hammer. But to get a view of the total house, the structure that will become someone's home, he must walk across the street. He has to step back, away from his detailed work, to see the shape of the whole.

What business is the carpenter in? Is he in the nail-driving business? The framing business? The home-building business? Or is he in the business of satisfying the age-old "nesting" need?

Only by stepping back can you answer the question of what business you are in. This is a very important question.

If you went far enough back in time in Action Step 10, you probably saw pictures of trains. Railroads used to be big business in America. Rail lines eventually linked the east and west coasts, and if you remember your American history, you probably remember the historic linkage at Promontory Point, Utah, in 1869, when the Union Pacific met the Central Pacific.

What has happened to the railroads since then? Well, the same thing that happens to lots of large business organizations. They downsized and lost their focus. And much of the track has been taken over by the government and run by Amtrak.

Why did this happen? Why was a huge, powerful industry forced to downsize?

The Railroads Forgot What Business They Were In

Okay, let's look back. Half a century ago, rail lines criss-crossed the continent. You could step onto a train in New York City and ride in safety, ease, and splendor all the way to California. Trains were the great movers of products and people. They owned timber, grazing land, mineral rights, country. Their names—*Chief, Super Chief, California Zephyr, Commodore Vanderbilt, New York Express, Texas Special*—had an aura of confidence, empire building, power, the grand strategy of efficient transportation. It was a magnificent era.

ACTION STEP 10

Travel back in time and observe a marketplace of the past.

Place yourself in a time warp and take a look at a marketplace of the past. What was selling 25 years ago? 50 years ago? 100 years ago?

To get this picture, look at old magazines, old catalogs, old movies, old TV shows, old high school yearbooks, and old family photographs. What do you see? Are all of the people dressed alike? Does everyone have the same smile, the same frown, the same serious look? How small is their world? How small is their horizon?

Study the advertisements in old magazines and newspapers and then make two lists:

1. List the products that are still around today.

2. List the products that are no longer on the market.

Which list is longer? What does this tell you about the changing marketplace?

define your business
develop a clear picture of what business you are really in

Yet, somewhere along the line, railroad magnates committed a grave error: they failed to **define their business.**

THE RR's SAID:	THE RR's MIGHT HAVE SAID:
"We're in the railroad business."	"We're in the transportation business."

life cycle
four stages, from birth to death, of a product, business, service, industry, location, and so on

That, coupled with the automobile, jumbo jets, interstate highways, and the general fickleness of consumers, was the beginning of the end for them. They entered the decline stage of their **life cycle.** Can they come back? As this book goes to press, America's major cities, caught in traffic gridlock, are asking the federal government for billions to build people-movers. There is talk of bullet trains like those in France and Japan. There is nostalgia about people-movers like the once-popular Los Angeles "Red Cars."

The lesson here is to know what business you are in—to know who your customers are and what satisfies their needs. Mary Clark's experience illustrates the importance of understanding what business you are really in.

> Mary Clark was a forty-year-old teacher who had always been more interested in riding her prize-winning saddle horses than in teaching school. When her grandmother died and left her $200,000, Mary made a down payment on a boarding stable and left teaching forever, she thought.
>
> The boarding stable was run down. It had stalls for 100 horses, but only forty of them were occupied. Mary did everything she could think of to make the place better for horses. She spent $57,000 rebuilding, painting, grading. She made Clark's Stables a very attractive place. She bought the highest quality of feed and gave the horses the best care money could buy.
>
> When the owners began to move their horses to other stables, Mary couldn't understand. She had not increased her fees, and she treated the horses like friends. In six months, only three customers remained. In nine months, she was behind on her mortgage payments. In her tenth month, Mary had to sell the stables.

Mary made the simple mistake of thinking horses were her target customers. Her real target customers were young girls between the ages of seven and fourteen. Mary thought she was in the business of stabling horses. The business she should have seen she was in was providing services for girls who rode horses. The girls wanted recreation, training, and social activities. Mary's customers left because other stables were providing lessons, trail rides, barbeques, and pony and horse shows. Today, Mary is back in the classroom wondering why people don't care more about their horses.

Define Your Real Business

What business are *you* really in? What business do you want to be in? Naming anything is a game of words, and a small business is no exception. The following examples can help you define your business. If you're hesitant about defining at this early stage, remember what happened to the railroads—and to Mary Clark's stable.

IF YOU'RE IN:	TRY SAYING:
Software sales	"I'm in the problem-solving business."
Pie baking	"I'm in the reward and satisfaction business."
College teaching	"I'm in the information business."
Medicine	"I'm in the healing business."
Auto manufacturing	"I'm in the ego-gratification business."
Mattresses	"I'm in the sound sleep business."
Cameras/camcorders	"I'm in the happy memory business."
Gourmet cookware	"I bring fun back into the kitchen."
Locksmithing	"I'm in the security business."
Badge manufacturing	"I'm in the recognition business."
Renters' guide publishing	"I help landlords find tenants."

Now complete this sentence:

I'm in the business of

_____

Explain why you chose this definition and how it relates to your target customer. (Include customer benefits.)

_____

Keep honing your definition of your business. Once a month is not too often to redefine it, especially before the start-up. Check your definition against the signals you get from your potential target customers, since they may perceive your business differently. You may have new letterhead stationery printed after you talk to them, but as business expenses go, that's a small price to pay to overcome customer confusion.

Now you're ready to do Action Step 11.

HOW TO MINIMIZE MARKETPLACE HEARTACHE—WATCH TRENDS

Let's say you've tried a small business and failed. Let's say you followed in the footsteps of Mary Clark, the teacher who loved horses; you opened a business out of love, and it fell apart. Your customers left you, and your creditors scared you to death. Okay, you failed once. Worse, you're still unhappy in your job. So, after licking your wounds, you've decided you'd like to try it again. After all, this is the Age of the Entrepreneur, right? So what's the next step?

Well, you look around with those new eyes. Study that list you made of products from 25 years ago and try to make some generalizations about how things have changed. Here's a quick overview.

ACTION STEP 11

Define your business and test your definition. Follow these steps:

1. Brainstorm what business you're really in. Let your mind play at this. Try to keep negative statements to a minimum.

2. Once you've decided what business you're in, visit your printer and order some one-color business letterhead stationery. (One-color is cheaper, so you save money right from the start.)

3. Next, go to the library and look for a thick publication called the *Encyclopedia of Associations*. Locate the name of a trade association your business would be a part of. Write down the address, phone number, and name of a contact person.

4. Before you leave the library, check the *Gale Directory of Publications* for a trade journal that covers your industry. Try to find one that's not connected to the association you found listed in the *Encyclopedia of Associations*. Write down the name of the publication; the publisher's name, address, and phone number; and the cost (if any) of a subscription.

5. Look in the *Thomas Register of American Manufacturers* for a company that manufactures a part or a product that you will need in your business. Note the specific name of the part or product and the manufacturer's, name, address, and phone number.

6. Finally, write letters to or telephone the publications and trade associations that are in your area of interest. Ask them for a "rate card" and for demographic studies. It's free because you are a prospective advertiser. The trade association will tell you about themselves and provide membership details.

You will soon be buried with useful information.

The Splintering of the Mass Market

Today's consumers are informed, individualistic, and demanding. Their buying habits are often difficult to isolate because they tend to buy at several levels of the market. For instance, many purchasing agents buy the office copier from Xerox but the paper from a discount office supply warehouse. High-fashion, high-income consumers patronize the up-scale boutiques and yet buy their household appliances at Kmart.

For the consumer, three key factors have splintered the mass market: (1) a shrinking middle class—there are both more high-end, affluent consumers and more consumers who live at or near the poverty level; (2) shifting sizes of age groups; (3) new living arrangements—including smaller houses, smaller furniture, enclosed patios, and twin master suites for working roommates. If you look around with new eyes, you can see major market segments emerging that were not here a decade ago: **baby boomers;** vigorous, healthy over-60-year-olds; teens; single parents; and affluent over-80-year-olds.

baby boom
the increase in the U.S. birthrate between 1946 and 1963

To get a better view of today's trends, contrast consumer values of the two decades between 1960 and 1980 with those we can project for the 1990s. Here's what you have:

Changing Consumer Values

1960–1980	1990–2000
Quantity	Quality
Things	Experiences
Initial cost	Total use cost
High expectations	Modified expectations
Liberal credit	Tightened credit
Conformity	Individuality
Impulse shopping	Planned expenditures
Experimental life-styles	Return to old values
Video games	Home entertainment
Car status	Home status
Stable middle class	Shrinking middle class
Child-oriented homes	Adult orientation
Throw away	Reuse

Action Step 12 will take you out into your community to conduct some trend research.

A List of Trends to Start You Off

Let's say you like taking care of people and you have worked for 10 years in an infant day-care center. However the neighborhood is aging, affluent families have moved away, and the day-care center has closed because of a lack of business. You decide to go into business for yourself. What business do you choose? How about a care center for elderly people?

Let's think about where other opportunities exist.

There is continued increase in dual-income families and single parents. That means no one is at home during the day. Obvious business opportunities are child care and home security systems.

With both adults working to pay the bills, no one has enough time (the "poverty of time" trend). Obvious business opportunities are easy-to-fix meals, fast food, teleconferences.

Ethnic diversity is expanding rapidly. The greater Los Angeles area is already the most ethnically diverse in the world. Opportunity: Helping schools and businesses integrate.

People are exercising for fitness and they want to look good while sweating. Opportunity: attractive sports clothes.

People must change jobs and they need retraining. Opportunity: education.

Continue the list here.

TREND	OPPORTUNITY

Some people make a business of trend watching. See Box 2.1.

THE LIFE-CYCLE STAGES

When you have produced a long list of trends, divide them into four groups according to the stage of their life cycle. See Figure 2.2. If a trend is just beginning, is in its formative stage, label it *Embryo*. If it's exploding, label it *Growth*. If it's no longer growing and is starting to cool, label it *Mature*. If it's beyond maturity and is feeling chilly, label it *Decline*. Think about these life-cycle stages often. Everything changes—products, needs, technology, neighborhoods.

Looking at the life-cycle diagram, you can see that the auto industry as a whole is very mature. Nonetheless, some of its segments are promising; for example, minivans, sports models, and upscale imports. Convertibles are back, and in the suburbs, you see young mothers driving around in Jeep 4 × 4s. Despite traffic jams, people are still driving. But the cars they drive reflect changing life-styles.

How do consumer habits determine trends? Well, people are keeping their cars longer, so one growth segment in the auto industry would be the **aftermarket**. Examples of businesses in that segment would be paint, detailing, electronic accessories, engine rebuilding. If you're interested in the auto industry, consider the aftermarket.

In the computer business, competition and the microchip have brought down the price of computer hardware. A personal computer system that sold for $5,000 three years ago can be purchased for one-third of that today. And that same $5,000 buys a system with more speed, more power, more bells and whistles. With the gain in power comes more sophisticated software. Some of the software, despite claims

ACTION STEP 12

What's new? What's hot? What's cooling down?

1. Take your new eyes out into the marketplace and observe what's happening at the local (or regional) level. Your community is a marketing lab. To discover what this means for you and your business, prowl around a supermarket and analyze what's going on. A locally owned store will give you a clearer picture than a chain will, because it serves the needs of your area. Chains only show you what the country is buying, and that's not much help for an entrepreneur.

   What's on sale? What's dusty? What's wilted? What is the store promoting? What conclusions can you draw about the store's marketing strategy? Which department has the most space? Which has the longest lines? Which has the most workers? Which has the highest prices? What products must move fast? Can you guesstimate the shelf velocities in the various departments?

   Move on to other locally owned stores—hardware stores, drugstores, restaurants, gift shops, and others.

2. Give your new-eyes research a data base by checking with the local newspaper. Visit the display advertising department and ask to see research they've compiled on the area.

3. Go to the public library and study last year's *Survey of Buying Power*, published by *Sales and Marketing Management* magazine. For your city or county, note:

   the total dollars spent, autos, related products

   the percentage of households with incomes above the national average

   the total city/county population.

   How do your new-eyes research findings correlate with what you found in the secondary sources?

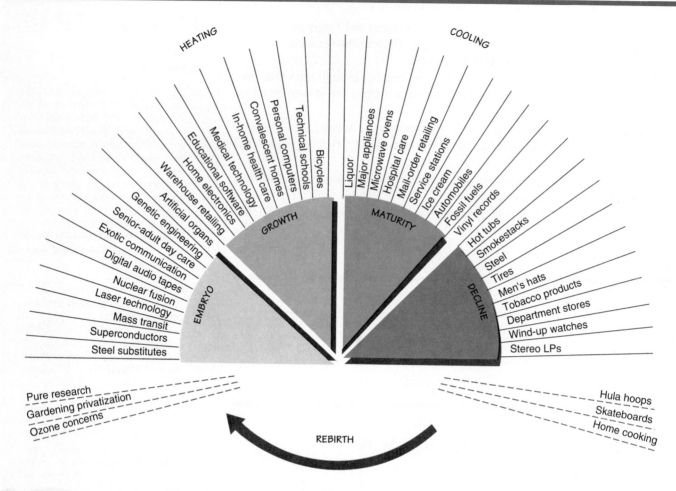

FIGURE 2.2   Every industry goes through a life cycle. You need to know where your business is in the cycle.

shelf velocity
the speed at which a product moves from storage to shelf to customer

aftermarket
the marketplace where replacement items can be purchased. Auto tires and sewing machine belts are examples.

deep discount
cutting a price to near cost, cost, or below cost

of being "user-friendly," has a long learning curve. So one opportunity in the computer field is computer instruction. In Chapter 3 you'll read a case study about a group of entrepreneurs who found a niche in computer instruction.

Where can you find gaps in the life-cycle diagram? Where is your business in its four-stage cycle?

Watch for Market Signals

Market signals are everywhere—in the newspaper (classified ads, bankruptcy notices, display ads), in the lines at the theatre, in the price-slashing after Christmas, in discount coupons, rebates, closings, grand openings. With practice, you can follow a product right through its life cycle.

For example, consider designer jeans. In the early 1980s, massive ad campaigns convinced otherwise-sane Americans they should pay $40 and up for jeans carrying designer labels. The jeans were available only in the posh stores. A year later, designer jeans had reached the discount stores. Jeans that had sold for $55 were now selling at **deep discount**—for $9.99. A bargain? Yes, and also a trend.

What items have you seen go through their life cycle, from upscale out of sight to deep discount?

Now go back to the life-cycle diagram and see if you can add some products and industries to it.

How Deep Is Deep?

When merchandise slides into deep discount, the profit party is over. The air is chilly. The market is flooded; sinking is likely, and drowning is possible. If that's happened to your job—or to your business—it's time for you to find a **growth segment** of a **growth industry**.

Experts tell us that the average working American will have at least five kinds of jobs in his or her lifetime. No one's job is completely secure. Rhonda Van Warden thought hers was, until her company eliminated her position. When that happened, she started to look at the trends in her community and in the nation. Rhonda has some great assets, including intelligence and being a good listener, and she has the flexibility to see herself in a totally new role when opportunity knocks.

> Rhonda was a great teacher. She had a warm personality, a terrific smile, and an intuitive understanding of what kids needed from a world of adults. When she was offered a job as a counselor in the school where she'd been teaching, she didn't hesitate. As a counselor, she knew she could reach more kids.
>
> Then the district cutbacks started. Due to forces beyond her control, Rhonda was furloughed. Naturally, she was very upset. Here she'd been working overtime, supporting the system, counseling her heart out, and what did she have to show for it? Not much.
>
> But Rhonda's a fighter who doesn't give up easily. She attended seminars, read books about job-hunting, and networked her friends for leads. One day she was talking to a couple of friends, and their conversation turned to lingerie.
>
> "What I wish," said Kary, "is that I could buy some of that semisexy stuff without having to go into Le Sex Shoppe to buy it."
>
> "There're always the catalogs," Marsha pointed out, "and there are ads in the back of every magazine I subscribe to."
>
> "I don't trust those catalogs," Kary replied. "When I pay that much money for something so small, I want to see what I'm getting!"
>
> Marsha turned to Rhonda. "You're sitting there not saying a word, Rhonda. What're you thinking about?"
>
> "I think," Rhonda said, smiling, "I've just discovered the business I want to be in."
>
> Rhonda's idea was to network her women friends for potential target customers who would like to come to her home for a private showing of women's intimate undergarments. Rhonda came up with the name for her business, "Private Screenings," and had letterhead stationery printed. Then she began to contact suppliers and manufacturer's reps. They were interested in her idea.
>
> Her first "private screening" was well-attended. Only women were present, and Rhonda sold almost a thousand dollars' worth of merchandise. The women loved what they saw and they had fun. Ten years earlier they probably wouldn't have considered buying the things they bought that night, but times and people change.
>
> Rhonda went on from her success in selling to develop a line of products that she sells through her own catalog. Her husband has joined her in the business, and she has hired a woman to present her intimate merchandise through seminars. (The seminars also are held in private homes.) Rhonda spends most of her time recruiting personnel and developing new products.

growth segment
an identifiable slice of an industry that is expanding more rapidly than the industry as a whole

growth industry
an industry whose annual sales increase is well above average

"When I started in this business," Rhonda admits, "I thought it might help to supplement my husband's income. But it's expanded so much that we have to scramble to keep up with orders. We travel a lot, talking to manufacturers about trends, picking up ideas. This business is a full-time job for *both* of us."

Rhonda was a sharp reader of market signals—the trends that reflect changes in how people think. What trends have helped to make Rhonda's business successful?

1. Specialized consumer tastes. Rhonda's target customers are discreet middle-class women in their forties and fifties, many of whom would be uncomfortable walking into a specialty shop to see intimate lingerie. When Rhonda brings the merchandise to them, they feel comfortable, special, and adventurous.

2. High-tech/high-touch. We can't stop the approach of computers and the Information Age. But we all try to balance the electronic effects of whirring machinery with human responses—EST, dance, the arts, feeding our fantasies. Private Screenings capitalizes on the desire for softness in these high-tech times.

3. Relaxing attitudes about sex. Private Screenings was founded in the early eighties, a time when attitudes toward sex were becoming more relaxed.

What other trends do you see contributing to the success of Private Screenings?

_____

_____

_____

CONDUCT YOUR OWN RESEARCH

This is a good time to take a walk. Action Step 13 will get you out into the neighborhood of your target customers. Take along your new eyes.

Rich Cameron is a very precise and careful person and he understands research *and* trends. If you're considering a venture you know very little about, you should work in that kind of business for a while to get experience. If you can't do that, then do what Rich did.

When Rich Cameron celebrated his thirty-fifth birthday, he was in the marketing end of the computer industry. The industry was doing all right, but Rich was frustrated with his job.

"I was your typical workaholic," Rich said. "I'd do overtime at the office, put out a lot of energy for the company, and then wonder why I didn't feel terrific. If someone had told me I was experiencing corporate burnout, I'd have laughed in his face."

Rich had been in the habit of changing jobs when he got frustrated. He started working as a grocery bagger when he was twelve, and since then he'd worked in sales, management, real estate, insurance, finance, research, and computer programming. Now he started to look around for something else to do. He arranged to work a 4-day work week—10 hours a day—and spent the 3 other days exploring.

"When I was a kid in high school, my dad took me aside and gave me some valuable advice. 'Son,' he said. 'Remember this. You are your greatest resource.' So one of the first things I did—before I checked out the marketplace—was take some aptitude tests. They told me three things: I'm good with spatial problems, I like being creative, and I like to play. The last one—play—is the one that threw me. I grew up in a family where we learned to work hard, and *play* is a word we didn't use much. It took me more than a year to accept the fact that I like to play."

ACTION STEP 13

Assess the life-style of your potential target customer by walking its neighborhood.

The best time to walk a target neighborhood is on the weekend, when the people are home and the garage doors are open. What you're looking for are clues to life-style.

How many cars? What makes and models? How old? What condition? Sports cars and low-slung two-door hatchbacks indicate owners who are young, or trying to be. Station wagons suggest families. Trucks, four-wheel drives, and luxury cars tell you other things.

Do you see any sports or recreation equipment? Any tools? Any pets, doghouses, stables?

What's the maintenance level of the homes? Are they patio homes, condos, townhouses, or single-family? Estimate the number of bedrooms, bathrooms, square feet, and so on.

Visit a real estate office and get a ballpark figure on housing costs in the neighborhood. Use these costs to estimate household income. (If the average price for a home in your target neighborhood is $300,000 and buyers can finance $200,000, the household income is probably $60,000–$90,000.)

If you don't have time to walk the neighborhood, bike it or drive it.

Commonly available secondary information can help you confirm your observations. See what data your community newspaper or cable station has already gathered. Also, review information from the latest census track. It's all free!

Study your target customer from all angles. You can't afford to make any blind guesses.

---

walk the neighborhood
tramp through the dust and gold of the marketplace

clues to life-style
things that indicate what's important to people

While Rich was digesting this news about himself, he attended some seminars, mostly in small business, and kept to his work schedule of 4 days for his boss and 3 days for himself. He walked more than a hundred neighborhoods and interviewed more than a hundred small business owners. He studied **traffic patterns**, shopping habits, and trends. After a year, he knew that he wanted to combine work and play by opening a toy store. He was about to settle on a location in a major shopping center when he happened to interview the owner of an antique store.

Rich asked the antique store owner why he'd chosen this location.

"We did research," the man said. "My wife is the mathematician of the family. She worked the whole thing out on paper."

"Great," Rich said. "I've been at it for more than a year, myself. What kinds of things did she do?"

"We counted the cars in the parking lot," the owner said. "We counted them every day for 2 weeks. This lot was packed solid from dawn to dark."

Rich looked out. Today, the parking lot was packed. "What about weekends?" he asked.

The antique store owner looked at the floor. "Now there," he admitted, "we've been having problems—ever since we lost our anchor tenant."

"How long ago was that?" Rich asked.

"Six months ago tomorrow," the man said.

Rich thanked the owner and kept on exploring. He had liked this center. It was close to a perfect target neighborhood. Yet, something was wrong. He could feel it.

Rich was still talking to store owners when evening rolled around and the parking lot began to empty, fast. He stopped his interviewing to do some "new-eyes" observing. Cars full of people kept pulling into the lot and stopping. Everyone except the drivers got out of the cars and walked to parked cars. None of the people went into the stores. Rich quickly deduced that this shopping center parking lot was being used by carpooling commuters.

"I'd been interviewing store owners all afternoon," Rich says, "and not one of them told me about this 'park and ride' situation. Maybe they didn't know it. Maybe they were hiding something. Either way, it was a signal for me to keep on looking."

It took Rich Cameron 2 years to find what he was looking for—a location close to a target neighborhood packed with kids, young parents, station wagons, and toys. He named his store "Toys from Middle Earth." He now works 70 hours a week until the Christmas season, and then he works 100 hours a week. He's not frustrated anymore.

"The main thing you've got to watch in the toy business," Rich says, "is how fast a trend can end. One week, you're selling hula hoops like crazy. The next week, hula hoops won't even move at deep discount and the kids are coming in the store asking for gear they've seen on a new TV show or in some movie. To make it in toys these days, you need to keep one eye on the kids, the other on the future." He grins. "If you'd told me this a couple years back, I wouldn't have believed you. But you learn to read the customers in this business, or you go under."

Rich Cameron won't go under. He likes to win too much.

Rich took a hard look "inside" and then spent two years researching the toy industry. Today, his toy business is growing steadily because he planned well and because he matched his skills with his business. Rich is a researcher to model yourself after. He integrated new-eyes research with hard data from secondary sources.

Secondary Sources

Now we're going to introduce you to some valuable secondary sources that you can use for gathering hard data.

Newspapers   John Naisbitt's Trend staff monitors 6,000 regional and daily newspapers. *Megatrends 2000* grew, in part, out of that research. Faith Popcorn's

traffic pattern
pathway of frequent travel

BrainReserve staff also does heavy research. Study the local newspaper, starting with the classifieds and display ads. For a bigger picture, read the *Wall Street Journal*.

Magazines   Faith Popcorn herself watches sitcoms and devours *People* magazine. The ads tell you what's hot and where the money is flowing. If you haven't looked at it already, check out *Sales and Marketing Management* magazine. *S & MM* also publishes two annual supplements of interest to small business pioneers: the *Survey of Buying Power* (lists results by counties all across the U.S.) and the *Budget Planner* (gives a dramatic big-picture look at regions, counties, industries, and metro areas). These *S & MM* supplements are definite must-reads.

trade journal
publication directed to the specific needs of an industry

Trade Journals   These are a valuable source once you know what industry you're in. Use your new business letterhead to write trade associations. You can find these listed with their addresses in the *Encyclopedia of Associations* and in the *Gale Directory of Publications*.

Banks   Banks are in the business of renting money, and any bank above medium size has a staff of economists, marketing experts, and so on, who research and write forecasts and reports of economic trends. Ask to see those reports.

Planning Offices   Cities and counties employ planners to chart the future and plan for growth. Check the city and county offices listings in the phone book to find out where these offices are. For the best service, however, you'll need to visit the office, make friends with the staff, and be pleasant and patient. Many counties use federal data to develop annual reports.

Reports from Colleges and Universities   State universities publish annual and semiannual reports on economic conditions in the state. You can probably get copies of these by writing to the university public relations office. Reports are also published by private institutions of higher learning with special interests in business. Inquire in your area.

Real Estate Firms   Large commercial and industrial real estate firms have access to developers' site research. The more specific you can be on your requirement, the easier it will be for them to help you. Familiarize yourself with the dynamics of the area. What firms are going into business? What firms are leaving business? (For more details on this, see Chapter 7.)

The SBA   The Small Business Administration of the U.S. government has tons of booklets. Call the nearest office or write to U.S. Small Business Administration, P.O. Box 15434, Fort Worth, TX 76119. Put tax dollars to work for yourself.

Federal Depositories   Scattered across the U.S. are special libraries that contain sources of census information on Consolidated Metropolitan Statistical Areas (CMSAs; for example, the New York–Long Island–Southwestern Connecticut–Northern New Jersey area, which has 17 million people), Primary Metropolitan Statistical Areas (PMSAs; for example, New York City), and Metropolitan Statistical Areas (MSAs; for example, Peoria, Fresno, and so on). These three were formerly grouped all together as Standard Metropolitan Statistical Areas (SMSAs), a category that will linger in the minds of marketeers for another decade or so. No matter what you call it, you can find census information in these Federal Depositories, where the 1980 SMSA for your area is probably still intact. Also look for a booklet called County Business Patterns. For the whereabouts of the nearest Depository, ask the friendly reference librarian at your public library.

SIC Codes

While you're scanning the big picture for trends, you might want to develop a feel for what you can do with SIC Codes. Starting with your own code will help you define your industry. It will give perspective to the big picture.

SIC stands for *Standard Industrial Classification.* It's a numerical system that assigns a number to almost every identifiable industry. SIC numbers come in three groups:

2-digit (for example, 36)—Major Group
3-digit (for example, 366)—Industry Group
4-digit (for example, 3662)—Specific Industry Group

SIC codes are contained in a government publication called *The Standard Industrial Classification Manual,* which is available at most libraries. To use it, first find the industry you think you're in in the alphabetical index. Then go to Major Group, Industry Group, and Specific Industry.

For example, let's say you're a creative entrepreneur who's just invented a device you can manufacture for $4.22 per unit that will make radio transmission easier. Your primary market will be manufacturers of radio equipment, and a secondary market might be telephone equipment makers. Before you start production, however, you want to assess the size of the market.

So you find your SIC classification in the alphabetical index under number 3662, "radio and TV communication equipment." That's you, all right. This number refers you to Major Group 36, "electrical, electronics," and then to Specific Industries under 3662. You notice that 3661 is "telephone and telegraph supplies," which is another industry category you need to explore.

You will notice that the manual will lead you only so far and no further. That's because the government does not release the sources of its data. So, where do you go from here? To private enterprise. Figure 2.3 shows three different tracks you can follow with your SIC code, depending on what you want to learn.

Track I   Track I leads to *S & MM's Budget Planner,* an annual study of markets that is available at most libraries. The *Budget Planner* gives you a big-picture look at business trends at the national level. It reports:

the major industry groups
the top 50 manufacturing counties
the 50 leading industrial metropolitan markets
regional and state summaries of manufacturing markets
profiles of the 50 largest manufacturing industries

Tables 2.1 through 2.7 illustrate the value of the data in the study. They are drawn from the *1991 Budget Planner* (published August 19, 1991).

If you're still following that SIC number 3662, you can get a breakdown, by employment totals, total shipments, percentages of SIC classifications, and so on, of the top seventy-one counties in the country. The *Survey* reports, for example, that Los Angeles County has eighty-three plants that make radio and TV equipment. Up above, in 3662, you'll notice that Cook County, Illinois, has eight companies that make telephone/telegraph gear.

Now, depending on your business and how widely you want to fling your marketing net, you take one or two more tracks. Track II leads to *Contacts Influential,* and Track III leads to Standard & Poor's *Register of Corporations, Directors, and Executives.*

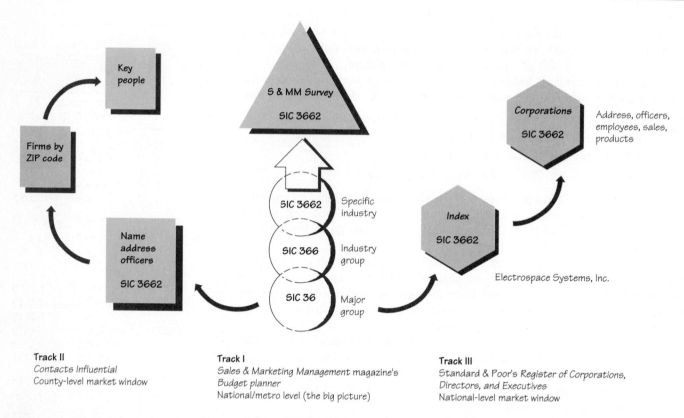

FIGURE 2.3 Working from the SIC codes, you can follow three different tracks to learn how your business relates to national and local markets.

Track II *Contacts Influential* gives information at the county level. Follow your SIC number (3662 in our example) to the first *Contacts* book, which gives you the name of a particular corporation, its address and phone number, and the names of the key officers. Next you double-check your data in the section where 3662 firms are listed by zip code. Finally, you look up the list of the key officers in their own section.

SIC 3662 has led you to some possible contacts in a specific county of interest. If you believe your device might be marketable at the national level, go on to Track III.

Track III SIC 3662 will lead you first to Standard & Poor's *Index,* where you locate the company you want, Electrospace Systems, Inc., located in Richardson, Texas. Then you move to another S&P volume, entitled *Corporations,* where you look up Electrospace Systems. Here you'll find the company's address and phone number, a list of its officers, the number of employees, regional contacts, its sales for the previous year, a list of its products, and your old friend SIC 3662.

Since the listings in *Corporations* are alphabetical, you'll find other interesting corporations beginning with *electro-*—Electronics Corporation of America, Electronics Corporation of Texas, Electronics Research, Inc. (which you learn makes FM broadcasting antennas—perhaps another market tie-in), and so on.

TABLE 2.1   Regional and State Summaries of Population as of December 31, 1990*

REGION/STATE	POPULATION			POPULATION BY AGE GROUP (Thousands)					HOUSEHOLDS	
	NUMBER (Thousands)	% OF U.S.	MEDIAN AGE	0–17 YEARS	18–24 YEARS	25–34 YEARS	35–49 YEARS	50 & OVER	NUMBER (Thousands)	% OF U.S.
New England	**13,285.7**	**5.2971**	**33.8**	**3,102.7**	**1,463.8**	**2,349.6**	**2,858.4**	**3,511.2**	**4,973.2**	**5.3628**
Connecticut	3,301.1	1.3162	34.5	758.2	341.7	579.2	724.9	897.1	1,236.0	1.3328
Maine	1,238.3	.4937	33.9	313.9	122.3	204.8	268.2	329.1	469.5	.5063
Massachusetts	6,042.2	2.4090	33.7	1,370.7	701.0	1,092.0	1,278.5	1,600.0	2,257.1	2.4340
New Hampshire	1,127.2	.4495	32.8	285.4	117.4	205.9	253.9	264.6	418.0	.4508
Rhode Island	1,008.9	.4023	34.1	229.0	118.9	172.5	204.9	283.6	380.0	.4097
Vermont	568.0	.2264	33.0	145.5	62.5	95.2	128.0	136.8	212.6	.2292
Middle Atlantic	**37,746.7**	**15.0498**	**34.5**	**8,954.9**	**3,907.2**	**6,360.8**	**7,981.5**	**10,542.3**	**13,984.8**	**15.0804**
New Jersey	7,768.8	3.0974	34.6	1,821.3	770.8	1,350.8	1,696.8	2,129.1	2,809.3	3.0294
New York	18,065.5	7.2029	34.0	4,309.6	1,929.2	3,114.1	3,840.8	4,871.8	6,668.4	7.1908
Pennsylvania	11,912.4	4.7495	35.2	2,824.0	1,207.2	1,895.9	2,443.9	3,541.4	4,507.1	4.8602
East North Central	**42,105.4**	**16.7876**	**33.0**	**11,057.5**	**4,399.9**	**7,033.1**	**8,748.1**	**10,866.8**	**15,631.0**	**16.8553**
Illinois	11,449.1	4.5648	32.9	2,973.6	1,194.0	1,972.3	2,376.8	2,932.4	4,207.6	4.5372
Indiana	5,556.7	2.2155	32.9	1,470.6	594.3	906.6	1,150.3	1,434.9	2,069.8	2.2319
Michigan	9,323.1	3.7172	32.6	2,484.6	988.7	1,561.1	1,964.5	2,324.2	3,429.6	3.6982
Ohio	10,864.4	4.3317	33.4	2,825.3	1,117.3	1,777.1	2,253.0	2,891.7	4,094.2	4.4149
Wisconsin	4,912.1	1.9584	32.9	1,303.4	505.6	816.0	1,003.5	1,283.6	1,829.8	1.9731
West North Central	**17,731.5**	**7.0696**	**33.1**	**4,717.5**	**1,766.5**	**2,924.4**	**3,579.9**	**4,743.2**	**6,745.7**	**7.2742**
Iowa	2,770.3	1.1046	34.1	722.2	277.8	423.1	548.2	799.0	1,061.7	1.1449
Kansas	2,491.1	.9932	32.9	669.9	251.8	411.1	499.9	658.4	949.6	1.0240
Minnesota	4,412.0	1.7591	32.5	1,185.1	439.4	778.0	924.2	1,085.3	1,661.6	1.7918
Missouri	5,145.1	2.0513	33.6	1,332.0	510.4	846.4	1,040.9	1,415.4	1,971.0	2.1254
Nebraska	1,579.4	.6297	33.0	432.2	153.4	254.7	314.1	425.0	602.6	.6498
North Dakota	636.2	.2537	32.4	175.9	66.6	102.6	121.8	169.3	239.8	.2586
South Dakota	697.4	.2780	32.5	200.2	67.1	108.5	130.8	190.8	259.4	.2797
South Atlantic	**44,186.1**	**17.6173**	**33.8**	**10,739.8**	**4,689.3**	**7,587.5**	**9,349.8**	**11,819.7**	**16,746.3**	**18.0583**
Delaware	673.2	.2684	32.9	166.4	75.8	118.8	140.0	172.2	250.2	.2698
District of Columbia	604.2	.2409	33.7	117.9	80.9	119.2	130.4	155.8	248.4	.2679
Florida	13,218.8	5.2704	36.6	2,948.4	1,221.7	2,135.0	2,601.5	4,312.2	5,250.4	5.6617
Georgia	6,586.6	2.6261	31.7	1,769.3	737.1	1,182.0	1,436.7	1,461.5	2,407.6	2.5962
Maryland	4,843.7	1.9312	33.1	1,185.9	504.2	901.0	1,100.8	1,151.8	1,771.9	1.9107
North Carolina	6,693.1	2.6685	33.2	1,634.8	775.2	1,142.0	1,424.6	1,716.5	2,542.7	2.7419
South Carolina	3,521.1	1.4039	32.1	936.6	402.7	590.4	737.6	853.8	1,271.3	1.3709
Virginia	6,265.1	2.4980	32.7	1,537.0	717.2	1,141.7	1,402.8	1,466.4	2,320.3	2.5021
West Virginia	1,780.3	.7099	35.5	443.5	174.5	257.4	375.4	529.5	683.5	.7371
East South Central	**15,225.0**	**6.0703**	**33.0**	**4,019.6**	**1,636.0**	**2,450.4**	**3,131.6**	**3,987.4**	**5,670.6**	**6.1150**
Alabama	4,056.1	1.6172	33.1	1,070.9	436.0	643.6	824.5	1,081.1	1,512.7	1.6312
Kentucky	3,687.3	1.4701	33.1	961.9	392.5	603.4	768.0	961.5	1,380.6	1.4888
Mississippi	2,575.3	1.0268	31.3	753.2	286.9	395.7	489.4	650.1	912.2	.9837
Tennessee	4,906.3	1.9562	33.7	1,233.6	520.6	807.7	1,049.7	1,294.7	1,865.1	2.0113
West South Central	**26,875.3**	**10.7154**	**31.3**	**7,626.3**	**2,881.4**	**4,636.4**	**5,475.4**	**6,255.8**	**9,729.5**	**10.4917**
Arkansas	2,358.0	.9402	34.0	627.2	232.9	355.9	467.6	674.4	894.3	.9644
Louisiana	4,206.7	1.6773	31.0	1,232.4	454.2	693.4	837.2	989.5	1,494.2	1.6112
Oklahoma	3,143.0	1.2531	33.2	842.2	315.1	503.1	636.7	845.9	1,204.9	1.2993
Texas	17,167.6	6.8448	30.8	4,924.5	1,879.2	3,084.0	3,533.9	3,746.0	6,136.1	6.6168

(continued)

TABLE 2.1 *Continued*

REGION/STATE	POPULATION			POPULATION BY AGE GROUP (Thousands)					HOUSEHOLDS	
	NUMBER (Thousands)	% OF U.S.	MEDIAN AGE	0–17 YEARS	18–24 YEARS	25–34 YEARS	35–49 YEARS	50 & OVER	NUMBER (Thousands)	% OF U.S.
Mountain	**13,834.0**	**5.5156**	**31.6**	**3,954.5**	**1,402.1**	**2,355.1**	**2,908.3**	**3,214.0**	**5,100.0**	**5.4996**
Arizona	3,740.0	1.4911	32.3	1,008.3	394.1	639.8	746.9	950.9	1,397.5	1.5070
Colorado	3,321.1	1.3241	32.4	874.5	332.7	610.9	774.4	728.6	1,292.6	1.3939
Idaho	1,009.4	.4024	31.4	311.2	96.3	151.7	207.3	242.9	361.9	.3903
Montana	797.2	.3179	33.8	222.9	68.4	121.6	174.0	210.3	305.1	.3290
Nevada	1,244.1	.4960	33.4	309.5	121.6	227.0	280.1	305.9	483.0	.5208
New Mexico	1,534.8	.6119	31.3	455.3	151.1	257.3	317.2	353.9	550.2	.5933
Utah	1,738.8	.6933	26.2	638.0	197.8	273.9	308.8	320.3	542.6	.5851
Wyoming	448.6	.1789	31.8	134.8	40.1	72.9	99.6	101.2	167.1	.1802
Pacific	**39,822.3**	**15.8773**	**31.9**	**10,450.9**	**4,357.9**	**7,348.8**	**8,626.8**	**9,037.9**	**14,153.8**	**15.2627**
Alaska	554.5	.2211	29.2	174.8	55.6	112.7	137.8	73.6	190.3	.2052
California	30,353.0	12.1019	31.6	7,970.7	3,430.5	5,727.1	6,470.0	6,754.7	10,593.6	11.4235
Hawaii	1,120.1	.4466	32.7	285.2	120.9	200.6	245.9	267.5	360.0	.3882
Oregon	2,863.5	1.1417	34.6	734.0	264.1	450.7	655.5	759.2	1,112.0	1.1992
Washington	4,931.2	1.9660	33.1	1,286.2	486.8	857.7	1,117.6	1,182.9	1,897.9	2.0466
Total United States	**250,812.0**	**100.0000**	**33.0**	**64,623.7**	**26,504.1**	**43,046.1**	**52,659.8**	**63,978.3**	**92,734.9**	**100.0000**

SOURCE: *Sales & Marketing Management; Budget Planner* (August 19, 1991), B-2.
*S & MM estimates

TABLE 2.2 State and Regional Population Growth 1980–1990

REGION/STATE	POPULATION (thousands)			PERCENT OF U.S. POPULATION		
	1990	1980	% CHANGE 1980–90	1970	1980	1990
New England	**13,285.7**	**12,386.1**	**+ 7.3%**	**5.78%**	**5.42%**	**5.36%**
Connecticut	3,301.1	3,109.0	+ 6.2	1.49	1.36	1.33
Maine	1,238.3	1,134.3	+ 9.2	.48	.50	.51
Massachusetts	6,042.2	5,741.1	+ 5.2	2.77	2.51	2.43
New Hampshire	1,127.2	935.5	+20.5	.35	.41	.45
Rhode Island	1,008.9	949.6	+ 6.2	.47	.42	.41
Vermont	568.0	516.6	+ 9.9	.22	.23	.23
Middle Atlantic	**37,746.7**	**36,779.6**	**+ 2.6%**	**18.19%**	**16.10%**	**15.08%**
New Jersey	7,768.8	7,380.2	+ 5.3	3.54	3.23	3.03
New York	18,065.5	17,526.3	+ 3.1	8.91	7.67	7.19
Pennsylvania	11,912.4	11,873.1	+ 0.3	5.74	5.20	4.86
East North Central	**42,105.4**	**41,800.9**	**+ 0.7%**	**19.76%**	**18.29%**	**16.86%**
Illinois	11,449.1	11,452.7	− 0.3	5.45	5.01	4.54
Indiana	5,556.7	5,512.9	+ 0.8	2.55	2.41	2.23
Michigan	9,323.1	9,287.9	+ 0.4	4.38	4.06	3.70
Ohio	10,864.4	10,813.3	+ 0.5	5.23	4.73	4.41
Wisconsin	4,912.1	4,734.1	+ 3.8	2.15	2.07	1.97

(continued)

TABLE 2.2   *Continued*

REGION/STATE	POPULATION (thousands)			PERCENT OF U.S. POPULATION		
	1990	1980	% CHANGE 1980–90	1970	1980	1990
West North Central	**17,731.5**	**17,281.8**	**+ 2.6%**	**8.02%**	**7.56%**	**7.27%**
Iowa	2,770.3	2,942.8	− 5.9	1.38	1.28	1.14
Kansas	2,491.1	2,374.9	+ 5.0	1.11	1.04	1.02
Minnesota	4,412.0	4,103.6	+ 7.5	1.86	1.80	1.79
Missouri	5,145.1	4,947.9	+ 4.0	2.31	2.17	2.13
Nebraska	1,579.4	1,579.6	N.C.	.73	.69	.65
North Dakota	636.2	657.1	− 3.2	.30	.29	.26
South Dakota	697.4	694.2	+ 0.5	.32	.30	.28
South Atlantic	**44,186.1**	**37,481.6**	**+17.8%**	**15.14%**	**16.40%**	**18.06%**
Delaware	673.2	599.4	+12.3	.27	.26	.27
District of Columbia	604.2	628.5	− 4.0	.37	.28	.24
Florida	13,218.8	10,026.0	+31.8	3.40	4.39	5.66
Georgia	6,586.6	5,536.4	+19.0	2.27	2.42	2.60
Maryland	4,843.7	4,236.8	+14.3	1.93	1.85	1.91
North Carolina	6,693.1	5,930.6	+12.9	2.50	2.60	2.74
South Carolina	3,521.1	3,157.7	+11.5	1.28	1.38	1.37
Virginia	6,265.1	5,399.0	+16.0	2.28	2.36	2.50
West Virginia	1,780.3	1,967.2	− 9.5	.84	.86	.74
East South Central	**15,225.0**	**14,801.0**	**+ 5.7%**	**6.30%**	**6.48%**	**6.12%**
Alabama	4,056.1	3,921.9	+ 3.4	1.69	1.72	1.63
Kentucky	3,687.3	3,698.4	− 0.3	1.58	1.62	1.49
Mississippi	2,575.3	2,540.2	+ 1.4	1.10	1.11	.98
Tennessee	4,906.3	4,640.5	+ 5.7	1.94	2.03	2.01
West South Central	**26,875.3**	**24,096.8**	**+11.5%**	**4.11%**	**5.09%**	**10.49%**
Arkansas	2,358.0	2,311.3	+ 2.0	.95	1.01	.96
Louisiana	4,206.7	4,251.2	− 1.0	1.80	1.86	1.61
Oklahoma	3,143.0	3,059.5	+ 2.7	1.26	1.34	1.30
Texas	17,167.6	14,474.8	+18.6	5.56	6.33	6.62
Mountain	**13,834.0**	**11,692.5**	**+18.3%**	**4.11%**	**5.09%**	**5.50%**
Arizona	3,740.0	2,805.6	+33.3	.88	1.23	1.51
Colorado	3,321.1	2,940.4	+12.9	1.10	1.29	1.39
Idaho	1,009.4	963.9	+ 4.7	.35	.42	.39
Montana	797.2	795.3	+ 0.2	.34	.35	.33
Nevada	1,244.1	822.0	+51.4	.24	.36	.52
New Mexico	1,534.8	1,323.1	+16.0	.54	.58	.59
Utah	1,738.8	1,487.1	+16.9	.52	.66	.59
Wyoming	448.6	482.1	− 6.9	.16	.21	.18
Pacific	**39,822.3**	**32,239.8**	**+23.5%**	**13.13%**	**14.11%**	**15.26%**
Alaska	554.5	410.2	+35.2	.15	.18	.21
California	30,353.0	23,979.8	+26.6	9.87	10.49	11.42
Hawaii	1,120.1	979.1	+14.4	.39	.43	.39
Oregon	2,863.5	2,678.4	+ 6.9	1.04	1.17	1.20
Washington	4,931.2	4,192.3	+17.6	1.68	1.83	2.05
Total U.S.	**250,812.0**	**228,497.1**	**+ 9.7%**	**100.00%**	**100.00%**	**100.00%**

Note: Changes of less than 0.1% are expressed as N.C. (no change).

SOURCE: *Sales & Marketing Management; Budget Planner* (August 19, 1991), A-22.

TABLE 2.3 Metropolitan Areas with the Highest and Lowest Median Household Effective Buying Income, 1990

METRO	1990 MEDIAN HOUSEHOLD EBI	METRO	1990 MEDIAN HOUSEHOLD EBI
Nassau-Suffolk, NY	$49,494	Monroe, LA	$20,020
Middlesex-Somerset-Hunterdon, NJ	48,591	Panama City, FL	19,920
San Jose, CA	45,662	Ocala, FL	19,616
Bergen-Passaic, NJ	44,360	Yuma, AZ	18,485
Bridgeport-Stamford-Norwalk-Danbury, CT	43,866	Gadsden, AL	18,290
Trenton, NJ	43,186	Las Cruces, NM	18,273
Washington, DC	42,929	Brownsville-Harlingen, TX	17,320
Lake County, IL	41,617	Jacksonville, NC	17,221
Anaheim-Santa Ana, CA	41,179	McAllen-Edinburg-Mission, TX	16,224
Oxnard-Ventura, CA	40,320	Laredo, TX	15,915

SOURCE: *Sales & Marketing Management; Budget Planner* (August 19, 1991), A-14

In summary, SIC codes can help you to:

1. discover what industry you're in,
2. define the boundaries of that industry,
3. locate customers and suppliers within that industry, and
4. reach out to other industries thoughtfully and systematically.

SEGMENTATION AND GAP ANALYSIS

The idea of market segmentation is to keep breaking down potential markets into as many "digestible" subsegments as possible. The more you learn about an industry, the farther you'll be able to go. This procedure will help you to isolate opportunity gaps and to see combinations of gaps that may constitute markets. Figure 2.4 illustrates a mind map that "explodes" one segment of the health-care industry into subsegments. This is the kind of thinking we want you to do in Action Step 14. It's another brainstorming activity, so have fun with it.

Entrepreneur Fred Hayes searched for gaps and opportunities by taking a long look at a major, far-reaching trend—the Baby Boom. Fred explains:

"I got into baby bedding by studying the home. What did it need? What would it be like in 5 years? Then I targeted the last wave of Baby Boomers—they were in their late twenties when I founded Sweet Dreams Bedding. My market research showed me that these people were having fewer kids but were spending more money on the ones they did have. That info told me to position my products in what we called "the New Nursery." My first year, sales were spotty. My second year, I grossed over a million dollars. I listen to my customers, and they tell me what they want me to produce. That nursery is my marketplace."

Fred Hayes is a big man, six-two, 210 pounds. He served in the Air Force, where he learned to sew on industrial machines and do construction work, and after that he made good money in commercial construction. An on-the-job accident put an end to that career, however.

Fred was in the hospital three weeks recuperating, and when he got out, the pain in his back told him he wouldn't be able to continue in construction work. Fred was bitter, but he was willing and able to shift careers.

TABLE 2.4   Percentage of Hispanic Population in the Nation's 50 Largest Metros

METRO	% HISPANIC POPULATION	HISPANIC POP. (THOUS.)
Miami-Hialeah, FL	50.0%	982.6
San Antonio, TX	47.8	633.0
Los Angeles-Long Beach, CA	38.4	3,447.9
Riverside-San Bernardino, CA	26.8	731.3
Anaheim-Santa Ana, CA	23.9	586.8
New York, NY	22.4	1,927.6
Houston, TX	21.8	727.5
San Jose, CA	21.2	321.2
San Diego, CA	20.8	532.0
Phoenix, AZ	16.4	356.8
San Francisco, CA	14.8	238.3
Dallas, TX	14.7	383.9
Oakland, CA	13.2	280.2
Denver, CO	13.1	214.1
Chicago, IL	12.4	751.5
Bergen-Passaic, NJ	11.9	152.1
Sacramento, CA	11.7	178.9
Fort Worth-Arlington, TX	11.5	156.2
Newark, NJ	10.6	193.0
Orlando, FL	9.2	102.1
Fort Lauderdale-Hollywood-Pompano Beach, FL	8.9	114.0
Middlesex-Somerset-Hunterdon, NJ	7.2	74.2
Hartford-New Britain-Middletown-Bristol, CT	7.0	79.2
Tampa-St. Petersburg-Clearwater, FL	6.8	144.4
Nassau-Suffolk, NY	6.5	170.4
Washington, DC	5.9	235.3
Salt Lake City-Ogden, UT	5.8	63.2
Cincinnati, OH	5.4	7.9
Boston-Lawrence-Salem-Lowell-Brockton, MA	5.1	93.7
New Orleans, LA	4.3	53.4
Monmouth-Ocean, NJ	3.8	37.7
Philadelphia, PA	3.7	179.0
Milwaukee, WI	3.7	52.6
Portland, OR	3.7	45.7
Rochester, NY	3.2	32.1
Kansas City, MO-KS	2.9	46.3
Seattle, WA	2.8	56.9
Norfolk-Virginia Beach-Newport News, VA	2.4	33.4
Atlanta, GA	2.1	60.3
Detroit, MI	2.0	86.4
Cleveland, OH	1.9	34.5
Minneapolis-St. Paul, MN	1.5	38.7
Baltimore, MD	1.3	30.9
St. Louis, MO	1.1	26.4
Indianapolis, IN	0.9	11.3
Charlotte-Gastonia-Rock Hill, NC-SC	0.9	11.0
Columbus, OH	0.8	11.6
Memphis, TN	0.8	8.0
Nashville, TN	0.8	7.8
Pittsburgh, PA	0.6	11.8

SOURCE: *Sales & Marketing Management; Budget Planner* (August 19, 1991), A-13.

TABLE 2.5   Percentage of Black Population in the Nation's 50 Largest Metros

METRO	BLACK POPULATION	BLACK POP. (THOUS.)
Memphis, TN	41.7%	403.1
New Orleans, LA	35.0	433.3
New York, NY	29.5	2,535.6
Norfolk-Virginia Beach-Newport News, VA	28.7	407.0
Washington, DC	26.8	1,067.5
Atlanta, GA	26.2	762.6
Baltimore, MD	25.9	622.9
Newark, NJ	23.8	433.7
Detroit, MI	21.7	952.0
Chicago, IL	22.3	1,352.6
Miami-Hialeah, FL	20.9	410.6
Charlotte-Gastonia-Rock Hill, NC-SC	20.0	236.1
Philadelphia, PA	19.7	961.3
Cleveland, OH	19.6	358.0
Houston, TX	19.0	632.0
St. Louis, MO	17.3	425.1
Dallas, TX	16.5	429.6
Fort Lauderdale-Hollywood-Pompano Beach, FL	15.8	201.4
Nashville, TN	15.5	153.9
Oakland, CA	14.9	314.2
Milwaukee, WI	14.1	202.6
Indianapolis, IN	13.8	174.0
Cincinnati, OH	13.2	191.9
Kansas City, MO-KS	12.9	203.9
Orlando, FL	12.6	138.7
Columbus, OH	12.0	167.3
Los Angeles-Long Beach, CA	11.9	1,070.2
Fort Worth-Arlington, TX	11.0	150.3
Rochester, NY	9.7	97.7
Hartford-New Britain-Middletown-Bristol, CT	9.2	104.1
Bergen-Passaic, NJ	9.1	116.0
Tampa-St. Petersburg-Clearwater, FL	9.0	190.2
Pittsburgh, PA	8.2	168.7
Nassau-Suffolk, NY	7.7	200.7
San Francisco, CA	7.7	124.9
Riverside-San Bernardino, CA	7.4	200.5
Middlesex-Somerset-Hunterdon, NJ	7.3	75.1
Sacramento, CA	7.1	108.8
San Antonio, TX	7.0	92.3
Boston-Lawrence-Salem-Lowell-Brockton, MA	6.8	256.6
San Diego, CA	6.8	173.8
Denver, CO	6.1	99.9
Monmouth-Ocean, NJ	6.0	61.0
Seattle, WA	4.2	83.9
San Jose, CA	4.0	60.1
Minneapolis-St. Paul, MN	3.8	94.0
Phoenix, AZ	3.7	79.9
Portland, OR	3.2	39.7
Anaheim-Santa Ana, CA	1.9	46.3
Salt Lake City-Ogden, UT	1.0	11.2

SOURCE: *Sales & Marketing Management; Budget Planner* (August 19, 1991), A-12.

TABLE 2.6   Metros with the Highest Percentage of Households with Incomes of $50,000 or More

METRO	% OF HOUSEHOLDS WITH EBIs OF $50,000 +	1990 MEDIAN HOUSEHOLD EBI
Nassau-Suffolk, NY	49.4%	$49,494
Middlesex-Somerset-Hunterdon, NJ	48.2	48,591
San Jose, CA	44.9	45,662
Bridgeport-Stamford-Norwalk-Danbury, CT	44.1	43,866
Bergen-Passaic, NJ	43.6	44,360
Trenton, NJ	42.3	43,186
Washington, DC	42.0	42,929
Anaheim-Santa Ana, CA	39.6	41,179
Lake County, IL	39.4	41,617
Newark, NJ	39.4	40,296
Oxnard-Ventura, CA	38.1	40,320
San Francisco, CA	37.4	38,826
Manchester-Nashua, NH	36.4	39,598
Oakland, CA	36.0	38,096
Monmouth-Ocean, NJ	35.4	37,880
Poughkeepsie, NY	35.1	38,897
Honolulu, HI	35.0	37,072
Anchorage, AK	33.5	36,633
Boston-Lawrence-Salem-Lowell-Brockton, MA	33.4	36,445
Hartford-New Britain-Middletown-Bristol, CT	31.9	36,477
Portsmouth-Dover-Rochester, NH	31.0	36,373
Santa Cruz, CA	31.0	33,294
New Haven-Waterbury-Meriden, CT	30.3	34,699
Los Angeles-Long Beach, CA	30.3	32,976
Joliet, IL	29.7	37,403
U.S. Total	21.5%	$27,912

SOURCE: *Sales & Marketing Management; Budget Planner* (August 19, 1991), A-8.

"Okay, I was forty-one years old. I had two great kids and a good marriage. I started collecting workmen's comp and looking around for a job, but it soon became clear that no one wanted to hire me.

"That meant I was going to have to work for *myself*.

"I signed up for a seminar in small business. I was a stand-up student, because it hurt to sit for more than 20 minutes at a stretch. But I got the message of small business loud and clear. . . .

" 'Know what business you're in,' the prof said. 'Scrounge up some customers who agree with you. Ask them what products they need and want. Find out what they can pay. Make the product. Ship it. Always pay your bills. And make sure you're pals with your banker before you run short of cash.' "

It was good advice, and Fred took it. Market research told him there was room in the baby bedding business, and he found a job sewing for a mattress manufacturer—to learn the business from the inside. In his spare time he designed a nursery set for some neighbors who had a new baby, and they were impressed. That's how Sweet Dreams Bedding began.

Fred worked out of his home the first year. When orders came in, he hired some help and moved into a small warehouse. As someone else took over the sewing, Fred went into sales. He kept an accurate customer file and was always careful to ask the customers what they liked about his product.

TABLE 2.7   Metros with the Highest (and Lowest) Median Age

RANK	METRO	MEDIAN AGE
1.	Sarasota, FL	48.9
2.	Bradenton, FL	43.3
3.	Fort Myers-Cape Coral, FL	42.3
4.	Naples, FL	41.1
5.	Fort Pierce, FL	40.8
6.	West Palm Beach-Boca Raton-Delray Beach, FL	40.3
7.	Ocala, FL	40.2
8.	Daytona Beach, FL	39.8
9.	Tampa-St. Petersburg-Clearwater, FL	38.9
10.	Fort Lauderdale-Hollywood-Pompano Beach, FL	38.0
307.	Salt Lake City-Ogden, UT	27.4
307.	Brownsville-Harlingen, TX	27.4
307.	Fayetteville, NC	27.4
307.	Grand Forks, ND	27.4
307.	Killeen-Temple, TX	27.4
312.	State College, PA	27.1
313.	Lafayette-West Lafayette, IN	26.9
314.	Bloomington, IN	26.6
315.	McAllen-Edinburg-Mission, TX	26.2
316.	Lawrence, KS	25.9
317.	Laredo, TX	25.5
318.	Jacksonville, NC	24.5
319.	Byran-College Station, TX	24.2
320.	Provo-Orem, UT	22.5

SOURCE: *Sales & Marketing Management; Budget Planner* (August 19, 1991), A-7.

ACTION STEP 15

Decode the secrets of the shopping cart.

Use your new eyes to uncover the life-style of your target customer by analyzing the contents of a supermarket shopping cart. Play detective the next time you're in a supermarket and make some deductions about life-styles as you observe the behaviors of shoppers.

Give each subject a fantasy name, perhaps associated with a product (Susan Cereal, Steve Steak, Eloise Sugar) so that you can remember your insights. What can you deduce about each shopper's life-style? What do their shoes say? Their clothes? What does their jewelry tell you? Or their hairstyle? Put these deductions together with a demographic checklist (sex, age, income, occupation, socioeconomic level), and then decide how many of these shoppers are potential target customers for your business.

Trained marketeers look for a category of buyer known as a "heavy user." A heavy user of apples would eat 20–30 a week. A heavy user of cigarettes would smoke two packs a day. A heavy user of airlines—called a "frequent flyer"—flies 10–30 times a year. Who are the heavy users in your business?

shopping-cart analysis
a process of primary research in which you observe purchases in a supermarket, drugstore, or other mass-market arena

"When you're in the baby business," Fred says, "and especially in the bedding segment, you study birthrates. I spent half my life in the library, looking at SIC codes and census tracts. I knew the Baby Boomers wouldn't have babies forever."

But business is funny. The second year Fred discovered that although young couples were having fewer children, they were spending a lot more money outfitting the children they did have. This gave Fred the clue that he should expand into coordinated nursery items—pillowcases, dust ruffles, and coverlets that go together.

" 'Trends are like customers,' my small business prof used to say. 'You can spot some of them by standing outside and staring through the window. But others don't show up until you're in business, working and sweating away, wondering whether or not you'll make it.' "

Action Step 15 can help you make some informal judgments about the marketplace. **Shopping cart analysis** is another window through which you can view the market.

Key Points from Another View

WINNING THE RACE

Striving for excellence should be the premise of all your endeavors, and the following 11 rules should guide you toward that goal:

1. Believe in yourself—belief in yourself keeps you on course and focused; it sets you up for the win.
2. Learn to motivate others to believe in you—excite others with your ideas.
3. Be a decision-maker—putting off decisions opens you up to failure.

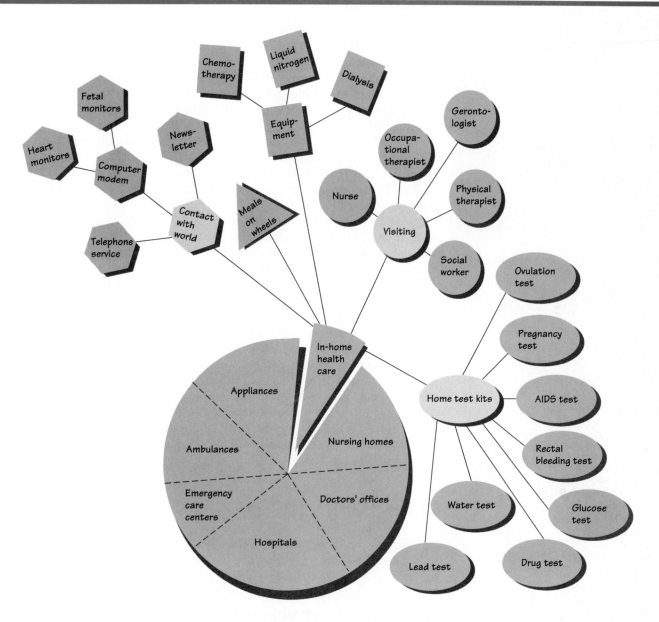

FIGURE 2.4   A mind-map analysis of just one segment of the health care industry. Use mind maps to explore *your* industry.

4. Set goals and objectives—make a list of goals and establish a time frame for each.
5. Don't quit—quitters never win; winners never quit.
6. Take a leadership role in your business—whenever the opportunity arises, be a leader.
7. Be informed—read professional publications that cover your field and related business.
8. Be an observer—watch and listen to successful people in your field.
9. Conduct yourself in a professional manner—be your professional best at all times.
10. Be a risk taker—success means taking risks.
11. If you fail, try again until you win—successes are cumulative; failures are not.

From: "Winning the Race," by Lyn St. James, *Entrepreneurial Woman,* July/August 1990, 128.

ACTION STEP REVIEW

10 Travel back in time and observe a marketplace of the past. How has it changed?

11 Define your business and test your definition by reaching out beyond the classroom.

12 What's new? What's hot? What's cooling down?

13 Assess the life-style of your potential target customer by walking its neighborhood.

14 Have some fun with segmentation and gap analysis.

15 Decode the secrets of the shopping cart using your new eyes.

SUMMARY

A trend is a direction of movement. For example, the trend of our present civilization is away from the smokestacks of the Industrial Age toward the computers of the Information Age. An easy way to start studying trends is to see what is happening in big business—since it is highly visible—and then move on to your own arena—the neighborhood, nearby shopping malls, Main Street, your trade association, your supermarket.

Two tools will help you chart trends: looking around with "new eyes" (that is, playing marketplace detective), and applying the life-cycle yardstick to products, industries, and so on. A life cycle has four phases: embryo, growth, maturity, and decline. Before you open the doors of your small business, you need to be aware of what phase your product is in. For example, if you think there's easy money in selling microcomputers, you need to know that this industry is now maturing. If you want to install security products, you need to know that this industry is between the embryonic stage and the growth stage. If you're thinking about opening a toy store, you need to know that the toy industry is mature and seems to be on the decline (see news articles on what happened at Mattel), and that you'll have to steal customers from other people.

Just for fun, select three to six businesses at random—for example, a foreign auto repair business, a restaurant–bar, a flower shop, a bedding manufacturer, a travel agent, and a computer school—and determine their life-cycle stages. While you're doing that, remember what happened to the railroad industry in the United States. Is the same thing happening to some of the smaller firms you know because they're failing to see what business they're really in?

Information on trends is all around you—on the freeways, in the stores in mid-December and after Christmas, in the headlines and classifieds, at government agencies, in the many trade associations. This information can give you the big picture if you know how to seek it out.

THINK POINTS FOR SUCCESS

◀ The most valuable tool you can use for charting trends is the four-stage life-cycle yardstick.

◀ The life-cycle yardstick helps you find a growth industry, decide what business you're really in, and discover gaps and segments that are promising.

◀ Once you know what segment you're in, you can focus on market research with new eyes.

◀ Try to latch onto a trend that will help you survive (in style) for the next 10–15 years.

◀ Trends don't develop overnight. The signs are out for all to read, months, and sometimes years, in advance.

REFERENCES

Akey, Denise, ed. *Encyclopedia of Associations*. Vol. 1, National Organizations of the U.S.; Vol. 2, Geographic and Executive Index; Vol. 3, New Associations and Projects. Detroit: Gale Research Co., Annual.

Coffee, Gerald. *Beyond Survival*. New York: G. P. Putnam Publishing Group, 1990.

Boyett, Joseph and Henry Conn. *Workplace 2000: The Revolution Reshaping American Business*. New York: NAL-Dutton, 1991.

Contacts Influential, 13132 Magnolia Street, Suite B, Garden Grove, CA 92644; 714-539-2032. [Publishes metropolitan-area business directories that takes off from SIC codes and lists firms by zip code. It names key individuals and gives telephone numbers. Currently covers the following metropolitan areas: Los Angeles County, Orange County (Ca.), San Diego County, San Francisco Bay Area, Denver, Kansas City, Minneapolis/St. Paul, Seattle/ Tacoma, Tampa/Orlando, Vancouver, and Calgary. Plans to expand into many other metropolitan areas.]

Davis, Stan and Bill Davison. *2020 Vision: Turbocharge Your Business Today to Survive in Tomorrow's Economy.* New York: Simon & Schuster, 1991.

Davis, Stanley. *Future Perfect.* Reading, Mass.: Addison-Wesley, 1987.

Dychtwald, Ken. *Age Wave: Choices and Challenges for Our New Future.* New York: Bantam, 1990.

Entrepreneur, monthly magazine. 2392 Morse Avenue, Irvine, CA 92714-6234.

Gale Directory of Publications, Detroit: Gale Research Co., Annual. [Good starting point for running down trade associations.]

Handy, Charles. *The Age of Unreason.* Boston: Harvard Business School Press, 1991.

Inc., monthly magazine. 38 Commercial Wharf, Boston, MA 02110.

Journal of Small Business Management, quarterly magazine. Bureau of Business Research, West Virginia University, P.O. Box 6025, Morgantown, WV 26505-6025.

Kanter, Rosabeth. *When Giants Learn to Dance: Mastering the Challenge of Strategy, Management and Careers in the 1990s.* New York: Simon & Schuster, 1990.

Krugman, Paul. *The Age of Diminished Expectations.* Cambridge, Mass.: MIT Press, 1990.

Market Guide. New York: Editor and Publisher (annual). [Provides market data for more than 1,500 U.S. and Canadian cities where a daily newspaper is published. Gives info on location, transportation, population, banks, climate, shopping centers, retail stores, etc.]

Merriam, John E., and Joel Makower. *Trend Watching: How the Media Create Trends and How to Be the First to Uncover Them.* New York: AMACOM, 1988. [An elaborate system for tracking media decisions to cover news. Uses Naisbitt as a whipping boy. Might be helpful to investors.]

National Trade and Professional Associations of the United States. Washington, D.C.: Columbia Books, Annual.

Ohmae, Kenichi. *The Borderless World: Power and Strategy in the Interlinked Economy.* New York: Harper Business, 1990.

Peters, Tom. *Thriving on Chaos: A Handbook for a Management Revolution.* New York: Knopf, 1987.

Rand McNally Commercial Atlas and Marketing Guide. Chicago: Rand McNally, Annual.

Slocum, Ken. "The Sun Belt Gains Manufacturing Jobs as Nation Loses Them." *Wall Street Journal,* April 1, 1988. [The Sun Belt has more manufacturing jobs—over five million since the slump of 1984–1987; the Rust Belt has fewer—down 392,000 to 7,701,700. Across the nation, we've lost 382,000 manufacturing jobs, mostly because of foreign inroads. It's a grim picture, because manufacturing creates other kinds of jobs. North Carolina now has 30% of its jobs in manufacturing.]

Standard and Poor's Register of Corporations, Directors, and Executives. New York: Standard and Poor's Corporation, Annual.

Survey of Buying Power. New York: Sales and Marketing Management Magazine, 1991. [S & MM publishes supplements to its magazine that are extremely helpful to the small business owner. We like the *Annual Survey of Buying Power* (August) and the *Budget Planner* (May). If your library doesn't carry these, you can inquire at the S & MM office, 633 Third Ave., New York, NY 10164-0563.]

Thomas Register of American Manufacturers. New York: Thomas Publishing Co., Annual. [If you're wondering whether your invention has already been invented, check the Thomas catalogs of manufacturers—complete with product descriptions, photos, and so on.]

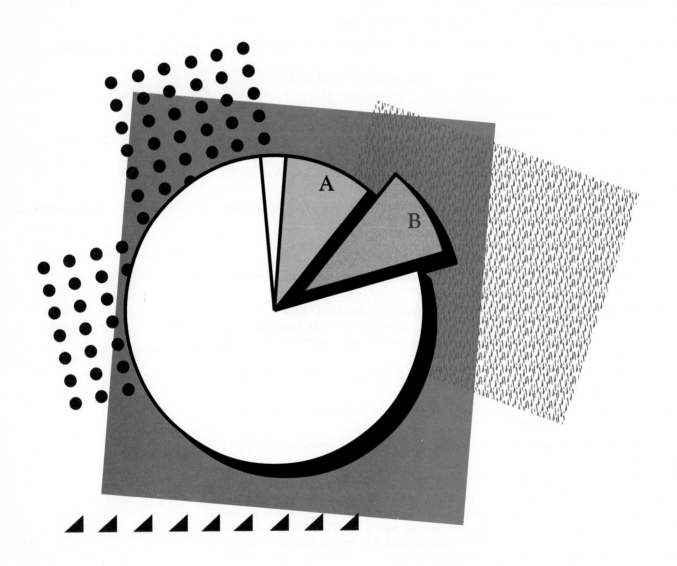

FIGURE 3.1
Chapter 3 will help you prepare part B of your Business Plan, "The Market and the Target Customer."

3 Power Marketing

▲ ▲ ▲ ▲ ▲ ▲ ▲

Learning Objectives

- To mesh your personal business objectives with one of the many opportunities in the marketplace.
- To understand that your business objectives provide a positive and unique thrust to your business.
- To narrow your industry research until viable gaps appear.
- To gain insight into hidden pockets of the life-cycle by using an industry chronology.
- To understand how problems can be turned into opportunities.
- To combine demographic (population) data with psychographic (picture of a life-style) data to produce a customer profile.
- To identify heavy users of your product or service.
- To brainstorm creatively.
- To use a matrix grid for blending your objectives with your research findings to produce a portrait of a business.
- To explore the fun of power pricing.

FUTURE FOCUS

Now that you have matched your aptitudes and values with emerging opportunities, you should be overwhelmed with the wealth of opportunity. This chapter will help you funnel and focus on the best options for you — now and in the next century.

ACTION STEP PREVIEW

16 List your business objectives.

17 Research your favorite industry.

18 Identify three or four segments that look promising.

19 List problems that need solutions.

20 Brainstorm for solutions.

21 Mesh possible solutions with your objectives by using a matrix grid.

22 Narrow the gaps and see your target customer emerge.

23 Try your hand at power pricing.

power marketing
seven-step process by which you select a market opportunity corresponding to your strengths and objectives.

As you head for one of the doorways to small business, you may notice that you feel weighted down with information. That's part of life in this Age of Information. Opportunities exist that were unheard of five years ago, and the speed of change is awesome. If you've done the research suggested in Chapter 2, you're probably experiencing information overload. That's understandable. In spite of the fact that you're a creative person and wound up and ready to charge, unless you live—vigorously—for two hundred years, you'll never be able to follow up on all the ideas you have.

What you need is a filter system, something like a wine press or a Moulie Mill, that kitchen machine that turns apples into applesauce. You have all this wonderful information and all these super ideas. To turn them into a business, you need a sifter. You need power marketing.

WELCOME TO POWER MARKETING

Power marketing is a tool that will help you exploit gaps—market segments—in the marketplace. It connects your skills to your research. It shows you what new skills you need to develop. It aims the power of your mind at a particular segment of small business.

Power marketing has seven steps (Figure 3.2). If you've been doing each action step as you move through the book, you're ahead of the game now. Here's a quick preview of the steps in power marketing:

1. Identify your business and personal objectives.
2. Learn more about your favorite industry.
3. Identify three to five promising industry segments.
4. Identify problems that need solutions.
5. Brainstorm for solutions.
6. Mesh possible solutions with your objectives.
7. Concentrate on the most promising opportunity.

At this point, you have just begun to plan. The marketplace lies open in all its excitement and confusion. The most important thing is not to lose your momentum. Momentum is related to confidence, and confidence helps you to win.

Power marketing is like a huge funnel equipped with a series of idea filters (Figure 3.3). You pour everything into this funnel—your goals, personality, problems, hopes, fears, industry data—and a viable business idea drains out at the bottom. Carrying out this process gives you the knowledge of where you're going. And that is *power.*

To illustrate how power marketing works, we've developed a case study that will lead you through the seven steps. The case study also introduces an important concept—teamwork.

Meet the Info Team

Three principals, friends from college, teamed together to explore business opportunities in some segment of the computer industry. They chose computers because they all had experience with different systems, and also because computers would continue to play a major role in shaping the future. While it was obvious to the three friends that opportunities were to be had in information and computers, they needed to narrow their focus and find a niche suitable for their goals, needs, and personalities. They were

1. LIST YOUR BUSINESS AND PERSONAL OBJECTIVES.
2. RESEARCH YOUR FAVORITE INDUSTRY.
3. IDENTIFY 3-5 PROMISING SEGMENTS.
4. LIST PROBLEMS THAT NEED SOLUTIONS.
5. BRAINSTORM FOR SOLUTIONS.
6. MESH POSSIBLE SOLUTIONS WITH YOUR OBJECTIVES BY USING A MATRIX GRID.
7. CONCENTRATE ON THE MOST PROMISING OPPORTUNITY.

FIGURE 3.2   The seven steps of power marketing.

smart people, quick, educated, gifted in their current professions. They still needed a systematic process for locating gaps in the marketplace.

Before we describe this process and how they used it, let's introduce the three friends:

Friend A—an advertising copywriter with a B.A. degree in English and minors in art and philosophy. Her experience included work at Apple in Silicon Valley and at Microsoft in Seattle. She was an expert with programs for the

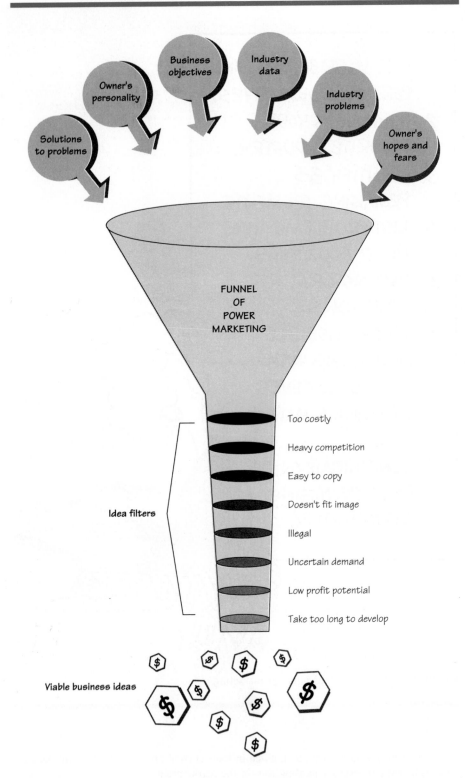

FIGURE 3.3   We can think of power marketing as a huge funnel that contains a series of idea filters.

Macintosh and had used desktop publishing to print books of poetry for some of her friends. She loved editing. Her greatest joy in life was consulting with a writer on a manuscript or a colleague with a problem.

Friend B—a helicopter pilot with military training. His background included a college degree in political science. His dream was to go into politics. He loved parties, which he labeled "bashes." He was very inventive by nature and had designed and sold three Quest-type computer games.

Friend C—a teacher and a commercial artist with a college degree in painting and computer graphics. In college, she worked part time at the campus computer store. As an adult, she married a man who owned a computer store, where she was responsible for the training.

IDENTIFYING OBJECTIVES

All members had extensive experience in owning and operating small businesses. Because of this, they knew very well that their first task was to list their **business objectives**.

The team argued a long time, but they finally agreed on nine objectives that sounded like heaven:

1. **Psychological Rewards**   They wanted to build something, to plant a seed, to watch it grow.
2. **Teamwork**   They wanted to be a part of something bigger than they could accomplish as individuals. Each member of the team had strengths and weaknesses. With luck, blending, and balancing, the team could be greater than the sum of its parts.
3. **Money**   They wanted to see a respectable return on their investment (ROI), a minimum of 25 percent per year.
4. **Safety**   They did not want to lose money.
5. **Growth Industry**   They wanted to find a booming segment of a growth industry.
6. **Time**   They knew that getting a business up and running takes a year at the very least. They decided they wanted a business that would make money in three years or one they could sell in five years for $20 million or more.
7. **Key People**   They wanted to attract the best people in the field.
8. **Fun, Adventure, Excitement**   From experience, they knew that starting a small business, even in a growth or glamour industry, would involve hassles, problems, and expensive surprises. So they decided to make sure their business would be one with which they would also have some fun.

That's why they chose the information industry. What industry will *you* choose? Action Step 16 will help prepare you for this decision.

INDUSTRY RESEARCH

As you searched for trends in Chapter 2, you probably found a dozen industries that seemed interesting. Now it's time to explore one of those industries in more depth. The industry that interests you the most might be genetics, robotics, entertainment,

---

business objectives
measurable goals a business is trying to reach

growth industry
an industry whose annual sales growth is considerably above average

---

ACTION STEP 16

List your business objectives.

What do you want from small business? Money? Fame? Job security? To be your own boss? Freedom to explore the marketplace? Control of your own destiny? Or maybe you just want to be a president.

Think back to the forces that made you interested in small business in the first place. What were those forces? Where were you when you first thought about owning the store? How have circumstances changed your goals?

You probably won't have trouble writing down objectives, but if you do, flip back to the notes you made for Action Step 4 and to your skills analysis (Action Step 8).

List everything you want, even if it seems unreasonable or is embarrassing to you. This is your personal list, after all, and you will sift through the ideas later.

food service, travel, education, publishing, retailing, construction, small manufacturing, or information; it should be something that looks interesting to *you*.

As you move into your favorite industry, collect information from your previous action steps. For secondary data, visit the library for a look at periodicals like the *Wall Street Journal, Inc.,* and *Entrepreneur* and at other, general business or news sources. Most libraries are equipped with computer data bases that will help you with your search. In addition, you can check through the *Reader's Guide to Periodical Literature* or the more specific *Business Periodicals Index.* What you're looking for is an accurate picture of trends in the industry that interests you. You need to learn what's breaking, what's cresting, and what's cooling down.

To focus on your industry, break down your search into categories such as life cycle, speed of change, history, competition, recent industry breakthroughs, costs of positioning yourself, target customers, and so on. Later, after you have gathered the data, you can use these categories as idea filters for sifting information through the power marketing funnel.

For example, using the life-cycle yardstick will sharpen a first look at any industry. When you're reading a newspaper and you see a headline that says CBS TRIES TO SHED STODGY IMAGE IN PRIME TIME—BUT CAN IT BE HIP?, you make three fast-reflex judgments. First, the industry is entertainment. Second, the segment is network television. Third, the shows are in the mature phase, on their way to decline.

And when you're driving down the street and you see a shopping mall being renovated, you know that the face-lift is an attempt to shove the mall back from a mature or decline phase into a growth phase. The point of all this is to find an industry segment where there is room for growth.

A second helpful category is **competition**, which we'll be analyzing in detail in Chapter 5. Competition varies with each stage of the life cycle. Using competition as an idea filter can save you years of grief.

A third category that might be helpful is the concept of the industry **breakthrough**. What is there in your industry or segment that really hums? Remember the first computers? They filled large rooms and ran on punch cards. The first industry breakthrough was the printed circuit. The second one was the microchip. And the third? Or picture yourself as a film director during the era of silent movies. What would have been your reaction to hearing Al Jolson in *The Jazz Singer*?

What breakthroughs are occurring in your industry? Does your business idea capitalize on the latest advances in technology and imagination? Put this kind of thinking into Action Step 17.

competition
a contestant in your arena who is fighting you for business

breakthrough
a new way through, over, under, or around an obstacle

IDENTIFYING MARKET GAPS

Now let's get back to our Info Team. Let's follow them through the process of industry research and see how they analyzed their data.

After gathering their research, the Info Team decided to focus on the changing role of the microcomputer within the information industry and to attempt to list some problems that need solutions. Here's what they found:

Life Cycle   The hardware keeps changing. From the simple microcomputer of the early eighties we've moved to numbers—286, 386, 486 indicate more power, speed, and sophistication—and to names like Quadra that smack of space-age mathematics.

New models with more power and more speed still push older models off the shelves, but you don't have to buy a system from Businessland, or even a computer store. Assemblers are everywhere. A computer technician in Telluride, Colorado, can assemble a personal computer for you, an IBM compatible with parts purchased at discount warehouses in St. Louis and Connecticut. The machine will have more capability at less cost to you, and the technician will still make money.

All this speed shortens the life cycle. Friend A kept her first computer, a Mac 512, for 7 years. It was user-friendly. She named it "Miss Macavity." When she upgraded to an LC, it went out of date in a matter of months. The newest versions of Microsoft Word and Quicken, a bookkeeping program, took ages to print a single page.

Friend B, a numbers wizard, missed the good old days of Supercalc, an early spreadsheet program. To run Lotus for Windows, or the newest version of D-Base or Quattro Pro, he had to buy a new machine, faster, with more disc space and more RAM (Random Access Memory).

The same thing happened to Friend C when she wanted to do desktop publishing that included better graphics. Because she worked at a computer store, she was current on all the possibilities in both hardware and software. Every time she decided on a system, something better would come along to delay her decision. If Friend C, who kept up on computers through trade magazines, found the industry mind-boggling, what about your average user in the street?

Friend A's dad, a journalist, was in distress because of the rapid changes in the industry that tossed good products onto the junk heap. (A junk heap, or second-hand retailing, is one clear sign of an industry in the mature phase.) When his dot-matrix printer stopped working, he decided to purchase a laser printer. But his word-processing software, an early version of Easy Writer, would not drive a laser. The company that made Easy Writer was out of business—Friend A's dad had been busy working, so he hadn't kept up—and all his data files (articles he was turning into a book) would have to be converted to a new program.

"When my dad tried WordPerfect," Friend A wrote, "he found it confusing, with simple things like a block move buried under the edit-copy function. So he's back with his old program and a used dot-matrix printer that he bought secondhand from a techie down the block."

(Problem: how to make use of this rapid life cycle, in which perfectly good products fall out of use, leaving customers unhappy and bewildered.)

Competition   Easy Writer, the program, used by Friend A's dad, lost market share to the survivors in the word-processing niche of the software market, like Microsoft Word and WordPerfect. A decade ago, WordStar was the bellwether word processor. If you go into a bookstore trying to find a WordStar manual, you won't find one.

At the consumer end, people want a product that works. When he lost support for Easy Writer, Friend A's dad, a journalist accustomed to this era of mergers and takeovers, understood what was happening. But that did not stop him from longing for the good old days when he could keep working with the same equipment and not take valuable time from his writing to learn a new set of skills.

Mergers and acquisitions make headlines in the business pages, but the competition between Apple and Microsoft, which resulted in a lengthy lawsuit, made the five o'clock news across the country. This major corporate battle was waged over icons like Apple's trash-can symbol, which act as one symbol in the graphics-driven interface between the user and the machine. On the screen of the Macintosh, when you want to delete a file, you drag it with the mouse down to the lower right-hand corner, where you drop it on top of this little trash-can symbol. Poof, it's gone.

Apple's lawsuit charged that the trash can and other icons were protected by copyright. A court decision in mid-1992, in favor of Microsoft, sent company stocks soaring.

(Problem: while the big boys are fighting for their share of the marketplace, what happens to customers like Friend A's dad?)

Industry Breakthrough   The biggest industry breakthrough in computers in the past few years is cheap memory. Friend B's Uncle Max, who was squeezed out of the marketplace by the Japanese competition, called chips toothpicks. "They were making them like toothpicks," Uncle Max said. "I went over there, saw their factories. They were using robots to do most of the work. Back home, I was paying good wages and my workers still staged a walkout. Overseas competition killed my business."

ACTION STEP 17

Research your favorite industry.

What industry really attracts you? What's out there that has a magnetic pull that you cannot resist? To help you get started, recall what you discovered in Action Steps 12 (What's New? What's Hot?) and 14 (segmentation, gap analysis) and dive in. Also, think aboutwhat you discovered when you interviewed small business owners in Action Step 11.

A good idea at this stage is to remember the American railroads and stay wide-angle in your views. Look at genetics, robotics, entertainment, food service, travel, education, publishing, the auto industry, retailing, construction, small manufacturing, information—anything that looks interesting.

After you've decided on "your" industry, research it like crazy. It might help to organize your research into categories like life cycle, speed of change, history, competition, recent industry breakthroughs, costs of positioning yourself, customer base, and so on.

If you're working alone, it will help to write your industry overview. If you're working with a team, you'll save yourself some confusion if everyone writes an overview, sharing his or her perspective with the others.

As a result of cheap memory from microchips, computers can get smaller while still having huge memory-storage capacities. As an offshoot of this huge capacity, program designers are able to write bulkier programs while they try to make the computer of the future so user-friendly that it's cuddly. Between the machine and the user is an interface. Lots of users find DOS (DOS is an acronym which stands for Disc Operating System), the main interface, to be clumsy, scary to use, and downright user-UNfriendly. Apple's Macintosh, small and compact and icon-driven, was an early industry break-through designed to solve this problem of UNfriendliness. But the Mac was slow. As Friend C's husband, the computer retailer, said: "You spend a lot of time watching that little old wristwatch. Our customers hate that. It reminds them of how much time they're killing just sitting there."

The latest attempt to solve the problem of the UNfriendly machine is a graphical user interface called Windows. Windows, which tries to turn an IBM computer or IBM clone into a Big Mac with turbo power, is a program controller that runs on top of DOS. Windows is made possible by hard drives enlarged by cheap memory.

The first hard drives, 10 megs, have ballooned to 120 megabytes, 200, 330—which seems like a lot until you load it up and watch Windows and the Windows applications gobble up space. Friend B found a paint program he liked for his IBM clone. The pro-gram wasn't expensive, just over a hundred dollars at the local discount software palace, but loading all fifteen discs onto his hard drive took 37 minutes and used up 3.3 mega-bytes of memory. "You just sit there," Friend B said, "and watch it eat."

Because of cheap memory, the biggest industry breakthrough that the three friends could remember, instructions on how to run the computer are embedded in the pro-gram itself, as well as in a handy manual. The idea is that you teach yourself how to use a new program, using an onscreen tutorial that guides you through. The docu-mentation, the printed booklet that accompanies the discs, looks great on the page. But when you hunt for a specific task—how to set margins in Microsoft Word, for example—you don't look under "margins."

"Microsoft has a number you can call," Friend B said.

"It's busy a lot," Friend A replied. "And my dad hates to ask for help. He's a loner. He has his pride."

"I hear you," Friend C said.

"Dad thinks that the only reason for the documentation is as a registration device."

"What kind of registration?"

"When you buy a software package, you have a registration number. You need the number to identify yourself as a buyer when you call the software company for support."

"Because of the computer pirates," Friend B said. "Now why didn't I think of that?"

"Because you're a techie," Friend A said. "You can figure things out for yourself."

"Hey," Friend B said. "Thanks. I needed that."

(Problem: how to take advantage of these twists and turns in the computer industry.)

Industry research will give you an overview of what's happening in the segment you have chosen. As you write down what you learn, do not be overly concerned with reaching final decisions. Nevertheless, you will probably feel yourself drawing closer.

Follow That Customer

When you write your Business Plan, you'll need to explain why you have chosen a particular market segment (gap). If you have chosen a promising segment and have communicated your excitement about it, you'll have developed a "hook" for the banker or venture capitalist who will read your plan.

The secret to focusing on gaps is to find a target customer, a person who needs a particular product or service that you could provide. Then you profile your target customer (we do this in detail in the next chapter), and that profile becomes one of your idea filters.

The Info Team made a few quick decisions that helped them to focus on a particular segment of the information industry.

"Okay," Principal A said, "we've done our research. Tons of the stuff. But what we haven't looked at is *people*. Who's using computers today? What are they using them for? Where do they work? How old are they? What are their problems, their needs?"

These questions helped the Info Team to develop their first customer profile, and doing that led them to a different market.

After looking hard at the information industry, the team drew some conclusions (see Figure 3.4):

Hardware production was out; too much competition.

Software writing/creation was possible, especially in the graphics segment, which was still in the growth phase.

Software users complained about the difficulty of getting up and running on applications software.

The hot growth area was desktop publishing, which combines graphics with text.

The biggest gap seemed to be in education and training.

Brainstorming began. Words flew around the room as the team identified computer users: "Businesspeople!" "Students!" "Educators!" "How about engineers and the CadCam?" "Secretaries!"

The next step was to rough out some customer profiles. One obvious problem was computerphobia—the fear of computers that many people feel. Another was the learning curve—it takes several days to get going on a piece of complex software. So the team did some primary research. They attempted to learn who's afraid of computers and who needs to get going. By doing this, they identified two target customers: Customer A and Customer B. Here are their profiles.

CUSTOMER A	CUSTOMER B
Where employed: in an office; clerical or analytical position	Where employed: at home or in a small office
Sex: female	Sex: male, 55%; female, 45%
Age: 20–55	Age: 30–60
Education: high school, limited college	Education: some college
Uses computer: at work	Uses computer: at home; small office situation
Income: $22,000	Income: $30,000 plus
Main computer use: word-processing, number-crunching	Main computer use: desktop publishing
Motivation to use computer: helps with workload; status symbol; in order to keep job or get a promotion; professional development	Motivation to use computer: joy of creativity; control; speed; superior reports; potential competitive advantage

Now it's your turn to focus on the segments within your industry and spot some that look promising. Complete Action Step 18.

computerphobia
fear of the tools of the Information Age

software
the information base that tells computer hardware what to do

ACTION STEP 18

Identify three or four segments that look promising.

Now that you're hip-deep in your industry, scrutinize segments where you think you could survive and prosper. It's time to begin to profile your target customer.

Prepare a combination demographic–psychographic checklist to help you explore target markets. Include items for evaluating:

Demographic data—age, sex, income, family size, education, socioeconomic status, place of residence, religion, political affiliation, and so on.

Psychographic data—occupation, life-style, buying habits, dreams, interests and leisure activities, ambitions, and so on.

Or, if you're going after a commercial/industrial market, use company size, type of industry, number of employees, location, departments of large companies, and so on.

Tailor your checklist to make it provide a thorough profile of your target customer.

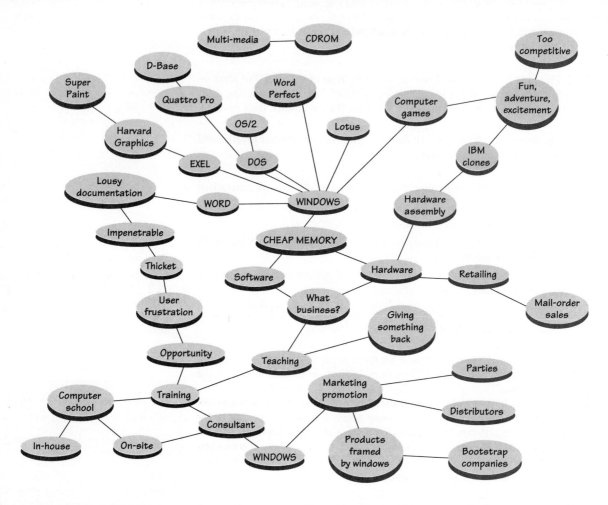

FIGURE 3.4 By segmenting the information industry, the team was able to identify the biggest gap with the greatest growth potential.

IDENTIFYING INDUSTRY PROBLEMS

After you have identified at least two major target customers, you need to identify **problems** that exist in the industry. *Turning problems into opportunities* is the key to small business success.

problems
turn them into opportunities

The Info Team made a list of problems they identified in their industry. It soon became obvious to them that some problems are common to many industries.

1. Product distrust   More people were using computers than ever before—word processing had replaced typing, and businesses were using desktop publishing to upgrade their presentation graphics—but new problems had emerged because of cheap memory.

Cheap memory allowed software writers to produce bulky software that failed to deliver on promises made by advertising and promotion. Let's say you buy a program that promises to sharpen up your graphics, but you can't make it work. You consult the manual, which is written in a language you can't understand. When you call the company for support, they log you on at the end of the line of callers while they play music at you. Waiting burns up long-distance dollars.

2. **Speed of change**   Just as you get used to a system, something better comes along. You study the possibilities—the industry term for this is *configuration*—and while you are deciding, or coming up with the money, something else enters the marketplace. This speed is confusing.

3. **Conditional support from software makers**   They're trying to help. Or they're trying to look like they're helping. And if you do get through to a help line at the company that made your product, the people are knowledgeable and pleasant. They really try. But at many software manufacturers, help is conditional on your ID number. Without it, software pirate or not, you won't get help.

4. **Minimal support from retailers**   Friend C, who's the trainer in charge of lessons on software and hardware for her husband's store, admits they can't afford the time it takes to do really careful teaching. Salespeople are great at sales but not so great at pacing learners through the steps. If you want good teaching, you have to hire good teachers.

5. **Mounting buyer resistance**   Friend A knows several users like her dad, who have decided to stick to an old applications program, one that they can manage, and not venture forth into a world of new-fangled gimmicks. "It's like my Volvo," her dad says. "It's got 175,000 miles, and I'm gonna keep getting her fixed and drive her the rest of my life."

6. **It's like we're living in a movie**   With so much to learn—TV, print, the changing world—buyers feel inundated by information. The computer should help us manage the information. Instead, it spews out more than we need. The documentation, which buries directions for simple tasks under stuff we don't need to know, mirrors this situation in miniature. Remember *2001: A Space Odyssey*, the movie in which the computer HAL got out of control because he wanted total control?

We're there, in the movie.

Action Step 19 will help you to see opportunities in *your* industry segment.

BRAINSTORMING FOR POSSIBLE SOLUTIONS

After listing the problems, the Info Team had mixed emotions. On one hand, they were pleasantly surprised at the depth of the problems. On the other hand, they were slowed by the fact that solutions were not bobbing to the surface. They decided to brainstorm.

Brainstorming is a process used by many groups—think tanks, middle management, small businesses, major corporations—to generate fresh ideas. The goal is to come up with lots of ideas, some that may seem far out or even erroneous, and then, as momentum grows, to see where concepts develop. The key to brainstorming is to reserve judgment initially so that creativity is not stifled.

What follows is a recap of a brainstorming session held by the Info Team as they began to transform problems into business opportunities. As you read, consider not only the information you gather but also the process involved.

Before they began, the three friends listed ideas for businesses that had come to them during the earlier steps of the Power Marketing process. Friend B, for example, wanted to start a company to design computer games, and go into head-to-head competition with Nintendo. Friend C, the graphic artist, said she could certainly help with the artwork. "You're a writer," Friend B said to Friend A. "You could write the copy."

ACTION STEP 19

List problems that need solutions.

When you surveyed your friends in Action Step 14 you were approaching the list of problems you need to develop now. The difference is that the problems you are seeking now are those that are unique to the industry you've been exploring.

Follow your success with Action Step 14 and get together with some people who know something about your industry. Ask them for input and write down everything. Use this input to develop your list.

Each problem you identify multiplies your opportunities to prosper in your segment.

On a flip chart, Friend A wrote down "Design Computer Games."

"Here's another," Friend B said. "Microsoft is the big player. Let's take them over." Friend A wrote it down: "Take Over Microsoft."

For a half hour, they transferred their ideas—game design, leveraged buyouts, a night commando raid on the Japanese microchip industry, software manufacture, hardware assembly, retailing, training end-users, marketing, parties for promotion and politics—onto the flip chart. Friend B, who was turning into a mad inventor, wanted to design a computer program that boiled all election data down into a single voter, who then made the decision on who became president.

"Time for a break," Friend A said.

They took a break. When they came back, Friend C flipped to a clean sheet on the chart, and proceeded to draw a mind map. Mind mapping, sometimes called clustering, is a sketch or diagram using words inside bubbles printed almost at random and then connected by lines to form units. (For an example, see Figure 3.4.)

As Friend C developed her mind map, five areas for a business emerged: hardware manufacture; software manufacture, including game design; retailing (both hardware and software); training, taking advantage of the speed of change in the industry, which left users in the dust; and marketing and promotion of software products.

Further refining of areas of the mind map brought training and marketing into the foreground, with the production of hardware and software receding into the background. With IBM and Apple and Microsoft battling it out, why get into that?

Retailing went into the background because Friend C wanted a change. The business belonged to her husband; she wanted something for herself.

Excitement built in the room as the ideas flowed, and soon all three friends were standing at the flip chart, adding their ideas and amendments to the mind map. As the brainstorming session wound down, they had identified two areas to explore.

The first area was computer training, taking up where the software makers left off, taking advantage of the impenetrable language of the software manuals. They could start their training in the computer store, renting space from Friend C's husband. They could branch out from there to do on-site training in businesses and corporations.

The second area was marketing and promotion. Friend A, who had worked for Microsoft, had watched Windows grow and finally blossom. "I haven't made a count," she said, "but it seems to me that half the software being developed today rides on the frame of Windows. These are small companies, bootstrap operations run by dreamers whose basic business skill is writing a check to pay a supplier. They have no idea about image, target customers, or promotion."

"You could consult," Friend C said. "You love that."

"I'd love to do the parties," Friend B said.

There was a silence. "So," Friend A said, "we've got two options that look pretty good. How do we decide?"

"How about a matrix," Friend B said.

"A what?"

"It's a way of weighting what you really want. I learned about it from one of my inventor buddies. He called it a matrix."

"Let's try it," they said.

It's helpful to summarize after a brainstorming session so that you can identify the most useful ideas. Let's summarize what happened in this session:

1. Using the mind-mapping device, the team identified problems and possible solutions

2. All ideas were good ideas.

3. The two ideas that looked good were computer training and software marketing and promotion.

4. Could they do them both at once? Or would one have to go on the back burner?

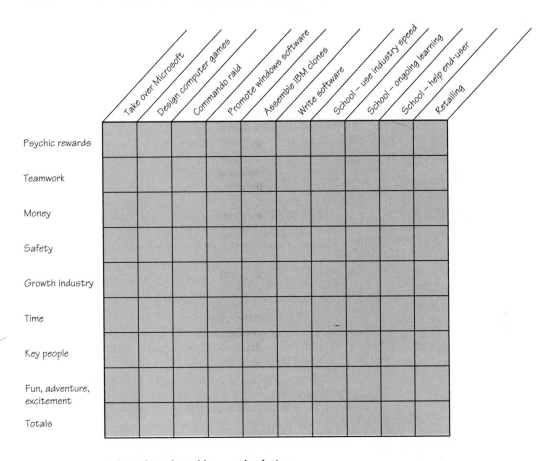

FIGURE 3.A Using a Matrix to mesh goals with problems and solutions.

Now that you understand what brainstorming is and what it can accomplish for a business, give it a try with your own business. Assemble your partners or some friends and go to it. Action Step 20 gives you some directions.

MATRIX ANALYSIS

Whereas some people like to use lists or mind maps for arriving at conclusions, others prefer a more systematic method. A **matrix grid** can provide the desired structure. After you have brainstormed some possible solutions, you need to improve your focus on them and evaluate them. The matrix grid in Figure 3.A helped the Info Team do this. At their next meeting they took a vote on each possible solution they'd brainstormed earlier.

matrix grid
a screen through which ideas are passed in order to find solutions

When the numbers were tallied, the team saw that:

Buying out Microsoft was a fine idea. They would all be rich and powerful. They could achieve their dreams and spend money to save the environment.

ACTION STEP 20

Brainstorm for solutions.

Okay, here's where you need to get creative. Dig out the list of problems in your industry that you made in Action Step 19. Every problem can be turned into an opportunity.

You'll generate better ideas in the long run if you just let your imagination roll. Don't be concerned with a lot of logic and reason—not at this stage; just let your mind run and leap. You might begin with a quick overview of what you know so far and then slide into possible (and impossible?) solutions. A cassette recorder can be useful.

Have fun.

---

psychological cushion
a unique, untouchable rung on the ladder in your target customer's mind

---

ACTION STEP 21

Mesh possible solutions with your objectives using a matrix grid.

A matrix analysis will help you focus, especially if you're working with a group and you have diverse objectives to satisfy. If you prepare a large grid and put it on the wall, all members of the team can participate.

Down the left side, list the objectives you brainstormed in Action Step 16. Along the top, list the possible solutions you came up with in Action Step 20. Select a rating system to use for evaluating the match of each possible solution with each of your objectives. It could be a ten-point scale or a plus-zero-minus system:

$$plus (+) = 3$$
$$zero (0) = 2$$
$$minus (-) = 1$$

When you've rated all of the combinations, find the total for each column. The totals will indicate your best prospects. The rest is up to you.

Friend B was the only vote for a night raid on microchip makers in Japan. He was an action guy who liked to keep busy.

Hardware assembly was out; software production could wait.

Everyone liked the idea of being in a business where you threw lots of parties. Promoting software companies felt like a good gap to investigate.

While they were investigating software promotion, they decided to start a computer school. They were all familiar with Windows, so they'd use it as a headliner concept for the school. Friend B knew Quattro Pro, and he'd always thought of being a teacher as well as a commando. They would start out by renting space from the store owned by Friend C's husband. Friend A, who was not wild about teaching, would coordinate activities while she researched the market for on-site Windows training in the business world. As trainers, they would have to:

Solve problems. People with computer systems have problems. Businesspeople have problems to solve and tasks to perform. The computer can take the load off. All you need is an open mind and the right software.

Provide clarity. Software documentation can be confusing. The school would devise a super-clear, streamlined, space-age teaching system.

Offer speed. Businesspeople are in a hurry, and time is money. Could the school teach software in a month? A week? A day? A half-day?

Build a psychological cushion. The founders would start a club. Once the students had taken a course, they'd be a club member for life and entitled to take the course over again at no charge.

Charge reasonable fees. Studies showed that businesspeople would pay $100 a day to learn software.

Be fun. If clients have fun learning, they'll relax and learn more. If they learn more, they'll spread the word about the school.

Now prepare a matrix grid to help you focus on the best course of action. Action Step 21 tells you how to do it.

Taking Stock

What have you learned about power marketing? Before you answer this, take a minute out to rethink what you want to achieve in small business. If you feel a little uneasy about how fast you've run the last couple of laps, perhaps it's because you haven't yet identified your industry. It's time to take stock.

What is your industry?

_____

What is your segment?

_____

What are some opportunities for you?

_____

_____

Now, before you lose the feel for the process of power marketing, try sketching out a rough picture of your journey through your favorite industry. If it doesn't feel like home, you should sense it now. Action Step 22 will help you to do this.

POWER PRICING

Think of the costs of producing a heart valve. The valve may contain only twenty dollars' worth of parts, but the amounts spent for developing and marketing it are staggering. But how much is it worth to the patient?

If you own a computer and you need a piece of software to solve a particular problem, how much are you willing to pay to solve the problem fast? How much did you pay for the cup of coffee or the soda you had with your lunch yesterday? How much did it cost to produce that beverage and get it to the café?

Look at the history of American business in the last 50 years. How many firms grew because they knew the value of their product/service in the eyes of their customers? How many made it big because they offered benefits?

The power-pricing way is to think of user benefits.

> The Info Team realized that the seats in their school were "perishable." Each unsold seat would represent unsold inventory that could never again be sold. Therefore it was important that they fill as many seats as possible and give the early impression of a big, successful operation. This philosophy had direct implications for their decisions about pricing.
>
> All pricing decisions hinge on the answer to the question "What is it worth to the customer?" A business or institution that has just invested $5,000 to $500,000 for computers might be willing to pay $100, per class, or even $1,000 per class, to get its employees trained as quickly as possible. A market survey showed that prices in the competition ranged from $59.00 per day—for classes in an old-fashioned classroom situation—to $500 for on-site training at the workplace. Because their equipment and training tools would be state-of-the-art, the team felt that they could test the market at $99 per day. This would make their break even point 3.5 students. To fill the classroom, however, they decided to offer two classes for the price of one.
>
> The strategy worked. Their classes filled. Many customers commented, "You people are too cheap!"
>
> Within nine months, they had moved the daily price to $199 and had dropped the two-for-one deal. In the slow seasons—summer and the month of December—they again offered the two-for-one special when attendance slacked off. They tested some classes at $299 and others at $399. Those prices worked for special programs that were not yet being offered by competitors.
>
> Because most classes at the new school were booked a month or more in advance, the team knew when it was time to offer a special to keep the classroom full—so as to minimize their "perishables."

Power-pricing decisions are not easy. Action Step 23 will help you begin testing the market for your own power pricing.

Key Points from Another View

Part I:
SELLING POINTS

If the thought of selling yourself, your company, and your product scares you, you're not alone in your fears. Selling is a national phobia. But you can overcome that and boost your sales skills by following these tips:

1. Appearances count—physical appearance is one key to success in sales.
2. Watch your mouth—although your appearance carries a lot of weight in any sales situation, a professional demeanor is equally important. As an

---

ACTION STEP 22

Narrow the gaps and see your target customer emerge.

All right, you've found your segment and you've tested parts of it. Now you need to stay with this segment until you know whether or not it will work for you.

One way to keep concentrating is to make a simple sketch or list that sums up what you've learned so far. Figures 3.2 and 3.4 may help guide you. Use a large sheet of paper, because you need to consider all the important things you've learned here. Begin with your objectives and move on through a review of what has happened.

After you've done your sketch, identify the gap in your industry that looks most promising for you.

ACTION STEP 23

Try your hand at power pricing.

Review the pricing policies of other people who sell your product or service. Do their customers respond to freebies? Discounts? Guarantees of outstanding service? Doing business with a firm they trust?

Call or visit three firms that offer products or services similar to yours. Attempt to learn which factors affect their pricing policies.

Then define *your* product and its benefits to the user. Check your prices against the competition's. Make every attempt to measure the value of your particular product or service. Is it faster, cleaner, more compact? How much more might the customer pay for such benefits? Ask for feedback on your product or service. Study all of your production and marketing costs. What margins do the resellers need? What is it worth to the customers?

Consider all of these things and establish a powerful price.

entrepreneur, your behavior should show that you take your business seriously and appreciate the professional relationship that might develop.

3. Be prepared—when dealing with potential clients, you'll benefit from a working knowledge of the company you're approaching. Learn about the business—what it's all about, what kinds of things they have done in the past, and what it might be seeking from you. Before you overwhelm clients with your ideas, listen carefully to their needs.

4. In the spotlight—your ability to present your case professionally is the key. Sell yourself by giving a little extra. Go the extra mile with clients. Go out of your way to be accommodating. After an appointment, always follow through with a letter or phone call.

5. Building a reputation—exposure is key to getting a business off the ground. Get your name known in the community. In addition to selling your product or service, you must also "sell" your company's reputation and image.

Entrepreneurs are often good at sales because they are passionate about their businesses. As an entrepreneur, you are responsible for your own success. It is important to build credibility, reputation, image, and professionalism, all of which are critical to your company's growth and success.

From: Christine Forbes, "Selling Points," *Entrepreneur,* July 1990, 96–100.

Part II:
HYPE YOURSELF

Marketing yourself and your business successfully is tricky. While marketing theory may seem incomprehensible, marketing practice can be straightforward and simple. The key is to recognize consumer needs that are not being met. Then you present a credible message explaining how you will meet these needs. Here are some key points to help you do the job:

1. Creating credibility—convincing others of your credibility requires three elements:
   a) knowledge—you must be seen as knowledgeable about the product or service you are promoting.
   b) trust—you must appear capable of providing expert information about your product or service.
   c) Other-orientation—customers must believe you will act with their best interests in mind.

2. Selling your image—to enhance your credibility and message, you need to create an image. Image determines how people view you, how much they value you, and whether they are attracted to you.
   Before you can create your image, ask yourself these questions.
   a) What does your business do?
   b) Who is your target audience?
   c) What do you want from your audience?
   d) What needs does your business meet? What problems does it solve?
   e) How will it benefit the consumer psychologically?
   f) What makes your business different from the competition?

3. Get the message across—once you have pinpointed your image and message, you need to project them continually.
   Here are six marketing rules to help you get across your image in speeches or informal talks:
   a) appearance—use your attire and posture to project confidence, competence, and status.

b) nonverbal behavior—make direct eye contact with your audience to reinforce your message.

c) verbal behavior—use simple, direct language, without jargon; speak clearly and concisely.

d) involvement—listen carefully; tailor your message to your audience's needs and interests

e) illustration—your language should create pictures in the audience's mind and appeal to the senses.

f) control—stay in control by deciding ahead of time exactly what you're going to say and how you're going to say it.

In today's competitive world, every entrepreneur must vie for the customer's attention. How you choose to create, project, and market your business image can mean the difference between success or failure.

From: Signe A. Dayhoff, Ph.D., "Hype Yourself," *Entrepreneurial Woman*, May/June 1990, 60–62.

SUMMARY

You've found the industry that interests you. You've applied the life-cycle yardstick to learn what stage the industry is in and how long you've got to make your business go. If your skills don't exactly guarantee success, you're sure of at least three things: you know where to acquire the skills you need, you know how long it will take to get them, and you're having fun exploring the marketplace.

To illustrate the seven steps of the power marketing process, we've followed the progress of a three-person team that founded a successful software school—a training facility that teaches people how to use complex computer programs in one day.

Step 1   The team held a group brainstorming session to develop a list of their business objectives. All members had read *Megatrends 2000* and were interested in the massive changes occurring in society because of the computer. Their brainstorming was very creative, and it helped weld them together as a team.

Step 2   Using three interlocking concepts—life cycle, competition, and industry breakthrough—the team researched the industry. Since all three had experience with computers, they focused on the computer segment of the information industry. Looking at life cycles of hardware and software reminded them that products whiz in and out of the marketplace with lightning speed. Ten years ago, the life cycle of a piece of hardware could be 6 years. Today you're lucky if it lasts 6 months before some competitor brings out an improved model. The big industry breakthrough was cheap memory, the invasion of the microchip from Japan, which changed the nature of software, which allowed the design of Windows, the latest attempt at a user-friendly interface between man and machine.

Step 3   Despite the apparent chaos in the industry, the team saw two promising segments: training and marketing. Game design, which had its appeal because of the inventive artistry of two of the team members, was shelved for the moment. The gap they found in education was produced by a combination of speed (products changing quickly) and complexity (programs with promise that failed to deliver). Their target customer would be businesses, both large and small, with interests in getting the most out of their software. The second promising segment, marketing, grew out of their investigation of all the new companies that had grown up around Windows. These companies needed help getting their products to market.

Step 4   The team listed industry problems—user frustration, poor documentation, minimal support from manufacturers, minimal support from retailers, and so on.

Step 5   Using lists and mind maps, they brainstormed for possible solutions—take over Microsoft, design computer games, help companies market better products, found a computer school.

Step 6   The team built a matrix grid that helped them evaluate the match of each of their objectives with each possible solution. Thus they discovered which solutions would satisfy which objectives. They could see that a software school would satisfy the most objectives.

Step 7   With the project firmly in mind, they began to define the chief element of their survival—the target customer.

As the customer profiles emerged, the team was able to do some market testing with power pricing. That's what you should do, too.

THINK POINTS FOR SUCCESS

◣ Be bold about brainstorming your business objectives. Who knows, some of them may take you through a doorway you didn't know existed.

◣ Build your business around your likes and your strengths.

◣ Power marketing aims the power of your mind at a particular segment of small business.

◣ The customer is always right.

◣ The target customer can always be profiled.

◣ Looking at businesses for sale is a great educational experience, but leave your checkbook at home. (We'll cover the tactics of this in Chapter 10.)

◣ Price according to the value as perceived by the buyer.

REFERENCES

Compuserve, Dialog, Dow Jones News/Retrieval, and The Source are a few of the major database distributors you can access with a PC and a modem. All of these services can provide you with an excellent way to do initial and ongoing research for both general and specific data. Costs are relatively low.

Elster, Robert. *Small Business Sourcebook.* Detroit: Gale Research, 1987. [A guide to more than 4,000 federal files and databases available at low or no cost.]

FIND/SVP, a major business-research company which will provide answers to questions, as well as locate very specific information for a fee. New York, NY (212) 645-4500.

Gershman, Michael. *Getting it Right the Second Time.* Reading, Mass.: Addison-Wesley, 1991. [Discusses the creative remarketing strategies for over 40 bestselling brands.]

Jennings, Diane. *Self-Made Women: Twelve of America's Leading Entrepreneurs Talk about Success, Self-Image, and the Superwoman.* Dallas: Taylor Publishing Co., 1987.

Kotler, Philip. *Marketing Management,* 6th ed. New York: Prentice-Hall, 1988.

Laumer, J. Ford, et al. *Researching Your Market.* Washington, D.C.: U.S. Small Business Administration, Office of Business Development, Management Aids No. 4.019, 1988.

Madden, Michael, ed. *Small Business Start-up Index.* Detroit: Gale Research, 1990. [Classifies information by type of business. Excellent source, periodically revised.]

Mancuso, Joseph. *Mancuso's Small Business Resource Guide.* New York: Prentice Hall, 1988. [Excellent sourcebook for references, with good selection of government listings.]

Morgan, James, and J. Jeffrey Morgan. *Cracking the Japanese Market: Strategies for Success in the New Global Economy.* New York: Free Press, 1991.

PREDICASTS, a research firm that publishes statistics. For a fee, provides specific research studies. Publications are available in major libraries.

Sobel, Robert. *The Entrepreneurs: An American Adventure.* Boston: Houghton Mifflin, 1986.

Wasserman, Paul, ed. *Small Business: An Information Sourcebook.* Phoenix, Ariz: Oryx Press, 1987.

APPENDIX 3.1 • Model Action Step 17: Research your favorite industry.

Professional desktop publishing for the graphics arts industry has magnetic attraction for me. From Action Step 17, I know it is emerging as a hot new technology, one that makes present typesetting equipment wholly obsolete.

For my own part, I have been involved in some portion of the graphics arts industry for the past 25 to 30 years. At present, I have three state-of-the-art page composition programs:

1. Front Page Plus, a program for precision control over one- and two-page documents that need careful layout and typography.
2. To supplement Front Page Plus, for which there no longer is support, I purchased Aldus Corporation's PageMaker PC program. It provides more precision control over single-page documents than Ventura Publisher.
3. Ventura Publisher, a fast generator of large documents, which offers good control over layout but lacks some of the finer points of typography.

All three page composition programs support PostScript, as does Microsoft Word 3.1, my choice of word processors. At the office, I have an IBM PC and HP LaserJet. I have become proficient on this "brain damaged" configuration, producing business documents that are superior to those produced on a Penta-Mergenthaler configuration and a Berthold forms production system.

Graphics Capabilities
At this stage, I am just beginning to become proficient in the graphics programs. Until recently, these programs were so rudimentary that I preferred to use clip art or custom art from a commercial designer or artist. My plans call for acquiring a Desk Scanner later on, perhaps this year if cash flow will support the purchase.

Life Cycle
This is definitely the growth stage of desktop publishing's life cycle. Until the late '80s, there were not enough elements in place to sustain it on an advanced or professional level. We are still awaiting major refinements in graphics programs. They are coming. So are scanners with better capabilities in reproducing halftones (photos).

Speed of Change
The speed of change is so rapid that it is almost physically impossible to keep up with the state of the art. Every week brings startling new announcements. Most of my weekends are devoted to incorporating significant developments into my *Graphic Arts Guide to Professional Desktop Publishing.* My present goal is not to publish this comprehensive report as a book, but rather, to sell it as an up-to-date report as of the week that I print out the document in Ventura Publisher. The list price will have to be at least $100, perhaps $250. That will be a small price to pay when planning the investment in a $20,000 desktop publishing system. My greatest known competitors in this arena readily concede that my knowledge of page composition software is superior to theirs. I know from seeing their printed output that my talents in typesetting and page design are superior to theirs, also.

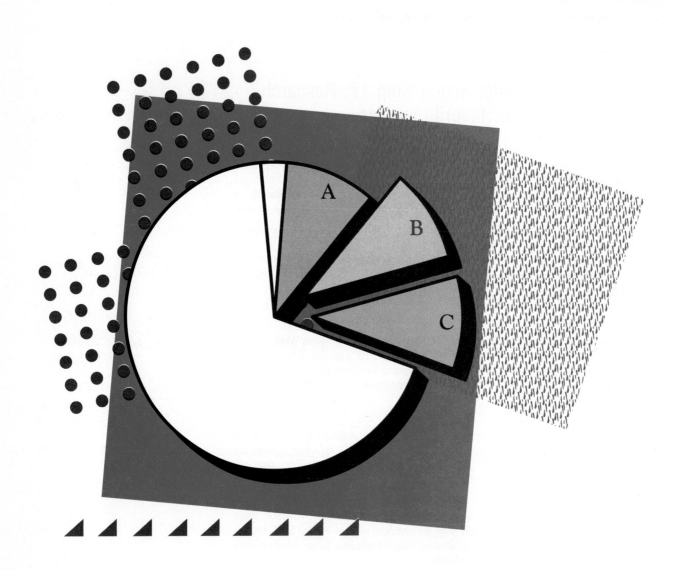

FIGURE 4.1
Chapter 4 will help you complete parts B and C of your Business Plan, "The Market and the Target Customer" and "The Competition."

4 Profiling the Target Customer

▲ ▲ ▲ ▲ ▲ ▲ ▲

LEARNING OBJECTIVES

● To understand that your key to survival in small business is the target customer.

● To develop your customer profiling ability into a reflex.

● To use your intuition to forecast what will happen in your industry.

● To use simple observation techniques to gain insight into consumer behavior.

● To simplify the messages you communicate through your business.

● To discover how popular magazines aim at the target customer.

● To match your target customer with what he or she reads, watches, and listens to.

● To know the heavy users of your product or service.

● To recognize the market, the target customer, and competitors who are about to surface.

● To gather critical market input from target customers through field interviews.

FUTURE FOCUS

The best ideas and products are worthless unless you have customers. This chapter will guide you to the discovery of where your target market (customers) is and how it can take you into the twenty-first century.

target customer
a person or type of person that has the highest probability of buying your product/ service

Flashback: Hefner sights his target customer and builds an empire.

It's the fifties. Americans in crew cuts are listening to a senator named Joe McCarthy. Ike is in the White House. Actress Rita Hayworth has astounded the world by marrying an Arabian prince. A young woman named Marilyn Monroe is about to become an important sex symbol. The movie houses are showing newsreels of a costly "police action" on a remote Asian peninsula called Korea. The Soviets are getting ready to launch Sputnik. Color TV is only a rumor on Madison Avenue.

And in snowy Chicago, a frustrated young writer named Hugh Hefner is sitting at his kitchen table, probing the future with the new eyes of an entrepreneur.

What did Hefner see when he looked out his kitchen window? He saw his **target customers**, lots of them, who would make him rich, famous, and envied around the world. Hefner believed his target customers would build him an empire.

And they did.

The entrepreneur with a dream can learn a lesson from Hugh Hefner's story. Your product will, no doubt, be much different from his, but study how he learned about his target customer, and use that knowledge to help *you* own the store.

THE POWER OF PROFILING

Hugh Hefner's message hasn't changed since the fifties. "Play," he says. "Play your ears off. You owe it to yourself to play. Play hard and never grow old, and find a playmate to keep you young."

Of course, anyone could say that, man or woman, of any age. But Hefner was careful to aim his message at a target audience that was superreceptive. Here's a quick profile of his target customer:

HEFNER'S TARGET CUSTOMER*

SEX: male

AGE: 18–34 (75%)

EDUCATION: some college (52%)

BACKGROUND: upper middle class

INCOME: $45,000 annually [adjusted to 1992]

MARRIED: 50%

RESIDENCE: urban/suburban (64%)

PURCHASING HABITS:

consume more than 7 drinks per week	25%
consume more than 10 drinks per week	18%
consume more than 15 drinks per week	12%
own 3 or more cars	17%
heavy smokers	21%
purchased car new	54%
purchased 7 or more dress shirts	17%
purchased 4 or more pairs of shoes	16%

---

*Material on the Playboy target reader has been adapted from *Subliminal Seduction: Ad Media's Seduction of a Not-So-Innocent America*, by Wilson Brian Key. Prentice Hall, Inc., 1972, pp. 118–119. Used by permission.

Hefner didn't pull these **demographics** out of thin air. He knew how to use secondary sources to help him complete his profile. You can do the same thing to learn about your target customer.

An easy way to understand the power of profiling is to analyze media sources that are aimed at different target markets. For example, what would you find if you contrasted *McCall's* magazine with *Playboy* magazine?

Often, we walk past magazines without giving them a sideways glance. That's unfortunate, because magazines hold the key to many questions about marketing. One way to regard a magazine is as a glossy cover wrapped around some pages of ads and editorial copy. With new eyes, however, you can see that a mass-market magazine exists because it is a channel to the subconscious of a certain type of reader.

That knowledge is power.

What can you learn about target markets, consumption patterns, and buying power from the advertisements in a magazine? Put yourself in an analytical frame of mind. Begin by counting the ads. Then notice the types of products that dominate the ads; these ads are probably aimed at the heavy users of those products. Next, study the models; they are fantasy images with which the target customer is expected to identify, connect, remember. The activities pictured in the ads enlarge the fantasy, and the words link it to real life. A good ad becomes a slice of life, a picture that beckons the customer inside, toward the product.

We took an issue of *Playboy* (it has a carefully profiled reader) and one of *McCall's* (a strikingly different target market) and did a new-eyes analysis. After we looked at the data, we drew a few conclusions. We developed categories as we went along (one of the nice things about **new-eyes research** is that you can expand the model as you collect data). Here is what we looked for:

> demographics
> key characteristics of a group of people—age, sex, income, where they live

> new-eyes research
> marketplace detective work; it's observation with intuition

  total number of ads one-third page or larger

  ads aimed at heavy users (type of products that are advertised the most)

  large ads (two pages or more)

  demographics of models (estimated age, income, and occupation; race)

  male

  female

  main activities depicted

  objects depicted (including mail order ads, if any)

Using the Model—An Analysis of *McCall's*

The total number of *McCall's* ads of one-third page or more was 80. Thirty-six of those were devoted to food, dieting, or eating, which suggests that the heavy users who read *McCall's* not only enjoy food, but they also cook and probably regard cooking as a way to express themselves creatively. Dieting is the escape hatch that attempts to balance any indiscretionary overindulgence in food. Five diet-food ads ran two pages; 21 ran a full page.

The next major product grouping was clothes; there were 2 double-page ads and 8 full page for clothes. After clothes came cigarettes, with 3 double-page ads and 5 full pagers. There were 6 ads for beauty/skin/hair care products, 3 for "intimate" products (bras, pantyliners), 5 for children's products (shoes, cereal, baby food, toothpaste), and 2 for headache pills.

A two-page ad for Kools cigarettes was dominated by a Porsche 928S equipped with a super-duper Blaupunkt audio system. Liquor was not advertised in this issue, nor were cars.

Female models seemed to range in age from their late teens to a couple of women in their late forties or early fifties. All models seemed to be comfortably middle class; none were portrayed as ostentatiously wealthy. All were white.

The major activity depicted was people smiling into the camera. One ad showed the lower three-fourths of a woman talking on the phone in an office as she advertised L'Eggs panty hose. Another showed a slender, slightly perspiring woman drinking Sprite with a background of weights and chrome barbells. In general, the ads with models pictured a world of charm and order, of women in control of themselves. Models were either young and famous, like Brooke Shields and Christie Brinkley, or they were aging gracefully.

Eight men, including Superman, made it into the *McCall's* ad stable: the Marlboro Man, the Barclay's Man, a Mazola Man, three musicians touting Kools, and Bill Cosby, advertising Jell-O. The median age of the men would be somewhere between 35 and 50. The Marlboro Man rides a spirited horse across an autumn landscape. The Barclay's Man lights his own cigarette while he cuts his eyes to the left, where an elegant female hand holds a glass of bubbly. The Mazola man—a husband archetype—is pictured with some apparatus to test blood pressure, suggesting a connection between eating Mazola and living longer. Bill Cosby—the only nonwhite adult in the magazine's ads—is surrounded by children munching Jell-O. (One of the six children is black.)

Conclusions   The objects depicted in these *McCall's* ads relate to the home, the hearth, the happy homemaker. A clean floor tied with a huge red ribbon extols the virtues of Brite. The glory of food is lauded with a plate of fancy spaghetti, cake mixes, frozen pie crust dough, a set of china, a perfect chocolate cream pie, and so on. Mail-order items were scarce. Most items advertised for mail order carried the magazine logo—for example, a *McCall's* pastry cloth set and a *McCall's* tart pan. What does this data tell us?

1. *McCall's* readers are predominantly female, age 19–55, with household incomes around $27,000. They live in metro-suburban areas. A high percentage are married, with children under 18. A high percentage are employed. The percentage of white readers far outweighs other racial groups.

2. The focus of *McCall's* readers is the home. Their adventures occur in the kitchen, when they get creative with food.

3. *McCall's* readers make decisions on lots of small purchases—Moisture Whip Maybelline foundation, Shaklee's Instant Protein, cigarettes, Sizzlelean.

4. *McCall's* readers are object-centered, private about bedrooms and intimate wear. If they dream about escape, they do so briefly, with lots of control. If they use alcohol, they use it sparingly or in secret.

We're on target. These conclusions have been confirmed by material we received from the *McCall's* **display ad department.** The point of our doing this new eyes-analysis is to show you how you can arrive at some exciting conclusions on your own. Let's apply the same kind of analysis to *Playboy* now.

display ad department
department of a magazine or newspaper publisher that can provide market data; it sells and produces "nonclassified" ads

Using the Model—An Analysis of *Playboy*

The issue of *Playboy* we studied contained 292 pages (the *McCall's* we studied had 158), with 79 ads one-third of a page or over, 33 of which were for hard liquor (Scotch, gin, brandy). This corroborates the findings reported in *Subliminal Seduc-*

tion about *Playboy* readers being heavy users of alcohol. Twenty-six of the liquor ads were full-page, 2 of them covered two pages, and 5 were half-pagers. The next cluster came with 22 for electronic entertainment gear—video, audio, camera, stereo, phones, fuzzbusters. There were 8 ads for cigarettes, which ties the *Playboy* smoker with the controlled smokers for *McCall's*. We found 8 ads for clothes and 4 each for perfume, cologne, and diamonds.

The largest ad was a five-page superspread for the newest Nissan "Z" model, a hummer of a car that would seem to guarantee to prolong the buyer's playing life, and suggesting that enough *Playboy* readers can afford a Nissan 300ZX to make advertising it this way worthwhile.

In contrast to *McCall's, Playboy* carried no food ads. The *Playboy* reader's attention is on a world beyond the hearth and family.

Except for a wry, satiric Santa Claus (advertising Crown Royal), the male models appeared to range in age from 25 to 45. Several were portrayed as indoorsy muscletypes working out on expensive exercise equipment. Most of the outdoorsy types wore work clothes, uniforms, heavy boots, and so on, and had mustaches. Female models appeared to range in age from 21 to 30; some were portrayed as girlish flirts and others as elegant, worldly women. In several of the ads, a man appeared between two women, suggesting an abundance of female companionship.

The only product strong enough to cross over from *McCall's* to *Playboy* was Marlboro. In *Playboy,* the Marlboro Man seems closer to us, less romantic, more rugged. He has replaced his *McCall's* horse with a macho calf-rope, symbolic of dexterity and control.

Playboy ads portray more action than *McCall's* ads. Examples include romantic settings at the top of the world (Hennessy cognac), adventure settings in the wilds (Camel), and rescue settings on isolated Arctic ice (Winston). The Gordon's gin ad portray two black models (male pianist, female dancer in white tights) in a tastefully austere, mirrored studio.

Many of the objects depicted in the *Playboy* ads are machines for grown-up play—Toyota trucks, a fire-engine red Nissan, radar detectors, videos, stereos, cameras. They project images of the indoor Good Life at night and the outdoor Rugged Life during the day. Night and day, the *Playboy* reader who can afford it can have the best of all possible worlds.

This issue contained one mail-order ad (800-number included) for Karess sheets. The other mail-order ads offered various products from the magazine—the "Playmate" calendar, "Playmate" and adventure videos, and so on.

Conclusions   We presented demographic data on the *Playboy* reader earlier in the chapter. Our new-eyes research supports the data; it tells us that:

1. The Good Life costs, but it's worth every penny. Female companionship is available if the "playboy" has the bucks. If he can't handle the fire-engine red Nissan right now, he'll have to settle for the tony grey VW Quantum until he can.

2. The *Playboy* reader makes big-purchase decisions—cars, stereos, phone systems, cameras, VCRs. He's a heavy user of hard liquor.

3. The *Playboy* reader spends hefty amounts of money on entertainment—some in his apartment, a lot more out in the playgrounds of the world. (In this issue, snow-covered mountains called to the winter sports nut: "Come and ski. Come and ski.")

4. *Playboy* readers are filled with hopes of achieving the Good Life permanently. Until they do, *Playboy* will line their dreams with products from the Playboy Information Empire.

Lesson from an Information Empire

Play is serious business, and it doesn't come cheap. If a *Playboy* advertiser spends $50,000+ for a full-page ad, the ad needs to generate a million dollars in gross sales—20 times the cost of the ad—for the advertiser to break even. What that means for you as a user of secondary research is that expensive ads are highly targeted. They must hit the target. If they do not, the advertiser takes his or her business elsewhere.

You can benefit from big business's advertising through new-eyes secondary research. Use it often; make it a habit.

You will certainly want to analyze the advertising in a magazine that your target customer reads soon. But first, get a feel for magazine advertising in general. Action Step 24 will help you do this. Have fun with this action step.

MOVING TARGETS: CONSUMERS ON THE LIFE-CYCLE YARDSTICK

What's become of the *Playboy* reader of the fifties? What is he reading today? Where does he live? Does he work, or is he retired? We can be pretty sure that his tastes have changed and that his income has quadrupled. He's probably changed jobs a couple of times. If he plays tennis, he's having trouble with tennis elbow, or maybe a trick knee. He travels more now. The world has changed, and his horizons have shifted dramatically.

What does this mean? It illustrates the fact that the target customer is always moving. There's a lesson in what happened to the *Playboy* empire; the lesson is *change:* watch the target customer.

The age range of *Playboy's* target customer has always been 18 to 34 years. That hasn't changed. The first *Playboy* readers started in the fifties, read the magazine for fifteen years, and then moved on to other magazines. Meanwhile, using the magazine as his cornerstone, Hefner built a diversified empire. What happened to the empire? Troubles developed after 15 or 20 years.

The fifties "playboy," Hefner's original target customer, grew up, perhaps still reading the magazine occasionally, but leaving the empire behind. The magazine, still the cornerstone, has not changed much in the thirty-five years.

In thirty-five years, tastes change and competitors emerge. As the life-cycle diagram in Figure 4.2 shows, *Playboy* magazine has moved from its embryo stage in the fifties to its maturity in the nineties. It's almost as if the Playboy empire has accompanied its target customer through those stages. The Playboy Clubs, which once symbolized male fun and male freedom, have closed their doors. Like much of corporate America, the Playboy empire is downsizing. Along those same lines, the young male reader of the fifties now has more money and more time. He now seeks fitness, a more realistic good life, and life extension.

People who began reading *Playboy* in 1953 at the age of 20 are in their mid fifties today and their magazine is likely to be *Modern Maturity*. With a present circulation of 17 million readers, *Modern Maturity* should soon have the largest circulation in the United States.

Now *there's* a market.

The *Sassy* Strategy

The publishers of *Sassy* have found a big pie. They estimate that total teen spending in 1990 was $57.4 billion. (Marketing data, which takes time to gather, runs a couple

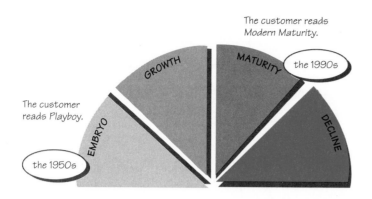

FIGURE 4.2   Life-cycle diagram of the moving target customer.

of years behind the world.) In 1985, for comparative purposes, total teen spending was $49.8 billion. Between 1970 and 1986, the number of teens owning cars tripled. By 1990, 28 percent of teenage girls—*Sassy*'s Target Market—owned cars. That's up from only 7 percent car ownership in 1980. Other ownership numbers: 72 percent of teenage girls own stereos; 86 percent own cameras; 92 percent own a watch; 81 percent own a bicycle. Knowing what your customers own helps you figure out what else you can sell them.

Once you get some data together, it's interesting to look at it in chart form. Figures 4.3 and 4.4 were originally done on a Macintosh computer, using a program called "Microsoft Chart." The bar graph, Figure 4.3, shows spending in billions of dollars by teenage girls, aged 13–19. The pie chart, Figure 4.4, gives the same information in percentage terms.

Use Action Step 25 to conduct some secondary research on your target customer at no cost.

Customer profiles are also available from newspapers and radio stations. For other specific data, you can contact trade associations through the Gale directory, which can be found in most libraries. Get into the habit of profiling. It's your key to success in small business. Box 4.1 gives you some guidelines.

Lessons from the Magazines

Display ad departments spend lots of money digging into the segment of their marketing pie. By tapping into their data base, you can save yourself months of market research. You can find new customers and glean hot ideas.

Just for fun, let's move the magazine life-cycle diagram into the nineties and use the *Playboy* strategy to gather new data in the marketplace. If you check your local newsstand or bookstore, you'll see that several flashy magazines are competing for the same readers. *Sassy* competes with *Elle* and *Seventeen*. *M* competes with *Playboy* and *Esquire*. (See Figure 4.5.)

Let's look for a moment at *M*. This magazines reaches the upscale male, average age 37.4 years, a decade older (and a decade richer) than the *Playboy* reader. The *M* reader is better educated: 92 percent attended college; 30 percent have master's degrees or more. The house owned by the *M* reader is twice as valuable as *Playboy*'s condo. He spends lots of money on collectibles: 32 percent buy one or more paintings a year; 24 percent buy antiques. He likes his plastic: 94 percent of *M* readers

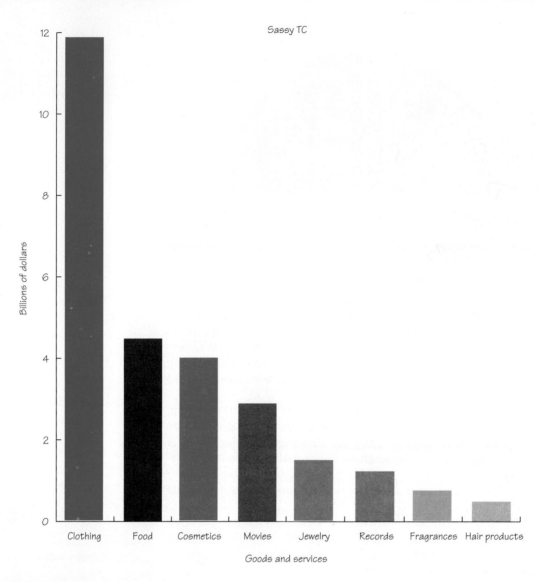

FIGURE 4.3   Where Teenage Girls Spend Their Money

use credit cards. As you might expect, *M* readers are part of the core market for yachts, classical music concerts, live theater, and memberships in tennis and boating clubs. They are users of catering services, tailors, specialty clothing stores, upscale travel agencies, auto detailers, fine restaurants, and the best wines.

For a Fun Profile, Find a Fun Magazine

By now, you've discovered the secret of profiling. What do *Playboy, M,* and *Esquire* have in common? What do *Vogue* and *McCall's,* and *Elle* and *Sassy* have in common? Answering these questions calls for analytical judgment. Marketeers call it

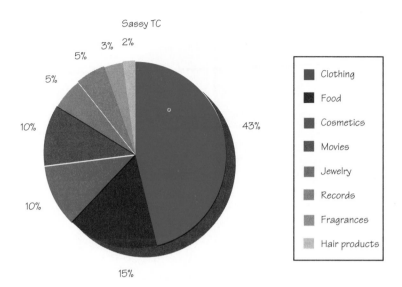

FIGURE 4.4 Spending Patterns of girls, ages 13–19

BOX 4.1   Getting a Handle on Profiling*

You can't profile your target customer too much. Here's a model to follow, from Chapter 8 of *Subliminal Seduction* by Wilson Brian Key.

The average age of *Vogue* readers is in the early thirties, and 72 percent are married. Some, at least the younger ones with high-upward-mobility husbands, work. The majority are married to men with managerial or executive responsibilities who are likely to be older than they. Men tend to hit their earnings peak in their mid to late forties.

A significant portion of *Vogue* readers are in their second marriages; their husbands, in their second, third, or fourth marriages.

The place of children in the life of the *Vogue* reader is curious. Two-thirds of *Vogue* families have no children under 18. This would not seem so surprising if the average age of the readers was over 40. At any rate, children do not play an important role in the typical *Vogue* reader's life.

Vogue readers are well educated: 78 percent attended college; 41 percent graduated. Of their husbands, 83 percent attended college, 64 percent graduated. As to their occupations (which tend to determine life-style, fashions, clubs, travel, sport, and amusements), 35 percent are professionals and 32 percent are executives, proprietors, managers, or officials.

Ninety-seven percent of *Vogue* readers belong to one or more clubs. They entertain frequently with dinner parties, buffets, and luncheons, and they are entertained by others as well; they average 6.4 social engagements monthly.

Adapted from *Subliminal Seduction: Ad Media's Manipulation of a Not-So Innocent America* by Wilson Brian Key, published by Prentice-Hall, Inc.

1950s

1990s

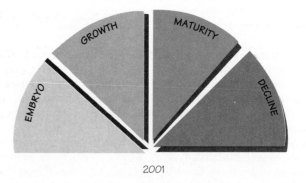

2001

FIGURE 4.5   Fill in the blanks. What magazines will be hot in 2001?

segmentation. You start with large classifications like sex (for example, *Esquire* for men and *McCall's* for women). You go on to age (*Modern Maturity* for seniors). And then you combine sex and age (*Sassy* for young women; *Lear's* for mature women). Then you keep adding layers of classification that leads you to numbers that allow you to make judgments. For example, here's a quick customer profile of *Sassy* readers:

Sassy's Target Customers

Age: 13–19
Sex: Female
Total females, age 13–19: 11.4 million
Employment: 41.9% are employed
Total Yearly Income: $21.7 billion from working; $14.2 billion from allowance
Total teen spending for 1991: $57 billion
Growth: by 2000, the teen population will grow to nearly 26 million

---

MAGAZINE SURVEY REVISITED

How many **general-interest magazines** did you spot on the racks you checked out? How many do you read? How many do you subscribe to? *Life, Look, Colliers, Coronet, Saturday Evening Post*—these were all general-interest magazines: they all aimed at the "general" reader. As you may suspect, they seem to have gone the way of the railroads. Table 4.1 shows you who's surviving in the magazine game these days. As you can see, segmentation means "money grooves."

No one can say if the phenomenon of the highly specialized audience is here to stay. *Saturday Evening Post* and *Life* have been revived, as monthlies. The new *Post's*

> general-interest magazine
> publication directed at a mass audience that crosses demographic lines

---

TABLE 4.1   Magazines, Target Readers, and Circulation

MAGAZINE	TARGET READER	CIRCULATION
D&B Reports	owners/top managers of small businesses with $9 million annual sales	71,000
Car & Driver	male; 34–35; college-educated professional	900,000
Money	middle-upper income bracket; sophisticated	1,100,000
Penthouse	male; 18–34; upper income brackets; college	5,300,000
Cosmopolitan	female; 18–34; middle-income bracket; career-minded	2,500,000
Sassy	99% female; 13–19; fun-loving, sophisticated young women seeking self-image	650,000
Esquire	64% male; 30–49; upper-middle income bracket; fashion, social issues	705,000
M	94% male; 33–49; top executives; 43% single; investments, collectibles, fine food, fine wine	200,000
Modern Maturity	male/female over 50; median age 63.4; family-oriented; socially active; 35% attended college; brand-loyal	17,000,000

circulation is around 700,000—slightly more than *EasyRider*'s—and *Life*'s is 1.5 million. Think about what this means for advertisers.

Modern Maturity data indicates that seniors over 50 control half of the disposable income in the United States. What does this tell you about surviving in the marketplace?

A Different Kind of Target Reader

"Our readers," a publisher of romance novels wrote, "are starved for the good life. Most of them will never see Europe, never eat in an elegant restaurant, never meet anyone famous or important. Their days are spent scrimping, watching the budget, doing dishes and the laundry. Their husbands are indifferent. If our readers work, they have jobs that are dull. They are going nowhere, and they want to read about women who have made it, who don't think twice about what something costs. Our readers live vicariously—they want to have the confidence of someone who has everything!"

Sarah was 52 when her husband died. They'd been married 30 years, and she missed him terribly. Her children lived three thousand miles away in California. They flew in for the funeral, looking fit, tanned, rushed, and happy with their lives. They both invited Sarah to come to visit them soon, which she did. However, after three days in her son's house in a smoggy southern California suburb, she went back home. She decided she belonged in New England.

Sarah grieved for her husband. To stay busy, she began to bake fine homemade pies for the Old New England restaurant down the road. The money helped to pay the bills, which were scary for Sarah. Her husband had always handled the money, and there had always been enough, even with the children, but now it seemed as if the insurance checks wouldn't quite stretch from month to month.

So Sarah baked more pies.

In the tourist season, business was brisk, so Sarah hired a teenage neighbor girl to help her. In a year, she had made enough money to pay all the bills, expand her kitchen, and hire another assistant. Sarah had some extra time now, so she went back to college. Since she'd always loved to read, she decided to take the course, How to Write a Mystery Novel.

Sarah's stories were set locally—old houses, dense forests, small New England towns—and they were pretty good stories. She did eight revisions of her final project before her professor was satisfied. When she was about to give up, the professor said she'd like to send it to a friend of hers in the publishing business in New York.

Sarah was nervous. She's always held publishers in high esteem. She didn't want to be hurt or disappointed.

Surprise—the publisher liked her story! They wanted to publish it, and they wanted to see more.

Sarah sold five mysteries in the next three years. She turned out to be a super storyteller, and she loved sitting at her desk with a fire in the fireplace, spinning out mysteries. She was paid an average of $3,000 for each book—not much, unless you're thrifty, which Sarah was.

Then one wintry November, Sarah's New York publisher broke her heart when he turned down her sixth novel. "The market's terrible for mysteries," he wrote. "Try me again when this has blown over."

Sarah was confused. She didn't understand. Market? What market? The only market she knew was Eldredge's, down the road, where she sold extra pies. Of course, she'd always heard people grousing about the *stock* market, but she'd never paid much attention. Markets were not her cup of tea.

A year passed, and she kept on writing. Two more mysteries were turned down, for the same vague reasons. Now Sarah was nervous. Her expenses in the pie business had increased, and she had a competitor now, a young woman who had just moved there from Boston. She'd come to rely on the money from her books, and that was now drying up.

Fighting back discouragement, Sarah began to study what goes on in the world of publishing. She read *Publisher's Weekly,* a trade journal. She read biographies, books by agents, books by publishers. She did not unearth any secrets.

Then, one day Sarah ran into a woman at the public library. Younger than Sarah, and heavier, she was carrying a stack of paperback romances. With gentle probing, Sarah learned from her that she read as many as ten romances a week and that she belonged to two romance book clubs and a romance readers' group.

"What organization," Sarah thought. Then she began to wonder how many romance readers there might be in New England, on the East Coast, and across the country.

That question was a turning point for Sarah. It directed her to a new set of target readers.

Working with New England diligence, Sarah did some research on the leisure activities of the American housewife. In an obscure marketing journal, she found a 1970 study that said housewives spend almost 70 percent of their leisure time reading. Not mysteries, Sarah thought. A *Publisher's Weekly* study reported that 37 percent of the fiction sold was romance fiction.

This helped to explain what her publisher had been talking about: market means *people.* In publishing, the market is *readers.* She wondered why he hadn't said that in the first place.

Sarah quickly wrote to romance publishers, requesting information on the mechanics of writing romance fiction. Practically immediately she received detailed reader profiles, plot suggestions, and length suggestions for each type of romance—in other words, blueprints for books.

"Our readers," one publisher wrote, "are starved for the Good Life. Most of them will never see Europe, never eat in an elegant restaurant, never meet anyone famous or important. . . ."

Sarah read through all of the material carefully. None of her friends read romances, and she wondered what they'd think if they learned she was writing them. She decided to use a pseudonym. Two days later she began to write her first romance novel, *Amelia Thorn.* A publisher snapped it up. It sold 300,000 copies and made more money in its first print run than all of Sarah's mysteries combined. Her second romance, *Rachel Duncan,* outsold *Amelia Thorn,* and forced her to find an honest lawyer who would help her incorporate.

Sarah's been a **corporation** for two years now. Six young women work for her, baking pies, and she's planning to start her own publishing operation—to do a cookbook called *Sarah's Pies.* One thing she learned from her research on publishing was that the bigger publishers don't like to do small print runs because they're not profitable for them. She regarded that as a market gap.

corporation
a legal entity that stands separate from its owners

Before Sarah finished the pie book, she hired a young man from one of the business schools to do some market research for her. He determined that there would be 25,000 readers for *Sarah's Pies.*

Sarah Routledge had discovered the key to small business.

"I think what helped me the most," she now says, "was discovering that I was in *business.* Because when you're in business, you think about *customers.* All I'd thought about before was pies and books. Customers are the key."

"Finding the right customers is like slicing a pie," Sarah goes on. "You take out only what you need for yourself. You leave the rest for somebody else. If someone comes along and wants the whole pie, then you have a choice—either you move on, or you dig in your heels and fight. The key to business, whether it's baking pies or writing books, is to know who's going to eat 'em or read 'em."

MAKE CUSTOMER PROFILING A REFLEX

We're trying to help you make customer profiling a reflex. If you keep at it, it will continually adjust your focus on the all-important marketplace.

ACTION STEP 26

Profile your target customer and try to identify the heavy users in your industry.

Prepare a checklist that will help you identify your target customer. Include *demographic* factors—age, sex, income level, household size, residence, and so on—and *psychographic* factors such as those described by Arnold Mitchell in *Nine American Lifestyles.* Psychographic factors include such considerations as what a person reads, eats, drinks, drives (What do cars tell you about people's self-images?), does in his or her leisure time, and so on. The more factors you include on your checklist, the better your profile will be—the clearer your picture of the person whose needs you want to serve. Add to your checklist as you continue to think about your TC. (You may want to look ahead to page 83; the VALS onion provides another way to classify life-styles.)

Now that you're deeper into your venture adventure, you'll have more information about the kinds of people at whom you should aim your product or service. Entrepreneurs we have known tell us you should watch for at least three TCs:

1. **Primary.** That's the one you just profiled with your checklist. It's the perfect target customer for your business, and he or she could be a heavy user. (The woman Sarah Routledge talked with at the public library was a heavy user of romance novels.)

2. **Secondary.** This one is not a heavy user, and may not be apparent at first, but is nonetheless "bread and butter." (The word processors in chapter 2 were the Info Team's secondary TCs.) Sometimes the secondary TC will lead you to the "invisible" customer.

3. **Invisible.** This customer appears after you open the doors, after you've mustered up the courage to go ahead and start up.

Think about your TC often. Dream about it. Your target customer is the key to your survival in small business. And you cannot do too many of these profiles.

Box 4.2 presents two contrasting profiles from *Nine American Lifestyles,* Arnold Mitchell's book about psychographics in America. For illustration purposes, we've selected just two of Mitchell's life-styles, "Belongers" and "Experientials." Belongers are outer-directed, whereas Experientials are inner-directed. It might help you to do a comparative chart that will highlight the differences in the two groups' consumption patterns. Read the profiles and then profile your own target customer by doing Action Step 26.

Invisible Customers

Some people go into business for themselves because they can't work for someone else. Some of them are mavericks who don't like to take orders. Others are dreamers who love their own ideas. Still others, like Fred Bowers, have some handicap that keeps them from getting a job with a large firm.

Fred's experience illustrates that customers sometimes "come out of the woodwork."

Fred Bowers had planned to be a career Marine until he was injured in a fall from a training helicopter. He could still walk, painfully, but his military career was over. With a medical discharge in his pocket, Fred looked around for work.

"I'd always loved soccer," Fred said. "I'd been a pretty fair player, and my coaching experience had given me a good understanding of kids. I thought there might be a place for a soccer specialty shop in our community, but before I went for financing I spent a year checking it out."

Fred found eighteen sporting good shops in the area he was interested in. None of them carried a full line of soccer products. When he began profiling his target customers, Fred came up with two easy targets:

Primary target: boys, age 6–17

Secondary target: girls, age 6–12

Household income (both targets): $28,000–$32,000

Socioeconomic level: middle, upper middle

Interest: sports

Then Fred segmented the youngsters into two groups: members of school teams, and members of American Youth Soccer Organization (AYSO) teams.

His description of his target customers was so good that when he showed his fifty-two-page Business Plan to a couple investors, they put up all the money he needed to start up Soccer City. Because of Fred's knowledge of the game, his store prospered. Schools counted on him for an honest deal, and parents of players counted on him for advice on equipment.

"I had thought I'd just be selling," Fred said. "What I was really doing was providing a service."

After he'd been in business a year, a third market began to emerge. The customers in this third group were adults, mostly foreign-born, from places like Great Britain, Germany, Mexico, and South America. They had grown up playing soccer and they loved the game. To them, it was a fiercely fought national sport, and they still liked to play. These heretofore invisible customers would drive 50–75 miles to Fred's shop for equipment they couldn't find anywhere else.

"They didn't show up in my research," Fred said. "If I hadn't opened up, I wouldn't have known about them. Now they make up at least 30 percent of my business. One day they weren't there; the next day, they were. I like that. I like it a *lot*. It makes this whole adventure more interesting."

BOX 4.2   Two Contrasting Target Customer Groups

While you're training your new eyes to zoom in on the marketplace, study these profiles of two very different target customers. *Nine American Lifestyles* analyzes the consumption patterns of nine distinctive customer groups. These descriptions will introduce you to two of those groups.

Belongers. Belonger households are major buyers of both large and compact American-made autos. Important purchase considerations for them are convenience of dealer location, cost of repairs and servicing, and safety features—the last probably reflecting concerns for the family. Exterior styling is relatively unimportant. They prefer American-made cars to imports.

In appliances, Belongers show a higher-than-average level of ownership of freezers and lower ownership levels for dishwashers, garbage disposals, food processors, and microwave ovens. These patterns possibly reflect their preference for doing things in the traditional way, as well as their tendency to live in older homes and rural areas.

Belonger women frequently wear slacks. Slacks appear to be sufficiently ingrained in their life-styles that it shows little relationship with employment status.

Belongers are substantially below average in consumption of all types of alcoholic beverages and regular carbonated soft drinks. A higher-than-average percentage consume fruit juices, as well as regular and decaffeinated coffee.

Experientials. Experiential households have among the highest incidence of ownership of compact, subcompact, and small specialty cars. They are the highest in ownership of, and preference for, foreign cars, and they show the highest ownership of European cars of all VALS types. (Box 4.3 gives short descriptions of the nine VALS types.)

Ownership of dishwashers and garbage disposals is high among this group, as is ownership of recreational equipment. Experiential households are substantially above average in owning camping and backpacking equipment and racing bicycles. In the home, higher-than-average ownership levels prevail for electronic games, and also for prerecorded and blank recording tapes.

Experiential women show an interesting pattern in their clothing preferences. Disproportionately more of them wear jeans, skirts, and dresses. They wear bras less frequently than the other VALS types, perhaps reflecting their "free spirits." Experiential men are among the most frequent wearers of jeans and sport and casual shirts, but they also wear suits more often than average.

Wines, including champagnes, and domestic and imported beers are the favored alcoholic beverages.

Source: Reprinted (with changes) by permission of Macmillan Publishing Company from *Nine American Lifestyles: Who We Are and Where We Are Going* by Arnold Mitchell, pp. 91–92, 132–133. Copyright © 1983 by Arnold Mitchell.

Placing Target Customers on the VALS Onion

VALS is an acronym for *v*alues *a*nd *l*ife-styles, a profiling system developed by SRI International, a Menlo Park, California, firm that specializes in market research. Arnold Mitchell, the author of *Nine American Lifestyles,* has developed an onion diagram that graphically relates the nine VALS life-styles; see Figure 4.6.

Note in the figure that the "Survivors" are at the bottom and "Integrateds" are at the top. Where are Fred's customers on the onion? To answer, study the figure for a moment and then read Box 4.3. After you find Fred's target customers, look for your own. Which part of the VALS onion will buy *your* product or service?

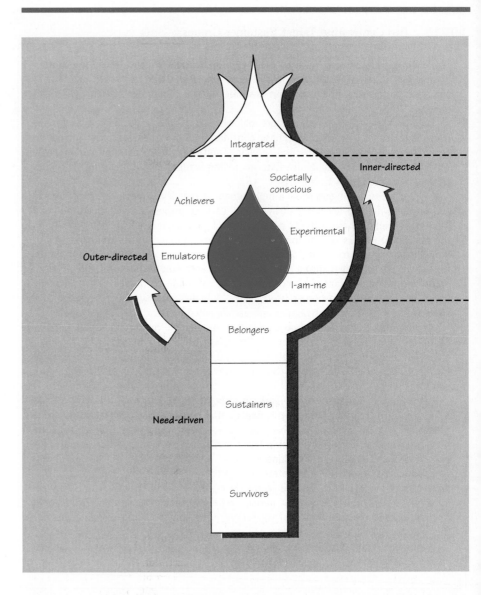

FIGURE 4.6   Where are you on the VALS onion? Where is your target customer? (Source: Adapted by permission of Macmillan Publishing Company from *Nine American Lifestyles: Who We Are and Where We Are Going* by Arnold Mitchell. © 1983 by Arnold Mitchell.)

Portrait of an Integrated   The VALS onion is actually an updated version of Abraham Maslow's "needs pyramid," which tops off with self-actualization. The VALS onion tops off with an individual called an "Integrated." There aren't a lot of Integrateds around—only three million or so, according to Mitchell. This is because it takes a lot of climbing to get there. You can find them on magazine covers, behind CEO desks, and heading up large organizations. Lee Iacocca is an Integrated, and so was Norman Cousins.

One clear portrait appeared in a 1988 issue of *The Wall Street Journal*, which profiled writer-producer-activist Norman Lear, creator of the controversial television show, "All in the Family," which gave us Archie Bunker. In 1985, he and cofounder Bud Yorkin sold Tandem Productions to Coca-Cola for $485 million.

BOX 4.3   Find Your Target Customers Here

Nine American Lifestyles is almost as helpful to the entrepreneur as *Megatrends*. Author Arnold Mitchell, director of the VALS Program at SRI International, gathered data for twenty years before writing the book. Locate your target customer in Mitchell's nine lifestyle groups.

Survivors   Old, very poor, fearful, depressed and despairing, far removed from the cultural mainstream; misfits. There are 6 million Survivors, most of whom are over 65; 77% are female, incomes are below $7,500, and the education median is 8th–9th grade.

Sustainers   Living on the edge of poverty, angry and resentful, streetwise, involved in an underground economy. There are 11 million Sustainers, 58% of whom are under 35; 55% are female; the median income is $11,000, and the education median is 11th grade.

Belongers   Aging, traditional and conventional, contented, intensely patriotic, sentimental, and very stable. There are 54 million Belongers, whose median age is 52; 65% are female; the median income is $17,500, and about 50% graduated from high school.

Emulators   Youthful and ambitious, macho, show-off, trying to break into the system and make it big. There are 16 million Emulators, whose median age is 27; 53% are male, the median income is $18,000, and many of them have some education beyond high school.

Achievers   Middle-aged, prosperous, self-assured, materialistic, able leaders, builders of the "American Dream." There are 37 million Achievers, whose median age is 37; 60% are male; the median income is $31,400, and 32% have graduated from college.

I-Am-Me   Transition state; exhibitionistic, narcissistic, young, impulsive, experimental, active, and inventive. There are 8 million I-Am-Mes, 91% of whom are under 25; 64% are male; the median income is $8,800, and most of them have some college.

Experiential   Youthful, person-centered, artistic, seek direct experience and inner growth. There are 11 million Experientials, whose median age is 27; 55% are female; the median income is $23,800, and 38% have graduated from college.

Societally Conscious   Mission-oriented, mature, successful, leaders of single-issue groups; some of them live lives of voluntary simplicity. There are 14 million SCs, whose median age is 39; 52% are male; the median income is $27,200, 58% are college graduates, and 39% have some graduate school.

Integrated   Psychologically mature, tolerant, and understanding, they have a large field of vision and a sense of fittingness. There are only 3.2 million Integrateds.

Source: Reprinted (with changes) by permission of Macmillan Publishing Company from *Nine American Lifestyles: Who We Are and Where We Are Going* by Arnold Mitchell, pp. 98–99, 176–179. Copyright © 1983 by Arnold Mitchell.

Lear, who will be in his seventies as we go to press, has become what the *Journal* calls "a savvy and unabashed capitalist." He is buying up movie theaters, magazines, and television stations. His business is called "Act III," for Act III of his life. Among his other media acquisitions are two movie theater chains in Texas for which he paid $47 million. Act III will not release figures, but experts estimate annual revenues of more than one hundred million dollars.

Norman Lear is a picture of intelligence, sharp taste, wit, and power. He's looking for gaps and buying up properties far away from the glitz of Hollywood and other media centers.

Doesn't it make you want to shinny up that onion?

Field Interviewing Target Customers

A lot of people go into small business because they don't have much choice. Many of them have to learn new skills and learn them fast. Fortunately, entrepreneurs tend to be bright, creative, and hard-working. Julia Gonzales is a good example.

It's no secret that I was distressed when my husband was transferred. I didn't blame him wanting the transfer; I would have wanted it, too. But I had a terrific job, as manager of a full-line baby furniture and bedding store, and to keep both job and husband I'd have had to commute over a hundred miles a day five days a week. So, I quit my job.

But I missed the store, and it was hard living on one salary when we'd gotten used to two. When I started to look for work, I found that my reputation had preceded me. Store owners knew of the store where I'd worked, and they were pretty sure that all I wanted to do was work for them to get a feel for the area so that I could open a store of my own and compete with them.

This gave me an idea. I hadn't *considered* doing that. So when I couldn't find work, I decided to go for it, to go ahead and compete with them. Their fear gave me confidence!

One thing I learned on my way up from stock clerk to store manager is that it pays to know your customer. So in the mornings I'd get the kids off to school, pick up the house a bit, and drive to a baby store. I'd park my car a block away and when customers came out of the store I'd strike up conversations with them.

"Hi!" I'd say. "My name's Julia Gonzales, and I'm doing market research for a major manufacturer who's interested in this area. I'm wondering if you might have a minute to answer a few questions about babies."

My enthusiasm must have helped. I like people and babies, and I guess it shows. Being a mother helps me understand other mothers, too. I always dressed up a little bit and carried a clipboard. I'd ask the obvious questions like:

What do you like about this store?

What things did you buy?

Were the people helpful and courteous?

And so on.

Sometimes, I parked in the alley, to research the delivery trucks. At the beach and the shopping malls, I would stop every pregnant woman I saw. I developed a separate list of questions for pregnant women:

Have you had a baby shower?

Which gifts did you like best?

Which gifts seemed most useful?

What things are you buying before your baby comes?

What things are you waiting to buy?

How are you going to decorate the baby's room?

What do you really need the most?

The research was time-consuming, but after thirty interviews I had enough information to make some very sound decisions. I also knew the weaknesses of my competition. And I located my new store right in the middle of a coming baby boom.

When Julia Gonzales discovered that she would have to work for herself, she quickly began to research her target customers. The method she chose was **interviewing**. You can do the same thing for your business. Action Step 27 tells you how to do it. Why not get out there and try a couple!

interview
a planned conversation with another person or group of persons for the purpose of eliciting specific information

KNOWLEDGE IS POWER

When Hugh Hefner had the vision about *Playboy,* he was alone in that market. His target customers were 17–34 years old. That was more than 30 years ago. Those same people are now 47–64 years old, and recent surveys suggest that *Playboy*'s readership is declining. Any product's life cycle is affected by the age of the customers. What is the life cycle of a magazine?

In autumn 1982 *Penthouse* magazine ran ads in major newspapers suggesting that it would run *Playboy* out of the arena. There is a word for the phenomenon of someone going after your target customers; it's *competition.* Competition is the topic of the next chapter.

Key Points from Another View
Part I:
KNOW THY CUSTOMER

Many business owners view market research as complex and confusing. Market research is a good, commonsense approach to how you plan to market a product or service.

Questions you need answers for:

- Who are your customers?
- How can you best reach them?
- Who makes the buying decision?
- What do customers like in a new product or service?
- What do they like in the current one?
- What need will your product or service fill?
  (For example, landscaping is not just mowing grass and trimming shrubs. Its major selling points are enhancing appearance and providing free time for the purchaser.)
- What are your competitors' strengths? What are their weaknesses?
  (A periodic walk through a competitor's store can generate insights on how to improve your own business. During your visit, take note of the decor, product line, price ranges, quality, and service. This helps you properly position yourself in the market.)

Effective market research can help you target rich niches and avoid stagnant ones. A visit to your local library or a call to your industry trade association brings a flood of statistics—geographic, demographic, industrial, ethnic—that helps you pinpoint growing markets.

You don't need the vast resources of a giant company behind you to engage in productive market research. Besides the library and trade associations, tap other resources: local Chamber of Commerce, National Chamber of Commerce, the U.S. Small Business Association (SBA), trade and industry magazines, business periodicals, government publications, and census data.

From: Richard J. Maturi, "Talking Shop," *Entrepreneur,* January, 1991, 44–47.

ACTION STEP 27

Interview prospective target customers.

Now that you've profiled several target customers, it's time for you to take a big step. It's time to move from the tidy world inside your head to the arena of the marketplace. It's time to rub elbows with the people who'll be buying your product or service.

You know where your TC hangs out, and you know its habits, income, sex, personality, and buying patterns. You can guess at this customer's dreams and aspirations, and you've identified the heavy users of your product or service. Now you're going to check out these things by interviewing your potential TCs—yes, through primary research.

Make up some questions in advance. Some of them should be open-ended questions, which call for more than just a simple yes or no. Here are some questions to help get you started:

Do you like to shop at this store?

What products did you buy today?

Are the salespeople helpful and courteous?

How did you learn about this store?

Is this your first visit? How often do you shop here?

What are you looking for that you didn't find in the store today?

Where do you live?

What do you read?

Remember, no one is totally happy with a particular store or business, and your questions may unearth some gaps that you didn't know of before.

Part II:

BREAKING IN: TEN WAYS TO CRACK THE COMPETITION— LEGALLY

Many small companies fail because the founder has not investigated how the competition is financed and organized.

Competitive Intelligence programs usually have these major objectives:

- Avoid surprises and decrease reaction time to competitors' strategies and tactics.
- Identify threats and opportunities.
- Improve planning skills.
- Help owner better understand their companies.

Here are ten inexpensive and legal ways entrepreneurs can find out virtually everything they to know about the competition.

1. Dedicate a specific time for evaluating the competition. Once a month, schedule a meeting to review activities of the competitors.
2. Organize a "Competitive Intelligence" file. Use this file to help you design products or services, to instruct your sales force, to create sales literature, and to address independent sales reps.
3. Scrutinize industry publications for information on competitors. You may be surprised to find stories that reveal important information about your competition.
4. Attend trade shows, exhibits, and conferences for your industry. It is also a good idea to participate in industry association activities.
5. Read the local papers where your major competitors are located. If you find one item that gives you an insight on a competitor—personnel, production, labor problems, litigation—it's worth the read.
6. Obtain and study competitors' literature. Brochures for sales, products, and services offer valuable insights into the image—how your competition presents itself to customers.
7. Poll "friendly" distributors, dealers and buyers of your products and services. Ask how they perceive your business.
8. Approach suppliers to find out what materials or services your competitors buy.
9. Analyze information you get from industry meetings and employee interviews.
10. Obtain credit reports on your competitors. Dun & Bradstreet, the world's largest business credit information company, has data on 9 million public and private companies.

From: Nathaniel Gilbert, "Breaking In," *Entrepreneur,* December, 1990, 147–153.

SUMMARY

Your target customer is your key to your survival in small business. Constructing a customer profile is like drawing a circle around that customer in order to turn the circle into a target at which you can aim your product or service. Before you open your doors, you should profile your target customer at least five times. After your doors are open, it's a good idea to gather data through surveys, interviews, and so on, and refine the profile monthly.

A profile combines demographic data (age, sex, income, education, residence, cultural roots, and so on) with psychographic insight (observations of life-style, buying habits, consumption patterns, attitudes, and so on). The magazines read by your target customer will reveal a well-drawn profile of your TC; this is because the purchasers of this very expensive advertising have already researched the customer very thoroughly.

Profiling your target customer is important because it shows you:

1. how to communicate your message with a minimum of confusion
2. what additional service your TC wants, such as delivery, credit, gift wrapping, installation, post-sale service, and so on
3. how much the TC can pay
4. what quality the TC wants
5. where large groups of TCs live
6. who else is after your TC

THINK POINTS FOR SUCCESS

◀ *Psychographics* is derived from *psyche* and *graphos,* Greek words for "life" or "soul" and for "written," respectively. Thus, psychographics is the charting of your customer's life, mind, soul, or spirit.

◀ Profiling draws a "magic" circle around your target customer. Placing the customer in the center of that circle transforms the whole arena into a bullseye.

◀ Segmenting is like slicing pie; it allows you to help yourself to a piece of the pie.

◀ You can save a lot of steps by using market research that has been done by others.

◀ Contact magazines and newspapers. They employ market researchers.

ACTION STEP REVIEW

Action Steps 24–27 help you zero in on your target customers.

24 Use your new eyes on some mass-market magazines to develop your profiling reflexes.

25 Do some secondary research on specific magazines.

26 Profile your target customer and try to identify the heavy users in your industry.

27 Back up your profile with primary data you collect by interviewing prospective target customers.

REFERENCES

Alsop, Ronald. "Advertisers Put Consumers on the Couch." *Wall Street Journal,* May 13, 1988. [Right brain/left brain moved into the world of advertising as the McCann–Erickson ad agency probed the reasons for an aerosol-spray roach killer's success. Researchers found that the women in the study identified roaches with men who had abandoned them. Spraying the roaches, the researchers concluded, was like spraying the men. What would Dr. Freud say?]

Balachandran, M. *State and Local Statistics Sources,* 2nd. ed. Detroit, Mich.: Gale Research, 1992.

Breen, George, and Albert Blankenship. *Do-It-Yourself Marketing Research,* 3rd. ed. New York: McGraw-Hill, 1989.

Brown, Paul, and Carl Sewell. *Customers for Life: How to Turn That One-Time Buyer into a Lifetime Customer.* New York: Doubleday, 1990.

Directory of Directories, Marlow, Cecilia, ed. Detroit: Gale Research, 1988.

Falk, Kathryn. *How to Write a Romance and Get It Published.* New York: NAL-Dutton, 1989.

Iacocca, Lee A. *Iacocca, An Autobiography.* New York: Bantam Books, 1984.

Key, Wilson Brian. *Subliminal Seduction: Ad Media's Manipulation of a Not-So-Innocent America.* New York: NAL-Dutton, 1974. [Fascinating study of methods used by the media to persuade us to buy things. Chapter 7, on *Playboy,* and Chapter 8, on *Cosmo* and *Vogue,* are especially valuable for helping you zero in on target markets.]

Kiam, Victor. *Going for It! How to Succeed as an Entrepreneur.* New York: NAL-Dutton, 1987.

Lauder, Estée. *Estée: A Success Story*. New York: Random House, 1985.

Lofflin, John. "Help from the 'Hidden Persuaders': What's New in Subliminal Messages." *New York Times,* March 20, 1988, 17.

Meyers, William. *The Image-Makers: Power and Persuasion on Madison Avenue*. New York: Times Books, 1984.

Mitchell, Arnold. *The Nine American Lifestyles: Who We Are and Where We Are Going*. New York: Warner Books, 1984. [A comprehensive, data-based study of psychographic patterns in America. Contains an illuminating chapter on Europe. Projects the future. Excellent to read in combination with *Megatrends 2000*.]

The National Directory of Addresses and Telephone Numbers. Omnigraphics Inc., Detroit, 1991.

The National Directory of Addresses and Telephone Numbers. Detroit: Gale Research, 1992.

Packard, Vance. *The Hidden Persuaders*. New York: Pocket Books, 1958.

Rice, Berkely. "The Selling of Life-Styles: Are You What You Buy? Madison Avenue Wants to Know." *Psychology Today,* March 1988.

Ries, Al, and Jack Trout. *Positioning: The Battle for your Mind*. New York: McGraw-Hill, 1988.
Marketing Warfare. New York: NAL-Dutton, 1990.
Bottom-Up Marketing. New York: McGraw-Hill, 1989.

Sewell, Carl. *Three Hundred Thirty-Two Thousand Dollar Customer*. New York: Doubleday, 1990.

Sherlock, Paul. *Rethinking Business-to-Business Marketing*. New York: Free Press, 1991.

Thomsett, Michael, C. *The Little Black Book of Business Statistics*. New York: AMACOM, 1990.

Townsend, Bickley. "Psychographic Glitter." *Across the Board,* March 1986, p. 41.

Van der Merwe, Sandra. "Grampies: A New Breed of Consumers Comes of Age." *Business Horizons,* November–December 1987, pp. 14–19.

Weiss, Michael. *The Clustering of America*. New York: Harper Collins, 1989.

Whitely, Richard C. *Customer Driven Company*. Reading, Mass.: Addison-Wesley, 1991.

NOTES _____
_____
_____
_____
_____
_____

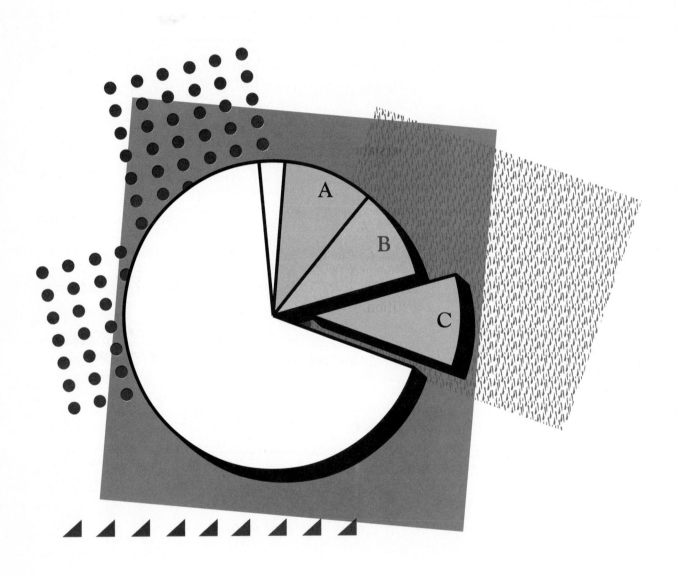

FIGURE 5.1
Chapter 5 will help you prepare part C of your Business Plan, "The Competition."

5 Reading the ▲▲▲▲ ▲ ▲ ▲ Competition

Learning Objectives

- To relate the four-phase life cycle to competition.
- To define the competitive arena in terms of size, growth, profitability, innovation, market leaders, market losers, and potential competitors.
- To understand the value of positive positioning.
- To view competition as a struggle inside the mind of the target customer.
- To evaluate competitors by all three kinds of research (primary, secondary, and new eyes).
- To develop skill as a marketplace detective.
- To use a competitor test matrix to determine the intensity of competition.
- To learn ways to disarm competitors.
- To see ways of changing the arena to your advantage.

FUTURE FOCUS

Every business has competition. You must develop your own unique monopoly to minimize competition and attract business. It's easier than you think. You simply must be better, faster, nicer, closer, more flexible, give something extra your customer doesn't expect or the competition can't deliver. These are the winning weapons you can use to disarm competitors in your own area.

penetration of the arena
a calculated thrust into the marketplace

conglomerate
an organization involved in several diverse businesses

Like everything else in life and business, competition has a life cycle of four stages: embryo, growth, maturity, and decline. In this chapter we will examine these stages and look at ways you can meet and beat your competition. Briefly, we can describe the four stages of the competition life cycle as follows:

1. In the *embryonic* stage, the arena's empty. There's just you and your idea for a product or service and a tiny core market.

2. As your industry *grows,* competitors smell money and attempt to **penetrate the arena** to take up positions they hope will turn to profit. Curious target customers come from all directions. You have visions of great success.

3. As the industry *matures,* competition gets fierce and you are forced to steal customers to survive. Shelf velocity slows. Production runs get longer. Prices begin to slide.

4. As the industry goes into *decline,* competition becomes desperate. Many businesses fail; weary competitors leave the arena, which is now silent except for the echoes of battle.

Figure 5.2 summarizes these stages.

A LIFE-CYCLE SCENARIO

The following scenario will help you understand the life cycle of a product. As a product progresses through the cycle, businesspeople vary their strategies to meet changing circumstances in the marketplace. This scenario, like the one in Chapter 3, emphasizes the importance of teamwork in small business. It shows you how a manufacturing team brainstormed its way to a brilliant success.

THE SETTING: The lunchroom at XRD, the giant telecommunications conglomerate.
THE PLAYERS:

> BETTY, a Wharton M.B.A. who worked in marketing and sales. Before coming on board at XRD, she had worked for Exxon, IBM, and TRW. Even though she had just received a promotion and a good raise, Betty was getting tired of having her marketing strategies shot down. She was ready to try entrepreneurship on her own.

> BRUCE, a junior vice-president. His favorite saying seemed to be "Let's have the bottom line, here." His dream was to be president of XRD, then chairman of

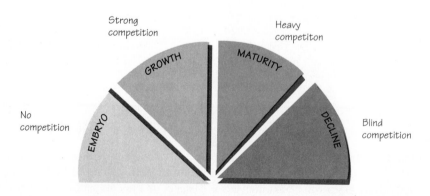

FIGURE 5.2   The product life cycle defines four stages in the intensity of competition.

the board, then U.S. senator, and then president of the United States. His hero was John DeLorean. "John was framed on the drug thing," Bruce was fond of saying. "It was an obvious case of entrapment. The company was his family. He was just trying to save his family." Bruce's desk was a paper jungle, and he was known for being impatient with subordinates. Though barely thirty-five, his hair was turning grey, and he suffered from a stomach ulcer.

HUGH, a designer who worked a flex-time schedule in the XRD "creative dungeon" and came to work in jeans, blue work shirts, and running shoes. Hugh could program a computer in his sleep. Because shaving took time away from his creative endeavors, he wore a beard. You could drive by his home any night or weekend and find him tinkering away. Hugh devoured books on art, computers, architecture, self-hypnosis, investing, and right-hemisphere power.

DAN, in Public Relations. He had a B.A. in journalism from Columbia University, and he'd worked for an ad agency for 10 years before coming to XRD. He dressed in three-piece suits from Brooks Brothers and drove a red convertible. He was always looking for a party; if someone else wasn't throwing one, Dan would throw one himself.

ACT I

"Listen, fellow inmates," Hugh said, finishing his cola. "Last night, I came up with an idea that could make us all rich."

Bruce's ulcer was bothering him. He glared at Hugh. "Spare us the details, Hughie. Let's just have the bottom line, okay?"

"Skates for ducks!" Hugh said, smiling like a mad inventor.

Betty's marketing intuition told her some exciting changes were about to take place. "Don't jump on him, Bruce," Betty said. "Go ahead, Hugh."

"*Ice skates?*" Dan asked. "Or *roller?*" Dan was already thinking of promotional angles.

"You're off the deep end, Hugh-Boy," Bruce said, looking around the table. "Why ruin another good lunch with your holistic nightmares?"

"Take the afternoon off, Bruce," Betty said. "Play some racquetball. They're working you too hard up there in the Executive Tower."

"I've got tennis elbow," Bruce said, "or I'd be on the court right now."

"You ever watch a duck?" Hugh asked. "They can stand on one foot. Their leg muscles are rock solid. And their feathers keep them warm, even when it's *really* cold."

"The **core market** is pretty thin," Betty said, "but I like the idea. It has an innovative touch that's almost sexy. Can we have something for the December Show?"

core market
customers whose perceived needs best fit a product's characteristics

"I'm testing the prototype Saturday at Dorman's Pond. It's a tame duck, of course, but you're all welcome to observe."

"The real market's in *wild* ducks," Betty said.

"The real promo angle is too," Dan said.

"You're all crazy," Bruce said, and he left the table.

So on Saturday, only Dan and Betty showed up for the test. They were amazed. Hugh's duck skated across the ice of Dorman's Pond serenely, like something out of a Walt Disney film. A gaggle of mallards gathered to watch the performance, and a young mallard came up afterward to try on the skates.

The mallard was a natural. He swirled out onto the ice, did figure eights and pirouettes. Betty was thrilled with what she saw. The ducks on the sidelines applauded. Betty sensed widespread customer interest.

"This is *exciting*!" Betty said.

"The PR possibilities are *endless*," Dan said. "We'll start with an autograph party this spring, as they fly north out of Mexico and South America."

The three friends had been in business before, so they started on a small scale. Hugh found a manufacturer in the next town who would make a hundred pairs of duck skates. They promoted the skates with a direct mail piece to duck owners in the local area. "Win a free pair of skates for your duck," the promo said. "Enter your duck in the Dorman's Pond Regional."

product innovation
improvement in the utility or design of a product

They developed an essay contest at the local high school. The topic was "Should American Ducks Have Access to Jet-Powered Ice Skates?" (The jet-powered models were still on Hugh's drawing board, but this was the moment to test the market for **product innovation**.)

The response from the students was an overwhelming *yes*.

Their skate manufacturer thought he had enough inventory to last until Christmas. Surprise. All 100 pairs were sold within a week. Catalog houses were calling, wanting the skates. The core market had emerged.

The three friends were excited. They hadn't lost a dime, and there was still no competition in sight.

One problem surfaced. At the duck races in West Ossipee, New Hampshire, three fleet mallards sustained severe injuries when they achieved speeds in excess of 237 m.p.h. and their skates flew off.

ACT II

Working late one night in his garage, Hugh developed an innovation: a Velcro heel strap that solved the flying skate problem. Endorsements by famous ducks quickly followed. Television networks began selling time for events featuring ducks on skates. As soon as Betty and Dan came up with a suitable company name—The Fire and Ice Skate Company—Bruce resigned from XRD and came on board as president.

distribution
the physical movement of the product from manufacturer to ultimate consumer

There was one ugly occurrence during **distribution**. A railroad car loaded with the all-new Luke Skywalker rocket-powered skates was hijacked by a gang of masked coots. Several coots were blown away when the skates they were wearing exploded. Editorials across the land carried the same message: Technology kills.

In Hollywood, celebrities that had never given a thought to ice-skating ducks were now sponsoring duck races, skate regattas, and skate ballets.

On New York's Publishers Row, major publishing houses entered a race to see who could bring out the definitive study of duck behavior. Would skating change the face of duckhood over the planet?

An entrepreneur at Texas A&M in College Station developed an "arctic refractor" that could freeze over a medium-sized lake in three hours flat. DuPont and GE put their plants into 24-hour R&D to show the world who would build the first arctic refractor. Meanwhile, the U.S. Government hired biologists to train ducks to stop migrating.

"We don't want them skating in Mexico," said one government spokesperson. "We need them up here—at home on our glorious lakes. It'll boost the national morale." All over the duck world, ducks were entering the work force. Parallax, Inc., the noted motivation research firm, stated that the major reason for this was that the ducks wanted to increase their income so that they could afford upgraded skates.

Wary of being exploited, ducks began to demand higher wages. They wanted their own show. In Pittsburgh, duck skaters' unions were founded, and they spread south and west.

Fire and Ice Skate Company had been in business only eighteen months when it declared an astronomical dividend. Hugh's new developments, coupled with aggressive management from Bruce, marketing expertise from Betty, and superpromotions from Dan, enabled the four friends to pay themselves two million dollars each in combined salary and executive perks. Bruce decided to fire their small accounting firm and sign with one of the Big Eight. Dan decided to throw a party.

With three scotches in him, Bruce slapped Hugh on the back and admitted he had been hasty in calling him crazy.

"*Time* wants me on their cover," Bruce said. "What's on the drawing board, anyway? Anything cooking?"

"Yes," Hugh said. "I'm off to Tibet."

"Tibet?" Bruce was shocked. "What for?"

"Ideas," Hugh said, pointing to his right brain. "Ideas."

ACT III

Price wars plagued the industry. Mallard Eski-Skates made cuts of 25 percent. Canadian Goose, Ltd., makers of the luxury Ugly Duckling model, slashed their prices by 40 percent. At Fire and Ice GHQ in Manhattan, Bruce took a look at the balance sheet and called down to Design with orders for seventeen new variations of the Fire and Ice turbo skate.

Betty came up with an idea for saving the firm—a duck skate palace in Armonk, New York—but the bank said Fire and Ice was already overextended as it was. Up in PR, Dan hadn't had an idea for media sizzle in days. The Fire and Ice computer told the story: the end was near.

"Where is Hugh when we need him?" Bruce asked at the group's regular Friday meeting. "We're in a trough. He could bail us out."

"Our marketing data says we've peaked," Betty said. "The Armonk skate palace was our last stand for this product."

"Show me that on the bottom line," Bruce said aggressively.

"I'm thinking about moving to Florida," Dan said. "According to this guy Naisbitt, that's where the action is."

The executive group meeting disintegrated into wild schemes and bickering. After the meeting broke up, Bruce kept the accounting department working through the night. "You people will stay here," Bruce said, "until you produce me a spreadsheet that does not forecast the end of my world."

But the numbers would not lie.

ACT IV

That year, Fire and Ice Skate Company tripled production to more than seventeen million pairs of duck skates. Prices were slashed. New colors were added. Velcro straps were striped with silver and gold. Five million pairs had to be sold at deep discount.

On December 26, Mallard Eski-Skates, the major competition, filed for Chapter Eleven. In January Fire and Ice closed its plants in California, Texas, Alabama, and southern New Hampshire.

DuPont's prototype arctic refractor blew up at a lake site in Louisiana, killing several hundred ducks and splattering more than a million fish across northern New Orleans. Ducks reacted by dropping their skates onto city streets at rush hour. The knife-sharp blades cut into the very heart of city traffic.

"How awful," Betty said.

"I'm off to Florida," Dan announced. "What will you give me for my stock?"

"Great news, men," Bruce said. "We just killed Canadian Goose, Ltd. They closed all their plants."

"We must do something," Betty said.

"I'm selling my car," Dan said. "Any takers?"

In the midst of chaos and depression, Hugh arrived from Tibet with an idea—a ten-speed turbo skate for people on the go.

As he was leaving, Dan met Hugh in the hall outside Executive Tower. Hugh had the sketches for the turbo skate in his shirt pocket. Dan noticed that Hugh's beard could use some immediate barbering.

"Great idea, Hugh!" Dan said. "Why didn't you think of this before?"

"It came to me on a mountaintop in Tibet," Hugh said, smiling peacefully. "How are things in the corporate universe?"

"I think," Dan said, "that we are back in business."

Dan promoted the turbo skate with a full-page four-color magazine ad. There was a photo of a young man in sweater and scarf sitting at the edge of a frozen pond. The ad copy read: "Romance fading? Dazzle her with the new F & I Turbo. With ten speeds, you can skate uphill, skate to work, or write her name in ice!"

Production geared up to make the Turbo. Bruce became F & I CEO and brought in a new man—a hotshot manager from the soft-drink industry—as president. Dan got busy making a documentary on the history of the skating duck movement. It would make great PR, he said, and enhance the company image. The documentary was set to air on network TV. Betty spent most of her time at trade shows, promoting the new ten-speed skates. She got an endorsement from a retired Olympic figure skater, which led to the idea to have a Turbo Skate Power Championship at the next Winter Olympics. Bruce, the competitor, fell in love with the idea and joined Betty on the road as they networked their way into the highest skating circles in the land. On their last joint report to the executive group, Betty and Bruce announced their engagement.

When last seen, a bearded, glassy-eyed Hugh was locked in the lab at Fire and Ice, working on an idea for two computer games—Skates in Space and The Duck in the Dungeon—and finalizing the sketches for his Hobby Skate model kit, which should be available in a toy store near you by Thanksgiving.

The Lessons to Be Learned

The moral of this scenario is that, to survive, you must know what stage of the life cycle you are in and compete accordingly. Figure 5.3 will help you to visualize this, and Box 5.1 will help you to *feel* each stage.

Life cycles exist for everything—industries, segments, products, locations, and so on; thus the life-cycle yardstick could be the most useful tool in your entrepreneur's toolkit. In Chapter 4 you saw the effect of the life cycle on Hugh Hefner's information empire. *Playboy* readers got older (the moving target concept), and the kingdom became a dukedom. It took Hefner and *Playboy* 30 years to move through

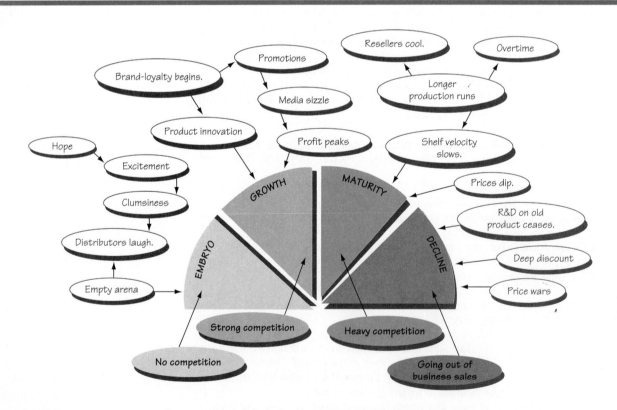

FIGURE 5.3   Different competitive strategies are needed at each stage of the product life cycle.

BOX 5.1   The Competition Life Cycle

THE EMBRYONIC STAGE

The embryonic stage is marked by excitement, naive euphoric thrust, clumsiness, a high failure rate, and much brainstorming. Pricing is experimental. Sales volume is low—because the market is very small and production and marketing costs are high. It's difficult to find distributors, and resellers demand huge gross margins. Profit is chancy and speculative. Shrewd entrepreneurs, however, can close their eyes and divine the presence of a core market. Competition has not yet appeared.

THE GROWTH STAGE

The growth stage is marked by product innovation, strong product acceptance, the beginnings of brand loyalty, promotion by media sizzle, and ballpark pricing. Product innovation occurs. Distribution becomes all-important. Resellers who laughed during the embryonic stage now clamor to distribute the product. Strong competitors, excited by the smell of money, enter the arena of the marketplace, as do new target customer groups. Profit shows signs of peaking.

THE MATURE STAGE

The mature stage is marked by peak customer numbers and zero product modifications. Design concentrates on product differentiation instead of product improvement. Competitors are going at it blindly now, running on momentum even as shelf velocity slows. Production runs get longer, so firms can take full advantage of capital equipment and experienced management. Resellers, sensing doom, are cool on the product. Advertising investments increase, in step with competition. Some firms go out of business. Prices are on a swift slide down. Any competitor who enters the market now is either dumb or overconfident or both. In the once-hot marketplace, there's a pervasive air of depression.

THE DECLINE STAGE

The decline stage is marked by extreme depression in the marketplace. Competition becomes desperate. A few firms still hang on. R&D ceases. Promotion vanishes. Price wars continue. Opportunities emerge for entrepreneurs in service and repair. Diehards fight for what remains of the core market. Resellers cannot be found; they've moved on.

---

the cycle, and that arc is smooth and even. Contrast the life-cycle arc of the hula hoop or the Pet Rock. They illustrate shorter life cycles, in which the movement from one phase to another is electric.

The other lesson in the Fire and Ice scenario is the value of teamwork. We'll cover teamwork in detail in Chapter 13, and we'll discuss the need for a balance of personalities and skills on a team. The "DISC scale" is used there to describe the ideal balance. According to the DISC theory of balance, the ideal team would have a Dominant member, an Influencing member, a Compliant one, and a Steady one. Fire and Ice had this combination:

Bruce is a no-nonsense hard driver; he's impatient and wants to be president of everything. Bruce is a *Dominant.*

Dan is a flashy, outgoing person who loves the spotlight and is good with words. Dan is an *Influencing.*

Betty is the manager/negotiator; she smoothes feathers. She's a *Compliant.*

Hugh is the individualistic inventor who can be counted on to come up with good new ideas. Furthermore, he's good with detail. Hugh is a *Steady.*

So Fire and Ice worked for two reasons: it found a segment that wasn't crowded, and it was a balanced team.

Where are your industry and your segment on the life cycle? What does this mean to you if you're a start-up venture? What are the implications for your survival? When your industry enters its maturity and decline, will you be ready with Plan B?

COMPETITION AND POSITIONING

Basically, competition is a mind game played out in the customers' minds, since that is where buying decisions are made. Inside customers' minds are many "ladders"—ladders for products, ladders for services, ladders for sports figures, TV programs, banks, wines, and rental cars. To compete for a position at the top of one of these ladders, a business must first of all get a foothold and then wrestle with other businesses to improve its position. It's that simple. Looking at competition from this perspective helps you focus on the mind of the target customer. To explore this idea, read *Positioning: The Battle for the Mind* by Al Ries and Jack Trout. Action Step 28 can help you get a foothold and improve your position on your ladder.

Competition in a Mature Industry

If you're in a mature industry, you're going to have to win customers away from competitors in order to survive. One way of doing this is by giving better service. That's what Roy Modell did.

> Roy Modell grew up in Arkansas. After he graduated from high school he took off to see the world. Ultimately, he wound up in Detroit. He was an independent kind of guy, and after working for someone else for awhile, he opened his own business—a gas station.
>
> "I did like a lot of guys in Motown," Roy says. "I just sort of jumped into something. It went along okay for a while, but one day I realized the business was broke."
>
> It took Roy five years to pay off his debts, but those years paid off. He built a solid reputation with three oil companies, and when he moved to the West Coast, that reputation followed him; oil company reps would come to him to give him first bid on station sites.
>
> He was in Orange County, running two stations near where a planned community was being developed. An oil company rep was pushing him to open a station there. Here's how Roy checked it out.
>
> Around 7:30 in the morning, he parked across the street from the only other station within three miles. He counted the cars buying gas for an hour. He developed a **competitor test matrix** to rate the station. For example, he noted the make of each car and correlated that with time at the pump. He had industry figures on tank capacity for all vehicles, and he knew from long experience the average amount of gas sold for each type of car. Roy had an insider's knowledge.
>
> He came back around noon, and then again during the evening rush hour. He compared weekday business with business on the weekends, just before people went out for some distance driving.
>
> In the employee sector, Roy saw a lot of opportunity for competition. "They were 'pump jockeys,'" Roy says. "They could have been a lot more courteous. They made five moves when one should have done. And there wasn't much attempt at selling tires, accessories, and batteries. That could have been because the owner wasn't around much."
>
> In any **mature industry**, Roy knew, you have to be ready to steal customers from your competition. He was prepared to do that with service.

ACTION STEP 28

Find your position in the marketplace.

Investigate your position on the competition ladder for your product or service by completing these steps:

1. Which firm is at the top? Why is it up there? What's unique about the firm? Who are its target customers? What are the company's strengths? Its weaknesses? Where is it vulnerable?

2. Who holds the number-two spot? The number-three spot? Ask the same questions about them.

3. Now look at your own business. What image are you trying to project? What is unique about your business? Where are you strong? Where are you weak? What are your major groups of target customers?

4. Ask yourself if you really want to compete on this ladder (in this arena)? Might a different ladder be better-suited—and thus more fun—for you?

A couple of tips: First, if you want to compete on this ladder, you must capitalize on your unique strengths as well as exploit the weaknesses of those above you—weaknesses such as age, size, and slow footwork. Second, evaluate your prospects on a different ladder by going through steps 1–4 with a different product or service in mind.

competitor test matrix
a grid used to get a clear picture of the strengths, weaknesses, and sales volume of your competitors

mature industry
growth has slowed here, few new competitors, strong competition, little real new product innovation

Roy put in his bid, and opened his station—at a great location: a busy corner in a medium-sized shopping center. Furthermore, his station had a good, efficient **layout**. The three service bays were always full, with two cars parked on the driveway outside, waiting to get in. After taking a good long look at the tire dealers in his area, Roy began running ads in the Sunday paper. In less than a year, he was outselling most of them.

Roy succeeded because he knew what business he was in and he knew how to compete. He knew how to wrestle his way to the top of the ladder.

layout
physical arrangement of a business

Scouting the Competition

The better you understand your competition, the more clearly you will see how you can position yourself for success. Figure 5.A is a sample competitor test matrix that will help you evaluate your potential competitors. Follow Roy Modell's example and study your competition. Action Step 29 will help you. Remember, work from your strengths, and strength is built on knowledge. Knowing your competitors will increase your confidence. Then you can win.

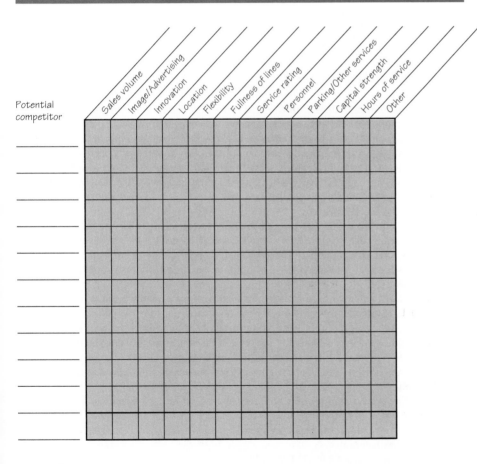

FIGURE 5.A

DISARMING THE COMPETITION

disarm the competition
cancel out competitors' strengths

Plan B
the counterattack blueprint that you have ready to implement in the event of shifts in the marketplace

image
the way a business is perceived

presence
a heightened awareness in the mind of the target customer

The two case studies that follow illustrate two tactics for **disarming the competition**. In the first case, Ben Jones grabs an exclusive rung on his target customer's ladder by being unique. In the second case, Ford Johnson is always one step ahead of the competition because he is ready with a **Plan B**.

Establishing Image and Presence

Every business projects an **image**. Some businesses are so concerned about theirs that they employ image consultants and store image designers. Image and **presence** help to establish a business in the minds of customers.

Ben Jones believes in keeping his image right up there. When he ships his expensive camera lenses (some wholesale for $2,000), he makes sure people who work in the shipping room will remember him—he packs the lenses in bags of popcorn or Virginia peanuts. And the bags are stamped with his company logo.

The people who work in the shipping room are Ben's target customers.

In addition, Ben sends out cards on April Fool's Day (instead of at Christmas), and when he visits clients he wears a Superman suit. He definitely maintains a presence. His clients remember him.

Being Ready for Change

Change is the most predictable element of competition. Because of this, the entrepreneur needs to keep one eye on the market and the other eye on Plan B.

Ford Johnson has been in the mail order business for a dozen years now. He says it gives him a lot of freedom to be creative. Ford was trained as an electrical engineer, and he spent 20 years in the aerospace industry before going into business for himself.

Ford has developed and marketed more than two hundred products—from a Mylar heat sheet (for pets) to Engine Coat (a motor lubricant using Teflon) to space monkeys (dried shrimp eggs that hatch when dropped into water). He's also developed a hundred strategies for handling his competitors. The best one is how he competes with himself. Here's the way it works:

He introduces a quality product in the marketplace. It retails for $12, which nets him a reasonable profit after overhead. Because he deals with established mail order houses (they ship to thousands and thousands of customers), Ford knows someone out there will copy his idea and try to ace him by bringing out a lower-quality product for less money.

So for the first couple of runs, Ford manufactures a quality product, using the best materials available. He charges full price for it, and waits for the phone to ring. When it does, he knows it's the buyer from the catalog house, telling him there's a competitor

inferior product
a product that is lower in utility than the product it's being compared to

waiting in the wings with an **inferior product** that will retail for $6—half of what Ford's costs. So Ford has a cheaper one ready to roll.

"When do you need them, and how many can you handle?" Ford asks.

"Wait," the buyer says. "What kind of numbers are we looking at?"

"Mine will retail for $5.75," Ford says. "And I can have 10,000 on your loading dock by two weeks from tomorrow."

"You're kidding," the buyer says. (He's new on the block. Other buyers have watched Ford work before.)

"Can you move 20,000?" Ford asks.

"Ten for sure," the buyer says. "And if we need more I'll get back to you in 2 weeks."

"Over and out," Ford says. "It's great doing business with you."

Now, let's really get an in-depth understanding of your competitors. When you understand your competitors, you'll be better able to visualize the position of your new company in the grand arena of the marketplace. Action Step 30 will help you dig.

If you're a potential buyer, everybody will compete for your dollar. If you change positions and become the store owner, you'll want to move fast to locate the ladder inside your TC's mind. If you can't locate the ladder or run into other difficulties, be ready to look for a different ladder.

CHANGING THE ARENA

Sometimes it becomes clear to a lone entrepreneur or a Big Business think tank that making a **change in the arena** can spell opportunity. The change may be very small—a slight change in some aspect of the product or service—but the effect on the market can be very large indeed. The world of business, large and small, is filled with stories of such breakthroughs, and the common thread of these stories is the discovery of an **area of vulnerability** in the existing product or service. Entrepreneurs love to hear these stories, and it's no wonder; the stories contain lessons and inspiration. That's why we include three of them here.

Bob and Ted Did It

IBM Corporation seems to have forgotten what made it one of the top ten largest corporations in America: customer service. Until it introduced the personal computer, IBM always dealt directly with customers. IBM employees sold and serviced IBM equipment. The customer could reach out and touch "Big Blue" through its employees.

Since the advent of the PC, however, IBM has effectively insulated itself from the customer. For example, IBM now sells its PCs through Sears, Businessland, Computerland, and other retail outlets. Then these computer retailers sell and service the IBM products along with the other products they handle. This represents a big change in the way IBM deals with the business community. And two sharp entrepreneurs believed it created a gap in the marketplace.

In 1990, Bob Ward and Ted Sundstrom got together and started brainstorming about the problems and opportunities in the computer industry. Bob had a degree in electronics from Cal Tech. Ted held a master's degree in computer science from the University of California at Irvine. While checking the ladder in the arena of business computers, they spotted the gap in the market abandoned by Big Blue—customer service. Checking around, they noted increased frustration when busy businesspeople dealt with retail employees.

They thought the opportunity was too good to pass up. But could they do it? Could they take the same approach IBM had used to score with the business community? Could a professional approach to service overcome their small size?

The partners each purchased a couple of "sincere" business suits. They incorporated, leased some office space, and had business cards and stationery printed. They named their firm Serich Computers: Professional Solutions to Business Problems.

Bob explains that they leased office space rather than retail space because their target customer likes to buy in a professional way. "We bring the prospect into a conference room and we sit down to discuss the problems they need to solve. After discussing the problems, we move to a demonstration room where we show them the equipment we believe will serve their needs. We wanted to distance ourselves from the "used car sales" image—an evolving image in the computer field—because we're in this for the long haul; we're not interested merely in moving a hunk of iron."

ACTION STEP 30

Use networking to learn about your competitors.

Leave your mystery shopper disguise at home and really dig into this competitor research. Some of it will be easy: yellow pages, newspapers, trade advertising, signs, former and present customers, and vendors/suppliers.

Interview everyone who will talk to you about them.

If your competitors have stock that is publicly traded, ask your stock broker about them or look them up yourself in Moody's or Standard and Poor's. Another neat trick is to ask your librarian to get you a 10K corporate report. (A 10K is required of public companies by the IRS and the Securities and Exchange Commission.) In addition, most firms are listed and rated by Dun & Bradstreet. Ask your friendly banker for a peek at the D&B reports.

Keep expanding your competitor test matrix. Use a 1–10 scale on everything you can see, hear about, touch (image, location, advertising, their signs, the way the employees dress, parking, target customers, product mix, pricing, hours of service, and so on). Whenever you unearth some hard data, compare it with industry averages.

Keep looking for those areas of vulnerability.

---

change the arena
transform a product or service by adding a simple benefit that has immediate customer appeal

area of vulnerability
your competitor's soft underbelly or Achilles' Heel—a weakness ready for you to exploit

Serich follows the same track with its employees. All the salespeople have degrees in computer science. Each employee has his or her own personal computer, and all of the PCs are networked.

In just 6 years, Serich has grown to $2.75 million in sales and has increased its staff every year. They now employ 19 people.

The moral here is, don't insulate yourself from your customers. Reach out and touch them. Listen to their problems, and then offer them solutions that are logical and effective.

Ted Turner Did It

If you were around in the winter of 1991, and if you had access to a TV set, there's a good chance you watched the action of Operation Desert Storm on CNN.

CNN, the Cable News Network, was started by entrepreneur Ted Turner, who used his new eyes to focus on opportunities in cable and satellite communications. Turner has four stations: WTBS (a "super station"); Headline News; TNT (a movie channel); and CNN.

CNN is beamed worldwide.

Turner is an entrepreneur who understands the rhythms of the life cycle. He was unable to buy a network, so he started one.

"Manufacturer B" Did It

"Manufacturer B," a very large electrical manufacturer, wanted to penetrate the market for movie projector lamps. The problem was that "Manufacturer A," another large company, had the market sewn up.

Manufacturer B's creative, entrepreneurial-type people went to work on the problem and discovered an area of vulnerability in Manufacturer A's bulbs. They then designed a new bulb with a four-prong locking flange pin. The new bulb was easy to install, it was safe, and the new design provided better focusing.

To promote the new bulb, Manufacturer B gave away the quarter-size sockets that were fitted to it and the bases into which to set the sockets. It was the system approach.

Because Manufacturer B's new system worked better and more smoothly than the piecemeal approach provided by Manufacturer A, the customers (Kodak, Bell and Howell, and other big companies) went for it. By the time Manufacturer A woke up to the change in the arena, it was almost too late, and when they started making bulbs with locking flange pins, they had to pay Manufacturer B, the owner of the patent, to produce them.

You Can Do It, Too

These are just three of many stories we could tell you about innovators who disarmed the competitors and brought about big changes in the marketplace. It's altogether possible that we may someday be telling such a story about *you*. Yes, you, too, can do it. You just need to:

> know what business you're in,
>
> know your target customer,
>
> know your competition,
>
> know your product, and then
>
> give rein to your creativity and your entrepreneurial spirit.

Go for it. Surprise us! Action Step 31 shows you how.

ACTION STEP 31

Formulate a plan for disarming your competitors.

Make this a brainstorming session with family or friends. Start with a novel idea (such as packing expensive gear in popcorn or competing with yourself) and let go with the wild ideas.

Keep your mind on the industry ladder as you brainstorm. What's unique about your product or service? Are you supplying something your target customer wants and/or needs? What tactics of your competitors can you utilize? Where are your competitors' areas of vulnerability? What might you do to establish presence? What image would be good for your business? Is there some way that you could become so unique that you would build your own little monopoly?

Consider what you might do if you start out in an embryonic industry and the arena soon becomes filled with competitors. Come up with a Plan B.

Think. Imagine. Create. Surprise. And have fun.

Key Points from Another View
Part I:
BUILDING A BETTER BUSINESS

The following basic ingredients can help boost a business from average to above average.

1. Customers always come first.
2. Your employees are valuable to your business.
3. Toot your own horn—free publicity is cheap.
4. Know when to do, and when to delegate.
5. Suppliers are your friends—treat them right and they will serve you better.
6. Make up your mind.
7. Do it today, not tomorrow.
8. Buy the best.
9. Consistency is key and makes for an organized, professional operation.
10. Dust off your goals.
11. Return phone calls.
12. Advance into high tech.
13. The temporary solution—consider temporary help.
14. Is anyone out there? Know your Target Market.
15. Remember your roots—keep your entrepreneurial spirit.
16. Complacency kills, so pay attention to what's going on.
17. School is still in session—you can never know enough.
18. Tactics for time off—every entrepreneur needs a vacation.
19. Getting to know you—participate in your community's activities.

From: Erike Kotite, "Building Blocks—Building a Better Business," *Entrepreneurial Woman*, Summer, 1989, 46–50.

Key Points from Another View
Part II:
MAGIC WORDS

The following ten phrases may be all that's standing between you and increased success.

1. How can I help?
2. I can solve that problem.
3. I don't know, but I'll find out.
4. I will take responsibility.
5. There will be no surprises.
6. I will keep you updated.
7. I will deliver on time.
8. It'll be just what you ordered.
9. The job will be complete.
10. I appreciate your business.

From: Dan Schreiner, "Building Blocks—Magic Words," *Entrepreneurial Woman*, March, 1991, 74–77.

SUMMARY

This chapter describes the competition life cycle and its implications for the entrepreneur.

In the *embryonic stage,* the arena is empty. Competitors are nonexistent. Your target customer is a dim profile on yellow paper. Potential customers ignore you. Suppliers and distributors laugh at you.

In the *growth stage,* competitors enter the arena and target customers surface. They have been waiting for your product for years! Smart distributors sign you up.

In the *mature stage,* competition makes shelf space scarce and you are forced to steal customers to survive.

In the *decline stage,* a few competitors hang on tenaciously. By then the sharp entrepreneur has moved to a new arena and a new enterprise.

Competition is a mind game, because buying decisions are made in the customers' minds. A number of case studies in the chapter show how successful entrepreneurs have disarmed the competition—by stealing customers, by scouting the competition for strengths and weaknesses, by establishing customer recognition with their image and presence, by being ready for changing conditions with a Plan B, and by changing the arena of competition.

THINK POINTS FOR SUCCESS

◀ Do it smarter.

◀ Do it faster.

◀ Do it with more style.

◀ Provide more features.

◀ Provide more service.

◀ Treat your target customers like family; consider their needs.

◀ Be unique.

◀ Change the arena through innovation.

◀ Keep your image in the prospect's mind.

◀ Compete with yourself if necessary.

◀ Disarm the competition by being better, faster, safer, and easier to use.

◀ A new firm cannot win a price war.

◀ Old habits are hard to break; give your TC *several* reasons to switch over to you.

◀ Develop your own monopoly.

REFERENCES

Albrecht, Karl, and Ron Zemke. *Service America: Doing Business in the New Economy.* Homewood, Ill.: Business One Irwin, 1985.

A Basic Guide to Exporting. U.S. Department of Commerce.

Cooper, Robert. *The Performance Edge.* Boston: Houghton Mifflin Company, 1991.

Davis, Stanley. *Future Perfect.* Reading, Mass.: Addison-Wesley, 1989.

De Cordoba, Jose. "Hollywood Finds Hispanic Audiences Are a Hot Ticket at the Movie Theater." *Wall Street Journal,* April 6, 1988. [Filmmakers discover that the simulreleases of a film in both English and Spanish can bump the gross up 5 to 10 percent. The new pie is the Hispanic audience—they go to movies more often than other customer groups. There's some distance to go, however, as advertisers try to sell ads in English to Spanish-language stations.]

Directory of Leading U.S. Export Management Companies. Bergano Book Co., P.O. Box 190, Fairfield, CT 06430.

Ingrassia, Lawrence. "Day-Care Business Lures Entrepreneurs: Market Growth, Fragmentation, Spur Ventures." *Wall Street Journal,* June 2, 1988. [A hot segment of a hot growth market, day-care centers are springing up across the country. The main competition is nonprofit centers that charge lower fees, so start-ups are claiming to offer high quality for the high price. Chains like Kinder-Care and La Petite Academy are entering the low end of the arena, which leaves to the entrepreneur the markets for the children of Yuppies, "New Homesteaders," "Towns and Gowns," "Young Suburbia," "Blue-Chip Blues," and "Baby Boom Again." For some explanation of these terms, see Chapter 7.]

Mackay, Harvey. *Beware the Naked Man Who Offers You His Shirt.* New York: Wm. Morrow, 1990.

Mackay, Harvey. *Swim with the Sharks without Being Eaten Alive.* New York: Wm. Morrow, 1988.

The 1990 Official Export Guide. Philadelphia: North American Publishing Co., 1990. [Order through publisher at 401 North Broad St., Philadelphia, PA 19108 ($479).]

Porter, Michael. *Competitive Advantage: Creating and Sustaining Superior Performance.* New York: Free Press, 1985.

Ries, Al, and Jack Trout. *Marketing Warfare.* New York: NAL-Dutton, 1990. [This is a follow-up book by the clever authors of *Positioning.* Examples: "Only the market leader should consider playing defense;" and "Find a weakness in the leader's strength and attack that point." They write well. If you're in business, read Ries and Trout.]

Ries, Al, and Jack Trout. *Positioning: The Battle for the Mind,* first edition revised. New York: Warner Books, 1988. [Update of the 1981 classic. Gives behind-the-scenes look at the details of many stunning business successes and failures.]

Secretary's Office, *Publications.* Washington, D.C.: Governmental Printing Office, periodically revised. [Request through U.S. International Trade Commission, 500 E St. S.W., Room 112A, Washington DC 20436. Little known source that provides free data and market research information on overseas markets.]

Standard & Poor's Industry Surveys. McGraw Hill, annual.

Thomas Register of American Manufacturers. New York: Thomas Publishing Co., annual.

Zemke, Ron, and Dick Schaaf. *The Service Edge.* New York: NAL-Dutton, 1989.

APPENDIX 5.1 • Model Action Step 28: Find your position in the marketplace.

Competition

The hottest competition is already appearing in the hardware, followed by the software market. Most of the competition in the field of software support and training is in the office-automation segment of the market, the low-technology area. I must further research the competition in the advanced arena. I have already referred to Epsilon Graphics as being a specialist in desktop publishing. This tiny, storefront operation will do little to win the confidence of Fortune 1,000 companies.

Cost of Positioning

At the present time, I have an open invitation from Nadek Computer Systems of Tustin, California, to enter a limited partnership in the sale, support, and training of in-plant employees for professional desktop publishing systems. Richard Sudek and Steve Natsuhara, principals at Nadek, wish to enter this potentially lucrative market. They know the hardware side and are proficient in local area network systems. But they readily acknowledge a complete lack of know-how in the area of typesetting, page composition, and graphics as they apply to desktop publishing. They are hesitant to enter this market unless they have instant access to in-depth desktop publishing know-how.

As for the cost of positioning ourselves, this should not be too expensive. A direct-mail program would suffice to get things started. Both Nadek and The Saddleback Scribe could embark on similar direct-mail programs, using computer-generated materials and mailing lists. Direct costs should not exceed $1,000, primarily for printing self-generated sales literature.

The only significant competition in desktop publishing that I am aware of at this point is Epsilon Graphics of Santa Ana. Dan Fili, the president, recently hired a typesetter, Dave Knoch, as a desktop publishing specialist. But Epsilon is targeting on the low-technology end of the market. That's office automation in disguise.

Since its founding, Nadek has depended on word-of-mouth advertising for new business referrals. That marketing effort has been highly successful. The technical proficiency of the Nadek employees is generally laudatory. The marketing proficiency still leaves something to be desired. Perhaps my capabilities would complement theirs to produce a successful combination. Later this year, Nadek will be moving to larger offices. That is one tribute to their success in expanding their penetration of the market.

Customer Spread

Desktop publishing is entering in-house graphic arts departments and spreading to the technical documentation departments of medium-size and large corporations. There are many of these in Orange County and southern Los Angeles County. I still have to complete my detailed research on this market. Other related markets include commercial typesetting houses, printing companies, advertising agencies, and art production houses.

NOTES

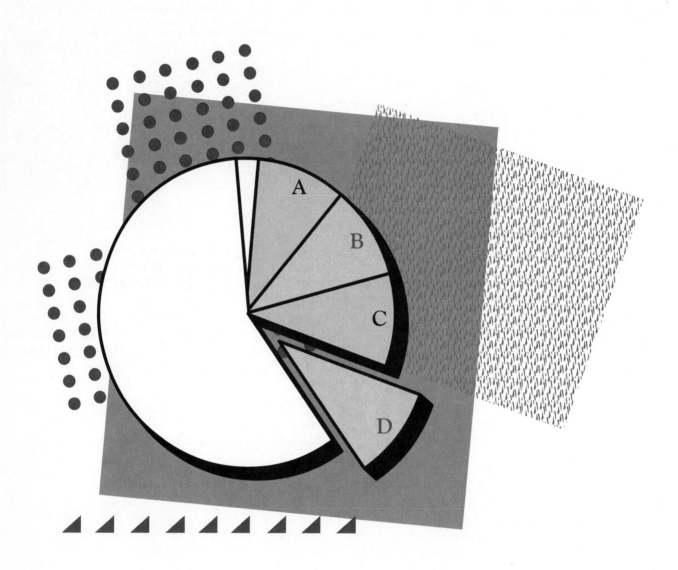

FIGURE 6.1
Chapter 6 will help you prepare part D of your Business Plan, "Marketing Strategy."

6 Promotion: Connecting with the Customer

▲ ▲ ▲ ▲ ▲ ▲ ▲

Learning Objectives

- To learn how to communicate with target customers using both conventional and creative promotional methods.
- To use research to determine a promotional strategy.
- To get free publicity.
- To maximize economy in advertising and promotion.
- To understand the value of personal selling.
- To use brainstorming techniques to arrive at the right promotional mix.
- To develop a customer list.
- To promote through networking.
- To build your own network.

FUTURE FOCUS

Don't keep your business a secret. There are thousands of way to communicate without spending money. Lack of imagination can kill you. Be audacious. Bite a bear! Tell your friends, family, people in supermarket lines about your business.

Now that you have profiled your target customer and gained a sense of competition and market niche, it's time to plan a promotional strategy. But each business is unique, and you don't want to throw away money on promotional schemes that don't work.

For example, if your target customer is college-educated, suburban female age 45–55, who makes over $100,000, owns three cars, rides horseback ten hours a week, and reads *Practical Horseman* and *Performance Horseman,* your best chance of reaching her is with direct mail.

If, on the other hand, your target customers are male and female, age 24–57, with a high-school education, and income of $17,000, you'll have to resort to some form of mass-market advertising or rethink your target market.

Promotion is the art or science of moving the image of your business into the prospect's mind. *Promotion* comes from the Latin verb *movere,* which means "to advance," "to move forward." It's an aggressive word, so learn to say it with a smile!

PROMOTIONAL STRATEGIES

The Promotional Mix

promotional mix
all the elements that you blend to maximize communication with your TC

The key to connecting with customers is to consider a wide variety of promotional strategies and then to pick the right **promotional mix.** Here's a list of some of the potential elements of that mix:

Paid media advertising
Point-of-purchase displays
Catalog sales
Direct mail
Money-back guarantees
Free ink/free air
Personal selling
Trade shows
Industry literature
Working visibility

All of these elements together make for a rich promotional mix. You may use some at one time or with one product, and others at another time or with a different product. For a closer look at each of these strategies, read on.

Potential Strategies

preferred placements
best locations within a publication, a store, or a business area; or the best time slots on TV or radio.

Paid Media Advertising   A surefire way to reach out is by ads in radio, newspaper, television, magazines, and trade journals. Advertising tickles the target customer's mind. With a good ad, you can reach right into your TC's mind and create the desire to buy from you.

Advertising has some obvious drawbacks: 1) it can cost plenty to create; 2) if you don't spend even more money, your ad won't get exposure; and 3) **preferred placements** go to big spenders.

Advice:

Make sure that a large percentage of the listeners, viewers, or readers are in one of your TC groups. Otherwise your message is wasted.

Your best ad is yourself. Stay visible.

Check with vendors. Ask for tear sheets, copy, cooperative advertising money, and help on layouts.

Check with marketing departments of newspapers. Ask for help, advice, information.

Newspapers often offer advertising in special supplements at reduced cost. The offer often includes free editorial copy.

Explore creative **co-op advertising**, in which suppliers share the cost.

Don't be afraid to **piggyback**. Let Madison Avenue build the market. Then use your promotional mix to tell the TC to buy at your place.

Start small, and test, test, test.

co-op advertising
when manufacturers cosponsor or contribute to the retailer's cost of advertising

piggyback
a technique that allows you to coordinate your local ad campaign with the hoopla generated by national advertising

P-O-P (point-of-purchase) display
a display that acts as a silent salesclerk for a specific product

Point-of-Purchase Displays   These encourage impulse purchases of last-minute stuff like paperbacks, pantyhose, candy, magazines, and gum. A sharp P-O-P can improve your image and it serves as a tireless silent salesperson, always on duty. A good P-O-P can be used for customer education. If it is hard to understand how to use your product or the benefits aren't clear to the TC, your silent salespeople can deliver the message.

There are problems with these displays: 1) you can't sell large items because they crowd customers at the cash register, and 2) the display must sell itself as well as the product. (A tacky P-O-P will turn prospective customers *off* instead of *on*.)

Advice:

Do weekly evaluations of all P-O-Ps. Make certain your silent salespeople are doing their work.

Catalogs   This sales tool is just right for isolated shoppers and shoppers in a hurry. Because we are becoming so "time poor," even general items are now being purchased via catalogs. A customer can shop at their convenience and not have to worry about store hours, parking, or traffic. **Catalog houses** such as Lillian Vernon don't usually manufacture anything, so they are always looking for good products. Use catalogs as another kind of silent salesperson to reach smaller customers.

If you try printing your own catalogs, you'll run into at least two problems: 1) cost (they are expensive to print and to mail); 2) size limitations (it's tough to sell anything by catalog that's big, bulky, or inconvenient to ship).

Advice:

catalog house
business that buys products and resells them via catalogs

Be prepared to take advantage of video catalogs. They are growing in number.

Let major catalog houses do your promotion, but make sure you can deliver if your product takes off.

Before you get in too deep, try a few major houses with a **product description** plus photographs. If they don't like your product, they may help you locate a catalog house that will. The feedback will be invaluable.

product description
a list of the features and benefits of a product

Direct Mail   This promotional tool lets you aim your brochures and flyers where they will do the most good. **Direct mail** is very important for small business, because it can go to the heart of your target market.

The success of direct mail depends on your ability to define the target market. If the market is too fragmented for you to do this, direct mail is not for you.

direct mail
advertisement or sales pitch that is mailed directly to TCs

Advice:

Stay up nights if you have to, but define the target market.

Develop customer lists. (Action Step 34 will help you do this later on in the chapter.)

Money-Back Guarantees   You may not have thought of a guarantee as a form of promotion, but it is. You can reach security-minded customers by emphasizing the no-risk features of your product.

The problem is that you must back up your guarantee with time and money.
Advice:

Figure 5 percent into your pricing to cover returned goods. If the product is fragile or easily misused—and people have been known to misuse just about everything—build in a higher figure.

press release
a news item written by a business about itself and sent to the media as an attempt to get free ink

free ink/free air
information about your business that is published or broadcasted free of charge

Free Ink and Free Air   Reviews, features, interview shows, **press releases**, and newspaper columns cost you nothing, and they are tremendously effective. **Free ink/ free air** is an excellent way to promote because it establishes your company in a believable way. The target customer is likely to attach more credence to words that are not paid advertising.

The obstacle here is getting media people to think your business is newsworthy.
Advice:

Every business is newsworthy in some way. Dig until you find something.

Know the media people. Aim your release at *their* target readers, viewers, or listeners.

Make your press kit visual. Send accompanying photos of your principals, your facility, and your product or service in use.

Present your press kit in an attractive folder to influential representatives of the media.

Personal Selling   It doesn't matter if you've never sold before; no one is a better salesperson than you are. You are the business. If you listen carefully, your target customers will *tell* you how to sell them your product or service. That's why a good salesperson is a creative listener, not a fast talker. Most customers like to talk with the owner of the business. Use that to your advantage.

personal selling
selling and taking orders by an individual salesperson

Unfortunately, **personal selling** is expensive, especially if you have to pay others to do it, and it will boost your overhead unless you pay your salespeople only by earned commission. And if you try to do it all yourself, you won't have the time and energy for other things that only *you* can do.
Advice:

Make everyone in your business a salesperson. Delivery people, warehouse people, computer programmers, bookkeepers, clerical people, switchboard operator. If nothing sells, they're out of a job. Remind everyone who works for you that your TC needs a lot of TLC.

network of sales reps
independent businesspeople who sell a number of noncompeting products and services in a specific geographic area on a commission-only basis

lead club
a group of business and professional people who meet regularly to exchange sales prospects and tips

Consider developing a **network of sales reps** who will work on a percentage of sales. Keep cheerleading. Reps need encouragement, too.

Increase your personal visibility. Join **leads clubs** in your area. Join service clubs and trade associations. Write a newspaper column. Be bold. (See Box 6.1.)

Don't ever get so big that you don't spend some time selling and talking with your customers. If you lose touch with your customer, you may lose your business.

BOX 6.1   Bite a Lion on the Tail

> For whatever reason, many people are afraid of personal selling. You can make that
> fear your challenge. Ever hear of the surefire cure for fear of lions? You just bite a lion
> on the tail.
>
> It's the same way with fear of elevators. The best cure is to ride in lots of elevators.
>
> If you're afraid of selling, go out and become your own best salesperson. *You can
> do it*—not only because you know the business better than anyone else, but because
> your very hesitancy indicates that you will be sensitive to your customers' needs.
>
> But don't just go out there and be sensitive. Go out and bite a lion on the tail.

Trade Shows   These shows display your product or service in a high-intensity way.
Trade shows develop a carnival, county-fair atmosphere, which can be so necessary
in business. Besides, your appearance at a trade show asserts your position in your
industry.

However, if the show is not in your area, you'll have transportation costs, and the
booths are expensive. Furthermore, unless you're careful and make a study of the
layout, you may rent a space that is thin on **traffic.** See Figure 6.2.

traffic
movement of vehicles and pedestrians

Advice:

Share booth space with another small business owner.

Combine functions by doing some market research while you're promoting.

Study the floor plan. Position yourself in a high-traffic area.

Industry Literature   Become a source of information in your industry by producing brochures, newsletters, handbooks, product documentation, annual reports,
newspaper columns for the layman, or even the "bible" for your industry. (How
would you like to be recognized as an expert in your field?) We think this is one of
the best promotional devices around.

You may balk if you're not handy with words, and that *can* be an obstacle, but
it's not an insurmountable obstacle. Remember that expertise is admired and sought
out by others. As you grow in expertise, you'll also grow in confidence and the ability
to communicate with words.

Advice:

Hire a writer.

Talk is cheap. If you get your thoughts down on paper, you're two steps ahead
    of the talkers.

Don't be afraid of audacity; it stirs the blood.

Working Visibility   In Chapter 5, our case study on Ben Jones painted a picture
of an entrepreneur who knew how to maintain a presence. You can do the same
thing even on a small budget. Most service firms display their presence as they work.
In other words, they put signs on everything: their business, their trucks, and their
work sites. Wherever they're busy, they let people know it. They make themselves
visible.

The drawback here is similar to one of the drawbacks with P-O-P displays. If the
presence you maintain doesn't sell itself—if it is unattractive, or if it calls attention
to an unsavory part of your business—you will lose potential customers rather than
gain them.

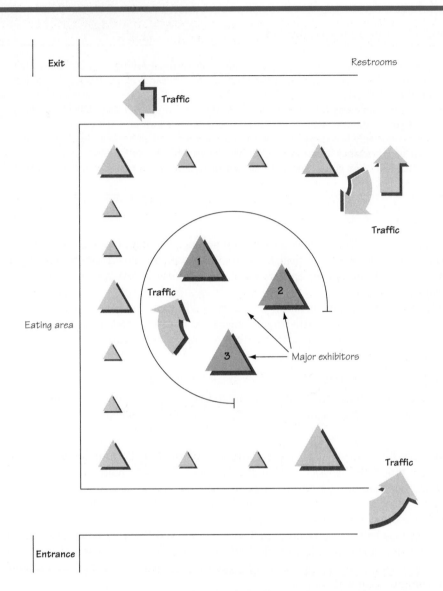

FIGURE 6.2   If you can preview the layout of a trade show for where the heaviest traffic flows will be, you can position your booth to take advantage of it.

Advice:

Exploit your public activities with signs that tell people who you are.

Review your displays weekly. Make sure the message is working.

How to Make the Right Decision

Any promotion or promotional mix that advances the image of your business is worth considering. You've just surveyed some of the most common and traditional means of promotion. Before you decide on your promotional strategy, make sure you're open to all options. That's why we ask you to keep an open mind throughout this chapter, as you brainstorm for strategies, examine promotion campaigns, and come to understand the importance of planning ahead. Then you will truly be able to make good decisions on how to connect with the customer.

SALES REPS AS CONNECTORS

Suppose you have a new product that has immediate sales potential across the country. How can you connect with the whole United States? Should you hire your younger brother to take care of it for you, or should you seek out a professional sales rep (who acts like a commissioned sales agent).

An army of sales reps awaits your call. However, a rep is not a rep is not a rep; select your reps carefully. Exercise caution because the reputation of your sales reps will become *your* reputation.

The best way to find good reps is to interview potential buyers of your goods. Ask them to recommend some reps who have impressed them. When the same name surfaces several times, you will know where to start your contacts.

Aggressive reps may contact you. Prepare yourself to ask them the right kinds of questions:

Who are your customers?

How many salespeople do you have?

What geographic areas do you cover?

What lines have you carried?

What help can you offer in collecting overdue accounts?

What ideas do you have for trade show presentations?

Do you have a showroom?

Could you work with us on a regional roll out, while we get ready for national coverage?

What percentage commission do you expect?

Can I participate in your sales meeting?

Do you handle competitive lines?

What kind of reports on your sales calls can I expect?

What kind of performance guarantees do you offer?

How can our agreement be terminated?

Can I pay you after I have collected from customers?

Provide all the encouragement and support to your reps that you can, and never stop being a cheerleader. Nonetheless, insist on sales call reports that will keep you informed on what is going on in the field, and pack your bags and make some calls with the reps. Write monthly sales letters and encourage feedback from both your reps and their customers. You *could* learn the worst—that a new line has taken your place or that the reps have been sleeping. This feedback will help you to evaluate your product line and your reps.

COURTESY AS PROMOTION

A luxury imported auto dealer mailed 5,000 postcards to prospects selected demographically according to high income. The message on the postcard read something like: "Come in and test-drive this road warrior and receive a nice gift."

ACTION STEP 32

Brainstorm a winning promotional campaign for your business.

Disregard all budgetary restraints. Pretend that money is no object. Close your eyes, sit back, and develop the ideal campaign for connecting with your target customers. It's okay to "get crazy" with this, because excellent, workable solutions often develop out of such bizarre mental activity!

If your product or service needs a multimillion-dollar advertising promotion with endorsements by your favorite movie star, fantasize that it's happening now.

If you need a customer list created in marketing heaven, specify exactly what you need and it is yours.

If you are looking for the services of a first-class catalog house, just whisper the name three times and you are in business.

If your business at its peak could use a thousand delivery trucks with smiling drivers who make your TC feel terrific, write down "1,000 smiling delivery people."

If your product is small, brainstorm the perfect point-of-purchase device, perhaps one with slot machines whose money-tubes are connected to your private bank vault.

Watch the money roll in.

This chance to ignore costs won't come around again. (Reality is right around the corner.) But for now, have fun.

One potential customer came from 40 miles away for his test drive. The gift was a good incentive, but he'd been looking at cars for a year and was about ready to make a decision, so he wanted the test drive. That morning he had transferred funds to his checking account. "Honey," he said to his wife as he left the house, "I'll be home with a car." His pink slip on his trade-in smoldered in the glove compartment.

Mr. Serious Prospect entered the dealer's showroom wearing old clothes and clutching his postcard. Four dapper salesmen in three-piece suits had seen him coming and had left the showroom quickly.

Without a salesperson in sight, the prospect spent 10 minutes waiting, reading the literature. The demos were locked, so he couldn't even sit behind the wheel for a fantasy drive. At last, a secretary entered the showroom, asked him for his postcard, and gave him the premium gift. About this time, one of the salesmen returned, hands in his pockets and looking bored. The prospect took the opportunity to ask some questions about the car, to which the salesman responded without enthusiasm in monosyllables—and with a yawn.

(Would *you* feel like doing business with such a place?)

Mr. Prospect took his business elsewhere that morning. He found the car he wanted and wrote a check for $25,000.

The objective was to bring in customers for a test drive—not to give away premiums. Everything worked except the last person in the chain. How many other deals did that dealer lose during the promotion?

Be dramatic. Impress your employees with the fact that you mean business about customer courtesy. Close down your business for a day and have all employees attend a sales retreat that stresses the importance of potential customers to your remaining in business. Follow up the retreat with incentive programs that reward employees for acts of exceptional courtesy to customers.

PLANNING AHEAD

You need to make a lot of intelligent noise before you open your doors for business. When you open, open with a bang. Start-ups are ironic—you need to spend bushels of money to overcome buyer inertia, yet you don't have those dollars to spend. What're you to do? Use your head instead of your checkbook.

Plan for your opening now. Few businesses are profitable at first, so yours probably will not be either. Many of the promotional tools we've just discussed cost very little. You will need to use those to lure customers and build confidence that you are in this game to win. Yes, use your head instead of your checkbook. And keep your target customers clearly in mind so that you'll be able to tell them how your product or service will benefit them.

Don't Keep Your Business a Secret

Earlier we said that if you fail to plan, you're planning to fail. When it comes to promotion, if you fail to plan you're planning to keep your business a secret.

One way to avoid keeping your business a secret is to brainstorm an ideal **promotional campaign** with no holds barred and with no worries about costs. Action Step 32 makes sure you consider all of your creative ideas before you discard them because you think they are unrealistic. Save the ideas you come up with in this action step, because we'll use them later. Box 6.2 shows how two entrepreneurs applied ingenious—and cost-effective—solutions to their promotional needs. Later in the chapter we share four case studies from our own file on creative promotions.

promotional campaign
a sales program designed to sell a specific product or service, or to establish an image/benefit/point

BOX 6.2   Creative Promotional Ideas from *Streetfighter*

Don't be afraid of being different. What's hot? What's cool? What's melting in your arms?

Problem: Salespeople at Wisman's Trusted Appliances & TV, Inc., feared that they were losing business when customers left the store to comparison-shop. *Solution:* The owner packed a freezer with ice cream. Every customer who looked at a freezer got a half-gallon carton, free. Instead of comparison shopping, the customers raced home to their refrigerators. That gimmick kept Wisman's in the mind of the prospect and helped increase sales by 11 percent.

Contest? Fat prize? Insure yourself with Lloyd's.
The owner of a small print shop was tapped for $750 by the organizers of a charity golf tournament. Wanting as much mileage as possible for his promotional dollar, he offered a hole-in-one contest prize of $10,000, to be split between the first golfer to ace the ninth hole and the charity. The owner's picture was taken with an oversize check, and the media kept cameras trained on the ninth hole. And if the golfer had sunk one? No problem. The shop owner was insured with Lloyd's of London against business loss with a premium of $450—$300 less than his name on the donors' board would have cost.

Source: Adapted by permission from *Streetfighter,* a newsletter published by RMI, P.O. Box 15719, Fort Wayne, IN 46885. Telephone (219) 485-7037. The *Streetfighter* motto is "Don't outspend the competition; out-think 'em."

As you'll see throughout this chapter, the entrepreneurs who succeed are the entrepreneurs who have the best fix on their target customers. They are also the entrepreneurs who understand the importance of market research.

PROMOTIONS AND MARKET RESEARCH

As you gain experience in promoting your small business, you'll see for yourself just how much promotional strategy and the target customer are interlocked. That's why you can't plan your promotional mix without dipping back into market research. The pros do both at the same time. But don't take our word for it—ask entrepreneur Frank Williams. He combined his research with promotion—a smart recipe. And he used a freebie for a come-on.

Frank Williams was really happy with his microcomputer until the switch went out two days after the 90-day warranty was up. Frank put the micro into his car and drove to the repair shop.

"You turn it on and off a lot?" the repairman asked.

"Of course," Frank said. "Several times a day. Why?"

"That's what wore it out," the repairman said. "The switch is the only moving part. The rest of this baby will last 10 years, at least."

The repair bill was $150, and when Frank got back home he gave the situation some thought. The reason he had to keep turning the machine off was so his youngest child wouldn't mess up his files. The easiest way to handle it was to turn the machine off.

The lock box idea came to Frank as he was dropping off to sleep that night. The next weekend he designed a prototype of wood. His model had a hinged lid, a brass lock, and a space-age look. Frank took it to a friend of his who was a manufacturer.

The friend thought it would fly. They consulted their wives on colors, and the group came up with eight colors—red, orange, yellow, black, beige, blue, white, and avocado.

"That's a lot of paint," the manufacturer said. "How can we narrow it down?"

"Market research," Frank said.

Frank took a prototype Lock Box to a computer trade show. He put up a large sign that said: **Register for a Free Micro Lock Box.** People crowded into Frank's booth to sign up for his drawing. The card had a place for their name, address, phone number, type of computer, and—what color they would like.

It worked. Frank's market research was cheap and fast. In a day and a half, he got 1,400 people to tell him what color Lock Box they wanted. The overwhelming favorite was beige. Furthermore, he had a good start on a customer mailing list.

By being curious and thorough, Frank Williams had discovered one of the secrets of the marketplace: You can promote and do market research at the same time. He also learned that if you don't know what your target customers want, all you have to do is ask them.

Ask the Customers Questions

When you're trying to brainstorm your promotional campaign, ask your customers how they perceive your business. Then ask them questions:

Is there anything they couldn't find?

Is this their first visit to your store? (or some other greeting that you can use instead of "Can I help you?")

What do they want?

Where are they from?

How did they find you?

How else might your company be of service?

Listen to the answers they give you, and value the information for what it is: primary market research data. Write down the customers' exact words in your Adventure Notebook.

Freebies in General

Freebies are a tremendously effective promotional gimmick. You can use them to get your customer's attention, to create interest in a new product, or (like Frank Williams) to gather market research. Freebies don't have to be expensive to help you connect with customers. Box 6.3 describes some inexpensive freebies that entrepreneurs have used to grab the mind of the target customer. (Note that many of the freebies are purely informational. Could you boost sales by offering free advice?)

Discount Coupons

Discount coupons are a special form of freebie because they give you positive feedback on your promotion. They should have an expiration date and multiple-use disclaimers (as, for example, a disclaimer that the coupon cannot be used in conjunction with other promotions or discounts). They should be coded to identify the source so that you can find out where your advertising is paying off, and they should be tested in small quantities before major use.

Everyone seems to like coupons. Even if your product or service is "upscale," consider trying coupons as an introduction or at your slow times of the year.

BOX 6.3   How Street-Smart Are Your Freebies?

Every business has a "freebie" that will help grab the mind of its target customer. This book is full of examples: the toy store retailer who gave away a large jar of pennies in exchange for a start on a customer mailing list; the inventor who gave away one computer lock box in exchange for a mailing list of 1,400 names. Here are some more examples of effective, street-smart freebies.

Orange Juice. A manufacturer of a new juice squeezer served freshly squeezed orange juice at a trade show.

Hot Dogs. A retailer obtained hot dogs and buns from a local hot dog maker, then advertised with promotions that read "Bring your buns to our August Sale at noon." At noon, the line of hot dog lovers stretched around the block. Curious customers, lured by free food and the carnival atmosphere, walked into the store to check out the sale. The cost of this promotion was $66.

Health Drink. The distributor of an expensive food blender gave away cups of a health drink and a booklet of recipes at a trade show. Salespeople were on hand to take orders for the blender.

Advice. A men's clothing store employed a woman fashion consultant during the month of December to give advice to women who came in to shop for presents for men.

A flower shop passed out "Green Thumb" information leaflets on plant care.

A hardware store expanded into the parking lot for a "home improvement weekend." Professionals were on hand to give tips and instruction on laying tile, repairing garden hoses, fixing leaky faucets, and installing dead-bolt locks.

Source: Adapted in part from *How to Get Free Press* by Toni Delacorte, Judy Kimsey, and Susan Halas (San Francisco: Harbor Publishing, 1981) pp. 120–121, 125, 127, 131–132.

MAKING DECISIONS

By now you should be ready to make a few decisions about your promotional mix. Let's begin with price.

Attach Price Tags to Your Promotion Strategies

A freebie, like other promotional strategy, costs money. Look at the ideal promotional strategies you came up with in Action Step 32 and pick the top four or five elements. Then determine the price of each. (For example, consider the difference in cost between a magazine ad and a press release.) Action Step 33 walks you through the process.

Don't be discouraged if price knocks out part of your ideal promotional mix. That's why we've filled this chapter with so many inexpensive promotional ideas. And in the meantime, you have used the powers of your imagination to brainstorm the best possible promotional effort for your business.

Even as you make decisions, keep thinking of that best possible effort—and of your target customer—and you can't go wrong.

Concentrate Your Efforts

One promotional strategy may prove to be a big winner for your business. The examples that follow show how several entrepreneurs discovered their winning strategies.

ACTION STEP 33

Attach a price tag to each item of your promotion package.

What will your Customer Connection cost? To get some idea, go back to Action Step 32 and list the top four or five connections you want with your customers. Then research what they cost.

Let's imagine that you have chosen this promotional mix:

1. **Magazine Ads.** This choice assumes you know what your TC reads. Good. Contact the display ad department of the magazines. Ask for their media kit and a reader profile. At the same time, ask for the rates for their mailing lists for the geographic areas you want to reach. Many magazines will sell lists by zip code.

2. **Direct Mail.** Look up mailing list brokers in the yellow pages under *Direct Mail*. Tell them what business you are in and ask for information and strategy tips. Ask for sample names so you can check mailing list accuracy against your TC profiles. Compare the cost of buying the lists from brokers with the cost of buying them from magazines.

3. **Press Releases.** Visit the marketing department of your local newspaper for information on targeting its readers. Use this information to angle your release. Type the release double-spaced. Make sure you catch the reader's attention. Keep the message simple. Be sure to wield the five W's (who, what, where, when, why) and the noble H (how) of journalism.

4. **Personal Selling.** If you cannot reach customers this way yourself, you will need to budget for someone who can. If you are planning on selling yourself, locate lead clubs in your area and start building a network of contacts. Figure your salary and expenses as a promotional cost. (For tips on how to profile your personality and how it can be balanced by others, see Chapter 13.)

Once you know what each item of your promotional package will cost, you can decide which of them you can afford.

While reading what these entrepreneurs have to say, you may discover your own winning strategy. Look for inspiration.

EARTH-TO-AIR TRAVEL, INC.—NEWSLETTER

Two years ago we missed the ironclad deadline for getting our ad in the phone book yellow pages, so we tried to make up for that by placing fun-type ads in community newsletters within a 2-mile radius of our agency. The ads didn't cost much, and we hoped they would help to keep our visibility high. Our best response came from a mobile home park less than a mile away. It's a gold mine of retirees with steady incomes who dearly love to travel.

By studying the community newsletters, we came up with our own format, and now we send out our own agency newsletter every couple of months. On the front page we feature a catchy travel theme, along with a picture of our employees. The picture helps us connect, especially with first-time customers. They see our smiling faces, and most of them feel they know us when they walk through our door.

We're already on the way to being friends.

THE SOFTWARE SCHOOL—DIRECT MAIL

When we started The Software School, we quickly discovered that the major local newspaper covered the northern half of the county, while the market we'd targeted—executives and small business microcomputer owners—lived in the southern half. The one sure way to reach the center of the market was with a direct mail piece. Our strategy was to buy a list from a magazine whose readers matched our customer profile—in this case, *Personal Computing*—and then we sent out our brochure.

The response was terrific. We generated enough business for a healthy start-up, and satisfied customers sold for us after that by talking up our 1-day teaching system.

Direct mail allowed us to go right to the heart of our market. When you're just starting out in a new venture, that kind of accuracy is worth every penny it costs.

ARGOSY AUTO PARTS—A SIGN ON YOUR CAR

sign on car
a simple promotional technique—you park your car or truck in a high-traffic area—the sign points the way to your business

The main reason we chose Argosy was because we thought it was a good name. My husband had thirty-two years of experience in the auto parts trade—in retailing and also in distribution—and when we opened our store in South Coast we felt it was a guaranteed money-maker.

We opened our new store in midsummer, but by September we were ready to call it quits. Sales had averaged only $2,000 a month, and that wasn't even enough to pay the rent.

Fortunately, we got help from a small business seminar. It was made clear to us that although everyone was familiar with the name Argosy, very few people knew we were Argosy in South Coast.

Our first step was simple—we parked our car on the main street near our store. On the back we placed a large sign, with an arrow pointing to our store. The sign read ARGOSY AUTO PARTS. Business picked up right away, and that gave us the confidence to make contact with service stations in the area.

Gradually, we built up our own network. I joined some local service clubs, and that led me to a sales lead club. We meet once a week, for breakfast, and if you don't bring someone a lead, you have to put a dollar into the kitty.

Things are all right now, but when I look back, I know that without that sign on the car we'd have been out of business in no time.

GARMENT GUIDE—FREE INK

When my partner and I got the idea for guiding shoppers through the L.A. garment district, we thought it would be so exciting we wouldn't have to do much except stop off once a week to make bank deposits.

Were we ever wrong.

We ran a good-sized ad in the local paper. It filled a couple of buses, but then our market ran out, because those customers didn't need a return trip on the bus. We had some flyers printed up and we covered every car in every parking lot in our community. Two thousand flyers netted us half a bus.

Then I just happened to read a feature story in the View section of the *L.A. Times* about a tour to Hollywood and Universal Studios. On an impulse I called the reporter up and told her about Garment Guide. It worked.

On the next trip, the reporter came along, and brought a staff photographer. Two weeks later, *our* story was on the *front page* of the View section—a beautiful third of a page—and customers began calling us! Our local papers followed a month or so later with features about the service, and after we got bigger, a TV reporter profiled us for one of the evening news magazines on television.

Now business is great. We haven't had to advertise for 18 months. When people ask me what kind of promotion I believe in, I tell them free ink!

We hope you found inspiration by reading about these entrepreneurs, who, through planning or perseverance, found successful promotional strategies. Now let's go on to two of the most useful promotional tools for *every* small business, mailing lists and networking.

MAILING LISTS

Sometimes the winning component of a promotional mix is a **mailing list** that goes to the heart of your target market. An accurate and up-to-date mailing list can mean money in the bank. Entrepreneur Mel Cartwright developed a database on his target customers in a fun and painless manner—in the midst of his Christmas promotion.

> **mailing list**
> names and addresses of potential customers

Mel Cartwright had worked for three large corporations before he decided to start a business of his own. He used some money of his own and founded Mel's Toys on the East Coast.

For the first six months, business was fair, and Mel broke even. Sales picked up dramatically the day after Thanksgiving. The parking lot in the shopping center was crammed with cars, and Christmas-conscious people came in hunting for gifts for their children. That Friday Mel made more money than he had in all of September.

"The toy business is seasonal," Mel said. "And with all those people coming through the door, I wanted to make sure I developed a solid customer base."

So for three weeks, Mel hired a Rent-a-Santa and a professional photographer. Every child that came into Mel's Toys was photographed, free, on Santa's knee. While the children were being photographed, the parents filled out information cards with their child's name, age, toy preferences, and date of birth.

At the end of the three weeks, Mel had developed a fine customer list. He also had one valuable piece of information—the birthday of every child who had been photographed.

> **customer file**
> a list of persons or firms that have purchased from you

So, every time a birthday rolled around, Mel mailed a small inexpensive toy along with some copies of the Santa photograph. As an added bonus, he made the negatives available to parents, many of whom ordered Christmas cards picturing their child talking to Santa.

As his mailing list grew, Mel came up with another idea.

"I was at the cash register one day when one of my employees was sick with the flu, and I noticed five customers in a row who spent more than $50. I kept those checks and credit card slips separate, and at the end of the day I photocopied them and started a Big Spender list. Today, my Big Spender list has grown to several hundred customers, and I've developed a special mailer aimed just at them."

I wish someone would have told me how important a mailing list would be in this business before I got into it. With what I know now, I think I could branch off into at least a dozen industries and do very well."

Mel smiles. "And to think it all began with a Rent-a-Santa."

ACTION STEP 34

Organize your files.

Begin with a study of what your target customer reads. Move from there to a reader profile and a mailing list, to find out where your TCs are concentrated.

For every customer you contact, make up a file card. Use your handy demographic set-up (sex, age, income, education, and residence—or size of company, type of industry, what department did the buying, and so forth) and launch yourself early into analyses of life-style or business style. If you have a microcomputer, this is a great time to use it.

Try to segment the big spenders and develop a special strategy for them. (Every industry has its heavy users. Who are the heavies in your industry?)

Start a media file by contacting all potential advertising media in your area. Ask for rate cards and demographics.

If you have not done it yet, start a file on your competitors and how they promote. Try to learn what is working. What ideas can you borrow?

Start a How-Can-They-Help-Me File on your vendors and suppliers. Action Step 53 in Chapter 11 will help you create your own vendor statement. Most vendors have been in the industry awhile. Get to know them, ask for advice, listen carefully. You may not buy from them, but the information you obtain could save your neck.

You may not need a Rent-a-Santa, but you do need well-organized information. Action Step 33 asks you to organize the information you already have. See how the concept of a mailing list may begin with a **customer file**, but expands to include your other contacts as well. You can't help but gather information as you operate your small business. With good files, that information becomes useful. Organized information is power. Action Step 34 shows you how to get that power.

NETWORKING

Another source of promotional power is the technique of **networking** (Figure 6.3). Networking carries the image of your business to a support group of noncompetitive helpers. It is the wave of the future in small business. Gena D'Angelo speaks for many when she gives this testimonial for networking.

> When Rob and I decided to go into business for ourselves, we looked around for more than a year. I had some training in graphics and Rob's good with numbers, and what we finally decided on was a franchised mail-box operation. We paid the franchisor a flat fee and agreed to pay them a percentage of our gross. They gave us aid and assistance and a well-developed business plan.
>
> What they didn't tell us about was networking.
>
> When you're in the mail-box business, giving good service is how you forge ahead. We knew we had to promote our image and we tried everything—brochures, leaflets, flyers, and full-page display ads in the local newspapers. But the business didn't start rolling in until I joined my first network.
>
> It's a sales lead club, and the membership is varied. We have a real estate broker, an insurance agent, the president of a small bank, the owner of a coffee service, a printer, a sign manufacturer, the owner of a chain of service stations, a sporting goods store owner, a travel agent, two small manufacturers, and a contractor. We meet once a week for breakfast. If you don't bring at least one sales lead for another club member, you have to put a dollar into the kitty. I've gotten more business from that club than from all my other promotional efforts combined.
>
> So I joined another one, and I used the contacts I made to build my own network.
>
> Business has been good ever since. We opened our second shop last April, put in a word processor to keep up with the typing, and added an answering service. That first year, we networked our way to even more business, and we're planning to open a third shop ten miles south of here by this time next year.
>
> Networking gives you confidence, and it allows you to pass on helpful information to people who aren't competing with you—as well as receive that kind of information.

networking
communicating through person-to-person channels in an attempt to sell or gain information

pyramid hierarchy
a form of bureaucratic organization with the Pharoah, Chief, King, President, Chairman, Chancellor, CEO, or Boss at the top, all others below

Why You Should Network

Look around you. The days of the **pyramid hierarchy** are drawing to a close, and it is sunset in the industrial desert. Church, state, corporation, and neighborhood—the old structures are crumbling, wheezing, and breaking apart.

One reason is what has come to be called "Toffler's trough." The old structures are wallowing in the cultural trough between the Industrial Age and the Information Age. As the engines of the industrial society slow down and break apart, they lose their efficiency. When that happens, people begin to ask questions and to cluster together for all kinds of reasons—to trade information, to solve problems, to nurture each other, to help each other survive. Networking is an example of this clustering.

You've probably been networking all your life. In school, you networked for information about teachers and courses. When you moved into a new community, you

FIGURE 6.3   Networking friends and acquaintances can produce a creative, vital flow of information; it can be used to gather sales leads and to carry the image of your business into the community.

networked for information about doctors, dentists, car service, babysitters, and bargains—all the life-supporting details that make up existence. On the job, you networked your way to sales leads, brainstormed your way to better designs, or got in a huddle with some fellow managers or co-workers to solve problems.

As a small business entrepreneur, you can network your way to a surprising number of new customer connections, which can spell success in big letters. If you don't have a network, use Action Step 35 to build one. Develop your network and build **core groups** of people within it. Because a network grows naturally from the loose association of people you already know, and because you are at the *center* of the net, it has to help you.

core groups
clusters of influential, key individuals that share a common area of interest

ACTION STEP 35

Build your network.

Visualize yourself as being in the center of a web of interpersonal contacts and associations. This web connects you with your family, friends, neighbors, acquaintances, business associates—everyone you know—and it is your potential network. Here's how to develop a functioning network for yourself.

Write down what you know about each person in your web—business, hobbies, residence, children, interests, and who they might know. Recall where you met the person. Does the meeting place tell you anything helpful? Are you members of the same group or club? What interests do you share? What, after all, is the connection between you and the person?

Now, from all these people, build a couple of core groups. Start with two or three people. Are they interested in networking? Are they diverse enough? (You'll need doers, stars, leaders, technicians, an organizer or two—people who will tend to "balance out" your own talents. See Chapter 13 on Team Building.) Make sure the people you contact are not competing for the same target customers. The members of a core group must *not* be competitors; if they are, the group won't function as it should.

Set up a meeting. If you are working, breakfast usually works best. If the core group catches on, you can share phone duties and arrange further meetings.

Before you know it, you will be networking your way through the channels of your community, business to business.

Key Points from Another View

ALL THE RIGHT PLACES

With careful preparation, your advertising efforts can earn high dividends.

1. The goal of advertising—to inform, persuade, and remind. In business, you use advertising to bring in orders to you instead of to your competitors.
2. Identify your objectives—they may be one or more of the following:
   - To develop new markets
   - To increase the awareness of your company name
   - To establish awareness of a new location
   - To increase sales
3. Who are your customers?
   - Who are you trying to reach?
   - When do you want to reach those customers?
   - Where do your prospects live?
   - How often do you want to reach your prospects?
4. Where should you advertise?
   - Newspapers—these have a special advantage for local advertisers.
   - Magazines—work because of their specialized content, also allow you to target the prospects who are most likely to be interested in your products.
   - Yellow Pages—people use the Yellow Pages when they know what they want to buy and just want to find out where to buy it.
   - Radio—advantageous because you're able to catch the listener's attention verbally.
   - Television—local stations and cable offer the advertiser a relatively low-cost, high-impact means of getting the advertising message to the potential customer.
   - Outdoor advertising—this method offers dramnatic impact and multiple exposure.
   - Direct Mail—mailing allows the advertiser to pinpoint specific target market segments; it allows personal, one-to-one communication; and it can be cost effective.
5. Making the choice—what you are looking for is the vehicle that is most likely to reach your target market in the most cost-effective way.

From: Lin Grensing, "All the Right Places," *New Business Opportunities*, April, 1991, 64–68.

SUMMARY

Promotion is the art or science of moving the image of your business into the prospect's mind. Anything that will advance that image is a good tactic to consider. We recommend that you survey the whole range of promotional strategies available to you and then choose the promotional mix that will work best for your unique business. Potential strategies include paid media advertising, point-of-purchase displays, catalog sales, direct mail, money-back guarantees, free ink and free air, personal selling, trade shows, industry literature, and working visibility.

We also recommend that you seek creative solutions to the problem of promoting within a small budget, and we give examples of how other entrepreneurs have responded to that challenge. Other topics covered include the proper place of freebies, the reasons why an accurate and up-to-date mailing list is a must for survival, and the importance of networking for sales leads and other information.

Throughout the chapter, we stress the relationship between market research—your strategy for locating target customers and learning their needs—and promotion—letting your customers know your business can serve their needs and make them happy in the process. The overall message of the chapter is to use your head as well as your checkbook in connecting with the customer.

THINK POINTS FOR SUCCESS

◀ Be unique with your promotions. Instead of Christmas cards, send Thanksgiving cards or April Fools' Day cards.

◀ Stand in your target customer's shoes. Think like your TC. Find the need. Find the "ladder" in the TC's mind.

◀ Maintain a visual presence.

◀ A world in transition means opportunities for entrepreneurship. Fast footwork can keep you in the game.

◀ To start your own mailing list, give away something for free. In return, potential customers will give you their names.

◀ Rent a Santa. Rent a robot. Rent a hot-air balloon. Rent a talking dolphin. Create some excitement, because excitement sells.

◀ When you think you have it made, keep connecting with that customer anyway. You will never be so big that you can afford to disconnect. Remember this and it will make you rich.

◀ Remember to promote the *benefits* of your product or service.

ACTION STEP REVIEW

32 Close your eyes and design the perfect promotional mix for your small business. For a moment, forget about budgetary restraints and go all out. Need a media blitz? You've got it. Need a thousand salespersons? You've got them.

33 Attach a price tag to each component of your promotional mix. You can do this by contacting display ad departments for magazines and newspapers, direct mail brokers, trade show organizers, and catalog houses.

34 Create a file for every contact you make in the promotional business. While you are creating these files, expand your efforts to a customer file, a vendor file, and (if you did not do it in the last chapter), a competitor file.

35 One of the best tools for making contacts with customers is a network. A network can be informal (friends, family, co-workers, people who share the same interests) or formal (service clubs and sales leads clubs).

REFERENCES

Advertising Your Small Business. Washington, D.C.: U.S. Small Business Administration, Office of Management Assistance, Small Business Management Training Instructors' Guide, No. 112, 1984. [Produced by the American Association of Community and Junior Colleges under contract to the U.S. Small Business Association, Contract No. SBA 4873-MA 89.]

Bacon's Publicity Checker, annual, Chicago, IL, Bacon's Publishing Co., Directory of magazines and newsletters.

Bencin, Richard, and Donald Jonovic. *Encyclopedia of Telemarketing.* Englewood Cliffs, N.J.: Prentice Hall, 1989. [Excellent and comprehensive look at use of telemarketing.]

Bennett, Steven J. *Playing Hardball with Soft Skills: How to Prosper with Nontechnical Skills in a High-Tech World.* New York: Bantam, 1986.

Blake, Gary, and Robert W. Bly. *How to Promote Your Own Business.* New York: NAL-Dutton, 1983. [A nicely written paperback. Good tips on trade shows and writing good ad copy and press releases.]

Delacorte, Toni, et al. *How to Get Free Press: A Do It Yourself Guide to Promote Your Interests, Organization or Business.* New York: Avon, 1984. [Contains an excellent chapter called "PR for Small Businesses," which has many solid ideas for promotions. May be hard to find. The 1981 edition, published by Kampmann, is apparently still in print.]

Directory of Manufacturer's Sales Agencies. Laguna Hills, CA 92654-3467, (714) 859-4040, annual directory listings by product/state/agents alphabetically.

Edwards, Paul, and Sarah Edwards. *Getting Business to Come to You.* Los Angeles: J. P. Tarcher, 1991.

Guiles, Melinda Greiner. "Why Melinda S. Gets Ads for Panty Hose, Melinda F. for Porsches." *Wall Street Journal,* May 6, 1988. [Fascinating study of the mailing list game by a veteran reporter. Guiles managed to get on various mailing lists by changing her middle initial. Melinda F. subscribed to *Fortune* and got an invitation to test-drive a Porsche. Melinda S. subscribed to *Savvy* and was barraged with ads for classes in upgrading her communications skills. Melinda O. subscribed to *Organic Gardening* and received ads for garden tillers.]

Harrell, Wilson. "Entrepreneurial Terror: Starting a Company? Get Ready for the Most Terrifying Experience of Your Life." *Inc.,* February 1987, 74.

Hawken, Paul. *Growing a Business.* New York: Simon & Schuster, 1988.

Husch, Tony. *That's a Great Idea! How to Get, Evaluate, Protect, Develop and Sell New Product Ideas.* Berkeley, Calif.: Ten Speed Press, 1987.

Laumer, J. Ford, Jr., et al. *Researching Your Market.* Washington, D.C.: U.S. Small Business Administration, Office of Business Development, Management Aids No. 4.019, 1988.

Levinson, Jay Conrad. *Guerrilla Marketing.* New York: Houghton Mifflin, 1985.

Levinson, Jay. *Guerrilla Marketing Attack.* Boston: Houghton Mifflin Company, 1989.

Levinson, Jay. *Guerrilla Marketing Weapons: 100 Affordable Marketing Methods for Maximizing Profits from Your Small Business.* New York: NAL-Dutton, 1991.

Naisbitt, John. *Megatrends.* New York: Avon, 1991. [Naisbitt devotes most of Chapter 8 to networking for the future. As we've said, this is must reading for any entrepreneur.]

Ross, Joyce. *Direct Sales: Be Better Than Good—Be Great!* Gretna, La.: Pelican Publishing Co., 1991.

Schonberger, Richard. *Building a Chain of Customers.* New York: Free Press, 1991.

Slutsky, Jeffrey, and Woody Woodruff. *Streetfighting.* Englewood Cliffs, N.J.: Prentice-Hall, 1984. *See also* Slutsky's *Streetsmart Marketing.* New York: Wiley, 1989. *See also* his *Streetsmart Teleselling.* Englewood Cliffs, N.J.: Prentice Hall, 1990.

The Sourcebook of Demographics and Buying Power for Every Zip Code in the USA. Fairfax, VA.: CACI, Inc. Annual. [For further information call 1-800-292-2224.]

Sroge, Maxwell. *The United States Mail Order Industry.* Homewood, Ill.: Business One Irwin, 1991.

Standard Rates & Data Services (consumer, business publication, TV, radio), Willmette, Ill. Annual.

Stone, Bob, *Successful Direct Marketing Methods.* Lincolnwood, Ill.: NTC Publishing Group, 1988.

Tradeshow Week Data Book, published by Trade Show Week. [For information, call (213) 826-5696.]

U.S. Department of Commerce, Bureau of the Census. *County Business Patterns,* Annual.

Wilson, Larry, and Hersch Wilson. *Changing the Game: The New Way to Sell.* New York: Simon & Schuster, 1987.

Zoble, Adrienne. *The Do-able Marketing Plan: Business Survival and Growth for the '90s.* Somerville, N.J.: Zoble Associates, 1991. [You can order direct at (908) 685-8008.]

APPENDIX 6.1 • Action Step 32: Brainstorm a winning promotional campaign for your business.

The Business Niche

For this action step, the proposed business is a limited-partnership joint venture with Nadek Computer Systems, Inc., of Tustin, California. The business niche is the sale, support, and training of desktop publishing systems to in-house graphic arts and public relations departments of medium to large corporations in Orange County, later expanding into southern Los Angeles and western Riverside counties.

Nadek Computers will sell the hardware and software. Jointly, we will determine the needs of the client and recommend the hardware and software configuration. Nadek will burn-in and install the hardware, which may include a large array of PCs on a Novell network. The Saddleback Scribe will install the software, get it running, and support the client with start-up training, customized style sheets, and printed instructions that supplement the tutorial materials supplied by the software maker. During a period that may last one to six months, The Saddleback Scribe will provide training and support to the client, with the work being billed directly to the client.

Rationale for the Business Niche

For the record, this is a proven business niche for Nadek Computers. The principals at Nadek have demonstrated expertise in hardware and networking systems. They readily acknowledge their lack of expertise in specialized software support, such as desktop publishing and accounting systems. To offer that expertise, they work with limited joint ventures. Kreisler Systems of Irvine provides a similar service in the area of business accounting systems.

The Perfect Promotion

The target customer group consists largely of people with VALS in the Achievers and Experimental segments, whose employees are in the Experimental and Societally Conscious segments. They will be highly responsive to direct mail.

The Guide to Desktop Publishing for Graphics Professionals

The Saddleback Scribe has nearly completed a comprehensive study of desktop publishing for graphic arts professionals (designers, artists, writers, publishers, typesetters, and printers) entitled *The Guide to Desktop Publishing for Graphics Professionals*. A working subtitle is "What Bove and Rhodes Failed to Tell You." (Even the second edition of their rapidly mass-produced book *Desktop Publishing* contains glaring errors and even more glaring omissions. And it is really targeted at nonprofessionals.) This guide will be offered to professionals for $100. It will be constantly updated—each copy being directly produced on a laser printer. It will launch The Saddleback Scribe as an expert in desktop publishing for professionals.

Direct Mail

From a list of Orange County's largest employers, we will develop a direct mail list, aiming for the in-plant graphic arts, public relations, or publications departments. The promotional package will include a letter, a flyer, and several samples comparing printed materials produced by professional typesetting equipment with those produced by desktop publishing. Most important, these samples will be accompanied by time sheets that show how much time was required to produce the similar documents by conventional and desktop methods. The time figures will be translated into dollar figures. The package will contain an offer for a larger kit of materials that can be obtained by returning a post-paid business reply card or by calling Nadek Computers directly. The promotional materials also will offer *The Guide to Desktop Publishing for Graphics Professionals* at a special price of $75. The goal is a joint sales call by Nadek and The Saddleback Scribe. (Nadek recently hired a very competent sales manager.) After a prudent time interval, a follow-up promotional package will be mailed.

Trade Association Memberships

The Saddleback Scribe will become active in the Orange County chapters of the business marketing and promotion trade association, the advertising association, the public relations association, and the editors' association. The Scribe will take copies of the promotional materials to the monthly meetings of these groups for distribution on a one-on-one basis to target customers. The Scribe also will offer *The Guide to Desktop Publishing for Graphics Professionals* at a reduced rate of $75. The joint venture also will buy ad space in the newsletters of those trade associations that publish them. This is a highly selective but highly effective medium.

Networking and Leads Clubs

The Saddleback Scribe will become active in several networking and leads clubs in the Irvine area with a goal of promoting this joint effort with Nadek.

Radio

Radio spots reach a large audience for a cost-effective investment. Our spots will run at varying times between 5:30 A.M. and 7:30 A.M., and 4:30 P.M. and 6:30 P.M. on radio stations that carry freeway Sig-Alert and traffic announcements.

Magazine Ads

During special promotions such as Printing Week, the joint venture will buy ad space in local and regional trade journals such as *Adweek* to promote their unique capabilities. The radio spots will be tailored in support of these special promotions.

Word of Mouth

Present heavy-user customers of Nadek will be polled directly for leads. Nadek has grown at a rapid rate in recent years strictly on the basis of word-of-mouth referrals.

Free Ink

To gain free ink for *The Guide to Desktop Publishing for Graphics Professionals,* The Saddleback Scribe will attempt to get the book reviewed, or get an interview into print in the business section of a daily newspaper or in one of the local business magazines.

P-O-P Display at Nadek Computers

Nadek Computer Systems will be moving to larger quarters soon. There will be an open house to announce the grand opening at the new location. Nadek will be mailing invitations to former, present, and potential clients. News of the desktop joint venture will be included in a special flyer inserted in the invitations. At the open house, a new point-of-purchase display that announces Nadek's new desktop publishing capabilities will be unveiled.

NOTES _____
_____
_____
_____
_____
_____

FIGURE 7.1
Chapter 7 will help you prepare part E of your Business Plan, "Location."

7 Location

Learning Objectives

- To understand the contribution of location to small business success.
- To understand the uniqueness of your business location needs.
- To develop skill in analyzing location dynamics.
- To develop a checklist for evaluating potential sites for your business.
- To use media demographic resources to refine your customer profile.
- To consult commercial real estate brokers in your search for a location.
- To negotiate a lease contract.
- To know when you need to consult an independent market research firm.

FUTURE FOCUS

You can operate out of your hat, the trunk of your car, a phone booth, a P.O. box. It depends on your customer's expectations and your pocketbook. Your business location may be the second most important decision you make.

perfect location
the optimum physical site for a business firm; its 100 percent location

ACTION STEP 36

Fantasize your 100 percent location.

Sit down where you won't be disturbed and brainstorm the ideal location for your small business. Get a pencil and paper and let yourself dream. Draw a mind map, or use a list format; the idea is to get your thinking on paper.

For example, if you were going to open a candy/cigarette/cigar stand, you might want to locate in the center of New York's Grand Central Station, where 10,000 people pass by every hour. If you were opening an extremely upscale boutique, you might visualize a location on Rodeo Drive in Beverly Hills.

Once you have the general idea of the type of neighborhood you have in mind, write down what else is terrific about this location. Writing everything down will give you a starting point as you move out to explore the world.

neighbor mix
the industrial/commercial makeup of nearby businesses

O ne of the most important decisions the entrepreneur makes is where to locate the business. Location is particularly important in retailing, and retail leases reflect that importance in their length and complexity; thirty to fifty pages is not unusual. This chapter will lead you through the processes of finding a good location for your business and negotiating a lease that will serve you well.

THE IMPORTANCE OF LOCATION

What Is the Perfect Location?

The **perfect location** is different for every enterprise. If you're in the housecleaning business, you can work out of a station wagon equipped with a cellular telephone. If you're in the mail-order business, you can work out of a "cocoon" or a post office box. Action Step 36 asks you to brainstorm the perfect location for *your* business.

A good location can make everything easier for a new business. A highly visible building that's easy for your customers to reach will save you advertising dollars. Once you've been discovered and your customer base is well established, however, location is less important. Nonetheless, for a retailing firm, a good location is absolutely essential.

For what kind of business would location be a secondary consideration? While you're thinking about this, work through Action Step 37. It will help you analyze the effect of location on your shopping habits. Use new eyes to examine your own consumer behavior.

A LOCATION FILTER

Before you charge out to scout possible locations for your business, you need to decide what you really need. This checklist will help you zero in on that. Use a scale of 1 to 10 to rate the relative importance of each item on this list. When you finish scoring, go back and note the high numbers, anything, say, above 5. Then after you've read the rest of the chapter, come back to this list to see if your priorities have changed.

_____ **Target Market.** How far will your customers be willing to travel to get you? Can your business travel/deliver to the customers (flowers, dry cleaning, plumbing, pizza, etc.) If so, how far can you travel and still make a profit?

_____ **Transportation Lines.** How much will your business depend on trucks, rail, buses, airports, shipping by water? If you're in manufacturing or distribution, you'll need to determine your major transportation channel. It's also a good idea to have a backup system. A good technique here is to make a diagram of the location and all the lines of transportation your business will use. (Common-carrier rate listings may help you.)

_____ **Neighbor Mix.** Who's next door? Who's down the street? Who's going to help pull your target customers to the area? Which nearby business pulls the most customers? If you're considering a shopping center, who's the anchor tenant (the big department store or supermarket that acts as a magnet for the center)?

_____ **Competition.** Do you want competitors miles away or right next door? Think about this one. If you're in the restaurant business, it can help you

BOX 7.1   Summary of Site-Selection Concerns

Ask these questions about a potential location:
How close is the target market?
How accessible is it to the transportation lines you will use?
What's the neighbor mix?
How close is it to competitors? (How close do you *want* to be?)
How safe is this location?
If you need labor, where's the nearest pool?
What ordinances will affect you?
What services are free (paid for by taxes), and what services would you have to pay for?
How much would it cost to rent (or buy)?
Who owns the property?
Would your customers be able to find you easily?
Could you expand here if you needed to?
Is there sufficient parking area?

to be on "restaurant row." (A good example of a working "competitor cluster" is San Diego's well-known Miles of Cars; having Nissans, Dodges, Chevrolets, Toyotas, and others all in one area cuts down customer driving time and allows for easy comparison shopping.)

_____ Security, Safety. How safe is the neighborhood? Is it as safe as a nursery at noon but an urban jungle at midnight? Is there anything you can do to increase the security?

_____ Labor Pool. Who's working for you, and how far will they have to commute? Does your business require more help at certain peak periods of the year? How easy will it be to find that kind of help? Will you need skilled labor? If so, where's the nearest pool of it? Is the site near a bus (train, subway)? Will you need technical people? How far will they travel? Don't overlook the potential of part-timers, teens, seniors, and homemakers.

_____ Restrictions. What local rules (state, county, city, merchants' association, and so on) will affect your location? For example, what are the restrictions on signage? Hours of business? Parking assignments? Deed restrictions? Zoning restrictions? Covenants and other conditions?

_____ Services. Police and fire protection, security, trash pickup, sewage, maintenance. What is included in the rent, and who pays for those services that are not?

_____ Costs. The purchase price if you're buying; otherwise, the rent or lease costs. (We advise against buying property and starting a business at the same time, because it diverts your precious energies and capital that you need for the business.) Taxes, insurance, utilities, improvements, association dues, routine maintenance. You need to know who pays for what. Can you negotiate a few months' free rent?

_____ Ownership. If you're still planning to buy the property, who will you get to advise you on real estate? Consider a lease with option to buy, but have the contract reviewed by a real estate attorney.

_____ Past tenants. What happened to the past tenants? What mistakes did they make, and how can you avoid those mistakes?

_____ Accessibility to customers. Will your target customers—lured by your terrific promotions—find you easily and then have a place to park when they

ACTION STEP 37

Use your new eyes to evaluate business locations.

Think about how location affects your spending habits. For example, where do you buy gas for your car? Do you buy it on your way to work or school, or on your way home? Why?

Now, with your Adventure Notebook in hand, look through your home. How important was the location of the retailer from which you purchased the items you see? For example,

cigarettes, candy, sodas
washing machine
paintings, wallhangings
carpeting, paint
dry-cleaning service
mail-order items such as books, magazines, clothing, CDs
custom-made golf clubs
eyeglasses
prescription drugs
designer clothes
wristwatch, jewelry
power tools, lawn and garden equipment
TV set, VCR
car, motorcycle
collectibles
your home itself

A random look through your checkbook might trigger your memory. Feel free to add to this list.

How far did you travel, for example, for your last dinner out with a friend? For a carton of milk? A magazine? A lounge chair? A video cassette rental? How far would you travel to use the services of a brain surgeon?

What conclusions can you draw about the importance of location in making a purchase?

You can expand upon this action step by interviewing purchasing agents and buyers of commercial and industrial goods. Ask them what impact location has on their choice of vendors or on their recruitment of employees

labor pool
qualified people who are available for employment near your business location

restrictions
city/county laws governing business
locations

location life cycle
the stages of a commercial/industrial area
from birth to death

get there? Consider highway access, and potential obstacles that could make coming to your place of business inconvenient or unpleasant.

_____ Space. If you need to expand, can you do it there, or will you have to move to a new site?

_____ History of the Property. How long has the landlord owned this property? Is it likely to be sold while you're a tenant? If the property is sold, what will happen to your business? What will happen to your tax obligations? If the property goes on the market, do you want the first right to meet an offer?

_____ Physical Visibility. Does your business need to be seen? If so, is this location easily visible? Can you make alterations to increase its visibility?

_____ Life-Cycle Stage of the Area. Is the site in an area that's embryonic (vacant lots, open space, emptiness), growing (high-rises, new schools, lots of construction), mature (building conversions, cracked streets, sluggish traffic), or declining (vacant buildings, emptiness)? What will the area be like in 5 years? What effect would that have on your business? What do the municipal planners have in mind for the area? When will the highway department tear up the street? (See Figure 7.2.)

_____ Image. Is the location consistent with your firm's image? How will nearby businesses affect your image? Is this an area where your customers would expect to find a business like yours? (Look for a place that reinforces your customers' perception of your business.)

Marcia Meadows's Story

Michael, my husband, had worked in the automotive industry for seventeen years—the last dozen in California—when his company decided to transfer him back to Buffalo. The new job would be a nice promotion, and for a while we were happily making

FIGURE 7.2   Evaluate the life-cycle stage of each potential location for your business.

plans. Then one day, coming back from the beach with the kids asleep in the backseat, I realized that I really didn't want to leave California. We had a lovely home, the children had good friends, and Michael and I both dreaded Buffalo's long winters.

So we decided to start our own Saab and Volvo repair business, since Michael knew a lot about servicing those makes of cars. I got busy and took a course in small business at the local community college.

The first thing we did was locate our competitors. We found three. The largest was in the north part of the county. The next-largest was west of here, a couple miles from the beach, and the other one was south of here. If you drew lines connecting them on a map, you'd have a wide-spread triangle. No one was in the middle, and Michael knew from experience that those three couldn't handle all the repair business in our area.

Our next step was to get a list of all the Volvo owners in the area. We contacted the Department of Motor Vehicles about this, and they were very helpful. For several days, we stuck little colored pins into our area map—one pin for each Volvo owner—and as the number of pins grew we noticed a growing cluster right in the middle of the three existing repair businesses. That's where we located *our* business.

Our research and planning worked. Now, when we hear of all that winter they're getting in Buffalo on television, we're very glad we're where we are.

Location was important to Marcia and Michael Meadows for a couple of reasons:

1. Convenience. Customers will drive only so many miles to have their cars repaired.
2. Equipment. A major expense in car repair service is equipment, and you don't want to have to move that from one location to another if a location doesn't work out.

An SBA booklet entitled "Starting and Managing a Small Business" tells how many people are needed to support particular businesses. A men's and boys' clothing store, for example, needs just under 12,000 people. A record shop needs 112,000; a toy store, 61,000. How many people does *your* business need to support it?

WHERE TO GO FOR LOCATION INFORMATION

Businesspeople tend to stay in a location for a while because it's expensive to pack up and move. Selection of a location is a *very* important decision. You need to make sure you're in the heart of your target market. So where do you go for information?

1. **Census tracts.** The most obvious place is a federal depository, where you look at census data from the federal government. Every 10 years, census takers walk through neighborhoods gathering data on household size, income, occupation, housing costs, and so on—things you need to know to start a small business. Your taxes pay for this service, so use it. It's readily available to you. The census data is a profile of the U.S.
2. **Zip codes.** Research firms have developed customer data based on zip codes. This data is similar to census-tract data but is more up to date. You can also request zip-code data from the research department of your local newspaper and from the public relations department of your local utility.
3. **Neighborhood clusters.** Firms like Equifax and National Decision Systems have extended their market research into smaller segments that might be helpful for the entrepreneur seeking a location. Much of this data was collected in a book called *The Clustering of America* by Michael J. Weiss.

Targeting by Census Tract

Every 10 years the government pulls together massive amounts of census data. Until 1982, this data was compiled for large population blocks known as Standard Metropolitan Statistical Areas (SMSAs) in statistical form broken down along demographic lines (age, income, cultural roots, and so on.) The data from the 1990 census—still trickling in as we rush to complete the third edition of this book—are so massive that they're being offered in electronic form: computer tape and compact disk (read only memory, CD-ROM). A visit to the nearest census office (see your business pages under federal government offices) will net you at least a dozen slick brochures offering products to help you use government-gathered statistics to locate your business. The one we found most helpful was ABC, an acronym for:

Applications in
Business and
Community

The ABC brochure takes you from the Area Level to the Tract Level to the Block Group to the Block. (see Fig. 7.3) Tracts in Metropolitan areas usually contain a large enough population sample (1,000–3,000 inhabitants) to give you a statistical picture that will help you decide on location. The sample graphic in the Census Bureau's most recent ABC booklet, which uses Blair County, Pennsylvania, is a model for your area. Locate your county-city-tract and go to work.

In the first two editions of this book, we used data from 1980 census tables for two tracts in Southern California. Tract 740.06, renamed Tract SA, is located in the city of Santa Ana. Tract 630.07, renamed Tract NB, is located in the city of Newport Beach. As of 1979, the tracts each had populations of between 2,700 and 3,000 people, a good number for a target market for almost any entrepreneurial start-up.

To find update information, we used two sources. First, we contacted the marketing department of a major local newspaper, *The Orange County Register* (circulation 300,000+), which provided us with a data-packed brochure called the Orange County Demographic Review. Second, we contacted the State Census Data Center in Sacramento. For a fee, the Data Center provided us with a six-page computer printout for both census tracts, SA and NB. For a slightly higher fee, you can have the Data Center generate a larger report.

Depending on the kind of information you want, and the state of the census when you research your 100 percent location, you'll have to do much the same thing to gather or update data. (The model tables in the current government brochures are from the 1980 census. Opinions differ on a publication date for 1990 tables in published form.) If you live in an urban area, you can go directly to your census bureau. If you live in unincorporated area, you might do better with some phone calls or a letter. Customer Service, Bureau of the Census, Washington, D.C., 20233 (301/763-4100).

For researching your location, you want data that gives you a picture of the lifestyles of your target customer: income, occupation, education, and housing.

In the pages that follow, we lead you from the 1980 census tables into the number-crunching maw of the information age. We launch our search from the graphic for the Metropolitan Statistical Area (MSA), moving quickly from the respective cities (Santa Ana, Newport Beach) to tract level (Tract SA, Tract NB). Let's look at income first, comparing it with an inset box to the 1980 table.

INCOME

Small business survival depends on accurate targeting, so one clue to life-style is discretionary income. If two households have income of $35,000 each, but household

Geographic Subdivisions in a Metropolitan County

AREA

Metropolitan Statistical Area (MSA) and Component Areas (central city and the surrounding metropolitan county(s); the Altoona, PA, MSA has only one county — "Blair" — part of which is shown here)

Census Designated Place

Incorporated Place (central city)

Urbanized Area (all shaded areas)

Incorporated Place

Minor Civil Division (MCD) or Census County Division (CCD)

POPULATION SIZE

These areas vary greatly in population size

Census Tract (small, homogeneous, relatively permanent area; MSA's are subdivided into census tracts)

Average 4,000

Block Group (BG; subdivision of census tracts or block numbering areas)

Average 1,000

Block (identified throughout the country; always identified with a 3-digit number, and some have an alphabetic suffix)

Average 85

FIGURE 7.3 The U.S Census subdivides metropolitan areas into tracts, block groups, and blocks.

SOURCE: Bureau of the Census, "Census ABC's: Applications in Business and Community," 6–7 (Washington, D.C.: U.S. Department of Commerce, 1989). Readers interested in a free copy should write or call Customer Services, Bureau of the Census, Washington, D.C. 20233–8300, (301) 763-4100.

A's income must support seven people and household B's must support only one, there's a good chance that household B has more discretionary dollars.

According to the 1980 census data, the median incomes for Tract SA and NB, respectively, were $18,264 and $51,061. In Table 7.1, from our 1990 computer printout, we see that incomes have jumped in the last decade. Tract SA's median income has doubled to $37,373; Tract NB's is up about 40 percent, to $91,703. In Tract SA, 152 households have incomes between $60,000 and $74,999. In Tract NB, 323 households have incomes between $75,000 and $99,999.

Income never tells the whole story of an area, of course, but it's a very good starting point. It's clear in the income data that households in Tract NB are likely to have more discretionary income than households in Tract SA.

OCCUPATION

A look at the 1990 Labor Force table (Table 7.2) shows that fewer people in Tract SA are working than in Tract NB, and the highest percentage of them (1,236 workers, or almost 44 percent) are in technical, sales, and administrative support. This category consists of three subcategories in our 1990 census computer printout: Technicians & Related Support (177); Sales (413); Administrative Support (646).

TABLE 7.1 Selected Census Data, Income and Poverty Status

HOUSEHOLD INCOME IN 1989 (P5/P80/P81/P107/P108)	[TRACT SA] (0740.06)	[TRACT NB] (0630.07)
Households	1,752	2,331
Less than $5,000	33	46
$5,000 to 9,999	61	29
$10,000 to 12,499	20	10
$12,500 to 14,999	57	13
$15,000 to 17,499	24	39
$17,500 to 19,999	23	17
$20,000 to 22,499	94	30
$22,500 to 24,999	133	18
$25,000 to 27,499	121	40
$27,500 to 29,999	104	43
$30,000 to 32,499	71	49
$32,500 to 34,999	79	21
$35,000 to 37,499	59	70
$37,500 to 39,999	104	27
$40,000 to 42,499	87	46
$42,500 to 44,999	83	27
$45,000 to 47,499	85	9
$47,500 to 49,999	75	39
$50,000 to 54,999	89	111
$55,000 to 59,999	95	22
$60,000 to 74,999	152	225
$75,000 to 99,999	63	323
$100,000 to 124,999	15	304
$125,000 to 149,999	19	162
$150,000 or more	6	611
Median	$37,373	$91,703
Mean	$39,808	$141,171

(continued)

TABLE 7.1 *Continued*

	[TRACT SA] (0740.06)	[TRACT NB] (0630.07)
HOUSING UNITS (H1-H3)		
Total	1,990	2,501
Occupied	1,752	2,342
Owner-occupied	748	1,552
Renter-occupied	1,004	790
Vacant	238	159
INCOME TYPE IN 1989 (P5/P89-P105/P114)		
Households	1,752	2,331
With earnings	1,642	1,936
Mean earnings	$38,002	$113,641
With Social Security income	86	342
Mean Social Security income	$6,134	$9,998
With public assistance	28	43
Mean public assistance	$8,824	$4,348
Per capita income	$17,306	$61,879
POVERTY STATUS IN 1989 BY FAMILY **TYPE AND AGE (P4/P126)**		
Total families	861	1,519
Above poverty/below poverty in families with children under 18 years	648/36	845/11
In married-couple family:		
under 5 years	248/0	220/0
5 years	39/4	40/0
6 to 17 years	214/13	449/0
In other family:		
Male householder, no spouse:		
under 5 years	21/5	0/0
5 years	4/0	0/0
6 to 17 years	19/14	0/0
Female householder, no spouse:		
under 5 years	14/0	27/0
5 years	18/0	0/0
6 to 17 years	71/0	59/11

Source: Adapted from 1990 U.S. census.
Note: Data are estimates based on a sample.

Back in 1980, the same category of workers was also the largest group at almost 41 percent.

In Tract NB, the highest percentage of workers (58 percent) in 1990 are in managerial and professional occupations. Of 3,026 people working, 1,010 are in Executive, Administrative & Managerial; 745 are in Professional Specialty. In 1980, 44 percent of the labor force was managerial and professional. Tract NB continues to have a higher percentage of people in sales: 671 to Tract SA's 413. (Keep in mind that many salespeople make good money.)

TABLE 7.2 Selected Census Data, Characteristics of Persons in Labor Force

LABOR FORCE STATUS (P70-P74)	[TRACT SA] (0740.06)	[TRACT NB] (0630.07)
Total males 16 years and over	1,729	2,127
Labor Force	1,609	1,758
Civilian labor force	1,602	1,758
Employed	1,576	1,725
Unemployed	26	33
Not in labor force	120	369
Total females 16 years and over	1,611	2,472
Labor Force	1,311	1,358
Civilian labor force	1,311	1,358
Employed	1,247	1,301
Unemployed	64	57
With own children under 6 years only	143	185
In labor force	125	94
With own childen 6 to 17 years only	132	258
In labor force	95	147
With own children under 6 years and 6 to 17 years	87	102
In labor force	53	11
No children under 18 years	1,249	1,927
In labor force	1,038	1,106
Not in labor force	300	1,114
OCCUPATION (P78)		
Employed persons 16 years and over	2,823	3,026
Managerial and professional specialty occupations:		
Executive, administrative, and managerial	330	1,010
Professional specialty	294	745
Technical, sales and administrative support:		
Technicians and related support	177	37
Sales	413	671
Administrative support, including clerical	646	179
Service occupations:		
Private household	15	28
Protective service	33	15
Service, except protective and household	364	122
Farming, forestry, and fishing occupations	18	14
Precision production, craft, and repair occupations	252	112
Operators, fabricators, and laborers:		
Machine operators, assemblers, and inspectors	169	0
Transportation and material moving	35	29
Handlers, equipment cleaners, helpers, and laborers	77	64

Source: Adapted from 1990 U.S. census.

Note: Data are estimates based on a sample.

EDUCATION

Education data is especially important if you're in entertainment, the arts, publishing, books, travel, recreation, or leisure-related fields. Table P-9 from the 1980 census told us that 91 percent of the residents of Tract SA and 95 percent in Tract NB were high school graduates. For the 1990 census (Table 7.3) the numbers widen between the tracts: in Tract SA, only 87 percent of the people have high school diplomas; in Tract NB, over 96 percent have them.

In years of college completed, Tract NB also stays ahead through the decade. In the old table from 1980, 911 people had finished college in Tract NB; 516 in Tract SA. By the 1990 census, according to our computer printout (again see Table 7.3), the numbers have jumped. Tract NB has 1,259 people with bachelor's degrees, 869 more with professional degrees. That's more than double Tract SA's 526 bachelor's degrees, and more than five times Tract SA's 162 professional degrees.

TABLE 7.3   Selected Census Data, Social Characteristics of Persons

	[TRACT SA]	[TRACT NB]
PLACE OF BIRTH (P42)	(0740.06)	(0630.07)
Total persons	2,818	2,766
Native:		
Born in state of residence	1,546	2,219
Born in other state in the U.S.:		
Northeast	344	810
Midwest	462	822
South	251	414
West	157	443
Born outside the U.S.:		
Puerto Rico	0	0
U.S. outlying area	0	0
Born abroad of American parent(s)	18	54
Foreign born	1,272	547
LANGUAGE SPOKEN AT HOME AND ABILITY TO SPEAK ENGLISH (P28)		
Persons 5 years and older	3,754	5,062
Speak only English	2,341	4,446
Speak Spanish:		
Speak English "very well"	299	149
Speak English "well"	278	42
Speak English "not well' or "not at all"	298	8
Speak Asian or Pac. Island Language:		
Speak English "very well"	116	108
Speak English "well"	96	51
Speak English "not well" or "not at all"	24	14
Speak other language:		
Speak English "very well"	224	200
Speak English "well"	53	36
Speak English "not well' or "not at all"	25	8
SCHOOL ENROLLMENT AND TYPE OF SCHOOL (P54)		
Persons 3 years and over	3,826	5,174
Enrolled in preprimary school:		
Public school	24	39
Private school	37	83
Enrolled in elementary or high school:		
Public school	398	461
Private school	11	95
Enrolled in college:		
Public school	502	362
Private school	68	74
Not enrolled in school	2,786	4,060

(continued)

TABLE 7.3 *Continued*

	[TRACT SA] (0740.06)	[TRACT NB] (0630.07)
EDUCATIONAL ATTAINMENT (P57-P60)		
Persons 25 years and older	2,684	4,014
Elementary (0 to 8 years)	174	56
High school (1 to 4 years), no diploma	176	81
High school diploma	516	390
Some college, no degree	781	1,097
Associate degree	349	262
Bachelor's degree	526	1,259
Graduate or professional degree	162	869
Percent high school graduates	87.0	96.6

Source: Adapted from 1990 U.S. census.

Note: Data are estimates based on a sample.

HOUSING

People are on the move in America, changing residences every 3–5 years, so you get more stability in your target market with owner-occupied housing. (Renters, as a group, tend to be more transient.) The 1980 census table on Occupancy, Utilization, and Financial Characteristics of Housing Units gave us not only the numbers of renter-occupied units (one clue to a shifting target market), but also gave us the value of specified owner-occupied housing units. Value was not available on our computer printout, so in Table 7.4 we have included data on gross rents and mortgage status and monthly owner costs. With government data, you take what you can get and go with it.

In the 1980 census, Tract SA had 1,082 renter-occupied housing units, while Tract NB had only 148. As we see in Table 7.4, in the latest census Tract SA has a total of 1,990 units, with 1,752 occupied, 748 by owners, 1,004 by renters. For Tract NB the 1990 census shows a total of 2,501 units, with 2,342 occupied, 1,552 by owners, 790 by renters.

Houses in Tract NB have more bedrooms (1,020 units have two bedrooms; 643 have three bedrooms) than houses in Tract SA (840 units have two; 163 have three).

THINKING ABOUT DATA

Think about your data this way. What do renters need? And what do homeowners need? Renters generally live in multiple dwellings (apartments, condos, and so on) where space is limited. Renters tend to buy portable things, smaller appliances they can carry with them when they move. (Limited space means renters will buy spacesavers.) Homeowners, on the other hand, will be a market for larger appliances and furniture—bigger-ticket items that are more difficult to move.

Table 7.5 summarizes some of the most important data from our search through the 1990 census printout.

Table 7.6, adapted from the Orange County Demographic Review, presents a cross-section of two zip code areas, one close to Tract SA (zip code 92701), the other close to Tract NB (zip code 92660). As you can see from the table, the data follows the same pattern, with more home ownership, more executives and professionals, and more education in the 92660 zip code. The 92701 zip code has more renters, more multifamily homes, more families with 2+ workers, and a higher percentage of blue-collar workers.

TABLE 7.4   Selected Census Data, Occupancy, Utilization, and Financial
Characteristics of Housing Units

	[TRACT SA]	[TRACT NB]
OCCUPANCY (H1-H3/H8-H12/H31)	(0740.06)	(0630.07)
Total housing units	**1,990**	**2,501**
Occupied	1,752	2,342
Owner-occupied	748	1,552
Renter-occupied	1,004	790
Vacant	238	159
Tenure by race and origin of householder		
Owner-occupied housing units	838	1,584
Percent of occupied housing units	40.7	65.7
White	624	1,531
Black	36	0
American Indian, Eskimo, and Aleut	0	0
Asian and Pacific Islander	68	21
Hispanic origin	90	32
Renter-occupied housing units	1,218	825
White	799	733
Black	40	0
American Indian, Eskimo, and Aleut	0	5
Asian and Pacific Islander	94	52
Hispanic origin	214	35
Bedrooms		
None	175	9
1 bedroom	696	162
2 bedrooms	840	1,020
3 bedrooms	163	643
4 bedrooms	116	467
5 or more bedrooms	0	200
MORTGAGE STATUS AND SELECTED MONTHLY OWNER COSTS (H52/H53)		
Specified owner-occupied housing units (with a mortgage)	174	1,191
Under $300	7	7
$300 to $499	7	40
$500 to $699	14	34
$700 to $899	29	20
$900 to $1,249	85	131
$1,250 to $1,499	14	86
$1,500 to $1,999	18	110
$2,000 or more	0	763
Median	$1,021	$2,001
Specified owner-occupied housing units (with no mortgage)	12	218
Under $300	0	0
$300 to $499	0	0
$500 to $699	0	23
$700 to $899	7	7
$900 to $1,249	5	16
$1,250 to $1,499	0	6
$1,500 to $1,999	0	0
$2,000 or more	0	166
Median	$243	$401

(continued)

TABLE 7.4 *Continued*

	[TRACT SA] (0740.06)	[TRACT NB] (0630.07)
GROSS RENT (H43)		
Specified renter-occupied housing units	1,004	790
Under $399	0	0
$400 to $449	16	4
$450 to $499	7	0
$500 to $549	16	4
$550 to $599	25	0
$600 to $649	18	0
$650 to $699	54	0
$700 to $749	166	20
$750 to $999	668	262
$1,000 or more	21	490
No cash rent	13	10
Median rent	$822	$1,001

Source: Adapted from 1990 U.S. census.

Note: Data are estimates based on a sample.

Author's Note: Totals under "Total housing units" (H1–H3) will vary from totals under category of "Tenure by race and origin of householder" (H8–H12). Different techniques were used to generate these numbers.

TABLE 7.5   Summary of Selected Census Data

	[TRACT SA] (0740.06)	[TRACT NB] (0630.07)
Median household income (P108)	$37,373	$91,703
Occupation (P78)		
Technicians/Support	177	37
Sales	413	671
Administrative Support	646	179
Exec./Managerial	330	1,010
Professional Specialty	294	745
Education (P57–P60)		
High school diploma	516	390
Bachelor's Degree	526	1,259
Professional Degree	162	869
Housing (H1–H3/H43)		
Renter Occupied	1,004	790
Owner Occupied	748	1,552
Median Rent	$822	$1,001

Source: Adopted from 1990 U.S. census.

Note: Data are estimates based on a sample.

TABLE 7.6   Demographics by Zip Code: Santa Ana and Newport Beach (92701 and 92660)

	92701	92660
POPULATION		
Total	48,573	29,014
Men	25,156	14,414
Women	23,417	14,600
HOUSEHOLDS	15,678	11,532
1–2 persons	60.4%	66.0%
3+ persons	39.6	34.0
AVERAGE HOUSEHOLD SIZE	2.75	2.44
Households with children	33.5%	28.2%
RACE		
White	91.7%	89.9%
Black	2.1	1.6
Other	6.2	8.6
(Asian/Pacific Islander)*	2.8	3.1
(American Indian/Other)*	0.7	0.4
Hispanic origin	76.8	6.2
AGE		
Under 18	30.1%	16.1%
18–34	33.8	33.1
35–54	22.9	26.0
55–64	5.6	10.9
65+	7.8	14.0
Median age	28.1	35.7
County median	32.9	32.9
HOUSEHOLD INCOME		
Less than $15,000	21.8%	14.0%
$15,000–$24,999	17.1	13.9
$25,000–$34,999	15.5	7.7
$35,000–$49,999	15.9	11.9
$50,000–$74,999	15.7	15.7
Over $75,000	14.0	36.8
Median household income	$31,828	$54,086
County median	$48,917	$48,917
HOME OWNERSHIP		
Own	32.8%	57.3%
Rent	67.2	42.7
Single units	53.0	78.0
Multifamily	46.6	19.2
Mobile homes	0.4	2.8
MARITAL STATUS		
Married	49.6%	51.5%
Single, never married	34.6	34.2
Divorced/Sep/Wid	15.8	14.3
MEDIAN YEARS SCHOOL	12.3	15.2
LABOR FORCE		
% Employed—Total	94.5%	96.7%
Families with 2+ workers	60.1	49.5

(continued)

TABLE 7.6 *Continued*

	92701	92660
OCCUPATION		
Exec/Admin/Mgmt	9.4%	24.5%
Prof/Specialty	8.5	22.1
Other white collar	25.5	35.7
Services	13.6	8.6
Blue collar	39.8	8.2
Forest/Farm/Fishing	3.2	0.9

Note: The numbers/percentages above the dotted line are based on 1990 census; below the dotted line represent 1989 estimates. 1990 census numbers should be available in 1992.

*These percentages represent 1989 estimates. 1990 census numbers have not been released.

Source: *The Orange County Register,* based on information from U.S. census, National Planning Data Corp., 1991, and Claritas Corp., 1989.

Targeting by City

The "pop facts" data in Table 7.7 come from National Decision Systems of Encinitas, California, which uses a system called "Vision." This kind of report is available for most of the United States. Vision divides the country into twelve demographic groups with designations like "Suburban Wealthy" and "Urban Affluence" at the top end of the scale, and "Rural Lower Income" and "Town Lower Income" at the bottom. The largest group is "Suburban Middle Class," which accounts for 23.1 percent of the households in the U.S. There are forty-eight subgroups in the Vision matrix. Subgroups within Suburban Middle Class (abbreviated *SM*) are

> Little League and Barbecues
> Baby Boom Again
> Industrial Upper Deck
> Porch Swings and Apple Pie
> Carports and Kids
> Declining Suburbia
> Ethnic Industrial

National Decision Systems prepared the material in Table 7.7 in response to information on a business site at the intersection of Baseline Road and Dobson Road in Phoenix, Arizona. The report was produced on a computer data base using nine information sources, which ranged from zip-code data to special Census Bureau data. As you can see in the table, the columns move out from the intersection in concentric circles—with radii of 1 mile, 3 miles, and 5 miles—to give a demographic profile of households surrounding it.

Targeting by Neighborhood Cluster—An Example

If you were planning to open a bookstore and you had $300,000 to invest, where would you go? The answer might lie in the Prizm "clustering" system developed by Claritas, a marketing research firm. Prizm has identified forty-eight "clusters"

TABLE 7.7   1980 Census Pro-Facts Profile Report, with Updates, Estimates, and Projections, for Baseline Road and Dobson Road, Phoenix, Arizona; coordinates 33:22.70, 111:52.60

DESCRIPTION	1.0-MILE RADIUS	3.0-MILE RADIUS	5.0-MILE RADIUS
Population			
1996 projection	15,759	170,949	395,138
1991 estimate	13,936	147,728	337,993
1980 census	9,695	95,954	212,039
1970 census	622	31,305	113,308
Growth 70–80	1,458.68%	206.51%	87.14%
Households			
1996 projection	5,948	68,012	155,154
1992 estimate	5,074	56,481	128,343
1980 census	3,212	32,866	72,668
1970 census	157	8,824	32,630
Growth 70–80	1,947.24%	272.47%	122.70%
Population by race and Spanish origin	9,695	95,954	212,039
White	93.01%	92.11%	90.11%
Black	1.77%	1.60%	1.75%
American Indian	0.43%	0.57%	0.96%
Asian and Pacific Islander	1.73%	1.38%	1.18%
Other races	3.06%	4.34%	6.00%
Spanish origin–new category	5.79%	8.35%	10.26%
Occupied Units	3,212	32,866	72,668
Owner occupied	79.95%	70.10%	63.43%
Renter occupied	20.05%	29.90%	36.57%
1980 persons per household	3.02	2.92	2.85
Year-round units at address	3,390	35,488	78,674
Single units	90.57%	76.72%	71.58%
2 to 9 units	2.49%	4.77%	7.33%
10+ units	6.88%	15.02%	16.07%
Mobile home or trailer	0.06%	3.50%	5.03%
Single multiple unit ratio	9.67	3.88	3.06
1991 estimated households by income	5,074	56,481	128,343
$75,000 or more	8.82%	9.91%	8.89%
$50,000 to $74,999	27.62%	22.34%	18.20%
$35,000 to $49,999	28.64%	23.70%	21.92%
$25,000 to $34,999	16.55%	16.37%	16.41%
$15,000 to $24,999	12.30%	14.88%	16.82%
$7,500 to $14,999	3.37%	7.36%	10.32%
Under $7,500	2.70%	5.44%	7.44%
Average	$44,129	$41,775	$38,752
Median	$43,540	$39,385	$35,482
Per capita income	$16,309	$16,095	$14,822
Population by age (years)	9,690	95,943	212,025
Under 5 years	10.57%	8.48%	8.34%
5 to 9	9.50%	8.52%	7.85%
10 to 14	8.79%	8.81%	7.93%
15 to 19	6.39%	8.83%	10.08%
20 to 24	8.85%	11.50%	13.98%
25 to 29	14.30%	11.62%	10.90%

(continued)

TABLE 7.7 *Continued*

DESCRIPTION	1.0-MILE RADIUS	3.0-MILE RADIUS	5.0-MILE RADIUS
Population by age (years) *(continued)*			
30 to 34	15.73%	11.23%	9.32%
35 to 44	13.59%	13.31%	11.40%
45 to 54	6.74%	8.07%	7.93%
55 to 59	2.41%	3.13%	3.53%
60 to 64	1.45%	2.26%	2.78%
65 to 74	1.20%	2.75%	3.69%
75+	0.47%	1.50%	2.28%
Median age	27.29	27.14	26.67
Average age	26.55	28.66	29.47
Populaton 25+ by education level	5,393	51,773	110,039
Elementary (0–8)	1.88%	4.81%	7.86%
Some high school (9–11)	4.01%	7.13%	8.72%
High school graduate (12)	29.32%	31.37%	32.68%
Some college (13–15)	29.03%	26.12%	25.12%
College graduate (16+)	35.76%	30.57%	25.62%
Populaton 16+ by occupation	5,038	48,898	103,398
Executive and managerial	16.48%	14.75%	12.58%
Professional specialty	21.20%	18.78%	16.56%
Technical support	4.33%	4.00%	3.79%
Sales	14.13%	13.90%	12.34%
Administrative support	17.51%	17.45%	16.92%
Service: private households	0.11%	0.35%	0.36%
Service: protective	1.75%	1.39%	1.47%
Service: other	6.38%	8.37%	10.25%
Farming, forestry and fishing	0.55%	1.08%	1.51%
Precision production and craft	10.28%	10.54%	12.08%
Machine operator	3.59%	4.45%	5.83%
Trans. and material moving	1.32%	2.24%	2.76%
Laborers	2.38%	2.70%	3.56%
Females 16+ with children 0–18	1,631	14,581	29,283
Working with child under 6	23.21%	21.72%	21.81%
Not working with child under 6	29.98%	25.97%	26.09%
Working with child 6–18	34.11%	36.50%	35.49%
Not working with child 6–18	12.71%	15.81%	16.60%
Households by number of vehicles	3,198	32,897	72,658
None	0.46%	2.66%	4.44%
1	21.58%	29.33%	33.18%
2	49.66%	41.25%	37.65%
3+	28.30%	26.76%	24.73%
Estimated total vehicles	6,764	64,960	136,330
Population by travel time to work (minutes)	5,011	47,887	101,524
Under 5 minutes	0.79%	1.92%	2.59%
5 to 9	10.20%	12.56%	13.08%
10 to 14	18.20%	17.83%	18.99%
15 to 19	15.62%	17.01%	17.09%
20 to 29	23.06%	21.39%	21.05%
30 to 44	23.20%	20.94%	18.98%
45 to 59	5.71%	4.59%	4.54%
60+	3.23%	3.76%	3.66%
Average travel time	22.15	21.31	20.65

(continued)

TABLE 7.7 *Continued*

DESCRIPTION	1.0-MILE RADIUS	3.0-MILE RADIUS	5.0-MILE RADIUS
Population by transportation to work	5,029	48,552	102,652
Drive alone	71.16%	71.26%	68.68%
Car pool	21.57%	18.93%	18.88%
Public transportation	0.87%	1.29%	1.05%
Walked only	1.43%	2.31%	3.75%
Other means	3.83%	4.75%	6.15%
Worked at home	1.14%	1.46%	1.49%
Housing units by year built	3,384	35,718	79,095
Built 1979 to March 1980	27.30%	15.51%	11.81%
Built 1975 to 1978	52.68%	29.44%	20.63%
Built 1970 to 1974	19.13%	31.43%	27.17%
Built 1960 to 1969	0.81%	17.47%	24.25%
Built 1950 to 1959	0.08%	4.34%	10.38%
Built 1940 to 1949	0.00%	1.32%	3.56%
Built 1939 or earlier	0.00%	0.49%	2.21%
1980 households by 1979 income	3,212	32,866	72,668
$75,000+	0.80%	0.95%	0.98%
$50,000 o $74,999	3.88%	4.05%	3.00%
$35,000 to $49,999	16.29%	12.71%	10.10%
$25,000 to $34,999	32.27%	24.23%	19.74%
$15,000 to $24,999	30.79%	29.32%	28.87%
$7,500 to $14,999	12.03%	18.17%	21.97%
Under $7,500	3.94%	10.57%	15.34%
1979 average household income	$26,790	$24,001	$21,472
1979 median household income	$25,828	$22,386	$19,575

among the 250,000 defined neighborhoods in the United States. Journalist Michael J. Weiss has related these clusters to four groups of book buyers:

Self-Help Buyers

Suburban Elite Business Buffs

Gardening and Home Repair Fans

Mature Mystery Mavens

Self-Help Buyers buy jazz records, drive convertibles, travel by cruise ship, enjoy sailing, drink imported beer, enjoy skiing, and belong to health clubs. They live in multiunit dwellings—usually in fringe areas—and are college educated. Some are single; others, divorced. They range in age from 25 to 34. They work at white-collar occupations, and there's a good chance they moved in the last year.

They're buying business books and self-improvement books. They're young and eager, and have money to spend. So you scout those locations.

If you're interested in Prizm, you can contact Claritas using the information in the reference section at the end of the chapter.

The Commercial Real Estate Agent

The numbers are always changing, so whether you go for the big picture through census tracts or the narrow picture through Vision or Prizm, you must keep searching for the latest data. There is so much to know, and you make location decisions very infrequently. An experienced real estate agent can save you time and money. He or she can guide you through the maze of what is available and advise you on rents, prices, terms, tenant improvement costs, financing, zoning, public transportation, and the availability of workers.

Real estate agents are paid by the landlord or seller and earn their commissions only when a deal is final and money changes hands. Don't let yourself be rushed by these people, but bear in mind that they are probably the best sources of free market information you can find. You can save an agent a lot of time if you have already defined your needs. If you compare each site against your ideal location, you will probably have several workable alternatives. Typically, on-site leasing people have different objectives because they are employees of the developer. They want to fill up the building. Most developers cooperate with real estate brokers, so a real estate agent can take you almost anywhere you want to go and, if asked, might help you negotiate more favorable terms.

Now you should be ready to complete Action Step 38.

ACTION STEP 38

Seek professional help in finding a location.

Visit to a commercial real estate office to gain information. Commercial real estate firms have access to planning reports and demographic information that will tell you a lot about growth in the community. Have your plan well in mind and make an appointment beforehand. Dress conservatively.

And leave your checkbook at home!

SOME THINGS YOU MUST KNOW ABOUT LEASES

lease
contract for occupancy

A **lease** document is drawn up by the property owner's lawyer. Although its language is very specific (see Box 7.2), the terms spelled out are *provisional;* that is, the terms are proposed as a starting point for negotiation. Nothing you see in the contract is cast in stone . . . unless you agree to it. Obviously, the terms proposed will probably favor the property owner. Consider the proposed lease seriously. Discuss it with your own lawyer and with others who have experience with leases, and determine how best to begin the negotiation. The following pages will guide you through this process.

Entrepreneur, Read Your Lease

landlord/landlady
a person/business you pay rent to

Entrepreneur Mick Beatty failed to read the terms of his lease. He thought he had a "gentlemen's agreement" with his **landlady,** but he was wrong. His story points up the importance of *assuming nothing* when it comes to leases.

I was on vacation when I discovered the perfect location for my business. It was in the sleepy tourist town of Laguna Beach, on the edge of the world in a fabulous part of Southern California. It was late summer, and I'd just spent a week driving down the coast from Washington State. When I saw Laguna, I felt like I'd come home.

I discovered Eddie's Pub my first evening in town. It faced the beach, and sitting there sipping a cool one, I watched the sun reflect off the water. From time to time, people would drift in for a casual drink, and while I sat there feeling like a million, I must have talked to twenty different folks. Most of them looked very upscale, and they all said they loved the place, too.

Vacations don't last forever, and when I got back home I kept thinking about Laguna and Eddie's. I worked for a large corporation, making good money in a pressure cooker of a job, and even though I was enough of a culture freak to appreciate New York City, I did not appreciate the winters and I wanted something more out of life. The first day it snowed, I sat in my office just staring out the window, thinking about the 3 days I'd spent on the beach in Laguna.

A business trip took me to Los Angeles the following spring, and I managed to get an extra day so I could stay overnight in Laguna and stop in at Eddie's.

I got the shock of my life when I got there. Eddie's Pub was for sale!

BOX 7.2   The Language of Leases

Before signing on the dotted line, be certain you understand the language of the lease. These terms will get you started:

building gross area—The total square-foot area of the building when the enclosing walls are measured from outside wall to outside wall.

usable building area—The square-foot area within the building actually occupied by tenants measured from center partition to center partition.

common area—The square-foot area of the building servicing all tenants in common, such as lobby, corridors, lavatories, elevators, stairs, and mechanical equipment rooms. The building common area is usually between 10% and 12% of the gross building area.

rentable area—A combination of the tenants' usable building area plus each tenant's pro rata share of the common area.

gross rent—A rental per square foot, multiplied by the rentable area, to determine the annual rent due on a lease where the landlord provides all services and utilities including tenant janitorial services.

net rent—A rent per square foot multiplied by the rentable area to determine the annual rent due under a lease whereby the tenant also pays, in addition to the rent, its pro rata share of all utilities and services and real estate taxes.

loss factor—The proportion of usable building area to total rentable area. The usable area is that in which you may put furniture and equipment for actual office use. The rentable area often includes a proportionate share of ancillary building services. The lower the loss factor, the more usable space there is. Loss factors can vary from floor to floor in the same building. Rentable area may be calculated in a different manner for one building than it is for another, and this will affect your comparison of rental proposals.

I called my banker in New York. He said I was crazy. I called two buddies—one from college, one from the Army. They thought it would be fun to be part of a new venture and they were ready to invest. I talked to Eddie, the owner, made a deal to pay him so much down and the rest out of profits, and there I was in business.

I phoned my boss, and he said I was crazy, too. "That whole beach is a dream," he said. "I was stationed there during the war, and I know. One day you'll wake up and it won't be there any more." Then he paused, and what he said next saved my life. "Tell you what, Mick. Don't pull the plug until you're absolutely sure. We'll give you 6 months. If you're still out there dreaming then, send me your resignation. Meanwhile, have fun. Every guy needs a fling before he settles down."

I said okay, and thanks, and that was that.

Eddie's Pub is only 450 square feet. The layout is long and narrow, and it has lots of mirrors and sort of a Gay Nineties atmosphere. The traffic is mostly walk-in—beach people, tourists—and the only promoting I did was to put up a sign that said HAPPY HOUR 4:00–6:30. I shook hands with the customers, gave some complimentary drinks, served the best espresso south of Los Angeles, and started making money my first day.

Then the trouble showed up. I'd been open a week when I got a call from my landlady. She was a crusty-voiced woman I'd barely talked to, and she told me there'd been some complaints about the music.

"Hey," I said, "I'm sorry. Who's complaining?"

"Your neighbors," she said. "They have rights, too, you know."

"Is it too loud?"

"No," she said, "it's not the volume. It's that rock stuff that's causing the trouble. It irritates the other tenants."

"Rock?" I said. "It's not rock, it's more like—"

"I don't know what you call it," she said, "but it's got to stop. And right now."

"My customers like it," I argued. "The music is part of the ambience of my place."

"Young man," she said, "What your customers like is neither here nor there. I own that property, and I have other tenants to think about. And if you have any questions, I'd advise you to read your lease." She hung up.

Well, I read the lease, carefully. And then I saw a lawyer. He confirmed what I'd read. According to the terms of the lease, my landlady had the power to tell me what kind of music I could play in my own small business. Incredible, but true.

So I turned off the music. Right away, my customers missed it. Drink orders fell off. I surveyed my neighbors and made a list of songs they didn't find offensive, but when I played that junk in the bar, my steady customers (who were becoming less steady) asked me to turn it off. As a last resort, I went to see my landlady and tried to renegotiate the lease. But she wouldn't budge.

There was only one thing to do. I sold the business and went back to my job on the East Coast. I still owe some money to my partners. When it snows I always think of the sun on the water at Laguna. Oh, I'll go back sometime, but right now I'm a little soured on the place. It's too bad. It's got a great beach . . . and a great little bar where you can sit and watch the sun go down. . . . My advice? Read the small print.

Anticipate the Unexpected

Bette Lindsay has always had a soft spot for books, and when she finally chose a business, it was a bookstore in a shopping center. She had researched everything—trends, census data, newspapers, reports from real estate firms, suppliers—but she failed to anticipate an important potential pitfall, dependency on an **anchor tenant**.

Few small businesses are themselves "destination locations." They must count on anchor tenants to draw traffic. Bette made an assumption that the anchor tenant in her center would be there forever. This case study shows the importance of having Plan B ready.

> My husband and I researched the small business field for almost 2 years, and my heart kept bringing me back to books. I've read voraciously since I was 7 years old, and I love a well-written story. So when a new shopping center was opening a mile from our home, I told my husband, "This is it."
>
> Everything looked perfect. They had a great anchor tenant coming in—a supermarket that would draw lots of traffic. The real estate agent we'd been working with during most of our search showed us the demographics of the area, which documented that we were smack in the middle of a well-educated market. According to statistics put out by the federal government, a book store needs a population of 27,000 people to support it. Our area had 62,000 people, and the closest bookstore was more than 5 miles away.
>
> Everything else looked good, too. We had lots of parking. The neighbors (three hardy pioneers like ourselves) were serious about their business and pleasant to work with.
>
> We wanted to be in for the Christmas season, because December is the peak season for bookstores, so we set a target date of mid-October. The contractor was still working when we opened a month later.
>
> We started off with an autograph party and we ran some best-seller specials. And even though construction work from our anchor tenant blocked our access, we had a very good Christmas that year. We started the new year feeling very optimistic.
>
> One day in mid-January, construction work stopped on our anchor tenant's new building. The next day we read in the paper that the company had gone bankrupt.
>
> Well, the first thing I did was call the landlord. He was out of town, and his answering service referred me to a property management company. They said they knew nothing about what was happening and that all they do is collect the rent. January was slow. So was February, and March. In April, two of our neighbors closed up. The construction debris was blocking customer access. It was a mess.
>
> In May, I finally succeeded in getting in touch with the owner and tried to **renegotiate the lease,** but his story was sadder than mine.

anchor tenant
a business firm in a commercial area that attracts customers

renegotiate a lease
obtaining a new/modified contract for occupancy

Fourteen months after we moved in we finally got our anchor tenant. If I'd suspected it'd take anything like that long I could have built some provision for it into our lease. That expensive mistake does not bear repeating.

How to Rewrite a Lease

You live with a lease (and a landlord) for a long time. If you're successful in a retail business, your landlord may want a percentage of your gross sales receipts. If you're not successful or if problems develop, you're going to want several Plan Bs and a **location escape hatch.** For example, your lease should protect your interests:

if the furnace or air-conditioning system breaks down

if the parking lot needs sweeping or resurfacing

if the anchor tenant goes under

if the building is sold

if half the other tenants move out

The possibility of such grief-producing eventualities needs to be dealt with with precise words and precise numbers in the lease.

Read the lease slowly and carefully. When you see something you don't understand or don't like, draw a line through it. Feel free to rewrite the sentences if you need to. It's *your* lease, too, you see. If you need help from a lawyer, get it. And make sure that the owner (or the leasing agent) indicates his or her agreement with your changes by initialing each one.

Here's a checklist to start you on your rewrite.

1. Escape Clause   If the building doesn't shape up or the area goes into eclipse, you will want to get out fast. Be specific. Write something like this into your lease: "If three or more vacancies occur in the center, tenant may terminate lease."

2. Option to Renew   Most businesses need at least 6 months to a year to get going. If your business does well, you will want to stay put. If it does not, you don't want to be saddled with a heavy lease payment every month. Get a lease for 1 year, with an **option to renew** for the next 2 or 3.

3. Right to Transfer   Circumstances might force you to sublet. In the trade, this is called "assigning." Make sure the lease allows you to transfer your lease without a heap of hassle if such circumstances arise.

4. Cost-of-living Cap   Most leases allow the owner to increase rents along with inflation according to the Consumer Price Index. To protect yourself, insist on a **cost-of-living cap** so that your base rate won't increase faster than your landlord's costs. Try for half of the amount of the CPI increase, a standard measure. Thus if the CPI rises 10 percent, your rate will go up only 5 percent. It's fair, because the owner's costs won't change much. Major tenants in your center will insist on a cap, so you should be able to negotiate one also. Proceed with confidence.

5. Percentage Lease   Percentage leases are common in larger retail centers. They specify that the tenant pays a base rate plus a percentage of the gross sales. An example: $3.00 per square foot per month plus 5 percent of gross sales over $500,000 per year.

6. Floating Rent Scale   If you're a pioneer tenant of a shopping center, negotiate a payment scale based on occupancy. For example, you may specify that you'll pay 50

rewrite a lease
alter the wording of a lease to make it protect your interests

location escape hatch
a way to cancel or modify your lease if the landlord fails to meet the specified terms

option to renew
a guaranteed opportunity at the end of your lease to extend for another specific period of time

cost-of-living cap
an agreement that the rent from one year to another cannot be increased by more than the CPI for the period

---

BOX 7.3   Before You Sign . . .

Before you sign a lease, ask these questions:
   Does the lease contain an escape clause?
   Does it have an option to renew?
   Can you "assign" the lease if you need to sublet?
   Do you have a ceiling on rent increases?
   Do you have a floating lease scale, according to how much of the center is occupied?
   Have you tried to negotiate a period of free rent while you are preparing to open the doors?
   Have you negotiated with the landlord to make the needed improvements and charge you for them over the total time of the lease?

---

percent of your lease payment when the center is 50 percent occupied, 70 percent when it's 70 percent occupied, and 100 percent when it's full. You can't build traffic to the center all by yourself, and motivation is healthy for everyone, including landlords.

7. Start-up Buffer   There's a good chance you'll be on location fixing up, remodeling, and so on, long before you open your doors and make your first sale. Make your landlord aware of this problem and negotiate a long period of free rent. The argument: if your business is successful, the landlord, who's taking a percentage, will make more money. If your business doesn't do well or if it fails, the landlord will have to find a new tenant. You need breathing space. You've signed on for the long haul. By not squeezing you to death for cash, the landlord allows you to put more money into inventory, equipment, service, atmosphere—the things that make a business go.

8. Improvements   Unless you're a super fixer-upper, you don't want to lease a place equipped with nothing but a dirt floor and a capped-off cold water pipe. You need a proper atmosphere for your business, but you don't want to use all your cash to pay for it before you open. Negotiate with the landlord to make the needed improvements and spread the cost of them over the total time of the lease. Otherwise, find a space that doesn't require heavy remodeling.

restrictive covenants
a list of things you can't do

9. Restrictive Covenants   If you're running a camera store and part of your income derives from developing film, you don't want a Fotomat booth to move into your center. If you're selling hearing aids, you don't want a stereo store next door. Build **restrictive covenants** into your lease to protect yourself.

10. Maintenance   When the parking lot needs sweeping, who pays for it? If the air-conditioner goes out, who pays? If the sewer stops up, who is responsible for the repairs? Get all of this written down in simple language. Your diligence with words and numbers will pay off.

A SUCCESS STORY

We close the chapter with Charlene Webb's success story because it illustrates very well the things we've discussed. You could almost use this case study as a checklist for small business success.

"My partner and I were both in education, so carrying out a lot of research for our gourmet cookware store didn't seem unnatural. We hoped to open in October in order to capitalize on the holidays, so we spent our week of spring vacation talking to owners of gourmet cookware shops in the Los Angeles area—where it seems there's one on every corner.

"We spent 5 days and visited an average of fifteen shops a day. The owners we talked to were helpful—since they knew our store would be 60 miles away.

"When spring vacation was over, we went back to our teaching jobs with our minds loaded with information and our hearts full of hope. Time pressures were heavy. If we were going to open in October, we knew we had to spend the summer on layout, image, and atmosphere. That meant we needed to find a good location very soon.

"Three days before the end of the school year we found a site—in a very safe and secure center near a convenient freeway off-ramp. Our nearest competition was 6 miles away, and a population study told us there were 55,000 people in the surrounding area to support us. It was perfect. All we had to do *now* was negotiate a lease we could live with.

"Perhaps it's because I was an English teacher, or because my dad's a lawyer, but whenever I came across a passage in the lease document I didn't like or didn't think was fair to us, I crossed it out. Several places I rewrote entire passages. When it was all over—after the landlord and I had discussed all my changes and we had both initialed the ones we agreed on—I had made four changes that really gave our business some flexibility and breathing space.

1. We got a 1-year lease with option to renew for the next 2. I knew if we were going to go under, it would be in the first year, and we certainly wouldn't want to have to continue paying a lease if our shop went under.

2. We got 3 months' free rent. I was very straightforward with the landlord on this. I said, "Look here, we can pay you 3 months' rent out of what cash we have left after fixing up the interior, or we can put that money into inventory that will help our start-up. I think it would be a benefit to both you and us if we put that money into inventory." The landlord agreed.

3. We got a 10 percent cost-of-living cap on the percentage the landlord can raise our rent each year. If I ever negotiate another lease, I'll go for 5 percent.

4. We refused to let the landlord or his representative look at our books."

Charlene and her partner's shop started off nicely, with a **grand opening** party for 500 friends and friends of friends. To bring in business, she started a cooking school, and her students have become good customers. Once a week she holds a special class called "Lunch and Learn."

grand opening
a splashy celebration announcing your entry into the market arena

For $10.00 and 50 minutes of their time, students get a glass of wine, a quick cooking lesson, and lunch they've just prepared for themselves. The heavy users in Charlene's business are women. "Lunch and Learn" is targeted at getting men into the store—so that they will see what's there and then come back to buy gifts or items they've learned to use in the classes.

Charlene has developed a customer list of 4,500 names, and she stays visible in the community by being actively involved in music activities, the Chamber of Commerce, and the bank (she's now on the Board of Directors) and by writing a gossip column for the newspaper.

Key Points from Another View

Part I:

ZERO IN ON THE RIGHT LOCATION

As a general guideline, you should determine your major markets and evaluate specific areas before selecting your site.

The key location issue is: Where will you be most effective? Remember, when you pick a location you are beginning to position yourself for your future.

1. Depending on what kind of company you have, scrutinize where you locate in relation to the competition. There are advantages and disadvantages to initially locating too close to the competition.

2. Determine your space needs—the top criteria for site selection are the cost of the space and the terms of the agreement.
   - First, draw up a simplified operational layout, whether it is for an office-oriented business, a retail showroom, or a service-related company.
   - Once you identify those offices or stores that match your needs, prepare a Request For Proposal (RFP) and present it to the owners or managers of the buildings. You'll have the strongest negotiating leverage if you go into a lease negotiation with at least three prospective buildings.
   - Also, insist that the landlord take on the bulk of tenant improvements so you do not have to spend your capital on office upkeep—that is, on things like getting door and windows fixed.

3. Hire a Helping Hand
   - Finding good help is critical. You want to find the best location to attract the best clerical, technical, or professional people you need.
   - Regardless of which business sector you are in—retail, service, or manufacturing—do a mini-analysis of the local labor market.

4. "X" Marks the Spot—three location aspects are critical for service and retail businesses.
   - First, research the local demographics: Is your business best suited for the city, an ethnic neighborhood, or the suburbs?
   - Second, consider accessibility by foot and auto traffic. Downtown storefronts must be practical for walking shoppers; suburban shops must provide sufficient parking.
   - Third, examine the lease, particularly in association with the land use plans for the surrounding blocks. What are the plans for the next city block—a jail or hotel?
   - For a light manufacturing operation, the availability of labor and labor expenses should be scrutinized. Also, find a spot that is convenient for commuting employees and close to the necessary modes of transportation: air, truck, rail, or sea.
   - Finally, location experts stress the need to avoid the high cost of moving within the first few years. Picking a suitable long-term location will help you avoid short-term solutions and the expense of relocating within the first few years.

Make Your First Move Your Best Move.

From: Kevin McLaughlin, "Zero in on the Right Location" *New Business Opportunities*, November, 1989, 66–70.

Part II:
IT'S YOUR MOVE

A move is not always necessary to accommodate growth. Often, more efficient use of existing space can eliminate the need for an expensive move.

Performing some preliminary research will help determine if a business needs to move, and if so, help select the right site.

1. First, interview your management and staff, especially the staff, to determine what each employee actually needs, in the way of furniture and equipment, to do their job.

2. Next, inventory your equipment. Then, further equipment needs must be considered. Look into the new (modular) work stations and overhead storage spaces.

3. Finally, if you need to move, put together a schematic floor plan that includes the locations for future floor plan that includes the locations for future employees and equipment. This way you can shop for what you need, not what you think you need.

Special Note: When looking for a new location, always take future growth into account. Don't spend too much for future growth, but you also don't want to outgrow your new location in 2 years instead of 5.

From: Frank Mixon, "Taking Charge—Tackling Management Matters" *Entrepreneur*, January 1990, 44.

SUMMARY

Some short journeys will help you see how important location is to a business. First, walk up and down the main business street of your town. Walk it on different days (weekend, weekday) and at different times of the day (midmorning, noon, afternoon, evening rush hour). Take some notes on what you see happening.

Second, explore a local shopping center on weekends, weekdays, and at different hours. Where is the action at these various times? Observe both vehicle and foot traffic, and what the people are buying. Locate the dead traffic zones. A poor location can kill a new business. Location is probably the most important decision a retailer can make.

THINK POINTS FOR SUCCESS

◢ The irony of the search for a start-up location is that you need the best site when you can least afford it.

◢ Take your time selecting a location. If you lose out on a hot site, don't worry; another one will turn up shortly.

◢ Begin with a regional analysis that will allow you to compare neighborhoods.

◢ A site analysis should include everything that is unique to a specific building or space. Many successful centers have some dead traffic areas.

◢ Who are your neighbors? Are they attracting *your* type of customers or clients? What will happen if they move or go out of business?

◢ Know the terms and buzz words—*CCOR, net, gross, triple net, industrial gross,* and so on—and be aware that they may mean slightly different things in each contract or lease agreement.

◢ Everything is negotiable: free rent, signage, improvement allowances, rates, maintenance. Don't be afraid to ask; a dollar saved in rental expenses can be worth more than ten dollars in sales.

◢ Talk to former tenants; you may be amazed at what you learn.

ACTION STEP REVIEW

Three action steps help you select a good location for your business.

36 Brainstorm your 100% location. Leave all geographic and budgetary restraints behind, and have some fun dreaming up the perfect site for your business.

37 Focus for a moment on your own buying habits. How far do you travel for candy, cigarettes, beer, a movie, car repairs, eyeglasses, a doctor, a dentist, a new car, a microcomputer? How far did you travel the last time you had dinner with a friend? If you needed brain surgery, how far would you be willing to travel?

38 Get a commercial real estate broker to help you check out locations, but leave your checkbook at home for now.

REFERENCES

Arden, Lynie. *The Work-at-Home Sourcebook*. Boulder: Live Oak Publications, 1990.

Black's Office Leasing Guide. New York: McGraw-Hill Publications Annual. [These guides are published annually for major metropolitan areas. They contain advertising by commercial and industrial developers and information on local rates and expenses. For information, contact McGraw-Hill Information Systems, P.O. Box 2090, Red Bank, NJ 07701.

Brabec, Barbara. *Help for Your Growing Homebased Business*. Naperville, Ill.: Brabec Productions, 1989.

Brabec, Barbara. *Homemade Money: The Definitive Guide to Success in a Home Business*. Naperville, Ill.: Brabec Productions, 1989.

Burstiner, Irving. *The Small Business Handbook: A Comprehensive Guide to Starting and Running Your Own Business*. Englewood Cliffs, N.J.: Prentice Hall, 1989. [Good, solid chapter on location.]

Edwards, Sarah, and Paul Edwards. *The Best Home Businesses for the '90s*. Los Angeles: J. P. Tarcher, 1991.

Garreau, Joel. *The Nine Nations of North America*. New York: Avon Books, 1982. [This is a landmark study of America's population that divides the continent into comprehensible chunks. It anticipates the year 2000, which can be called "the year of demographics."]

MPA (Market Profile Analysis), published by Donnelly Marketing Information Services. Provides information by county, city, town, zip code, or census tract. Also, gives retail market indicators, business market indicators, new construction activity, and financial factors.

National Decision Systems. Encinitas, CA: National Decision Systems, 1988. [NDS is a market consulting company that develops targeting plans for large and small business. You can phone them at 619-942-7000.]

National Home Business Reports. Quarterly, published by Brabec Productions. Write to P.O. Box 2137, Naperville, Illinois, 60567, for more information. Free catalog on request.

National Retail Federation. [This not-for-profit trade association will provide you with information on retail locations and operations. (212) 244-8780.]

Pinson, Linda, and Jerry Jinnet. *The Home-Based Entrepreneur*. Tustin, Calif.: Out of Your Mind and into the Marketplace, 1989.

"Restaurants & Institutions," publication providing an excellent source of industry statistics.

Weber, Fred. *Locating or Relocating Your Business*. Washington, D.C. U.S. Small Business Administration, Office of Business Development, Management Aids no. 2.002, 1988.

Weiss, Michael J. *The Clustering of America*. New York: Harper Collins, 1989. [Weiss discusses Prizm, a target marketing technique that focuses on forty neighborhood clusters in the United States. His classifications and their names—"Blue-Blood Estates," "Furs and Station Wagons," "Sharecroppers," "Downtown Dixie-Style," and so on—are perceptive and memorable.]

APPENDIX 7.1 • Action Step 36: Fantasize your 100 percent location.

In the past, because my free-lance work as a writer has been service-oriented, location has been of little immediate concern. My telephone number has usually been more important than where my "shop" was located. I've never advertised, or even produced a brochure on my business. It has been all word-of-mouth, and I usually get as much work as I can handle on weekends. Now my new eyes are beginning to open and widen in anticipation of a business where image is an important perception to medium-to-big business clients.

My choice of location will be only a recommendation to Nadek Computer Systems, Inc., as they are the major partner in our joint-venture association. Based upon what I have learned in this class and from my own experience in shopping for computer equipment, I wholeheartedly endorse the Main and Red Hill location that Joe Ryan suggested.

Main and Red Hill Businesses

I have personally found the Main and Red Hill location to be convenient. Here are some companies I have called on in that vicinity since 1982.

The Learning Shack. This was a computer school and software sales business situated on Fitch, just off Main and south of Red Hill. The building was one of those all-glass, mirrored structures, quite impressive. Although I did not attend the school (no need to), I did buy my 1982 and 1983 federal income tax programs from the company. The cost was only $65, in a period when a typical word-processing program cost $700. Perhaps that's why the company went into Chapter 7 liquidation and I was unable to buy my 1984 income tax update program from them.

Studio Software. After considerable research and investigation, I concluded that the page-composition program called Do-It was the best answer for desktop publishing at my employer, Santa Fe International. When the company declined to buy it, I purchased the program myself. The original cost of the software was $2,850. Through competition from Aldus PageMaker on the Macintosh, the cost of Do-It began dropping. When it got down to $1,295, I bought the program and a PostScript laser printer. Studio Software later renamed Do-It as Front Page ($695), Front Page Plus ($1,295), and Front Page to Type ($1,495). The latter contained a PostScript printer driver for the Mergenthaler 101 and 202. In February 1987, shortly after Xerox Corporation released Ventura Publisher, the backers of Studio Software closed the doors and dismissed the employees. After five years of effort, the company had never made a profit. Do-It and Front Page are difficult programs to learn and somewhat quirky to operate, but they are still my choices as the best page composition programs under $5,000. I wonder if the high rent in the Main and Red Hill area were contributing factors in the demise of Studio Software and The Learning Shack. In my own opinion, a wholly inept tutorial, poor after-sales support, and downright terrible advertising and promotion were the major reasons for Studio Software's untimely expiration.

Priority 1 Electronics. The brains behind Priority 1 Electronics are in the Chatsworth area. They do have a knack for picking winning products, discounting them, and promoting them through catalogs and flyers. But how the store on McDurmott near Main and Red Hill remains open is a mystery to me. When I call there, I'm usually in the market to buy something. I have researched the product thoroughly and gone there because of a favorable price. Invariably, I must lasso and hog-tie a salesman to get waited on. I wanted a 20-megabyte hardcard disk there, but it was out of stock. Delivery was promised the following Monday. It did not arrive, though I was billed on my Visa card. I finally gave up on Priority 1 Electronics and bought a 21-megabyte HardCard by Plus Development from Inacomp. Location might be important, but so is service. At Priority 1 Electronics, all the salespeople seem to be on the telephone making pitches to heavy users. Because of that competition, I couldn't even get to be a heavy user!

Quality Micro Systems. Until recently, few people had heard of QMS, but they make one of the widest-range laser printers of all manufacturers. These are quality products. The QMS-PS 800 is a PostScript printer in the same market with the Apple LaserWriter. For reasons irrelevant to this Action Step, the QMS product is demonstrably superior to the Apple product. So is the service, as evidenced by the QMS Western Regional Service Center on McDurmott just a few feet from Priority 1 Electronics. The service manager, Gary Casper, is a superior person who projects a superior image for the QMS organization. His shop is small, but the employees are friendly and they remember their customers by name. I can't possibly say too much for the service. (They replaced the defective motherboard on my PS-800 laser printer 5 days after the warranty had expired.)

Conclusions

Everything about the Main and Red Hill location bespeaks quality and positive image for someone in the microcomputer business. If space could be found at a reasonable price, I would highly recommend to Nadek Computer Systems, Inc., that they take space there, even if only for a sales office. Perhaps they could keep the present location on Myford Road near MAI/Basic Four as a service center, warehouse, and business office.

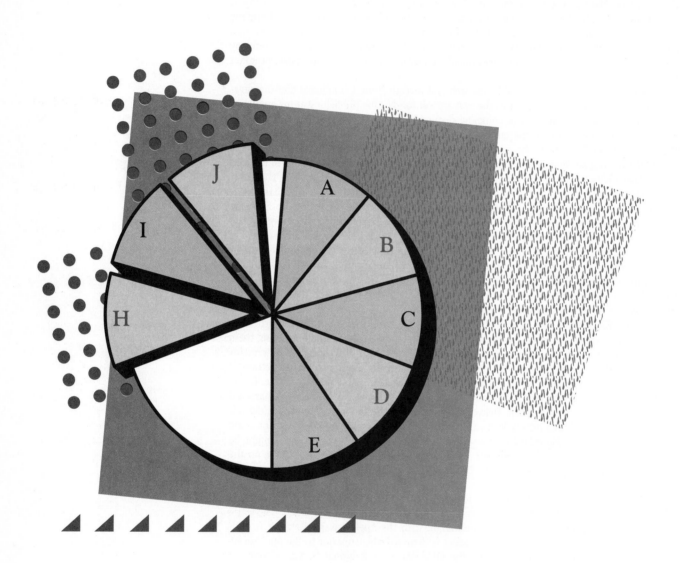

FIGURE 8.1
Chapter 8 will help you prepare parts H, I, and J of your Business Plan—the financial section.

8 Surprises You Can't Afford

▲ ▲ ▲ ▲ ▲ ▲ ▲

Learning Objectives

● To anticipate potential troublesome events that could occur in your business.

● To develop Plan B (C, D, . . .) in order to minimize the ill effects of unfortunate surprises.

● To learn the cost of each item you will need to do business, so that you know your total start-up expenses.

● To develop a personal financial statement in order to know how much you will have to borrow to go into business.

● To weigh the opportunity costs of going into business.

FUTURE FOCUS

Surprises can kill you. Do your homework and you will be able to keep them to a minimum. Make your mistakes on paper and learn from the mistakes of others. New eyes and ears will help you stay alert.

In earlier chapters, we've talked about the need for Plan B—an alternate strategy for bailing your business out of a tight spot created by some unforeseen, unfortunate occurrence. Having at least one Plan B is a must for every entrepreneur. Developing one can start with a list of potential problems and their solutions. We will help you develop such a list in this chapter. This kind of thinking can help you cut down your surprises by half.

EXPECT THE UNEXPECTED

Nonetheless, there's always something coming that you can't see, perhaps something like this case study illustrates.

Tommy Mankiewicz was in playing poker with a couple of his Army buddies when the idea of starting a small business came up.

"Dry cleaning," Rick said. "You can work out of the garage. All you need's a panel truck and a customer list. It's like coining money, right from the start."

"Sandwiches," George said. "And I know just the place. Traffic 25 hours a day—beach traffic, commercial, commuters, blue-collar workers, school kids. Gimme two cards." George had been in sandwiches in Florida. After a couple beers, Rick and Tommy often called him George the King of Sandwich. They assumed he knew a lot about Business.

"How much would it cost?" Tommy asked.

George whipped out a pencil and paper and pushed some numbers around. "Figure twenty grand apiece, tops," he said. "Plan to double your twenty in 18 months, easy."

"Those are nice numbers at the end," Tommy said. "But which one of you big spenders can loan me the twenty at the beginning?"

"Hey," George said, "no problem! They don't call me the Sandwich King of Pampano Beach for nothing. Give me a handshake now and your name on a paper later, and we're in business."

So Tommy and Rick shook hands with George.

George was between jobs, so he handled lots of the details. He found the location, negotiated with the owner of the building, talked to equipment vendors, bought a great-looking sign. Tommy and Rick prepared financial statements to give to the banker George knew, and Tommy contacted relatives and friends to ask for start-up money.

Tommy and Rick and their wives spent some weekends fixing up the place. Tommy worked hard. He was handy with tools, and he built cabinets and shelves. But what really excited him was making interesting sandwiches.

"Hey!" Rick said. "This tastes great! Serve enough of these and we'll be famous!"

Everyone agreed that Tommy made the best sandwiches in the world. Tommy was encouraged by their support. He'd always been creative, and now he had a new arena in which to use his creativity. He bought books and researched the history of sandwiches. He dreamed about quitting his job with the state and teaching some seminars on the art of the sandwich. He began making notes for a book, a small book to start with, called *Cosmic Sandwiches: Secrets of the Universe,* although he didn't tell anyone about it.

Tommy was building one of his creations the day the city inspector dropped in at the shop to make his inspection. He was a heavy-set man with beady eyes and was carrying a clipboard. He walked around the place frowning and making notes. After awhile he asked Tommy, "Where's the restroom for the disabled?"

"What?" Tommy said, feeling a chill on the back of his neck.

"The disabled restroom. You know, wide enough for a wheelchair, regulation railing along the wall, special raised toilet facility. You gotta have one."

"Can you wait for my partner to come back?" Tommy asked. "He just stepped out. If you'll talk to him, I'm sure he—"

But the inspector just stood there, shaking his head. And Tommy knew that George hadn't taken care of it, and even when George did get there, all the inspector did was read them chapter and verse of the city code. *Every public place must have a restroom for the disabled.* They had to tear out a wall, put in a drain, move some machinery around in the kitchen, and replumb everything. It cost $12,000.

The inspector came back to check the work when they'd finished. He sat down at the counter, and Tommy brought him one of his finest creations. He told Tommy that they were lucky not to have been fined. The inspector paused and then said, "Your sandwiches are great. Once you guys get going, they'll make you famous."

The work on the new restroom delayed the opening of Tommy's shop more than a month.

Reading about these fellas' experience, it's all too easy to say "I told you so." It's easy to second-guess in such a situation and to say to yourself, "They should have known about that requirement. They just didn't do their homework."

But Tommy and his partners were experiencing the heady excitement of entrepreneurship. They were having fun and were caught up in the busy work of opening a business.

The same thing could happen to you. That's why you've got to plan for everything, even surprises.

A Plan B Checklist

Here's a checklist of some obvious start-up concerns. Add to this list as you think of things.

I. Taxi Squad
   A. Lawyer
   B. Banker
   C. Accountant/bookkeeper
   D. Insurance agent
   E. Commercial real estate agent
   F. Mentor
   G. Consultant(s)
   H. Suppliers
   I. Chamber of Commerce
   J. Other organizations
   K. Other

II. Organization
   A. Federal I.D. number
   B. DBA ("Doing business as" = fictitious business name)
   C. Partnership agreement
   D. Corporation
   E. Other

III. Licenses, Permits
   A. Business license
   B. Resale permit
   C. Department of Health
   D. Beer, wine, liquor
   E. Fire inspection permit
   F. Other

(continued)

  IV. Location
- A. Lease review (lawyer)
- B. First and last month's rent
  (Rent has to be paid while making improvements. Estimate time needed to do improvements.)
- C. Security deposit
- D. Leasehold improvements
- E. Insurance
- F. Security system
- G. Utilities, deposits, estimated monthly costs
  1. Electric
  2. Gas
  3. Water
  4. Phone installation
- H. Other

  V. Auto (Consider new, used, leased)
- A. Auto(s)
  1. New/used
  2. Lease/purchase
- B. Truck(s)
  1. New/used
  2. Lease/purchase
- C. Insurance
- D. Maintenance, repairs

  VI. Equipment
- A. Office
- B. Retail space
- C. Warehouse
- D. Manufacturing area
- E. Kitchen
- F. Dining area
- G. Communication
- H. Other

  VII. Fixtures
- A. Tables
- B. Chairs
- C. Desks
- D. File cabinets
- E. Work benches
- F. Storage cabinets
- G. Display cases
- H. Lighting
- I. Shelving/storage

  VIII. Supplies
Business cards, pencils, pens, notepaper, tape, letterheads, dictionary, calendar, appointment book, coffee, tea, soft drinks, bottled water, and so on.

IX. Inventory

What are the minimum/maximum average inventory requirements needed on hand in order to do business on your first day?

X. Advertising/Promotion

    A.   Signs

    B.   Business cards

    C.   Fliers/brochures

    D.   Displays

    E.   Ad layouts

    F.   Media (newspaper, radio, other) costs

    G.   Name tags

    H. Other

XI. Banking

    A.   Checking account

        1.   Check charges

        2.   Interest on account

    B.   One-write checking/bookkeeping system

    C.   Deposit box

    D.   Savings/money market account

    E.   Credit

        1.   Credit cards

        2.   Personal lines of credit

        3.   Loans

        4.   Credit from suppliers/vendors

XII. Employees

    A.   Application/employment forms completed

    B.   Training program

Following is a list developed by the founders of a solar energy business (installation of hot water systems). They didn't need any start-up inventory as they would only order solar equipment after selling the system.

Equipment and Office Furniture

    Desk chair

    Two guest chairs

    Lamp and table

    Potted plant

    Credenza

    Secretary desk and chair

    Locking file, two drawer

    File systems, folders

    Typewriter/computer/software

    Copier

    Facsimile machine

    Phone

    Rolodex file

    3×5 tickler file

    In & out box (2)

Pager
Answering machine
Petty cash box
Postage meter (application for permit)
Postage scale
Coffee machine

Miscellaneous

Post office box
Instruction booklet
Tax deduction tables
Federal employer ID number
State employer ID number
Bank account
Check book
One-write checking/bookkeeping system
Utilities—telephone, water, gas, electricity
Insurance
Business license
Air-postal-post-zone rates
Telephone directory

Supplies

Letterhead
Personal size pager
Envelopes/letterhead
Business cards
Second sheets for letterhead
Copy paper
Invoices/letterhead
Mail register
Organizer for mail
Ribbons for typewriter, printer
Pencils, pens
Pencil holders
Tape
Stapler and staples
Staple remover
Rulers
Hole punch (2/3 hole)
Scissors
Colored tabs
Erasers, paper clips
Telephone message pads
Minute book for corporation
Pocket appointment book
Desk appointment book
Dictionary
Reference book

Calendars

Long distance call record

Clients and projects directory

Correction supplies

Steno pads

Scratch paper

Coffee supplies

File folders and labels

Mileage log

Local area wall map

Local area map for truck

If you get into the habit of making lists, doing mind maps, writing everything down, you'll improve your chances of surviving in small business. Action Step 39 will help you anticipate potential surprises.

Paying the Piper when the Purse Is Thin

Small businesses are especially vulnerable at start-up time, because that's when they're least able to afford surprises. If Ginny Henshaw had anticipated possible surprises, she'd have been better prepared for what happened to her.

> The reason I decided to start a day care center was because I really like kids. I talked it over with my husband, who said he'd help out if I got in over my head.
>
> I think we planned things pretty well. We found a good location—smack in the middle of a neighborhood of young families with an average 2.3 children—and then we spent weekends painting and fixing up. We worked hard, but it was fun, and it made us feel a part of something warm and cozy.
>
> Well, about three weeks before our opening, we called the light and power people to ask them to turn on the lights. "Sure thing," they said. "Just send us a check for $700, and the lights will be on in a jiffy."
>
> "What?" I asked. "Did you say $700?" We had around $800 in the kitty, but that was earmarked for emergencies.
>
> "That's right. You're a new commercial customer with a good credit rating. That's the reason the figure's so low."
>
> "You think $700 is low?" I asked. I was shocked.
>
> "For your tonnage," they said, "it's right on the money."
>
> "Tonnage? What tonnage?"
>
> "Your air conditioner," they said. "You have a 5-ton unit on your roof. Figure you run it for a month, that's $310. The other $40 is for lights and gas."
>
> "But we're not planning to run it!" I said. "The breeze here is terrific. We don't need the air conditioner."
>
> "Sorry, ma'am. Our policy is pretty clear. As I said, sometimes we get 3 months' deposit, but for your business, we'll only require the 2. Is there anything else I can help you with today?"
>
> "No," I said. "Nothing."

MANAGING THE UNEXPECTED

Risk management is old stuff. For example, how would you have protected yourself against unfortunate surprises if you were a fig trader in Damascus two thousand years ago and your main problem was brigands who robbed your caravan? You'd probably have hired guards to protect the merchandise.

risk management

transferring risks to an underwriter and/or setting aside funds to meet deductible amounts

ACTION STEP 40

Attach price tags to your business.

Sit down at your desk and look around with new eyes.

A. List the items on your desk. Pencils, paper, telephone, typewriter, microcomputer, business cards, calendar, and so on. List the desk itself, the lamp, chair, bookcase, filing cabinet, coffee machine. Now go through the drawers, writing down every item you use to make your work run easier and smoother.

When you finish the list of things you can see and feel, make another list—a list of your expenditures for things you cannot see, some of which you might take for granted. These include such things as insurance protection, rent, utilities, taxes, legal services, accounting services, and so on.

B. Beside each tangible item and each intangible expense, write down how much it cost(s) you. If you don't know precisely, jot down a ballpark figure and move on. You can learn the exact amount later. Then add up those amounts.

C. Move all your items to the SBA data sheet (Figure 8.2). Note that the SBA differentiates costs as either start-up expenses or operating expenses. This is an easy way to think about costs.

As you gather more information, you'll be able to refine the numbers on this sheet.

small business guru
a wise person on the sidelines who can help you with advice and counsel

How would you have protected yourself if you were a New Bedford whale oil dealer in 1845 whose underwriters were getting testy about financing another voyage because of your past losses due to shipwreck? You'd have hired better ship captains.

Most business surprises will cost you money, and your ability to cope with them will depend upon your ability to pay for them. The worksheet in Figure 8.2 and Action Step 40 will help you see how well prepared you are for the risks of doing business.

Getting Advice

Yes, you must be prepared, because there's a boatload of surprises awaiting every entrepreneur who enters the marketplace. We've talked about Plan B, formulating your strategy, checking and double-checking your market, and peering into the future to see what lies ahead. There's another angle to planning; it's called seeking advice.

Think for a moment about where you are right now on your road to the marketplace. You're halfway through this book. You've analyzed your skills and needs. You've probed your past and surveyed your friends. You've discovered what success means to you, and you've plotted trends and found your industry segment. You've profiled your target customer, and studied the demographics, and developed a promotion campaign. You've examined the competition. You've used your new eyes to find a dynamite location. Now you need to find a **small business guru** and get some advice.

Where might you find a business guru? Well, what about your banker? Many people come to him or her for money—some of them carrying Business Plans, others not knowing a spreadsheet from a bed sheet. What about your accountant? What about the real estate broker who helped you with your search for a location? What about your business insurance specialist? Have you contacted your local SBA office? Have you contacted SCORE?

You can use your network to find other people who may help you. Show them your list of potential surprises and ask for their advice. Ask them for their ideas about what other surprises might be in store for you. If one of those persons gives you wonderful advice, consider putting him or her on your board of directors.

The Risk of Dishonest Employees

One of the nastiest surprises for a budding entrepreneur is employee dishonesty. You might think that because you're small, employees won't steal from you, but that is wrong. Small firms get hit more often than big ones. Here's a list of precautions that will help minimize the opportunities for employee theft and fraud.

Sign all the checks yourself.

Don't let any one employee handle all the aspects of bookkeeping.

Insist that all bookkeeping is done clearly and neatly.

Insist that your bookkeeper(s) take scheduled vacations.

Do regular physical inventories.

Open all mail containing payments yourself.

Track all cash transactions.

Use numbered order forms, and don't tolerate missing slips.

Insist on fidelity bonds for every employee who handles cash.

ESTIMATED MONTHLY EXPENSES			
Item	Your estimate of monthly expenses based on sales of $_____ per year	Your estimate of how much cash you need to start your business (see column 3.)	What to put in column 2 (these figures are typical for one kind of businesss. You will have to decide how many months to allow for in your business.)
	Column 1	Column 2	Column 3
Salary of owner-manager	$	$	2 times column 1
All other salaries and wages			3 times column 1
Rent			3 times column 1
Advertising			3 times column 1
Delivery expense			3 times column 1
Supplies			3 times column 1
Telephone and telegraph			3 times column 1
Other utilites			3 times column 1
Insurance			Payment required by insurance company
Taxes, including Social Security			4 times column 1
Interest			3 times column 1
Maintenance			3 times column 1
Legal and other professional fees			3 times column 1
Miscellaneous			3 times column 1
STARTING COST YOU ONLY HAVE TO PAY ONCE			Leave column 2 blank
Fixtures and equipment			Fill in worksheet 3 on page 12 and put the total here
Decorating and remodeling			Talk it over with a contractor
Installation of fixtures and equipment			Talk to suppliers from whom you buy these
Starting inventory			Suppliers will probably help you estimate this
Deposits with public utilities			Find out from utility companies
Legal and other professional fees			Lawyer, accountant, and so on
Licenses and permits			Find out from city offices what you have to have
Advertising and promotion for opening			Estimate what you'll use
Accounts receivable			What you need to buy more stock until credit customers pay
Cash			For unexpected expenses or losses, special purchases, etc.
Other			Make a seperate list and enter total
TOTAL ESTIMATED CASH YOU NEED TO START WITH		$	Add up all the numbers in column 2

FIGURE 8.2   This SBA worksheet will help you estimate how much cash you need to open your business.

Triple-check references on resumes and employment applications.

If your business is a cash business, be there. Absentee owners, beware!

The Bottom Line

Although financial return may not be the number-one reason you want to start your own business, it should be high on your list. Money is a strong motivating factor; just thinking about it will help you keep your business on the success track. Here are some things to think about:

Income stream. What can you count on from your business? How much salary? How much profit? What benefits? Company car? Insurance? Travel? Retirement fund?

Profit from sale. What is the potential profit if the business is sold? What could you make if you took the company public via a stock offering?

Life cycle. How long will it take for your business to move from start-up to a profit position? Most businesses take at least 2 years, even 3, to show a profit. What happens to your investment if you project it 2 or 3 years down the road?

The rule: Every business should provide the owner with two sources of financial return: an income stream and growing equity. If you have income without equity, you're in trouble. If you have equity without income, you could starve to death.

THE PERSONAL FINANCIAL STATEMENT

financial statement
a list of assets and liabilities that will show your net worth

How Much Money Do You Have Now?

start-up money
all funds necessary to open the doors and to keep them open until you have a positive cash flow

The next question to ask yourself is: Do you have enough **start-up money**? You can find out by getting a total for your assets (what you own), getting a total for your liabilities (what you owe), and then doing the easy arithmetic to determine your net worth—in other words, you need to see what you are worth right now by preparing a personal financial statement.

An easy way to do this is to ask your banker for a form for doing it. It will look something like the one in Figure 8.3. Pulling together a financial statement is important because it tells you where you are with money now, and it forces you to get organized.

Get some practice by doing Action Step 41.

Are You Prepared to Wait?

time lags
periods of waiting—for mail deliveries, business cycles, and accounts receivable—that test the patience of an entrepreneur

We've said before that it's going to be a while before your business starts making money. In small business, you don't just rent a location, throw open the doors, and begin to show a profit. You need to be aware of **time lags**.

What does this awareness mean? It means you've planned everything down to the doorknobs. It means you don't quit your job until you've finished your Business Plan and checked with your banker (and your backup banker) and know that you have enough money to withstand whatever surprises await you. It means you're not

ASSETS		LIABILITIES	
Cash in Wells Fargo	$	Notes Payable Banks–Schedule I	$
Cash in other–identify		Secured	
Stocks and Bonds–Schedule II		Unsecured	
Accounts Receivable		Accounts/Bills Payable–Schedule I	
Cash Surrender Value Life Insurance			
Face Value $			
Real Estate–Schedule III		Mortages Payable on Real Estate–Schedule III	
Automobiles		Other Debts–itemize	
Other Assets–Itemize			
		Total Liabilites	
		Net worth (total assets less total liabilities)	
TOTAL ASSETS	$	**TOTAL LIABILITIES PLUS NET WORTH**	$

SOURCES OF INCOME		SCHEDULE I–DEBTS AND CREDIT REFERENCES		
Salary	$	Notes Payable, Banks, Credit Cards, Dept. Stores, etc. itemized		
Spouse's Salary–(if applicable)		(All debts are listed ☐ Yes ☐ No)		
Bonus and Commissions		**NAME AND ADDRESS OF CREDITOR**	**BALANCE**	**MO. PMT.**
Real Estate Income–Net				
Dividends				
Other Source (**Note:** You need not list income from alimony, child support or maintenance unless you wish it to be considered				
		Alimony, Child Support, Maintenance		
Total	$	Totals	$	$

SCHEDULE II–STOCKS AND BONDS					
DESCRIPTION	**WHERE QUOTED**	**COST OR MARKET**	**TITLE IN NAME OF**	**QUANTITY**	**VALUE**

SCHEDULE III–REAL ESTATE							
DESCRIPTION/ADDRESS	**DATE ACQUIRED**	**TITLE IN NAME OF**	**COST**	**MARKET VALUE**	**MORTGAGE**		
					DUE TO	**AMOUNT**	**MO. PMT.**

SCHEDULE IV–SEPARATE PROPERTY		
Complete if married, and any assets listed above are separate property.		
DESCRIPTION	**TITLE IN NAME**	**VALUE**

GENERAL INFORMATION–CONTINGENT LIABILITIES

Have you ever had a repossession? ☐Yes ☐No   Have you ever declared bankruptcy? ☐Yes ☐No

Are you an Endorser, Guarantor, Co-maker? ☐Yes ☐No

Are you a party to any Claims or Suits?   ☐Yes ☐No

Do you owe any taxes for years prior to the current year?
☐YES   ☐NO   AMOUNT: $

FIGURE 8.3   A personal financial statement form—available at any bank—will help you construct an accurate picture of your net worth.

opportunity cost
the cost of making an investment

projection
an intelligent forecast

ACTION STEP 41

Develop a personal financial statement.

Sit down with a pencil and paper and do some figuring.

1. List everything you own that has **cash value** and estimate its worth. Include: cash, securities, life insurance, accounts receivable, notes receivable, rebates/refunds, autos and other vehicles, real estate, vested pension, Keogh or IRA funds, and so on.

   Don't stop now. Go on to list the market values of your home furnishings, household goods, major appliances, sports equipment, collectibles, jewelry, tools, livestock, trusts, patents, memberships, business interests, investment clubs, and so on.

   Add up the amounts you've written down. The total represents your *assets*.

2. List every dime you owe to someone or something. Accounts payable. Contracts payable. Notes payable (such as car loans). Taxes. Insurance (life, health, car, liability, etc.). Mortgages/Real Estate Loans. Anything else you owe. These are your **liabilities**.

3. Subtract your liabilities from your assets to find your net worth. It's that simple.

   Now you know how much you have and, thus, how much you need to raise so that you can start your business.

cash value
the value of tangible and intangible items when converted to cash

liabilities
a sum total of what you owe

surprised when your business does not support you (right away) in the manner to which you've become accustomed.

A business is a living, breathing entity, and it takes time for the golden egg to hatch. Be prepared to wait awhile.

OPPORTUNITY COSTS

Before You Take the Plunge

Before you jump into your own venture, make sure that you are being honest with yourself. What are the **opportunity costs**? What would your financial situation be if you kept working for someone else and did not go into business?

Any new business will take time—50 to 100 hours per week—so you will have to love what you're doing in order to succeed. Box 8.1 will help you measure the value of that time if you spent it elsewhere. It will also force you to consider the value of the fringe benefits you are probably earning while you work for someone else.

Complete Action Step 42. The dollar **projection** you come up with should let you know precisely what you're getting into. If it hurts you to think about what you'll be giving up if you go into business, maybe you're not ready for the plunge.

BOX 8.1 How to Project Opportunity Cost

Project your salary for the next 12 months. _____
Add in benefits from your employer:
  Life insurance _____
  Disability insurance _____
  Health insurance _____
  Pension plan _____
  Company car _____
  Social Security (employer's contribution) _____
  Expense account _____
  Bonuses _____
  Other _____
    Total _____
Calculate the interest you could earn in the 12 months on the capital you're planning to invest in your business. *Example:* $25,000 × 7.75% = $1,937.50. _____
Add in your time.
  Hours per week you plan to work in your new business: _____
  Subtract the number of hours you now work. _____
  Hours available for moonlighting: _____
  Multiply moonlighting hours by hourly rate and then by 50 weeks. _____
Total opportunity cost (your potential income for the next year) _____

In weighing the opportunity costs of going into business, ask yourself questions such as these:

Can you afford to leave your job?

What are your gut feelings as you approach the point of no return?

How comfortable are those "golden handcuffs"?

Think Again about What Success Means to You

As we've pointed out before, money isn't the only measure of success. You need to keep your focus on what you really want. Make a list. Do a mind map. Dig deep into yourself and learn what makes you tick.

AN OUNCE OF PREVENTION

When survivors from any field or profession get together, they like to share horror stories. We have collected a few of these in the small-business surprise area and come up with some **preventive actions** for them. They're listed here. You can probably think of more.

preventive action
positive steps taken to minimize risk of potential adversities

SURPRISE	PREVENTION
Your landlord decides to evict you and your business.	Get a lease. Rewrite the lease to favor your business. Keep in contact with the landlord. Make sure you have a renewal clause.
The newspaper does not run the ad for your grand opening.	Make connections with all media. Develop a **tickler file**. Make sure you see proof sheets. Withhold payment until they do it right.
An hour after you sign your name to guarantee the lease, your best friend and partner gets cold feet and pulls out. You do not have a thing in writing to protect you against **partner's remorse**.	Line up partnership commitments before the big day. Open a special **escrow account**. Everybody deposits. Everybody signs.
For eight weeks, during your peak season, the city has the sidewalk in front of your store torn up. The noise is deafening.	Network your way into city hall. Make sure you know your councilman. Try to rally media sympathy. Use the underdog angle.
Your general contractor goes bankrupt.	Get a **completion bond**. Ask the bonding agency to expedite.
Your bookkeeper disappears with $100,000, your books, two trade secrets from the company safe, and your spouse.	A fidelity bond would have protected you. Join a singles club.
Your best salesperson is hired away by the competition.	Woo **key employees**. Keep them involved and informed. Don't take them for granted. Think about giving them a piece of the business. Check the horizon for pirates.

tickler file
a calendar-based reminder system

escrow account
funds held by a neutral, state-regulated third party until the stated conditions are met

partner's remorse
backing out of a deal before the business gets rolling

completion bond
an insurance policy that will pay for finishing a project

key employee
a worker whose loss would seriously affect the future of your business

(continued)

Continued

backup banker
banker who would like to have your
business and is ready to help

SURPRISE	PREVENTION
Due to an administrative error, the bank calls your loan. It is payable in 30 days. If you would like to cash out, they will give you 25 cents on the dollar.	Take a banker to lunch. Take a **backup banker** to lunch. Back up the backup banker with a backup.
A new customer pays you by check, takes delivery of the goods, and then stops payment on the check before you get it to the bank. You were too busy to get check verification/authorization.	No matter how busy you are, take time for important survival tasks.
Your largest customer declares bankruptcy. The money owed you in receivables is 77% of your gross annual sales.	Don't keep all your eggs in one basket.
The bank where you have your checking account refuses to extend you a $3,300 line of credit to buy a piece of equipment that will double your business. The bank has a policy of not lending money to small firms.	Keep your banker in your information loop. Make sure you give your banker updates on your Business Plan. Get a backup bank. Discuss money long before you need it.

ACTION STEP 42

Determine how much you can make
if you do not go into business.

Calculate what will happen, money-
wise, if you keep on with what you are
doing and attach a value to the extra
time you're going to have to spend in
your new business. Box 8.1 can help
you.
   A. Project your salary for the next
12 months.
   B. Add in the value of the fringe
benefits you receive from your
employer—insurance, pension plan,
company car, expense account,
bonuses, Social Security (employer's
contribution), parking, free photocop-
ying, complimentary paperclips, and
so on.
   C. Now figure in the capital you're
planning to invest in the business.
What would you make on this money
if you invested it in a no-load family of
money-market funds that allows you
to switch from stocks to money markets and back to stocks when interest
rates change?
   D. Add in the value of your time. If
you're planning to work 60 hours a
week in your new business (many
entrepreneurs work 100 during peak
seasons), subtract 40 (your normal
work week) from 60. That would leave
you 20 hours a week available for
moonlighting. Say you could make
$7.50 per hour moonlighting. Then,
20 hours a week times 50 weeks a year
times $7.50 equals $7,500.
   E. Find the total.

Turn a Lemon into Lemonade

At some time in your business life, you're going to need to find a way to capitalize
on one of those unfortunate surprises. When that time comes, we hope you will be
as resourceful as Terry Adkins.

Terry and Susan Adkins' Donut Place got off to a slow start. They grossed only $275
a day the first month, when what they needed was closer to $700. But then things
started picking up. They had weeks that averaged $310, $380, and then $475, and they
could see that they were going to make it after all.

By Easter of the second year, they were pulling in $850 on weekdays and $600 on
weekends, when trade naturally slowed down. They were beginning to look forward to
taking their first vacation in 6 years when the Energy Crisis hit.

It didn't get as nasty in their community as it did in the big cities, but it was bad
enough. Cars lined up for blocks to wait for available gas. Terry and Susan's business
fell off dramatically because a major oil company station was on the nearby corner.
Their customers were either waiting in line for gas, or they couldn't drive in for their
morning doughnuts without having to break through the lines of waiting cars. If the
shop took in $200 a day, they called it profit. It wasn't profit, of course; it didn't come
anywhere near paying the bills. Needless to say, they were in despair.

After a week of no business, they had an idea. They borrowed a shopping cart from
the supermarket and bought a fifty-cup coffee urn. They put the urn—full of steaming
coffee—onto the grocery cart and stacked boxes of doughnuts, disposable cups, cream
and sugar packets, and napkins around the urn. And then Terry took their doughnuts
to the street.

While he sold doughnuts, Terry got to know the people in the cars. The second day
he went out, he took along a paper and pencil. He wrote down the people's names and
what kinds of doughnuts they liked. He didn't know that this is called "market
research"; it just seemed like the smart thing to do.

Terry and Susan didn't make as much money as they had before the Energy Crisis,
but they made enough to keep going until things got sorted out in the Persian Gulf.
And when the Energy Crisis was over, they had more than a hundred new customers.
And because of Terry's market research, they knew what kinds of doughnuts the new
customers liked.

moonlighting
holding down a second job

After Plan B

The reason for many small business successes is fast footwork. A small business can move more quickly than a big business. The idea is to keep informed, alert, and flexible. After you develop Plan B, work on Plans C and D.

Key Points from Another View
Part I:
THE BASICS OF BONDING

What is bonding? Basically, bonding is a guarantee in which the bonding company promises to cover any losses to the business or its customers.

Types of Bonds

1. Bonds on employees are called *fidelity* bonds.
   - You can cover an individual employee.
   - You can cover all employees with one bond.
     - Named schedule bond. Each employee is listed by name and may have a separate amount of coverage.
     - Position schedule bond. Positions or employee titles, rather than employee names, are listed.
   - There are alternatives to fidelity bonds. You may opt for employee dishonesty insurance, which is usually carried in a "package" of commercial crime insurance (for example, burglary, robbery, other).
2. On the other hand, *surety* bonds are usually purchased because they are required. Surety bonds are used in businesses that work under contract. They ensure that if the business does not carry out the contract, the bonding company will. This does not financially protect the bonded business, because the bonding company covers the loss to the customer. It seeks repayment from the business.

How to Get Bonded

1. Any insurance agent who handles casualty insurance sells bonds, but few agents would issue a fidelity bond only—it's usually part of a "package" of business insurance.
2. There are also companies that specialize in bonding, called surety and fidelity companies.
3. The first step in getting bonded is determining the type of bond you need.
4. Next, you need to determine the amount of the bond. To determine the size of bond you should carry on your employee(s), you need to consider the amount of money or goods they could steal.
5. Finally, do the paperwork. Both you and your employees need to fill out applications for fidelity bonds. The complicated applications are used in classifying the type of business and determining the risk of the employee.

To Bond or Not to Bond

1. In the case of surety bonds, you probably won't have a choice of whether to get bonded. In many fields, you are required to purchase surety bonds.

In other cases, bonding is not legally required, but is the accepted norm in the field.

2. Bonding gives clients peace of mind.

3. Bonding is also good protection against employee theft and embezzlement. Studies have shown that in almost all cases of embezzlement, the embezzler was a "trusted employee."

4. Any business with employees should consider bonding. Bonding is relatively inexpensive protection and is simple to obtain.

From: Denise Osburn, "The Basics of Bonding," *New Business Opportunities*, September, 1990, 80–82.

Part II:

RISKY BUSINESS—INSURANCE CAN BE THE MOST VITAL TOOL IN YOUR BUSINESS SURVIVAL KIT

All too frequently, small business owners either haven't planned ways to cope with a loss or find that their insurance policies don't cover their particular loss.

For many entrepreneurs, lining up adequate insurance is the last thing on their minds.

Despite frustrations, it is crucial for businesses to reduce their risk of catastrophic loss. Business owners need to understand what their risks are, how to reduce them, and when it's a good idea to insure.

Risk Management

- Frequently, though, it makes more sense to reduce risks in other ways, or even to assume some of them, than to put the money into insurance policies.
- Insurance is only one of the options—and it should be the last resort. Other options include eliminating the risk, reducing it, assuming it, or transferring it to someone else.
  - If one of your products generates low profits but exposes you to substantial liability for personal injury, consider eliminating the product.
- Insurance can reimburse you only for unintentional, unforeseen and uncontrollable losses or liabilities—not for everyday business risks.
  - Because it is impossible to insure against every possibility of harm, business owners need to do all they can to prevent accidents from happening in the first place. You can install a sprinkler system, put in burglar alarms, provide protective gear for employees, store and dispose of waste safely, maintain vehicles in good condition, install handrails, and empty cash registers regularly.
  - A third option is to assume the risk. Many companies assume part of the risk by agreeing to large deductibles. For small businesses, self-insurance is generally not workable.
  - In some cases, a fourth option is to transfer the risk. For example, if you're worried about sending drivers out on the highway to deliver your merchandise, consider hiring a delivery company instead and letting that company assume the risk.

Shopping For Insurance

- A good starting place is a business package policy, which offers a range of property and liability coverage considered essential for small business.
  - Insurance companies frequently put together packages for particular types of businesses, such as retail, wholesale, service, and restaurants.

- A typical catastrophe package would include fire, lightning, windstorm, explosion, smoke, vandalism, and other basic coverage, plus options such as full-value building replacement and insurance of valuable papers.
- Don't overlook one of the most important business risks: the danger that you or one of your key employees will die or become disabled suddenly, seriously crippling the business. Look into term life insurance, payable to the company, on the life of anyone whose death or disability would seriously damage the company.

Finding an Agent

- A good agent knows the market, understands all the different types of coverage available, and can put together a favorable policy.
- Ask friends and business associates for their recommendations.
- Ask questions to make sure the agent is familiar with your business and knowledgeable about what various companies can offer.
- Once you've chosen an agent, make sure he or she understands your business and can paint a good picture when applying to insurance companies for coverage.

When to Switch

- If a company is offering good coverage and good service, it is generally a bad idea to switch just to save a few dollars on premiums.
- Insurance companies, like anyone else, look for loyalty and consistency. If you have done business with me for a long time, I'll want to take care of you.

Living with Insurance

- In a typical insurance policy, there's more print telling what the policy doesn't cover than describing what it does cover.
- It's important for you and your agent to be aware of every exclusion, so that you don't leave gaps in your coverage or pay twice for overlapping coverage.
- To avoid problems, review your coverage periodically to make sure all of the exposures you're not willing to assume are adequately covered.
- Finally, make sure you abide by any restrictions in your policy, or you may find yourself holding the bag.

With a top-notch agent and some good risk-management practices, though, you can avoid catastrophic losses without having to pour all your profits into premiums.

From: Jane Easter Bahls, "Risky Business—Insurance Can Be The Most Vital Tool In Your Business Survival Kit," *Entrepreneur*, September, 1989, 66–76.

SUMMARY

Start-up needs to go smoothly. What you don't need then is expensive surprises that knock you and your business for a loop. So before you open your doors, you need to have anticipated as many potential unpleasant surprises as possible and have a plan of action for each one of them. For example, what will you do if:

your landlord decides to evict your business?

your yellow pages ad stinks?

the customer that accounts for 75 percent of your business declares bankruptcy?

ACTION STEP REVIEW

Four action steps help you anticipate surprises:

39 Use your new eyes to develop strategies for dealing with unforeseen events that could cripple you.

40 Make a list of all your business needs and estimate their costs. List *everything*, the tangibles first and then the intangibles.

41 Develop a personal financial statement to learn your net worth. Look closely at your assets and your liabilities.

42 Assess the opportunity costs of going into business for yourself. Determine how much you will make if you do *not* go into business. If what you learn is painful, perhaps you're not ready to make the plunge into small business.

Expecting and *planning for* the unexpected can make the difference between life and death in business. Looking closely at your present assets and liabilities—by developing a personal financial statement—and calculating the opportunity costs of going into business for yourself will help you eliminate some surprises, and they may cause you to question whether you're truly ready to take the plunge. Just remember two things: no one can anticipate everything, and it will probably cost more and take longer than your planning indicates.

THINK POINTS FOR SUCCESS

◢ Be prepared for your competition to counterattack.

◢ Be aware of closing dates for yellow page advertising and other key media.

◢ Keep a time log that tells everyone (you, your founders, your key employees) how you are progressing on the Plan.

◢ Make sure your partners are as committed to the business as you are.

◢ Keep an ongoing list of unfortunate surprises that could hurt your business.

◢ Always have a Plan B. And a Plan C. And a Plan D.

◢ Let some key customers in on your planning; let them see it with their own eyes.

REFERENCES

Delsack, Katherine. *The Small Business Form Book*. Newport Beach, Calif.: Law Prep Press, 1990.

Financial Management: How to Make a Go of Your Business. Washington, D.C.: U.S. Small Business Administration, Office of Management Assistance. Small Business Management Training Instructors' Guide No. 106, 1984.

"General Information Concerning Patents." US Patent and Trademark Office, Superintendent of Documents number 003-004-00651-0. [Available from the Government Printing Office, (202) 783-3238, for $2.00.]

Mastering Business Writing. National Institute of Business Management, 1989.

"OSHA Handbook for Small Business." [Contact (202) 523-7266.]

Recordkeeping in Small Business. Washington, D.C.: U.S. Small Business Administration, Office of Business Development. Management Aid No. 1.017, 1987.

Walton, Mary. *Deming Management at Work*. New York: Putnam Publishing Group, 1991.

APPENDIX 8.1 • Action Step 40: Attach price tags to your business.

The Saddleback Scribe soon will be 5 years old. The Saddleback Scribe is used for public relations and editorial work, such as writing and editing *NavCom World* magazine for Gould, Inc., in El Monte.

The Saddleback Scribe has invested and basically written off through Schedule 173 and ACRS depreciation about $25,000 worth of computers and office equipment, including: two computers, three printers, a suitable supply of stationery, lamps, fixtures, desks, tables, and office supplies, and a large assortment of software programs. I have the most important software programs for desktop publishing (investment of $3,600). I also have the usual spread-sheet programs, data-base management programs, project management programs, at least four accounting programs, and a word-processing program.

Because these investments are behind me and paid in full, and because I plan to enter what is essentially a consulting business, my start-up costs should be minimal. I can work out of my home, using Nadek Computer Systems, Inc., as my unpaid storefront. The main expense will be the salary I pay myself until cash flow can generate profits. All expenses item-ized in the table are available to me at this time.

Estimated Expenses

MONTHLY ITEM	MONTHLY COST	AMOUNT NEEDED TO START
Salary of owner–manager	$3,000	$6,000
Other salaries/wages	none	none
Rent	none	none
Advertising	500	1,000
Delivery, supplies	none	none
Telephone	100	200
Other utilities	none	none
Insurance	50	100
Taxes, including FICA	360	720
Interest	none	none
Maintenance	none	none
Professional fees	100	200
Miscellaneous	500	1,000
START-UP ITEM		
Fixtures, equipment: scanner		$4,000*
Decorating, remodeling		none
Installation of fixtures		none
Starting inventory		none
Utilities deposits		none
Professional fees		none
Licenses, permits		none
Advertising for opening		1,000
Accounts receivable		1,000
Cash		1,000
Other: flyer, newsletter		1,000
TOTAL CASH NEEDED TO START		$17,220
Total if the scanner is leased		$14,020
Reserve for emergencies		$10,000

*I can lease a scanner on a lease–buy plan for 10% down and $150 a month.

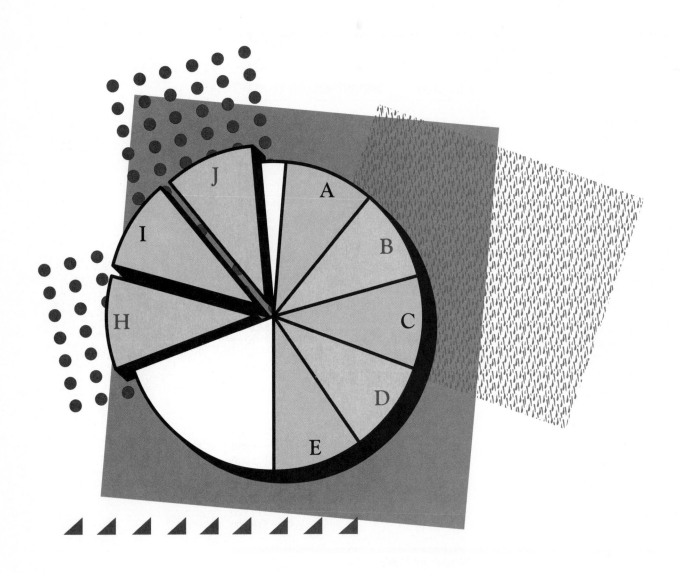

FIGURE 9.1
Chapter 9 will help you prepare parts H, I, and J of your Business Plan—the
financial section.

9 Numbers and Shoebox Accounting

Learning Objectives

- To be able to use numbers to project your business future.
- To develop strategies for managing cash.
- To project monthly sales.
- To search your own financial history for creative ways to deal with shortfalls.
- To understand that bills are paid with cash, not profit.
- To understand that the government taxes *paper* profit.
- To be able to use ratios as a cash management tool.
- To create an income statement.
- To create a cash flow projection.
- To consider numerical projections in choosing a legal form for your business.
- To know how to use shoebox accounting.

FUTURE FOCUS

Cash management need not be complicated. But you need to pay attention. Cash is the lifeblood of your business. Here is how to stay in control of the flow.

I n this chapter, we urge you to move beyond your start-up plans and venture out into the uncertain future. It's time to set some numerical goals for your first year of operation. Running out of money in business is the end of the business. This chapter will show you how to avoid running out of money.

CHART YOUR BUSINESS FUTURE WITH NUMBERS

Which months will be strong in your particular business and which will be weak? What will be your gross sales the first year? The second? The third? How much profit will you make? Or how much will you lose? How can you project cash flow, bank loans, lines of credit, vendor credit? Can you add some people to the team who will bring in some cash? What will your cash picture look like when your start-up dollars are spread over a full year? How fast will your business grow? What would rapid growth do to your cash picture? Have any of your life experiences prepared you for handling money in business?

Start with the Past

Looking at your past can help you chart your business future. Money does indeed make the world go 'round, and up and down. Everyone has financial ups and downs. When were some of your "down" times? Action Step 43 directs your thinking to the past and to the future.

Collect Survival Information

In Chapter 8 you worked out a personal financial statement. In Action Step 43 you recalled personal survival tactics—how you dealt with money problems in the past. Your next step is to begin building a business budget. There are four things you need to think about, generally, before you plunge into the numbers of business management: sales forecasting, seasonality, cash management, and profit and loss. We discuss each of these briefly here.

Sales Forecast   Before you jump into a business, you need to figure out how much it will produce in a given period of time. You can pull a first-year forecast together by combining information on sales from business owners and trade associations.

seasonality
the recognition that business, like life, flows in cycles connected to the four seasons

Seasonality Scenario   Almost every business experiences peaks and valleys. What will be your best month? Your worst? Attempt to develop a seasonality scenario for the first year of your particular business.

cash management
the tightrope balancing of liquid money resources to obtain maximum benefit from each dollar

Cash Management   Because of time lags (checks clearing, dating, credit sales, credit cards, bad risks, human factors, paperwork, weekends, and so on), you probably will not get paid the same day you make a sale. Meanwhile, you will have to pay out cash for labor, taxes, rent, utilities, inventory, and other expenses. If your business is to stay afloat in the interim, you're going to have to know where every dollar is. Long before the dollars stop trickling in, you must make arrangements for help.

Cash management involves knowing where the dollars are every month and maximizing the benefits of the money you are holding. The idea is to speed up the inflow and slow down the outflow. Remember, your expenses are someone else's sales.

Profit and Loss   Unless you are the exception to the rule, you are not going to make lots of money your first week in business, and if you do get rich, it will happen slowly. A projected profit and loss statement will tell you when you should start making a profit—which has to happen before you can start getting rich. If you're not going to make a profit for a while, you might want to structure your business so that your losses can be deducted from personal taxable income.

Forecast Sales

The following case study about a bookstore operation illustrates the value of planning. The owners, Patricia and Don French, carried out three important steps:

1. They developed a seasonal scenario so that they were not surprised by the Christmas crush and the February slump.
2. They gathered data from their trade association that gave them ballpark numbers.
3. They projected their sales by using ratios.

In any retail operation, you want to distinguish your product mix according to how fast it moves—that is, by its "shelf velocity." Industry data told Patricia and Don to separate paperbacks from hardbacks, because the shelf velocity for each category was different.

We planned every phase of our bookstore operation. My husband, Don, has always been a great reader, and my friends in college used to accuse me of being a bibliophile—but we quickly discovered when we did our research that a bookstore is a business. In business, you either grow fast or you die, so we needed to master a lot of new skills, fast.

Running a bookstore is not the same as being a happy-go-lucky English major in college.

We worked and saved for several years—in bookstores, teaching, advertising—and when we started our business we had over $30,000. In addition, we got our friends interested, and they contributed $50,000 more. With that in hand, we wrote up an eighty-page Business Plan and went to our banker, who extended us a line of credit for $25,000.

The location we found had about 2,500 square feet of floor space, and data from the ABA [American Booksellers' Association, the major trade association] indicated that sales for that size store in this demographic area would be around $130,000 annually. Our major competitor had done $150,000 the year before.

Our first question was how much to spend on inventory. To answer that, we used a ratio method of inventory projection. First, we found the annual **turn ratio** for hardbacks, which was 3. Then we found the annual turn ratio for paperbacks, which sell faster. That was 6.

To find the amount we needed for initial inventory, we first multiplied the annual sales figure by the percentage for gross sales. Industry figures told us hardbacks would account for 60 percent of sales and paperbacks, 40 percent. Thus,

60% × $130,000 = $78,000 annual hardback sales

Next, we figured cost of goods sold, which has gone up. It's now 65%. We multiplied $78,000 by 65%. That came to $50,700 for our annual cost of hardback goods sold.

To estimate what our start-up hardback inventory would cost us, we divided the cost of goods sold by the annual turn ratio, which for hardbacks was 3.

$$\frac{\$50,700}{3} = \$16,900$$

ACTION STEP 43

Recall hard times and look to the future.

A. Your Personal Money Past. Look back over your life, to times when you have been pressed for cash. List the times in your life when you ran out of money.

Where were you, and what were you doing? How old were you? How much job training and experience did you have? Who were you with? Did you have any dependents? How did you feel about running out of money? (Angry? Sick? Depressed? Victimized?)

How did you solve the problem? (Moonlight? Borrow money? Take out another mortgage? Tighten your belt and run leaner?)

B. Your Personal Money Future. Look ahead into the next year and list your expenses (shelter, food, medical expenses, transportation, insurance, phone, school, clothes, utilities, and so on). (If you need a form with blanks to fill in, ask your banker. Most banks have personal budget forms to give their customers.) Add up all the amounts and add 10 percent for a contingency fund.

Now, write down how you will handle these expenses. If it looks like you're not going to have enough money, what will you do?

turn ratio
a measurement obtained by dividing the average inventory into annual sales

So we knew our cost for the initial hardback inventory would be about $16,900.

We went through the same procedure for paperbacks—multiplying the annual sales by percentage of gross sales and by the cost of goods sold, and then dividing by the turn ratio:

$$\frac{40\% \times \$130,000 \times 65\%}{6}$$

or, simplified,

$$\frac{\$52,000 \times 65\%}{6} = \frac{\$33,800}{6} = \$5,630$$

Adding the two figures, we came up with $22,530, almost $23,000, that we needed for initial inventory. This seemed like a lot of money, but it was a relief to know where we were going.

After we'd been in business for a year, we did something we should have done before. We plotted out a **scenario for a year** and assigned percentages of sales to each month. This gave us a feel for the future, based on the past.

Before we opened, we knew that December would be our **peak time**, but we didn't realize the extent of the peak. The holiday season accounts for at least a third of our business. Here's our scenario:

January (6.5%). "January is an anticlimax to Christmas, but it's still busy because of gift certificates and exchanges. Don and I run some good specials at the end of January, prior to taking our yearly inventory. Even though sales are slowing down, we have to order new titles, because publishers (our suppliers) are giving us advance notice on their lists for spring."

February (4.5%) and March (5%). "Very quiet. We take inventory, weed out stuff that didn't sell, send it back. We meet a lot of publishers' reps, who are out on the road pushing new titles. On March 15th we have an Ides of March sale. Next year we're planning a St. Patrick's Day tie-in."

April (5%). "Still slow. We get a slight jump in sales after the 15th, mostly because spring vacations give some people time to read."

May (8%) and June (8%). "Two holidays—Mother's Day and Father's Day—plus weddings and graduations give us our second-busiest season. Art books and gift editions do well, also encyclopedias and how-to's."

July (6%) and August (7%). "We're not in a tourist area, and summers for us are slow. We sell mostly easy-to-read paperbacks. Our minds are on ordering books for Christmas."

September (9%). "Saved by back-to-school purchases. We're interviewing people for Christmas jobs and making last-minute purchases of gift items."

October (10%) and November (12%). "The start of the busy season. Customers sense it, and we can feel the momentum. The rush is just around the corner. We usually hire more sales help at this time."

December (19%). "The crush. I work the front while Don stations himself in back, inputting our sales into the computer. We gather information daily so we can spot the direction holiday sales will take. It's different every year, but with two years of data gathering behind us, we're getting a feel for what really happens. And that helps us plan ahead for the next year."

Don and Patricia prepared Tables 9.1 and 9.2 before they opened their doors and Table 9.3 after their first year in business. These tables can serve as examples for you to follow.

After the first year of business, sales forecasting will become easier. Keep very careful records that first year, so that you'll know how your own peaks and valleys correlate with the seasonality of your industry.

scenario for a year
combining seasonality with sales percentages to produce a picture of the peaks and valleys of the business cycle

peak time
a high-volume period when maximum inventory and resources are needed

TABLE 9.1   Bookstore Income and Expense Forecast, First Year*

	JULY	AUG	SEPT	OCT	NOV	DEC	JAN	FEB	MAR	APR	MAY	JUNE	TOTAL
Sales	7,800	9,100	11,700	13,000	15,600	24,700	8,450	5,850	6,500	6,500	10,400	10,400	130,000
Cost of Goods Sold	5,070	5,915	7,605	8,450	10,140	16,055	5,495	3,800	4,225	4,225	6,760	6,760	8,450
Gross Profit	2,730	3,185	4,095	4,550	5,460	8,645	2,955	2,050	2,275	2,275	3,640	3,640	45,500
Expenses													
Rent		1,875	1,875	1,875	1,875	1,875	1,875	1,875	1,875	1,875	1,875	1,875	20,625
Utilities	200	200	200	200	200	200	200	200	200	200	200	200	2,400
Adv./PR/4%	310	365	470	520	625	990	340	235	260	260	415	415	5,205
Insurance	75	75	75	75	75	75	75	75	75	75	75	75	900
Supplies/1%	80	90	115	130	155	245	85	60	65	65	105	105	1,300
Misc./5%	390	455	585	650	780	1235	425	295	325	325	520	520	6,505
Credit card fees	70	80	105	120	140	225	75	55	60	60	95	95	1,180
Loan interest				10									10
Total Expenses	1,125	3,140	3,425	3,580	3,850	4,845	3,075	2,795	2,860	2,860	3,285	3,285	38,125
Net Profit/Loss	1,605	45	670	970	1,610	3,800	−120	−745	−585	−585	355	355	7,375

*Sales: the first-year forecast of $130,000 is based on industry information gathered by the owners.
Cost of Goods Sold: Estimated at 65% of sales.
Rent: 75 cents per square foot × 2,500 square feet; no rent charged for the first two months; the owners used the first month to get ready for their opening.
Utilities: Figures are estimates from the local utility company.
Advertising and Promotion: Estimated at 4% of sales based on information from other bookstore owners.
Insurance: $900 per year is the rate quoted by owners' insurance agent.
Supplies: Estimated at 1% of sales based on interviews.
Miscellaneous: Estimated at 5% of sales based on interviews; added a fudge factor to cover unexpected expenses.
Loan Interest: This represents interest on the line of credit at 1% per month of the unpaid balance.
Credit Card Fees: Projected on the basis of 30% of sales being credit-card sales; the credit card company charges 3%.

TABLE 9.2   Bookstore Cash Flow Forecast, First Year

	JULY	AUG	SEPT	OCT	NOV	DEC	JAN	FEB	MAR	APR	MAY	JUNE
Cash on hand	1,900	3,945	100	145	610	5,715	21,070	20,990	20,360	22,030	21,200	20,950
Sales	7,800	9,100	11,700	13,000	15,600	24,700	8,450	5,850	6,500	6,500	10,400	10,400
Less: Credit fees	−70	−80	−105	−120	−140	−225	−75	−55	−60	−60	−95	−95
Loan			1,000									
Total	9,360	12,965	12,965	13,025	16,070	30,190	29,445	26,785	26,800	28,470	31,505	31,255
Disbursements												
Book purchases	4,255	9,880	9,305	8,030	6,720	4,575	5,080	3,760	2,045	4,545	7,440	8,420
Rent		1,875	1,875	1,875	1,875	1,875	1,875	1,875	1,875	1,875	1,875	1,875
Utilities	200	200	200	200	200	200	200	200	200	200	200	200
Adv./PR/4%	310	365	470	520	625	990	340	235	260	260	415	415
Insurance	450											
Supplies/1%	80	90	115	130	155	245	85	60	65	65	105	105
Misc./5%	390	455	585	650	780	1,235	425	295	325	325	520	520
Interest				10								
Loan payment				1,000								
Total	5,685	12,865	12,550	12,415	10,355	9,120	8,455	6,425	4,770	7,270	10,555	11,535
Net Cash Flow	3,945	100	145	610	5,715	21,070	20,990	20,360	22,030	21,200	20,950	19,720

TABLE 9.3 Bookstore Income and Expense Forecast, 2nd–5th Years*

| | 2ND YEAR | | | | | 3RD YEAR | 4TH YEAR | 5TH YEAR |
	1ST QTR	2ND QTR	3RD QTR	4TH QTR	TOTAL	TOTAL	TOTAL	TOTAL
Sales	34,320	63,960	24,960	32,760	156,000	201,175	210,800	237,200
Cost of Goods Sold	22,310	41,575	16,225	21,295	101,405	137,020	137,020	154,180
Gross Profit	12,010	22,385	8,735	11,465	54,595	64,155	73,780	83,020
Expenses								
Rent	5,905	5,905	5,905	5,910	23,625	24,805	26,045	27,350
Utilities	630	630	630	630	2,520	2,645	2,780	2,920
Adv./PR	1,375	2,545	1,000	1,310	6,230	7,330	8,430	9,490
Insurance	235	235	235	240	945	990	1,040	1,090
Supplies	345	640	250	330	1,565	1,835	2,110	2,370
Misc.	1,785	3,200	1,250	1,640	7,875	9,215	10,540	11,860
Credit card fees	310	575	225	295	1,405	1,650	1,900	2,135
Loan interest								
Total Expenses	10,585	13,730	9,495	10,355	44,165	48,470	52,845	57,215
Net Profit/Loss	1,425	8,655	−760	1,110	10,430	15,685	20,935	25,805

*2nd year: 20% growth
3rd year: 17.5% growth
4th year: 15% growth
5th year: 12.5% growth

Most businesses are seasonal, and you'll need to develop strong control systems to manage your financial resources. Start now to identify alternate sources of credit and find ways to collect cash from customers before all of your products or services are delivered.

Forecast Collections

If you're in the ice cream business, your sales will heat up in summer. The same is true of hardware (especially home improvement supplies) and auto parts, since people tend to drive more in the summer months. If you run a ski shop, you might have to order your skis at a summer trade show, pay for them when they arrive in September, and then wait until late March to sell the last of them.

If, on the other hand, you're in the bed-and-breakfast business, you can collect your money ahead of time—sometimes as far ahead as 6 months—and have it spent or invested long before you have to provide the bed and breakfast. The same is true for airlines, insurance companies, magazines, newspapers, advertising agencies, travel agents, universities that charge tuition, printers, and caterers. If you do business with such businesses as these, keep this in mind.

Develop an Income Scenario

Now it's time for you to project an income scenario. Action Step 44 takes you through the process. Note that more than just sales are involved; you also need to project times of collection and other time lags so you can get a feel for the way cash will flow through your business. The action step winds up by asking you a pointed question: Now that you have seen your sales percentages, what **management strat-**

management strategies
making directional decisions

egies will you develop to get more control of your business? You need to tackle that question *before* you open your doors.

Think about that as you read the following case study. It tells the story of how Laserian, Ltd., a flashy company in a glamorous growth industry, got into money trouble because its CEO was too busy to attend to cash management.

Jerry Fiske's Laserian, Ltd., a manufacturer of laser optics, was entering its second year of operation when it started to run out of money.

Jerry was an engineer and an inventor, and he had fooled around with lasers for twenty years before he got some backers together to found Laserian, Ltd. He knew lasers, and every instinct told him it was the hottest growth industry going. So when he solved one of the tricky problems in the industry, he knew he would become rich and famous.

The problem Jerry solved was the problem of light leakage. Big communications companies were experimenting with sending messages through glass fiber tubes, which are a lot more efficient for carrying information than metal wires. The messages traveled without a hitch as long as the tubes were straight, but whenever there was a bend in the tube, some of the light would continue on in a straight line, resulting in light leakage and a garbled message.

Jerry's solution was to coat the inside of the tube with a substance that would bounce the light into a graceful curve, and thus help it to glide around corners.

At the moment he ran short of cash, Jerry was developing a dozen applications of his discovery, and other Laserian engineer–inventors were designing a scanner that would read labels for the food industry. Nonetheless, his research and development people told him the company needed a **cash injection**.

"We're out of money, Jerry. What's the story?"

Jerry didn't know. So he put on his coat and tie and went to see Phil Brill, his banker.

FIRST VISIT

"Jerry," Phil said, shaking hands. "Glad you called. Long time no see."

Jerry handed Phil a profit and loss statement he had roughed out on the back of an envelope. Phil took the envelope, glanced at the figures, then looked at Jerry.

"How's the laser business, anyway?"

"Booming," Jerry said. "We've got orders pouring in for our scanner. Every food chain in the country wants one the day before yesterday. We're starting up production of a holographic camera—one that will take pictures of automobile tires to check for defects. The Air Force has sent six guys out to see us about signing a contract to work on a new cryptographic device. The numbers speak for themselves, Phil. We did three hundred thousand dollars in sales this month and had a profit of more than fifty-two thousand."

The banker looked at the numbers on the envelope:

Sales: $300K

Cost of Goods Sold: $172K

Gross Profit: $128K

Expenses: $76K

Profit: $52K plus

"How much do you need?"

"Thirty thou should do it, Phil. Just for odds and ends until our receivables start pouring in." (Jerry is a person who can pick up key words and use them right away. *Receivables* was one of those words.)

"From the look of these numbers," Phil said, "I'd say you'd be good for it."

Jerry smiled. This was easy street. "I never argue about money," he said.

Later that week, he had a check for $30,000. He turned the check over to his manager and got back into the lab, where he was happy.

A month later, Laserian ran short of cash again.

cash injection
infusion of dollars into a business, usually at a critical point to help meet cyclical needs

SECOND VISIT

"Sorry to bother you again, Phil," Jerry said. "But we need another green transfusion." Jerry was smiling. He had received money before, and he knew this was a piece of cake.

"How much this time?" the banker said.

"What about ninety grand?" Jerry asked.

"Sounds steep," Phil said. "What's your cash picture?"

Jerry smiled. "We're in terrific shape, Phil." He handed Phil a sheet of graph paper that contained a short column of numbers. "Take a look at this month."

	FEB
Sales	$320,000
Cost of Goods Sold	184,000
Gross Profit	136,000
Expenses	87,000
Profit	49,000

The banker studied the figures without saying anything.

"Feast your eyes, Phil. Sales are up over last month. The total profit for the last 2 months is over a hundred grand. If things keep up at this rate, we'll have five million dollars in sales by the end of the year. And that means a million in profits."

The banker looked up at Jerry. "What's the money for?" he asked.

"Plastic," Jerry said. "Everything we build is housed in plastic, and my purchasing guy found a real deal. That stuff's made with oil, you know, and if the world runs short of oil, we've got to have enough plastic to get us through."

"A sound point," Phil said.

"I'm in kind of a hurry, Phil. When can I get the check?"

"Can you have your accountant get me a completed profit and loss statement?" Phil asked. "And do something on **cash flow**?"

"Can do," Jerry said. "I'll get my people right on it."

"Let us see the numbers," Phil said. "I'll get back to you."

Walking out of the bank, Jerry was disappointed in the banker's conservative attitude. He thought briefly of changing banks, then swung his mind back to the excitement of lasers.

Back at the plant, he told his manager to do up a profit and loss statement and a cash flow projection, and then he got back to his inventing.

This time, it took the bank almost three weeks to approve the loan, and two loan officers came out to have a look at Laserian, Ltd. Apparently they liked what they saw, because the check came through, just in time.

The $90,000 lasted a couple of months, and then Jerry had to go back to the bank a third time.

THIRD VISIT

"I'll bet you know why I'm here," Jerry said.

"You'd better tell me, just the same," Phil said.

This time, Jerry had brought along computerized **spreadsheets**. He unrolled them for the banker. "Look at those numbers, Phil! Feast your eyes. That's over a million in sales you're looking at! It's also over $220,000 in profits, counting next month. The sales are already on the books, and we're showing a backlog that will carry us for two more months."

The banker studied the spreadsheets [see Table 9.4]. He noticed that they covered only the first four months.

cash flow
the lifeblood of any business

spreadsheets
displays of critical accounting data

TABLE 9.4   Laserian Income Statement

	JAN	FEB	MAR	APR	TOTAL
Sales	300,000	320,000	360,000	380,000	1,360,000
Cost of Goods Sold	172,500	184,000	207,000	218,500	782,000
Gross Profit	127,500	136,000	153,000	161,500	578,000
Expenses					
Sales/Commissions	27,000	28,800	32,400	34,100	
Advertising/Promotion	1,500	1,600	1,800	1,900	
Travel	500	5,000	2,000	5,000	
Equipment rental	800	800	800	800	
Auto/Truck	1,300	1,300	1,300	1,300	
Repair/Maintenance	800	800	900	900	
Rent	12,000	12,000	12,000	12,000	
Supplies	1,500	1,600	1,800	1,900	
Telephone	4,000	4,400	4,900	5,300	
Utilities	1,200	1,200	1,200	1,200	
Insurance	1,700	1,700	1,700	1,700	
Legal/Accounting	2,500	2,500	2,500	2,500	
Dues/Subscriptions	250	400	400	400	
Salary, management	15,000	16,000	17,000	18,000	
Salary, staff	3,000	5,000	7,000	9,000	
Miscellaneous	1,000	1,100	1,100	1,200	
Interest on bank loan		1,900	1,900	1,900	
Payroll taxes	1,300	1,500	1,700	1,900	
Total Expenses	75,350	87,600	92,400	101,000	356,350
Net before Taxes	52,150	48,400	60,600	60,500	221,650
Tax Reserve	23,450	21,800	27,300	27,300	99,850
Net Profit after Taxes	28,700	26,600	33,300	33,200	121,800

Phil was a banker. Numbers were his business; he'd seen thousands of spreadsheets, and he knew that fast growth could kill a company that wasn't ready for it. "How much do you need this time, Jerry?"

Jerry smiled. He thought he'd found a money tree. "Thirteen thousand looks like what we need, but I thought we could double that, just to be on the safe side." Jerry paused. "Let's say $30,000."

"You're already into us for $120,000," the banker said. "Before you get any more, I'd like to discuss how we're getting the one-twenty back."

"Hey," Jerry said. "I'm good for it. Look at those numbers!"

The room was silent. For a long time, the banker didn't say anything. When he finally said something, it was no.

What Went Wrong?

Bankers don't like surprises. The banker's job is to protect bank depositors, and bankers all over the world worry about small firms that don't plan in advance. Jerry Fiske's banker did not feel that the bank could afford to underwrite Laserian's prosperity, which was based on uncontrolled growth, regardless of Laserian's **gross profit**.

gross profit
net sales minus cost of goods sold

TABLE 9.5 Ideal Laserian Statement of Cash Flow

	JAN	FEB	MAR	APR
Cash on Hand at Start of Month	10,000	170,800	74,900	52,100
Cash Received/Accounts Receivable	210,000	280,000	316,000	352,000
Three-Year Bank Loan	200,000			
Total Cash Available	420,000	450,800	390,900	404,100
Cash Disbursements				
Manufacturing Disbursements				
Packing, etc.	18,000	19,000	21,000	23,000
Material	123,000	224,000	172,000	198,000
Outside labor	44,000	49,000	53,000	57,800
Other Disbursements				
Sales/Commissions	14,000	27,000	28,800	32,400
Salary, management	12,000	12,800	13,600	14,400
Salary, staff	2,700	4,500	6,000	7,600
Payroll taxes	4,500	4,500	5,300	6,000
Advertising/Promotion	1,400	1,500	1,600	1,800
Travel	500	500	5,000	2,000
Auto/Truck	1,300	1,300	1,300	1,300
Equipment rental	2,400			2,400
Repair/Maintenance	800	800	900	900
Rent	12,000	12,000	12,000	12,000
Supplies	1,400	1,500	1,600	1,800
Telephone	2,500	4,000	4,400	4,900
Utilities	1,200	1,200	1,200	1,200
Insurance	4,000			
Legal/Accounting	2,500	2,500	2,500	2,500
Dues/Subscriptions		1,200		
Miscellaneous	1,000	1,100	1,100	1,200
Interest on bank loan		7,500	7,500	7,500
Total Disbursements	249,200	375,900	338,800	378,700
Cash Flow for Month	170,800	74,900	52,100	25,400

Therefore, Jerry Fiske did not get the money he needed to sustain the rapid growth of his company. The company was out of control, and Jerry didn't see it even when the numbers were down on paper.

What could Jerry have done differently? If he had prepared a cash flow projection ahead of time, his shortfall would have been predicted—and he could have applied for one big loan instead of a series of smaller, haphazard loans. Table 9.5 shows what that ideal cash flow would look like with an adequate loan of $200,000 in place. Note that the bottom line in Table 9.5 is "Cash Flow for Month."

What you need to aim for—over and above paper profits—is positive cash flow. Enough money should be available for you to buy what you need in order to stay in business.

Now let's revise Table 9.5 by taking away Jerry's one-time loan of $200,000 and see why Jerry had to run to the banker so often. January's cash flow becomes negative ($170,800 − $200,000 = −$29,200). No wonder Jerry needed to borrow $30,000 in a hurry! This negative cash flow carries on through. If we assume that Jerry wasn't able to borrow any money at all, our revised cash flows for each month would look like this:

	JAN	FEB	MAR	APR
Cash on Hand at Start of Month	$ 10,000	$(29,200)	$(117,600)	$(132,900)
Cash Received/ Accounts Receivable	210,000	280,000	316,000	352,000
Bank Loans	—	—	—	—
Total Cash Available	220,000	250,800	198,400	219,100
Total Disbursements	249,200	368,400	331,300	371,200
Cash Flow for Month	$(29,200)	$(117,600)	$(132,900)	$(152,100)

If you're figuring along, you'll notice that Total Disbursements now differ from the Total Disbursements in Table 9.5. This is because there won't be loan payments of $7,500 in February, March, and April if there is no loan. Note also that in spreadsheets, a negative amount like −$29,000 is often shown in parentheses, as $(29,000).

Fortunately, Jerry bagged a few loans, but another quick revision of the cash flow shows why $30,000 in January and $90,000 in February weren't enough:

	JAN	FEB	MAR	APR
Cash on Hand at Start of Month	$ 10,000	$ 800	$ 2,400	$(12,900)
Cash Received/ Accounts Receivable	210,000	280,000	316,000	352,000
Bank Loans	30,000	90,000	—	—
Total Cash Available	250,000	370,800	318,400	339,100
Total Disbursements	249,200	368,400	331,300	371,200
Cash Flow for Month	$ 800	$ 2,400	$(12,900)	$(32,100)

And remember, Laserian showed $121,800 of net profit after taxes during these 4 months.

The Moral of the Story

Although Laserian was profitable on paper (as shown in Table 9.4), every month that sales increased, accounts receivable (money owed the company but not yet paid) also increased. Because the company was expanding, the money that came in had to go for inventory. Past sales could not generate enough cash to support the growth. Without outside sources of cash, the company could not keep up.

Project your income and cash flow before you open your doors—for at least a year in advance. If your Business Plan and numerical projections are sound, your banker is likely to loan you the amount needed to cover any negative cash flow.

INCOME STATEMENT AND CASH FLOW PROJECTION

A projected income statement tells you when you're going to make a profit on paper. A cash flow projection tells you whether or not you can pay the bills and when you'll have to visit the banker. Both of these projections are essential to the survival of your business.

Projected Income Statement

Projecting your income is like projecting a moving picture of your business. If you're careful in how you prepare your numbers, that movie will be reasonably accurate. Action Step 45 leads you through this projection step by step. You already have a head start because you forecasted your sales in Action Step 44. A worksheet from the SBA (Table 9.6) will help you, too.

If you discover that you won't show a profit for two years, you're going to need a very good plan, a team of terrific investors, and an understanding banker. A case study later in this chapter will suggest something you can do if your Business Plan forecasts losses for the first year or so of operation.

Cash Flow Projection

As Jerry Fiske's experience illustrates, an income statement doesn't tell the whole story. (Even a documentary movie is shot from only one angle at a time.) It's nice

TABLE 9.6   Projected Sales and Expenses for One Year

	Total	JAN	FEB	MAR	APR	MAY	JUN	JUL	AUG	SEP	OCT	NOV	DEC
A. Net Sales													
B. Cost of Goods Sold													
1. Raw Materials													
2. Direct Labor													
3. Manufacturing Overhead													
Indirect Labor													
Heat, Light, and Power													
Insurance and Taxes													
Depreciation													
C. Gross Margin (A − B)													
D. Selling and Administrative Expenses													
4. Salaries and Commissions													
5. Advertising Expenses													
6. Miscellaneous Expenses													
E. Net Operating Profit (C − D)													
F. Interest Expense													
G. Net Profit before Taxes (E − F)													
H. Estimated Income Tax													
I. Net Profit after Income Tax (G − H)													

Source: Small Business Administration, *Business Plan for Small Manufacturers*, SBA Management Aid 2.007 (Small Business Administration: Washington, D.C., 1981), 8.

FIGURE 9.2   This simple cash flow diagram shows the typical time lag between paper profits and the flow of real profits. Plan ahead for this lag.

to watch paper profits, but you must be alert to what is happening to real cash. Figure 9.2 shows the typical pattern of cash flows.

Cash flow projection is a tool for helping you control money. Action Step 46 leads you through a monthly cash flow projection. An SBA worksheet, Table 9.7, will help you. When you have finished, show the results to an expert. Ask him or her if it looks accurate. It's better to know the truth now, while you're working on paper; paper truth is a lot easier on the pocketbook than real truth.

Break-Even Analysis

Knowing a few key numbers can help you avoid painful surprises. If you know your costs (variable and fixed) and your gross sales, you can use a couple of break-even formulas to tell you when you will start making money. Break-even analysis is useful

TABLE 9.7   Projected Cash Flow

	JAN	FEB	MAR	APR	MAY	JUN	JUL	AUG	SEP	OCT	NOV	DEC
1. Cash in Bank at Start of Month												
2. Petty Cash at Start of Month												
3. Total Cash (1 + 2)												
4. Expected Accounts Receivable												
5. Other Money Expected												
6. Total Receipts (4 + 5)												
7. Total Cash and Receipts (3 + 6)												
8. Disbursements (for month)												
9. Cash in Bank and Petty Cash at End of Month (7 − 8)*												

Source: Small Business Administration, *Business Plan for Small Manufacturers*, SBA Management Aid 2.007 (Small Business Administration: Washington, D.C., 1981), 9.
*This is your Total Cash balance for the start of the next month.

at start-up time, when you have completed your income and expense projections, and when you are considering launching a new product or service.

A small manufacturing company was completing a plan for its second year of operation. Its first-year sales were $177,000, and a sales breakdown for the last 3 months of their first year looked like this:

October	$24,000
November	29,000
December	15,000
	$68,000

The owners took a look at the numbers and called in a consultant to help. The consultant gathered information from sales reps, owners, and customers and then projected that sales for the second year would be a whopping $562,000. The owners reacted with disbelief.

"You're crazy," they said. "That's more than three times what we did last year."

The consultant smiled. "Didn't you tell me you were going to add three new products?"

"Yes."

"And new reps in March, June, and September?"

"Yes, but—"

"And what about those big promotions you've got planned?"

"Well, sure, we've planned some promotions, but that doesn't get us anywhere near three times last year."

"All right," the accountant said. "Can you do $275,000?"

The owners got into a huddle. Based on the fourth quarter, they were sure they could stay even, and four times $68,000 (the fourth-quarter sales) was $272,000. They knew they had to do better than last year.

"Sure, no problem. We can do $272,000."

"All right," said the consultant, rolling out his break-even chart. "I've just projected $562,000 in sales for the year. To break even, you only need $275,000."

"Hey," the owners said, "we're projecting $90,000 the first quarter."

ACTION STEP 45

Project an income statement to get a moving picture of your business.

Adapt Table 9.6 for this action step.
Part A. Generate your numbers for the year as follows:

1. Using data from trade associations and small business owners, forecast your sales for the year.

2. Figure your cost of goods sold and subtract figure from your sales. This gives you your gross profit.

3. Add up all expenses and subtract them from gross profit. This gives you the net profit before taxes.

4. Subtract taxes. (Uncle Sam uses what we might call "old eyes." You will be taxed on paper profit, so you have to build this figure in.) The figure you get is your net profit after taxes for the year.

Part B. Now spread out these figures month by month to create a kind of moving picture of your business. Will your net profit, after taxes, be negative for awhile? How long?

"I'm glad you're thinking my way," the consultant said. "Because if you don't believe you can reach a goal, you'll never get there." He paused, then said, "By the way, that $90,000 is three times what you did your first quarter last year!"

"Just tell us what to do," the owners said.

Based on a careful cash-flow analysis, the consultant determined that the company would need to borrow money. The owners knew their business—industry trends, product line, competitors, sales and promotion plans—but what banker would believe such growth? The key to getting the loan would be to convince the banker that the company could do better than break even. The consultant prepared a break-even chart on the $562,000 sales figure. [See Figure 9.3.] Note in the chart that after $280,000 in sales, the firm will have passed its break-even point and be making a profit.

The banker did grant them the loan, because he realized the company could pass the break-even point, and then some. The key, as usual in business, was a combination of numbers and human confidence.

PROJECTIONS HELP DECIDE YOUR BUSINESS FORM

Working with sales projections and cash flow numbers can help you decide the legal form your business takes. The three partners in the next case were smart. Numerical projections told them they would not make a profit for several months after they opened the doors. So they held onto their jobs and used the losses to offset their regular income.

Once they understood that their break-even point would not occur until the first eight months, they chose to form a subchapter S corporation—a legal form that gives you some protection while allowing you to write losses off on your personal income tax.

Herman, Terry, and Mitch were having some beers one night after a big win over the best team in their bowling league, and they started griping about their jobs.

"My boss hates my guts," Herman said. "I feed him great ideas and he just shoots them down. Boom!"

"Yeah," Terry said. "I came up with a boiler plate that would save my company 50K per annum, and they just smiled me out the door."

"Both of you should quit," Mitch said, "and go into the pizza business with me."

"Too risky," Terry said. "Statistics show you can lose your house and everything when you start too small."

"I worked in a restaurant once," Herman said, "back in high school. For the people who owned it, it was like coining money. Especially during the season."

"Does that mean you're interested?" Mitch asked. "Or are you just being your old late-fifties self?"

"I'm interested," Herman said, draining his glass, "and so is Terry the Numbers Man."

Terry worked in his company's accounting department. He knew the ins and outs of pro forma statements and cash flow management. "I think there's room in this town for an innovative pizza parlor," Terry said. "My brother-in-law's into one in Duluth, and I've seen the books for his second year. He's making a profit just on the write-off."

"I like it," Herman said. "I like the sound of being my own boss."

"Herman Smith," Mitch said, "the Great Entrepreneur."

"My advice," Terry said, "is to hang on to your jobs while I pull some numbers together. They'll tell us a lot."

"Well, hurry it up," Herman said. "My boss is on my nerves."

Terry worked four weeks on the numbers. Herman and Mitch couldn't believe it took so long. Both of them had drawn up personal financial statements, and each was ready to put $20,000 into Three-Way Pizza—the name they'd settled on.

ACTION STEP 46

Project your cash flow.

If you don't have access to a computer and an electronic spreadsheet program, get a spreadsheet from your bank or adapt Table 9.7 to project your cash flow across the first year of your business.

1. Write down the amount of cash you'll start the year with as the amount on hand (or in the bank) at the beginning of the first month.

2. For each month, enter the amount of cash you'll receive from sales or accounts receivable.

3. Enter any loans in the month you receive the cash from the lender.

4. Total the above items to learn how much cash will be available each month.

5. Now list all disbursements (cash going out). Spread these out, too.

6. Subtract disbursements from cash available for each month. This gives you a monthly cash flow. Carry this figure forward (to point one for each succeeding month).

Now examine your work. Have you explored the quirks of seasonality? Have you discovered the minimum and maximum time lags between when you make a sale and when you get paid (in cash) for that sale? Does the picture look accurate? Have an expert check it for you.

Try the "what-if test": If your cash-flow picture looks good, introduce a couple of what-ifs. What surprise expenses could throw a monkey wrench into your new business?

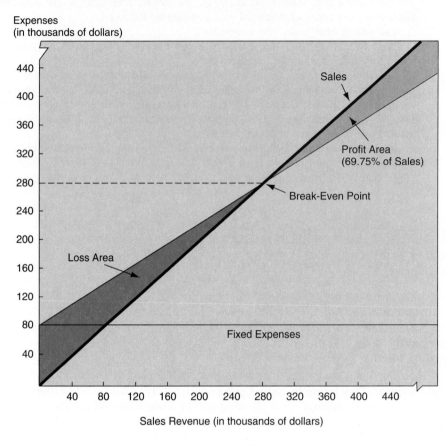

Projected Sales: $562,000
Projected fixed expenses: $82,750
Projected variable expenses: $392,000

Total sales needed to break even:

$$\text{Fixed Expenses} \div \left(1 - \frac{\text{Variable expenses}}{\text{Sales}}\right)$$

$$\$83,000 \div \left(1 - \frac{\$392,000}{\$562,000}\right)$$

$$\$83,000 \div (1 - .6975)$$

$$\$83,000 \div .3025$$

$$\$274,380$$

Break-even range: $270,000 to $280,000

FIGURE 9.3   A simple break-even chart like this may be all it takes to convince your banker that a small loan now means big profits later.

Then Terry came back with the bad news. He showed them the computer printouts. All Herman and Mitch could understand were the totals.

Three partners putting in $20,000 apiece would give them a total of $60,000 to start a business. Just the sound made them feel rich.

In addition, they would borrow $30,000 from family and friends, to give them $90,000 total start-up capital. A king's ransom.

"Expenses will eat us alive the first year," Terry explained, "even with the leased equipment. As you can see, the big expenses are salaries and supplies. We've got to have a first-rate hostess, and they don't come cheap. And if we go into the pizza delivery business—where the money is—we won't reach the break-even point for at least eight months."

"Lucky for me I didn't kiss off my boss," Herman said. He felt depressed.

"Ninety grand," Mitch said, "is just a drop in the bucket."

"There is a way," Terry said. "Let me talk to my buddy, John. He's a tax lawyer who specializes in small businesses."

"All lawyers are crooks," Herman said. "Why, I remember, back in Oshkosh, there was this lawyer who. . . ."

Terry and Mitch met with John, the tax lawyer, while Herman went bowling alone. The lawyer told them that Three-Way Pizza should be chartered as a **subchapter S corporation**. (The *S* stands for *small*.) All three partners were in a top tax bracket, and except for their families, they had few deductions. As founders of a subchapter S corporation, they could deduct early business losses on their personal income tax returns.

> **subchapter S corporation**
> a small, closely held corporation that is taxed like a sole proprietorship

"Hey," Herman said when he heard the good news, "this is better than my crummy tax shelter plan at work. Why didn't you guys think of this in the first place?"

Three-Way Pizza opened in February, 3 months before the start of the summer season. It lost money for seven and a half months, but then began making a small profit. The partners were better off at tax time, and by the second year, they were realizing a nice profit.

SHOEBOX ACCOUNTING: LEAVING A PAPER TRAIL

If you're the typical entrepreneur, you're not real big on details and you're very busy; nonetheless, you know it's important to keep good records. One solution for you is shoebox accounting—a simple procedure that will give your accountant or bookkeeper a chance to put together financial statements and prepare your tax returns. The idea of the system is to leave a paper trail.

How to Implement the System

Open a business checking account—even if you are just doing business under your own name. Deposit all business income into this account, making a note in the checkbook (or check register) as to the source of the deposit: for example, "Sat., 10/21, Swap Meet Sales." Write a check for each business expenditure, even if it's only one dollar. Enter in the checkbook what the check was for. Get a receipt and write the check number on the receipt. During the first few weeks, toss everything into a shoebox. When the shoebox begins to fill up, purchase an alphabetical file folder—one of those brown accordion jobs—and file all receipts there according to some system. (Ask your accountant or bookkeeper.)

If you must pay for items with cash, use a petty cash box or a bank bag. Get a receipt for every cash purchase, also, and clip all of the receipts for cash purchases together. When you have made enough cash purchases that it makes sense to write a business check to yourself—perhaps $10–$20 or so—write yourself a check, being careful to record the check number on each cash receipt.

Together, the business checkbook and the file folder are the paper trail you leave for your accountant or bookkeeper—and for the IRS. This trail could save your neck in an IRS audit. The system is a step up from the "pocket" system—that is, in one pocket and out the other—and only a stopgap until you move into a one-write bookkeeping system, which is explained in Appendix A.

Key Points from Another View

Part I:

AVOIDING A CASH CRUNCH

The most likely cause of a severe cash shortage is the success of your company. Rapid growth could send your business venture right down the tubes.

Rapidly growing entrepreneurial businesses often end up in a situation where the success of their products creates exploding sales. This culminates in a severe cash crunch, since inventories, accounts receivable, and other expenses must expand rapidly to deliver the goods to customers.

1. Planning Ahead
   - To avoid a cash emergency, your strategic business plan must include realistic cash-flow projections that detail when the cash that drives your business will arrive and where that cash comes from.
   - All of the following questions and more need to be addressed to prevent a cash crunch:
     - How much cash will derive from sales?
     - Will you need to ante up more capital in the future?
     - Is your personal financial condition stable and flexible enough to meet cash demands?
     - Do outside sources of capital, such as bank financing or venture capital, enter the picture?
     - Have you kept your banker or venture capital partners informed of future cash requirements?

2. Surviving a cash crisis
   - Customers may slow down payments to your firm, or the cost of raw materials may rise suddenly. What can you do if you find yourself in this situation?
     - Immediately start to concentrate your efforts on collecting accounts receivable.
     - Get rid of excess assets, such as slow-moving inventory and underused equipment, to free up cash.
     - Factoring receivables is a good way for some businesses to free up cash, because you are paid immediately.
     - Other options include reviewing your total operating plan to see where costs can be cut or whether your growth plans need to be scaled back to match available case sources.

Make cash-flow forecasting a regular part of your long-range strategic planning and avoid getting caught in a case crunch.

From: Richard J. Maturi, "Management Smarts—Avoiding a Cash Crunch," Entrepreneurial Woman, May/June 1990, 12–15.

Part II:

KEEPING YOUR BALANCE

Running a successful business requires more than a good concept and a knack for marketing—it also takes sound financial management.

1. Working out the Basics
   - How much money venture?
   - Make a detailed list of everything you'll need to get your business going.
   - Estimate your start-up costs and monthly expenses.
   - Next, estimate your sales for the first year or so.
   - If you don't think your sales will be adequate to cover expenses, consider your options. Even if you do have adequate capital, it's wise to make contingency plans.

2. Monitor Your Working Capital
   - Once your business is running, studying your working capital regularly lets you know where your business stands financially.
   - There are six components that make up your working capital:
     - Cash and liquid assets
     - Accounts receivable
     - Inventory
     - Trade credit
     - Debts
     - Operating expenses and taxes

3. Accounting and Record-Keeping
   - Keeping accurate records helps you manage your cash flow—and comply with tax laws.
   - Setting up a record-keeping system needs to be done only once. Do it right from the start, and avoid problems in the future.
   - Businesses with few bookkeeping requirements might consider a one-write system [See Appendix A].
   - Opening a separate bank account for your business is a must.
   - Also, set up a petty-cash fund for incidental expenses and remember to retain a receipt or memorandum so your expense is documented for tax purposes.

4. Save It for Later
   - You are responsible for retaining records for taxes.
   - The following should be retained in a safe place for tax and/or legal purposes:
     - Canceled checks
     - Paid bills
     - Duplicate deposit slips
     - Purchase invoices
     - Receiving reports
     - Copies of sales slips
     - Invoices sent to customers
     - Receipts for cash paid out
     - Cash registers tapes
     - Any documents that substantiate entries in your records
   - For a complete list of all employment records you must maintain in your files, contact state and federal tax authorities.

5. Beyond Accurate Records: Analysis
   - Once you've established a good system for recording income and expenditures, you're ready to examine your financial situation.

- Following is a short explanation of your financial statements:
  - A *balance sheet* tells you what your business is worth to you at any given time. From the balance sheet, you learn what your business has and what it is worth (its assets), how the assets were financed (liabilities), and to whom they belong (capital claim).
  - The *statement of earnings,* or profit and loss statement, measures the economic performance of your business over time. Your statement of earnings tells you how profitable your business is after subtracting the cost of sales, operating expenses, and other costs of doing business.
  - If your business is goods-oriented, take a close look at the cost of holding inventory.
6. Choosing the Right Professional
  - A good accountant is the single most important outside adviser a business owner has.
  - The first step is finding prospective accountants to contact. Ask associates for referrals.
  - Next, examine each accountant's credentials and experience.
  - Lastly, shop around for an accountant who inspires your confidence and trust.

With the right guidance, careful planning, and constant attention, you can manage your finances ably and help make your business the success you want it to be.

From: "Keeping Your Balance" from *Entrepreneur* Magazine's *Complete Guide to Owning a Homebased Business,* by the Editors of *Entrepreneur.* Copyright 1990 by *Entrepreneur,* Reprinted by permission of Bantam Books, Homebased Business, Winter, 1991, 68–70.

SUMMARY

Not surprisingly, many entrepreneurs find it difficult to project numbers for their businesses. There are several explanations for this:

> They're action people who are in a hurry; they don't think they have time to sit down and *think*.

> They're creative; their strengths are greater in the innovation area than in the justification area.

> They tend to think in visual terms, rather than in terms of numbers or words.

Nonetheless, business is a numbers game, and in spite of the entrepreneur's feelings about numbers and projections, survival in the marketplace depends upon having the right numbers in the right color of ink. This chapter helps you get those kinds of numbers down on paper.

The idea in projecting numbers is to make them as realistic as possible. You need to relate each projection to your specific business and to industry standards, and then to *document* them (tell where they came from) in your Business Plan. The case studies and the examples in this chapter will help you make your projections believable to your banker as well as to yourself.

That is the key. Your numbers may seem reasonable to you, but you must make them seem reasonable to others as well. You make them believable by keeping them realistic and by documenting them properly.

THINK POINTS FOR SUCCESS

◣ It's cheaper to make mistakes on a spreadsheet before you go into business.

◣ When you work out numbers for your Business Plan, hit the return-on-investment section with underlines.

◣ When you visit your banker to ask for money, make sure you know how much you're going to need for the long run.

◣ Projecting will help you control the variables of your business—numbers, employees, promotion mix, product mix, and the peaks and valleys of seasonality.

◣ At the very *least,* leave a "shoebox" paper trail of your business dealings so that a professional accountant or bookkeeper can bail you out.

REFERENCES

Cash Flow Problem Solver. Sourcebooks. [For information, contact (800) 798-2475.]

Donnahoe, Alan S. *What Every Manager Should Know about Financial Analysis.* New York: Simon & Schuster, 1989.

Helfert, Erich A. *Techniques of Financial Analysis.* Homewood, Ill.: Business One Irwin, 1986.

"How to Choose and Use a CPA." AICPA Communications Division, 1211 Ave. of the Americas, New York, NY 10036-8775.

Robert Morris Associates, *Statement Studies.* Annual. Median values of various financial ratios for about 300 different lines of businesses.

Siegel, Joel, and J. Shim. *Accounting Handbook.* New York: Barron's, 1990.

ACTION STEP REVIEW

43 Close your eyes and recall a couple of times in your life when you ran out of money, or when you had to scratch for money. How did you solve the problem? What did you learn from the experience that can help you in the future?

44 Develop a typical income scenario for your business for one year. Using industry data, plot out percentages of sales for each month of the year.

45 Develop an income statement. This shows you when you are going to start making a profit.

46 Make a cash flow projection. This will tell you whether or not you can pay the bills. If you are going to run out of money seven months after you open the doors, you need to know about it so that you can plan for it. Be sure to add in an emergency fund for unforeseen surprises and to have your work checked by an expert.

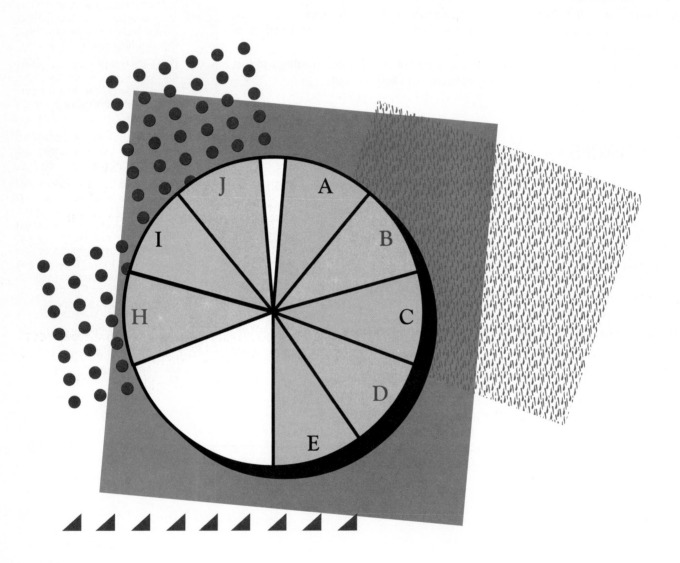

FIGURE 10.1
Chapter 10 investigates the alternative of buying an ongoing business.

10 Buying a Business

Learning Objectives

- To grow in your understanding of the big world of small business.
- To recognize a dishonest seller.
- To discover the secrets of business-opportunity brokers.
- To evaluate objectively businesses that are for sale.
- To understand the pros and cons of purchasing an ongoing business.
- To assess the market value of an ongoing business.
- To sense when you need professional help.
- To assess the market value of goodwill.
- To decide whether it is better for you to buy an ongoing business or to begin from scratch.

FUTURE FOCUS

Buying a business "right" may be the best way to get started in small business. But be careful that you don't just end up buying yourself a job. Proceed only with great caution. Hide your checkbook until you have finished this chapter. Where will the business be in the 21st century? This is a very good question to ask even if you start a business from scratch.

I n this chapter, you'll learn some ways to evaluate businesses that are up for sale. Although we focus on ongoing, independent operations, many of the tactics are the same for evaluating franchise opportunities. We'll discuss franchising more specifically in Chapter 15.

When you buy an ongoing business, you're buying an income stream. You may also be buying inventory, a location, goodwill, and an agreement that the seller will not compete with you. When you buy a franchise, you're primarily buying the right to use a name. In addition, you may also be buying a training program, a Business Plan, advertising assistance, lease negotiation assistance, and purchasing advantages.

You should explore businesses for sale whether you're serious about buying or not. By now, you're far enough along on your quest to sense the atmosphere of the marketplace. Talking to sellers is just one more step in your education in entrepreneurship.

So have fun, but leave your checkbook at home.

WHY BUY AN ONGOING BUSINESS?

The overwhelming reason for buying an ongoing business is *money*, primarily the income stream. If you do your research and strike a good deal, you can start making money the day you take over an ongoing business. Since most start-ups must plug along for months (even years) before showing a profit, it's smart to consider this doorway to business ownership.

If you find a "hungry seller," you should be able to negotiate good terms. You might get into the business for very little cash up front, and you might also get a good deal on the fixtures and equipment. (See Figure 10.2.)

How to Buy and How Not to Buy

Smart buyers scrutinize everything about a business with microscope, geiger counter, computer analysis, clipboard, and sage advice from business gurus. They do not plunge into a business for emotional reasons. For example, you may have eaten lunch around the corner at Millie's Cafeteria with your pals for years, and when the place goes up for sale, nostalgia may make you want to write out a check for it on the spot. That would be a wrong reason to buy. *Don't* buy a business that way.

Every business in the country is for sale sometime. Deals are like planes. If you miss one, another one will be along soon.

Good buys are always available to the informed and careful buyer, but they may be difficult to discover. Seeking the right business to buy is much like an employment search: the best deals are seldom advertised. In contrast, the worst business opportunities are advertised widely, usually in the classified sections of newspapers. When you see several ads for a particular type of business, you know where the unhappy businesspeople are.

Running your own ad can be a good idea, however. A man ran this ad in the business section (not the classifieds) of a large-circulation Midwestern newspaper:

> Sold out at 30. Now I'm tired of retirement and ready to start again. Want to buy business with over 1 million dollars in annual sales. Write me at Box XXXX. H. G.

H. G. received more than one hundred replies and he says that reading the proposals was one of the most educational and entertaining experiences he's ever had. Five of

AN INCOME STREAM

POSSIBILITY OF GOOD TERMS

INVENTORY

GALLERY

FIXTURES AND EQUIPMENT

ACME PIZZA OVEN

FIGURE 10.2   Four reasons to consider buying an ongoing business.

them looked like good deals, but only one fit his talents and interests. After 3 months of investigation, he decided he would rather start his next venture from scratch. (The firm he almost bought was a beer distributorship whose supplier went out of business the following year. Perhaps the seller knew something.)

Getting the Word Out

Once you're ready to look for a business to buy, you'll need to learn what's for sale. These tips will help you do that:

1. Spread the word that you are a potential buyer.
2. Contact everyone you can in your chosen industry—manufacturers, resellers, agents, dealers, trade associations, and so on; let them know you are looking.
3. Ask your network of bankers, attorneys, CPAs, and community leaders to help you in your search.
4. Advertise your needs in trade journals.
5. Send letters of inquiry to potential sellers. (See Action Step 47.)
6. Knock on doors.
7. Check with business-opportunities brokers.
8. Talk with firms that deal in mergers and acquisitions.
9. Don't allow yourself to be rushed; time is your ally, and the deals will get better.

Action Step 47 will help you get the word out. It should be quite interesting to read the letters you receive in response to your form letter.

ACTION STEP 47

Prepare a letter of inquiry.

Write a form letter of inquiry and send it to three to five firms that you may be interested in buying. Keep it open-ended; let them make the disclosures.

It's best to learn of businesses being for sale by networking, but you can find some of the most eager sellers by their advertising in the newspaper classified section.

Leave your checkbook right where it is for now. This action step will cost you practically nothing. The goal is to learn what's out there and how sellers talk about their businesses.

INVESTIGATE THE BUSINESS FROM THE OUTSIDE

Once you've found a business that looks promising, check it out by playing marketplace detective. This section will suggest some techniques that will make you feel like a super spy. After checking it out from the outside, you'll be ready to move inside, to check the books and talk to the owner and attempt to learn the real reasons he or she is selling. But the first step is to get your telescope and your telephoto camera and gather as much information as you can from the exterior. Unfortunately, Ben and Sally Raymundo didn't do this, and they learned about fraud the hard way.

A Horror Story from the Suburbs

Ben and Sally Raymundo bought a women's sportswear store in a thriving community about two miles from a regional shopping mall. They learned too late that the seller had a more profitable store in another part of the county and that she had used that store's records to misrepresent the store they bought. Here are the particulars:

1. The seller moved the cash registers from the higher-volume store to the store she wanted to sell so that the store's sales were greatly inflated.
2. The price was fixed at inventory plus $10,000 for goodwill. This seemed a bargain for a store whose cash register records showed it was grossing $300,000 per year at a 40 percent average gross margin.
3. Ben and Sally paid full wholesale value ($60,000) for goods that had been shipped there from the other store. The goods were already shopworn and out of date and eventually had to be marked down to less than $20,000.

4. Ben and Sally assumed the remainder of an iron-clad lease at $5,000 per month, and the landlord made them sign a personal guarantee that pledged their home as security on the lease.
5. The location proved to be a dead foot-traffic location in a marginally successful center.

Fortunately, Ben had kept his regular job. Sally worked at selling off the unwanted inventory and replaced it with more salable stock. They spent another $50,000 for advertising during the twelve months they stayed in business. It was another year before the landlord found a new tenant and Ben and Sally could get out of the lease.

Learn from Others' Mistakes

What could Ben and Sally have done to avoid this fiasco? Many things. They could have asked the mall merchants how well the shopping center was doing. They could have spent some time observing the store and the shopping mall before they committed. They could have insisted that Sally be allowed to work in the store prior to or during the escrow period, with a clause that would have allowed them to bail out.

Ben and Sally were honest, hard-working people who took the seller at face value. This was a huge mistake. A talk with suppliers might have uncovered the seller's fraud. They are now suing, and the CPA and attorney they have hired could have helped them before they purchased the business. It's only going to get more expensive for them, and their chance of recovery is slim.

Some sellers don't count the value of their own time as a cost of doing business. This makes the firm show an inflated return on investment (ROI). Let's say such a firm earns $60,000 per year and has an inventory of $100,000. This could be a bad buy if the seller, his spouse, and their two children work a total of 200 hours per week and if a $100,000 investment could earn 10 percent or more per year in high-yield bonds.

Look at each deal from the viewpoint of what it would cost to hire a competent manager and help at market wage rates. In this case, let's suppose you had to pay $30,000 a year for a manager, $20,000 a year for an assistant, and $20,000 a year for two hourly employees. You would have spent $70,000 and lost the opportunity to earn another $10,000 on your investment. Yes, this would be a "no-brainer," but a lot of businesses are bought with even less going for them.

It's time now to go out and investigate a business on your own. Remember what you've learned from Ben and Sally's bad experience, and take along your new eyes and your camera. You'll be surprised how much there is to see. Action Step 48 tells you how to do it.

Know when You Need Outside Help

We've already discussed the need for a team of small business gurus to help you realize your dream of small business ownership. When you evaluate a small business for purchase, however, you may need a special kind of outside help. If you have any lingering doubts about the business you are researching, you may need the perspective of someone who is more objective than one of your team players. If you're not the Sherlock Holmes type yourself, hire someone who is. Your dream may be shattered by this kind of investigation, but you'll save money in the long run.

Georgia Webster had some doubts about the business she and her husband were considering. See what you can learn from her experiences.

I'd worked for a large ad agency in New York for twelve years before I gave it up and moved west, to the Bay Area. I couldn't believe it—no snow, no grey-black winter slush, no icicles in April—and I soon became a sports freak, to make up for all the years I'd spent indoors, I guess. I took up tennis, then racquetball, then biking, then volleyball, then hiking.

I met Fred on the tennis court. It was love at first sight, for both of us, and we were married 6 months later. Fred is really creative, and he'd always wanted to have a business of his own. Since we both loved sports, we decided to look around for a sporting goods store to buy.

We found the perfect store by networking with our sports-minded friends. It was called The Sports Factory, and it was located a block from a complex of tennis courts, three blocks from a new racquetball club, and a quarter-mile from a park where volleyball tournaments are held every other month.

A friend of ours who's an accountant checked over the books. He said they looked perfect. "Great P and L," he said, "and accounting ratios you wouldn't believe for this business. If you get the right terms, you could clear fifty G's every quarter, and *that's* only the beginning. This guy doesn't even advertise."

We learned that the owner wanted to sell the store because he was tired of it—the long hours, being tied down, and so on. He'd been doing that for a dozen years and he wanted to start enjoying life.

But I'm from New York, and I wasn't so sure. I sensed we needed help—some sort of Sam Spade of the business world—but Fred was in a hurry to close the deal.

"This is our golden opportunity, Georgie," he kept saying, "a real opportunity. We'd never find such a good deal again."

I knew Fred was unhappy in his job, but half the money we were going to invest was mine, and I felt something was not quite right. Frankly, the owner of The Sports Factory didn't look all that tired to me.

So I asked around—networking again—and I located a community college professor who knows a lot about small business. His name is Harry Henkel, and he's written a book about going into small business. I called him, and he listened very patiently when I told him our story. Then we made an appointment to talk some more. After 15 minutes he told me he'd be glad to check things out for us for a small fee. I told him to go ahead, but I didn't tell Fred about it.

Two days later, my marketplace detective called and said he had some news.

"Oh?" I said. "So soon?"

"Yes. Do you remember seeing a bulldozer working across the street from The Sports Factory?"

"No, I don't. *What* bulldozer?"

"It started grading last week. Right across the street."

"We were just there Sunday," I told him, "and we didn't notice anything like that."

"Well," he said, "I talked to the driver on his lunch break. It seems a developer is putting in a seven-store complex, and one of the stores is going to be a discount sporting goods store." He paused.

"Oh, no," I said. "Are you sure?"

He explained that the store going in was part of a monster **chain**. I could see that we would have a hard time competing with them. I asked him if the owner knew, and if maybe that's why he's so "tired."

"Yes," Harry said, "I double-checked at the city planning office, where building permits are issued." And he paused again.

I was having trouble catching my breath. "Could I get this in writing," I asked, "so that I can show my husband? He likes everything documented."

Harry chuckled. "No problem," he said. "I'll get it in the mail tomorrow. Let me know what you decide, okay?"

"Don't worry," I said. "And thank you. Thank you very much."

This marketplace detective work cost us $475, but it saved us thousands of dollars and years of heartache. Armed with what we learned through that experience, we examined almost a hundred businesses before we found the right one for us. It pays to investigate.

chain
two or more stores operating under the same name and owner

Georgia and Fred Webster came very close to buying the wrong business. The outsider's perspective helped them avoid making a very terrible mistake. Now it's time to get some inside perspectives.

INVESTIGATE THE BUSINESS FROM THE INSIDE

Once you've learned all you can from the outside, it's time to cross the threshold for a look at the interior. This is an important, time-consuming process, and it's an important milestone in your quest.

There are two ways to get inside the business: you can either contact the owner yourself, or you can get assistance from a business-opportunity broker. We recommend that you use a broker, because brokers have access to a lot of listings. You can locate them in the yellow pages under *Real Estate* or *Business Brokers* and in the newspaper classifieds.

Call some brokers to learn if they have any listings in your area of interest. If so, check out the ones that appear interesting. Be prepared for disappointment. You will probably look at a great many businesses before you find anything close to your requirements. Nevertheless, you will learn a lot from the experience.

Dealing with Brokers

Business-opportunity brokers are active in most communities and they often play an important role in matching up sellers with buyers. Their level of competency ranges from specialists who know as much about fast-food franchises as McDonald's, Inc., to part-timers who know so little about business that they will only waste your time. A good broker can save you time and be very helpful in playing a third-party role in negotiations.

A broker has a fiduciary responsibility to represent the seller and is not paid unless he or she sells something. Typically, the broker's commission is around 10 percent, but it's less on bigger deals, and everything is open to negotiation.

Some sellers list with brokers because they do not want it generally known (to their customers, employees, competitors) that they want to sell their business. Most sellers who list with brokers, however, do so out of desperation because they've already tried to sell their business to everyone they know. Probably nine out of ten fall into this category.

Spending time with a skilled broker can be a fascinating educational experience. If you want a particular type of business and are able to examine a half-dozen that are on the market, you will probably end up with a better grasp of the business than the owners. Network your business contacts to locate a competent broker. Ask brokers for referrals from their former clients. Quiz their business knowledge. (Can they explain a cash-flow forecast, an earn-out, the bulk sales law?) And as we've said so many times before, leave your checkbook at home. Don't let anyone rush you.

> **business-opportunity broker**
> a real estate broker who specializes in representing people who want to sell businesses

How to Look at the Inside of a Business

Once you have gotten your foot in the door and established yourself as a potential buyer, you will be able to study the inner workings of the business. Take full advantage of this opportunity.

Study the Financial History.   What you need to learn from the financial history is where the money comes from and where it goes. Ask to see all financial records, for at least 5 years back if they're available, and take your time studying them. If you don't understand financial records, hire someone who does. Your aim in buying an ongoing business is to step into an income stream. The financial records give a picture of that stream.

Look at the history of cash flow, profit and loss, and accounts receivable. If the seller has a stack of accounts receivable a foot high, remember that:

After three months, the value of a current accounts dollar will have shrunk to 90 cents;

after six months, it will be worth 50 cents;

after a year, it will be worth 30 cents.

Review every receipt you can find. If a tavern owner tells you he sells 30–40 kegs of beer per week, ask to see the receipts from the suppliers. If none is offered, ask permission to contact the suppliers for records of shipment. Make him prove to you what he has bought from suppliers. You can then accurately measure sales. If the seller won't cooperate, run—don't walk—away; he's hiding something. You can use this technique with any firm that is buying and marking up material or merchandise.

Evaluate closely any personal expenses that are being charged to the business. (Your CPA will help you determine a course of action that will keep you out of trouble.) This allows you to get a clearer picture of the firm's true profits.

It's also a good idea to look at canceled checks, income tax returns (probably for the last 5 years), and the amount of salary the seller has been paying himself. If your seller was stingy with his own salary, decide whether you could live on that amount.

Tip: You can use the seller's accounts receivable as a point for negotiation, but don't take over the job of collecting them.

Compare What Your Money Could Do Elsewhere.   How much money would you be putting into the business? How long would it take you to make it back? Have you figured in your time?

Let's say you would need to put $50,000 into this business, and that the business will give you a 33.3 percent return, which is full payback in 3 years. Are there other investments you could make that would yield the same amount on your $50,000?

If you will be working in the business, you need to add in the cost of your time; that's $25,000 per year (your present salary) over the 3-year period, or $75,000 (assuming no raises). In 3 years, the business would need to return $125,000 after expenses and taxes in order to cover the risks involved with your $50,000 investment and to compensate you for the loss of $25,000 in annual salary.

tangible assets
things you can see and touch

Evaluate the Tangible Assets.   If the numbers look good, move on to assess the value of everything you can touch, specifically the real estate, the equipment and fixtures, and the inventory.

1. **Real Estate**   Get an outside, professional appraisal of the building and the land.

2. **Equipment and Fixtures**   Remember, this stuff is used. You can get a good idea of current market values by asking equipment dealers and reading the want ads. Scour your area for the best deals, because you don't want to tie up too much capital in equipment that's outmoded or about to come apart. Suppliers have lots of leads on used equipment, so check with them. If you're not an expert in the equipment field, get help from someone who is.

inventory
items carried in stock

3. **Inventory**   Count the inventory yourself, and make sure the boxes are packed with what you think they are. Make certain you specify the exact contents of shelves and cabinets in the purchase agreement. Don't get careless and write in something vague like "All shelves are to be filled"; specify what goes on the shelves.

    Once you've made your count, contact suppliers to learn the current prices.

If you find merchandise that is damaged, out-of-date, out-of-style, soiled, worn, or not ready to sell as is, don't pay full price for it. *Negotiate.* This is sacrifice merchandise and it should have a sacrifice price tag.

Talk to Insiders.   There's no substitute for inside information. Every detective takes it seriously.

Suppliers   Will suppliers agree to keep supplying you? Are there past difficulties between seller and supplier that you would inherit as the new owner? Remember, you're dependent on your suppliers.

Employees   Identify the key employees early, and talk to the credit manager. In small business, success can rest on the shoulders of one or two persons, and you don't want them to walk out the day you sign the papers and present the seller with a fat check.

Competitors   Identify the major competitors and interview them to learn what goes on from their perspective. Expect some bias, but watch for a pattern to develop. (Chapter 5 tells how to identify the competitors; refer to that discussion if you need to.)

Get a Noncompetition Covenant.   Once you buy a business, you don't want the seller to set up the same kind of business across the street. Customers are hard to come by, and you don't want to pay for them and have them spirited away by a cagey seller. So get an agreement, in writing, that the seller will not set up in competition with you—or work for a competitor, or help a friend or relative set up a competitive business—for the next 5 years. You may need a lawyer to help you.

Whether you get a lawyer or do it yourself, be sure to specify the exact amount you're paying for the noncompetition covenant. That way, the IRS will allow you to deduct it against ordinary income over the life of the covenant.

Analyze the Seller's Motives.   People have all kinds of reasons for selling their businesses. Some of these reasons favor the buyer, and others favor the seller. Here are some reasons for selling that can favor the buyer:

1. retirement, ill health
2. too busy to manage—seller has other investments
3. divorce, family problems
4. disgruntled partners
5. expanded too fast—out of cash
6. poor management
7. burned out, lost interest

These reasons for selling will favor the seller (Buyer beware.):

1. local economy in a decline
2. specific industry declining
3. intense competition
4. high insurance costs
5. increasing litigation
6. skyrocketing rents
7. technological obsolescence
8. problems with suppliers

9. high-crime-rate location
10. lease not being renewed
11. location in a decline

Examine the Asking Price. Many sellers view selling their firms as they would view selling their children; that is, they are emotionally attached to the business and they overvalue its worth. Pride also plays a role; they might want to tell their friends that they started from scratch and sold out for a million. If you run into irrational and emotional obstacles, walk away or counter with unreasonable terms—such as $100 down and 10 percent of the net profits for the next 4 years, limit one million dollars.

Some industries have rule-of-thumb bench marks for pricing. For example, a service firm might be priced at 6–12 months of its total revenue. Such pricing formulas are often unwise. The only formula that makes sense is the return on your investment minus the value of your management time.

$$\text{R.O.I.} - (\text{Hours spent} \times \text{Value of your time per hour})$$

price/earnings ratio
a measure of the value of a share of common stock; the ratio of its market price to its earnings per share

If you can earn 10 percent without sweating on high-grade bonds, you should earn at least a 30 percent return on a business that will make you sweat.

It can be useful to consult the newspaper financial pages to learn the **price to earnings ratios** of publicly traded firms. Firms whose P/E ratios are low (the stock price is less than 10 times its earnings) are not regarded as growth opportunities by sophisticated investors. Firms with above-average P/E ratios (price is more than 25 times its earnings) are regarded as having above-average growth potential. Thus, you should be willing to pay a higher price for a firm with above-average growth potential than for one that is declining. In fact, you should not buy a declining business unless you think you can either purchase it very inexpensively and turn it around or dispose of its assets at a profit.

goodwill
an invisible commodity used by sellers to increase the asking price for a business

ill will
all the negative feelings about a business; the opposite of goodwill

Negotiate the Value of Goodwill. If the firm has a strong customer base with deeply ingrained purchasing habits, this has value. It takes a while for any start-up to build a client base, and the wait for profitability can be costly.

Some firms have built up a great deal of **ill will**—customers who have vowed never to trade with them again. A large proportion of the businesses on the market have this problem. If the amount of ill will is great, the business will have little value; it may be that *any* price would be too high.

A smart seller will ask you to pay something for goodwill. Thus you'll need to play detective and find out *how much* goodwill there is and *where* it is. For example, consider the seller who has extended credit loosely. Customers are responding, but there's no cash in the bank. If you were to continue that policy and keep granting easy credit, you could be in the red in a couple of months. Or maybe the seller is one of those very special people who is loved by everyone and will take the goodwill with him—like a halo—when he walks out the door.

So negotiate.

Let's say the asking price for the business you'd like to buy is $100,000 and that its tangible assets (equipment, inventory, and so on) are worth $50,000. In other words, the seller is trying to charge you $50,000 for goodwill. Before you negotiate, do these things:

1. Compare the goodwill you're being asked to buy to the goodwill of a similar business on the market.
2. Figure out how long it would take you to pay that amount. Remember, goodwill is intangible; you'll be unhappy if it takes you years to pay for it. Even the most cheerful goodwill comes out of profit.

3. Estimate how much you could make if you invested that $50,000 in T-bills.

This gives you a context in which to judge the seller's assessment of the value of goodwill, and you can use the hard data you have generated to negotiate a realistic—and no doubt, more favorable—price.

Learn if Bulk Sales Escrow Is Needed.   You need to know if any inventory you would buy is tied up by creditors. If it is, the instrument you'll use to cut those strings is a bulk sales transfer, a process that will transfer the goods from the seller to you through a qualified third party. In most states, bulk sales transfer is specified under a series of regulations known as the Uniform Commercial Code.

If there are no claims by creditors, the transfer of inventory should go smoothly. If there are claims, you'll want to be protected by law. Either consult an attorney who has experience in making bulk sales transfers, or get an **escrow company** to act as the neutral party in the transfer. The quickest way to find an escrow company is to look in the yellow pages under *escrow*. A *better* way is to ask your banker or CPA to recommend one. Try to find one that specializes in bulk sales escrows.

(*Escrow* comes from *escroe,* Old French for "parchment," "deed," or "scroll." The distant Indo-European root is *skeru-,* which means "to cut"—and you'll need an expert to help you cut off creditors who have strings attached. For a look at the jungle of documents you can encounter in buying a business, read pages 169–221 of *Buying and Selling Business Opportunities* by Wilfred E. Tetreault.)

bulk sales escrow
an examination process intended to protect buyers from unknown liabilities

escrow company
a neutral third party that holds deposits and deeds until all agreed-upon conditions are met

An Earn-Out Success Story

Sam Wilson had held several key executive positions in large manufacturing firms after receiving his M.BA in the 1950s. His last position was as president of a medium-size U.S. firm with branch offices throughout the Free World. Sam got squeezed out when a large conglomerate purchased the firm and moved the headquarters to London.

After doing some free-lance management consulting, Sam arranged to purchase an executive search firm that specialized in finding engineering talent in the aerospace industry. Buying the business seemed like a good idea to Sam because the business had been profitable for more than 20 years. The key personnel agreed to stay with the firm. It had loyal customers, a solid reputation, and Sam knew it would take him years to build a similar business from scratch, even though he understood the business.

He purchased the business for no cash down and agreed to pay off the entire purchase price from the earnings over the next 5 years. [This is called an **earn out.**] The seller was an older man who had known of Sam's reputation as a winner. Sam was one of the few prospective buyers who were willing to pay full price for the business and seemed qualified to continue the growth of the firm. The business did prosper, but its growth was somewhat limited to what could be achieved while keeping a watchful eye on cash flow. Sam had to pay the salaries long before he received payment from clients.

Sam worked in the firm 1 to 2 days a week, and monitored activities by daily reports. He had plenty of time to run another business, but it would have to be a type of business whose cash flow is "front-loaded," rather than "back-loaded" like the search firm. Front-loaded businesses are those whose customers pay cash up front before the product or service is delivered. They include such businesses as hotels, bed and breakfast inns, bridal shops, custom printers, magazine publishers, and so on.

Sam chose to purchase a travel agency. He found a medium-size firm that had five excellent travel agents but was only slightly profitable. He purchased it for a low six-digit figure on a no-money-down, earn-out basis.

The travel agency cash flow was positive, and Sam saw some opportunities to make the firm more profitable. Observing that many travel agencies are run by "hobbyists" who know little about marketing and management, he refocused the agency efforts on exotic cruises and up-scale vacation adventures. The agency was located in a very affluent

earn out
the seller agrees to accept (a portion of) his payment for the business from the business's future earnings

area, and yet none of the competitors were specializing like this. He also knew that volume is the key to profit; some of the large chain agencies were earning 17 percent commissions on trips that paid small firms only 10 percent. Sam is now in the process of purchasing four more good agencies on an earn-out basis so that he can take advantage of the larger commissions.

Buying a business on an earn-out basis is an option only if the seller has great confidence in the buyer's skills and knowledge of the business. Thus the burden of convincing the seller to agree to such terms is on the buyer. It's necessary to show the seller that the business will continue to show a profit.

Sam conducted both transactions described in the case study by developing a detailed Business Plan that demonstrated to the sellers that he was an expert—and his track record and references backed him up.

Few people are able to manage more than one business at a time. Sam can, however, because he knows how to set up controls. He stays in daily contact with his key people, and perhaps most importantly, he spends a lot of time talking to customers—which ensures him of the highest level of feedback.

Too many people purchase businesses emotionally. They buy a business as if it were a home, a car, or a suit. They are drawn to businesses that they think will enhance their image—that will impress their friends and relatives. Physically attractive businesses are often the worst investments, because "image-conscious" buyers have bid the price up to an unreasonable figure. The "ugly" business or the "invisible business" often provides the best return on time and investment.

Many people view buying a business as buying a *job;* they look at it as providing them with "employment." (Sam's experience demonstrates that this is a narrow view.) Such people lack the experience to make a good choice, and they often invest their life savings in ventures that demand 70–100 hours per week to run and pay them less than their 40-hour-week jobs did.

Does the thought of walking into someone's business for the purpose of "snooping" around, looking at the books, and asking the owner probing questions fill you with anxiety and make you nervous? It shouldn't. Sellers expect prospective buyers to do those things, and you are seriously looking for a business to buy. What's more, you are now *prepared* to investigate a business close up—and to enjoy it. You are ready for Action Step 49.

ACTION STEP 49

Study a business inside out.

Looking at a business from the inside enables you to determine its real worth and to see what it would be like to own it. Make an appointment–or have a business-opportunity broker arrange it–to take a serious inside look at the business you think you want to buy. Before you go, review everything we've explained in this section and write down a list of things you hope to learn while you're there. Don't allow anyone to rush you. Leave the checkbook at home; this fun is free.

THE DECISION TO BUY

Even if you think you're ready to make your decision, don't do it—not yet. Read the checklist in Box 10.1 first. It reminds you of thirty-three important details you might have overlooked. Even if you *know* you've found your dream business, complete this checklist before you sign the papers.

Prepare for the Negotiations

Let's say you know you're ready to buy. You've raised the money, and the numbers say you can't lose, so you're ready to start negotiating. (If you're an experienced entrepreneur, you already know how to negotiate. If not, some good books on the fine art of haggling are listed in the Reference section at the end of the chapter.)

We suggest two things about negotiations. First, when it comes time to talk meaningful numbers, the most important area to concentrate on is *terms*—not ask-

BOX 10.1 Final Checklist

_____ How long do you plan to own this business?

_____ How old is this business? Can you sketch its history?

_____ Is this business in the embryonic stage, the growth stage, the mature stage, or the decline stage?

_____ Has your accountant reviewed the books and made a sales projection for you?

_____ How long will it take for this business to show a *complete* recovery on your investment?

_____ What reasons does the owner give for selling?

_____ Will the owner let you see bank deposit records? (If not, why not?)

_____ Have you calculated utility costs for the first 3–5 years?

_____ What does a review of tax records tell you?

_____ How complete is the insurance coverage?

_____ How old are receivables? (Remember, age decreases their value.)

_____ What is the seller paying himself? Is it low, or high?

_____ Have you interviewed your prospective landlord?

_____ What happens when a new tenant takes over the lease?

_____ Have you made spot checks on the currency of the customer list?

_____ Who are your top 20 customers? Your top 50?

_____ Is the seller locked into 1–3 major customers who control the business?

_____ Are you buying inventory? What is the seller asking?

_____ Have you checked the value of the inventory with vendors?

_____ Have you checked the value of the equipment against the price of used equipment from another source?

_____ Who does your seller owe money to?

_____ Has your attorney checked for liens on the seller's equipment?

_____ Do you have maintenance contracts on the equipment you're buying?

_____ Has your attorney or escrow company gone through bulk sales escrow?

_____ Have you made certain that:

    _____ you're getting all brand names, logos, trademarks, and so on, you need?

    _____ the seller has signed a noncompetition covenant?

    _____ the key lines of supply will stay intact when you take over?

    _____ the key employees will stay?

    _____ the seller isn't leaving because of stiff competition?

    _____ you aren't paying for goodwill but taking delivery on ill will?

    _____ you're getting the best terms possible?

    _____ you're buying an income stream?

ing price. Favorable terms will give you the cash flow you need to survive the first year and then move from survival into success. Unfavorable terms can torpedo your chances for success, even when the total asking price is well below market value.

Second, when the seller brings up the subject of goodwill, be ready for it. Goodwill is a "slippery" commodity; it can make the asking price soar. It's only natural for the seller to attempt to get as much as possible for goodwill. Because you know this ahead of time, you can do your homework and go in primed to deal. Action Step 50 will help you do your homework. When the seller starts talking about goodwill, you can flip the coin over and discuss ill will—which hangs on longer, like a cloud above the business.

Only you can negotiate out a high price for goodwill, the intangible commodity. You're going to be on your own. Action Step 50 will help you. Go for it!

ACTION STEP 50

Probe the depths of ill will.

How many products have you vowed never to use again? How many places of business have you vowed never to patronize again? Why?

Make a list of the products and services you won't buy or use again. Next to each item, write the reason. Does it make you sick? Does it offend your sensibilities? Was the service awful?

After you've completed your list, ask your friends what their negative feelings about particular businesses are. Take notes.

Study the two lists you've made. What are the common components of ill will? How long does ill will last? Is there a remedy for it, or is a business plagued by ill will cursed forever?

Now turn your attention to the business you want to buy. Survey your target customers. How do you feel about the business? You need to learn as much as you can about the ill will that exists toward the business.

Have fun with this step, but take it seriously—and think about the nature of ill will when your seller starts asking you to pay for goodwill.

lien
a legal obligation filed against a piece of property

Protect Yourself

Evaluate each business opportunity by the criteria we present in this chapter. When you find one you think is right for you, start negotiating. Your goal is the lowest possible *price* with the best possible *terms*. Start low; you can then negotiate up if necessary.

If you are asked to put down a deposit, handle it this way:

Deposit the money in an escrow account, and

Include a stipulation in your offer that says the offer is *subject to your inspection and approval* of all financial records and all aspects of the business.

Doing this gives you an escape hatch so that you can get your deposit back—and back out of the deal—if things don't look good. Also, consider working in the business for a few weeks with the option to back out if you have a change of heart.

Expect Some Pleasant Surprises

Well, you've come a long way and you've worked hard on your research. You may be wondering if the digging was worth it. Only you can answer that. There *are* bargains to be found out there—businesses like Woolett's Hardware. For hunter–buyers with vision and persistence, beautiful opportunities are waiting behind ugly facades.

I heard about Woolett's being up for sale more than a year ago. I'd just opened up my second store at the time—it's also in the hardware line—and it took me just about a year—April to April—to streamline the paperwork. Thanks to a computer and a good manager, my sanity remained intact.

So when I finally got over there to check things out, Woolett's had been on the market a year and a half or so. One look from the street, and I could see why.

The store was a mess. The building was pre–World War II, and so was the paint. Out front, the sign was sagging. The parking lot needed lots of work; there were potholes 6 inches deep. The entryway was littered with scraps of paper, and the front door was boarded up.

Inside, things weren't much better. The floor needed a good sweeping. The merchandise was covered with dust. And all around there was this feeling of mildew, age, and disuse. It was dark—like a *cave*. It was tough finding a salesperson, and when you did, you couldn't get much help. Yet there were customers all over the place.

After you've been in business a while, you develop a sort of sixth sense about things. And the minute I stepped into the store, I knew there was something special about it—something hidden, something the eye couldn't see right off. I knew I had to dig deeper.

A visit to the listing real estate broker didn't help much. "Make us an offer," he said. "We just dropped the price yesterday. To $400,000."

"What do the numbers look like?" I asked.

He dug into a slim manila folder. "Last year," he said, "they grossed just under $600,000. The net was around $200,000."

"What about inventory?" I asked. "What about loans and liens and accounts receivable? When can I interview the manager? And why is the owner selling?"

"Are you just asking that," he said, "or is this for real?"

"This is for my son," I said. "He's new to the business, and we don't want a lot of surprises."

"Like I said, make us an offer."

"Let me check the books," I said. I deposited five hundred dollars with an escrow company, making sure I got my usual escape clause—a deposit receipt saying my offer for the business is contingent upon my inspection of all assets and my approval of all financial records. Doing this has saved me tons of heartburn over the years.

The minute they got wind of a buyer, the manager and two of the employees up and quit. The back office was a mess, and it took me three days of searching to find something that would tell me I was on the right track. I found a supply of rolled steel. It was on the books at $12,000, but I knew it was worth $150,000. I took that as a buy signal.

The next day, I made an offer—$12,000 down, with the balance to be paid out of profits over the next five years. The owner accepted, and we cleared escrow in 30 days.

The first thing we did was clean the place up. We surfaced the parking lot with asphalt, added a coat of paint, fixed the door, added lighting.

Business picked up right away. My son, newly married, was settling down and learning the business. He seemed to have managerial talents.

Then we found another set of records that had been hidden away in a safe. They showed us that the Woolett Corporation owned a bank account containing $180,000 and five acres of land, mostly along the road leading to town, right in the path of future growth! We had bought the *whole corporation*.

The first year we did just over a million dollars in sales. And there was every indication that we would do better from then on.

People who come into the store now hardly recognize the place. We've spent some more money on new lighting fixtures and we've added a large kitchen section—to appeal to the yuppies. And in the summer we're staying open until eight.

If you're in the area, stop by.

Key Points From Another View
Part I:
GET IT IN WRITING

Stock in closely held companies is difficult to sell. Without a ready market for the stock, shareholders and their heirs may find their investment in the company "locked in" when they retire, otherwise leave the business, or upon their death.

I. Buy–Sell Agreement
   A. You can protect the interests of both your company and your shareholders by using a "buy–sell agreement."
   B. Under such an agreement, either the company (in a redemption agreement) or the remaining shareholders (in a cross-purchase agreement) have an option or an obligation to purchase the departing shareholder's stock in certain situations.

II. Understanding the Agreement
   A. A buy–sell agreement can be mandatory or optional.
   B. Mandatory
      1. If you want to ensure a market for the departing shareholder's stock, your company or your remaining shareholders *must* purchase that stock.
      2. If you want to avoid taking on a new shareholder, the departing shareholder must sell his stock either to the company or to an existing shareholder.
      3. Optional agreement simply gives the purchaser a "right of first refusal" to buy the stock if the departing shareholder or his estate wants to sell.

    C. The buy–sell agreement is typically triggered by the shareholder's death, retirement, disability, or termination, or the transfer of stock to a new stockholder.

III. Determining the Price

    A. In the past, a business's "book value" was frequently used to set a price in buy–sell agreements, but it is rarely used now because it usually understates a company's true value.

    B. A more common pricing mechanism is to use a formula based on earnings or cash flow.

    C. You can also use appraisers to set a buy–sell price. Your agreement should clarify how you will select the appraiser(s).

IV. Funding the Purchase

    A. The purchaser in a buy–sell agreement can't always afford a large cash payment to the selling shareholder. For this reason, payment is usually deferred.

    B. Sometimes, neither party wants a deferred payment plan. Instead, the purchase obligation may be funded by insurance.

        1. With both the cross-purchase agreement and the redemption agreement, insurance is purchased on the lives of the potential sell-shareholders.

        2. The potential purchaser (your company or your other shareholders) is generally the owner and beneficiary of the policy.

From: Frank J. O'Connell, Jr., "Tax Talk—A Professional's Approach to Taxing Matters—Get It in Writing," *Entrepreneur,* July, 1991, 24–26.

Part II:

A NEW CHAPTER—SNATCHING VICTORY FROM THE JAWS OF DEFEAT

You can own the company you have always wanted, at a discount price, and with some built-in advantages over your competitors, if you know how to buy a business out of bankruptcy.

    I. One of the big pluses of buying a bankrupt business is a chance to obtain assets at a real bargain price.

    II. Another major plus: Filing for bankruptcy clears out all a business's old debts, so you'll start with a clean balance sheet.

    III. However, buying out a bankruptcy can be time-consuming and require staggering legal fees.

    IV. And turning a bankrupt business around is no cakewalk.

        A. You'll have to deal with suppliers still steaming about your predecessor's failure to pay bills.

        B. It's likely the plant and equipment are in bad shape, having been neglected as the operation spiraled into bankruptcy.

        C. You'll have to rebuild trust in the minds of customers soured by deteriorating service or products.

    V. Getting Ready to Buy

        A. You'll need good legal and financial support.

B. Looking for a business to buy:
  1. Consult legal notices posted in your local newspaper.
  2. Talk to the workout department of a bank that advises companies having problems.
  3. Look up attorneys who specialize in bankruptcies.
  4. If you are interested in buying a bankrupt company, look everywhere, talk to everyone, and be ready to move when you see something you want.

C. Speed and timing are critical when you're trying to purchase something out of bankruptcy.

VI. You'll want the services of a good attorney, and, because a bankruptcy deal is more than a legal matter, be discriminating about who you hire.
  A. You need a deal-making attorney.
  B. Choose somebody with a track record in bankruptcy court negotiations, who has been through the process and knows the ins and outs.

VII. After getting your legal arsenal in order, the next thing you'll need to think about is financing.
  A. Venture capitalists, private investors and even bankers can be willing to fund the right deal.
  B. The person buying the company has to understand the business well, have a good relationship with the company, and be buying a decent operation. If you have that, and you can explain your plans, you can probably get your deal financed.

VIII. Making a Bankruptcy Bid—There are all kinds of bankrupt companies, and several different ways you can buy one.
  A. The classic way is to find a company that has filed Chapter 11 but is still operating, then approach the company's current owner and the court with a definite plan.
  B. Chapter 7 always leads to liquidation, in which the company's assets are auctioned off under the supervision of a court appointed trustee, and the business ceases to exist.
    1. Liquidation can be an excellent opportunity to pick up underpriced assets.
    2. Any cash offer gets serious consideration.
  C. You can also buy part of a company's assets out of Chapter 11 bankruptcy proceedings by simply contacting the business owner and offering to buy.
  D. One thing you should almost never do is buy the stock of a company in bankruptcy or about to go bankrupt.

IX. Turning it Around
  A. Your main problem will be fixing all the things a foundering business neglects as it is going under for the third time.
  B. The very first task the new buyers have is to repair relationships that have been damaged.
  C. Don't make wholesale exchanges, even in a failed enterprise, without checking with customers first.

From: Mark Henricks, "A New Chapter—Snatching Victory from the Jaws of Defeat," *Entrepreneur*, April, 1991, 163–166.

SUMMARY

There are two good reasons to explore businesses for sale: you'll learn a lot by exploring the marketplace, and you might find a gem like Woolett's Hardware—a business that will make money right from the start.

If the seller is "hungry," you may be able to obtain terrific terms. For example, let's say you find a business for sale with an asking price of a million dollars. Its profit last year was $50,000. You and the seller agree on

$20,000 down

a no-interest loan of $980,000

payments of 20 percent of net profits each year until the loan is paid off

Result: each year you'd have an ROI of 200 percent. Your loan payment would be 20 percent of $50,000, or $10,000 a year. You'd have a profit of $40,000 left each year. After ten years, you'd have paid the owner $100,000, and your profit would have been $400,000. With such good terms, you wouldn't need to think about paying off the loan for a long, long time.

THINK POINTS FOR SUCCESS

◄ Stick to what you know. Don't buy a business you know nothing about.

◄ Don't let a seller or a broker rush you. A business is not a used car.

◄ If your seller looks absolutely honest, check him out anyway.

◄ Worry less about price; work harder on terms.

◄ Most good businesses are sold behind the scenes, before they reach the open market.

◄ Make sure you're there when the physical inventory takes place. Look in those boxes yourself.

◄ Get everything in writing. Be specific.

◄ Always go through bulk sales escrow.

◄ Buying a corporation is tricky. Have an experienced attorney help you.

ACTION STEP REVIEW

Four action steps help you investigate the alternative of buying an ongoing business:

47 Prepare a letter of inquiry. Learn what's out there and how sellers talk about their businesses.

48 Study a business from the outside. Determine whether it's worth your time to pursue this option.

49 Study a business inside out. Talk to the owner, look at the books, be alert, and learn a lot.

50 Probe the depths of ill will. Learn all you can about the ill will that exists toward the business you're interested in.

REFERENCES

Benguai, August. "Making Noncompete Agreements Stick." *Small Business Reports,* February, 1991, 66–69.

Buying and Selling a Small Business. Washington, D.C.: Superintendent of Documents. Stock #045-000-00003-6, 122.

Choosing a Retail Location. Washington, D.C.: U.S. Small Business Administration, Office of Business Development. Management Aid No. 2.021, 1988.

Cohen, Herb. *You Can Negotiate Anything: How to Get What You Want.* New York: Bantam Books, 1983. [An intriguing look at the tactics of wheeling and dealing, with case studies and scenarios for working the marketplace.]

Finegan, Jay. "The Insider's Guide," *Inc.,* October, 1991, 26–37.

Fisher, Roger, and William Ury. *Getting to Yes: Negotiating Agreements Without Giving In.* New York: Viking Penguin, 1991. [An excellent source on how to negotiate.]

Franchise Opportunities Handbook. Washington, D.C.: U.S. Department of Commerce, Industry and Trade Administration, Office of Minority Business Enterprise, Annual.

Horn, Thomas W. *The Business Valuation Manual: An Understandable, Step-by-Step Guide to Finding the Value of a Business.* P.O. Box 7783, Lancaster, PA 17604, Charter Oak Press, 1990.

Jurek, Walter. *A Reference Manual on Buying and Selling a Business.* Quality Services, Inc., 3887 State Street, Santa Barbara, CA 93105.

Knight, Brian and the Associates of Country Business, Inc. Staff. *Buy the Right Business at the Right Price.* Dover, N.H.: Upstart Publishing, 1990.

Mancuso, Joseph, and Douglas Germann. *Buying a Business: For Very Little Cash.* New York: Simon & Schuster, 1991. [An excellent general guide to buying a business, with additional information on franchising.]

Niemann, Hiendrix, "Buying a Business." *Inc.,* February, 1990, 28–38. [An excellent story of the process of buying a business.]

Niemann, Hiendrix. "The Rest of the Story." *Inc.,* October, 1991, 38–46. [An update to the story above—both of these are must reading.]

Pratt, Shannon. *Valuing a Small Business and Professional Practices.* Homewood, Ill.: Business One Irwin, 1985.

Tetreault, Wilfred F. *Buying and Selling Business Opportunities: A Sales Transaction Handbook.* Reading, Mass.: Addison-Wesley Publishing Company, 1981. [Explains the overwhelming number of documents needed to buy a business. One look at this book may convince you to handle your own start-up.]

Wright, Jeffrey P. *What Is a Business Worth?* P.O. Box 5268, Scottsdale, AZ, 85261, E.V.S. Publications, 1990.

ASSOCIATIONS
Institute of Business Appraisers
American Society of Appraisers
International Business Brokers Association

TRADE PUBLICATIONS (may be available at large business libraries)
The National Review of Corporate Acquisitions
Buyouts
Mergers and Acquisitions

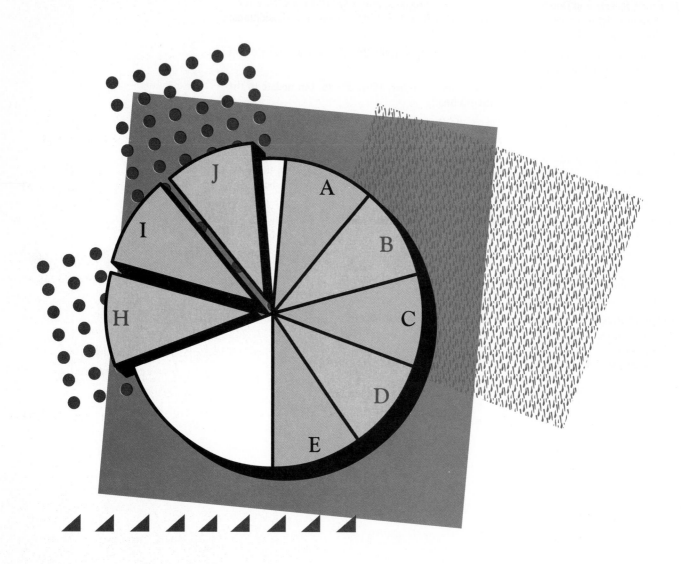

FIGURE 11.1
Chapter 11 will help you prepare parts H, I, and J of your Business Plan—the financial section.

11 Shaking the Money Tree

Learning Objectives

- To understand that you need to establish connections in the world of money.
- To understand that your banker is a gatekeeper to the world of money.
- To develop strategies for working with your banker.
- To develop a more sophisticated concept of money and its power.
- To develop confidence and street survival skills in the worlds of high and low finance.
- To learn how to seek out potential lenders.
- To learn how to generate cash from customers.
- To develop a vendor statement that will allow you to make intelligent purchasing decisions quickly.
- To scour the lending arena for money to fund your new business.

FUTURE FOCUS

Even if you have a ton of cash, you need to know the rules for getting the most out of lenders, customers, vendors, and investors. If you are broke, you still might find a way. The easiest time to borrow money is when you don't need it. Build a solid relationship with your banker for the long-term success of your business.

Would it sound too easy if we told you to go out and simply shake a money tree to get financing for your business? Yes, of course. You know it will not be that easy. First you must become familiar with the world of money. Then you must learn to tell the forest from the trees. And then you must find the right tree. Once you've accomplished these things, you might be surprised how money turns up.

LOOKING FOR MONEY

Before we get to specifics, let's see how Alexander Adams learned some things about the world of money.

Alexander Adams worked for a giant telecommunications conglomerate as "Assistant to the Associate Vice-President for Region X, Subsection C, Department of Marketing and Market Research." His forte was product development. His territory was the East Coast, from New England to South Carolina. He worked 50–70 hours a week and traveled two weeks out of three. Alex was valuable to his company because his innovative ideas allowed his employer to change the competitive arena.

Down deep, however, Alex felt that the computer was a toy and that international electronic networking was just so much gossip at light-speed. But money was money, so he kept cranking out new ideas for his employer.

One day after he had presented yet another terrific idea to his superiors and they had once again failed to see the value of it, Alex made a decision. He told his wife, Jayne, about it at dinner. "I'm getting out," he said. "I've had enough. Remember the idea I had last night? The one about the double mini-disks in one slot and the Winchester in the other?"

"Of course," Jayne lied.

"Well, they shot it down. Bang-bang. Just like that. This is the fifth time in two months. I feel strangled. I feel caged. If I don't get out, I'll go crazy."

"It scares me to hear you talk that way, Alex."

"It scares me *not* to," he said, and he left the table.

Alex got most of his good ideas in dreams. That night he dreamed about a man on a shady park bench. The man wore a Palm Beach suit. A straw boater rested on the bench beside him, on top of a folded copy of *The Wall Street Journal*. The man was feeding the pigeons, and he—Alex—was one of the pigeons. When he recognized his own face above the plump body of a pigeon eating corn nuts, he woke up.

On his next business trip, Alex found himself in New York. He had twenty minutes between meetings, so he went to Central Park for a walk. As he came around a bend in the walk, he saw the man in the Palm Beach suit feeding pigeons. As Alex walked toward him, the man smiled, said hello, and held out his hand. Alex took it. For some reason the man reminded Alex of his grandfather. They talked. The man seemed to know a lot about finance. He hinted that he had been an unofficial adviser to three U.S. presidents. Alex told the man about his job, his feeling of being caged, and his desire to escape. The man offered Alex some advice.

"I felt that way once," he said, "when they wanted me to go into the family business. I was afraid to go out on my own, and yet I heard the call of adventure. If I'd worked in the family business, I'd have gone crazy early. It should be easier now, because the financial market is so splintered, and there are a lot of opportunities. Here's what I'd do if I were your age—first, hang onto your job while you build up some personal credit. Do you get those offers in the mail—just sign your name here for credit?"

"Sure. I throw them away."

"Well, start gathering them together. You can probably get a hundred thousand in credit just by signing your John Henry. You own your house?" the man continued.

"Yes," Alex smiled, "and so does the bank."

"Use your house as collateral to open another line of personal credit. Where do you bank?"

"One of the big interstates."

"All right. Find out if they lend money to small operators. If they don't, find a smaller bank—one where you can shake hands with the president. What's your cash position?"

"Eleven thousand," Alex said. "In CDs. It's our emergency fund."

"How much can you borrow, short term?"

"I don't know. Why should I?"

"Because you want to open your new account with a big bankroll. Try to open with a minimum of $10,000. Then when potential creditors ask your bank about your credit, the bank will only say that you opened with a five-figure amount. You want to make their eyes pop. Get ahold of your friends and relatives. Offer them a half-percent over what they're making, for just long enough to open the account. Pay them back as soon as you get the account opened."

"That's a great idea!" Alex said.

The man talked for several more minutes, giving Alex more good ideas. Then he asked: "How will you make money once you've quit your job?"

"I'm good at marketing," Alex said. "I won't have any problem finding something else."

"That's just another cage, isn't it?"

"No," Alex said. But he knew it was, and the idea made him sad.

A pigeon waddled up. The man reached for a handful of corn nuts. As he dropped them one at a time, he said something to Alex that struck home: "Life's pretty simple. There are the pigeons waiting to be fed, and there are the feeders. It's all in deciding what end of the corn nut you want to be on."

Alex said nothing. He just thought about his dream, when his face had been attached to the body of a feeding pigeon.

Well, by this time he was late for his appointment so had to run. As the men shook hands, the older man handed Alex a package. Alex hurried off. When he opened the package later, he found two books, a clipping from the *Wall Street Journal*, and the stranger's business card. One book was *Megatrends 2000*; the other, *Nine American Lifestyles*.

Alex put the facts together: Florida, elderly population increasing, household size decreasing. He linked them to some personal considerations—his need for escape, his plan to retire in Florida, his need for a job, his creativity. Then he thought of people he knew. His father had just been mugged two blocks from his home in a St. Louis suburb. His mother hated the Midwest cold. Some of their friends had retired to Orlando.

His excitement kept him awake that night. He called his parents early in the morning. He explained his idea: "Emerson Landing," condo complex for seniors. It would contain medium-priced living quarters, social areas, easy access to markets, an infirmary, and a wellness clinic.

Alex's parents weren't wealthy, but they offered to loan him $47,000 up front and $90,000 more when their house was sold. Furthermore, they volunteered to help him raise funds among their friends, in return for a small percentage off the top.

Alex's escape machine was in motion.

He returned home and went to see his banker, who liked the idea and offered to help him develop a Business Plan. His bank was interested in Florida developments, he said, and they loved real estate projects created by innovative people who had their numbers together.

Jayne liked the idea, too.

Alex made a phone call before going to bed. He called the man he'd met on the park bench to thank him.

"Is there room for another investor?" the man asked him. "This city's too cold, and I've been wanting to get my teeth into a project."

"You don't mean—?" Alex cried.

"Why don't we have lunch and talk about it? I can free up some capital. How does twenty-two million sound?"

"Ulp," Alex said. "I mean, it sounds terrific."

"Let's get rolling," the man said. "These old fires have been banked too long."

"Yes, sir," Alex said.

That night, Alex's dreams were in Technicolor.

What Can You Learn from Alex?

When Alex needed to escape from the golden handcuffs of the large corporation, what did he do? Did he insult his boss? No. Did he march into his bank and demand $100,000 in seed capital? No. What Alex did was *plan*:

1. He located someone who knew more about money than he did and learned from him.
2. He kept abreast of trends in the marketplace. He read and he used his new eyes to analyze and sense what was going on around him.
3. He lined up banking connections and lines of credit before quitting his job.
4. He started looking for money close to home—his parents, friends of his parents. People who knew him were eager to invest in his good idea.
5. He opened his business bank account with an impressive dollar figure. Later, when he went to the bank for a credit line, it was smooth sailing.

Learn How Much Money You Need Each Month

Lenders will want to know as much as possible about your money management skills, so it's a good idea to concentrate first on your personal, household budget. After all, personal money management and business money management involve the same skills. You need to determine how much money you need each month and what you have coming in each month. Table 11.1 will help you do this. Notice that the table asks you to give a high figure and a low figure for each item. Budgeting this way will give you two budgets: a fat budget and a bare-bones budget. Try not to overlook anything, because surprises are dangerous to your financial health.

The time to think about your personal financial status is right now. Down the road a ways you're going to need to show lenders that you will have enough money to live on when you open the doors of your new cash-hungry business.

Learn How Much Credit You Have

Now it is time to have a little fun. Let's find out how much unsecured credit you have. This will give you a very general picture of how the financial world rates you at this time. On the business side, once you've done this, you can determine if there are any untapped sources of funds for your start-up, or fall-backs and emergency sources for your business or personal expenses. Use Table 11.2 or a sheet of blank paper. To learn your credit limits on your charge accounts, look at your most recent statements. You may need to call or write to some businesses for this information. When you've filled in the amounts for each account you have, add them up.

Surprised? Few people are aware of how much credit they have. However, before you tell your boss what he can do with his job, there are some things you may want to do while you still have a job, a steady income, and a benefits package. For example,

TABLE 11.1   Your Monthly Income and Outgo

ITEM	HIGH	LOW
Expenses, monthly		
Food		
Clothing		
Shelter: mortgage/rent		
utilities		
maintenance, cleaning, other		
Car payments		
Insurance		
Dependents' expenses		
Contributions, dues		
Credit card bills		
Other		
Expenses, periodic *(Convert these to monthly amounts.)*		
Taxes		
Auto registration, maintenance		
Holidays, gifts, vacations		
Other		
TOTAL monthly expenses		
Income *(Convert these to monthly amounts if necessary.)*		
Your income (if it will continue)		
Your spouse's income		
Interest on savings		
Stock/bond dividends		
Retirement		
Insurance payments		
Trust fund		
Other		
TOTAL monthly income		

1. Get complete medical checkups for the entire family—whatever is covered by your current insurance—vision, dental, general medical. (Health insurance for a family of four may run $400 per month.)

2. Check on the cost of continuing the insurance coverage provided by your employer—life, dental, vision, disability, medical, retirement, other.

3. Apply for two (additional) credit cards—one Visa and one MasterCard. Set them aside to use only for business expenses when you start. Pay the bills when they come due with a company check. The banks don't care who writes the check, as long as it clears. In addition, it will give you good documentation for your bookkeeper and the IRS. Plus you will have some additional credit for your business.

4. Consider applying for a personal line of credit. Usually, depending on the four C's of credit (your capital, character, capacity, and collateral), you can obtain anywhere from $5,000 to $50,000 of unsecured credit at very attrac-

TABLE 11.2   Your Current Unsecured Financial Sources

SOURCE	AMOUNT/LIMIT
Department Stores	
Sears	
JC Penney	
Others	
Oil Companies	
Exxon	
Standard Oil	
Mobil	
Texaco	
Shell	
Others	
Bank Credit Cards	
American Express	
Diner's Club	
Visa	
MasterCard	
Discover Card	
Others	
Personal Lines of Credit	
Bank	
Savings & Loan	
Credit Union	
Others	
Any Other Unsecured Credit	
TOTAL Credit Available	

tive rates. If you have a personal line of credit, you are in a much more flexible position with your new business. If you need it to finance the new business, it's available. If not, it can be your security blanket, to be there for you if unexpected expenses should pop up.

With regard to points 3 and 4 above, bankers are much more relaxed about extending credit to a "steady citizen": a person with steady employment income. Also, you would be making arrangements for the money when you don't need it. Bankers tend to like lending money to people who don't really need it.

One reason we suggest that you obtain two bank cards is that your business will have at least limited sources of credit for which payments can be delayed up to 45 or even 60 days without interest. This can be a big help with cash flow. See Table 11.3. Notice that the two cards in the example complement each other in that they allow the holder to get 45 to 60 days of free credit on charge purchases made any day of the month, provided the proper card is used. As you can see, the technique provides the maximum credit when purchases are charged early in the billing cycle. Warning: payments must be in the bank's hand on or by the payment due dates. This technique will also work with suppliers who offer credit terms.

TABLE 11.3   How to Get 45 to 60 Days' Free Credit with Two Credit Cards

| CARD | CLOSING DATE OF BILLING CYCLE | WHEN TO USE | | TIME FROM PURCHASE TO PAYMENT (EXAMPLE) |
		START	STOP	
Visa	4th of the month	5th	19th	Charge July 5th, pay September 3rd (60 days)
MasterCard	19th of the month	20th	4th	Charge July 20th, pay September 18th (60 days)

Collin Smith financed his business with $8,500 in cash and some bank credit cards. His history may inspire you.

> Collin was 21 years old when he had the idea to start his own limousine service. He had been working for Big Orange Lincoln/Mercury for 5 years. For the last 6 months, he had been the assistant manager in the parts department.
>
> After being turned down by his bank for a start-up loan for his limo business, he sat down to review his finances. When he completed his credit list he found that he had had two car loans, one for a stereo, three department store charge cards and both a Visa and MasterCard. He also noted that he had never been late with a payment. A pretty good credit history, he thought.
>
> He had been talking with Chuck Miller, the owner of Custom Limo Mortgage, and knew that he could get an 85 percent loan on a good used limo. Collin has $8,500 in savings and would have $4,000 left after a $4,500 down payment on a good $30,000 used limo.
>
> Because of the limo industry's track record, the insurance company wanted the full year's premium of $2,500 up front. That would leave only $1,500 for all the other start-up expenses, permits, phones, and so on, but Collin believed the $1,500 would just about do it. That would be cutting it pretty close.
>
> His Visa and MasterCard accounts had credit limits of $1,000 and $1,500, respectively, and he owed only $200. If he could get both cards to raise their limits by $500 and get cards from two other banks, he might have up to $5,500 or $6,000 of credit. He figured that if he applied while he still had $8,500 in the bank and his good job, he shouldn't have any trouble.
>
> Things worked out even better than he'd thought they would. The current credit cards raised his limits to $2,000 and $3,000, and the new card companies came through with $1,500 each. This gave him a total of $8,000 of credit! That was more than enough to cover the first few months' operating expenses plus some unfortunate surprises if they should occur.
>
> So with $8,500 in cash and $8,000 in bank card credit, Collin bought a used limo and launched Royal Class Limo Service.
>
> Seven years later, Royal Class Limo has twelve limos (four of them brand new), over a million dollars a year in sales, and ten credit cards with a little over $50,000 in loans. "I don't like paying 18 percent interest on those credit-card loans," said Collin, "but even with my seven profitable years, the banks aren't interested in lending money to my limo business. Without credit cards, I wouldn't be drawing a high five-figure salary from a business that's worth somewhere between $500,000 and $750,000. Plus, I just bought a condo a block from the beach. Not bad for a 28-year-old former assistant parts manager who had $8,500 to invest!"

When you own a business, your financial return comes from two sources. One source is some type of steady income/benefits stream. This may be in the form of a

ACTION STEP 51

Make a money list.

Before starting to look for outside money, review the personal financial statement you developed in Action Step 41. Figure out how much money you will need to cover your personal expenses each month. (If there's more than one owner, each owner should do this.)

Once you have this worked out, determine where you will get money to live on for at least six months—in some cases 12 or 18 months. The longer you can go without drawing money out of your business for your living expenses, the higher the probability of success.

bank

a place where some people park their money

bankers

gateways to the world of money

salary, owner's draw, a company car, insurance, and a retirement plan. The second source is what you realize from the sale of the business, a merger, or taking it public.

In Collin's case, the two sources total approximately $200,000 more than his salary would have been the past seven years, even with raises and promotions—a difference of about $30,000 per year. Plus, if he sold out today, he could walk away with at least a half-million dollars. This would bring his total to $700,000, or $100,000 per year. Not bad for an $8,500 investment!

There's no dollar figure for the fun and excitement Collin has had building his business. He says he wouldn't trade the past 7 years for anything. "What I have done and how I feel can only be compared to being the winning quarterback in the Super Bowl."

It's time to look at your personal financial situation and your life-style. Figure out how you can go into business *and* keep a roof over your head. Do Action Step 51 now.

BEFORE YOU SHAKE THAT TREE

What action do you take when you need money to start a business? Do you ask the bank? Do you ask Aunt Alice, or your co-workers? Do you write to your congressman? Do you refinance your home?

Most new ventures begin with the entrepreneur's own capital. Funds can usually be borrowed if you have other sources of income and collateral—such as good equity in a home.

Although **banks** are in the business of lending money, they also have a responsibility to their depositors. Thus **bankers** tend to choose the safest deals. They want to help businesses expand, but they have to be picky. Banks can help you in many areas, but they are not investors, so don't expect them to take risks.

Piggy-Bank Blues

Suppose you worked 10 years for a well-known firm and are now out on your own working as a consultant. Last year, your first year in business, you made three times your former salary. You can now afford a nicer house, but lenders say you don't qualify. The reason: you're self-employed. You now have an erratic income stream, and you can't provide two years of self-employed income tax returns.

Welcome to the world of the independent contractor! A lender may treat you like a pal while you're employed by XIT, the megacorporation up the freeway, and then when you go to work for yourself, give you the cold shoulder.

So how can this be avoided? By building lender relationships. Take a banker to lunch. Get to know the officers of your bank. Ask your banker for advice on pulling together your Business Plan. If you build a relationship before you need cash or credit, you'll save yourself much aggravation.

Also, think about what kind of bank you want to do business with. In large banks, for example, loan officers move around from branch to branch. In a small bank, the chief loan officer may be a part-owner. You're hunting for a permanent relationship, not merely a place to park your money. Bear in mind that your business could outgrow a small bank and that some firms need support services that only a large business bank can offer, such as import–export assistance.

Few bankers are thrilled about lending to start-ups. Nonetheless, bankers are *people*, so start seeking a banker who understands you and your needs. Network your attorney, your tax person, the Chamber of Commerce, civic clubs, lead clubs, and people in your trade association for recommendations. Ask your accountant to accompany you on your introductory visit to the bank, especially if you are fuzzy about the details of your financial statement. Be prepared to spend a lot of time on this search. Nurture the relationship, and keep your banker informed of changes and updates. But also, find a backup banker.

Preparing for the Search

Before hunting the money tree, prepare, prepare, prepare.

Research the World of Money.   Money creates its own world, with its own customs, myths, and rules. Before you go around with your hand out asking for money, spend three or four months studying the **world of money**. If you are new at this, a good place to start is *Money* magazine. Then go on to books like those listed in the reference section at the end of this chapter.

world of money
a strange and mysterious place where the signposts are written in dollar signs

Sit at the Feet of a Money Guru.   Think of three people who know more about money than you do. Seek out one of those persons. Begin to build a money network.

Buy Some Stock.   Invest a small amount of money in a few shares of **common stock** of a business you want to know about. When you read its financial reports, monitor your emotions. Write down how you feel as you open up the *Wall Street Journal* to check the roller-coaster of your ups and downs. When it comes time to ask people to invest in *your* business, read over what you wrote.

common stock
a certificate of equity ownership representing a certain number of shares

Watch Your Four C's.   Continually ask yourself these questions:

1. *Capital.* How much liquid cash (savings and checking accounts) do I have?
2. *Character.* Do I pay my bills on time?
3. *Capacity.* Do I have the ability to repay the loan out of the profits of the business?
4. *Collateral.* Which of my tangible assets—such as my car, securities, condo, life insurance—can I use to secure a loan?

the four C's
a classical series of questions lenders use to screen potential borrowers

Check out Your Personal Credit.   Ask the credit bureau for a copy of your credit report. The cost is minimal, and they are required by law to make it available to you. You may find some surprises, such as black marks that were posted in error. Make sure your credit report is clean or explainable before you go to the bank.

Sketch out Your Business Plan Now.   The Business Plan is your showcase for displaying all the ideas and information you've gathered in your venture adventure. A suggested format for the plan appears in Chapter 16. Start thinking about your plan now and test it on family, friends, and bankers.

Befriend a Banker, and a Backup Banker.   Banks are conservative, and they probably will not want to lend you start-up money unless you pledge real property or security. However, bankers can lead you to money sources you hadn't considered. Seek your banker's advice on pulling your Business Plan together. If you get your banker's input, he will have a hard time refusing help later on. Your banker is one gateway to the world of money, but you should know more than one banker.

YOUR BANKER

information loop
a network of people who need to be kept informed about your business successes

Bring your banker into your **information loop** and involve him or her in your business idea. People lend money to people, and bankers are people. They get excited about good ideas. Stop thinking about a banker as someone who will lend you an umbrella only on a sunny day. *You* would not lend money to a stranger, so make sure your banker knows what you are up to.

How to Deal with a Banker

Here are some strategies for dealing with bankers.

1. Never ask a banker for money; ask for *advice* and *information*. Ideally, a banker will *tell you* when it is the right time to seek money.

2. A bank may seem like a formidable medieval fortress or a modern cathedral. Cut through this symbolism and mythology with new eyes. If you choose to see a banker on his or her own turf, always: 1) make an appointment (it's polite; it also makes the banker feel worthwhile); 2) dress conservatively (nothing impresses a banker like order and neatness); 3) act as if you don't need any money.

your turf
a place where you invite your banker when you want advice and information

3. Lure a banker to **your turf**. Say: "It's difficult to explain to you exactly what my shop is like. Why not come out for a look-see? We could have lunch. How's Thursday around noon?" On your own turf, you will be in a stronger position. You should feel more at ease, and communication will probably flow more easily for both parties.

4. Once you have your loan or line of credit, stay in touch with your banker. Keep your Business Plan up to date and keep your banker friend informed about how things are going in your business. Keep positioning yourself on the ladder in your banker's mind.

5. While you're negotiating with one bank, get yourself a backup bank. You can use information from one bank to cross-check the other bank. Shop for money like you would shop for any major purchase. The deals could surprise you.

6. Negotiate for your line of credit or loan while you are still employed. A personal line of credit is often reviewed annually. You may have to prove that you are still a good credit risk after you are in your own business. If you keep up a good credit rating, however, the chances are good that you will be able to keep the personal lines of credit.

Keep a running list of questions to ask prospective bankers. These will get you started:

What are your lending limits?

Who makes the decisions on loans?

What are your views on my industry?

What experience do you have in working with businesses like mine?

Could you recommend a highly qualified lawyer? Bookkeeper? Accountant? Computer consultant?

equipment lease
long-term arrangement with a bank or leasing company for renting capital equipment

Are you interested in writing **equipment leases**?

accounts receivable
what is owed to a firm

What kind of terms do you give on **accounts receivable** financing?

Does your bank offer businesses Visa and MasterCard accounts? What credit limit could I expect for my business credit cards?

What handling charge would I have to pay on credit card receipts?

What interest can I earn on my business checking account?

Do you have a merchants' or commercial window?

Do you have a night depository?

If you can't lend me money, can you direct me to people who might be interested in doing it?

Do you make **SBA-guaranteed loans?**

If I open up a business checking account here, what else can you do for me?

Make Your Banker a Member of Your Team

A helpful banker can be an entrepreneur's best friend and a member of his or her auxiliary management team or "taxi squad." Business growth demands money from external sources. The more successful you become, the more likely you will need a close bank relationship to help you finance prosperity. If you grow more than 25 percent a year, you'll need lots of financing help. Manufacturers get into trouble fast, but even service firms have to wait for their customers to make payments. Your creditors and employees will want their money when it's due them. So keep your banker in your information loop. Bankers are more willing to help if they understand your needs and know you are trying to anticipate your needs.

Now read about how Steve McWhorter handled his cash flow problems by helping a banker to understand the business he was in.

line of credit
an unsecured lending limit

> Things went really well our first year. My third invention—a battery-operated fuel monitor for the new diesel turbos being made in Germany—was selling like hotcakes, and I'd found a great production manager to keep things going down on the line.
>
> Then cash flow troubles developed.
>
> It happened in February of our second year when a couple of the big car makers—customers that purchased at least half of our product—slowed down on their payments. Some payments were more than 90 days past due.
>
> I stay pretty much in the lab and the shop, because that's the fun part of the business for me, so I didn't find out about the cash problems for almost three weeks. When I did find out, we invoiced the customers again. Still no money. The first week in March, I had trouble meeting the payroll. The second week I had to pay a couple of crucial supplier accounts. The third week, except for petty cash, the company was almost out of money.
>
> I gave my banker a call. We were on good terms, and I had four accounts at her bank. When I told her my problem, she simply asked me how much I needed and for how long. Instant **line of credit.** What a relief.
>
> Well, we got that squared away, and when things were rolling smoothly again, my banker sat down with me and the company books, and we worked out a strategy for bridging the gap between billing and customer payment.
>
> Those sessions really bored me, so I started looking around for someone to help out on the numbers. My banker helped here, too, with advice and recommendations about what kind of person would be best at keeping track of money.
>
> When I worked for someone else, I never thought of a banker at all. Since I've been in business, I've come to realize a banker can be a businessperson's best friend.

Action Step 52 will get you started in your developing relationship with a banker.

SECRETS OF SMALL BUSINESS SURVIVAL

Make Your Dollars Work Overtime

Steve McWhorter discovered the art of managing money in the eleventh hour. It's no secret that start-ups are expensive, and those first few months can be a make-or-break time for the entrepreneur. You want to make your dollars work efficiently. Here are some tips:

1. Find out who you have to pay right now.
2. Find out who can wait awhile.
3. Keep asking what you're getting for your money.

How to Save Money

If you work the dollars you do have, you won't have to shake the money tree so hard. Here are some tips that could save you money. Read through the list. How many of these ideas have you thought of? How many are new to you?

cash deposits
funds paid in advance of delivery

trade credit or dating
a vendor's extension of the payment term into the near future

on-site improvements
modifications to real estate to accommodate the special needs of the business

dead goods
merchandise no longer in demand

liquid cash
funds that can be used immediately, usually held in checking or other accounts

nonbank lenders
institutional lenders other than banks

1. Ask your customers for **cash deposits** when they place orders.
2. Persuade your vendors to give you more **trade credit** or **dating** and more time to pay.
3. Lease your equipment.
4. Run a lean operation; do not waste anything.
5. Work out of your home if you can.
6. Get your landlord to make **on-site improvements** and finance the cost over the term of the lease.
7. Stay on top of your receivables. Be aggressive.
8. Keep track of everything. Try to resell whatever waste or by-products you have in your business.
9. Return goods that aren't selling.
10. Take markdowns quickly on **dead goods**.
11. Use as little commercial space as you can.
12. If your customers do not visit your business facility, it does not have to be highly visible or attractive.
13. When you have to borrow money, shop around.
14. Make sure your **liquid cash** is earning interest.
15. Shop **nonbank lenders** like commercial credit firms.
16. Do not collateralize your loans unless you have no other alternative.
17. Survey your friends and relatives for loans. They might lend you money at rates higher than they would get in the money markets but lower than you would have to pay institutional lenders.
18. Befriend a venture capitalist who funds your type of firm.
19. Consider selling limited partnerships. You could become the general partner with little or none of your own capital invested.
20. Consider selling stock. (Consult an attorney.)

The Vendor Statement Form

An often overlooked technique for reducing your capital requirement is to probe your vendors (major suppliers) for the best prices and terms available. Professional buyers and purchasing agents ask their vendors to fill out an information sheet that forces them to write down the terms and conditions of their sales plans. This is a good idea for you as well.

A small business must buy professionally, and a **vendor statement** will help you do just that. With this form, your vendors' verbal promises become written promises. How well you buy is as important as how well you sell, because every dollar you save by "buying right" drops directly to the bottom line. To compete in your arena, you need the best terms and prices you can get. The statement will help you get the best.

Personalize your form by putting your business name at the top. Then list the information you need and provide blanks for them to write on. This list provides some of the basics for you:

> **vendor statement**
> a personally designed form that allows you to negotiate with each vendor from a position of informed strength

1. Vendor's name
2. Vendor's address and phone number
3. Sales rep's name
4. Business phone (Will vendor accept collect calls?)
5. Home phone (for emergencies)
6. Amount of minimum purchase
7. Quantity discounts? How much? What must you do to earn?
8. Are dating or extended payments terms available?
9. Advertising/promotion allowances
10. Policies on returns for defective goods (Who pays the freight?)
11. Delivery times
12. Assistance (technical, sales, and so on)
13. Product literature available
14. Point-of-purchase material provided
15. Support for grand opening (Will supplier donate prize or other support?)
16. Nearest other dealer handling this particular line
17. Special services the sales rep can provide
18. Vendor's signature, the date, and some kind of agreement that you will be notified of any changes

Remember, the information the vendor writes on this statement is the starting point for negotiations. You should be able to negotiate more favorable terms with some vendors, because these people want your business. Revise your application form as you learn from experience how vendors can help you.

A Success Story

You met Rich Cameron in an earlier chapter. He was in marketing, working for a large firm, when he decided to go into business for himself. He attended seminars, interviewed owners, walked neighborhoods, and read trade journals for quite awhile before opening his toy store.

The store opened in May, but Rich knew from doing industry research that he would have to start placing orders for the Christmas season right away. The problem was that his store would hold $100,000 worth of toys, but Rich had only $30,000 to use for his inventory. He knew he would have to be well-stocked by Thanksgiving or miss out on the profitable holiday business.

The unwritten rule in a new business is that suppliers want you to pay cash up front—for everything. You are a new account, unproven in the grand arena of trade and commerce. They want to wait and see how well you do before they extend credit.

Rich found a way to get around this. He showed his Business Plan to his suppliers' credit managers.

What happened?

"They were amazed," Rich says. "They'd been dealing with toy store owners for years, and mine was the first Business Plan they'd seen from a toy store owner. I showed them everything in black and white—industry trends, projections, marketing plan, management-team statistics, promotion strategy, everything—and when they had read it, they gave me extended dating terms."

The Business Plan didn't do all Rich's work for him. He also bought merchandise for his store very carefully (see Box 11.1) and he developed his own personalized vendor statement to use when he spoke to sales reps.

"A vendor statement really helps," Rich says, "because the survival items are written down. It puts sales reps on the spot. If they want your business to succeed, they have to deal with the questions.

"I got some strong resistance when I brought out my vendor statement form. One guy spent 30 minutes on long distance, telling me why he wouldn't sign it. He wanted all cash up front for the first sale, 75 percent cash for the second, 50 percent for the third, and 30 percent of net after that. But using the statement, backed by my Business Plan, I was able to negotiate him into dating, which means I bought toys in early summer and didn't have to pay for them until December 10. Dating saved my business."

Rich smiles as he recalls those early days. "The interesting thing about negotiating is that it gets you in close enough so you can ask for other assistance. A lot of my advertising and promotion comes free through the vendors because they want my store to be a success. If I hadn't gone in to deal, they wouldn't have known I was going to be a major customer for the long run. And I couldn't have moved confidently without that vendor form."

If you're a new account, flash 'em your Business Plan. Then flash 'em your vendor form. Tell them you're going to be a very important customer very soon.

Now it's time to prepare your own vendor statement form. Action Step 53 will help you.

ACTION STEP 53

Design a vendor statement form.

One of the best ways to save money is to get help from your vendor/supplier. To do that, you will need to create your own special form that specifies, in writing, the terms to be negotiated.

Be tough. Be firm. Be pleasant.

Personalize this form by putting the name of your business at the top. Prepare your list of needed information using the list of eighteen suggestions we've given you.

The vendor form will give you talking points. Most vendors hold something back; design your form to help you learn what those things are and get the best deal for your business.

When negotiating, use a lot of open-ended questions like "What else can you do for me?"

BOX 11.1 **Merchandise Buying Tips for the First-Time Buyer**

1. Attend seasonal merchandise shows at your local fashion market center. Here, you can review merchandise from competing manufacturers. You can compare price points and delivery availability. You can see what you are buying.

2. Start small. You want to test items while minimizing your risk. Manufacturers will try to sell you more by offering large-lot discounts. Beware.

3. Do not allow any vendor to ship an assorted selection. If you choose the widgets, you know what you're buying; if they choose the widgets, they'll send you the stuff that's just passed into the decline stage.

4. Don't pay for merchandise until it's delivered. C.O.D. is a good way to go. Check the packing slip before you pay to ensure that you got what you ordered.

5. One of your protections when you place an order is a cancellation date. Set a date beyond which you will not accept merchandise.

6. As you are buying, think of your target customers. Buy for them, not for the world. Don't try to please everyone.

7. Watch what is moving; this will tell you what your customers want.

SHAKING THE MONEY TREE

SCOUTING THE FOREST

By now you've befriended a banker, you've increased your money savvy, and you have prepared a vendor statement form. Now is time to zero in on your **lenders**. Action Step 54 asks you to prepare on paper by listing potential lenders and investors and by developing your persuasive tactics ahead of time. Without persuasive **inducements to lenders**, they have no reason to invest in your business. If you need help in listing your reasons, you might begin by profiling your target customer, the one who's out there waiting for your product or service. You might list industry trends, and dovetail them with a scenario of where your product or service fits. Move from there to marketing strategy, selling, the profit picture, and return on investment.

In the final part of Action Step 54 you test your tactics on friends. Ask your friends to respond as though they were potential investors. You *want* to hear their objections so that you can answer their objections on paper. When you have completed this action step, you will be truly prepared to meet your lender.

lender
person or firm who advances money

inducement to a lender
an extra benefit offered to a lender—can be a stock warrant, discount, or control of company

SHAKING THE MONEY TREE

In Action Step 41, you prepared a personal financial statement that gave you an idea of your net worth. You will use that information as you shake the money tree.

Face it. It is your business, and you are going to have to use some money of your own. That's only fair. But you might be surprised at how money turns up when you start looking around with new eyes.

second mortgage
a second lien or note on real property that is subordinate to the first mortgage

Sources of Capital

Make a list of potential sources of capital for your business, and add to it when you think of a new source. Here's a list to get you started.

1. Savings.
2. Borrow on your life insurance.
3. Refinance your car, boat, camper.
4. Take out a **second mortgage**. A third? A fourth?
5. Get a line of unsecured personal credit from your bank, credit union, or other financial institution.
6. Research your assets (coin collections, old baseball cards, or whatever).
7. Sell that crummy stock you have been holding and write off the loss. Or get a loan on the securities you want to retain.
8. Get a part-time job; moonlight your way to more money.
9. Network with your friends and family. You may be surprised at the nest eggs lying there.
10. Look at nonbank sources (Figure 11.2):
    a. savings and loan associations
    b. credit unions
    c. insurance companies (They prefer to make big loans—starting at a million dollars.)
    d. commercial credit corporations. (The Money Store, for example, makes SBA-guaranteed loans.)

Prepare to meet your lenders.

Know who your potential lenders are and why they should want to help you.

Part A. List potential lenders and investors. Begin with your family and friends and move on to business acquaintances and colleagues. Don't forget institutional leaders.

Part B. Now quickly list some reasons why lenders should want to invest in your business. What inducements are you offering potential investors? If you're offering them a very small ROI, what are you offering that will offset that?

Think about the legal form of your business. Would you attract more investors if you incorporated?

Part C. Test your tactics by talking to a few friends. Tell them: "This is just a test, and I'd like your reactions to my new business venture." Watch their reactions, and make a list of the objections they give you—the reasons why they cannot loan you money.

Using your list of your friends' objections, write down your answers to those objections. Are there any you cannot answer? What does this mean for your business?

FIGURE 11.2   When seeking out institutional lenders, don't stop with just one bank. Lenders come in many shapes and forms.

e. cooperative venture with customers
f. stock brokerage houses
g. the SBA
h. SBICs
i. venture capitalists
j. BDCs

Let's look at several of these potential money trees.

cooperative venture with a customer
a lucky break where you find a major user
who will finance your business

Small Business Administration

The Small Business Administration (SBA) of the U.S. government has two major categories of loans, guaranteed and direct. The guaranteed loans are made by banks and nonbank lenders. The direct loans are made directly to businesspeople by the federal government. Direct loans are scarce. Guaranteed loans are changing.

The guarantee is between the SBA, an arm of Congress, and the bank. If the business goes under, up to 90 percent of the loan is repaid by the government. (This figure is dropping, perhaps to 75 percent. Get the latest information at your nearest SBA office.)

SBA
federal agency whose mission is to help small business

Small Business Investment Companies

Small Business Investment Companies (SBICs) are privately operated companies that are licensed by the SBA to provide money to small firms. Most SBICs are owned by banks or groups of individuals. The money for loans comes from the SBA, which gets it from the U.S. Treasury, which gets it from you.

SBICs
nonbank lending institutions licensed by the SBA to provide money to small business

Venture Capital Firms

With venture capital firms we enter an area of myth, the world of high rollers and higher flyers. Unlike banks, which lend money that is secured, usually by real estate, venture capitalists don't lend money; they buy a piece of the business. They gamble on the business's rapid growth, hoping to reap a three- to five-hundred percent return on their investment. The payoff for most venture capital firms occurs when the company interests enough investors for a public issue of common stock or when it is purchased by a larger business. When the business "goes public," the venture capital people take their money out.

Venture capital people prefer to enter the financial picture at the second stage of a firm's development—when the business has proven its potential and needs a large infusion of cash to support growth. They tend to like high-tech concepts in embryonic industries with high growth potential. As we move toward the year 2000, venture capital companies will grow in number and become more significant in financing entrepreneurial America.

Venture capitalists come in lots of shapes. For example, there are family firms (Rockefeller), industrial firms (GE), bank firms (Bank of America), and other firms (insurance companies, finance companies). These people will let you run the show if you give them a healthy ROI.

There's a good list of names and addresses of venture capital firms in *The Guide to Venture Capital Sources*, listed in the reference section at the end of this chapter. Names of local and regional venture capital firms are sometimes compiled by business editors of newspapers. *Inc.* magazine publishes an updated list in December.

Business Development Corporations

Business Development Corporations (BDCs) are private concerns that operate at the state level. Their goal is to increase employment within their specific state. New York has the largest BDC in the country.

You can locate your state's BDC by contacting your state economic development agency. Try the government information number in the phone book white pages.

Key Points From Another View
Part I:
IS LEASE BEST?

Entrepreneurs who want to enter an industry as lowest-cost providers have to be the least-cost producers. How do you get the best equipment with the least outlay?

You have three options: renting, leasing, or buying.

- Ownership is invariably more expensive in the short run.
- Leasing or renting, while far less expensive at first, are more expensive in the long run.

  I. Weighing the Factors
- A. The crucial questions are:
  1. Do you have the money for an outright purchase?
  2. Do you have enough money for a down payment (usually 20 percent) for a financed purchase?
  3. Will you earn a better rate of return on an asset that appreciates, rather than on standard equipment you can rent or lease?
  4. Does the equipment allow you to earn more than you will be paying for the loans or credit?
- B. Good reasons to consider leasing
  1. It keeps existing lines of credit untouched.
  2. In times of inflation, leasing lets you pay for today's equipment with tomorrow's cheaper dollars.

 II. Last, but Not Leased
- A. There are some cases, however, in which leasing is not the ideal solution. Sometimes, technology may change so rapidly and prices drop so quickly that the system you buy today may be obsolete in a few months, and its market-worth may drop 50 percent. In this case, it may be better to rent.
- B. Balancing cash flow requirements against the acquisition of assets, lease credit liabilities against unreported rentals, all within time frames and market opportunities, is not easy. The decision process requires careful investigation and patience.

Nathaniel Gilbert, "Open for Debate—Exploring Issues Affecting Your Business—Is Leased Best?" *Entrepreneur*, July, 1991, 200–203.

Part II:

Money at Your Fingertips

Going after the ideal amount of financing, rather than the lowest practical amount, is probably the most common mistake start-up entrepreneurs make. The next most common mistake is thinking that raising money for the venture will be relatively easy.

The range of financial sources willing to fund start-up businesses is quite broad; however, each source of capital is usually directed to a specific niche.

I. Leveraging Your Assets

    A. Despite everything you've heard about making your fortune with other people's money, you will have to provide a substantial portion of the start-up capital.

    B. Some bankers expect to see the owner contribute more than half the needed capital. If the business is a start-up, they also want a lot of collateral, such as a deed of trust against a piece of real estate.

II. Friendly Funds

    A. Your family and friends are the most likely source of secondary start-up and expansion capital.

    B. Friendly funds may come in the form of equity investments where no return is expected for 4 to 6 years, or in the form of a subordinated loan (meaning that any bank loan would be paid off first).

III. Business "Angels"

    A. Each year, more than 490,000 private venture capitalists, or business "angels," commit $56 billion to new and expanding firms owned by 87,000 entrepreneurs.

    B. Research shows that a business angel interested in your venture very often lives within 10 miles of you, and is probably already familiar with your type of business.

    C. Since business angels are invariably valued as much for their wisdom as for their cash, your best strategy for finding one is to look for a mentor.

    D. Start by networking at your chamber of commerce or trade association meetings; ask your accountant, banker, and attorney for referrals.

    E. When you tell people about your business, you can mention that there may be "an investment opportunity" for the right person.

IV. Seller Financing—If you are buying a new franchise or business opportunity, one of your first questions should be, "What financing will the seller provide?"

V. Financial Institutions

    A. Banks very seldom make start-up loans.

    B. When they do, they expect:

        1. A very solid Business Plan with good projections.

        2. Experience in managing a business.

        3. Background in the industry.

        4. Enough other assets for the borrower to live on while the business is growing.

     C. If other people are interested and putting their money in, then the venture appears far more attractive to bankers.

     D. Bankers look for at least two reliable sources of repayment and a start-up business is not considered a reliable source.

        1. Second salary in the family

        2. A co-signer who guarantees your loan

        3. An assortment of solid or liquid assets, such as real estate or stocks and bonds

  VI. Federal Government Programs

     A. SBA (Small Business Administration) Direct Loans

     B. SBA Guaranteed Loans—usually written for longer terms than banks prefer.

 VII. State Government Programs

     A. For lucky entrepreneurs who live in states that have instituted their own financing programs, financing sponsored by the state government might be the most exciting alternative available.

     B. To find out if your state has a suitable financial program, call your local Small Business Development Center (SBDC).

VIII. Innovative Funds—getting a loan or an investment is not the only way to finance your new business.

     A. Could you make deliveries for a local business in return for rent-free use of their conference room?

     B. Would your printer agree to wait for payment until you have completed a graphics layout for him?

     C. Can you convince any of your suppliers to give you credit for 90 days, instead of 30 days?

From: Iris Lorenz-Fife, "Money at Your Fingertips," *Homebased Business,* Summer 1990, 28–32.

SUMMARY

Money creates its own world. It has its own customs, rituals, and rules. Before you start asking people for money for your business, spend 3 to 4 months researching the world of money. Here are some things you can do to streamline your research:

1. Read back issues of *Money* magazine.

2. Find someone who knows more about money than you do, and ask questions.

3. Invest a little money in a few shares of stock in a business you want to know about. Read the stockholders' reports.

4. Know that loans are made on the basis of the four C's—Capital, Character, Capacity (to repay), and Collateral.

5. Start to outline your Business Plan. You will need the plan to show to bankers, vendors, and lenders. For now, an outline is good enough. (See Chapter 16 for a model plan.)

6. Begin thinking of a banker as your gateway to the world of money.

THINK POINTS FOR SUCCESS

◣ Your banker can be a doorway to the world of money. Use that door.

◣ How well you buy is as important as how well you sell.

◣ Business is a game. Vendors enjoy having secrets. Try to learn those secrets so that you can get the best deal.

◣ In dealing with bankers and vendors, use lots of open-ended questions like "What else can you do for me?"

REFERENCES

Blechman, Bruce, and Jay Conrad Levinson. *Guerrilla Financing: How to Get All the Money You Need to Start, Buy, or Expand Any Business without Banks, Collateral, or Cash!* Boston: Houghton Mifflin Company, 1991.

Fenn, Donna. "Raising Money—Lots of Money: How One Entrepreneur Got the Venture Capital She Needed to Grow." *Working Woman*, January, 1988, 35.

Fenn, Donna. "What to Do Before You Even Think about Venture Capital—and Where to Find It when You're Really Ready." *Working Woman*, January, 1988, 40.

Gladstone, David. *Venture Capital Investing: The Complete Handbook for Investing in Small Private Businesses for Outstanding Profits.* Englewood Cliffs, N.J.: Prentice-Hall, 1987.

Hicks, Tyler G. *Business Capital Sources*, fourth edition. Rockville Centre, N.Y.: International Wealth, 1990.

Malone, Michael S. *Going Public: MIPS Computer and the Entrepreneurial Dream.* New York: Harper Collins, 1991.

Manko, Joseph M., and Robert Kant. *Going Public: Practice, Procedure, and Consequences.* Director of Publications, Bowne & Co., 345 Hudson St., New York, NY 10014.

National Venture Capital Association Directory, NVCA, 1655 N. Fort Myer Dr., Suite 700, Arlington, VA 22209.

Posner, Bruce. "Laughing All the Way from the Bank: How a Few Clever Companies Finance Their Growth without Relying on Those Undependable Lenders." *Inc.*, December, 1987, 56.

Pratt, Stanley E., and Jane K. Morris, eds. *Pratt's Guide to Venture Capital Success*, Phoenix, Arizona: Oryx Press. Annual. [This guide is very expensive, so try your library first.]

Rennhoff, Harley A. *Get That Business Loan: Convince Your Banker to Say Yes.* Gretna, La.: Pelican, 1987.

Rich, Stanley R., and David E. Gumpert. "Business Plans: What Turns Investors on, What Turns Them off: Eight Key Do's and Don'ts to Make Your Business Plan a Winner." *Working Woman*, January, 1986, 38.

Stevens, Mark. "Boost Your Borrowing Power: When the Banks Balk, Here's where to Go." *Sylvia Porter's Personal Finance Magazine*, December, 1987, 88.

Stevens, Mark. "Negotiating a Loan: How to Bargain with Your Banker for Better Terms." *Sylvia Porter's Personal Finance Magazine*, July–August, 1987, 20.

Tuller, Lawrence. *When the Bank Says No!: Creative Financing for Closely Held Businesses.* Blue Ridge Summit, Penn.: Liberty Hall Press, 1991.

Woeltjen, Lance, and Thomas Sanders. *Surviving the Credit Crunch of the '90s.* Radnor, Penn.: Chilton Book Co., 1990.

ACTION STEP REVIEW

Four action steps help you focus on the world of money and what it means to you:

51 Make a money list. Take stock of what you need and where you can get it.

52 Befriend a banker and use him or her as a resource to help you design your Business Plan. Remember, always ask for advice; never for money.

53 Develop your own vendor statement, a form that allows you to negotiate important survival assistance and to get it in writing.

54 List reasons why lenders would give you money for your business. Test your persuasive powers on your friends and prepare answers to the objections they raise.

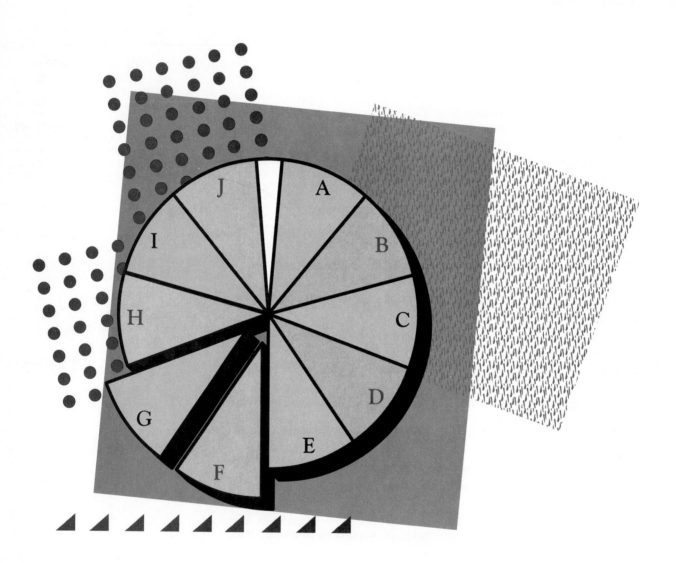

FIGURE 12.1
Chapter 12 will help you complete parts F and G of your Business Plan,
"Management" and "Personnel."

12 Legal Concerns

Learning Objectives

- To decide which legal form (sole proprietorship, partnership, corporation) is best for your business.
- To understand the importance of getting everything in writing.
- To anticipate potential surprises of your going into business with someone else.
- To understand the power of psychological forces and the need for appropriate escape routes for yourself.
- To understand legal escape routes.
- To develop tactics for finding the right attorney.
- To develop questions for probing the mind of an attorney.
- To explore the reasons for incorporating.
- To recognize signals that you should incorporate.
- To explore the pitfalls of "offshore" incorporation.
- To get assistance in writing leases, contracts, labor policies, and other legal documents.
- To conduct secondary research into corporations and incorporating.

FUTURE FOCUS

Keeping it legal takes thought and planning. Why take on a partner? Why incorporate? Be careful of contracts. How do you stay out of the courthouse? Network your way to a good lawyer, then ask him or her to become a member of your Taxi Squad.

ACTION STEP PREVIEW

55   Take a lawyer to lunch.

56   Do some secondary research on corporations.

In your interviews of successful entrepreneurs, you've probably run across the three main legal forms for small business: sole proprietorship, partnership, and corporation. It's common for a small business to start out as a sole proprietorship or a partnership and then become a corporation later. The Tax Reform Act of 1986 is making the shift to a corporation tricky. A lawyer is needed for that. This chapter is about the care and feeding of your attorney. By now your new eyes should be pretty sharp. Use them now to look ahead.

IT PAYS TO LOOK AHEAD

incorporate
form an artificial, immortal business entity

Imagine that you are in a great business with a partner you trust and respect. When should you **incorporate**? Perhaps sooner than you think. That's what Phil Johnson would tell you now.

The power sailer was my idea. My partner, Steve Savitch, said it would break us, and I should have listened to him. Steve's an engineer and inventor. He's great with numbers and computers, but he doesn't know much about people, which is my department. We'd been friends for a dozen years, at least, and we'd been partners—Savitch and Johnson, Business Consultants—for the past 3. We were each going to clear over eighty thousand dollars this year.

money market fund
a pool of managed money secured by short-term corporate IOUs

Steve's tight with a nickel. I knew he'd sock his money away in a **money market fund** at a conservative rate. But I had this idea that we could buy a boat for the partnership, write off the down payment as an expense, and do our company image a world of good.

Selling is 50 percent sweat, 40 percent image, and 10 percent product. I've been in sales all my life. I know.

"I don't know, Phil," Steve said when he saw the boat. Her name was *The Ninja*. She was forty-six feet long, with polished brass fittings and wood that gleamed back at you when you smiled. "What does a fancy rig like that have to do with anything?"

"Image, Steve," I said. "Image."

"Uh-oh," Steve said. "Here we go with the unmeasurable intangibles."

"It's not intangible when you think about those prospects coming from Chicago next week," I said. "A cruise to Catalina should soften them up, don't you think?"

"Maybe," Steve sighed. He gave me his engineer's thin smile. "I trust you, Phil. You're the people person."

Steve's reluctance faded some when he saw the numbers. The power sailer was listed at 25 percent below market, and the owner was eager to carry back some paper. We took our banker for a sail that weekend, and by Monday noon, we had a check for the difference. The first payment wasn't due for a month, and when Steve and I took it out with our wives, I tell you, I felt like a prince of the sea. We'd pulled off a smooth deal, and I patted myself on the back every time I thought about the **write-offs**.

write-offs
legitimate business deductions you can report to the IRS

The Ninja boosted business, just like I'd thought it would. We closed the Chicago deal and we were busy on a couple of others that looked promising. We made the first payment with no trouble, and when Steve **counter-signed** the check, he admitted he was beginning to like the boat.

countersigning
a situation in which two or more signatures are required before action can occur

"If it's okay with you, Phil, I'm going to sleep there a couple nights this week. My house is full of in-laws, and I've got to get my projections done for those guys from St. Louis.

"Be my guest," I said.

So for a couple of weeks, Steve took his portable computer and slept on *The Ninja*. We took her out that weekend, with four prospects from St. Louis, and Steve seemed a little preoccupied. I closed the deal with them Sunday, fifteen minutes before putting them on the plane for home, but when I called Steve's house to tell him the good news, his wife, Mary, told me he was still at the boat.

Thinking back later, I remembered hearing something funny in Mary's voice. But at the time, I was so excited I didn't think anything about it.

Monday, Steve didn't come to work until almost noon. He looked hung over, but he handed me his projections and we got on with planning our strategy for the next couple of weeks.

"Anything wrong, partner?" I asked. "You seem a little far-off today."

"Sorry," Steve said. He was never one to admit to having emotions. "My mind wandered a bit there. Where were we?"

I should have gotten suspicious right then. But I'm not one to pry, so I didn't. We all like our privacy.

On Tuesday and Wednesday, Steve was at the office when I got there, working away at his computer. On Thursday, the first thing I saw when I got to work was a stack of computer printouts two inches high. It was Steve's half of the next three jobs.

By noon, Steve still hadn't made it to work. I called his house. No answer. I thought of driving down to the dock to check the boat, but I had to pick up a couple of clients at the airport. They were flying in from Minneapolis. We were scheduled for an evening aboard *The Ninja*. When we arrived at our dock, around 4:30 that afternoon, there was no sign of *The Ninja*. Someone on the next boat said Steve had taken off early this morning with a woman on board.

I was in shock. There I stood, with two clients in deck shoes and Bermuda shorts.

Then Joey, the guy who pumps gas, came up waving a gas bill for eight hundred dollars—one I'd thought Steve had paid. And the bad news didn't end there. The next day, a fellow who sells radar equipment called me. Seems Steve had bought two thousand dollars' worth of radar, and this fellow was wondering when he would be paid.

As I hung up the phone, my secretary buzzed me. It was Mary, Steve's wife, wanting to know where Steve was.

Now my stomach was really hurting. My partner Steve was gone—no one knew where—and I was liable for all his business debts, including the payments on *The Ninja*. Terrific.

The problem was that Steve and I had never seen the need for having anything in writing. We were both men of good faith. We had each pulled our weight in the business, and we had balanced each other's skills.

Now that Steve was gone, I felt lost, angry, and betrayed. For the first time in twenty-two years of business, I made an appointment to talk to a lawyer. He just shook his head.

"You should have come to me sooner, Phil," he said. "A lot sooner."

Last week when I was closing the place down and getting ready to go back to work for my old boss, I got a postcard from Steve, from Tahiti. "Sorry, Phil," it read. "Didn't mean to run out on you. It was the only way I could handle it. These things happen. Wanda says hi. Your pal, Steve."

The Good and Bad of Partnerships

A **partnership**, as lots of people find out too late, is only an accounting entity. It does not shield you from trouble. It won't make your business immortal or continuous, and it's taxed at the same rate you are.

The great thing about partnerships is that they're warm, easy to form, and feel good right from the start. You can form a partnership with a handshake, and **dissolve** it without one. A partnership is dissolved when one of the partners dies or when some easy legal steps are taken. The best thing about a partnership is that it allows the financial and moral support of a teammate.

A partnership is somewhat of a paradox. In a legal sense the partnership doesn't do much for you, but as many partners admit, there are sound psychological reasons for going into business with someone else.

What are some of those reasons? Let's say you've analyzed your personal skills and you realize you need balance in a couple of critical areas. For example, you may be an engineer who can come up with twenty original ideas a day but couldn't sell canned heat in an Arctic snowstorm. Or maybe you don't have much money so you

partnership
an enterprise in which two or more people are engaged as owners or owner/operators

dissolution of a partnership
the separation of partners; an eventuality that needs to be prepared for with intricate planning and much thought

need a partner who can supply your new business with capital. Or maybe you get along with people and love to sell and you need to team up with an inventor/producer who can supply you with products to sell. Many successful business owners would never have started a business without a partner.

Before you commit yourself to a partnership, read the rest of this chapter. Then project your cash flow and your P and L to get a ballpark look at your first couple of years. Then, on the basis of a careful business analysis, decide which legal form is best for your business.

The legal form of your business is just that—a form, a shape. To your customers, the particular form you choose will make no difference, but to you, the right shape is absolutely essential. You want your business to be rock-solid, stable, and protected—and you want to be able to change the form if it doesn't work.

THE THREE LEGAL FORMS FOR SMALL BUSINESS

Your small business can exist in one of three legal forms: a sole proprietorship, a partnership, or a corporation. Beyond the mental images we have of these forms of ownership (Figure 12.2), there are business realities—and various amounts of paperwork—that you should know about. Table 12.1 summarizes the differences.

The Sole Proprietorship

Most small businesses start as sole proprietorships. If you start a business on your own—without partners—you will be a sole proprietor. If this form is your choice, the paperwork will be relatively easy. You might get by with a city business license,

TABLE 12.1   Comparison of Business Legal Forms

FORM	WHO'S IN CONTROL	PAPERWORK REQUIRED	SOURCES OF CAPITAL	TAX BURDEN	OWNERS' PERSONAL LIABILITY	CONTINUITY
Sole proprietorship	The owner	None	Limited	Personal rate	Total	Uncertain
Partnership, general	The general partner(s)	None, but written agreement is advised	Greater	Shared by all partners; personal rate	Unlimited	Depends on buy–sell agreement
Partnership, limited	The general partner(s)	Agreement should be drawn up by attorney and filed with the state	Greater	Shared by all partners; personal rate	Limited to the amount invested	Terminated by death
Corporation	Stockholders, board of directors	Much (need attorney and CPA)	Can sell stock; relatively unlimited	Corporate rate, may be higher than personal rate	None unless owners sign a personal guarantee	Potential for immortality
S corporation	Stockholders, board of directors	Much (need attorney and CPA)	Can have no more than 35 stockholders	Gains or losses passed on to stockholders	None unless owners sign a personal guarantee	Potential for immortality

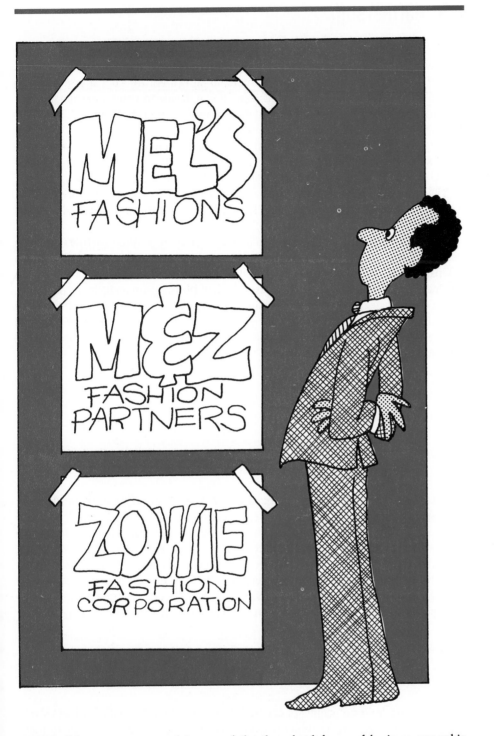

FIGURE 12.2 Common mental images of the three legal forms of business ownership. Beyond these images there are business realities that you should investigate before you decide which form is right for you.

a resale license, and a "doing-business-as" or fictitious business statement (a "DBA"). If you use your own name, you won't need the DBA. But you may discover that your business is sending you signals that another form would better suit your needs.

The Partnership

Many small businesses start as partnerships and it works out great. The start-up paperwork may be as easy as for a small proprietorship. Although *you* would want a good lawyer to put together the partnership agreement for you, it is possible to form a valid partnership with a handshake. If you decide to enter a partnership, get a partnership agreement; you'll be glad you did in the long run. Figure 12.3 presents a sample partnership agreement.

A partnership is made up of at least two parties. There can be more—six, ten, a baker's dozen—but the more partners a business has, the more tricky are the decisions. Think of a ship with a dozen captains. Who makes the decisions?

There are two types of partnerships: limited and general. In a general partnership, each partner has a hand in managing the business and assumes unlimited personal liability for any debts.

In a limited partnership—composed of two or more limited partners and one general partner—the general partner assumes both management duties and the downside risk. A limited partners' liability is limited to the *amount* of his or her original investment as long as he or she has had no role in management decisions.

On the surface, partnerships make a lot of sense. Two or more entrepreneurs face the unknown together and pool their skills. They can raise more capital than one person could alone. But forming a good partnership is more difficult than forming a good marriage.

The Corporation

A corporation is a legal entity created by the state. It stands legally separate from the owners and it does business in the name of the corporation. It can sue and be sued.

Because a corporation is an artificial entity, a creation on paper, it needs more paperwork to justify its existence. There are fees required, and meetings of the Board of Directors. The secretary of the corporation must keep accurate, complete records of what transpires at meetings. Nonetheless, for many businesses, it's worth going to the trouble to form a corporation because a shield is created between the creditors and the owners' personal wealth. To keep the shield in place, active owners become *employees* of the corporation; their business cards have the corporate name and logo and specify their job title. Owners sign contracts as *officers* of the corporation.

GET A LAWYER

Businesses are built on people, of course, and this is why you need a business structure that will gives you flexibility when the people in your business want to make a change. Don't underestimate the power of psychological forces. This chapter is designed to help you anticipate those internal forces that can make you wish you had planned escape routes ahead of time.

A good **small business attorney** can help you create the right business structure for a partnership or a corporation—a structure that gives you the flexibility you'll need. Network your contacts for a lawyer with experience in your industry. You need to have a lawyer on your **taxi squad**. Once you've found one you think might be right for you, make an appointment with him or her.

small business attorney
an attorney who specializes in small business

taxi squad
human resources outside your business that you can call upon as needed

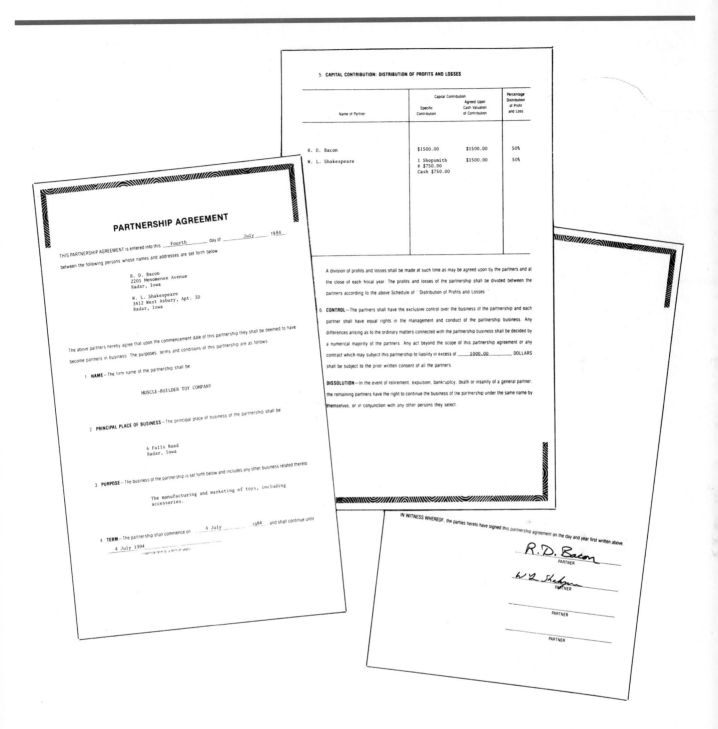

FIGURE 12.3   A sample partnership agreement between R. D. Bacon and W. L. Shakespeare, both of Radar, Iowa.

ACTION STEP 55

Take a lawyer to lunch.

Network your business contacts for the names of three to five attorneys with experience in forming small business corporations and partnerships. Concentrate on those who have worked in your industry.

Check them out on the phone and then take the most promising candidates to lunch. (Lunch is optional—but your inquiries are vital.)

The first thing you're looking for is someone you can get along with. Then look for experience in the world of small business. A hot trial lawyer may have a lot of charisma, but you want a nuts-and-bolts small business specialist who can save you time, pain, and money.

During lunch, find out about fees and costs. Compare the cost, for example, of having your lawyer write up a complex partnership buy-out agreement with the cost of setting up a corporation. This section of this book lists some questions to start you off in your discussions with your prospective attorney.

A good lawyer will offer perspectives that will be helpful in the formation of your business. You may have to look awhile, and it may cost you some dollars up front, but there's no substitute for good legal help.

contingencies
unforeseen events in the future that alert you to prepare Plan B

Questions to Ask a Prospective Lawyer

The answers to these questions will help you know which legal form of business ownership is best for you and your business.

1. During your first phone conversation: Do you offer a free get-acquainted session? If the answer is yes, make an appointment. If the answer is no, ask about lunch. (Many lawyers can't afford to give free sessions, but most of them eat lunch. If you buy lunch, you can get 45 minutes of free advice.)

2. On the phone, before the first meeting: What information do you need in order to help me decide what legal form of business will be best? Do you have a list of questions for prospective business owners that you can mail me? Where can I get sample partnership agreements?

3. At the first meeting, after the lawyer knows exactly what kind of business you're in: What would be the pros and cons of sole proprietorship, partnership, and incorporation for me with regard to liability, tax burden, raising money, paperwork, and control.

4. If there will be more than one owner: What are the pros and cons of our forming a general partnership/a limited partnership/a corporation/a subchapter S corporation? What are the setup costs? What does it cost to change from one form to another? Are there time restrictions on when I could change forms?

Be sure to prepare your own agenda for each conversation with the lawyer. If you're organized you will save money on your fee.

Now you're ready to do Action Step 55.

Provide for Contingencies: Look Ahead

If you don't use a good lawyer to help you structure your business, you probably won't have a plan to handle **contingencies**, and unforeseen events can take you by surprise. If Paul Webber had used his imagination to look ahead, his story might have turned out differently.

Paul was a computer programmer when he met Jerry Dominic. Jerry was a likable guy and a dynamite salesman—and after reading *Megatrends 2000* he knew there was money to be made in the information business—so he got together with Paul and formed a software consulting business. They specialized in microcomputers, because that's where the action was. Their first year was okay—they netted over $40,000 apiece—but their second year was looking even better.

By May of their second year, their projections told them they could make a hundred thousand each before the end of summer. They thought it felt great to be rich.

To celebrate, they went to a neighborhood bar for a couple of drinks. Jerry got into an argument with a bald-headed guy about politics. There was a fistfight and Jerry ended up on the floor. As Paul stooped down to help Jerry up, he noticed his partner felt heavy, like dead weight.

At forty-nine years old, Jerry Dominic was dead of a heart attack.

Two days after the funeral, Paul was on the phone with a customer when Jerry's widow walked in. Mildred had just inherited Jerry's half of the business.

Paul didn't like Mildred being his partner, but there was nothing he could do. He knew he would have to break his back to teach her the business. Computer software was fast-track and competitive—it changed before you could take a breath—and Mildred would have to learn an awful lot in a short time.

Paul was a good guy, so he tried. The first week, he was extra tired because he was handling his own customers while he spent long hours trying to teach Mildred the business. The second week, two of Paul's customers on hold defected to a competitor. Paul heard about it on the grapevine. The third week, the company almost ran out of cash, and Paul had to dump in $5,000 from his personal account to keep suppliers happy.

The other problem was that Mildred wasn't learning the business. She was getting in Paul's hair, and she was spending money. But she wasn't able to hold up her end, and there was no improvement in sight.

Paul hung on for a couple more weeks. Then he did the only thing he could do for his own survival: he took what customers he had left and rented an office six blocks away and tried to keep going. He figured he had paid his dues to Jerry. He hoped Jerry understood, wherever he was.

Sometimes, Paul wishes he and Jerry had had something in writing to cover *contingencies*. In business, you always need a Plan B.

If you still want to form a partnership, get a lawyer to draw up a **partnership agreement** and consult your insurance agent about getting some protective insurance. If you're able to look ahead, you'll avoid problems regardless of the legal form of your business.

partnership agreement
a written agreement between two or more partners that should specify profit sharing, capital gains distribution, and tactics for painless dissolution

CORPORATIONS AND SMALL BUSINESS

There are at least seven good reasons for incorporating. In general, we think most owners of small businesses fail to incorporate because they don't see the signals their businesses are giving. If you don't see the signals, don't incorporate. If you do, check it out with an attorney. (See Box 12.1.)

Seven Reasons for Incorporating

1. You Limit Your Liability. A corporation acts like a shield between you and the world. If your business fails, your creditors can't come after your house, your condo, your Porsche, your first-born, and your hard-won collectibles—provided you've done it right. Fortunately for Henry Bemis, he'd done it right.

Henry Bemis was going great guns with his coffee service when a piece of his equipment spewed boiling water all over the hands of Jody Dawn, a professional model.

BOX 12.1   Two Clear Signals that You Should Incorporate

If you are in business now and are thinking about incorporation, answer these two questions. Your business may be giving you signals that you should incorporate.

1. Could you be sued? If you are vulnerable to litigation, then incorporate or buy lots of protective insurance.
2. Do you want a different, more prestigious image? Again, if the answer is yes, incorporate.

Miss Dawn's hands earned her over $200,000 a year. The day her hands were burnt, she was at a branch of a major bank, doing a DeBeers-sponsored commercial for diamond rings and safety-deposit boxes.

Her hands were her living and her future. On the advice of her attorney, Miss Dawn sued Henry Bemis and his Easy-Cup Coffee Service.

Henry had insurance, of course. But it stopped at $350,000, and the courts were about to award Miss Dawn 2 million dollars. Here's the way they figured it:

> She had been earning $200,000 a year.
>
> She could figure on an active career of at least 10 years.
>
> Ten years × $200,000 = $2,000,000.

Luckily, Henry had had the good sense to incorporate when he went into business. So while the courts went after Easy-Cup Coffee Service, Inc., Henry's house and car and personal properties were safe.

Also, because he'd gotten into a couple of networks, Henry was able to start another business right away.

This time, he didn't go into coffee.

To keep your corporate shield up, make sure you: (1) hold scheduled board of directors meetings, (2) keep up the minutes book, and (3) act as if you are an employee of the corporation.

Here's an example that illustrates the corporate shield: your secretary gets into a fender-bender while driving on company business. If you're a corporation, the injured parties will come after your corporation, not you. (If your employees use their own cars on company business, make sure they're insured for a minimum of one million dollars.)

2. You Change Your Tax Picture.   Consult the current IRS schedule or ask a CPA for advice.

3. You Upgrade Your Image.   What does the word *corporation* mean to you? IBM? Exxon? TRW? Texaco? TWA? GM?

Heavy hitters, right?

Let's look at that word. It comes from the Latin *corpus,* which means "body." *To incorporate* means to make or form or shape into a body. Looked at from that angle, *incorporating* starts to sound creative.

It will sound that way to lots of your target customers, too. As a corporation, you may:

> have more clout and solidity in the world,
>
> attract better employees, and
>
> enjoy more prestige.

4. You Have the Opportunity to Channel Some Heavy Expenses.   With some legal help, you can write a medical assistance clause into your by-laws. Here's the way it works:

1. Your corporation pays your health insurance **premiums**.
2. Your corporation reimburses you for the deductible.
   a. Your corporation writes off the money paid to you as a business expense.
   b. You aren't liable for taxes on the reimbursement.
3. You can deduct **F.I.C.A.** payments as a business expense.

insurance premium
a rated payment on insurance coverage

F.I.C.A.
contribution to federal government for Social Security

5. **You Simplify the Division of Multiple Ownership.**   For example, say you're going into the printing and graphics business with two good friends. The business needs $100,000 to get started.

You can put your hands on $60,000.
Friend A delivers $25,000.
Friend B delivers $15,000.

The way to handle the ownership is with stock. You get 60 percent, Friend A gets 25 percent, and Friend B gets 15 percent.

6. **You Guarantee Continuity.**   If one of the owners skips town, the corporation keeps on chugging. That's because you've gone through a lot of red tape and planning to set it up that way. It's one of the few justifications for red tape we know.

7. **You Can Offer Internal Incentives.**   When you want to reward a special employee, you can offer some stock or a promotion (for example, a vice presidency) in addition to (or in place of) pay raises. Becoming a corporate officer carries its own special excitement, and this gives you flexibility.

What a Corporation Will Not Do

Becoming a corporation won't solve all your problems. For example, a corporation will not:

- immunize you against all creditors (The bankers and creditors will still want a personal guarantee—which could mean your collateral.)
- make *you* immortal
- protect you if you fail to hold meetings, keep minutes, and keep your state corporate records current

Subchapter S Corporations

Subchapter S corporations are semicorporate bodies that limit the owner's liability while still allowing a pass-through of business losses to the personal income statements of the owners, founders, and others. *Subchapter S* refers to the section of the 1958 IRS code that describes it.

The number of stockholders is limited to thirty-five, and corporate income (or loss) is allowed to be passed directly to the stockholders. There is no corporate tax. The IRS has specific time requirements for filing, and some states do not recognize the tax aspects of the Sub S category. Check out these things for your state. Your attorney can help you.

Do Research Now

We've told you a lot of what you need to know about corporations, but it's not enough. You need to start reading widely on the subject. Action Step 56 will get you started. It takes time to incorporate properly, so it pays to get started early.

ACTION STEP 56

Do some secondary research on corporations.

Before you take any action about legal forms you need a lot of information. Go to the library and the bookstore, and start reading books like *Inc. Yourself* by Judith McQuown, *How to Form Your Own Corporation without a Lawyer for Under $50* by Ted Nicholas, and *Incorporating Your Business* by John Kirk. See the reference section at the end of the chapter.

When you have become familiar with the broad concepts, do some research on specific corporations in your industry. (Start with your incorporated competitors.) You can get information from the library, from a stockbroker, or by writing to the corporations.

While you're doing this research, keep looking around with new eyes.

Key Points from Another View
Part I:
THE LAW REVIEW

With the legal maze facing small businesses these days every entrepreneur needs a good attorney.

I. When to Use a Lawyer

    A. It's generally worthwhile to consult an attorney before making any decision that could have legal ramifications.

    B. As a small-business owner, you'll probably consult your attorney primarily on business matters.

        1. Setting up a partnership or corporation

        2. Checking for compliance with regulations

        3. Negotiating loans

        4. Obtaining trademarks or patents

        5. Preparing buy–sell agreements

        6. Assisting with tax planning

        7. Drawing up pension plans

        8. Reviewing business forms

        9. Negotiating and drawing up documents for the purchase and sale of real estate

       10. Reviewing employee contracts

       11. Dismissal procedures

       12. Collecting bad debts

II. Choosing an Attorney

    A. Ask for recommendations from business owners in your industry, or from professionals such as your accountant or banker.

    B. Look for an attorney whose personal style matches—or complements—your own.

    C. Before retaining an attorney, arrange a conference in which you can describe your business and its legal needs. Take note of what the attorney says and does, and look for the following qualities:

        1. Experience

        2. Understanding

        3. Ability to communicate

        4. Availability

        5. Rapport

        6. Reasonable fees

III. Controlling Costs

    A. Because sound legal advice can prevent expensive mistakes, the money you pay your attorney is generally well spent.

    B. On some matters, though, attorney's fees can add up to more than you stand to gain. To keep a lid on costs, learn how lawyers bill their time.

        1. Hourly or per diem rate

        2. Flat fee

  3. Monthly retainer

  4. Contingent fee

  5. Value billing—try to avoid lawyers who use this method.

 C. When you hire an attorney, draw up an agreement detailing the billing method.

 D. Beyond the basic agreement, take the following steps to control legal costs:

  1. Estimate the cost of each matter in writing

  2. What expenses you're expected to reimburse

  3. Learn what increment of time the firm uses to calculate bills.

  4. Request monthly, itemized bills and review them.

IV. Making the Most of Your Lawyer

 A. Use your attorney's time efficiently by preparing ahead of time.

 B. Sit down with your attorney once a year to discuss the past year's progress and your goals for the coming year.

 C. In evaluating the attorney's performance on any matter, consider whether you've been able to meet your goals. If you've met your goals without undue costs, the attorney is probably doing a good job.

From Jane Easter Bahls,"The Law Review," *Entrepreneurial Woman,* July/August, 1990, 62–65.

Part II:
LEGAL-EASE—AN ENTREPRENEUR'S CRASH COURSE IN BUSINESS LAW

It's important that every entrepreneur be familiar with basic legal concepts, as well as with some of the special problems that can arise in particular areas of their business. The following general guide to small-business law will help you formulate sensible questions to ask your attorney.

 I. Structuring Your Business

 A. Sole Proprietorship

  1. Sole proprietor means that you alone own and control the business.

  2. You are personally responsible for all of its debts, and if someone sues your business over a defective product or an employment grievance, all of your business and personal assets are on the line.

 B. Partnership

  1. A partnership gives each partner a say in the management of the business and a stake in both profit and losses.

  2. Each partner is fully responsible for the debts of the partnership—including any debts his or her partner incurs in the regular course of business.

  3. You can be prepared for problems by drawing up a partnership agreement specifying what rights each partner has, how disputes will be settled, and how the business will be transferred if one partner quits.

C. Corporation
1. The chief advantage of operating as a corporation is that the owners aren't personally liable for the company debts.
2. It usually costs several hundred dollars in legal fees to set up a corporation, and the law requires corporations to elect officers and directors, keep records, and file separate tax returns.

II. Your Ads
A. The ground rules are fairly simple: Avoid misleading or deceptive ads. The FTC (Federal Trade Commission) has labeled ads deceptive for implying:
1. That a company squeezed juice straight from the orange into the carton when they actually pasteurized and froze it first.
2. That a brand of liquor was Scotch when it wasn't made in Scotland.
3. That doctors recommend a particular brand of aspirin instead of aspirin in general.
B. Truth is your best defense, so keep a file of evidence to substantiate your advertising claims.
C. For advertising guidelines, contact the Federal Trade Commission, Pennsylvania Ave. and 6th St. N. W., Washington, D.C. 20580

III. Price Fixing
A. If you think the Sherman Antitrust Act applies only to big corporations, you're mistaken. Every year, many small businesses face lawsuits or even criminal investigations for entering "contracts, combinations or conspiracies" in restraint of trade.
B. Sitting down with your competitors to set prices is against the law.

IV. Employment Law
In addition to the familiar prohibitions against various kinds of discrimination, be aware of the following trouble spots and take steps to avoid them.
A. Sexual harassment—The Equal Employment Opportunity Commission (EEOC) defines sexual harassment as "unwelcome sexual advances, requests for sexual favors and other . . . conduct of a sexual nature."
B. Employee Handbooks
1. Some employees have convinced courts that the handbook also functions as a contract.
2. If you don't intend your handbook to be a contract, print a disclaimer in bold letters in the front.
3. Before discharging an employee, keep a record of job-related incidents that support your decision.
C. Defamation—In order to qualify as defamation, a statement about an employee must:
1. Be false
2. Tend to harm the employee's reputation, and
3. Be communicated to someone other than the employee.
4. Consider meeting with every terminated employee to compose a statement explaining the reason for dismissal, and use that statement in future references.

V. Trademarks and Copyrights

    A. In an expanding legal trend, courts have also granted protection under the Lanham Act, a federal statute designed to protect the rights of artists and entrepreneurs, to some companies' distinctive "trade dress"—referring to the total image.

    B. If you've created an innovative product, the corporate giants may soon be on your heels with a lower-priced imitation.

       1. File a copyright before it is too late.

       2. Likewise, if you've designed a trademark, be sure to register it properly.

VI. Credit Problems

Legally, you have a right to be paid for the goods or services you've provided, but whether you'll ever actually see the money depends on how well you've protected yourself.

    A. Investigate the customer; keep a record of the buyer's name, address, bank, and type of business.

    B. Include a due date on your bill of sale, and specify how much interest is owed on overdue payments.

    C. For larger trade sales, such as equipment, insist on a lien on the property sold. Then, you'll need to "perfect" the lien by filling a financing statement with the state or county.

From: Jane Easter Bahls, "Legal-Ease—An Entrepreneur's Crash Course in Business Law," *Entrepreneur,* March, 1990, 96–101.

SUMMARY

There are three basic legal forms for a small business: sole proprietorship, partnership, corporation.

You can start doing business as a sole proprietorship with a minimum of hassle. You might need only a city license, a resale license, and perhaps a DBA (fictitious name) statement.

The legal paperwork for a partnership is almost as simple. You can form a partnership with a handshake and dissolve it without one. There are good psychological reasons for forming a partnership. Only 8 percent of the small businesses in the U.S. are partnerships. If you decide a partnership is right for you, get a lawyer to prepare a partnership agreement to protect you against trouble.

Forming a corporation takes the most paperwork, but it gives you more flexibility, as well as a shield to protect you in case your business hurts someone. With a corporation, you:

1. limit your liability
2. change your tax picture
3. upgrade your company image
4. can rechannel some expenses (like medical)
5. can simplify multiple ownership by apportioning company stock
6. can guarantee continuity
7. can offer internal incentives to key employees

ACTION STEP REVIEW

Two action steps teach you more about legal forms.

55 Take a lawyer to lunch. Use the time to determine the lawyer's personality and his or her ability to help you.

56 Read some books about corporations and the art of incorporating. Learn all you can now.

THINK POINTS FOR SUCCESS

◤ We only remember what we want to. Get everything in writing.

◤ If your business is small and you like it that way, keep it simple—like your hobby.

◤ Most growth businesses need outside infusions of cash. Don't pay Uncle Sam more than you have to.

◤ When you create corporate stock in your by-laws, think about creating at least ten times more than you intend to sell at start-up.

◤ Even if you incorporate, a banker may still want a personal guarantee for loans.

◤ Forget about incorporating in Nevada or Delaware (unless you live there), or in exotic offshore locations. You'll be a foreign corporation (out-of-state) and you'll have to pay extra to do business at home.

REFERENCES

Clifford, Denis and Ralph Warner. *The Partnership Book.* Berkeley, Calif.: Nolo Press, 1991.

Cook, Wade B. *Incorporation Handbook for Small Business Owners.* Scottsdale, Ariz.: Regency Books, 1986.

Diamond, Michael. *How to Incorporate: A Manual for Entrepreneurs and Professionals.* New York: Wiley, 1987.

Flamholtz, Eric. *Growing Pains: How to Make the Transition from an Entrepreneurship to a Professionally Managed Firm.* San Francisco: Jossey-Bass, 1990.

Krasnow, Erwin, and Robin Conrad. *100 Ways to Cut Legal Fees & Manage Your Lawyer.* National Chamber Litigation Center, 1615 H St. N.W., Washington DC 20062.

Mancuso, Anthony. *How to Form Your Own California Corporation,* 7th ed. Berkeley, Calif.: Nolo Press, 1988. [Now also available for Texas and Florida.]

Mancuso, Anthony. *The California Professional Corporation Handbook,* 4th revised edition. Berkeley, Calif.: Nolo Press, 1989.

Murray, Mark. "Organizational Documents: A Guide for Partnerships and Professional Corporations," AICPA, (800) 334-6961 to order.

Professional Report Editors and John Kirk. *Incorporating Your Business.* Chicago: Contemporary Books, 1986.

Wasserman, Paul, Gary McCann, and Patricia Tobin. *Encyclopedia of Legal Information Sources.* Detroit: Gale Research, 1988. (Excellent resource on over 460 law-related topics).

Whitmeyer, Claude, et al. *Running a One Person Business.* Berkeley, Calif.: Ten Speed Press, 1988.

NOTES

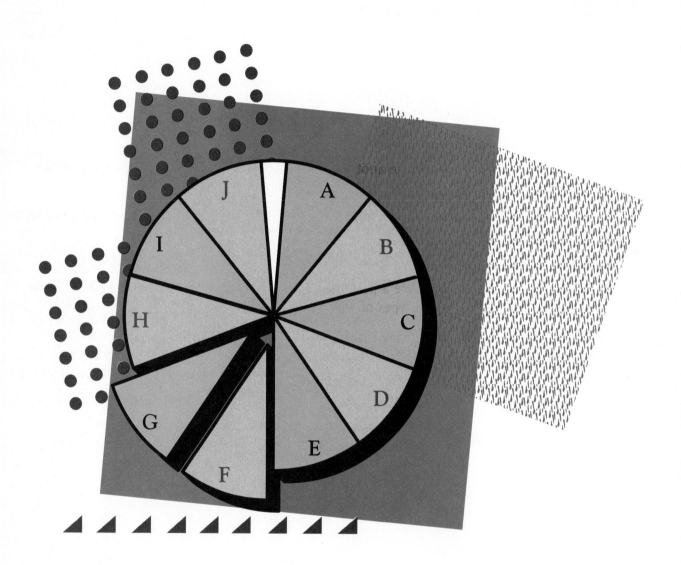

FIGURE 13.1
Chapter 13 will help you prepare the Management and Personnel parts of your
Business Plan, parts F and G.

13 Building a Winning Team

Learning Objectives

- To accept that you probably can't do everything well.
- To understand the importance of balance to the survival of your business.
- To take another look at yourself and identify your weaknesses.
- To explore new ways of putting together a team.
- To look back, and see if there's anyone you wish could work with you in this venture.
- To use brainstorming techniques to assemble a team.
- To use a personality profile system to identify who you are and the types of people you need for balance.
- To survey your competitors and network your vendors for potential team members.
- To brainstorm with your new team *before* you open the doors, so you can take advantage of your people resource.

FUTURE FOCUS

Sooner or later you will need teammates and helpers. Building a winning team means having the right people doing the right job. You can't afford a misfit. Who do you know that would be on your team? It's never too early to make a list. The basic difference between successful and unsuccessful businesses is their people. Never just settle for an employee; hire the very best to be a teammate.

DISC
a system for profiling prospective or existing team members

Building a winning team can be one of the most enjoyable tasks you face. To do this, you must first look at yourself objectively, and then build your team around your business and psychological needs. That's what the successful entrepreneur does. This chapter will show you how to build to win.

BUILDING BALANCE INTO YOUR TEAM

Balance is essential to a team. You may think you already understand everything you need to know about balance. If you're a person who tries to solve every problem yourself, it may be a while before you admit you need help. Fortunately, tools are available to give you perspective.

One such tool is the DISC system of personality profiling, an outgrowth of William Marston's research on human behavior and recorded in his book, *Emotions of Normal People*. DISC is easy to remember because it is an acronym (uses the first letter of each word in a string) based on these four personality types:

D = Dominant
I = Influencing
S = Steady
C = Compliant

Think about these personality types as you read the following case study. Four people go on vacation. Who has control? Who does the planning? Who reads the map when they get lost? Who cools the arguments down? Who wants to lead all the time? Try to categorize Ted, Carol, Alice and Bob.

Friends as Team Members

Four friends decided to spend vacation at Bufadora, a small fishing village on the coast of Baja California. They drove down in two vehicles. Carol and Bob drove Carol's Mercedes, and Ted and Alice drove their Chevy Blazer with four-wheel drive.

The house they rented overlooked the ocean. Carol, an expressive person, kept exclaiming how beautiful it was. "Have you ever seen anything," Carol said, "as lovely, as beautiful, as gorgeous as that blue?"

The thirteenth time she said it, Ted became irritated and began to snipe. "How about the desert outside Las Vegas?" he said. "You've just won a million dollars, and the world is your oyster."

"Las Vegas is ugly," Carol said, "but I did enjoy hearing Frank Sinatra. He was wonderful!"

"That guy," Ted said.

They went on arguing until Alice got them organized on lunch. She sent Ted off to the market for some matches. She assigned Carol the job of assembling a platter of fruit. She asked Bob to figure out how to light the gas-fired barbecue. He had to take it apart and clean the feeder lines to make it work. Thus, lunch was delayed.

When the barbecue was working again, Ted cooked the meat to perfection. Everyone enjoyed the meal. Carol ate mostly fruit. Bob and Ted ate mostly meat. Alice ate a balanced meal of meat, fruit, and vegetables.

After lunch, the four went for a drive in the Mercedes. Carol drove with a lot of flair, tooting at people in the street. Ted didn't think she drove very well and told her so. Bob frowned at him for badgering Carol, while Alice did her best to smooth things over for everyone's sake.

Six miles outside town, Carol saw a sign pointing to a church she was sure would be charming and turned off the main highway. Dust boiled up around the car. A mud hole soon appeared in the road. Carol decided to drive through it, disregarding Ted's warning to slow down. The Mercedes ground to a halt.

"What on earth happened?" Carol said.

"You got us stuck!" Ted said.

"I'm sure it's not a big problem," Alice said.

Ted and Bob worked for an hour but could not free the rear wheel of the car. During this time Carol sat in the shade, and Alice cheered the men on and tried to be helpful.

"Okay," Ted said, "enough! We're going to have to hike back to town."

"In these shoes?" Carol said, pointing to her new pumps from Saks Fifth Avenue.

"It does seem a little far," Alice said.

"Six point two miles to be exact," Bob said.

"The road curved around," Ted said. "The town is just over this hill about a mile as the crow flies."

"Let's wait for someone to come along," Carol suggested.

"You can wait if you want," Ted said, "but I'm hiking over that hill."

An argument ensued. While Bob studied a map of the area, Alice, the perpetual peacemaker, attempted to come up with some compromise that would please everyone.

In the end, Ted and Alice hiked up the hill. At the top, they saw the ragged string of Bufadora rooftops. They waved to Carol and Bob back at the car, but Carol was listening to the car stereo and Bob was studying alternate routes on the map.

Ted and Alice walked to the village and got help, and the Mercedes was towed out by sunset.

That evening they went out to dinner. Carol was glitteringly beautiful—the belle of the cafe. She ordered a bottle of champagne for Ted and Alice and toasted them as the world's greatest explorers. Bob spent dinnertime analyzing why the car had gotten stuck.

Let's Analyze This Team

Ted is pushy. He knows he's right, and he's ready for adventure—or an argument; he doesn't mind confrontation. Under stress, he must take action, whether it's right or not; he cannot sit still and wait for a plan. On the DISC scale, Ted is a Dominant.

Carol is glib, pretty, and glittery. She enjoys the spotlight, speaks in superlatives, and dresses to impress. Under stress, she needs lots of people around her. She likes to persuade people to her point of view. On the DISC scale, she's an Influencer.

Alice is sweet. Her main goal is to keep things moving, and pleasant. She hates confrontation and spends her energy negotiating the energies of others. Alice is a Compliant.

Bob is precise. He likes numbers and measurements. He has the best mind of the four and he keeps it in shape by analyzing things. Bob loves to tinker with machinery. Under stress, he probes the situation with careful analysis before taking any action. Of course, Bob is a Steady.

D's need other people, other types. Ted, a flaming D, is married to Alice, a cool C. They make a good team because their personalities balance each other. Carol, a flamboyant I, is married to Bob, a precise fellow who keeps things under control.

How Does This Relate to Your Small Business?

If you're an entrepreneur, there's a good chance you're a Dominant. You probably like adventure, and thrive on challenges. Management, however, may bore you. You may be able to motivate people when you're in the mood, but when you're not in the mood, forget it. You're maybe not so great at sales, either. (After all, why should you have to sell anyone on a product that is obviously superior?) If you're a D, you probably think people who don't see things your way are dumb, or stupid. If you're

ACTION STEP 57

Categorize your friends and acquaintances.

Make a list of your friends, acquaintances, and people you've met in the previous action steps. Classify these people into four groups:

Adventurers are pushy, always looking for the next horizon. Adventurers must lead and be in control, even when they're wrong. They question procedures and are always creating new procedures.

Spotlighters love to talk, tell stories, amuse. They hog the spotlight. They need people and more people. They have lots of charm and are often physically attractive.

Negotiators smooth things over, make groups cohesive. They smile a lot while they are introducing Adventurers to Spotlighters. They feel best in situations where everything is nailed down by rules and regulations.

Handlers get their kicks from handling details. To a Handler there is no such thing as too much detail. They take their time assessing, studying, examining, and probing. They also take a long time to reach a decision.

Now, from each category, select one person who could help you in your small business. List three skills the person has that could help balance your entrepreneurial team. Transfer the list of skills to a separate sheet of paper. Keep your list in pencil and prepare to make adjustments as you learn more about your potential team members. The decisions you make in building your founding team are among the most important decisions you will make.

balanced team
a group of individuals with complementary skills, aptitudes, and strengths

balance sheet
a financial tool that gives you a picture of your business at one point in time

a D, you most likely lack the patience to repair broken equipment; instead, you have someone else repair it or you replace it. D's, like so many entrepreneurs, must get on with it.

But to do that, you need a balanced team. Here's how it works:

> For management, negotiations, smoothing over, you need a Compliant.
>
> For sales, advertising, promotion, anything flashy, you need an Influencer. You need someone with pizzazz and spark.
>
> For the precise tasks like accounting, engineering, computer work, operating a switchboard, you need a Steady.

DISC is not the only quadrant-oriented profiling program. There are others, and large organizations use them to help people connect in more fruitful ways. If you're coming out of a large organization into small business, you've probably had experience with one or more of these profiling systems. You're bringing a lot of skills and experience with you to the world of small business. You might not have the time for elaborate testing when you're building a team for your own business, but you can still use the insights gained from the research that has gone into shaping these systems.

This is a good time for you to practice profiling some personalities you know well by doing Action Step 57. The system we want you to use is similar to the DISC system.

An Example

Harry Marquez needed a **balanced team** and didn't know it.

> Harry was a terrible student in high school. His grades in English were rotten and he couldn't spell. To him, history was a laugh, government a lie, and science an unimaginative way of looking at the world.
>
> Harry did all right in three courses: art, physics (he liked electricity), and Latin. But you can't graduate with three strong subjects and ten weak ones, so Harry joined the Army. The Army sent him to Germany, and he quickly became invaluable as a tank repair specialist. He fixed tanks, and the Army gave him weekend passes.
>
> At the end of his tour, Harry married Liliane, a young model he'd met in Germany, and they moved to Harry's home town. Harry looked up his old physics teacher. After a lot of scrambling and maneuvering, Harry made it into a good university.
>
> There, he could choose courses he could handle, and he met an English teacher who taught him how to write. Harry finished his electrical engineering degree in 3 years. In two more, he had his doctorate. And along the way, he had discovered a field that looked hot: industrial robots.
>
> Harry landed a job with a *Fortune* 500 firm. The pay was good, but he hated the lack of freedom. When he couldn't create, his mind slowed down and he felt dead. Working at night, he developed an idea to make a two-armed robot. When he presented the idea to a vice-president, he was told that the company wasn't interested. So Harry formed his own company.
>
> He didn't know the first thing about business, but he hired a man who did. Fred Winslow had a sales background, a sincere smile, a warm handshake, and a way with words that could have made him a preacher or politician. Winslow told him the only place for this kind of firm was the Silicon Valley, so that's where they went.
>
> Harry and Liliane owned all the stock of Marquez Robotics. Their first year, they grossed just under a million. Harry loved it. He didn't understand a **balance sheet**, and talk about cash flow put him right to sleep, but he loved having money to spend.
>
> They bought a Turbo Porsche and an Eldorado. Harry had worked hard, and now that they could afford it, he wanted all the creature comforts. He also wanted stimulation, and that meant people like himself, who were loaded with ideas, people who could work through the night on a project and cap it off with a party. So Harry hired

a lot of people like himself, and lots of times the phones would ring like crazy and no one would answer them.

The second year, Winslow wanted a piece of the company, but Harry didn't want to let go. He felt it was *his* company—built with his Army money plus the money he and Liliane had saved while he was breaking his back in big business—and it was *his* two-armed robot. So Harry said no.

Then two things happened. Liliane decided she wanted a divorce, and Winslow left the company. Liliane went to San Francisco, and Winslow went down the road a half-mile and founded Winslow Electromagnetic. With him went two of Harry's key employees—both inventor–engineers, and seventeen of Harry's largest customer accounts.

One by one, the wild-and-crazy engineer–inventors left when Harry didn't have enough cash to meet his payroll. Meanwhile, Harry was busy in his lab, working night and day on an electric motor that would take the place of the hydraulic engines used in most robots.

There was no one in the front office, no one to answer the phones. The books went from bad to worse. Harry was in a race with his creditors, who would ship only with a C.O.D., but he was so involved with his new invention that he hardly noticed.

What Can Harry Marquez Teach Us?

Harry's business failed for at least two reasons. Number one, he could design great equipment, but he could not design a winning team. True, he did hire Winslow, who in many ways was his perfect complement, but Harry couldn't read the man's drives for power and control.

Number two, Harry didn't take time to listen to his employees. The people he hired did not fill real business needs. In business, that's fatal. It's important to hire good people and then listen to them. A company is no more than its people. Successful businesses of all sizes view their employees as resources.

Let's go back and try a **personality analysis** of Harry. We can say that he:

personality analysis
an enlightening way of looking at yourself and at the people around you

- was bright, creative
- was impatient with day-to-day operations
- was a dreamer
- was a quick learner, but a terrible student
- was able to fix almost anything mechanical or electrical
- liked to be surrounded by attractive people (his model wife, the people he hired)
- needed a certain amount of flash in the world (the cars he bought)
- didn't want to give up even a very small piece of his company (He felt like a proud parent.)
- didn't understand the power drives of Fred Winslow
- went back to his lab (womb, retreat from the world) when the going got tough, to perfect yet another dazzling invention

It's probably obvious to you that Harry's team needed balancing, but it wasn't obvious to him. He needed the DISC system.

THE DISC SYSTEM

Yes, Harry needed something like the DISC system to help him understand people and how people can balance each other. The DISC system, developed by John Geier, is owned by Performax Systems International. It's inexpensive and thorough, and it can give the busy entrepreneur insight and quick perspective on people. DISC takes about 25 minutes, and it's easy to analyze. Reminder:

D = Dominance
I = Influencing
S = Steadiness
C = Compliance

Look at the grid in Figure 13.2. Where would you put Harry? Where would you put Fred Winslow? See Figure 13.3.

The Right Kind of Help

top-heavy team
a team composed mostly of chiefs

The DISC grid can show at a glance where you are. Harry's was a **top-heavy team**. He didn't have anyone to handle day-to-day operations. He didn't have anyone to answer the phones. In fact, when it came to phones, Harry was the caller, not the answerer. Harry needed help, but he didn't know it. What sort of help did he need?

Janet Ames is a capable woman in her mid thirties who has two well-behaved children. When her youngest reached the age of 10, Janet went back to work.

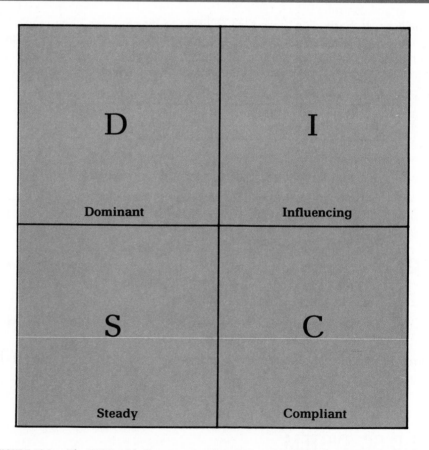

FIGURE 13.2 The DISC grid allows you to classify an individual's personality as one of four types.

FIGURE 13.3   Harry's team was top-heavy.

Janet began working for Marquez Robotics 3 weeks after the previous vice-president for marketing, a Mr. Winslow, went off with several key employees and some very influential customers.

Janet went right to work as the new vice-president for marketing. It took her just two full working days to shape up the front office. The first thing she did was to hire Rudy to handle the telephones. He was a fussy young man who kept a very tidy desk. Before noon on his first day, Rudy had established his own territory in one corner of the front office. He had his own desk, his own nameplate, and a wastepaper basket with his initials monogrammed on it in large letters. Janet liked that. It bespoke order.

Once she got the phone question settled, she began networking with her contacts for someone to straighten out the books. Janet was a good bookkeeper, but she knew a mess when she saw one, and off in the distance she could smell tax problems for her new boss. In this instance, an expert was definitely called for.

Janet saw Dr. Marquez, the president and CEO, the day she was hired, and then she didn't see him again for 11 days. Although that might have bothered someone else, it suited the very stable Mrs. Ames just fine. One of her philosophies was that it takes all kinds.

To her, Dr. Marquez and the men in the lab seemed like playful children; they needed freedom to create. If they had been real children, of course, she would have applied some well-needed discipline. But they were adults, and you don't tell adults when it's time to scrub behind their ears, especially if you are employed by them. So Janet worked hard at being diplomatic, at smoothing over rifts in the company surface, at helping and counseling and controlling.

Nine months after Janet came to work, the company was again in the black. She celebrated by hiring a young woman to help out in the front office. Her name was Sandra Star, and she wanted to be an actress. Her smile made the customers happy, and she took the office PR load off Rudy, who was promoted to Communications Chief.

Rudy spent three entire weekends personalizing his new office. With his name on the door lettered in gold, he was delighted with his new title, and he felt a renewed loyalty and devotion to Janet and the company.

Portrait of a Balanced Team

Turn to the DISC grid (Figure 13.2). We have already placed Harry as a **Dominant**. Where would you put Janet Ames? Rudy? Sandra, the secretary–receptionist?

Let's do a quick DISC analysis of Janet Ames. She:

> understands the need for control
>
> is diplomatic with everyone
>
> checks for accuracy
>
> is good at analysis, critical thinking, and sizing up situations
>
> complies with authority
>
> gets the job done
>
> likes standard operating procedures (If there aren't any, she can establish them.)
>
> enjoys being part of a group

You can see that Janet is probably a **Compliant**. Such people make good managers, and that's what Marquez Robotics needed.

Rudy Bowman, a classic **Steady**, is no slouch as a team member, either. Steadies love to sit in one place and control a very small turf. They are invaluable for specialized skills, listening, doing the books, security tasks. They get to work on time; they leave on time. Treat a Steady right and you'll be rewarded with tons of loyalty and fidelity.

Dominant
a person who shapes the environment by overcoming the opposition

Compliant
a person who works with existing circumstances to promote quality in products or services

Steady
a person who cooperates with others to carry out the task

And finally, Sandra Star, the secretary–receptionist, is an **Influencer**. She's the neon entertainment—great for the front office as long as the working conditions are favorable. A ripple or two and she'll be off to another adventure. Figure 13.4 shows the completed team picture.

Action Step 58 asks you to do some **self-analysis** and to think about the types of people that could complement your personality and skills. Think about what kinds of help you need.

Influencer
a person who shapes the environment by bringing others into alliance

self-analysis
an introspective look at your strengths and weaknesses

Another Look at the Team's Founder

Take a minute to think about the personality of Harry Marquez. Do any of his traits remind you of your own?

We can't reproduce all the DISC profiles here, but we can summarize Harry's personality briefly. Harry is a creative achiever who likes to dominate and control. In many ways, he is the typical entrepreneur:

1. *He operates from internal motivation and deeply felt goals.* Harry's main **joy in life** was to invent. He set and met his own goals and was surprised when others in the organization didn't do the same. He was unaware that some people need goals set for them. He did his work and expected everyone else to do theirs.

2. *He is bored with routine work.* Harry couldn't believe that some people actually thrive on routine tasks. People like Harry are so busy setting their own pace that they seldom look back. Under pressure, they become aggressive and competitive. They like the limelight, and when they don't get it they can get sulky.

3. *He judges others by concrete results.* Harry couldn't believe Fred Winslow wanted a piece of the company because he couldn't see that Fred had accomplished anything. To an inventor, sales is invisible and insubstantial. Money exists, but the sales and **marketing** functions of a business seem like mumbo jumbo and double-talk. From Harry's point of view, Fred Winslow never really did anything except smile and glad-hand and take customers to lunch on company time. This shows Harry's limited point of view.

4. *He is a super-quick thinker.* When he was on his own turf, Harry had the fastest feet in the business. He was inventive, and if led along the right path, he could have invented a system to handle the problems of his organization. But business matters bored Harry, so the best thing for him to do was to hire someone to manage the day-to-day affairs, negotiate, and smooth over the rough spots.

Without a balanced team, Harry Marquez would have been out of business fast. Since he didn't want to work for someone else, he would have been in trouble. Remember this: the smaller an organization is, the more important is the team. **Team building** is important.

SCOUTING AND HIRING

In Action Step 59 you use the idea of balance to scout potential team members. If you're able to imagine how each candidate would work out in your new business, you'll be well on your way to building a **winning team**. Do Action Step 59 now.

ACTION STEP 58

Brainstorm your ideal team.

What do you need to win at the game of small business? Money, of course. And energy, tremendous energy. (You've got that or you wouldn't have read this far.) You also need footwork, a terrific idea, intensity, the ability to concentrate, a sense of industry and thrift, and the curiosity of a Sherlock Holmes.

And you need people. People to support your effort. People to balance your skills. People to take up the slack. People to help you with tasks you find distasteful or don't understand.

So analyze yourself first. What do you like? What are you good at? What do you hate? What does your business need that you cannot provide yourself? Who can fill that need for you?

This one idea alone will get you started on building your ideal team.

---

joy in life
where you get your main reason for being

marketing
all the activities that take place between identification of the need for a product or service and its delivery

team building
the orderly procurement of a group of people who together can achieve maximum results for the firm

winning team
what you must build to succeed in business

FIGURE 13.4 Janet Ames instinctively hired people who balanced Harry's team.

Later, when you're hiring, try to hire the best-quality people you can find. There's wisdom in this old adage:

> If you're first rate, you hire first-rate people.
>
> If you're second rate, you hire third-rate people.
>
> If you're third rate, you hire fourth-rate people.

How long can you make it with anything but a first-rate team? With what kind of materials do you want to build your business?

In a large firm, a poorly placed employee or one who's not pulling his or her weight can be transferred to a different job. There are lots of jobs, lots of slots. If you've got a "Driver" answering phones, you can move her to R&D. If you've got a "Steady" going crazy in a leadership position, you can move him to a job that requires attention to detail. On the other hand, in a firm with only three employees, for example, one weak employee makes you 25 percent less effective. Two weak employees will cut your effectiveness in half. Choosing the right team is one of the most important decisions you will make.

A Team of Part-Timers

Charlene Webb has built a winning team of part-time employees.

> After Charlene Webb sold her gourmet cookware shop, she opened a women's specialty store. The shop is small—about 3,000 square feet—and is located in a neighborhood center in an upscale community of about 10,000 people.
>
> Charlene discovered that her ideal employees were local women who are active in the community life and who prefer to work only one day a week. Monday's help is a golfer whose country-club friends come in to visit and buy from her on her day of work. Tuesday the tennis player is on, and her friends have followed her to the store. Wednesday is the yacht club member; Thursday, a leader of hospital volunteers; Friday, a well-known club woman; and Saturday, an attorney's wife. All of them are friendly women who know a lot about fashion and have a lot of energy, because they never have a chance to tire from the routine.
>
> Charlene, who writes a society column (as free PR) in the community newspaper, has positioned herself as a social force, and many women have come to view her shop as *the one* to buy from for formal events at the country club and the nearby Ritz Carlton Hotel.
>
> Her part-time helpers are not only an effective marketing tool; they also serve as local fashion consultants. They help Charlene make wise purchasing decisions. They are valuable members of her team, and her friends as well.

Get a Mentor

If you're starting up a business for the first time, there's a good chance you need a mentor—a person who can give you advice and encouragement. Perhaps you have a mentor already. If not, how can you find such help? First, network with your friends, co-workers, and business associates. Tell them what you're looking for— that is, a successful business owner with a good track record. The perfect mentor would be one with experience in your particular segment. Second, join the Chamber of Commerce and one or more civic clubs. Third, keep your new eyes peeled for a mentor appearing on that horizon. If your community has a chapter of SCORE (Service Corps of Retired Executives), contact them to see if you can find a match.

ACTION STEP 59

Network your competitors and vendors to build a winning team.

After you've taken the time to do some research into your own personality (your strengths and weaknesses), you'll begin to get the feel for what kind of help you need in your venture.

Start with the list you made in Action Step 57. Is there anyone there who can balance some of your skills?

Now make a list of the people you know. Beside each name, make a note about where that person fits on the DISC grid.

If you're a D-intensive entrepreneur, how many more D's can you take on and still have a winning team?

Now that you have the idea of balance firmly in mind, network your vendors and your competitors for potential team members. Whenever you meet someone new, try to apply DISC (or one of the other balancing systems). Keep asking yourself: "How would this person work out in my new business?"

Keep looking for your future team with new eyes.

Once you've located some candidates, develop a set of questions and set up a meeting. You want to pick the brains of all the candidates. Here are some things to consider in selecting a mentor:

Do you feel comfortable with this person?

Can you trust him or her?

Is he (she) easy to communicate with?

Does he (she) have experience and contacts that can help your new business?

Once you've made your choice and the person has agreed to help you, keep in close contact. See the person at least once a month, and use phone calls to smooth out rough spots. Your mentor may be able to help you establish banking connections and vendor–supplier relationships. A good mentor can be invaluable for checking your leases and contracts.

Here's a story that illustrates the kinds of assistance mentors can provide.

> Dick Knox is the proud owner of a 7-year-old, three-million-dollar company, Personal Computers, Inc. Dick started selling from his garage and moved to a warehouse facility. Filling a gap left by IBM, he sells personal computers in an office environment, with full-service follow-up to every customer. Dick's training was in computer programming. He had the energy but not the knowledge to start up a small business, so he kept his eyes open for a mentor.
>
> Enter Bob Redman. Bob's computer programming firm had just been purchased by a *Fortune* 500 company. The deal required that Bob stay on for 2 years as president. He wasn't happy in this role, so when Dick approached him with the mentor offer, he jumped at it. He loved being associated with a start-up, and the day he left his president's chair he was ready to step into his own business—a five-person computer consulting firm. [Mentoring works both ways, you see. Dick gave Bob a new angle on a tired life; Bob gave Dick almost a million dollars in sales leads.]
>
> Dick's second mentor was Mickey McCarthy, a wild and crazy entrepreneur who had sold his last venture for forty million dollars. Mickey was tired. Starting businesses took energy and he was ready to retire to a cottage in the mountains. Before he packed his bags, however, he agreed to be a mentor to Dick.
>
> A month later, Dick was having cash-flow problems. He was meeting payroll but had not taken a salary himself for 3 months. The cupboard was bare, and Dick had lost 8 pounds.
>
> Over the next couple months, Mickey worked with Dick on a complete Business Plan/bank package with projections for the next 5 years. These projections in hand, Dick met with Mickey's banker. Three weeks later, he had a credit line of $100,000 and the provision that he could expand it to $300,000 when he needed it.

With mentors like Bob and Mickey, how could Dick lose?

INTERNAL UNDERSTANDING MAKES A STRONGER TEAM

Many bright, intelligent, energetic entrepreneurs lack self-knowledge. One such entrepreneur was E. G. Bogard, a world-beater, CEO, and adventurer whose business was growing beyond the world of small business. Bogard had come up the hard way—a one-man shop, a disastrous partnership, a small corporation. As we arrive on the scene, the growth of Bogard's company threatens to undermine his spectacular success. He has no idea how to handle it. He can barely admit there's a problem, and the problem is with himself.

E. G. Bogard's corporate family didn't understand him. If they had, they would have known better than to waste his valuable time.

Bogard was a self-made man. He'd started 14 years earlier in his garage workshop in Skokie, and this year his Chicago manufacturing firm, which employed 200 people, was about to gross $17 million.

In his industry, Bogard had a reputation for running a **lean operation**. Three of his toughest competitors had gone down during the last recession, but Bogard had not only stayed afloat, he'd managed to make a profit by trimming fat. By laying off employees and giving minimal raises, Bogard trimmed selling costs by 7 percent in one year.

Inc. magazine wrote him up as "Jack Sprat Bogard: The CEO with the Seven per Cent Solution," but the article hadn't done much to help internal understanding. Just yesterday, the **executive committee** had come in with a recommendation about company cars, company blazers, and all-expenses-paid trips to Hawaii—and it had taken them six pages, single-spaced, to get their message across.

Bogard hated waste.

Bogard was thinking about firing the lot when he went off for his regular Thursday game of handball. That was one ritual he never missed. His opponent was Maury Applebaum. Maury was in advertising, a dozen years younger than Bogard, and the only fellow around who could give Bogard a game. Bogard was ferocious that day. He took three straight games. After the match, Maury asked him what was going on.

"It's nothing," Bogard snapped.

"Hey. Come on, E. G. This is Maury, remember? You were crazy out there today. You were wild."

"It's nothing," Bogard said.

But finally, over his one beer for the day, Bogard admitted what was going on. "It's my gang at the plant," he said. "They don't understand me. Maybe it's time to cash out and spend my days on the beach in Miami."

"You wouldn't last a week," Maury said.

"Probably not," Bogard said. "But lately I just can't seem to communicate to my people."

"I may have an answer for you," Maury said. "Can you give me half an hour tomorrow morning?"

"Where would I find a half-hour?"

"Fifteen minutes, then."

Reluctantly, Bogard agreed.

The next morning, Maury Applebaum arrived, accompanied by a woman named Mary White, an intelligent, no-nonsense person. Mary took one look at E. G. Bogard's desk—the high D's **paper jungle**—and went right to work.

"Mr. Bogard, I realize you're a busy man, so we'll get right to it. This is a **measurement tool** that can increase communication inside your company." Mary held out a light-blue folder. Bogard eyed it with suspicion.

"How long?" he asked. "And how much?"

"Fifteen minutes," she answered. "Eight dollars."

Bogard gave her a flinty smile. "Time me, Maury," he said, and dove into the folder.

The pale-blue folder contained a personality measuring tool called DISC. Bogard turned out to be high in D (Dominance), low on I (Influencing others), medium high on S (Steady) and very low on C (Compliance).

His personality was categorized as "Developer." A breakdown of the Developer traits showed:

Strong individuality

Self-reliance

Bypasses convention, comes up with innovative solutions

Forceful behavior

Can be shrewd at manipulating people and situations

lean operation
using the talents of a very few hard-working people to achieve business objectives

executive committee
advisers to the chief executive

paper jungle
the mark of a Dominant person on the DISC scale

measurement tool
any device that allows management to assess productivity

Hates boredom most of all

Lacks empathy

Wants to get things done

"Hey," Bogard said, "that's *me!*"

Mary smiled at Maury, who pointed at his watch. More than 30 minutes had passed since Bogard had begun his profile, but the CEO, intent on the DISC instrument, hadn't noticed.

He looked up. "How soon can we get a couple hundred of these?" he asked. "I want to shoot them down to my people."

"How about Monday?" she said.

"How about this afternoon. I'll have the comptroller issue a check now." Bogard reached for the phone.

Almost all Bogard's employees were delighted with the **profiling system**. At first, a few people felt threatened, but taking the test proved to be fun, and when the employees began to compare notes, they reached insights about themselves and others.

The best thing to come out of the experience was a new understanding of the boss. All memos were now triple-spaced, short, and easy to read. The memos actually felt lean.

Bogard was happy. He was no longer misunderstood. He knew his family, and they knew him. There were still differences among people—nothing can do away with that—but somehow, everyone was working together with a lot more efficiency.

profiling system
a system that measures differences between people

GETTING HELP

If you are an entrepreneur, you like to move fast. You want quick answers and quick action. You've studied the marketplace. You've found your market niche. You didn't think you'd need much of a team, but now you're growing so quickly that you have to do some team building. You're an entrepreneur, so you want to move fast building this team. To do so, you must need a key to human behavior. You want people who can help you, not hurt you, because evey person counts in small business. A test—called an assessment instrument in the training field—might help you locate the key that unlocks the door that leads to the room where your team awaits.

We would like to point out that the search for the key to human behavior is not a recent phenomenon. In the earliest civilizations, astrologers and star-gazers tried to explain human behavior based on the four elements: earth, air, fire, and water. In the fourth century, B.C., Hippocrates, who gave us the Hippocratic Oath, kept the four-part framework developed by the astrologers but changed the labels: choleric, phlegmatic, sanguine, and melancholic.

The four-part grid continued on into the Middle Ages, where physicians treated patients based on which of the Four Humours—blood, phlegm, choler, and black bile—dominated the bloodstream.

In the 20th century, Carl Jung left us with his Big Four—feeler, thinker, sensor, intuitor—and then William Marston gave us the basis for the DISC scale with his four: dominance, inducement of others, steadiness, and compliance.

As the century comes to a close, we find other behaviorists renaming the quadrants again, calling them driver, expressive, amiable, and analytical. Or, again, controller, organizer, analyzer, and persuader.

Our device is to leave the name-calling to the experts and to get help building your team. If you are an entrepreneur, there's a good chance you are either a Dominant Driver-Controller or an Expressive Inducer-Persuader. In either case, you're busy leading and charging, so you need help with details and organization. Find a simple test. Take it yourself. Use it to build your team. It might slow you down before you hurtle into a skid.

Think of these sources for help:

1. The counseling-testing center of your local community college.
2. The Yellow Pages. Look under Training.
3. A book called *Tests in Print,* published by Buros (Lincoln, Nebraska), and updated each year in *Mental Measurement Yearbook,* also published by Buros. See the reference section for a complete listing.

Now it's your turn. Action Step 60 is to be completed once you have built your team. It's your chance to brainstorm for ways to win. Make the most of all the creative human resources you've just brought on board! We think this action step is a great way to end this chapter on team building, and a great way to start your new business.

Key Points from Another View
Part I
BUILDING A WINNING TEAM

A. Winning teams have six basic characteristics in common:
   1. Players focus on a common purpose.
   2. In addition to the larger purpose, players share smaller, specific goals.
   3. Winning teams keep score.
   4. Winning teams share the rewards of success.
   5. Every players knows his or her role and how to play that role to perfection.
   6. Every player is expected to be involved in winning all the time.

B. Creating a Winning Environment. You must create an environment where your employees—your players—can develop the characteristics of a winning team. Here are some suggestions:
   1. Clearly define the mission of your business.
   2. Make sure every employee understands the mission.
      a. Prepare a written statement of your business mission and distribute it to your employees.
      b. Develop a motto and post it everywhere.
      c. Live the mission.
   3. Develop specific goals—you should identify five to ten measurable areas of performance that are critical for achieving your business mission. To identify these areas, do the following:
      a. Review your mission statement—break into specific, measurable areas of performance.
      b. Make a list of your competitors or potential competitors.
      c. Set long-term goals to beat your competition.
   4. Develop and implement a scorekeeping system.
   5. Make performance matter by sharing the rewards.
   6. Make sure employees understand their roles and have a chance to become involved in improving performance.

From: Fran Tarkenton and Joseph H. Boyett, "The Competitive Edge—Winning Strategies from a Pro—Building a Winning Team" *Entrepreneur,* May, 1989, 14–21.

ACTION STEP 60

Tap your people resources by brainstorming with your team.

Before you sign a lease, go into the hole for $50,000 worth of equipment, hire a lot of people, or spend $2,000 for six-line telephone service, get your new team together and brainstorm the organization and objectives of your new business. A blackboard is a handy tool here, so that everyone can follow the track of the session. One way to begin is to ask every member of your team to write down what they believe would be good objectives for the business.

You've found some good people, and it's taken some hard work. Make that work pay off by tapping your human resources. Brainstorming will get you going. You'll be surprised at what develops.

If you have trouble narrowing down after the ideas start flowing, go back and review the seven-step procedure in Chapter 3.

Part II
THE OUTSIDERS

Despite the dangers inherent in the outside contractor arrangement, for many entrepreneurs it means the difference between gaining new business and flat growth.

I.   An Irresistible Lure—the trick to being successful is to understand all the issues involved.

  A.   There is a good chance to be successful in using outsiders when the work is a self-contained entity and not part of an ongoing project.

  B.   The key to achieving results is to structure the job carefully ahead of time.

  C.   By putting your objectives in writing and communicating them fully, you set the stage for success.

  D.   Rather than settle on an in-house jack-of-all-trades/master-of-none to fulfill a variety of functions, you can pick and choose who best satisfies a need and then contract out that specific work.

  E.   You eliminate all the cost associated with having an employee, from vacation pay to Social Security.

II. Handle with Care

  A.   The flip side of the flexibility to hire and fire on demand is the lack of control.

  B.   Another problem with relying on outsiders is that they're not always available when you want them.

  C.   A business's greatest risk is in the area of payroll taxes; the IRS is closely scrutinizing who really qualifies.

III. Play It Safe

  A.   A worker is considered an employee if he/she meets all the following criteria:

    1.   He/she must comply with your detailed directions about when, where, and how to work.

    2.   It is necessary to provide training before he/she can perform their duties.

    3.   You have established a prolonged, ongoing relationship.

    4.   He/she is required to devote all their work time to your operation rather than accept additional clients.

    5.   He/she is paid exactly like your other staff.

    6.   He/she must use your tools or materials rather than bringing supplies.

    7.   You want him/her working within your range of vision—at your place of business.

    8.   He/she needs to have their performance periodically checked as the job progresses.

  B.   The key to whether someone is your employee or an outside contractor revolves around job control. If you have it, you're the boss.

  C.   You should formally draw up a letter of engagement spelling out in detail the exact nature of the contractor relationship.

IV. Showing Proper Form

  A.   Once you hire an independent contractor, you are required to fill out two tax forms by February 28th of the following year.

1. 1099-Misc. (Statement for Recipients of Miscellaneous Income), is sent by the business to every independent whose fee totaled $600.00 or more.

2. A copy is also sent to the IRS, accompanied by Form 1096 (Annual Summary and Transmittal of U.S. Information Returns).

B. The choice of whether or not to use an outside contractor is not always easy, but whatever you decide, make sure it's legal and prudent, or what began as a cost-effective measure could end up costing a bundle.

From: Janine S. Pouliot, "Management Smarts—The Outsiders," *Entrepreneurial Woman,* April, 1991, 12–15.

SUMMARY

It's fun being an entrepreneur. You're on your own, doing your own thing, running your own show. And one of the toughest things you have to admit is that you can't perform all business tasks with the same success. This chapter helps you focus on what you can do and where you need help.

This chapter provides tools to help you learn more about yourself and how you relate to people. One tool is the DISC Personality Profile. We like DISC because it is relatively inexpensive and quick to take. Once you've spent 20–30 minutes with it, insights begin to flow, and there's enough explanatory material to guide you through your own interpretation. If you don't like the DISC system, others are available.

Another tool is the concept of balance. You want to construct a team in which people's skills and personalities are complementary. The case studies of Harry Marquez and Janet Ames illustrate the way different personality types can balance each other. Harry, a typical entrepreneur, is energetic, creative, forceful, single-minded, and impatient with detail. Janet, an excellent manager, is calm, organized, supportive, and patient. She plans well and will see to it that the bills are paid and the phones answered.

We touch on how to scout and hire the members of your team and stress the importance of internal understanding for a stronger team.

Balance, proportion, the right materials, and the structural forces of personality—all of these are important in building a winning team.

THINK POINTS FOR SUCCESS

◤ People tend to "hire themselves." How many more like you can the business take?

◤ A winning team is lurking in your network.

◤ Look to your competitors and vendors for team members.

◤ Your company is *people*.

◤ Balance the people on your team.

◤ Have each team member write objectives for his or her responsibilities within the business. Set up your own internal **MBO** (management by objectives) system.

◤ You can't grow until you have the right people.

◤ How much of your team can be built of part-timers and moonlighters?

ACTION STEP REVIEW

No matter what personality type you are, four action steps get you into the spirit of creative team building:

57 Look at the people you know and categorize them by their personalities.

58 Brainstorm your ideal team. What kind of help do you need to win at the game of small business?

59 Network your competitors and vendors for team members. It's time to try to make that ideal team reality.

60 After you've assembled a winning team, set aside a couple of hours to brainstorm ways you're going to win.

MBO
establishing measurable objectives for a specified time period

REFERENCES

Alessandra, Anthony, et al. *Non-Manipulative Selling,* second edition. Englewood Cliffs, N.J.: Prentice-Hall, 1987.

Benson, Benjamin, and Edwin T. Crego. *Your Family Business: A Success Guide for Growth and Survival.* Homewood, Ill.: Business One Irwin, 1989.

Bucholz, Barbara, and Margaret Crane. *Corporate Bloodlines: The Future of the Family Firm.* New York: Carol Publishing Group, 1989.

"Business Week Newsletter for Family-Owned Business." (202) 463-1611.

Case, John. "The Knowledge Factory," *Inc.,* October, 1991, 54–59. [An excellent article on building a team by sharing numbers.]

Center for Family Business, P.O. Box 24268, Cleveland, OH 44124.

Conoley, Jane C., and Jack L. Kramer, eds. *The Tenth Mental Measurements Yearbook.* Lincoln, Nebr.: Buros Institute of Mental Measurements, 1989. [Critiques vocational, personality, and similar tests used in hiring and promoting.]

Feingold, S. Norman, and Leonard G. Perlman. "A Quiz for Would-Be Entrepreneurs." *Nation's Business,* March, 1986, 26.

Goleman, Daniel. "The Psyche of the Entrepreneur." *New York Times Magazine,* February 2, 1986, 30.

Jaffe, Dennis. *Working with the Ones You Love: Strategies for a Successful Family Business.* Berkeley, Calif.: Conari Press, 1991.

Keirsey, David, and Marilyn Bates. *Please Understand Me: Character and Temperament Types.* Del Mar, Calif.: Prometheus Nemesis Book Co., 1990.

Nelton, Sharon. *In Love and in Business: How Entrepreneurial Couples are Changing the Rules of Business and Marriage.* New York: Wiley, 1986.

Peters, Thomas J., and Nancy K. Peters. *A Passion for Excellence: The Leadership Difference.* New York: Random House, 1985.

Peters, Tom. *Thriving on Chaos: Handbook for a Management Revolution.* New York: Knopf, 1987.

Peters, Thomas J., and Robert H. Waterman, Jr. *In Search of Excellence: Lessons from America's Best-Run Companies.* New York: Harper Collins, 1988. [Not really in the area of small business, but has good advice for every business on action, autonomy, the customer, running lean, and so on.]

"Problems in Managing a Family-Owned Business," U.S. Small Business Administration, Order No. MP 3.

Steck, Robert N. "Why New Businesses Fail: A Conversation with Peter Drucker." *D&B Reports,* November–December 1985, 35.

Tannen, Deborah. *You Just Don't Understand: Men and Women in Conversation.* New York: Ballantine Books, 1991.

NOTES

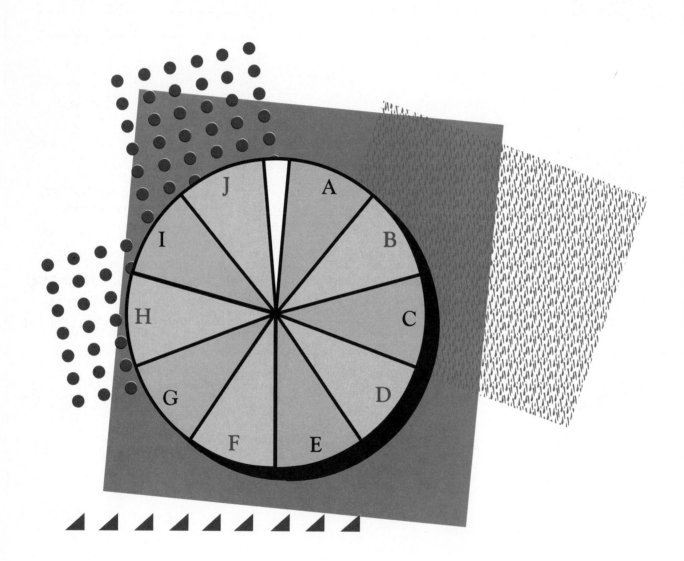

FIGURE 14.1
Chapter 14 will acquaint you with ways the computer can help you plan and manage your small business.

14 The Entrepreneur's Toolkit

Learning Objectives

- To determine how badly you need a computer for your small business.
- To identify tasks in your business that can be done better with the aid of a computer.
- To become aware of what is going on in the computer industry and how it affects your selection of a small-business system.
- To know what questions to ask, and to distinguish between who wants to help you and who is out to take your money and run.
- To learn reliable sources of information about what is happening in information processing.
- To resolve to keep learning about computers, even if the speed at which they change makes you dizzy.

FUTURE FOCUS

Know your needs and the tools of the trade. Computers, phones, office/car appliances all beckon. You can blow all your money if you are not careful. Stay flexible. Keep your sights on the 21st century. The right tools can help propel you there.

T his chapter will help you investigate the tools you will need for operating and controlling your new and growing business. The entrepreneur's toolkit must also be adequate to accommodate changing customer needs. For example, to prosper in the Information Age, businesses are using the telephone for more than conversation; many customers want to send orders on fax machines, leave messages on answering machines, and send data via computer modem.

Your toolkit may need to include a laptop computer, a cash register, a "one-write" bookkeeping system (see Appendix A), and special equipment unique to your type of business. The most important item in your toolkit, however, will probably be a computer.

INVENTORY YOUR TOOLKIT

computer
a machine that processes information

Throughout this book, we have encouraged you to use your head. "Think," we say. "Plan, plan, plan. Make a list. Get out a pencil and paper and do a mind map. Before you plunge into the marketplace, use your new eyes. Before you design the machine to build your product, profile your target customer. Before you sign a lease, play marketplace detective and check out the neighborhood. Brainstorm. Do interviews. Ask questions. Make a list. Make a chart. Make another list."

The reason for this advice is simple: the road to success is in your mind, so to reach success, you need to use your mind. Your most basic tools are pencils and lots of paper, of course, but a computer also is helpful. Later in this chapter we'll lead you through the process of selecting a computer for your small business. For right now, however, take stock of the tools you have already used in exploring small business by doing Action Step 61. Figure 14.2 may help you.

ACTION STEP 61

List the tools that have been helpful to you in planning your business.

Beginning with the simplest tools— that is, pencil and paper—make a list or a mind map of the tools you already have in your toolkit. For example, you might list the future wheel, the life-cycle yardstick, matrixes, the customer profile, the profit profile, and the market-position ladder that exists in your target customer's mind. If you use a mind map, your evolving list might look like Figure 14.2. We started by putting the word *toolkit* in the center, and then branched out from there. One branch leads to the future wheel, which leads to the cocooning trend, which leads to home-based business. If you operate a business from your home, your problem will be that of reaching out to connect with customers. In that event, your toolkit might need to include a telephone, a pegboard bookkeeping system, a computer, a modem, and a printer. If you have an office in your home, you might need a copy machine, a fax machine, and a postage meter.

So brainstorm your toolkit. What do you need for your small business, and how much will it cost? Make *yet another* list.

COMPUTERS AND SMALL BUSINESS

The Computer as a Symbol

In his book *The Third Wave*, futurist Alvin Toffler writes about the shift we're making, as a nation and as a people, from the Industrial Age to the Information Age.

The First Wave, Toffler says, was agriculture: farms, livestock, harvest. The Second Wave was industry: machinery, smokestacks, factories, robber barons. The Third Wave is electronic; that is, the Age of Information is based on the pulsing beat of the computer. The Third Wave has come about relatively quickly; whereas the shift from agriculture to industry took at least one hundred years, the shift from industry to the Information Society has taken place in a few lightning-fast years.

The Third Wave is symbolized by the **computer**, a machine that has already reorganized our lives and our minds. If you have a digital watch, you're computerized. If you drive a new car, you're computerized. When you receive a phone bill, a light bill, or a personalized letter you know went to a million other folks, you've been computerized.

The computer is quiet, unidirectional, unemotional, tireless, error-free. And it's here to stay.

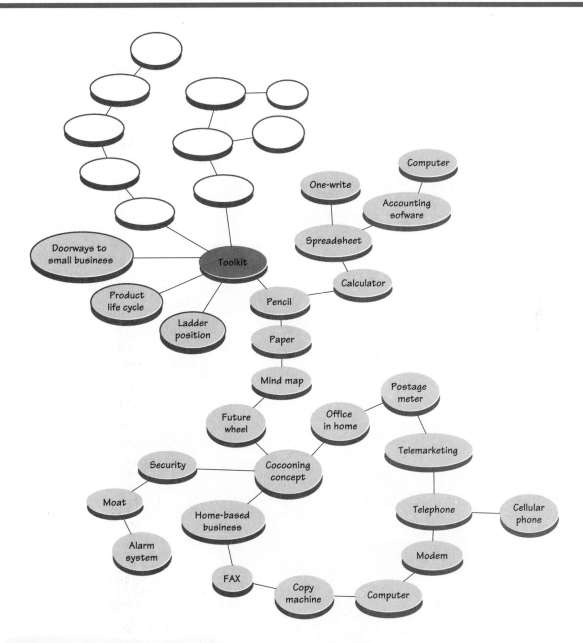

FIGURE 14.2   **Mind map of small business tools. See Action Step 61.**

The Computer as a Tool

The **microcomputer** seems to have been created especially for the entrepreneur. The right micro, with the right software, can make all the difference in the world in your small business. It can become an electronic extension of your mind and personality. It will take orders, handle details, print while you're doing something else, do your filing, cross-check files, probe the future of profit and cash flow, print payroll checks, and put you in touch with business information that will help you survive (Figure 14.3).

microcomputer
a desk-top information processor that has sparked an entire industry

FIGURE 14.3 The microcomputer seems to have been created especially for the entrepreneur.

The micro is amazing. It sits on a table, or desk, or your lap. It doesn't cost an arm and a leg. If it needs moving, you can move it. It can handle any repetitious detail in your business and thus leave your hands and your head free for entrepreneurial creativity. It will do accounting, word-processing, **general ledger,** mailing lists, customer (patient, client, student) files, flyers, inventory control, newsletters, memos, and so on.

> **general ledger**
> a master collection of all accounting transactions

The mark of an entrepreneur is fast footwork. The reason you can succeed is not because your advertising budget can compete with the hefty purses of Madison Avenue. The reason is because you can spot an opportunity and get tooled up to deliver faster than the big guys can. And with a micro on your desk, you can be even quicker.

Where to Begin

The computer selection process consists of three steps:

1. First, identify problems that need solving and tasks you want done.
2. Next, locate software programs that will solve the problems and do the tasks.
3. Finally, find hardware that will:
   a. accommodate the software,
   b. keep you happy punching keys and studying the screen, and
   c. not shatter your pocketbook.

Before and After

If you talk to successful entrepreneurs who have computerized their small businesses, you soon learn that a business itself may tell the entrepreneur why the business needs a computer. The information is after the fact. Business owners often kick themselves for not acting sooner—and with more strategic planning. You may be able to learn from the entrepreneurs in the following case studies and avert the marketplace crises that forced them to rush into computerization.

ARLENE JAMESON—PROPERTY MANAGEMENT

"The reason we finally decided to computerize was because the business was exploding. We'd started it 4 years earlier—just my husband and myself, doing property management—working out of our home. As we expanded, we bought a trailer that we'd park at construction sites. Then we hired someone and bought another trailer, and by the fourth year we knew we'd either have to find a way to control the business or stop writing management contracts. We could tell we were at a decision crossroads in our business.

"So we consulted a **computer consultant.** He told us what kind of software we needed, and what kind of hardware would go best with the software, and we got our system.

> **computer consultant**
> a specialist who can help you solve problems with the computer

"For 2 weeks, I almost went crazy learning it. Converting our books was the hardest part. It took me three months, and all that time I was still doing books manually, with a pencil and a calculator.

"Now that I understand the electronic spreadsheet method, I'll never go back to the old way. Computers saved our business."

PAUL TAKAHASHI—CONSULTANT

"I had $500 in the bank when I was laid off. Like a lot of guys in that position, I went into the consulting business. After I'd been in business about a year, I knew I wasn't going to survive if I didn't get some help, especially with the repetitive parts of my business. That means numbers, of course, keeping the records straight. But it also means newsletters, flyers, printed invoices, and such things as that all-important letter that I'd been meaning to revise that was sitting there, in the typewriter, waiting.

> **cross-filing**
> a reference system in which information is listed by two or more categories

ACTION STEP 62

Identify your problems and tasks.

Take a minute to list some problems and tasks in your small business. Think first about *repetition*. What things do you do over and over? Think next about *detail*. What do you do that has to be precise? Think next about monitoring *time*. Where are the time lags in your business, and how can they be tracked? Accuracy and efficiency are the computer's main contributions, you see.

Use these questions to trigger your thoughts:

1. What are the demographic characteristics of your ten top customers? The top 20? The top 100?

2. Is there a time lag between a sale and when you bill the customer?

3. Do you pay overtime? Do you pay hourly overtime to salaried employees?

4. Do you have a list of your most active customers and another list of customers who make fewer purchases but who are still important to your business?

5. Would you like to update your profit and loss statement without having to consult your accountant?

6. Do you have trouble managing inventory?

7. Do you have 100 or more vendors? Does your buying produce more than 100 purchase orders per month?

8. Do you write more than 100 checks per month?

9. Would you like to do your own spreadsheet analysis so that you can get your financial picture on your own?

10. When you update your Business Plan, would you like to be able to change a few numbers and have the new version printed while you're doing something else?

11. Do you write the same business letter to several customers?

12. Would you like to be able to coordinate your customer mailing list with a program that corrects your typos and spelling errors?

"Well, the computer did all that, and more. I couldn't have survived without it. It gives my one-man show the capabilities of a much larger outfit."

RON TERKEL—INSURANCE AGENT

"The thing that sold me on computers was a file program called the Data Factory.

"I'm an independent insurance agent, and one of the problems we have is **cross-filing**. We've got at least twenty different categories of claims and an incredible variety of possible adjustments. Sometimes it takes hours for my staff to locate vital information.

"Well, with this computer system, backed up by the Data Factory, we can search from one file to another. It's great. It's like having X-ray vision and being able to see through a hundred manila folders all at once. Now that we're on the system, I don't know how we ever did without it."

JIM WINNER—TOY CROSSROADS

The toy business had been flat for 3 years, and new competition had come into town. Through a lot of hustle Jim was able to keep his sales about level, but because of increasing costs, his profits slipped.

Finally, Jim computerized last year, and it made a big difference. The smile on Jim's face after the winter holiday season was ear-to-ear. When asked why, Jim explained, "Our sales were down for the year but profits were the highest in our history. We ran out of inventory on several popular items the day before Christmas. With the new computer system, my buying skills improved 110 percent. The system tells me quickly how a new toy is doing, and I just increase, decrease, or cancel orders accordingly. End result: less inventory to sell at reduced prices, and fewer dollars tied up in inventory. It was a great year. You know, it's still fun to be in the toy business."

Action Step 62 will help you take the first step toward computerization. It asks you to list problems and tasks in your business. The list of questions will help you focus on your business's needs.

HOW TO SHOP FOR A MICROCOMPUTER

Gather Information

Once you have identified the tasks you need help with and the problems you want to solve, you are ready to learn more about available **computer systems**. A computer system is composed of hardware and the software to make it go. Think back to the three steps. Remember that you need to focus on software first. This may seem strange to you. Just remember, every machine in the marketplace is limited in the kinds of software it can use. If you go out shopping for hardware before you have identified what software will be best for you, you're putting the cart before the horse.

To make the best decision, you must have information, and one of the best places to get it is the very marketplace where salespeople are pushing computer systems. (See Box 14.1.)

Mentally Prepare Yourself

We're going to help you prepare for your first visit to a computer systems store by having you imagine yourself in a scenario. The action takes place in a large computer emporium, and you are just beginning to investigate computer systems.

> SALESPERSON: How can I help you?
> YOU: I'm looking for a computer system.
> SALES: You've come to the right place, dude. What capabilities do you want?

YOU: Well, I'm in business for myself. I've got a PC at home, a Sperry that I love, but I want to upgrade. I think I want a 486/33 with 8 megabytes of **RAM**. I want to run **Windows** and it takes 4 megs, which doesn't leave me much left over to run **CAD**.

SALES: For that, man, you'll need 16 megs.

YOU: No kidding?

SALES: This new software, we call it the Memory Hog. It gobbles memory. Want to walk over here? Micro-Batics has this deal going.

[The salesperson leads you to a desk loaded with computer equipment. You sit at the screen. Your monitor is black and white. This one is colored, very jazzy.]

SALES: This is the Micro-Batics Vision Saver, easy on the eyes, with a built-in screen to protect sensitive vision. Windows comes bundled on. It's basically your one-button system now. Just lock onto an icon with the mouse and it goes.

YOU: How much RAM in this one?

SALES: Sixteen megs, like the one we're talking for you.

YOU: Micro-Batics. I never heard of them.

SALES: You will.

YOU: What happened to some of the old established names? Kaypro, for example.

SALES: My Uncle Chuck had a Kaypro. I was just a kid.

YOU: What do you use?

SALES: I'm packing a Mac, man. I'd recommend it to you, but you seem hooked on an IBM clone.

YOU: What is this going to set me back?

[Whipping out a calculator powered by light, the salesperson taps in numbers. Surprise: the total figure for a complete system is one-third the price you paid 3 years ago for a system with less capability. This one has more RAM and a 200 megabyte hard drive. It's faster and runs a whole load of games. In computers, at least, you're getting more for your money.]

YOU: Is there training?

SALES: We're always here, dude. But with Windows and what goes with it, you've got built-in help. It practically teaches you how to use it. You want help, just pull down the menu and select Help. You want answers, just call the 800 number.

[After haggling a while, you buy the system. The salesperson throws in two boxes of diskettes and a package of paper for your new laser printer. Leaving the computer store, you feel you have linked up, not only with the Information Age, but also with the future.]

RAM
an acronym for Random Access Memory

Windows
a graphical user interface that runs on top of DOS

CAD
an acronym for Computer Aided Design

BOX 14.1   Free Help and Information

You can find lots of free offers of help and small business information in the ads in your local newspaper and *The Wall Street Journal*. The ads are placed by firms that have something to sell, but almost all companies are willing to give help and advice to gain customers. Hunt through the ads for the information you need.

Computers have changed, but computer salespersons stay the same. Remember, you're not buying hardware. You're buying a link to the Information Age. Your job is to shop for solutions to problems in business.

If you need information before buying a computer, you have a couple of choices. One, you can read books and magazines. Two, you can hire a computer consultant, who will help you develop a Needs List. The field changes so fast that there's no hope of keeping up. By the time this book gets into print, another sweeping change will have altered the face of the computer industry. For instance, they're already talking about an Intel 80586 superchip running above 50 megaherz. This one will be designed for voice control. It's like having the command deck of Captain Kirk's starship, *The Enterprise,* on your desk.

Before You Buy a Microcomputer

If you have found a computer system (software and hardware) that seems right for you, no doubt you're eager to test-drive your micro. Before you close the sale, however, we want to give you a little advice.

software cost
ideally, at least 50 percent of the total system budget

1. Think problem first, software second, hardware third.   Invest a lot of time listing your problems and tasks. Invest a lot more locating software that will do the job. Work those computer salespeople. Read the trade magazine evaluations.

2. Don't buy for forever.   Once you've identified your immediate needs, buy a system for the next 18 months or so, but make sure it's expandable. This is the Age of Information, and the computer will change your life; a fancier system with more bells, more whistles, and more power is already on its way from some new Silicon Valley somewhere.

3. Expand, expand, expand.   Buy a system you can expand. Research the components you might need at some future date (things like printer and modem), and then check each system for the ports you plug into and the possibilities for upgrading when you need more power.

4. Buy locally, from a reputable dealer; you get what you pay for.   If it's your first computer system, buy from a local dealer who will throw in training, support, service, and hand-holding. During the first 200 hours of initiation into the World of Computers, the hand-holding is essential. (It's true—you can get some good deals out there, price-wise. But a dealer who's pulling in business with loss leaders is not going to help out when your computer says SYNTAX ERROR CAN'T READ DRIVE ONE NO FILE OPEN. Because you're in business, you don't want to be asking your computer for favors. Remember the movie *2001*? "Open the pod door, Hal.")

5. Hire a consultant.   If this is your first system, you can save yourself lots of grief by hiring a computer consultant. A good consultant will help you identify what your problems are and how to solve them. Get references.

6. Budget for software.   Budget at least 50 percent of your total system cost for **software cost**. The right software means the difference between happiness and despair.

7. Experience pays; innocence hurts.   After you've learned thoroughly what your system can do, then you can start shopping around for discount software in the mail-order market. But remember, with mail-order shopping you are on your own and without dealer support, so be careful.

8. Educate yourself.   Keep taking computer classes. Knowledge will keep you on the leading edge.

Learning from Others' Mistakes

Fortunately, we learn things from our mistakes. Nonetheless, what's even better than learning from our mistakes is learning from the mistakes *others* make. That's why we think you'll appreciate this true story about a *Fortune* 500 company. Remember, you as a small business operator have the opportunity to be more astute than many of the big guys. Big does not mean smart.

In the early seventies, just before the great computer boom, the management of a well-known *Fortune* 500 company decided to make the transformation from caveman bookkeeping to computer bookkeeping. They bought a mainframe plus terminals for all of their telephone order clerks.

The caveman method was characterized by primitive tools: pencils, paper, carboned order forms, typewriters, and an intricate network of grey tunnels (or chutes). The tunnels were about three inches in diameter, and they connected departments with other departments in the corporate headquarters building. The order clerks would place the order forms inside message cylinders, snap the little metal doors shut, and then insert the cylinders into an entry port, from where they would be whisked away by air pressure.

Exciting.

Because of **bureaucratic lag**, it took several months of negotiation and research before management could agree on the best replacement for the system of grey tunnels. The system that was finally chosen, a combination in-house mainframe computer with peripherals from other *Fortune* 500 giants, was magnificent.

"This system, without a doubt, will serve our firm until at least 1990," said one of the top managers.

"Yes," said another manager, "and perhaps beyond."

"Agreed," intoned a third. "The system has great capacity. We'll interface with markets everywhere. For us, it's perfect."

At the end of the first week, everyone was delighted with the system. Furthermore, everyone was using it like crazy because it was so useful, and so fast.

During the second week, the system was showing signs of overload. People were having to stand in line to use it. They had discovered the computer could save them time, which they could use for phone calls, conferences, and thinking.

By the end of the third week, the system was overloaded beyond its capacity.

Moral: Even if you're a big hitter, the computer will change your life in ways you never imagined. Buy a system you can expand.

> **bureaucratic lag**
> the span of time in the corporate world when things should get done (but often do not, which drives entrepreneurs crazy)

Some Final Thoughts

The microcomputer can help you complete your Business Plan in two ways. (1) If you create your Plan on a word processor, you'll be able to make changes easily, and (2) if you use an electronic spreadsheet, you will be able to speed up your financial projections. The sample Business Plan in Chapter 16 contains several financial statements generated using an electronic spreadsheet.

As we end this chapter on microcomputers, we want to refer you to one of the best places to learn the latest trends in the fast-moving microcomputer field: the yearly Comdex trade show. Comdex shows are announced in *The Wall Street Journal* and other national business and computer publications, and usually are held in the fall.

Key Points from Another View
Part I
CHANGING THE WAY WE DO BUSINESS

Computerizing small business has increased productivity, reduced overhead, and opened the doors to many new and exciting opportunities.

Even in the smallest firm, do-it-yourself fliers, graphics, newsletters, invitations, slide shows, and menus are all in a day's work . . . with a PC.

Computerization offers something for everyone—no matter what the industry.

For example, computerized retailers, armed with detailed purchasing knowledge of what each customer purchases—item, color, size, cost, frequency—can do a better job of planning their product orders. The ability to track inventory instantly with point-of-sale software is probably the biggest advantage to retailers.

Computers have allowed service entrepreneurs to do their work faster, better, and smarter. A fast-food restaurant, for example, can use innovations to turn itself into a high-tech eatery. Employees use hand-held computers to take orders in a drive-through line. Machines dispense beverages. Cash registers transmit food orders to a display screen in the kitchen, where fryers are timed by computers.

In the manufacturing sector, computers help in two areas:

1. In manufacturing, CADD, which means Computer-Aided Drafting and Design, allows design engineers to make detailed drawings of a product idea from scratch. They use 3-D graphics and the mathematical calculations are done right now. On the production line, computer-controlled machines cut and stitch and glue and weld to a preset pattern.

2. In operations, computers keep track of orders coming in from customers, which enables the factory owner to estimate manufacturing requirements. A good accounting system might be all a company needs to stay on top of payables and receivables, and to know which products are profitable.

In small business, computers make life easier. They make staffs more productive. They make profit margins bigger.

From: "Computer Revolution: Changing the Way We Do Business," *Entrepreneur,* November, 1991, 79–82.

SUMMARY

Computers are here to stay. If you are going into small business, you need to consider getting one. Two questions will arise:

1. How badly do I need a computer?
2. What model do I need, and where should I buy it?

This chapter discusses the computer as a business tool and as a symbol of the future. Here's some advice to think about before you start searching with new eyes for your computer:

1. Think of computer acquisition as a three-step process—define your tasks and problems; locate software to do the job; locate hardware to run the software.
2. Buy a good computer, but do not lock yourself in with overpriced hardware. The computer industry changes fast, and fancier, more powerful products will be coming along soon.
3. Buy a system you can expand.
4. Buy your first system locally, from a reputable dealer. You'll spend more money up front, but you're going to need dealer support during your first days, weeks, and months of operation.
5. Think about hiring a consultant.
6. Budget at least 50 percent of your total system cost for software.
7. Wait until you're familiar with your machine and with software programs before you start buying discounted programs through the mail.
8. Keep taking computer courses, and keep reading.

THINK POINTS FOR SUCCESS

◄ A computer can be an extension of your creative, entrepreneurial personality.

◄ The hardware for your computer system will be relatively easy to select—if you work from problems to solutions to software. Software needs determine hardware needs.

◄ Take a computer course. Educate yourself about the Information Society.

ACTION STEP REVIEW

The three action steps in this chapter help you inventory your entrepreneurial toolkit.

61   List the tools that have been helpful to you as you've been examining the world of small business. Move from simple to complex, starting with *pencils* and *paper.*

62   Identify problems and tasks in your small business that might better be handled by a computer. Look for tasks that are *repetitive,* that demand attention to *detail,* and that relate to monitoring *time* (schedules).

63   Once you've identified tasks the computer might help you accomplish, hit the streets and check out systems—software first, and then hardware. Find software that will solve your problems and be easy to use. Find a computer that's compatible with other computers.

◀ If you find yourself balking at computers because you don't know how they work, analyze your feelings about driving a car. You probably don't know how the internal combustion engine works, but that didn't keep you from learning to drive.

◀ You've got to compute to compete.

REFERENCES

Banks, Michael, et al. "Software Secrets: Boost Windows 3.0 Efficiency." *PC-Computing,* May, 1991, 166.

"Best of the Rest: The Pop Ten Products for Your Home Computers." *Compute,* January, 1989, 36.

Burgard, Michael. "Quattro Pro 3.0: Making a Great Spreadsheet Even Better." *PC-Computing,* May, 1991, 40.

Ferranti, Marc. "Early Praise Sets Stage for Debut of Mac 1-2-3." *PC Week,* June 3, 1991, 6.

Ferranti, Marc. "PC Business Programs Share Comdex Spotlight." *PC Week,* November 12, 1990, 47.

Gajeway, Charles. "The Pros Have It: FileMaker, Quattro, and MacLabel: Plus: Personal R:Base and Framework XE." *Home Office Computing,* May, 1991, 66.

Korngold, Bob. "Building a Check Register into a General Ledger." *Small Business Computers,* March/April, 1983, 50–53. [Takes the beginner through a simple program in *VisiCalc.*]

Landis, Ken. "Quicken: The Best Home-Finance Package of 1988 Just Got Even Better." *MacUser,* December, 1989, 68.

McGrath, Jack. "Forecasting Add-ins: Garbage in, Gospel out." *PC Magazine,* April 16, 1991, 119.

McWilliams, Peter. *The Personal Computer Book.* New York: Doubleday (Quantum Press), 1984.

McWilliams, Peter. *The Word Processing Book.* New York: Doubleday (Quantum Press), 1984.

Micro-Computers for Use in Small Business. Small Business Management Training Instructors' Guide No. 108. Washington, D.C.: U.S. Small Business Administration, Office of Management Assistance, 1984. [Produced by the American Association of Community and Junior Colleges under contract to the U.S. Small Business Administration, Contract No. 4873-MA 80.]

Milenback, Julian. "1-2-3 for Windows Beta Rivals Microsoft Excel." *PC Week,* May 20, 1991, 8.

Naiman, Arthur. *Word Processing Buyer's Guide.* New York: McGraw-Hill, 1983. [Naiman developed a 100-point checklist, which he uses to evaluate 14 programs exhaustively and another 104 programs briefly. Naiman gives prices, addresses, and sharp advice on word processors. He can't keep up with the industry, but who can?]

Nelson, Stephen L. "Use Your PC to Track Impact of Inflation on Your Finances." *PC Computing,* May, 1991, 237.

"Sales and Marketing Software." *Sales and Marketing Management,* December, 1990, 69–111.

Stetson, Christopher, and Eamonn Sullivan. "1-2-3 for Windows Offers Easy Upgrade." *PC Week,* August 26, 1991, 1.

Stevens, Mark. "Six Small Business Problems Computers Can Solve." *Working Woman,* September, 1987, 33.

Stewart, Michael M., and Alan C. Shulman. *How to Get Started with a Small Business Computer,* Management Aid No. 2.027. Washington, D.C.: U.S. Small Business Administration, Office of Business Development, 1987.

Stinson, Craig. "$99 Laptop Tool Cuts Dead Weight from Worksheets." *PC Magazine,* June 11, 1991. 49.

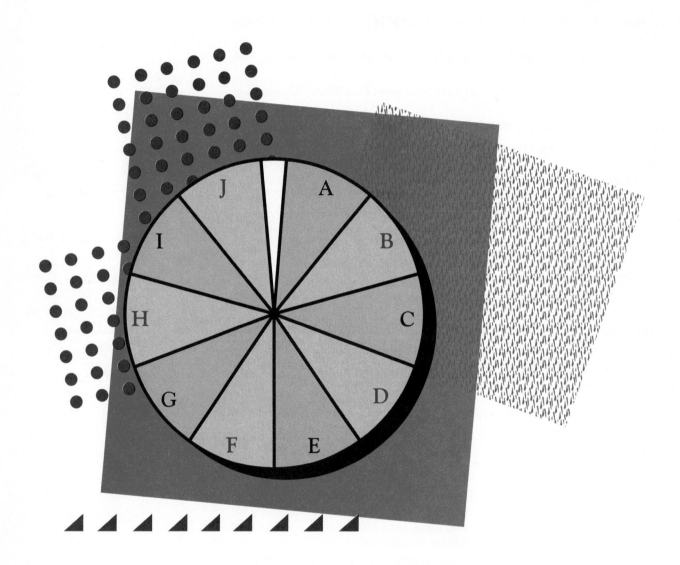

FIGURE 15.1
Chapter 15 investigates franchising, an important doorway to small business.

15 Buying a Franchise ▲ ▲ ▲ ▲ ▲ ▲ ▲ ▲

Learning Objectives

- To explore the vast world of franchising.
- To develop techniques for examining franchises.
- To understand the relationship between franchisor and franchisee.
- To learn the benefits and liabilities of owning and operating a franchise.
- To understand the risk–reward relationship of a ground-floor opportunity.
- To learn why the stronger franchises tend to operate an "insiders only" game.
- To learn why some people should consider *only* franchises.
- To understand why the true entrepreneur is always the *franchisor*.
- To decide if buying a franchise is the right step for you.

FUTURE FOCUS

Is a franchise for you? When does it make sense? Are you ready to surrender your independence? Is this where you want to be 10 years from now? Is this a good first business; a stepping stone to the future entrepreneurship you seek? Franchising can provide education, experience, and capital for your future.

ACTION STEP PREVIEW

64   Investigate the franchise system by interviewing franchisors and franchisees.

65   Visit a franchise exposition.

Our walk-through of opportunities in small business is almost finished. Decision time approaches. If you've followed the action steps, you've spent several months gathering data and talking to people in small business. You have spent some time exploring businesses that are up for sale and talking to sellers. If you wanted to write a Business Plan now, you could sit down and do it. Before you do that, however, there is one other doorway to explore, the doorway to a franchised business.

The franchise industry is enormous. If you were to buy or rent a car tomorrow morning, put gas in it, and then drive it to a fast-food restaurant for lunch, you might be supporting a franchise at every stop.

WHY BUY A FRANCHISE?

The overwhelming reason for buying a franchise is to benefit from name recognition. Consumers grow to trust brand-name products and services. Look at the places where you do business. Do you drink Coca-Cola? The Coca-Cola headquarters are in Atlanta, but the beverage is bottled by regional franchisees. Do you buy gas at a Mobil, Texaco, Exxon, or Shell station? They're franchises, too. If you buy milk at 7-Eleven, buy hamburgers at Burger King, purchase books at Little Professor, or use a Century 21 Realtor, you're into the franchise system. Franchised products and services are predictable and reliable. Many consumers go out of their way to do business with franchisors. This customer loyalty is worth paying for.

What the Franchisee Gets

franchisor
the firm that sells the rights to do business under its name and continues to control the business

franchise
authorization granted by a manufacturer or distributor to sell its products/services

franchisee
the individual operator who is licensed to operate under the franchisor's rules and directives

Let's examine what you can get when you pay money to a **franchisor** for a **franchise**—that is, when you become a **franchisee**. A franchise can provide:

1. Brand-name recognition. If you ask the right questions and pick the right franchise, the marketing boost you get from the name of your franchise might be worth what it will cost you.
2. Support from corporate. Corporate services can include help with selecting a site, employee training, inventory control, vendor connections, a corporate-produced Business Plan, and more.
3. Training. The franchisor will teach you the business.
4. Money. Lenders prefer to lend to new franchisees over new start-ups.
5. Planning. You are buying a proven Business Plan.
6. Bargains. You may share in economies of scale in purchasing goods, services, and promotion.
7. Continuous training.
8. Psychological hand-holding and field visits from the franchisor.
9. Assistance in layout and design.
10. Location and leasing assistance.
11. Reduced odds of failure.
12. Pretested products and promotion.
13. The opportunity to buy another franchise in your area.
14. Assistance of a store-opening specialist. This person can help get you off to a running start.

BRAND·NAME RECOGNITION · HELP WITH INTERIOR LAYOUT · VENDOR CONNECTIONS · HELP WITH SITE SELECTION · HELP WITH INVENTORY CONTROL · READY-MADE BUSINESS PLAN · A PROVEN WINNER · TECHNICAL ASSISTANCE · PROFESSIONAL DEVELOPMENT · ·ADVERTISING + PROMOTION · INVOLUNTARY SERVITUDE · BOOKKEEPING + ACCOUNTING · FINANCING · TRAINING · A LOSS OF INDEPENDENCE

FIGURE 15.2   A franchise can provide you with a number of things.

Figure 15.2 illustrates some of these benefits of franchising, as well as a couple of its drawbacks.

When you buy a franchise, you're really buying a license. If you wanted to bottle Coca-Cola—the best-known franchise in the world—you'd have to negotiate for a license from the Coca-Cola Bottling Company. You might find a bottler who wanted to sell you his license, but you'd still have to negotiate with Coke. In some cases, buying a franchise is like buying a supplier for eternity. Nonetheless, many people have been happy to do that, because approximately 20 percent of the small businesses in the country are franchises.

Franchisors often sell the rights to a region, state, or county to a master franchisor, who in turn sells and manages franchise sales to individuals.

What the Franchisor Gets

Franchisors earn money in several ways:

1. They collect a **franchise fee** for the rights to use their name and system. This ranges from $3,000 for a small service firm to over $100,000 for a well-established name such as that of a hotel, auto dealership, or major restaurant.

franchise fee
fee paid by a franchisee for the rights to represent the franchisor in a given geographic area for a specified length of time, commonly 5–10 years

royalty fee
ongoing obligation to pay the franchisor a percentage of the gross sales; may or may not include advertising fee

2. They collect a **royalty fee**, which ranges from 2 percent to 15 pecent of gross sales.
3. They may make a profit on items they sell to franchisees.

In addition, franchisees commonly pay franchisors advertising and promotion fees. These generally range from 2 percent to 5 percent of a franchise's gross sales.

Some of the fees may be open to negotiation—especially with a new franchisor. For example, it might be possible to delay the royalty fee for six months or until the franchise is profitable. It's always a good idea to ask for concessions.

Franchising Growth and Trends

Table 15.1 documents the phenomenal growth of franchising from 1970 to 1987. In 1987, 499,000 franchise outlets provided a whopping $591 billion in revenues. Comparing that with 396,000 outlets (generating $120 billion) in 1970, you can see how franchising has mushroomed.

In Table 15.2, figures for individual industries help you add to your knowledge of trends, which you began thinking about in Chapter 2. If you're interested in becoming an auto or truck dealer, your window of opportunity has grown smaller (from 37,200 franchises down to 27,800). But if you're in business aids and services, the window has grown in size (from 10,500 to 61,300).

It's certainly not necessary to memorize these tables. They are included here to show you the vast range of opportunity in franchising, which seems to be moving from smokestacks and manufacturing to information and services. Franchises in the service sector are enjoying a lot of growth now. Real estate, for example, is a natural. Others that share a network of technology or body of information include Century 21 and Dale Carnegie.

TABLE 15.1   Franchising in the United States, 1980–1990

ITEM	UNIT	1970	1980	1983	1984	1985	1986	1987	1988	1989[1]	1990[1]
DOMESTIC[2]											
Number of franchised establishments	**1,000**	**396**	**442**	**442**	**444**	**455**	**462**	**479**	**481**	**499**	**533**
Company-owned[3]	1,000	72	85	86	87	86	88	89	94	95	98
Franchisee-owned	1,000	324	357	355	357	369	374	390	387	404	435
Sales of products and services	**Bil. dol.**	**120**	**336**	**423**	**492**	**543**	**569**	**599**	**648**	**679**	**716**
Company-owned[3]	Bil. dol.	23	47	59	64	68	85	90	98	104	112
Franchisee-owned	Bil. dol.	96	289	364	428	475	484	509	550	575	604
Average sales per establishment	$1,000	302	760	958	1,108	1,193	1,231	1,251	1,348	1,360	1,344
Employment	1,000	(NA)	4,668	5,165	5,671	6,283	6,501	(NA)	(NA)	(NA)	(NA)
INTERNATIONAL											
U.S. companies operating foreign outlets	Number	[4]156	279	305	328	342	354	(NA)	374	(NA)	(NA)
Foreign outlets	1,000	[4]3.4	20.4	25.7	27.0	30.2	31.6	(NA)	35.0	(NA)	(NA)

Source: *Statistical Abstract of the United States*, 111th ed. (Washington, D.C.: U.S. Department of Commerce, 1991), p. 778; based on data in International Trade Association, *Franchising in the Economy, 1986–88* (Dept. of Commerce, 1988) and beginning 1988, *Franchising in the Economy, 1988–1990* (Washington, D.C.: Intl. Franchise Assoc. Foundation; New York: Horwath Intl.; 1990).

NA Not available.   [1]Estimated by respondents to annual survey of franchisors.   [2]Excludes foreign outlets of U.S. companies.   [3]Represents establishments owned by the parent company.   [4]1971 data.

TABLE 15.2 Number of Establishments and Sales by Kind of Franchised Business, 1980–1990

KIND OF FRANCHISED BUSINESS	NUMBER OF ESTABLISHMENTS (1,000)						SALES (bil. dol.)					
	1980	1985	1987	1988	1989[1]	1990[1]	1980	1985	1987	1988	1989[1]	1990[1]
All franchising, total	**442.4**	**455.2**	**479.1**	**480.8**	**498.8**	**533.0**	**336.2**	**543.0**	**599.4**	**648.1**	**678.8**	**716.4**
Auto and truck dealers[2]	29.4	27.5	27.6	27.8	27.6	27.6	143.9	282.6	319.7	345.1	353.6	362.3
Percent	6.6	6.0	5.8	5.8	5.5	5.2	42.8	52.0	53.3	53.2	52.1	50.6
Restaurants (all types)	60.0	73.9	83.3	90.3	94.3	102.1	27.9	47.7	56.8	64.3	69.1	76.5
Percent	13.6	16.2	17.4	18.8	18.9	19.2	8.3	8.8	9.5	9.9	10.2	10.7
Gasoline service stations[2]	158.5	124.6	115.9	113.2	112.0	111.7	94.5	100.8	89.2	101.9	108.5	115.1
Percent	35.8	27.4	24.2	23.5	22.1	20.9	28.1	18.6	14.9	15.7	16.0	16.1
Retailing (nonfood)	35.2	45.1	47.9	46.2	49.2	54.1	10.5	20.6	25.4	23.3	26.0	28.6
Percent	8.0	9.9	10.0	9.6	9.7	10.2	3.1	3.8	4.2	3.6	3.8	4.0
Auto, truck rental services	7.3	11.2	10.0	9.5	9.9	10.6	3.1	5.7	6.5	6.6	7.0	7.6
Automotive products and services[3]	40.2	36.5	39.3	34.7	35.8	38.6	7.1	10.7	12.3	11.4	12.2	13.6
Business aids and services	40.7	49.8	56.7	55.6	59.8	67.3	6.7	12.0	14.7	15.7	17.1	19.5
Employment services	4.4	4.8	6.1	6.5	6.6	7.4	1.6	2.7	3.7	4.7	5.0	5.8
Tax preparation services	9.2	8.1	8.5	8.3	8.2	8.5	0.3	0.4	0.5	0.6	0.7	0.7
Accounting, credit, collection, and general	2.4	2.1	2.0	1.7	1.7	1.9	0.1	0.2	0.2	0.2	0.2	0.2
Real estate[4]	17.3	13.9	15.2	15.3	16.0	17.0	3.6	4.6	5.6	5.9	6.2	6.8
Printing and copying	2.8	4.5	5.6	5.9	6.5	7.4	0.4	0.9	1.2	1.5	1.6	1.9
Other	4.8	16.4	19.4	17.9	20.8	25.1	0.8	3.1	3.5	3.0	3.4	4.1
Construction, home improvement, maintenance, and cleaning	14.3	17.5	21.7	22.0	24.7	28.3	1.5	4.1	5.2	5.3	6.0	6.8
Convenience stores	15.6	15.1	16.3	17.2	17.3	17.5	7.8	10.8	12.3	13.9	14.1	14.4
Educational products and services	3.2	8.2	9.6	11.6	11.9	13.3	0.3	0.8	1.0	1.7	1.9	2.3
Equipment rental services	2.2	2.5	2.8	3.0	3.0	3.4	0.4	0.7	0.7	0.7	0.7	0.8
Food retailing[5]	15.5	18.7	20.5	21.6	23.0	25.4	7.4	10.1	11.1	10.2	10.9	11.9
Hotels and motels[6]	6.4	7.5	9.3	9.3	10.1	11.1	9.5	14.8	17.7	19.7	21.3	23.9
Laundry, dry cleaning services	3.4	2.3	2.2	2.3	2.5	2.6	0.3	0.3	0.3	0.3	0.3	0.3
Recreation, entertainment, travel	4.6	7.8	8.2	8.8	9.5	10.3	0.5	2.3	4.0	3.5	4.1	4.7
Soft drink bottlers[2][7]	1.9	1.4	1.1	0.9	0.8	0.8	14.4	18.3	20.9	22.7	24.2	25.8
Miscellaneous	3.6	5.5	6.8	6.9	7.3	8.4	0.4	0.9	1.5	1.7	1.9	2.2

Source: *Statistical Abstract of the United States,* 111th ed. (Washington, D.C.: U.S. Department of Commerce, 1991), p. 778; based on data in International Trade Association, *Franchising in the Economy, 1986–88* (Dept. of Commerce, 1988) and, beginning 1988, *Franchising in the Economy, 1988–1990* (Washington, D.C.: Intl. Franchise Assoc. Foundation; and New York: Horwath Intl.; 1990).

[1]Estimated by respondents.   [2]Estimated by source on basis on Bureau of the Census and trade association dates.   [3]Includes some establishments with significant sales of nonautomotive products such as household appliances, garden supplies, etc.   [4]Gross commissions   [5]Excludes convenience stores.   [6]Includes campgrounds.   [7]Includes soft drinks, fruit drinks and ades, syrups, flavoring agents and bases. Excludes independent private label and contract-filler bottling companies, which accounted for 22 percent of the value of shipments of the total industry in recent years.

INVESTIGATING FRANCHISE OPPORTUNITIES

As you can see from Tables 15.1 and 15.2, franchising is a major force in the U.S. economy. You can learn a lot about small business by investigating franchises. We recommend that you talk with franchisors and franchisees to get a feel for the world of franchising.

It may be that you would not be comfortable operating by the rules and regulations set down by franchisors—many entrepreneur-types are not. Nonetheless, it makes good sense to check out franchise opportunities (especially those in your industry), because it will give you a better picture of the marketplace. Action Step 64 will get you started on this.

ACTION STEP 64

Investigate the franchise system by interviewing franchisors and franchisees.

Franchises are everywhere—McDonald's, Roto-Rooter, Dale Carnegie, RE/MAX, Holiday Inn, Exxon, Midas, Hertz, and many, many others. To learn more about the system, interview people on both sides of the franchise agreement.

Part A. Franchisors. Leave your checkbook at home and interview at least three franchisors. Here are some questions to start you off:

What's included in the franchise fee?

What's the duration of the agreement?

How can the agreement be bought back or canceled?

What are the royalty fees and other assessments?

What level of training and service could I expect?

Is the territory well-defined?

What are the minimum volume requirements?

How much help could I expect with advertising and promotion?

Part B. Franchisees. Now interview several franchisees. Ask them the same questions.

A handy reference is the *Franchise Opportunities Handbook* published by the U.S. Department of Commerce.

voluntary chain
wholesaling organization established by wholesalers or retailers to gain purchasing power and other economies of scale

corporate
the franchisor

Franchise Problems

Some notable pitfalls plague franchising in general:

1. Competition is becoming intense among competitive franchisors. Franchisors of fast-food outlets, quick-printing shops, and specialty retailers often oversaturate markets, which causes many failures.
2. Many of the training programs are poor or nonexistent.
3. Multilevel distributorships and pyramid sales schemes may benefit only the promoters.
4. The best opportunities are seldom offered to outsiders.

Beware of "ground-floor" franchise opportunities; it's pretty risky to be an early franchisee. A franchisor offering such an "opportunity" would be experimenting with *your money*. You want to buy a recognized brand name, a proven Business Plan, excellent field support, and experience that demonstrates the particular franchise will work in your location.

Voluntary chains—such as True Value and Ace hardware stores, for example—are often a more desirable option. Members of those chains remain independent and pay no royalty or franchise fee. Look for more such organizations in the near future.

A Franchising Success Story

Susan Moore and her husband were lucky when it came time to investigate franchises; they had a source of inside information right in the family. They were also lucky because the franchisor they chose provided excellent support. Note that corporate support was more important than name-brand recognition to Susan and her husband.

Three years ago, my husband was having to travel a lot in his job and I was working very hard for a large company. While we were both drawing good salaries, we felt we had what it took to succeed in small business. We decided to go the franchising route.

We were both interested in the printing industry, and we chose a medium-sized national chain that seemed to have a franchise package we could live with. We did have some inside information on this particular franchisor. My brother had been with them for 3 years, in the Pacific Northwest area, and he was making a good living.

While we were interested in the quick-print industry, we weren't experts, so the two weeks of training was incredibly valuable. In addition, the people from **corporate** helped us with site selection, market analysis, negotiating the lease, and the layout and design of our shop. There are so many details to think of when you're starting a business; it's very helpful to have experts take over some of the tasks.

Another good feature of this franchise is that corporate will allow you to finance up to 80 percent of your start-up costs. This particular franchise can run as high as $100,000 up front, so that helped us.

We opened a second shop last January, and both stores are doing nicely. We print stationery, business cards, flyers, invitations—and we're developing a reputation for being on time in an industry known for being perpetually late.

A good way to learn a lot about franchising in a short time is to attend a franchise exposition. You can learn when and where they are to be held in your area by watching for announcements in major newspapers. Go and enjoy yourself (leaving your checkbook at home), and complete Action Step 65.

As you look for a good franchise opportunity, bear in mind that the best opportunity may lie with a young franchise that has proven its concept, has 20 to 30 winners, and is looking for growth in an area with which you are familiar.

EVALUATING A FRANCHISE

Evaluating a franchise opportunity is much like evaluating any other business that's up for sale, but because of the nature of franchisors, you need to ask some additional questions. For example:

How long has this franchise been in business?

Who are the officers? What is their track record?

How many franchise outlets are operating right now?

How well does this franchise compete with similar franchises?

Where is this franchise in its life cycle?

What will this franchise do for me?

In Chapter 10 we presented a checklist to use in evaluating an ongoing business you are considering buying. That checklist applies to franchises as well. To supplement it, we're giving you a checklist prepared specifically for evaluating franchise opportunities; see Box 15.1. The questions will help you generate a profile of the franchise and make a wise decision.

Typically, current franchisees are offered new locations before they are offered to outsiders. Rarely is a new player offered a sure thing. New players are offered those that have already been passed over. This was Myron Bailey's introduction to franchising.

> By the time Myron was 29 years old he'd made a lot of money in the stock market, but he felt he was too young to retire. After making several attempts to purchase one of the better known fast-food franchises and waiting almost a year, he was offered a location in another state.
>
> The store had been open for 3 years and not yet turned a profit. Other franchise owners had already turned down the opportunity to take over the operation. Myron liked what he saw and made an offer. The unsuccessful franchisee welcomed his offer as a graceful exit, and the franchisor could hardly wait to see if a new franchisee could turn the loser around.
>
> Myron is a "people person" and a strong manager. His employees followed his enthusiastic leadership, and new customers came in droves. In less than a year the store became very profitable, and the franchisor offered Myron three new locations, all of which he accepted.
>
> Myron's touch was magic; two of the three new stores also became very successful. But try as he would, he couldn't make money on the third one. After 3 more years, Myron decided that too much of his time was being drained by the one loser. He called the franchisor and asked them to assist him in selling it. They found several prospective buyers and chose the one they thought was the best operator. He wasn't able to turn it around either. Myron now devotes all his time to working with his winners.

Reasons for Not Buying a Franchise

Many entrepreneurs have decided against buying franchises. Here are some of the reasons they have given:

1. I know the business as well as they do.
2. My name is as well known as theirs.
3. Why pay a franchise fee?
4. Why pay a royalty fee and advertising fee?
5. My individuality would have been stifled.
6. I don't want others to tell me how to run my business.

ACTION STEP 65

Visit a franchise exposition.

Most major cities have at least one franchise show a year. Attend one and visit with the exhibitors. Learn what you can from their sales presentations.

Collect their literature and select one that seems worth a second look. Write up a brief summary of your findings to present as an oral report to your class. Have your classmates evaluate the franchise.

Remember, it's usually the small and new franchisors that exhibit at the shows, and their salespeople work on commission. Don't allow yourself to be pursued; you are there to observe and evaluate. You are probably not yet ready to buy.

BOX 15.1   Franchise Evaluation Checklist

GENERAL

	yes	*no*
1. Is the product or service:		
a. considered reputable?	___	___
b. part of a growing market?	___	___
c. needed in your area?	___	___
d. of interest to you?	___	___
e. safe,	___	___
protected,	___	___
covered by guarantee?	___	___
2. Is the franchise:		
a. local?	___	___
regional?	___	___
national?	___	___
international?	___	___
b. full-time?	___	___
part-time?	___	___
possible full-time in the future?	___	___

3. Existing franchises

a. Date the company was founded _____

Date the first franchise was awarded _____

b. Number of franchises currently in operation or under construction _____

c. References

Franchise 1: owner _____

address _____

telephone _____ date started _____

Franchise 2: owner _____

address _____

telephone _____ date started _____

Franchise 3: owner _____

address _____

telephone _____ date started _____

Franchise 4: owner _____

address _____

telephone _____ date started _____

d. Additional franchises planned for the next twelve months _____

4. Failed franchises

a. How many franchises have failed? _____ How many in the last two years? ____

b. Why have they failed?

Franchisor reasons: _____

_____

Better Business Bureau reasons: _____

_____

Franchisee reasons: _____

_____

continued

BOX 15.1, *continued*

5. Franchise in local market area
   a. Has a franchise ever been awarded in this area? _____
   b. If so, and if it is still in operation:
      owner _____
      address _____
      telephone _____ date started _____
   c. If so, and if it is no longer in operation:
      person involved _____
      address _____
      date started _____ date ended _____
      reasons for failure _____
      _____
   d. How many inquiries have there been for the franchise from the area in the past 6 months? _____
6. What product or service will be added to the franchise package:
   a. within 12 months? _____
   _____
   b. within 2 years? _____
   _____
   c. within 2 to 5 years? _____
   _____
7. Competition
   a. What is the competition? _____
   _____
   _____
8. Are all franchises independently owned?
   a. Of the total outlets, _____ are franchised, and _____ are company-owned.
   b. If some outlets are company owned did they start out this way, _____ or were they purchased from a franchisee? _____
   c. Date of most recent company acquisition _____
9. Franchise operations
   a. What facilities are required, and do I lease or build?

	build	lease
office	____	____
building	____	____
manufacturing facility	____	____
warehouse	____	____
_____	____	____
_____	____	____

   b. Getting started—Who is responsible for:

	franchisor	franchisee
feasibility study?	____	____
design?	____	____
construction?	____	____
furnishings and equipment?	____	____
financing?	____	____
employee training?	____	____
lease negotiation?	____	____

continued

BOX 15.1, *continued*

FRANCHISE COMPANY

1. The company
   a. Name and address of the parent company, if different from the franchise company:
      name _____
      address_____
   b. Is the parent company public, ___ or private? ___
   c. If the company is public, where is the stock traded?
      New York Stock Exchange ___
      American Stock Exchange ___
      over-the-counter   ___

      _____   ___

2. Forecast of income and expenses
   a. Is a forecast of income and expenses provided? _____
   b. Is it:
      based on actual franchisee operations? ___
      based on a franchisor outlet? ___
      purely estimated? ___
   c. Does it:

	yes	no
relate to your market area?	___	___
meet your personal goals?	___	___
provide adequate return on investment?	___	___
provide for adequate promotion and personnel?	___	___

3. What is the best legal structure for my company?
   proprietorship ___
   partnership ___
   corporation ___

4. The franchise contract
   a. Is there a written contract? _____ (Get a copy for lawyer and accountant to review.)
   b. Does it specify:

	yes	no
franchise fee?	___	___
termination?	___	___
selling and renewal?	___	___
advertising and promotion?	___	___
patent and liability protection?	___	___
home office services?	___	___
commissions and royalties?	___	___
training?	___	___
financing?	___	___
territory?	___	___
exclusivity?	___	___

Source: Adapted from C. R. Stigelman, *Franchise Index/Profile*, Small Business Management Series, No. 35 (Washington, D.C.: Small Business Administration, 1973), pp. 31–41.

7. I didn't want a ground-floor opportunity where I'd be the guinea pig.
8. I'd have been committed for the rest of my life.
9. There were restrictions on selling out.
10. If I didn't do as I was told, I would lose my franchise.
11. The specified hours of business did not suit my location.
12. The franchisor's promotions and products did not fit my customers' needs or tastes.
13. They offered no territory protection.
14. I would not be in control of my business.

If you can develop a winning formula, you can become a franchisor yourself. Many entrepreneurs have done this. This is another reason to learn all you can about franchising now.

A Final Word about Franchises

If you have few business skills, or perhaps little business experience, then your chances of succeeding are far greater as a franchisee. A franchisor with a well-developed Business Plan will keep you on track. Ask to see that Business Plan.

The key here is gut feeling. If you should decide to buy a franchise and then feel like an employee of the franchisor, strike out on your own. Develop your own Plan, and go for it. Look at franchising as an option—an example to learn from—and then blend that knowledge into a unique business that explores the gaps exposed back in Chapter 3, "Power Marketing."

If you're not ready to be on your own yet, franchising may be the way for you to start.

Key Points from Another View
Part I
FRANCHISE PRIMER

The main reason franchises succeed is that the franchisor has a knowledge of the industry, and is selling a proven training system, distribution knowledge, and merchandising methods. The word "franchise" literally means to be free from servitude.

I. The players in the game are:
   A. The franchisor, who owns the right to the name or trademark
   B. The franchisee, who purchases the rights to use the trademark and system of doing business
II. These players work within the confines of three basic kinds of franchises:
   A. Entire business format
   B. Trademark and brand-name format
   C. Product distribution format
III. Types of franchises:
   A. A franchise to operate a single business, often at a specific location, may be referred to as a *unit franchise, individual franchise,* or simply as a *franchise.*

B. The term *area franchise* can refer to the right to develop a franchise in a specific area or to a franchise that is operated in a specified territory; or it may be used in a multi-layered franchise structure.

C. A *subfranchisor* holds the master license rights to sell subfranchises, a right assigned from the franchisor.

IV. Tools of the Trade

    A. Products

        1. There may be trademarked products that are available to the franchisee only from the franchisor or suppliers select by the franchisor (designated supplier).

        2. Other times, products used or sold by the franchisee must conform with the franchisor's standards, but may be purchased from any "approved supplier."

    B. Exclusive territory is generally understood to mean a geographic area in which no one else will be authorized by the franchisor to do the same kind of business as the franchisee.

    C. An "Operating Manual," "Confidential Manual," or "Policy and Procedure Manual" is one of the fundamental tools for communicating details about the day-to-day operation.

    D. Find out what types of "ongoing support" the franchise offers.

        1. Monthly newsletter

        2. "800" number

        3. Monthly visits from a franchisor's representative

        4. Special advertising and marketing support

    E. It's essential to understand what factors are being included in the costs.

V. Decoding the UFOC (Uniform Franchise Offering Circular)

    A. State registration and disclosure laws require that unless a statutory exemption is available, a franchise cannot be offered or sold in the regulating state unless a prospectus detailing all the material facts of the franchise sales transaction has been approved by the appropriate state agency.

    B. The UFOC contains information concerning:

        1. Past history of the franchisee

        2. Initial franchise fee or other payments

        3. Obligations of the franchisee

        4. Financing arrangements

        5. Trademark information

        6. Restrictions on the goods/services offered by the franchisee

        7. Earnings claims

        8. Other information

    C. When evaluating a franchise, pay attention to the following:

        1. The background and the overview of the franchisor's business

        2. The experience of the individuals affiliated with the franchisor's business

        3. Any past or pending litigation against the franchisor or its principals

        4. All fees required to establish and operate the business over a given time period

5. The franchisee's initial investment
6. Franchisor-franchisee obligations
7. Exclusive areas or territories
8. Termination and renewal rights for both parties
9. Earnings claims
10. The franchisor's financial statements (check footnotes)

VI. Making the Right Choise

A. Before you consider signing, visit as many franchises as possible.

B. Once you have narrowed down your choice to a specific industry sector, identify the leaders in the field.

C. By carefully examining your options, you can save yourself a lot of aggravation.

From: Kevin McLaughlin, "Franchise Primer," *New Business Opportunities*, November, 1989, 32–39.

Part II
BUYING A FRANCHISE?
INVESTIGATE BEFORE IT'S TOO LATE

The best system for the franchisee is one in which the franchisor looks to the same source as you do for his profits; the ongoing royalties from your sales.

Evaluating a Franchise—the following steps will help you choose the right franchise for you:

I. Assess Yourself

A. The first year, you will work harder than you've ever worked in your life. Are you ready for that?

B. You need to put pride of ownership and the rewards of personal achievement first.

C. Making a financial success of a business is key, but money alone is not.

II. Research the Industry

A. It is far easier to evaluate a franchise if you are already familiar with the industry it represents.

B. Many people do look outside their field of experience for a franchise; in that case, it pays to investigate the industry very carefully before you examine the particular franchise.

III. Research the Company

A. The franchisor is required by law to give the prospective franchisee detailed information about the company.

B. Not only should you read this information yourself, but you should also have a lawyer specializing in franchising look it over.

IV. Visit the Corporate Staff—most franchisees agree about the importance of making a personal visit to a potential franchisor.

V. Talk to Franchisees—not only should you talk to and visit other franchisees and former franchisees, but you should also find out how satisfied their customers are.

VI. Check out the Territory

    A. Most franchisees assume that their franchise comes with a guarantee of exclusivity within a certain territory, but unless exclusivity is specified, assume the worst.

    B. Check not only the territory, but also the demographics. Make sure the demographics matches the franchisor's Target Customer Profile.

VII. Negotiate—you should feel free to negotiate points in the contract that confuse or disturb you, but don't expect to be able to rewrite the franchise agreement entirely.

VIII. Have Realistic Financial Goals—have a realistic sense of what will happen, and beware of the salesperson who overpromises.

IX. Guarantee Long-Term Security—there are, alas, no guarantees. All you can do is choose a franchisor who is concerned about the welfare of its franchisees.

- There's a good living to be made franchising for those who choose wisely and work hard.
- Do your homework before, not after, you sign the franchise document.

From: Geraldine M. Strozier, "Buying A Franchise? Investigate Before It's Too Late—It's Not So Elementary, Watson," *Entrepreneur*, January, 1990, 69–73.

SUMMARY

There are two good reasons to consider buying a franchise: first, if the brand name is respected, you'll already be positioned in the marketplace; second, if the franchisor is sharp, you'll inherit a Business Plan that works. Examine the franchise's appeal with consumers carefully; you want to get a marketing boost from the name. Depending on the franchise, you may also get other services for your money (for example, help on site selection, help on interior layout, and vendor connections), but the main thing you're buying is brand-name recognition.

Just as if you were investigating an ongoing, independent business, study the opportunity thoroughly. Examine the financial history, and compare what you'd make if you bought the business to what you'd make if you invested the same money elsewhere.

ACTION STEP REVIEW

We suggest you examine franchising in two steps.

64 Investigate the franchise system by interviewing franchisors and franchisees. Ask a lot of questions.

65 Visit a franchise exposition. Talk to franchisors and see how they operate.

THINK POINTS FOR SUCCESS

◣ Avoid ground-floor opportunities. "Grow with us" can mean *caveat emptor* ("Let the buyer beware").

◣ Talk to franchisees.

◣ The franchisor gets a percentage of gross sales for advertising and royalty fees whether the franchisee is profitable or not.

◣ Do you really need the security blanket of a franchise?

◣ Read the proposed agreements carefully.

◣ Would you be comfortable relinquishing your independence?

REFERENCES

Brown, Buck. "Small Business: Testing Psyches of Future Franchisees." *Wall Street Journal,* May 20, 1988. [If you're independent and creative, the chances are good that you'll be screened out by this 2½-hour test. Developed by Franchise Developments, Inc., of Pittsburgh, the test selects people who will work well within the system. Entrepreneurs, pass by.]

Business Planning: Road Map to Success. Small Business Management Training Instructors' Guide, No. 102. Washington, D.C.: U.S. Small Business Administration, Office of Management Assistance, 1984. [Produced by the American Association of Community and Junior Colleges under contract to the U.S. SBA, Contract No. SBA 4873-MA 80.]

Evaluating Franchise Opportunities. Management Aid No. 7.007. Washington, D.C.: U.S. Small Business Administration, Office of Business Development, 1987.

Info Franchise Newsletter, monthly, Lewiston, N.Y. (716) 754-4669.

Kostecka, Andrew. *Franchising in the Economy, 1986–1988.* U.S. Department of Commerce. [Send $4.75 to the Superintendant of Documents, U.S. Government Printing Office, Washington, DC 20402.]

Small Business Incubator Handbook: A Guide for Start-Up and Management. Washington, D.C.: U.S. Small Business Administration, Office of Private-Sector Initiatives, 1986.

Tetreault, Wilfred F. *Buying and Selling Business Opportunities: A Sales Transaction Handbook.* Reading, Mass.: Addison-Wesley, 1981. [Contains an overwhelming set of documents needed when buying a business. One look at this book, and you'll decide to handle your own start-up.]

United States Department of Commerce. *Franchise Opportunities Handbook.* Washington, D.C., Annual.

The following books and magazines are available through the International Franchise Association, 1350 New York Avenue, NW, Suite 900, Washington, DC 20005 [(202) 628-8000]:

The Franchise Advantage [by Donald D. and Patrick Boroian, franchise consultants; $18.95].

The Franchise Option: How to Expand Your Business through Franchising [by William Ginalski and DeBanks M. Henward III and revised by Kathryn L. Boe, Assistant Dean, Creighton University School of Law; $20 paperback, $26 hard cover].

Franchising: The How-To Book [by Lloyd Tarbutton, cofounder of EconoLodges of America; $24.95]

Franchising World [bimonthly magazine of the I.F.A.; $12 a year]

How to Be a Franchisor [by Robert E. Kushell, franchising attorney, $8]

FIGURE 16.1
Chapter 16 tells you how to draw on all of the materials you have generated in the earlier chapters to create your finished Business Plan. Each wedge of the pie chart represents a part of your complete Business Plan—a portable showcase for your business as well as a personal road map to small business success.

16 Pulling the Plan Together

▲ ▲ ▲ ▲ ▲ ▲ ▲

Learning Objectives

- To pull all the information together into one coherent unit, which becomes a portable showcase for your business.
- To study a sample Business Plan to see how one group of entrepreneurs defined and showed off their business.
- To match or surpass the sample Business Plan in power and effectiveness.
- To put your finished Business Plan to work.

FUTURE FOCUS

Putting all your information together proves or disproves the business concept. Chart the pathway and you and your team members can follow into the twenty-first century.

Business Plan
a portable document that becomes the blueprint for your business

Your Business Plan could be the most important document you've ever pulled together. It will help keep you focused while you're out there doing the work on your start-up, researching, finding the gaps, interviewing small business owners, profiling your target customers, and so on. Staying focused is important because you're going to get a lot of distracting ideas for more new businesses while you're out there hunting.

A **Business Plan** will keep your creativity on track and your power grooved. How? By being a constant reminder of who you are and where you are going.

When you've finished your Plan, you've got something in writing to show to the people who are important to your business: your banker, lenders, relatives, venture capitalists, vendors, suppliers, key employees, friends, the SBA, and others. The Plan is portable, and you can make as many copies as you need to show to the people who can help you succeed. You can even mail it to contacts clear across the country.

Planning is hard work. You'll stay up nights over this, maybe lose some sleep, but you'll save time in the end. Just as a pilot would not consider a long flight without a plan, neither should you consider a business venture without a Business Plan.

HOW TO WRITE YOUR BUSINESS PLAN

Two-Part Structure: Words and Numbers

Your Business Plan tells the world what kind of business you're in. For ease of handling, divide your plan into two sections, and provide the needed documentation in appendixes at the end. In Section I use *words* to briefly introduce your strategies for marketing and management. Try to "hook" your reader with the excitement of creating a business, assessing the competition, designing a marketing plan, targeting customers, finding the right location, and building a team—all those human things that most people can relate to, even if they're not in business.

In Section II present *numbers:* income statement, cash flow projection, and projected balance sheet. This section is aimed primarily at bankers, credit managers, venture capitalists, vendors, SBICs, commercial credit lenders. At the same time, you've got to make it accessible to the casual reader who searches for the bottom line.

Support the two sections with *appendixes*. This is where you put resumes, maps, diagrams, photographs, tables, reprints from industry journals, letters from customers, letters from vendors, credit reports, personal financial statements, bids from contractors, and other documentation that demonstrates the viability of your plan. Note that in most cases, material in the appendixes comes from existing sources. You're not stating anything new here; you're just supporting what you've already said. (Appendixes vary according to each business; for that reason sample appendixes are not included in this book.)

By following the action steps in this chapter, you will complete all the components you need to make a winning Business Plan. If you want to jump ahead for a quick overview of your Plan, take a look at our sample table of contents in Figure 16.3.

The Relationship of Your Plan to This Book

You may be closer to your Business Plan than you think. If you have completed the action steps in the preceding chapters, you already have the major components of your Plan. The earlier chapters gave you the materials, and this chapter gives you the structure.

Section I, the description of your business, draws its parts directly from Chapters 2 through 7 and 12 and 13. For example, Chapter 2 helps you prepare Part A, "The Product or Service."

Section II draws from Chapters 8, 9, and 11. Those chapters give you the background and the skills to crunch numbers for the three financial statements that compose this section. The same chapters prepare you for writing good explanatory notes to accompany each financial statement. These notes will make the statements meaningful to readers who don't relate to the numbers so easily.

How to Start Writing

If you're a creative thinker, chances are your thought processes don't always follow a linear sequence. That's great—it will help you as an entrepreneur! Nonetheless, the action steps in this chapter *do* follow a linear sequence, the sequence of the parts of a finished Business Plan. This is a matter of convenience—you get to see an example of each part as it would appear in the finished product. Bear in mind, however, that we don't expect you to write each part directly in sequence.

The best way to start writing a Business Plan is to begin with the material with which you feel most comfortable. For example, if you really enjoyed interviewing target customers, you might begin with Part B, "The Market and the Target Customers," referring to Chapters 3 and 4 for boosts. Once you have a foothold, the other parts will seem easier to reach.

In this chapter the action steps can serve as a checklist for keeping track of which parts of the Plan you have written. For example, in practice you would probably write the **cover letter** last of all, although that is the first action step we present. Think of the writing of this first cover letter as a valuable exercise. The more cover letters you write, the easier it becomes to write them effectively.

cover letter
a tailored introduction to your Business Plan

THE COVER LETTER

To aim your Plan so that it will achieve the most good, you use a cover letter. Each time you send the Plan to someone, you write a special cover letter addressed to that specific reader. The cover letter introduces the excitement of your Plan, and it tells the person why you are sending it to him or her.

Read the sample cover letter in Figure 16.2 now.

Let's summarize what's good about our sample cover letter. We can see that:

1. The writer is making use of a previous contact.
2. The writer tells his reader—the manager of a bank—that he is in the market for a loan. He does not put her on the spot by asking for money.
3. Instead, he asks for advice on where to find sources of capital.
4. The writer struck the right tone. (To do that, he rewrote the letter several times.)

You can do as well or better—and it's worth the effort! As you draft your cover letter, remember that the reader will pass judgment on your Business Plan (and on your business ability) on the basis of the letter. Do you want your small business to look bright, attractive, and welcoming? Your cover letter needs to give the same impression. A good cover letter will make its readers want to become involved in your venture.

Action Step 66 will help you write your cover letter.

ACTION STEP 66

Write a cover letter for your plan.

Address your letter to a specific person who can help your business. Be brief; aim for about 200 words.

State the reason you are sending the plan. If you are asking for money, tell the person what you want it for and how much you need. One well-written paragraph should be all you need to do this.

Your purpose in writing the cover letter is to open the door gently and prepare the way for further negotiations. The cover letter is bait on your hook.

If you are putting money into the business, or if you have already donated, indicate how much.

The tone you are after in this opening move is confident and slightly formal. You want to appear neat, bright, organized, and in control of your venture.

Be certain to explain briefly how you will repay the money.

Refer to the sample letter in Figure 16.2.

THE SOFTWARE SCHOOL

Mrs. Deborah Wallis
Manager, Franchise National Bank
1400 Market Circle
Anytown, USA

Dear Mrs. Wallis:

I've been meaning to write a formal thank you for the immense help you provided on revising and updating the enclosed Business Plan. Your input was helpful in the marketing area and invaluable on the Financial Section. Everyone here at The Software School appreciates the care you took reading over those early drafts.

Thanks very much.

We're now in the market for a loan of $50,000 (the figure you suggested) to be used for capital expenditures--microcomputers, desks, chairs, and upgrading our curriculum--and we'd appreciate any guidance you could give us concerning sources of capital. (As I'm sure you'll recall, our venture was launched without any equity debt whatsoever, with each of our five principals putting up $20,000 apiece. And the present Turbo Drive location already has space available for the second classroom.)

We're planning to repay the loan out of new profit over the next three years. (For more information, please refer to Financial Section, beginning on page 14.)

Thank you very much for your help and advice. We couldn't have done it without you.

Cordially,

Derek Campbell

Derek Campbell, CEO

47 TURBO DRIVE,
SUITES 108-110
NEWPORT BEACH
CALIFORNIA

FIGURE 16.2   In this sample cover letter, The Software School's CEO introduces his company's Business Plan to a potential lender.

PRELIMINARIES

The Table of Contents

Figure 16.3 provides a sample table of contents to give you a quick overview of a finished Business Plan. In practice, the table of contents is prepared last.

The Executive Summary

The executive summary serves as an introduction to the Business Plan. In function, it is similar to the preface of this book: it is written to acquaint the reader with the subject of the material that follows, to direct the reader's attention to whatever strengths the author (entrepreneur) wants to emphasize, and to make the reader want to turn the page and read, read, read. Because the executive summary gives perspective to the entire Business Plan, it needs to be written last—after Parts A through J are written.

As you write your executive summary, remember that lenders prefer "hard," numerical data and facts; they cannot take speculations about things real seriously. Therefore, such phrases as "50 percent return on the original investment" and "secured agreements from 17 area businesses" make the following example a strong executive summary. They help to paint a picture of good management and solid growth for The Software School.

Executive Summary

The Software School is a user-friendly, state-of-the-art microcomputer training center. In our first 6 months of operation, we demonstrated our unique and profitable way of exploiting a strong and growing market within a fast-growing industry. The Software School's sophisticated electronic classroom provides "hands-on" education that teaches computer users how to use new software programs. By January 2, 19XX, we were operating at 92 percent capacity (50 percent is break-even) and had a waiting list of 168 students.

We plan to add a second classroom in order to double our capacity. This expansion will allow us to attain $400,000 in sales by the end of our 18th month. At that time, our pretax profits will have reached almost $50,000, representing a 50 percent return on our original $100,000 investment.

Our target customers seem to have insatiable appetites for software application knowledge, and The Software School anticipates an annual compound growth rate of 50 percent over the next 5 years. We have secured training agreements from 17 retail computer stores in the area and firm contracts for more than 700 employees from 84 industrial users.

Our competitors continue to train in the traditional classroom style and currently show no sign of copying our unique instructional approach. Occasional price-cutting by competitors has had no effect on our enrollment.

Management, led by Derek Campbell, has demonstrated how to offer superior training at competitive prices. Our plans for the future include developing additional profit centers by providing on-site counseling and training for firms throughout Southern California. Research and customer surveys indicate that we have just begun to satisfy the ever-increasing need for software education.

TABLE OF CONTENTS

*The need for specific appendixes varies greatly from Business Plan to Business Plan. For that reason, this chapter does not include sample appendixes. As you draft your Plan, you will see needs to document and substantiate your business strategies; this kind of documentation is best included as appendixes.

FIGURE 16.3   The table of contents page of The Software School's Business Plan.

ACTION STEP 67

Write an executive summary.

Imagine you had two minutes to explain your business venture to a complete stranger.... This gives you an idea of what information you need to put into writing for your executive summary.

Practice explaining your venture to friends and strangers, limiting yourself to two minutes. Ask them to raise questions, and use their questions to guide you as you revise, and hone, your presentation.

When you are satisfied with your oral summary, write it down and type it up. It should not exceed three typed pages. (The Software School's executive summary that serves as our example was less than one page, single-spaced.) This may constitute a very small portion of your Business Plan, but it could be the most important part of it.

You, too, can write an effective executive summary. Action Step 67 will help you to decide which facts and numbers will portray you and your business venture as credible and promising and then to summarize them on paper.

SECTION I: DESCRIPTION OF THE BUSINESS

Do you know your business? You need to prove it with words and numbers. By the time your reader finishes your Business Plan, you should have a convert to your side. To give you examples to follow, we reprint key sections from the Business Plan (newly revised and updated) for The Software School, an ongoing business that is seeking financing for acquiring more equipment. Regardless of whether your business is ongoing or just starting up, the goals of Section I are the same—to demonstrate that you know your business and that you're a winner.

Part A: The Product or Service

Here's how The Software School tackled this part of Section I.

The Service We Provide

The Software School, a California Corporation, is a microcomputer training facility located in Newport Beach, between John Wayne Airport and a high-density executive business complex. It's the heart of Orange County's microcomputer users. Now in its seventh month of operation, the school has a waiting list of 168 students (67 percent of whom have put down deposits).

We train people in computer software systems from the Top Ten List of best-selling microcomputer software packages. Because of their power, these systems are complex. They provide a learning hurdle, especially at first.

Students are drawn to our teaching method because it gives them **hands-on experience** and because it's fast. Working people are busy, and a student can upgrade a given software skill by 80 percent in 8 hours. (Slower learners are guaranteed a second try, and a third, at no cost.) Most of our courses can be completed in one day or two evenings. In contrast, the average college course (which emphasizes concepts, rather than hands-on software systems) takes 12 to 18 weeks. Our price is $100 for most courses, and so far no one has complained about the cost.

The Software School achieves this space-age learning speed with a sophisticated electronic teaching system adapted from flight-simulation techniques used by airlines for training pilots. We are constantly streamlining and upgrading the system, using funds already allocated in our start-up budget.

One especially bright note: We have done far better than we had hoped. Our actual income figures average 24 percent above our original projections. Projected income for the first six months, with an assumed **occupancy rate** of 50 percent, was just over $10,000 a month. The actual occupancy has not peaked, and for the past two months we have operated at 92 percent capacity.

As a service business, we sell seats as well as skills and information, and as Appendix 1 shows, our promotion has generated a heavy demand for present courses like Computer Fundamentals, Lotus 1-2-3, and Windows. At the same time, customers are asking for courses to meet their needs—for example, a course in Lotus desktop publishing.

Until the end of our fifth month, we were open six days a week from 8 A.M. to 10 P.M. To meet demand with our current classroom facilities, we are now open on Sundays from 9 A.M. to 6 P.M., and the Sunday classes are full.

The demand increased dramatically when we contracted with some of Southern California's large computer retailers to develop a training program. (See Appendix 2 for letters from specific sales managers.) These retailers sent us their salespeople for training; the salespeople, in turn, have referred their customers to us. Computer retailers quickly discovered they can sell better systems to buyers who are not afraid of computers, and they are in the business of selling, not training. We combat customers' fears in a logical way, with knowledge.

Our equipment (IBM PCs) is top-quality. Our staff combines excellent training skills with attention to people and their needs. We have launched a solid start-up in a heated growth industry, and we plan to continue our growth and success.

---

hands-on experience
nonacademic exposure to real life

occupancy rate
the percentage of a commercial property or development that is occupied

ACTION STEP 68

Describe your product or service.

Excite your reader about your business. Excitement is contagious. If you can get your reader going, there's a good chance you'll be offered money. Investors love hot ideas.

If this is a start-up, explain your product or service fully. What makes it unique? What industry is it in? Where does the industry fit in the big picture?

Mention numbers wherever you can. Percentages and dollar amounts are more meaningful than words like *lots* and *many*.

If this is a going business, your records of sales, costs, and profit and loss will substantiate your need for money.

Keep the words going and the typewriter smoking. You need to convince the reader to keep reading.

The Software School will get its funding because the writer of the Plan proves that his business is a winning concern. The writer has:

1. let the facts speak for themselves,
2. supported all claims with numbers,
3. avoided hard-sell tactics, and
4. refused to puff the product.

The writer does a terrific selling job without appearing to be selling at all. Now it's your turn. Do Action Step 68.

Part B: The Market and the Target Customer

Knowledge is power, especially in the Information Age. The Software School—an information business—capitalized on expert knowledge to define the marketplace. In the same way, if your research is sound, it will show up in your writing.

As you continue to read The Software School's Business Plan, remember:

1. This is a revised Business Plan, so the writing is smooth. You will need to do several revisions in order to smooth out your writing. (How many revisions are you planning?)
2. The reader of your Business Plan is a special kind of target customer. (How can you use your marketing abilities to look at this reader with new eyes? Have you developed a profile of this very special target customer?)

The Market and Our Target Customer

INDUSTRY OVERVIEW

Fifteen years ago, the personal computer did not exist in the U. S. marketplace. There were **mainframes**, of course, and terminals linked to invisible data banks—but nothing you could carry home in a suitcase.

Things are different today. Approximately 200 firms are making personal computers. The lion's share of the market goes to Apple, IBM, AST Research, Dell Computers, Compaq, and so forth, and yet someone brings out a new PC (personal computer) almost every day of the year. The microcomputer industry is moving so fast that statistics can't keep pace. In 1981, the one-millionth computer was sold. The next year, 1982, a million computers were sold. It's projected that 2 million computers will be sold in 1990, and 3 million in the year 2000.

With all this sales flurry and emphasis on space-aged speed, some people are being left behind because they don't know how to use computers. A computer can be your best friend, but only if you learn how to use it. This makes training people to use computers a booming industry, and The Software School is on the **leading edge** of a major growth segment.

TARGET MARKET

Our potential **total market** is Southern California, with a logical concentration in Orange County—which will increase in population from 2,800,000 in 1991 to 3,500,000 in the year 2000.

Geographically, our target market encompasses Long Beach, La Habra, and Brea on the north; San Clemente on the south; Huntington and Newport Beaches on the west; and Orange, Fullerton, and Mission Viejo on the east. We are looking ahead to possible future expansion through the Southwestern United States.

For now, our focus is Orange County. Within this highly concentrated population area, our target customer is the small business person. Latest statistics show 76,000 small businesses in Orange County.

mainframes
massive hardware for processing data

leading edge
the latest state of the art

total market
every person or business that might need a product or service

continued

OUR TARGET CUSTOMER

Our primary target customer is the small business, profiled here:

    Size: 1–30 employees
    Annual sales: $250,000 to $5,000,000
    Type of business: service industry
    Major output: paper (reports, letters, documents, etc.)

Our secondary target customer is the home user:

    Sex: 50% male, 50% female
    Age: 18–45
    Education: some college
    Owns PC: 22%
    Access to computer at work: 52%
    Lives near computer store: 73%
    Household income: $55,000 plus
    Occupation: professional, managerial, executive, entrepreneurial

Action Step 69 gives you a chance to show what you know about your market and your target customer. If you need help getting started, review your work in Chapters 3 and 4. You can also review what the Business Plan for The Software School says about its market and TCs. Be sure to use secondary sources (like documents, tables, and quotes) to lend this portion credibility.

Part C: The Competition

Obviously, if you know who your competitors are and how they fail to meet market needs, you are well on your way to strategic competition. You need to persuade your reader how great your competitive tactics are. (If you need a reminder, reread Chapters 4 and 5. Competition changes according to the life-cycle stage of the industry, so a good way to begin your section on competition is to place your industry in the proper life-cycle phase.)

How tough do your competitors look? As you read The Software School's assessment of its competition, note that the writer takes a cool, objective look at the competition. He does not belittle them, and he certainly doesn't underestimate them.

ACTION STEP 69

Describe the market and the target customer.

Bring all of your marketing research into this section and wow your reader with a picture of your target customer just sitting there waiting for your product or service.

    Use data from secondary sources to give credibility to the picture you are painting.

The Competition

The competition for computer training in Orange County is minimal at this time. The Software School has four main competitors:

Traherne Schools.   Our oldest, most entrenched competitor. Three locations in Orange County: Brea, Garden Grove, and South Coast Plaza. Traherne's conducts a 6-hour course on Introduction to Microprocessors for $95. They currently run a course on desktop publishing for the Mac, and they have been planning to introduce a word-processing course for some time.

    Traherne's target market is on the north rim of ours. Their South Coast Plaza operation is closed on Saturdays.

Big Micro Computer Instruction.   Excellent classroom facilities, located in El Toro, near the San Diego Freeway. All instruction is tied to MacIntosh machines, and is free if you buy your hardware from Big Micro. Otherwise, courses usually cost around $95, and take 6–8 hours.

continued

The instructors try hard, but Big Micro is really in the business of pushing hardware.

Micro Hut Computer Center.   Friendly salespeople with teaching skills double as teachers. Courses at Micro Hut are divided between Compaq and Apple. Costs: VisiCalc, $89; Word Processing, $149. The Word-Processing course takes about 12 hours of classroom time and is available only on Apple computers.

Micro Hut is not in the education business. They offer courses only to help sell systems.

Your Micro and You.   Local facility developed by professional educators. The atmosphere of YMAY is excellent. They offer a normal range of programs and a course in using the computer in a small business, each course costing about $125. All instruction is tied to the Apple. Their market seems to be divided between adults with a casual interest in computers and children aged 10 to 15.

These people have done it right.

MEETING THE COMPETITION

The Software School is in the computer education business. We do not sell hardware or software.

Our program of instruction is geared to the times. We teach popular software, and we are constantly on the lookout for trends that will lead us to new markets. Furthermore, our prices are competitive, and we teach classes 7 days a week.

ACTION STEP 70

Describe your major competitors.

Briefly profile the businesses that compete with you directly. Try to be objective as you assess their operations.

What are their strengths? What are their weaknesses? What can you learn from them?

After you've described your competitors, indicate how you're going to ace them out of the picture.

The Software School's Business Plan leaves no doubt that management is exploiting a market gap that is ignored by the competition—training people how to use popular software on the emerging industry leader, the IBM PC and IBM PS/2. This is more than a matter of writing skill. Early on, the entrepreneurs who founded The Software School did the right research so they could make decisions ahead of time—just as you were asked to do in the earlier chapters.

How will you handle the competition in your Business Plan? Your readers will expect you to be cool and objective. Now you're ready to complete Action Step 70.

Part D: Marketing Strategy

Now it's time to describe your marketing strategy. Need a reminder? Look back at your work in Chapter 6.

The Marketing Strategy excerpt from The Software School's Business Plan demonstrates a carefully reasoned approach. The excerpt describes conscious marketing policies that will help this small business be competitive. If you read a Business Plan in which the writer did not demonstrate this care and deliberation, how much faith would you have in the writer's business abilities?

Note that The Software School uses a three-pronged approach to reaching the public. This business understands the importance of finding a good promotional mix.

Marketing Strategy

An analysis of our competitors indicates that our price—$99 for a 1-day course, $198 for a 2-day course—is between two extremes. These prices are competitive but still maintain our image of quality.

continued

We use a wide range of strategies to let our customers know where we are: **mass-media advertising** (newspapers, television, and radio), special promotions (press releases, brochures, newsletter, etc.), and personal selling (commissioned salespeople, networking, corporate contracts, trade shows, etc.)

MASS-MEDIA ADVERTISING

The Software School has been placing ads in the *Los Angeles Times* and smaller, area newspapers to keep a continuous presence in front of our target customers. In the beginning, we used inducements (two-for-one offers, 15 percent reductions, etc.), but that is no longer necessary as our waiting lists grow.

As we continue to expand, we will develop advertising on radio and TV.

CREATIVE PROMOTIONS / INK / FREE INK

In our first month of operation, we sponsored a scholarship contest in the local high schools, which resulted in some very positive press. In addition, the school has been featured in several local newspapers.

We are in the Information business, and toward that end we are presently developing three different publications—a computer handbook, a newsletter, and a brief history of the founding of The Software School. In time, we hope that this history (a how-to for computer educators) will become a guide for the industry.

Our mailing list grows daily. We log all incoming phone calls with information on the callers and how they found out about us. This information helps us define our target market.

PERSONAL SELLING

Personal contact has gained us our largest accounts so far. (Please refer to letters from computer retailers in Appendix 2.) We intend to intensify our efforts along these lines. Fortunately, our directors have experience and talent in the area of personal selling.

We maintain a booth at the major computer trade shows in the area. Approximately 17 percent of our hobbyist/home-user business has been generated this way.

mass-media advertising
reaching unselected hordes of people through print, sound, or visuals

The entrepreneurs who run The Software School stay on top of the changing market picture. They have demonstrated this by:

1. dropping discount inducements from their continuous print campaign,
2. looking ahead to radio and TV exposure,
3. logging calls and gathering information on the callers to maintain a base of up-to-date information on their target market, and
4. determining how they have gained their largest accounts and planning to intensify their efforts in that area.

Action Step 71 will help you to refine your marketing strategy. Note that you must continue to focus on the target customer.

ACTION STEP 71

Describe your marketing strategy.

Now that you've profiled your target customer and assessed your competition, take some time to develop the thrust of your market strategy. Which techniques will get the best and most cost-effective response?

Because pricing is such an important consideration, you might start with what your TC sees as a good value, and then develop your marketing mix.

Part E: Location

The next part of your Business Plan is the one on location. You may want to review your work in Chapter 7 now.

Read how The Software School shows off its location to advantage.

business zoning
legal designation of property for business use

ACTION STEP 72

Show off your location.

The great thing about a location is that it's so *tangible*. A potential lender can visit your site and get a feel for what's going on.

A banker will often visit your business site. That's good news for you because now the banker is on your turf.

Clean up the place before your banker arrives.

In this section, you want to persuade potential lenders to visit your site. Describe what goes on here. Use photographs and diagrams and illustrations to make it feel almost like home.

Our Location

The Software School is currently in the first year of a 3-year lease at 47 Turbo Drive, Newport Beach, California. The facility is all on the ground floor and occupies 2,100 square feet. The area, which is **zoned for business use**, is a hotbed of high-technology activity. Within the immediate area, there are 2 computer stores, 1 computer furniture store, 1 software dealer, an electronics store, and 2 printers, one of which does typesetting work directly from software diskettes. Within a 4-mile radius are 27 computer dealers.

During our lease negotiations, we persuaded the landlord to make extensive improvements in the interior, and to spread the cost out over the 3-year term of the lease. The decor—blue carpet, white walls, orange furniture—gives the effect of a solid, logical, somewhat plush business environment in which our target customer will be comfortable and learn fast.

The building is divided into 5 areas: a reception area (300 square feet), a director's office (100 square feet), a classroom (700 square feet), a lounge (200 square feet), and a storage area (800 square feet).

The principals envision the storage area as a second classroom. See diagram in Appendix 9.

You need to paint an attractive picture of your business site and, at the same time, keep your reader interested by inspiring confidence in your choice. Location takes a tremendous amount of analysis. The Software School writer gives himself a subtle pat on the back by describing the lease arrangements and by identifying the need for a second classroom. If the reader needs more, he or she is referred to the appendix. This is smart writing.

Your Plan will become very real when you showcase your physical facility. Complete Action Step 72.

Part F: Management

Management will make or break your small business. You are a member of the management team, and you want this Business Plan to inspire confidence in your team. Writing this section will help you focus more closely on your management team members. (If you need a refresher, review your work in Chapters 12 and 13.)

Now let's see how The Software School introduces *its* management.

Management

Derek Campbell.   Mr. Campbell was born in Shaker Heights, Ohio, in 19—. He took a B.S. degree in Industrial Engineering at Purdue University and then spent 5 years in the Marine Corps, where he was a flight instructor, a check pilot, and a maintenance officer. While in the service, Mr. Campbell completed an M.A. degree in Marketing, Management, and Human Relations.

Following military service, Mr. Campbell was employed as a pilot for United Airlines. He is currently the CEO of EuroSource, a software importing company. He is the author of several articles on computers and the Information Age and is listed in *Who's Who in California*.

continued

Robert Jericho.   Mr. Jericho was born in Dallas, Texas, in 19—. He has a B.S. degree in Geology and Physical Sciences at the University of Oklahoma and served 6 years in the Marine Corps, where he was a flight instructor, flight operations officer, and schedules officer.

Following military service, Mr. Jericho was a pilot for Trans World Airlines. He has completed training in the Nestar system managers' course, the Apple computer maintenance course, and has been working as an accountant and comptroller for Euro-Source for the past 2 years.

DIRECTORS

C. Hughes Smith.   Mr. Smith was born in Corpus Christi, Texas, in 19—. He has a B.A. degree from Tulane University in political science and philosophy, a M.A. degree in business administration from Stanford, and a law degree from the University of Texas at Austin.

Mr. Smith is a senior vice-president of Lowes and Lockwood, a residential home-building firm, and a partner in Graebner and Ashe, a Houston law firm. He is the author of numerous articles in the field of corporate planning and taxes. (Please see Personal Resumes in Appendix 4.)

Phil Carpenter.   Mr. Carpenter was born in Duluth, Minnesota, in 19—. His B.A. degree is from the University of Kansas and his M.B.A., with a marketing specialty, is from the University of Wisconsin.

Mr. Carpenter spent 20 years in the corporate world (IBM, TRW, Inter-Comp, etc.), where he worked in marketing and industrial sales. Currently a professor of Business at Huntington Beach Community College, Mr. Carpenter is the general partner in 2 businesses and a small business consultant. He has written and lectured widely in the area of small business.

Dan Masters.   Mr. Masters was born in Palo Alto, California, in 19—. His degrees (B.A., M.B.A.) are from Stanford, where he specialized in marketing and finance. Mr. Masters served his Army duty in Korea, where he worked on the United Nations Korean Civil Assistance Program, a long-term plan for making Korea economically independent. Following his military service, Mr. Masters worked for Kodak and then for Sylvania (senior account sales executive, sales manager, and so on) for a total of 25 years.

Mr. Masters is currently an associate professor of Business at San Juan Capistrano Institute of Business Science. He is active in several small businesses, lectures widely, and has published numerous articles in the field of small business.

OTHER AVAILABLE RESOURCES

The Software School has retained the legal firm of Farney and Shields and the accounting firm of Hancock, Hancock, and Craig. Our insurance broker is Sharon Mandel of Fireman's Fund. Our advertising agency is George Friend and Associates.

This management team shows balance, diversity, experience (some interesting track records), the will to succeed, and above all, a love of adventure. Robert Jericho and Derek Campbell were both flight instructors. Now they're using space-age industrial training techniques in the computer classroom. In addition, pilots must plan and must take responsibility—good experience for running their own show.

Balance is important too, and this shows up in the short resumes. Jericho is the technician who handles systems management. Campbell is the marketeer and manager. Both have good people skills. Who do you suppose is the idea man?

The Software School is a corporation, and the authors of the Business Plan were wise to include resumes of the directors. In this case, the background of the directors enhances the balance of the team. All three directors have admirable depth in their business careers, with two of them sharing a combined 45 years of experience in the corporate world. Campbell very wisely uses his directors to assist him in the sales function.

The listing of the legal counsel, accounting firm, an insurance broker, and advertising agency also adds to the impression of solid business practices. We sometimes refer to these people as the "taxi-squad," but in a Business Plan, the language is more formal.

Nothing is more important than the people who will make your business work. Present their pedigrees, and focus on their track records and accomplishments as you complete Action Step 73.

Part G: Personnel

Part G of your Plan shows off your personnel. For a start-up business, you're peering into the future with confidence—doing informal job analyses for key employees who will help you to succeed. For an ongoing business, you need to list your present employees and anticipate your future personnel needs. If you have five employees now and you want to indicate growth, try to project how many jobs you'll be creating in the next 5 years.

When you start thinking about tasks and people to do them, review your work in Chapters 12 and 13. Preparing this part of your Plan is important because it gives you one more chance to analyze job functions before you start interviewing, hiring, and paying benefits—all of which are expensive.

You'll notice that The Software School gives a very brief rundown of its personnel situation.

Personnel

At the end of 6 months of operation, The Software School has 3 full-time employees and 14 part-time employees. The full-time employees include:

1. Manager, salaried at $3,000 per month
2. Receptionist, salaried at $8 per hour
3. Training Director, salaried at $1,500 per month

The part-time employees include 3 directors, who assist in the marketing function, 3 outside commissioned salespeople, and 8 part-time instructors. According to our plan, 1 salesperson will become full-time at the end of the seventh month.

We will continue to hold down overhead with part-time employees as long as it is feasible. We believe that running a lean operation is important to our success.

In describing their lean operation, the entrepreneurs who run The Software School keep their description lean as well. They show good sense when they express a commitment to hold down operating costs. Their decision reflects business discipline and foresight. If you were a potential investor in this business, wouldn't you appreciate some tight purse strings?

Every person on your team is important. Action Step 74 will help you describe the kinds of people you will need and how you will help them to become productive.

SECTION II: FINANCIAL SECTION

Good Numbers

The financial section is the heart of your Business Plan. It is aimed at lenders—bankers, credit managers, venture capitalists, vendors, SBICs, commercial credit lenders—people who think in numbers. Lenders are professional skeptics by trade; they will not be swayed by the enthusiasm of your writing in Section I. Your job, therefore, is to make your numbers do the talking. This is easier than you may think.

You started jotting down numbers in Chapter 8, when you began thinking about money. You projected cash flow and income in Chapter 9. In Chapter 10, you tested your numbers on real lenders in the real world. Now you're ready to organize your numbers into three standard instruments:

1. the projected income statement,
2. the cash flow projection (also called a "pro forma"), and
3. the projected balance sheet.

Examples from The Software School will serve as models for you. You can adapt them to fit your business.

The idea is to know where every nickel is going. You need to show when you'll make a profit and appear neat, orderly, in control, and conservative. You'll know you've succeeded when a skeptical lender looks up from your Business Plan and says, "You know, these numbers look good."

Good Notes

One way to spot a professional lender is to hand over your Business Plan and watch to see which section he or she reads first. Most lenders study the notes that accompany income and cash flow projections first. Knowing this allows you to be forewarned. Use these notes to tell potential lenders how you generated your numbers (for example, "Advertising is projected at 5 percent of sales") and to explain specific entries (for example, "Leased Equipment—monthly lease costs on IBM microcomputers").

Make these notes easy to read, with headings that start your readers off in the upper left-hand corner and march them down the page, step-by-step, to the bottom line. (Some sample projection charts use tiny footnotes, on the same page. We prefer *large* notes on a separate page. Notes are important, so they should be big.)

Creating your Business Plan takes a lot of time. It's only natural for you to hope that lenders will read it, get excited, and ask questions. These notes can help you accomplish that, even if you haven't started up and the numbers are projections into the future.

Part H: Projected Income Statement

Your next task is to put together your projected income statement (sometimes called a "profit and loss" statement). With the information you've gathered so far, it shouldn't be too hard. In fact, it will be enjoyable—if the numbers look good.

The Software School's projected income statement is shown in Table 16.1, and the careful documentation of each item is reprinted here. For instance, if a lender

TABLE 16.1 The Software School's projected income statement

INCOME STATEMENT/SOFTWARE SCHOOL

	7th Month	8th Month	9th Month	10th Month	11th Month	12th Month
SALES						
Instruction	$23,285	$24,950	$26,630	$28,215	$29,900	$31,580
Books	215	250	270	285	300	320
TOTAL SALES	$23,500	$25,200	$26,900	$28,500	$30,200	$31,900
Cost of Instruction						
Clssrm. Matrls.	$1,765	$1,890	$2,020	$2,140	$2,265	$2,395
Inst./Personnel	2,500	2,500	2,600	2,600	2,700	2,700
Books	150	175	190	200	210	225
TOTAL COST/ INSTR/BOOKS	4,415	4,565	4,810	4,940	5,175	5,320
GROSS PROFIT	$19,085	$20,635	$22,090	$23,560	$25,025	$26,580
EXPENSES						
SALES:						
Commissions	$2,330	$2,495	$2,665	$2,820	$2,990	$3,160
Advertising	1,175	1,250	1,335	1,410	1,495	1,580
Credit Cards	295	315	335	355	380	400
ADMINISTRATIVE:						
Salaries	3,300	3,300	3,300	4,500	4,500	4,500
Payroll Taxes	570	580	600	695	715	725
Leased Equip.	1,270	1,270	1,270	1,270	1,270	1,270
Licenses/fees	2,330	2,495	2,665	2,820	2,990	3,160
Accounting	500	500	500	500	500	500
Rent	3,890	3,890	3,890	3,890	3,890	3,890
Office Supplies	60	65	65	70	75	80
Dues/Subscript.	20	20	20	20	20	20
Repair/Maint.	235	250	265	285	300	320
Insurance	80	80	80	80	80	80
Telephone	355	380	405	430	455	480
Utilities	470	505	540	570	605	640
Depreciation	1,170	1,170	1,170	1,335	1,335	1,335
Interest				650	650	650
Miscellaneous	705	755	805	855	905	955
TOTAL EXPENSES	$18,755	$19,320	$19,910	$22,555	$23,155	$23,745
NET PROFIT	$330	$1,315	$2,180	$1,005	$1,870	$2,835
Reserve for taxes	65	265	435	200	375	565
NET PROFIT AFTER TAXES	$265	$1,050	$1,745	$805	$1,495	$2,270

TABLE 16.1   *Continued*

INCOME STATEMENT/SOFTWARE SCHOOL

	13th Month	14th Month	15th Month	16th Month	17th Month	18th Month	TOTAL
SALES							
Instruction	$33,265	$34,945	37915	$39,600	$42,770	$42,770	$395,825
Books	335	355	435	500	530	530	4,325
TOTAL SALES	$33,600	$35,300	$38,350	$40,100	$43,300	$43,300	$400,150
Cost of Instruction							
Clssrm. Matrls.	$2,520	$2,650	$2,875	$3,000	$3,240	$3,240	$30,000
Inst./Personnel	2,800	2,800	2,900	2,900	3,000	3,000	33,000
Books	235	250	305	350	370	370	3,030
TOTAL COST/ INSTR/BOOKS	5,555	5,700	6,080	6,250	6,610	6,610	66,030
GROSS PROFIT	$28,045	$29,600	$32,270	$33,850	$36,690	$36,690	$334,120
EXPENSES							
SALES:							
Commissions	$3,325	$3,495	$3,790	$3,960	$4,275	$4,275	$39,580
Advertising	1,660	1,750	1,895	1,980	2,135	2,135	19,800
Credit Cards	420	440	480	500	540	540	5,000
ADMINISTRATIVE:							
Salaries	4,500	4,500	4,500	4,500	4,500	4,500	50,400
Payroll Taxes	745	755	785	795	825	825	8,615
Leased Equip.	1,270	1,270	1,270	1,270	1,270	1,270	15,240
Licenses/fees	3,325	3,495	3,790	3,960	4,275	4,275	39,580
Accounting	500	500	500	500	500	500	6,000
Rent	3,890	3,890	3,890	3,890	3,890	3,890	46,680
Office Supplies	85	90	95	100	110	110	1,005
Dues/Subscript.	200	20	20	20	20	20	420
Repair/Maint.	335	355	385	395	435	435	3,995
Insurance	80	80	80	80	80	80	960
Telephone	505	530	575	600	650	650	6,015
Utilities	670	705	765	800	865	865	8,000
Depreciation	1,335	1,335	1,335	1,335	1,335	1,335	15,525
Interest	650	650	650	595	595	595	5,685
Miscellaneous	1,010	1,060	1,150	1,205	1,300	1,300	12,005
TOTAL EXPENSES	$24,505	$24,920	$25,955	$26,485	$27,600	$27,600	$284,505
NET PROFIT	$3,540	$4,680	$6,315	$7,365	$9,090	$9,090	$49,615
Reserve for taxes	710	935	1,265	1,475	1,820	1,820	9,930
NET PROFIT AFTER TAXES	$2,830	$3,745	$5,050	$5,890	$7,270	$7,270	$39,685

wanted to know how the figures for commissions were generated, Note 6 explains that they are estimated as 10 percent of sales.

Notes for Projected Income Statement

1. **Instruction.** Based on 2.5% occupancy growth per month, starting at 35% (235 students) and growing to 60%. Students pay $99 per course.
2. **Books.** Revenue from books sold averages approximately 1% of instructional sales, rounded to bring total sales to an even $100 figure.
3. **Classroom Materials.** $7.50 per student.
4. **Instruction Personnel.** Instructor cost is $100 per 8-hour class, starting with 25 classes and growing to 30 classes by the end of the year.
5. **Books.** Cost of books is 70% of selling price.
6. **Commissions.** Average 10% of instructional sales.
7. **Advertising.** Projected at 5% of sales.
8. **Credit Cards.** Approximately 50% of sales are paid with credit cards. The cost is 2.5% of the sale.
9. **Salaries.** Start with 3 full-time employees. Bring on one additional person beginning the 10th month.
10. **Payroll Taxes.** The company's share of employee taxes averages 7% of commissions and salaries.
11. **Leased Equipment.** Monthly lease costs on IBM microcomputers.
12. **Licenses and Fees.** 10% of instruction sales paid for license (right to use copyrighted material).
13. **Accounting.** Average accounting and bookkeeping costs for the area and size of the business.
14. **Rent.** Based on 3-year lease.
15. **Office Supplies.** Estimated at 0.25% of sales.
16. **Dues and Subscriptions.** Estimated costs for magazines, newspapers, and membership in organizations.
17. **Repair and Maintenance.** Projected to be 1% of sales.
18. **Insurance.** Based on current insurance contract for next 12 months, payable every 6 months.
19. **Telephone.** Figured at 1.5% of sales.
20. **Utilities.** Figured at 2% of sales.
21. **Depreciation.** Schedule established by accounting firm.
22. **Interest.** Loan at 13% with $5,000 payments due every 6 months until paid off.
23. **Miscellaneous.** Figured at 3% of sales.
24. **Reserve for Taxes.** State and federal taxes estimated at 20% of net profit.

ACTION STEP 75

Project your income statement.

What you're driving at here is *net profit*—what's left in the kitty after expenses—for each month and for the year.

First, you figure your *sales*. The first big bite out of that figure is the *cost of goods sold*. (In a service business, the big cost is labor.) Subtracting that gives you a figure called *gross margin*.

Now add up all your *expenses* (rent, utilities, insurance, etc.), and subtract them from gross margin. This gives you *net profit before taxes*. (Businesses pay quarterly installments.)

Subtract taxes. There's your net profit.

Action Step 75 will help you project your own monthly profits and losses for 12 months. Refer to Table 16.1 as you predict your income.

Part I: Projected Cash Flow

Next focus your attention on the projected cash flow— the lifeblood of your business. By projecting cash flow figures out across the year, you get a month-by-month picture of how healthy your business will be.

The Software School's cash flow projection is set out in Table 16.2. The notes for these numbers are reprinted here. If you compare the projected income statement (Table 16.1) with the cash flow projection, you will see that some items are treated differently in the tables. For example, expenses in the projected income statement are divided into monthly installments, whereas the same expenses in the cash flow projection are shown as bulk payments when due. Now look at insurance expense. In the projected income statement we find a total expense of $960 shown as twelve monthly debits of $80 each. The same expense in the cash flow projection is shown as two payments of $480 each, falling due in the seventh and thirteenth months. If the entrepreneurs running the business had only $80 available to pay for insurance in the seventh month—that is what is shown in the income statement—they would be in trouble.

Notes for Cash Flow Projection

1. **Beginning of the Month.** Cash available as the month begins.
2. **Sales.** Includes all sales paid by cash, check, or credit card at the time the class is taken. Does not include accounts receivable.
3. **Credit Card Expense.** Fees of 2.5% paid to credit card companies. Approximately 50% of customers use charge cards.
4. **Loans.** Loan for new course development and audiovisual equipment.
5. **Total Cash Available.** Sum of all money available during the month.
6. **Books.** Books for sale are ordered and paid for one month in advance of projected sale.
7. **Instructional Materials.** Covers course materials purchased from licenser.
8. **Salaries.** Net salaries paid employees approximate 80% of gross salaries paid.
9. **Payroll Taxes.** Total of amount withhold from employees, plus Income Statement payroll tax item.
10. **Advertising.** Established as 30-day accounts with all media companies.
11. **Leased Equipment.** Lease payments are due the first of each month.
12. **Licenses and Fees.** License fees are due the 15th of the following month.
13. **Legal and Accounting.** Due 30 days after bill is received.
14. **Rent.** Due the first of each month.
15. **Office Supplies.** Paid at time of purchase or with subscription. No credit.
16. **Insurance.** Paid every 6 months in advance.
17. **Telephone and Utilities.** Paid within 30 days of receipt of bill.
18. **Interest.** Interest only, paid each month.
19. **Loan Payback.** $5,000 loan payment due every 6 months.
20. **Miscellaneous.** Paid in month expense occurs.
21. **Income Tax Reserve.** Paid into a special tax account at the bank.
22. **Total Disbursements.** Total cash expended during the month.
23. **Net Cash before Capital Investment.** Cash balance before capital investment payments.
24. **Capital Equipment.** Purchase of additional audiovisual equipment.
25. **Contracted Course Development.** Contract payments due for new course development.
26. **Monthly Cash Flow.** Cash balance after all payments at the end of the month.

ACTION STEP 76

Project your cash flow.

Get used to doing cash flow. Once a month is not too often to do it. If you prepared a cash flow for your business back in Chapter 9, bring those numbers forward. If you skipped that step do it now. Here's how it's done:

1. Write down all the cash you will have for one year.
2. Add net profit.
3. Add any loans.
4. Figure your total cash needs for the year.
5. Spread these numbers out across the year. You may have a lot of cash at the start of the year; you want to make sure you have enough to get all the way through.
6. Now list all disbursements. Spread these out, too.
7. Now examine the figures. Is there any time during the year when you will run short of cash? It's better to know the truth now, when you're still working on paper.
8. If your cash picture looks good, drop in a couple of what-ifs. (Let's say you've budgeted $300 for utilities, and the air-conditioner goes out. It will cost $200 to repair it, and the lease says it is your expense. Or let's say you see an opportunity for a sale, but you would have to hire someone to handle it for you. Can your cash flow handle such surprises?)

Profits don't pay the bills and the payroll; cash flow does. Potential lenders look at cash flow projections first, so Action Step 76 can make or break you.

TABLE 16.2   The Software School's cash flow projection

CASH FLOW/SOFTWARE SCHOOL

	7th Month	8th Month	9th Month	10th Month	11th Month	12th Month
CASH-RECEIPTS						
Beginning of Month	$3,970	$7,365	$6,015	$51,575	$47,060	$35,275
Sales	23,500	25,200	26,900	28,500	30,200	31,900
Less: Credit Card Expense	(295)	(315)	(335)	(355)	(380)	(400)
Loan			60,000			
TOTAL SALES	$27,175	$32,250	$92,580	$79,720	$76,880	$66,775
DISBURSEMENTS						
Books	$175	$190	$200	$210	$225	$235
Inst./Materials		6,000			7,500	
Salaries:						
Instruction	2,000	2,000	2,040	2,080	2,120	2,160
Administration	2,640	2,640	2,640	3,120	3,600	3,600
Commissions	1,730	1,865	1,995	2,130	2,255	2,390
Payroll Taxes	2,045	2,195	2,250	2,435	2,690	2,755
Advertising	1,080	1,175	1,250	1,335	1,410	1,495
Leased Equip.	1,270	1,270	1,270	1,270	1,270	1,270
Licenses/fees	2,160	2,330	2,495	2,665	2,820	2,990
Accounting	500	500	500	500	500	500
Rent	3,890	3,890	3,890	3,890	3,890	3,890
Office Supplies	60	65	65	70	75	80
Dues/Subscript.	20	20	20	20	20	20
Repair/Maint.	235	250	265	285	300	320
Insurance	480					
Telephone	325	355	380	405	430	455
Utilities	430	470	505	540	570	605
Interest				650	650	650
Loan Payback						
Miscellaneous	705	755	805	855	905	955
Inc. Tax Reserve	65	265	435	200	375	565
TOTAL DISBURSEMNTS	$19,810	$26,235	$21,005	$22,660	$31,605	$24,935
Net Cash Before Capital Invest.	$7,365	$6,015	$71,575	$57,060	$45,275	$41,840
Capital Equipment			10,000			
Contracted Course Development			10,000	10,000	10,000	10,000
	$7,365	$6,015	$51,575	$47,060	$35,275	$31,840

Part J: Projected Balance Sheet

The professionals will look at your balance sheet (sometimes called a "statement of financial position") to analyze the state of your finances at a given point in time. They are looking at things like **liquidity** (how easily your assets can be converted

liquidity
convertibility to cash

TABLE 16.2   *Continued*

CASH FLOW/SOFTWARE SCHOOL

	13th Month	14th Month	15th Month	16th Month	17th Month	18th Month	TOTAL
CASH-RECEIPTS							
Beginning of Month	$31,840	$28,645	$27,900	$33,115	$43,895	$47,800	$364,455
Sales	33,600	35,300	38,350	40,100	43,300	43,300	400,150
Less: Credit Card Expense	(420)	(440)	(480)	(500)	(540)	(540)	(5,000)
Loan							60,000
TOTAL SALES	$65,020	$63,505	$65,770	$72,715	$86,655	$90,560	$819,605
DISBURSEMENTS							
Books	$250	$305	$350	$370	$370	$385	$3,265
Inst./Materials		9,000			9,000		31,500
Salaries:							
Instruction	2,200	2,240	2,280	2,320	2360	2360	26,160
Administration	3,600	3,600	3,600	3,600	3,600	3,600	39,840
Commissions	2,530	2,660	2,795	3,030	3,170	3,420	29,970
Payroll Taxes	2,805	2,870	2,925	3,025	3,075	3,170	32,240
Advertising	1,580	1,660	1,750	1,895	1,980	2,135	18,745
Leased Equip.	1,270	1,270	1,270	1,270	1,270	1,270	15,240
Licenses/fees	3,160	3,325	3,495	3,790	3,960	4,275	35,305
Accounting	500	500	500	500	500	500	6,000
Rent	3,890	3,890	3,890	3,890	3,890	3,890	46,680
Office Supplies	85	90	95	100	110	110	1,005
Dues/Subscript.	200	20	20	20	20	20	420
Repair/Maint.	335	355	385	395	435	435	3,995
Insurance	480						960
Telephone	480	505	530	575	600	650	5,690
Utilities	640	670	705	765	800	865	7,565
Interest	650	650	650	595	595	595	5,685
Loan Payback			5,000				
Miscellaneous	1,010	1,060	1,150	1,205	1,300	1,300	12,005
Inc. Tax Reserve	710	935	1,265	1,475	1,820	1,820	9,930
TOTAL DISBURSEMNTS	$26,375	$35,605	$32,655	$28,820	$38,855	$30,800	$339,360
Net Cash Before Capital Invest.	$38,645	$27,900	$33,115	$43,895	$47,800	$59,760	$480,245
Capital Equipment							10,000
Contracted Course Development	10,000						50,000
	$28,645	$27,900	$33,115	$43,895	$47,800	$59,760	$420,245

into cash) and **capital structure** (what sources of financing have been used, how much was borrowed, and so on). Professional lenders will use such factors to evaluate your ability to manage your business.

Table 16.3 shows two balance sheets for The Software School. Note that the first one shows its actual position at the end of its first 6 months and the second is a

capital structure
source of funds; debt vs. equity capital

TABLE 16.3   The Software School's balance sheet

	ACTUAL BALANCE SHEET SOFTWARE SCHOOL AS OF SEPTEMBER 30, 19XX (AFTER FIRST 6 MONTHS)			PROJECTED BALANCE SHEET SOFTWARE SCHOOL AS OF SEPTEMBER 30, 19XX (AFTER FIRST 18 MONTHS)		
ASSETS						
Cash	$3,970			$59,670		
Instr. Materials & Books	2,500			4,495		
	--------			--------		
TOTAL CURRENT ASSETS			$6,470			$64,165
Leasehold Improvements	$41,000			$41,000		
Furniture	15,100			15,100		
Audio/Visual	10,600			20,600		
Office Equipment	3,600	$70,300		3,600	$80,300	
Less Depreciation	--------	7,020	63,280	--------	22,545	57,755
		--------			--------	
License Agreement			25,000	$25,000		
New Courses			-0-	50,000		75,000
			---------			---------
TOTAL ASSETS			$94,750			$196,920
			========			=========
LIABILITIES						
Instructor's Salaries	$1,250			$1,500		
Administrative Salaries	1,650			2,250		
Commissions	2,165			4,275		
Accounts Payable	4,495			9,020		
Current Liabilities	--------	$9,560		--------	$17,045	
Long-Term Debt		-0-			55,000	
		--------			--------	
Total Liabilities			$9,560			$72,045
NET WORTH (OWNER'S EQUITY)						
Capital Stock	$100,000			$100,000		
Retained Earnings	(14,810)		85,190	24,875		124,875
	--------		---------	--------		---------
TOTAL LIABILITIES & NET WORTH			$94,750			$196,920
			=========			=========

ROI

$$\frac{\text{net profit}}{\text{owner's investment}}$$

projection of where it will be at the end of its first 18 months. If you're just starting up, *all* figures will be projections.

Let's talk for a minute about ROI, return on investment. ROI is a bottom-line figure that shows how much is earned on the total dollars invested in the business. You have this kind of information up front if you invest money in bonds. The interest tells you your return on investment. Imagine that you had two funds, Bond A and Bond B, and Bond A paid you a 4 percent return and Bond B paid you 25 percent. Which bond would have the better ROI?

You compute ROI for a business by dividing the net profit by investment dollars. For The Software School, the profit after taxes is $39,685 (from Table 16.1). Divide that by the owner's investment of $100,000 (from Table 16.3):

$$\frac{\$39,685}{\$100,000} = 39.7\%$$

Could you get 39.7 percent from a savings account or a bond fund? It's not a bad ROI. It would dazzle lenders and probably draw the attention of a venture capitalist.

The Software School did not provide notes to its balance sheets, because in this case no notes are needed. In conjunction with the income statement and the cash flow projection, all the entries in the balance sheet will make sense to your professional readers. Under some circumstances, you would want to note unusual features of a balance sheet for an actual fiscal year, but in most cases—and in most projections—this won't be necessary.

Now project a balance sheet for your business. Action Step 77 will help you.

What I hear, I forget.
What I see, I remember.
What I do, I understand.
—Old Entrepreneur

EPILOGUE: ACT ON WHAT YOU KNOW

Well, do you feel like you're ready? You are. You have thoroughly researched your product or your service, your market and your target customer, your competition, your marketing strategy, and your location. You've discovered how to prepare for surprises you can't afford, how to handle numbers, how to pursue financing, when and why you should incorporate, how to build a winning team, and whether you should buy, franchise, or start on your own. You've surveyed the vistas that a small business computer can open up for you. And you've written it all up in a beautiful showcase: your winning Business Plan.

Before you take off running, we want to give you one more tool that we think every entrepreneur should have—a tool to help you put your Business Plan to work. It's called **PERT**—an acronym for *Program Evaluation and Review Technique*—and it's often used to establish schedules for large projects. It was pioneered in military research and development as an aid for identifying activities and their optimal sequence, and then monitoring progress. The aerospace industry, the construction industry, and other big businesses that must plan complicated projects use PERT charts, and so can you.

A PERT chart is just the thing if you feel overwhelmed by the tasks of starting up and don't know where to begin. If you're a person who sometimes tries to do everything at once, PERT is also recommended. It will help you focus your energy on the right job at the right time. A sample PERT chart is provided in Table 16.4. Yours will need to be bigger and more detailed. You can use days, weeks, or months to plot the tasks ahead. (If you think you should use years, reassess your industry.)

Action Step 78 is the last one we give you in this book, and it symbolizes the first one you take on your own as an entrepreneur. It's the end, yes, but also the beginning. All our best wishes go with you as you embark on your great adventure. We hope that this book and its action steps have convinced you that you can achieve success—whatever it means to *you*—and have fun at the same time. Good luck! Work smart, and enjoy your adventure!

PERT
Program Evaluation and Review Technique

Key Points from Another View

Like a headline in a newspaper, the Executive Summary is the section that pulls your reader into the Business Plan. It is your crown jewel, the promise that catches the eye of the investor. Here are tips for writing a winning Executive Summary:

1. Compare your product with a known product. (Your information software does for your industry what the VHS camcorder does for the family photographer. The camcorder simplifies the recording process; your software handles tough problems with one simple-to-use tool.)

ACTION STEP 77

Project your balance sheet.

A projected balance sheet is simply a prediction, on paper, of what your business will be worth at the end of a certain period of time. This prediction allows you to figure your actual and projected ROI, which is the real bottom line.

1. Add up your assets. For convenience, divide these into *Current* (cash, notes receivables, etc.), *Fixed* (land, equipment, buildings, etc.), and *Other* (intangibles like patents, royalty deals, copyrights, goodwill, contracts for exclusive use, and so on). You'll need to depreciate fixed assets that wear out. As value, you show the net of cost minus the accumulated depreciation.

2. Add up your liabilities. For convenience, divide these into *Current* (accounts payable, notes payable, accrued expenses, interest on loans, etc.), and *Long-Term* (trust deeds, bank loans, equipment loans, balloons, etc.)

3. Subtract the smaller figure from the larger one.

You now have a prediction of your net worth. Will you be in the red or in the black?

ACTION STEP 78

Construct a PERT chart and go for it.

Rehearsal is over. Now it's time to step onto the stage and get the drama under way. One way to shift from planning into action is to develop your own personal PERT chart. A PERT chart will serve as a script for you. It also will tell you and the other members of your team how long certain jobs should take.

List the tasks you need to accomplish—befriending a banker, filing a fictitious name statement, taking a lawyer to lunch, ordering business letterhead, selecting a site, contacting vendors, and so on—and set your deadlines.

As you already know, a successful package is made up of many, many details. If you take the details one at a time, you'll get there without being overwhelmed. The sample PERT chart in Table 16.4 can guide you.

2. Emphasize the benefits, not the product itself. (Better information management control gives you better control over assets and inventory.)

3. Use simple language to summarize where you are with production. (Test users like the product. You'll have a complete product line in 4 months.)

4. Identify your marketing strategy. (Direct mail, magazine advertising, telemarketing.)

5. Project your sales goals. ($820,000 in sales the first year produces a net income of $269,000 or 32 percent of sales.)

6. Summarize the experience of your management team. (Each of the 5 owners will participate in management. Three will participate in sales.)

7. Summarize your cash-flow picture. (An investment of $125,000 will sustain our business through the 4 months prior to opening.)

Even if you feel you have no need for outside capital, a well-crafted executive summary will keep you and the founding team on track. Vendors, lenders, and especially venture capitalists save time by reading your executive summary.

From: "Creative Financing," by Bruce Blechman, *Entrepreneur Magazine*, March 1992, 25–27.

SUMMARY

It's been a long haul, and you're now ready to create your Business Plan. The Business Plan is a portable showcase for your business. When you visit vendors, bankers,

TABLE 16.4   A Sample PERT Chart

TASK	WEEK					
	1	2	3	4	5	6
Befriend banker	x	x	x	x	x	x
Order letterhead		x				
Select site	x					
Get fictional name statement	x					
Bulk mail permit			x			
Ad agency	x					
Lunch, lawyer			x			
Appointment, accountant				x		
Vendor statement					x	
Utilities deposits					x	
Review promotional material					x	
Survey phone system			x	x	x	
Order phone system						x
Open house						x

and potential lenders, you can take along a copy of your Business Plan to speak for you, to show them you've got a blueprint for success.

Begin writing by starting with the material you feel most comfortable with. Once you have finished one part of the Plan, the other parts will fall into place more easily. Fortunately, your work in earlier chapters has prepared you for each section.

You'll need to write a cover letter for each copy of the Plan you send out. The cover letter will personalize the Plan and aim it so that it does the most good.

THINK POINTS FOR SUCCESS

◀ Section I should generate excitement for your business. Section II should substantiate the excitement with numbers.

◀ Be sure to use sufficient footnotes to explain the numbers in your financial statements—Parts H, I, and J.

◀ The Executive Summary should read like ad copy. Hone it till it's tight and convincing.

◀ Now that you have Plan A, have you thought about Plan B?

REFERENCES

Bangs, David H., Jr. *Business Planning Guide,* rev. ed. Portsmouth, New Hampshire: Upstart Publishing Co., 1989. [An excellent handbook for structuring a Business Plan. Clear writing, humorous examples. Their model business is Finestkind, a retail fish market located in York, Maine. Copies of the book can be ordered from Upstart Publishing Co., P.O. Box 323, Portsmouth, NH 13801; (603) 749-5071.]

Business Plan for Retailers. Management Aid No. 2.020. Washington, D.C.: U. S. Small Business Administration, Office of Business Development, 1987.

Business Plan for Small Manufacturers. Management Aid No. 2.007. Washington, D.C.: U. S. Small Business Administration, Office of Business Development, 1987.

Eliason, Carol. *The Business Plan for Home-based Business.* Management Aid No. 2.028. Washington, D.C.: U. S. Small Business Administration, Office of Business Development, 1986.

Ernst & Young staff et al. *Ernst & Young Business Plan Guide.* New York: Wiley, 1991. [Excellent detailed business plan outline. See also the following.]

Ernst & Young's Preparing a Business Plan. Ernst & Young at 1300 Huntington Building, Cleveland, OH 44115.

Hiebing, Roman G. and Scott W. Cooper. *How to Write a Successful Marketing Plan.* Lincolnwood, Ill.: National Textbooks, no date given.

J.K. Lasser Tax Institute staff. *How to Run a Small Business,* 6th ed. New York: McGraw-Hill, 1989.

Kingstone, Brett. *Student Entrepreneur's Guide: How to Start and Run Your Own Business.* New York: McGraw-Hill, 1990.

Maul, Lyle R., and Dianne C. Mayfield. *The Entrepreneur's Road Map.* Alexandria, Va.: Saxtons River Publications, 1990.

ACTION STEP REVIEW

66 Write a cover letter that will open the door for future business transactions.

67 Grab attention with your executive summary.

68 Describe your product or service against the backdrop of industry. You want to excite your reader without being flamboyant.

69 Discuss your target market and profile your target customer.

70 List your major competitors and tell how you will disarm them.

71 Describe your marketing strategies. What techniques will best serve your small business?

72 Discuss your site and explain how it will contribute to your success.

73 Introduce your management team. Depict a great management track record in your industry.

74 Describe the kinds of employees you will need. Emphasize that you'll run lean.

75 Project an income statement to give an idea about net profit for your first year—and then for the next three, if possible.

76 Project your cash flow to learn when you're going to need money.

77 Show your potential investors and lenders what they can expect for an ROI by projecting balance sheets.

78 Construct a PERT chart and go for it.

Policastro, Michael L. *Developing a Strategic Business Plan.* Management Aid No. 2.035. Washington, D.C.: U. S. Small Business Administration, Office of Business Development, 1987.

Schilit, W. Keith. "How to Write a Winning Business Plan." *Business Horizons,* September–October, 1987, 13.

Sears, Marion, and Thomas Navin. "The Rise of a Market for Industrial Securities, 1887–1902." *Business History Review* (1955), 112–116.

Siegel, Eric, et al. *The Arthur Young Business Plan Guide.* New York: John Wiley and Sons, 1991.

Small Business Reporter series. San Francisco: Bank of America, 1988. [The series consists of sixteen excellent booklets on entrepreneurship, management, computers, franchising, financing, marketing, personnel, and accounting. They may be ordered (obtain an order form and prices at any B of A branch) from Small Business Reporter, Bank of America, Dept. 3631, P.O. Box 37000, San Francisco, CA 94137.]

Sobel, Robert. *The Age of Giant Corporations: A Microeconomic History of American Business 1914–1970,* 2nd ed. Westport, Conn.: Greenwood, 1984.

Spencer, Austin H. "Relative Downward Industrial Price Flexibility, 1870–1921." *Explorations in Economic History,* vol. 14, no. 1, January, 1977.

Stevens, Mark. *The Macmillan Small Business Handbook.* New York: Macmillan, 1988.

Tarbell, Ida. *The History of the Standard Oil Company.* Cutchogue, N.Y.: Buccaneer Books, 1987.

Temin, Peter. *Iron and Steel in Nineteenth-Century America: An Economic Inquiry.* Cambridge, Mass.: MIT Press, 1964.

NOTES _____
_____
_____
_____
_____
_____

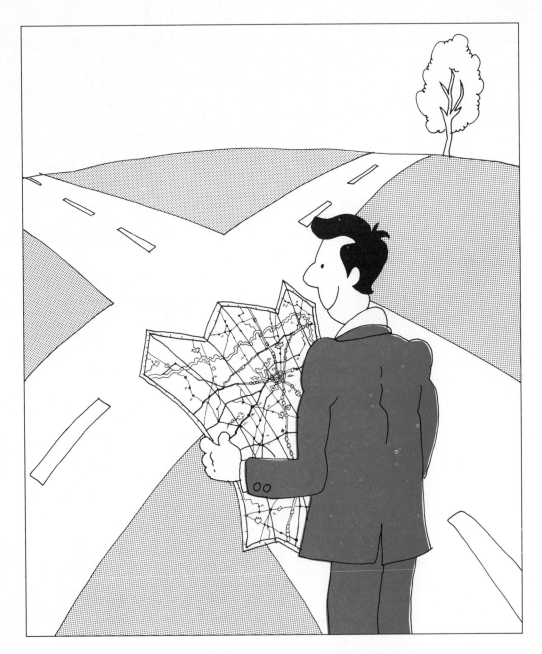

FIGURE 17.1
Chapter 17 hands you a mini-Business Plan that is almost ready to fly.

17 Fast-Start Business Plan

Learning Objectives

- To admit that you're in a hurry.
- To launch a start-up without getting help from bankers.
- To capitalize on a hot opportunity in the marketplace.
- To start small while you explore the possibilities of growing larger.
- To work with numbers so that you can keep going when the going gets tough.
- To make some money now.
- To plan as you work in your new business.

FUTURE FOCUS

If you don't want to or don't have to write a comprehensive Business Plan because yours is a simple venture, then the "Fast-Start Mini-Business Plan" is for you.

There are millions of possible low-risk ventures out there—some short-term, others long-term moonlighting ideas, and some simply designed to raise cash so you can move up to a better venture.

You still need to pay attention when getting your feet wet—or you could drown in debt. The Mini-Plan will keep you on track and out of trouble.

Maybe you're in a hurry. If so, we have some help. But first you need to make sure the fast start is the right start for you. In this chapter, we help you give thought to your big decision, your business description, your start-up costs, and your final pass. We also provide a model business plan.

THE BIG DECISION

If you're going it alone, with money you can afford to lose ($500, $1,000, even $5,000), and if the loss of that money won't jeopardize your loved ones and make wolves howl at your door, use the Fast-Start Plan.

If other people are involved—investors, bankers, advisors, company officers—then return to Chapter 16 and write a comprehensive plan.

The comprehensive plan gives you a blueprint to follow month by month through the first year. It gives you the framework to go for a 4-year projection following that first year. It tracks your business through seasonal ups and downs. It allows for contingencies.

The Fast-Start Plan lets you get going now. It's great if you've been in business before and know the footwork of entrepreneurship. With the Fast-Start Plan, you're using the business as a probe into the marketplace. You can start quickly because you have an instinct for beating out the competition. You have a market sense. You have a good sense of the business you are starting.

The Fast-Start Plan is quicker to write. Marketing, pricing, and advertising employ a low key approach. As you gain experience, you fold that experience into a rolling projection. You can write the fast-start in 1 to 3 months. The full Business Plan, because of the extensive data gathering and passing through many hands, takes 6 months to a year.

Quick Checklist

Here's a quick checklist for implementing the Fast-Start Plan:

1. Can you afford to lose your dollar investment? How much money can you afford to lose at the slots in Reno or Las Vegas or Atlantic City? Can you lose $100? $500? $1,000? $5,000? More? What's your deductible on your car insurance? Your boat? Your major medical? Write down the amount you can afford to lose. If you have excess money to speculate with, then the Fast-Start Plan is for you.

2. How easy is it to enter this business? Is it easy to talk to owners? Are role models in great abundance? Do the prospective customers have a clear understanding of the goods and services provided? Examples of businesses with wide doors: window washing, auto detailing, landscape maintenance, vacation pet-sitting, house-sitting.

3. Can you start this business on a part-time basis? Starting part time lessens your risk. You have a chance to prove the business. You see how much you really like it. You keep a running tally of customer responses. You keep your other job.

4. How tough is it to gather the data needed to formulate a Fast-Start Business Plan? In breaking new ground, be careful. In a venture like this, the market is not clearly defined. There are very few competitors. Pricing is

not clear. Remaining part time is essential. You must make certain you've got a market out there.

5. Can you start using only your own funds? Bill Gates, the founder of MicroSoft, could use the Fast-Start Plan for a business start-up costing $50,000 to $1,000,000. A single parent of two with rent and car loan to pay might afford much less. Be honest with yourself. Be honest with your family.

Structuring Your Plan

Use these questions to structure your Fast-Start Plan:

1. How do you describe your business?
2. What business are you really in?
3. Who is your competition? How are they doing?
4. What is your pricing strategy?
5. Who is your target customer? Why should they buy from you?
6. How will you advertise?
7. What are your start-up costs?
8. What are your sales goals for the first 3 months?
9. What are your operating expenses for the first 3 months?
10. If you crash and burn, what can you salvage for cash?
11. What have you forgotten?

BUSINESS DESCRIPTION

It's night. The family's gone to bed. The house is quiet. The pets are snoozing.

It's time to sit back in your favorite chair, time to relax, time to dream about your new business. So dream awhile and then write down your dream:

> You step out of your van. It's a handsome vehicle, spotless, white, and gleaming. On the side, in red letters, is your sign: MY CARPET CLEANERS—QUALITY AND SERVICE IS OUR NUMBER ONE JOB. Your company phone number is underneath. You are all in white, white jumpsuit, white shoes. The starched look gives you the image of the best carpet cleaner in town. You catch your reflection in the mirror. The jumpsuit makes you look taller. The company logo stitched on your breast pocket makes you proud.
>
> The house of your prospect is large. Three stories, well-kept lawn, a three-car garage, a curved driveway. The walkway leading to the front door is paved. The doorway is large enough to drive a truck through. Out back, you can hear the happy shrieks of children as they splash in the pool.
>
> Cut to the job. You're in a big room with wall-to-wall carpet. Your machine sucks up the dirt. The customer enters, walking on a drop cloth you laid down for your equipment. Pointing to a transparent tube attached to your super-steam vacuum, you show the customer the dirt coming out of her carpet. The carpet sparkles in the sunlight as you go after those drapes. The customer, overwhelmed with such service, hands you the biggest check you've ever seen.
>
> This check is 4-feet long and 2-feet high. The customer smiles. You read the amount—fantastic money for a fantastic job—and dance your way out of the house and down the walkway to your van.

ACTION STEP 79

Describe your new business:

What will your business look like?
  To your customers?
  To your competitors?
  To yourself?

Write quick descriptions of your products and/or services. What do they look like? How do they feel? How much time do they take? How much do they cost? Next, describe them in terms of benefits to your customers. How will Target Customer A benefit from buying your product or service?

Keep going.

What is unique about your product/service? What separates you from your competitors?

Research the marketplace. Is your type of business growing? If so, how fast? Where are you on the Life Cycle chart? Is your market area growing?

Try to describe your business in fifty words or less. When you tell people about your business, you want to have a clear, crisp picture. You want to use the right words.

This is your business. You want to know exactly what it is.

Great Dream Equals Great Business

A business dream separates your business from everyone else who's out there trying to clean carpets.

You're clean and you're in the cleaning business. You're proud of being in business. You care. The customer, owner of expensive things, cares that you care. We like to do business with people who care about what they're doing. Such people take pride in a job well done.

By being spotless when you enter this home, you show the customer respect. Your equipment is spotless. You're not dragging someone else's dirt into this place. The drop cloth is a nice touch.

You look like a carpet cleaner. You act like a carpet cleaner. Your dream gives you a jump start. Now you add in details.

What products and/or services will you offer? Will you limit yourself to carpets? Or will you clean chairs and drapes? Will you specialize in homes? Or will you do offices? Will you provide a simple service? Or will you also sell spot remover, touch-up cleaners, other extras?

What Business Are You Really In?

Are you selling clean carpets? Are you selling a better looking home or office? Are you selling better health? Are you helping the customer preserve an investment?

To help you get a handle on this, let's profile two different businesses in the same industry.

Business A is a family restaurant. It's open 24 hours. There's nothing on the menu over $9.95. The menu for children is extensive. On each table is a digital clock and a sign that says you eat free if your meal is not on the table within 10 minutes of being ordered. The clock invites the customer to set it, invites the waiter to beat the clock.

Business B is a restaurant with limited hours. Weekdays it's open from 11 A.M. to 2 P.M. and from 5 P.M. to 10 P.M. Weekends it's open from 5 P.M. until midnight. Each table features large, comfortable chairs. The lighting is soft. The china is fine, the silverware first cabin. The waiters wear tuxes and their manners are impeccable, right on the edge of snooty. The wine list contains fine vintages from Europe and California. If you can stump the bartender by requesting a drink she cannot mix, your drink is served free by the maitre d' hotel. The cheapest entree on the menu is $25. (This restaurant rounds prices off.)

Both A and B are in the food service business. You can find both in the restaurant section in the Yellow Pages. But are they both in the same business?

For your answer, look at the customers.

Customers go to Business A for fast service. Their desire is to feed the whole family without going broke. They don't want a long travel time, so Business A is close to home. The food is good. Not wonderful, not divine, but good.

Customers go to Business B for excellent food and superior service. They go to relax, to enjoy a perfect moment over a rare vintage. They may be driven by fantasy or romance or escape. They may go just to watch the staff perform. That's entertainment.

What business is A in? What business is B in?

Business A is in the family-feeding business. By B is in the entertainment business. A provides nourishment at affordable prices. B provides more than food—B provides a dining experience.

ACTION STEP 80

What business are you really in?

This is a tough question.

Start by interviewing customers of your competitors. Why do they buy what they buy? Why do they shop here instead of somewhere else? What are they after? What are they trying to satisfy? What itch does this business scratch?

Stimulate your thinking by analogy. What, for example, do you get when you have your car washed? It costs you anywhere from $5 to $25, and for what? A clean car? A savings in time? Pride of ownership? A car your customers will ride in? Does washing the car make you feel clean? Or maybe it's maintenance: Do you live near the beach, where the salt air eats your chrome?

Where do you buy clothes? Why? Where do you buy gas? Why? Who cleans your carpet? Why?

Probe your own buying habits. Probe the buying habits of your friends. Keep an open mind. Gather data. All this will lead you to discover what business you're really in.

If you were the manager of Business A, you would do these things:

> purchase good food in quantity
> get it at the lowest price
> control waste in the kitchen
> develop a fast and efficient delivery system
> turn those tables

If you were the manager of Business B, you would do these things:

> retrain all employees to fit the upscale image
> "fancy up" your interior
> select quality food, rare food, specialty food
> find a bartender who knows the latest mixes and can smile

To figure out what business you're in, take a couple of steps back. Look at your business from the viewpoint of the customer. Then plan your course of action.

Who Are Your Competitors?

This is a good time to try out your New Eyes. How much can you learn from your competitors?

How do you find them? If you're hunting for retailers or restaurant owners, you hop in your car and drive around. But how do you find a home-based word-processing business? How do you find a home-based cleaning service? How do you find a mobile auto detailer?

You know this: in order to stay in business, a business must communicate with potential customers. So you tune in your entrepreneurial radar. Check your Yellow Pages. Check area newspapers. Look for business cards in copy services, in service stations, in local food stores, on kiosks.

Once you find your competitors, take a closer look. Were they easy to find? How visible was their advertising? As you study their advertising strategy, what kind of a customer profile can you draw? Are they spending a lot on their advertising? Are they working on a shoestring?

What can you tell from their pricing? Are prices firm? Are they negotiable? Are they high, low, or competitive? What kind of customer will go for these prices? Who will get shut out? Do your competitors understand the marketplace? Is their pricing structure positioned properly?

Are your competitors zeroed in on a specific Target Customer, or are they using the shotgun approach? Just for practice, profile the Target Customer of your competitors.

Which of your competitors are successful? Can you tell why? Which are just hanging in there? Why? If a business has been operating for some time, there's a good chance the owner's doing something right. What is it? Nose around. What customer benefits do they offer? Fast service? Quality work? Free delivery and pick up? Low prices?

Even the most successful business overlooks something. Find out what they missed. Did they overlook a market segment? Did they get sloppy with their advertising? Is their range of services actually limited? Is their inventory sparse? Thousands of businesses have been built on the weaknesses of competition.

Take the time to chat with the customers of your competitors. Are they satisfied? If not, why not? How do they see the competition? What image does the competition project? How do customers feel about price, quality, timeliness, and so on?

ACTION STEP 81

What do your competitors look like?

Are they winners? Losers? Why?

What things are they doing right? What are they doing wrong?

How many competitors do you have? What customer groups are they serving? Whom are they overlooking? Where do they advertise? Where do they promote? What do you think of their location? What market area do they cover?

If you owned a competitor's business, what would you change?

What can you learn from studying your competitors? After you have opened your business, do some more marketplace detecting as you study your competitors. You'll learn more because you know more. A veteran entrepreneur knows what to look for.

Take the time to chat with competitors outside your area. Is there a gap no one has thought to close?

How Much Should You Charge?

Pricing is key. Don't be misled by thinking you can whisk customers away from established competitors by charging less for the same thing. It didn't work for now bankrupt department stores. It won't work for you.

Find out what is important to the customers. It's probably time or dependability or quality or convenience. Then learn to see the value of your product or service through your customers' eyes.

For example, when you eat lunch at a fast-food restaurant, you buy french fries, coffee, tea, a soft drink. You pay fifty cents or more for each of these items. The cost to the seller is a nickel or a dime. Within limits, these items are not price-sensitive. The question is, what is the customer's perception of value?

When you shop, train yourself to make price comparisons:

a. Pricing newspapers at the newsstand:

The Wall Street Journal	75 cents
USA Today	50 cents
local paper	25 cents

b. Coffee:

at local doughnut shop	45 cents
at a luxury hotel	$2

c. Car wash:

high school students Saturday special	$1
do it yourself	$2
you watch them	$5–10

d. Transportation:

Ford	$10,000
Mercedes	$40,000
Bentley	$275,000

e. Education

a year at Stanford	$20,000
a year at state college	$8,000

Profile Your Target Customer

Who will receive the biggest benefit from your business? Who can pay the price? Who can you target? Where do they live? What's their income range? What do they need? What work do they do? Are they married? Single? Divorced? Retired?

To profile your customers, become a marketplace detective. To practice, study the customers that buy from your competitors.

Do the women outnumber the men? What's the average age? What cars do they drive? Make? Year? Price range? How are the customers dressed? How expensive are their shoes? If you can get inside, check out methods of payment. Do they use cash? Checks? Credit? How expensive are the items they're buying?

Practice trains your eye to consider the person as a prospect.

ACTION STEP 82

What is your pricing strategy? Why?

What does your target customer see as good value?

What is most important to your target customer? Convenience? Quality? On-time delivery? Image? Price?

What stage of the product/service life cycle are you in? How many competitors do you have? How close are they?

If price is the main decision factor, try to add something a little extra. What's unique about your product? Is it unique enough so that you can charge a little extra?

ACTION STEP 83

Describe your target customer and your main market area.

Who is your primary target customer? Do a profile: sex, age, income, occupation, residence, vehicle(s)—anything that gives you a picture of needs and wants. What do they read? What do they watch? What do they listen to?

When you have profiled your primary customer, do the same thing for secondary customers.

How large is your main market area? Will you sell in one section of town? The whole town? The county? The state? The region? If you're driving around to service accounts, how far will you have to drive?

How Do You Make that Customer Connection?

Before you spend a bundle on a TV ad, or 3 months knocking on doors of houses along Golf Course Drive, take some time to put together a message.

What image do you want to project? How do you want the marketplace to receive your product or service? What position do you want to assume among your competitors? What are the key benefits your business will offer customers? How soon do you want to start? How many autos can you detail—or homes can you clean—in 1 day?

Once you answer these questions, design your business card. Use a logo that offers an insight into your business. If you're starting a word-processing business, use something along the lines of "On Time Quality Service." If you're thinking of house cleaning: "Only Sparkle—Not a Speck of Dust." Always carry lots of business cards. They're inexpensive memory seeds, handy reminders, and often your most cost effective advertising.

Once your business cards are done, research ways of reaching customers. Do they gather at church? At school? At football games? At Little League? What do they read? Watch? Listen to? Could you reach them best through the Yellow Pages? Through radio? On a billboard? What can you afford? Match that up with the most effective communications channel.

Stay visible. If your Target Customers gather in groups, try to reach them there. Attend their meetings. Get on their list of speakers. Give a demonstration. Hand out business cards. Offer a freebie.

If you must find your customers one at a time, spend a few hours each day knocking on doors. Telephone prospects. Work your mailing list. If you use mail contacts, be sure you do phone follow-ups.

Join the local Chamber of Commerce. If you're lucky, your Chamber will run a short piece about you, the newcomer, in their newsletter. Stay visible at Chamber meetings. Don't get pushy with your business cards, but have them handy.

While you're connecting with customers, don't overlook organizations that might act as your sales force. For example, let's say you've found a school where the parents' group is trying to raise funds to support an athletic endeavor. Put together a flyer for students to take home. In return for each sale from the flyer, your business will donate 10 to 25 percent to the fund-raising group. Consider the donation a part of your promotional budget.

WHAT ARE YOUR START-UP COSTS?

At your local office supply store, make these purchases: a mileage log, an expense journal, and a folder to hold receipts. You can deduct mileage and expenses related to your business start-up.

List everything that you need to get started. Don't worry if the list would cost a bundle. You're brainstorming at this point. The key here is not to overlook anything. A visit to your competitors will add ideas to your list. An interview with an owner will trigger new items. When you're chatting with business people, ask questions: What kind of cash register do you use? What kind of bookkeeping system do you have? What's the cost of a start-up inventory? When your list is fat, add price tags.

When you start purchasing, check the large discount stores. Also investigate mail-order houses, especially for personal computers. If one company in your area can supply most of your needs, try to make a package deal and develop a long-term relationship.

ACTION STEP 84

Describe your advertising and sales program.

How will you let potential customers know that you are open for business? How will you let them discover the benefits of buying from you?

Start with budget. How much money can you spend on promotion? Once you know what you can afford, select the advertising to match your budget.

As part of your plan, set up a evaluation procedure. You want to know how well each promotion works.

ACTION STEP 85

What will it cost to open your doors?

List your expenses, equipment, rentals, inventory—everything you'll need to start your business. Start your list with business cards. End with the key for the front door. What comes in between?

When you have listed all the items, give each one an estimated cost. On equipment, buy used. If you can't buy used, try leasing. On inventory, negotiate with each supplier to see if you can get credit terms right from the start. If you can't get credit, find out how you can qualify.

When the list is complete—items and costs—go through it with a black marker, deleting items you can do without for a month or so. You are trying to keep your up-front cash outlay to a minimum.

On equipment items, save by buying used. Used equipment might be scratched or dented, but you stand to save 50 to 90 percent. Check the newspaper classifieds under "Equipment for Sale" or "Office Furniture." Talk with potential suppliers—they usually know someone who's going out of business. You can find good deals from an owner who's folding.

You should also consider leasing your equipment. Leasing costs more in the long run, less when you're getting started. As your business grows, and your leases expire, you can decide whether to replace by buying new or used. Leasing provides you a lot of flexibility up front.

Divide your start-up list into two columns. Column 1 should contain items that are absolutely necessary. Column 2 contains "nice-to-haves."

Check Column 1. Is there anything you can borrow from home, parents, friends? Scrape to the bottom of the barrel here. Your goal is to cut costs so you'll have cash to run the business.

ACTION STEP 86

How much will you sell in your first month? How much will you spend?

Your goal in this Action Step is to set realistic goals. To do that, you need to know your maximum capacity. For example, how many houses with an area of 1,500 to 2,000 square feet can you clean in one day? One week? One month? This will give you the top sales figure you could reach. That's your ideal.

Fixed expenses don't change with sales volume. List those first. Then list the variable expenses.

For fixed expenses, check with people who can give you answers: public utility companies (water, gas, electricity, natural gas); leasing agent for rental rates; insurance agent for estimated insurance costs.

For variable expenses, those that change with sales volume, figure out how far they go up relative to some fixed unit of change. For example, $100 of sales per house cleaned. If you can establish a percentage relationship between sales and each individual variable expense, then it will be easy to fill in your projections each month.

Charting Your Sales Goals for the First Three Months

How much would you like to sell the first month? The second? The third? How much can you afford to sell? What is a realistic target for your new business?

Sales goals provide the information you need to forecast your variable expenses—those expenses forced to change in relation to sales volume. If you are selling a product, sales goals will allow you to estimate the cost of goods sold.

Sales goals provide the driving force for you and your team. They help you focus on your target for the month. When the month is finished, compare how you did with your initial sales goals. Did you make it? If not, why not? Did you exceed your goal by 25 percent? Why? What worked well? What didn't? As you evaluate, decide how to improve next month, and how to keep improving.

To chart a reasonable sales goal, focus on three factors:

1. The weight of your advertising program. Do you plan a wide-area campaign? Or will you start by calling on friends and neighbors, counting on them to spread the word slowly? How much energy are you putting into this? Will you start full-time? Will you keep your job? If you're in school, will you stay enrolled?

2. The experience of entrepreneurs in businesses like yours who operate in a noncompeting area. How much effort does Entrepreneur A have to put out to make a $100 sale in his or her area?

3. The capacity you have to deliver the product or service. What do you need to make this venture go? If it costs you $500 for materials to build one computer cabinet and you only have $500 worth of capital, then you will be limited to building one cabinet at a time. You have to get paid before you can build a second cabinet.

Or let's say you're starting a part-time business detailing autos. Detailing one auto takes 3 hours. Driving time takes almost a half hour per auto. Your maximum sales activity per week will be based on the number of hours you can devote to your business after you put in your hours at your full-time job. If you can devote 20 hours a week, then your sales would be 20 hours, divided by time, multiplied by your charge. Let's try that:

20 divided by 3.5 = 6 autos per week
Your charge per auto is $60.
6 times $60 = $360 per week.

	1	2	3	4	5	6	7	8	9
1									
2	First Sales Forecast								
3									
4		1st Month		2nd Month		3rd Month		4th Month	
5	Monthly Detailing (2)	240	(4)	240	(4)	300	(5)	360	(6)
6	Quarterly Detailing (3)	180	(3)	180	(3)	0		180	(3)
7	Rest of 18 Prospects (4)	180	(3)	300	(5)	0			
8	Need to Find (5)			360	(6)	1500	(25)		
9	Sales	600		1080		1800			
10									
11									
12									

FIGURE 17.2   First Sales Forecast

Make a list of your friends and relatives. Find out how many of them have their autos detailed. Add the repeat factor: how often do they want detailing? Once a month? Once every quarter? Once a year? When your list is finished you have twenty-four prospects. You have a realistic shot at eighteen of those prospects. For your business, that's enough for a start-up.

As a wise entrepreneur, you know that your first few jobs will take longer than later ones. You're new. You're learning the business. You want to make sure you do a super job. You have four prospects who want monthly detailing. You have six who want it quarterly. Start with these ten prospects and lay out a chart. (See Figure 17.2.)

Make these assumptions:

1. Assume that the first and second months contain 4 weeks and the third month has 5 weeks.

2. Assume sign-ups of four monthly detailing prospects from your list of 24. Add one new monthly prospect out of every six new customers from the Need to Find group.

3. Assume a sign-up of six quarterly customers from our list of 24 prospects. Add one new quarterly customer out of every six new customers from the Need to Find group.

4. Assume a sign-up of eight one-time prospects from our list of 24 prospects.

5. Action: must find new customers from the remaining six prospects on the 24 names list. Other sources are referrals, sales calls, and advertising.

6. We only plan for the first 3 months. The fourth month is easy to start building from monthly and quarterly customers.

Expense Forecast

List everything you'll need to pay for on a regular basis to operate your business, for example, phone, supplies, truck, advertising/promotion. Next, list everything you can think of under each heading. Here's a partial example:

SUPPLIES	TRUCK
rags	gas
soap	oil/maintenance
wax	insurance
cleaner	
Q-tips	

Now consider each specific item. Which ones can you tie to the detailing job? For example, for each auto detailing job, you use two packages of rental rags: one-half can of wax; one-quarter can of cleaner; ten Q-tips; $1 for gas, and so on.

Add these expenses to your first sales forecast. Also add expense items that don't change. See Figure 17.3.

Assumptions:

1. Monthly basic rate, plus pager.
2. $20 per month, plus $1 per job.
3. $10 per month toward oil change, tires, maintenance, plus 50 cents per job.

	1	2	3	4	5	6	7
1	First Income Statement Forecast						
2							
3		1st Month	2nd Month	3rd Month			
4	Sales						
5	Monthly	240	240	300			
6	Quarterly	180	180				
7	Original Prospects	180	300				
8	Need to Find		360	1500			
9							
10	Sales Total	600	1080	1800			
11							
12	Expenses:						
13	Phone (1)	20	20	20			
14	Gasoline (2)	30	38	50			
15	Oil/Maint (3)	15	19	25			
16	Insurance (4)	100	100	100			
17	Supplies (5)	100	180	300			
18	Ad/Promotion (6)	50	75	75			
19	Depreciation (7)						
20	Miscellaneous (8)	50	50	50			
21							
22	Expense Total	365	482	620			
23	Profit (9)	235	598	1180			
24							
25							

FIGURE 17.3   **First Income Statement Forecast**

4. $1,200 a year, $100/mo. expense paid quarterly.
5. Estimated at $10 per job.
6. Yellow Page ad at $35 a month, plus $15 a month for 4-line ad in weekly paper for the first month and $25 for flyers and business cards in the second and third month.
7. Depreciation should be factored in for truck and buffer.
8. Set aside: plan for surprise expenses.
9. Profit before depreciation (a noncash expense). In time, you should get an estimate from your accountant for depreciation.

FINAL PASS

Out of the twenty-four prospects, you manage to sign up fifteen for auto detailing. That's good. Six of those who want monthly detailing bargained you down to $50. Two of those six agreed to a weekly hand wash at $12. Five prospects agreed to a quarterly detailing and one of those five agreed to a weekly hand wash. Five prospects decided on a one-time trial. You'd like to snag twenty-five new customers by the third month. A more reasonable estimate, however, is fifteen new customers.

New expenses include $5 a week for a Leads Club breakfast; $75 to join the Chamber of Commerce; $2 for the car washes; $1 for gas. The new numbers go into your forecast. (See Figure 17.4.)

"Things to Do" List

Now that your plan is complete, act on it. Your first step is to write up a list of things that need doing. You need this list for at least three reasons:

1. It gives you easy steps to follow.
2. It keeps you on target.
3. It gives you a sense of getting there at last.

Following is a sample "Things to Do" List from a catering service started by Doris and Mike in a mid-sized city on the East Coast.

List of Necessities Before Opening Day—Catering Service

1. Talk with experienced caterers.
2. Prepare Fast-Start Mini-Business Plan.
3. Stay organized.
4. Choose a business name.
5. File for fictitious business name.
6. Make arrangements to use pizza or other food service kitchen.
7. Determine what area to service.
8. Have business phone installed. Purchase answering machine.
9. Set up business checking account.
10. Locate suppliers: refrigeration, cooking, baking, utensils, cash register, tables, chairs, other.

	1	2	3	4	5	6	7
1	Start–Up Income Statement Forecast						
2							
3		1st Month	2nd Month	3rd Month			
4							
5	Sales						
6	Monthly	250	250	300			
7	Car Washes	108	120	156			
8	Quarterly	180	120				
9	Rest of 15	120	180				
10	Need to Find		360	900			
11							
12	Sales Total	658	1030	1356			
13							
14							
15	Expenses:						
16	Phone	20	20	20			
17	Gas	39	41	54			
18	Oil/Maint	19.5	23	27			
19	Insurance	100	100	100			
20	Supplies	100	180	236			
21	Ad/Promotion	145	95	95			
22	Depreciation						
23	Miscellaneous	50	50	50			
24							
25	Expense Total	491.5	510	582			
26	Profit	166.5	520	774			
27							

FIGURE 17.4   Start-up Income Statement Forecast

11. Check city and county business license regulations.

12. Get Federal I.D. number—needed by all employers.

13. Get an insurance agent.

14. Hire employees. Full-time or part-time? How many? Make sure to get all information: Social Security number, correct name and address, phone, citizenship. Develop application form. Have each employee fill out a W-4.

15. Complete advertising before the opening so people will know opening date.

16. Join a discount price warehouse.

17. Choose food suppliers.

18. Support business contracts:
    a. Rental tents, equipment.
    b. Florists.
    c. Entertainment.
    d. Service staff.
    e. Other bakeries, specialty suppliers, ice carvers, props, lighting, etc.

19. Business cards should be ordered and ready to hand out.
20. Preprinted billing statements for customers who do not pay upon receipt. Preferably get money up front.
21. Record all income and expenses daily in a ledger.
22. Find a bookkeeper to prepare financial statements. Check out computerized accounting systems.
23. Get an attorney.
24. Network with friends, relatives, other caterers.
25. Join Chamber of Commerce. Good place to meet potential customers.
26. Do projected profit and loss statement for 3 months.

SUMMARY

The Fast-Start Mini-Business Plan is not a substitute for preparing a full-fledged plan. Use the fast-start for a specific venture that is easy to start, carrying minimal risk. Also use it for a business that's breaking new ground, where there is little data available.

The key to any business, and to any Business Plan, is how well you understand the needs of your Target Customer. Find an itch that isn't being scratched and you can ace your competitors.

Write your own Fast-Start Plan. Keep it handy. Refer to it often. Use it to keep your business on track in those early months of operation. When you've been in business for 3 months, use your Fast-Start Plan as a launching pad for your next 9 months of operation. For your second year, write a full-fledged Business Plan.

THINK POINTS FOR SUCCESS

◣ Your Business Plan, fast-start or full-fledged, is your pathway to success.

◣ Looking at your competition helps you see your Target Customer. Seeing your Target Customer clearly helps you position your business strategically in the marketplace.

◣ Building a plan builds confidence. Confidence breeds excitement. If you don't feel excited and confident about your business, bail out now.

◣ Once you get started heading around the track, don't forget to keep your New Eyes on the marketplace.

ACTION STEP REVIEW

79 Paint a word picture of your new business in brief economical strokes so you and others can see it clearly.

80 Like a difficult riddle, the true identity of the business you're in will yield only to prolonged effort. (Hint: What needs does your business satisfy?)

81 Know your competitors to discover which choices to avoid and which to make.

82 You need to know both the costs and the value of your product to price it strategically.

83 If you know your target customers and where they live, it will be easier to make the right decisions on running your business.

84 Make more of your business with an appropriate advertising and sales program.

85 List the costs of starting your business—and then plan a strategy to lower them.

86 Estimate how much money will be coming in and going out. You must set realistic goals.

87 Listing the things to do helps you stay in charge.

MODEL BUSINESS PLAN

Yes, We Do Windows

1. Definition of your business.
2. What business am I really in?
3. Competition
4. Pricing
5. Target Customer
6. Ad/Sales program
7. Start-up costs
8. Sales goals/expenses/first 3 months
9. "To do" list

1. Definition of the Business.

I have been a window washer for 3 years. For 2 years I worked for Windowlite Ltd., a large organization with over 250 satellites across three states. For the next year, I worked for a local operator who owned a truck and three squeegees. I feel that I know the business from both ends.

My plan—and the subject of this plan—is to do window and house cleaning.

> Window Cleaning. I will clean windows, screens, and window casings.
>
> Housecleaning: I will vacuum, dust, polish/wax, mop. I will do bathrooms, mirrors, kitchens, range tops, ovens.

A customer may contract for one or more services. Housecleaning will be offered on a once-a-week or once-every-two-weeks basis. Window cleaning will be offered monthly, quarterly, twice a year, or as needed.

2. What business I am really in?

Determine the answer by identifying customer benefits:

a. Pride of ownership—a home is a person's most expensive investment. Keeping it clean makes the customer proud.

b. Time-saving—homeowners work hard to pay for their investment; many homes today are supported by double incomes; few homeowners have the time to do their own cleaning.

c. Preserving the value of the investment—dirt and grime damage the home. Cleaning on a regular basis enhances and preserves the value of the home.

d. Comfortable, healthy living area—a clean home is a healthier home. Who wants to live with dirt?

The business I am really in: "providing a clean and healthy environment while at the same time preserving the value of an investment and deepening pride of ownership."

3. Competition

At this writing there are 77 window cleaning services and 102 housecleaning services listed in my metropolitan area Yellow Pages.

Taking the time to make phone calls to these competitors made me feel even better about my idea for a business. Their phone skills need retooling. The clerks who answered were impolite. They didn't seem interested in the prospect of making money. Out of fifty-nine businesses polled, a hefty 68 percent charged for an on-site estimate.

The phone bids were vague. When pressed, the people who answered the phone said they would have to call me back. Very few did call back.

I can see two "musts" for the business. (1) My bids must be firm. (2) My phone skills must be customer-oriented. If I can't answer the phone, I must find a phone person who can fulfill these two musts. The image we're presenting here is "We aim to please. We're interested in servicing your home."

One question I asked was: "Will the same person be in my home?" A mere 6 percent said yes. The other respondents were vague. That indicated a problem in scheduling.

Measuring the competition has given my start-up a real advantage. Since I'll be doing all the work myself, I can gather customer data as I work. As I expand, I shall match employees to homeowners. A home is a private place. It's a place where you go to escape from the day. You don't want it invaded by different strangers every week. My plan is to expand only when I find the right employees.

4. Pricing

My strategy is to price my services just slightly higher than the current competitor's rates. Every 3 months, to stay current, I will survey the competition.

Basic Rates for Housecleaning:

1ST CLEANING—CHECKSHEET ITEMS ONLY

Square Feet	Price
1,000	$ 50
1,000–1,500	75
1,500–2,000	100
2,000 +	100 + $25 per 1,000 sq. ft.

Weekly Cleaning	
1,000	$ 35
1,000–1,500	55
1,500–2,000	75
2,000 +	75 + $15 per 1,000 sq. ft.

Bi-monthly	
1,000	$ 45
1,000–1,500	70
1,500–2,000	90
2,000 +	90 + $20 per 1,000 sq. ft.

WINDOW WASHING

One-story house	
up to 15 windows	$ 25
each additional 5 windows	10

Two-story house	
up to 25 windows	$ 60
each additional 5 windows	10

5. Target Customer

I can classify three types of Target Customers for my business:

Customer A—Family Dwelling.

A married couple with one or more children. The household income is $75,000 or more. Two vehicles. Both parents work. Reason for the service: spare time is at a premium for child care, recreation, and entertainment. Parents cannot spare the time to do windows or other cleaning.

Customer B—Single Person Condo.

Customer B is a single or divorced person living alone, usually in an apartment or waterside condo. Age range from 28 to 40. The income here runs from $32,000 to $50,000. Time is at a premium. Customers are seldom at home on nights or weekends.

Customer C—High Roller.

Customer C is distinguished by incomes in the six-figure range. Home values start at $400,000 and move up the scale to $1.0 million. Customer C has high standards, wants a spotless home. Has zero desire to perform menial tasks. As long as the work is excellent and they feel they're not getting ripped off, price is no object.

6. Ad/Sales Program

A. I will maintain an image of high visibility. My truck is washed daily. The color is white. If there is mud on the tires after a job, the mud is washed off before the next job. I wear a white jumpsuit that bears the company logo. My employees wear similar jumpsuits. Our footgear is white sneakers. They're easy on the feet and look professional, almost a sporty image.

B. My business cards are white with blue lettering. On the reverse side is a list of my services. I make it a habit to get a business card whenever I hand one out. Data from these cards is entered into a computer. Names are added to a master list.

C. Flyers will be placed door to door in target neighborhoods. I plan to do one neighborhood of 100 to 200 homes, and then evaluate the response. I ask questions of each person who calls about the flyer: What did they like? What was missing? From this marketing survey, I'll redesign the flyer before approaching a second neighborhood.

I make a habit of leaving flyers and business cards at all day-care centers in the area. In exchange for each customer I gain, I donate to a fund for school books or toys.

7. Start-Up Costs

Truck	$6,000*
Paint truck white	800
Ladder rack (custom-made)	350
Ladders	412
Supplies—windows	400
Supplies—housecleaning	500
Signs for new truck	195
Advertising	250
Answering machine	75
Phone and pager installation	200
P.O. box per month—first and last month	40

(continued)

Continued

Chamber of Commerce	200
Fictitious business name	65
Business license	55
Used desk and chair	275
Desk calendar	6
Date book, home	65
Date book, truck	15
Rolodex, supplies, file system	50
Bank account and one-write system	125
Total Estimate Start-up Expenses	10,078*

*You should be able to buy this for $1,000 down and $175 to $200 per month for 36 months. Thus, start-up cash may be as low as $5,078.

8. Sales Goals and Expenses, First Three Months

My plan is to work 6 days per week. Until I gain experience, I can work a maximum of three jobs per day. As a carrot for customers, I will do windows at half price with the first house cleaning. I will devote two full weeks to marketing my new business. On the schedule at present, I have four weekly customers and two bimonthly scheduled for the third week. When not on the job, I plan a strong marketing effort, so that I can add one customer per week until I'm up to eighteen customers, my maximum for the week. At that time, I will evaluate my ability to add additional customers and/or hire a part-time employee. (See Figure 17.5).

	1	2	3	4	5	6	7
1	Sales Goals and Expenses						
2							
3		1st Month	2nd Month	3rd Month			
4							
5	Sales (1)	1087.5	2580	4580.5			
6							
7	Expenses:						
8	Gas (2)	73	91	115			
9	Maintenance (3)	25	25	25			
10	Insurance (4)	125	125	125			
11	Phone (5)	45	45	45			
12	Advertising (6)	80	80	80			
13	Supplies (7)	65	155	275			
14	Truck Loan Interest	60	60	60			
15		473	581	725			
16	Expense Total	614.5	1999	3855.5			
17	Profit						

FIGURE 17.5   Sales Goals and Expenses

NOTES FOR FIGURE 17.5

1. Average customer will be a one-story house of 2,000 square feet with 15 windows. Month 1 = 4 weeks. Month 2 = 4 weeks. Month 3 = 5 weeks. Every other new customer bi-monthly. All window washing contracts on a quarterly basis.
2. Gas, $15 per week plus $1 per job.
3. Maintenance—mainly a reserve for tires, repairs, oil changes, $25 per month.
4. Auto insurance and bonding, $1,500 per year.
5. Basic phone, pager, post office box.
6. Approximately 400 flyers per month comes to $55, plus $25 for distribution.
7. Approximately $5 per job.

"Things to Do" List

File for fictitious business name.
Design business logo, cards, and flyer.
Order phone installation.
Purchase phone.
Lease pager.
Set up bank account.
Order one-write check system.
Order business cards.
Set up post office box.
Locate source of supplies.
Purchase supplies.
Purchase truck.
Get it painted white.
Order signs for truck.
Purchase answering machine.
Buy ladder rack for truck.
Buy ladders.
Join Chamber of Commerce.
Purchase desk, chair, and office supplies.

NOTES

APPENDIX A
One-Write Bookkeeping

NECESSITY'S GIFT TO THE SMALL-BUSINESSPERSON

Though the one-write bookkeeping system may have been patented in Europe in 1916, it took World War II to explode its popularity.

When the war effort drastically curtailed the manufacture of bookkeeping machines, the "poster" or "writing board" came into common use as a temporary replacement. These were familiarly referred to as "pegboard" systems, because some form of pegs was used to align the multiple forms involved. No longer a stop-gap innovation, pegboard bookkeeping has been shaped and reshaped through the years until it has become a basic tool in thousands of today's small businesses and branch offices of large corporations.

The present-day version, usually referred to as *one-write,* is the simplest of all bookkeeping methods and has proven more than adequate in meeting the record-keeping requirements of most small firms—quite inexpensively. This is not surprising, because it's the one bookkeeping system designed specifically for small businesses and professional offices.

SAVES TIME AND ELIMINATES MISTAKE-PRONE REPETITIVE STEPS

A check or receipt, a journal, an earnings record, or a ledger all require the same information. Instead of completing each record individually, this system allows them to be completed in one writing. See Figure A.1.

The poster holds two or more forms in alignment so that one writing simultaneously produces multiple records. Through precision forms design and the use of Waxspot® carbon or sensitized paper, the desired information—and only that—transfers through from the form being filled out. The forms themselves overlap like shingles on a roof and can be inserted or removed with ease. The design of the poster or "pegboard" facilitates alignment.

> One-write eliminates the need for multiple postings.

> One-write eliminates the errors inherent in reposting numbers.

Because only a single posting is required, there's just one record to balance. One proof reconciles all records, and these are both accurate and up-to-date.

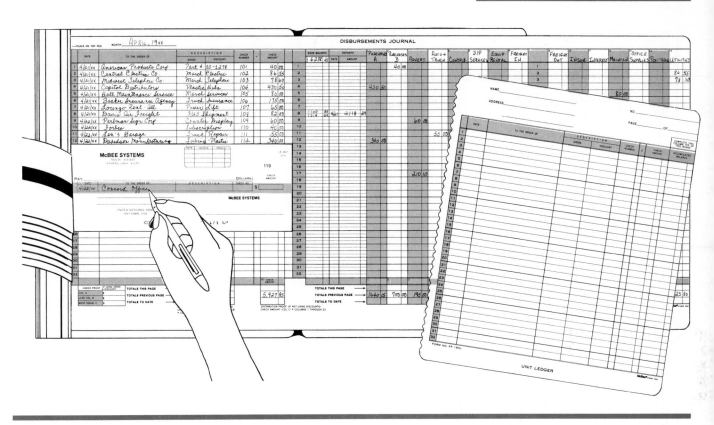

The system makes balancing the books a simple affair. After completing entries, you only need to run adding machine totals to check the balance. Yet such a set of books provides ongoing positive control in both check-writing and receipting functions.

Far simpler than a purely manual set of spread sheets, a three-up checkbook and separate ledgers, a one-write system costs just about the same. More important, it's so simple that anyone can use it proficiently with only a few minutes of instruction.

A one-write system likewise helps you gain greater use of your accountant's time and expertise. It gives your accountant organized journals to work with instead of having to ride herd on loose vouchers and check stubs. Knowing that the subsidiary books balance and that possible transcription errors are eliminated speeds and simplifies the preparation of your financial statements. With less time needed to straighten out the books, one-write frees more time for your accountant to spend analyzing them and advising you.

FIGURE A.1 Though just two pieces of paper, a check and a journal, this disbursements system, the simplest of all one-writes, provides all the benefits of sound bookkeeping: known distribution, sequential check control, an audit trail, balanced totals, a running bank balance, instant review. In a word, *accountability.*

CASH DISBURSEMENTS SYSTEM FOR USE WITH COMPUTERS

This system provides a well-organized, preproven document—namely, the journal—precisely for data processing purposes. See Figure A.2. The sequencing of "Check Number," "Account," and "Check Amount" makes it an ideal source of client input. The journal is coated to allow for a duplicate copy. Because both you and your accountant have a copy, the time constraints of having to return data and respond to questions, phone calls, and mailings are eliminated.

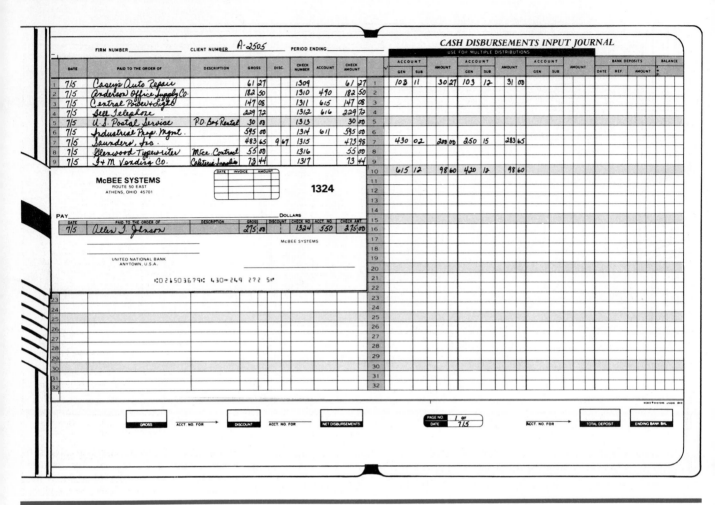

	DATE	PAID TO THE ORDER OF	DESCRIPTION	GROSS	DISC.	CHECK NUMBER	ACCOUNT	CHECK AMOUNT		GEN	SUB	AMOUNT	GEN	SUB	AMOUNT	GEN	SUB	AMOUNT	DATE	REF.	AMOUNT	
1	7/5	Casey's Auto Repair		61 27		1309		61 27	1	103	11	30 27	103	12	31 00							
2	7/5	Anderson Office Supply Co.		182 50		1310	490	182 50	2													
3	7/5	Central Power + Light		147 08		1311	615	147 08	3													
4	7/5	Bell Telephone		229 72		1312	616	229 72	4													
5	7/5	U.S. Postal Service	P.O. Box Rental	30 00		1313		30 00	5													
6	7/5	Industrial Prop. Mgmt.		595 00		1314	611	595 00	6													
7	7/5	Saunders, Inc.		483 65	9 67	1315		473 98	7	430 02		200 00	250 15		283 65							
8	7/5	Glenwood Typewriter	Mtce. Contract	55 00		1316		55 00	8													
9	7/5	J + M Vending Co.	Cafeteria Supplies	73 44		1317		73 44	9													
10									10	615 12		98 60	420 12		98 60							

CASH DISBURSEMENTS INPUT JOURNAL

FIRM NUMBER _____ CLIENT NUMBER A-2505 PERIOD ENDING _____

FIGURE A.2 Three sets of columns have been provided to accommodate multiple expense distributions when the amount cannot be expensed properly to a single G/L account.

The Account Number column is divided into "General" and "Sub" accounts for departmental or branch accounting.

When posting is finished, you simply down-add and balance the journal and update the bank balance. Two proofing checks are printed on the journal as reminders.

PAYROLL SYSTEM

Accurate and auditable payroll accounting records are a must for all businesses. The one-write version is well suited for the small- to medium-size company or for the executive payroll of a corporation. The Employee Earnings Record is simply slipped between the check and the journal. In this case, a top-write check is used with a detachable stub serving as the employee's record of earnings. See Figure A.3.

Because the Earnings Record, the Statement of Earnings, and the Journal are all automatically posted in a single writing, they can be balanced in a single proofing, saving additional time and eliminating possible transcription errors.

CASH DISBURSEMENTS/PAYROLL COMBINATION SYSTEM

Here you can switch from writing disbursements to writing payroll simply by inserting the employee earnings record between the check and the journal: the same check is used, the same journal is used, the same writing board is used. See Figure A.4. With either application, one-write completes all records simultaneously. It's the ideal system for the small business that does not need to maintain separate bank accounts for general disbursements and payroll.

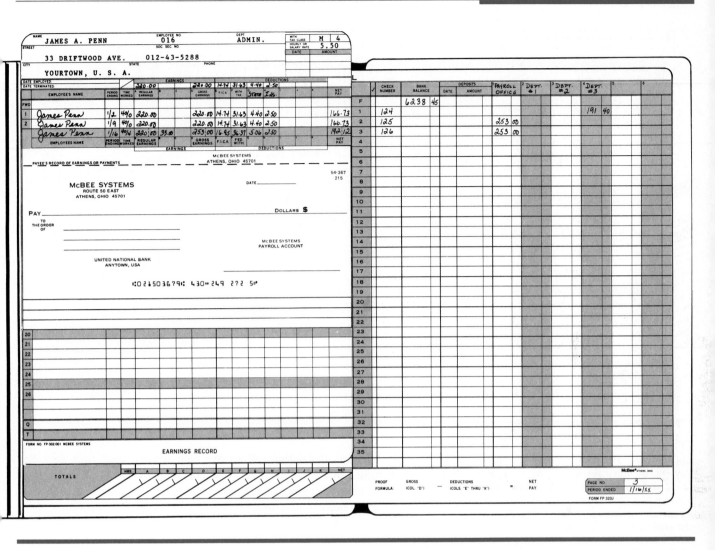

FIGURE A.3 The Earnings Record, divided into quarters, facilitates the preparation of federal, state and local required reports. In addition to "F.I.C.A." and "Fed. With.," two earnings and five deduction boxes can be overprinted with the headings of your choice, illustrative of the flexibility of one-write. The journal offers twenty or more columns of distribution for breaking down individual employee pay by job, product, department, and so on.

A journal featuring Sales and Cash Receipts information on the back flap is an available option. It's perfect for the business that keeps daily register totals and/or totals from individual sales tickets.

ACCOUNTS PAYABLE

For a business to be able to sell on credit, it normally must buy on credit because of limited working capital. Therefore, accounts-payable (accrual) accounting is an almost universal business function. It gives you an up-to-date picture of your firm's liabilities.

However, its terminology and the variety of ways of handling payables often make this the most "mysterious" phase of accounting. The result is that many businesses neglect to have a systemized approach. One-write simplifies the mechanics. See Figure A.5.

ACCOUNTS RECEIVABLE

Needed cash won't flow in unless your firm's billing flows out—smoothly and regularly. This calls for a *system,* not just repetitive paperwork.

FIGURE A.4 The Center-Write Check is available in duplicate form. The duplicate serves as a handy proof of payment when attached to a paid invoice, as well as providing an easy means of auditing the records. The duplicate copy plays an important role in payroll preparations because it serves as the employee's statement of earnings.

A one-write Accounts Receivable system can help smooth your cash flow. See Figure A.6. Customer Statements and A/R Ledgers are prepared as *by-products* of posting daily sales slips. Therefore, statements are ready to be mailed at any time, and overdue balances become easy to spot.

CASH RECEIPTS SYSTEM

It's easy for cash to fall through the cracks. That's why it's important to use some form of receipting system. Each transaction should be recorded. One-write takes this a step further—offering tighter control over your cash payments, and it's more efficient than the receipt book method. See Figure A.7.

HAS ONE-WRITE BEEN BURYING ITS LIGHT UNDER A BUSHEL BASKET?

If one-write bookkeeping is such a boon to small business, why isn't it more widely known?

It's not that one-write is one of America's best-kept secrets. It's more the case that its popularity cannot keep abreast of that eye-opening number of new business start-ups year after year. It's not the type of product that's nationally advertised or talked about on the computer platform.

ACCOUNTS PAYABLE LEDGER

The rule of thumb is that any firm with less than twenty-five people on the payroll and/or that writes as few as twenty-five checks a month is a candidate for one-write bookkeeping. The estimate is that almost 80 percent of the small business market does not use a one-write system. Rather than having rejected it, most of these firms have yet to learn about it—for several reasons:

1. Old-line accountants have never used one-write and they are reluctant to change.
2. Though many accountants praise it, many new businesses exist for years before hiring an accountant.
3. Rarely is it found in the college curriculum, even for accounting majors.
4. Only recently have some banks started promoting one-write, and then only small, nonmetropolitan institutions.

This last point is worth amplifying. The new owner of a small business, upon opening a commercial account at a bank, invariably winds up ordering a three-up checkbook. Most of the time is spent discussing the desired color of the checks and whether or not a logo is to be printed on them. Little or no attention is given to the idea of check writing *as a system*.

Yet, that's exactly what the check with the "black strip on the back" is all about: a check-writing and record-keeping system all in one. In fact, because of its flexibility, one-write offers the assurance that each entrepreneur can have the check writing system best suited to his or her firm's needs.

Regrettably, one-write is just one of dozens of products the bank's busy New Account Representative has to deal with. However, in today's heated competition for retail banking business, the accent falls heavily on *customer service,* which is where one-write belongs. Banks small enough to change without layers of committee meetings are beginning to think of one-write as a viable check alternative.

FIGURE A.5 *Incurring the Expense* (illustrated here): Invoices are posted to the Accounts Payable Ledger and to the Purchase Journal simultaneously.

Paying the Bills (not shown): As checks are written, entries are simultaneously posted to the Accounts Payable Ledger and to the Disbursements Journal.

This plan forces the bookkeeper to maintain accurate figures so that the status of payables is always known. Peak work loads are avoided. Multiple postings are eliminated. And one balancing proves all records—journals, ledgers, and checks are posted correctly.

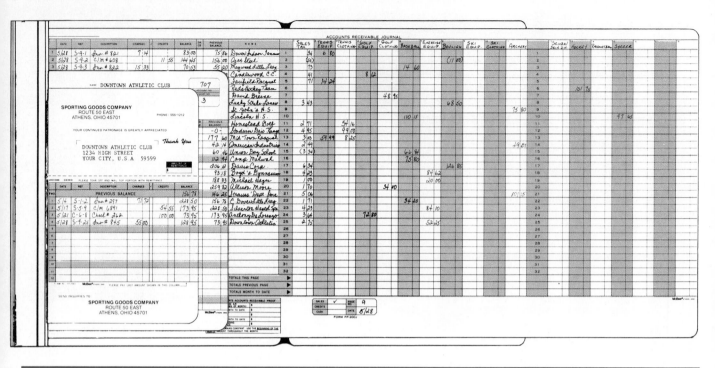

FIGURE A.6 When posting charges, the Accounts Receivable Journal, the A/R Ledger, and the Customer Statement are put in position on the "pegboard."

For payments received, the Cash Receipts Journal is used along with the A/R Ledger and Statement.

You can get a custom designed sales ticket, invoice, or receipt as part of your A/R one-write system at surprisingly little cost.

HALLMARKS OF ONE-WRITE: SIMPLICITY AND FLEXIBILITY

The one-write systems described in this appendix represent only a few basic accounting applications. Bear in mind, there are dozens of simple, flexible one-write systems or plans. Generally speaking, there are three categories of one-write systems:

1. Off-the-shelf or stock plans
2. Custom-designed systems
3. Between these ends of the spectrum, there are a whole range of individualized plans.

By design, one-write can handle four forms at the same time. The wide version of the poster board, for example, can accommodate two different ledgers simultaneously. You can have journals with preprinted column headings of your choice. There are duplicate journals and duplicate checks. The permutations are practically endless. The significant point is that a one-write system can be assembled to fit a need.

HOW AND WHERE TO FIND THE RIGHT ONE-WRITE FOR YOUR BUSINESS

Though they are still not available at your local stationery store, one-write bookkeeping systems are easily attainable through forms distributors and mail-order catalogs—provided you want a basic or "stock" system and you already know how to use it.

FIGURE A.7 *Cash Receipts Journal* provides a chronological listing of all cash receipts. You are given a choice of five or twenty-three columns, for example, for analysis purposes, and a General Ledger column for miscellaneous income.

Cash Receipts are offered in single or duplicate format. The duplicate copy can be retained for auditing reference.

Bank Deposit Slip, created as a by-product of posting the receipts, assures all payments are deposited in the bank.

However, there are a few companies that specialize in one-writes. These are national concerns selling through a distributor or their own national sales force. Such companies offer a catalog of one-write systems covering all basic accounting functions and designed for a number of different businesses. Here's a partial list of such applications:

- Cash Disbursements
- Accounts Payable
- Payroll
- Accounts Receivable
- Combination PR/Disbursements
- Combination AP/Payroll
- AR/Aged Trial Balance
- Cash Receipts
- General Ledger
- Organized Computer Input
- Inventory Control
- Time Control
- Telephone Message

And specially designed plans for the particular needs of:

- Accountants
- Builders, Remodelers
- Franchise Operators
- Insurance Agents
- Lawyers
- Medical Offices and Labs
- Property Management Firms
- Real Estate Offices
- Restaurants
- Schools
- Self-Storage Facilities

There's also a Personal Income Control system for home use to help organize your personal finances.

Equally important, these companies are continuously developing new versions to meet the changing needs of the marketplace. In real estate, for example, there are now more than a dozen one-write systems ranging from property management to rent collection and from escrow/trust to commission settlement.

One-write likewise offers unique advantages to national franchise chains by unifying the record keeping in a way that's compatible with the needs of corporate headquarters. Whether it's hamburgers or health clinics, whether you're building homes or selling them, it doesn't matter. That's why household names like Burger King®, Century 21®, the U.S. Department of Health and Human Services, and the National Association of Home Builders all offer and encourage their branches or franchisees to employ one-write bookkeeping.

APPENDIX B
Small Business
Start-Up Forms

INFORMATION NEEDED FOR SELLER'S PERMIT AND/ OR USE FUEL PERMIT*

When applying for a Use Fuel Permit, you will need to show the registrations for all diesel vehicles. If you have just recently purchased the vehicle, also take along a copy of the bill of sale, signed by the seller.

Sole Ownership or Partnership

You must apply for a permit in person. At least one partner is required to apply.

1. Business address and phone number
2. Owner or owners' Social Security number(s) and drivers license number(s)
3. Residence address(es) and phone number(s) of owner(s)
4. Estimated monthly expenses and sales (Seller's Permit only)
5. Three personal references with names, complete addresses, and phone numbers
6. Names and addresses of banks—both personal and business

Corporation

At least one corporate officer is required to apply for the permit. If one is not available, a notarized power of attorney is required.

1. Articles of incorporation
2. Business address
3. Estimated monthly sales and expense figures (Seller's Permit only)
4. Federal Identification Number
5. Corporate Number
6. Names, residence addresses, phone numbers, driver's license numbers, and Social Security numbers of all corporate officers
7. Bank name, location and corporate account number
8. Names of corporate stockholders and percentages held

---

*Authors' Note: If your business requires the collection of sales tax, contact the closest state tax office and be prepared to offer the same information.

A	MAIL CERTIFIED COPIES TO:	B	PUBLISH IN NEWSPAPER:

A MAIL CERTIFIED COPIES TO:

NAME _____

ADDRESS _____

_____

☐ First Filing . Renewal Filing

Current Registration No. _____

B PUBLISH IN NEWSPAPER:

COUNTY CLERK'S FILING STAMP

FICTITIOUS BUSINESS NAME STATEMENT
THE FOLLOWING PERSON(S) IS (ARE) DOING BUSINESS AS:

1. Fictitious Business Name(s)

2. Street Address, City & State of Principal place of Business in California   Zip Code

3.
Full name of Registrant   (if corporation - show state of incorporation)

Residence Address	City	State	Zip Code

Full name of Registrant   (if corporation - show state of incorporation)

Residence Address	City	State	Zip Code

Full name of Registrant   (if corporation - show state of incorporation)

Residence Address	City	State	Zip Code

Full name of Registrant   (if corporation - show state of incorporation)

Residence Address	City	State	Zip Code

4. This Business is conducted by: (CHECK ONE ONLY)
( ) an individual   ( ) a general partnership   ( ) joint venture   ( ) a business trust
( ) co-partners   ( ) husband and wife   ( ) a corporation   ( ) a limited partnership
( ) an unincorporated association other than a partnership   ( ) other—*please specify* _____

5. The registrant commenced to transact business under the fictitious business name or names listed above on _____

6A.
Signed _____

Typed or Printed _____

6B. If Registrant a corporation sign below:

Corporation Name _____

Signature & Title _____

Type or Print
Officer's Name & Title _____

This statement was filed with the County Clerk of _____ County on date indicated by file stamp above.

NOTICE

THIS FICTITIOUS NAME STATEMENT EXPIRES ON DECEMBER 31, 19_____. A NEW FICTITIOUS BUSINESS NAME STATEMENT MUST BE FILED PRIOR TO DECEMBER 31, 19_____.

I HEREBY CERTIFY THAT THIS COPY IS A CORRECT COPY OF THE ORIGINAL STATEMENT ON FILE IN MY OFFICE.

_____
COUNTY CLERK

BY _____ DEPUTY

File No. _____

Fictitious Business Name Statement

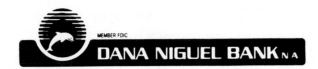

DANA NIGUEL BANK N A

34180 PACIFIC COAST HIGHWAY • DANA POINT, CA 92629 • 714/661-4100

Bank use only
Sic.# _____
Officer _____
Initial _____

BUSINESS LOAN APPLICATION INSTRUCTIONS

Date _____

Please fill in all blanks, and answer all questions. Please print or type. All information requested is needed to properly process this application and only for this purpose. Failure to complete all items, particularly full names and address, may result in delay and inconvenience to you. Please be assured that all information will be held in strictest confidence.

Firm Name: _____ Phone: (___) _____

Address: _____ City: _____ State: _____ Zip: _____

Equipment
Located at: _____ City: _____ State: _____ Zip: _____

Type of Business: _____ Fed. Tax No: _____

No. of years
in Business: _____   Corporation ☐   Insurance Carrier: _____ Agent: _____
                        Sole Owner ☐ Partnership ☐   Address: _____

OWNERSHIP

Principal: (1) _____ Title: _____   Own ☐ Rent ☐

Home Address: _____
                                      CITY   STATE   ZIP
                     1st ☐ Mortgage

Lender _____ Indicate 2nd ☐ Mortgage   Cost _____   Present Market Value _____

Loan No. _____ Year acquired _____   Total Balance owed _____

S.S. # _____ D.L.# _____ Exp. Date _____ State _____ Phone # (___) _____

Principal: (2) _____ Title: _____   Own ☐ Rent ☐

Home Address: _____
                                      CITY   STATE   ZIP
                     1st ☐ Mortgage

Lender _____ Indicate 2nd ☐ Mortgage   Cost _____   Present Market Value _____

Loan No. _____ Year acquired _____   Total Balance owed _____

S.S. # _____ D.L.# _____ Exp. Date _____ State _____ Phone # (___) _____

BANK

Name of
Bank (1): _____   ☐ Checking Acct. # _____
                                      ☐ Savings Acct. # _____
Address: _____ City: _____   ☐ Loan # _____ Amt. _____
                    Bank
Phone: (___) _____ Officer: _____   Past Loan # _____ Amt. _____

Name of
Bank (2): _____   ☐ Checking Acct. # _____
                                      ☐ Savings Acct. # _____
Address: _____ City: _____   ☐ Loan # _____ Amt. _____
                    Bank
Phone: (___) _____ Officer: _____   Past Loan # _____ Amt. _____

Name of
Bank (3): _____   ☐ Checking Acct. # _____
                                      ☐ Savings Acct. # _____
Address: _____ City: _____   ☐ Loan # _____ Amt. _____
                    Bank
Phone: (___) _____ Officer: _____   Past Loan # _____ Amt. _____

TRADE

CREDIT REFERENCES

Name: (1) _____ Address: _____   Phone No.: _____

Name: (2) _____ Address: _____   Phone No.: _____

Name: (3) _____ Address: _____   Phone No.: _____

EQUIPMENT

EQUIPMENT

Vendor: _____ Contact: _____

Address: _____ Phone: (___) _____

Type of Equip.: _____ Amount _____ Tax _____ Total _____

Terms _____ MOS.@ _____ Deposit _____

Sample Business Loan Application   *continued*

Are there any unsatisfied judgments against the business or principal owner(s)? Yes ___ No ___

If "yes": Amount $ _____ to whom owed: _____

has the company or principal owner(s) declared bankruptcy in the last 10 years? Yes ___ No ___

If "yes" give details on a separate form.

Banking Relationship

Are you willing to change your prime banking relationship if the subject loan is approved?

Yes___ No___If "no" why? _____

LIST FIVE MAJOR CUSTOMERS

Name	Address	Telephone	Account Officer
1.			
2.			
3.			
4.			
5.			

──────────────── **REQUIRED FINANCIAL INFORMATION** ────────────────

Last Fiscal year-end Business Statement of Condition including Profit and Loss statement.

Last Interim Business Statement of Condition if fiscal year end is more than 90 days from date of this application; include Ageings of Accounts Receivable and Accounts Payable, Profit and Loss Statement.

Complete Copy of last two years Federal Tax returns on the Business.

Personal financial statement on each principal owner.

Complete Copy of last year's Federal Tax Return on each principal owner.

OWNERSHIP additional principal(s) not listed on the reverse side of this application with ownership of 20% or more; use a separate Business loan application form.

The information contained in this statement is provided to induce you to extend or to continue the extension of credit to the undersigned or to others upon the guaranty of the undersigned. The undersigned acknowledge and understand that you are relying on the information provided herein in deciding to grant or continue credit or to accept a guaranty thereof. Each of the undersigned agrees to notify you immediately and in writing of any change in name, address, or employment and of any material adverse change (1) in any of the information contained in this statement or (2) in the financial condition of any of the undersigned or (3) in the ability of any of the undersigned to perform its (or their) obligations to you. In the absence of such notice or a new and full written statement, this should be considered as a continuing statement and substantially correct. You are authorized to make all inquiries you deem necessary to verify the accuracy of the information contained herein, and to determine the credit-worthiness of the undersigned. Each of the undersigned authorizes you to answer questions about your credit experience with the undersigned.

Business Name: _____

By: _____
        Name   Title

Date: _____   By: _____
                                            Name   Title

Sample Business Loan Application, page 2

PERSONAL FINANCIAL STATEMENT

Submitted to: **DANA NIGUEL BANK N.A.**

34180 Pacific Coast Hwy., Dana Point, CA. 92629

• IMPORTANT: Read these directions before completing this Statement

☐ If you are applying for individual credit in your own name and are relying on your own income, or assets and not the income or assets of another person as the basis for repayment of the credit requested, complete only Sections 1, 3 and 4.

☐ If you are applying for joint credit with another person, complete all Sections and provide information in Section 2 about the joint applicant. If appropriate, the joint applicant may complete a separate personal financial statement (C-100), and the applications may be submitted together.

☐ If you are applying for individual credit but are relying on income from alimony, child support, or separate maintenance or on the income or assets of another person as a basis for repayment of the credit requested, complete all Sections. Provide information in Section 2 about the person whose alimony, support, or maintenance payments or income or assets you are relying on. Alimony, child support, or separate maintenance income, need not be revealed if you do not wish to have it considered as a basis for repaying this obligation.

☐ If this statement relates to your guaranty of the indebtedness of other person(s), firm(s), or corporation(s), complete Sections 1, 3 and 4.

Section 1 - Individual Information (type or print)	Section 2 - Other Party Information (type or print)
Name	Name
Address	Address
City, state & zip	City, state & zip
Position or occupation	Position or occupation
Business name	Business name
Business address	Business address
City, state & zip	City, state & zip
Length of employment	Length of employment
Res. phone Bus. phone	Res. phone Bus. phone

Section 3 - Statement of Financial Condition as of _____ 19 _____

Assets (Do not include assets of doubtful value)	In dollars (omit cents)	Liabilities	In dollars (omit cents)
Cash on hand and in this bank		Notes payable to banks-see Schedule E	
Cash in other banks		Notes payable to other institutions-see Schedule E	
U.S. Gov't & marketable securities-see Schedule A		Due to brokers	
Non-marketable securities-see Schedule B		Amounts payable to others-secured	
Securities held by broker in margin accounts		Amounts payable to others-unsecured	
Restricted, control, or margin account stocks		Accounts and bills due	
Real estate-see Schedule C		Unpaid income tax	
Accounts, loans, and notes receivable		Other unpaid taxes and interest	
Automobiles		Real estate mortgages payable-see Schedules C & E	
Other personal property		Other debts (car payments, credit cards, etc.)-itemize	
Cash surrender value-life insurance-see Schedule D			
Other assets-itemize-see Schedule F if applicable			
		Total Liabilities	
		Net Worth	
Total Assets		Total Liabilities and Net Worth	

Section 4 - Annual Income For Year Ended _____ 19 _____		Annual Expenditures		Contingent Liabilities	Yes	No	Estimated Amounts
Salary, bonuses & commissions $ _____		Mortgage/rental payments $ _____		Do you have any			$ _____
Dividends & interest _____		Real estate taxes & assessments _____		Contingent liabilities (as endorser, co-maker or guarantor? On leases? on contracts?)	☐	☐	_____
Real estate income _____		Taxes- federal, state & local _____		Involvement in pending legal actions?	☐	☐	_____
Other income (alimony, child support, or separate maintenance income need not be revealed if you do not wish to have it considered as a basis for repaying this obligation) _____		Insurance payments _____		Other special debt or circumstances?	☐	☐	
		Other contract payments (car payments, charge cards etc) _____		Contested income tax liens?	☐	☐	
		Alimony, child support maintenance _____		If "yes" to any question(s) describe			
		Other expenses _____					
Total $ Income		Total $ Expenditures		Total $ Contingent Liabilities			

(COMPLETE SCHEDULES AND SIGN ON REVERSE SIDE)

Sample Personal Financial Statement   *continued*

SCHEDULE A - U.S. GOVERNMENT & MARKETABLE SECURITIES

Number of Shares or Face Value of Bonds	Description	In Name of	Are These Registered Pledged or Held by others?	Market Value

SCHEDULE B - NON-MARKETABLE SECURITIES

Number Of Shares	Description	In Name of	Are These Registered Pledged or Held by Others?	Value	Source Of Value

SCHEDULE C - RESIDENCES AND OTHER REAL ESTATE EQUITIES (PARTIALLY OR WHOLLY OWNED)

Address and Type of Property	Title in Name of	% of Ownership	Date Acquired	Cost	Market Value	Monthly Payment	Mortgage Amount	Mortgage Holder
Residence(s)								
Residence(s)								
Other								
Other								

SCHEDULE D - LIFE INSURANCE CARRIED, INCLUDING GROUP INSURANCE

Name of Insurance Company	Owner of Policy	Beneficiary and Relationship	Face Amount	Policy Loans	Cash Surrender Value

SCHEDULE E - BANK AND OTHER INSTITUTIONAL RELATIONSHIPS

Name and Address of Creditor	Original Loan Line Amount	Date of Loan	Maturity Date	Unsecured or Secured (List Collateral)	Monthly Payment	Amount Owed

SCHEDULE F - BUSINESS VENTURES

List Name and Address of Any Business Venture in Which You Are a Principal or Partner	Total Assets Listed In Section 3	Your % of Ownership	Your Position/Title In the Business	Total Assets Of Business	Line of Business	Years in Business

(USE ADDITIONAL SCHEDULES IF NECESSARY)

The information contained in this statement is provided to induce you to extend or to continue the extension of credit to the undersigned or to others upon the guaranty of the undersigned. The undersigned acknowledge and understand that you are relying on the information provided herein in deciding to grant or continue credit or to accept a guaranty thereof. Each of the undersigned represents, warrants and certifies that the information provided herein is true, correct and complete. Each of the undersigned agrees to notify you immediately and in writing of any change in name, address, or employment and of any material adverse change (1) in any of the information contained in this statement or (2) in the financial condition of any of the undersigned or (3) in the ability of any of the undersigned to perform its (or their) obligations to you. In the absence of such notice or a new and full written statement, this should be considered as a continuing statement and substantially correct. You are authorized to make all inquiries you deem necessary to verify the accuracy of the information contained herein, and to determine the credit-worthiness of the undersigned. Each of the undersigned authorizes you to answer questions about your credit experience with the undersigned.

Signature (individual) _____

Social Security Number_____

Date signed _____, 19_____   Date of Birth _____

Signature (other party)_____

Social Security Number_____

Date Signed_____, 19_____   Date of Birth _____

Sample Personal Financial Statement, page 2

OMB Approval No. 3245-0016
Expiration Date: 10-31-93

U.S. Small Business Administration
APPLICATION FOR BUSINESS LOAN

Individual	Full Address	

Name of Applicant Business		Tax I.D. No. or SSN

Full Street Address of Business		Tel. No. (inc. A/C)

City	County	State	Zip	Number of Employees (Including subsidiaries and affiliates)

Type of Business		Date Business Established	At Time of Application _____

Bank of Business Account and Address	If Loan is Approved _____
	Subsidiaries or Affiliates _____ (Separate from above)

Use of Proceeds: (Enter Gross Dollar Amounts Rounded to the Nearest Hundreds)	Loan Requested		Loan Requested
Land Acquisition		Payoff SBA Loan	
New Construction/ Expansion Repair		Payoff Bank Loan (Non SBA Associated)	
Acquisition and/or Repair of Machinery and Equipment		Other Debt Payment (Non SBA Associated)	
Inventory Purchase		All Other	
Working Capital (Including Accounts Payable)		Total Loan Requested	
Acquisition of Existing Business		Term of Loan - (Requested Mat.)	_____ Yrs.

PREVIOUS SBA OR OTHER FEDERAL GOVERNMENT DEBT: If you or any principals or affiliates have 1) ever requested Government Financing or 2) are delinquent on the repayment of any Federal Debt complete the following:

Name of Agency	Original Amount of Loan	Date of Request	Approved or Declined	Balance	Current or Past Due
	$			$	
	$			$	

ASSISTANCE   List the names(s) and occupations of any who assisted in the preparation of this form, other than applicant.

Name and Occupation	Address	Total Fees Paid	Fees Due
Name and Occupation	Address	Total Fees Paid	Fees Due

PLEASE NOTE: The estimated burden hours for the completion of this form is 19.8 hours per response. If you have any questions or comments concerning this estimate or any other aspect of this information collection please contact, Chief Administrative Information Branch, U.S. Small Business Administration, Washington, D.C. 20416 and Gary Waxman, Clearance Officer, Paperwork Reduction Project (3245-0016), Office of Management and Budget, Washington, D.C. 20503

SBA Form 4 (12-91) Previous Edition is Obsolete

Application for SBA Loan   *continued*

ALL EXHIBITS MUST BE SIGNED AND DATED BY PERSON SIGNING THIS FORM

BUSINESS INDEBTEDNESS: Furnish the following information on all installment debts, contracts, notes, and mortgages payable. Indicate by an asterisk(*) items to be paid by loan proceeds and reason for paying same (present balance should agree with the latest balance sheet submitted).

To Whom Payable	Original Amount	Original Date	Present Balance	Rate of Interest	Maturity Date	Monthly Payment	Security	Current or Past Due
	$		$			$		
Acct. #								
	$		$			$		
Acct. #								
	$		$			$		
Acct. #								
	$		$			$		
Acct. #								

MANAGEMENT (Proprietor, partners, officers, directors all holders of outstanding stock - **100% of ownership must be shown**). Use separate sheet if necessary.

Name and Social Security Number and Position Title	Complete Address	% Owned	*Military Service From	To	*Race	*Sex

*This data is collected for statistical purpose only. It has no bearing on the credit decision to approve or decline this application.

THE FOLLOWING EXHIBITS MUST BE COMPLETED WHERE APPLICABLE . ALL QUESTIONS ANSWERED ARE MADE A PART OF THE APPLICATION.

For Guaranty Loans please provide an original and one copy (Photocopy is Acceptable) of the Application Form, and all Exhibits to the participating lender. For Direct Loans submit one original copy of the application and Exhibits to SBA.

1. Submit SBA Form 912 (Personal History Statement) for each person e.g. owners, partners, officers, directors, major stockholders, etc ; the instructions are on SBA Form 912.

2. If your collateral consists of (A) Land and Building, (B) Machinery and Equipment, (C)Furniture and Fixtures, (D) Accounts Receivable (E) Inventory, (F) Other, please provide an itemized list (labeled Exhibit A) that contains serial and identification numbers for all articles that had an original value greater than $500. Include a legal description of Real Estate offered as collateral.

3. Furnish a signed current personal balance sheet (SBA Form 413 may be used for this purpose) for each stockholder (with 20% or greater ownership), partner, officer, and owner. Social Security number should be included on personal financial statement. It should be as of the same date as the most recent business financial statements. Label this Exhibit B.

4. Include the statements listed below: 1,2,3 for the last three years; also 1,2,3, 4 as of the same date, which are current within 90 days of filing the application; and statement 5, if applicable. This is Exhibit C (SBA has Management Aids that help in the preparation of financial statements) All information must be **signed and dated**

1. Balance Sheet   2. Profit and Loss Statement
3. Reconciliation of Net Worth
4. Aging of Accounts Receivable and Payable
5. Earnings projects for a least one year where financial statements for the last three years are unavailable or where requested by District Office.
    (If Profit and Loss Statement is not available, explain why and substitute Federal Income Tax Forms.)

5. Provide a brief history of your company and a paragraph describing the expected benefits it will receive from the loan. Label it Exhibit D.

6. Provide a brief description similar to a resume of the education, technical and business background for all the people listed under Management Please mark it Exhibit E.

SBA Form 4 (12-91) Previous Edition is Obsolete

Application for SBA Loan, page 2

ALL EXHIBITS MUST BE SIGNED AND DATED BY PERSON SIGNING THIS FORM

7. Do you have any co-signers and/or guarantors for this loan? If so, please submit their names, addresses, tax Id Numbers, and current personal balance sheet(s) as Exhibit F.

8. Are you buying machinery or equipment with your loan money? If so, you must include a list of equipment and cost as quoted by the seller and his name and address. This is Exhibit G.

9. Have you or any officer of your company ever been involved in bankruptcy or insolvency proceedings? If so, please provide the details as Exhibit H. If none, check here: ☐ Yes ☐ No

10. Are you or your business involved in any pending lawsuits? If yes, provide the details as Exhibit I. If none, check here: ☐ Yes ☐ No

11. Do you or your spouse or any member of your household, or anyone who owns, manages, or directs your business or their spouses or members of their households work for the Small Business Administration, Small Business Advisory Council, SCORE or ACE, any Federal Agency, or the participating lender? If so, please provide the name and address of the person and the office where employed. Label this Exhibit J. If none, check here: ☐ Yes ☐ No

12. Does your business, its owners or majority stockholders own or have a controlling interest in other businesses? If yes, please provide their names and the relationship with your company along with a current balance sheet and operating statement for each. This should be Exhibit K.

13. Do you buy from, sell to, or use the services of any concern in which someone in your company has a significant financial interest? If yes, provide details on a separate sheet of paper labeled Exhibit L.

14. If your business is a franchise, include a copy of the franchise agreement and a copy of the FTC disclosure statement supplied to you by the Franchisor. Please include it as Exhibit M.

CONSTRUCTION LOANS ONLY

15. Include a separate exhibit (Exhibit N) the estimated cost of the project and a statement of the source of any additional funds.

16. Provide copies of preliminary construction plans and specifications. Include them as Exhibit O. Final plans will be required prior to disbursement.

DIRECT LOANS ONLY

17. Include two bank declination letters with your application. (In cities with 200,000 people or less, one letter will be sufficient.) These letters should include the name and telephone number of the persons contacted at the banks, the amount and terms of the loan, the reason for decline and whether or not the bank will participate with SBA.

EXPORT LOANS

18. Does your business presently engage in Export Trade? Check here: ☐ Yes ☐ No

19. Do you have plans to begin exporting as a result of this loan? Check here: ☐ Yes ☐ No

20. Would you like information on Exporting? Check here: ☐ Yes ☐ No

AGREEMENTS AND CERTIFICATIONS

Agreements of non-employment of SBA Personnel: I agree that if SBA approves this loan application I will not, for at least two years, hire as an employee or consultant anyone that was employed by the SBA during the one year period prior to the disbursement of the loan.

Certification: I certify: (a) I have not paid anyone connected with the Federal Government for help in getting this loan. I also agree to report to the SBA office of the Inspector General, Washington, D.C. 20416 any Federal Government employee who offers, in return for any type of compensation, to help get this loan approved.

(b) All information in this application and the Exhibits are true and complete to the best of my knowledge and are submitted to SBA so SBA can decide whether to grant a loan or participate with a lending institution in a loan to me. I agree to pay for or reimburse SBA for the cost of any surveys, title or mortgage examinations, appraisals credit reports, etc., performed by non-SBA personnel provided I have given my consent.

(c) I understand that I need not pay anybody to deal with SBA. I have read and understand SBA Form 159 which explains SBA policy on representatives and their fees.

(d) As consideration for any Management, Technical, and Business Development Assistance that may be provided, I waive all claims against SBA and its consultants.

If you make a statement that you know to be false or if you over value a security in order to help obtain a loan under the provisions of the Small Business Act, you can be fined up to $5,000 or be put in jail for up to two years, or both.

If Applicant is a proprietor or general partner, sign below.

By:_____

Date

If Applicant is a Corporation, sign below:

Corporate Name and Seal   Date

_____

By:_____

Signature of President

Attested by:_____

Signature of Corporate Secretary

SBA Form 4 (12-91) Previous Edition is Obsolete

Application for SBA Loan, page 3

See Reverse Side for Instructions and Public Comment Information

MONTHLY CASH

NAME OF BUSINESS	ADDRESS		OWNER	

	Pre-Start-up Position		1		2		3		4		5	
YEAR MONTH	Estimate	Actual	Estimate	Actual	Estimate	Actual	Estimate	Actual	Estimate	Actual	Estimate	Actual
1. CASH ON HAND (Beginning of month)												
2. CASH RECEIPTS (a) Cash Sales												
(b) Collections from Credit Accounts												
(c) Loan or Other Cash injection (Specify)												
3. TOTAL CASH RECEIPTS (2a + 2b + 2c = 3)												
4. TOTAL CASH AVAILABLE (Before cash out) (1 + 3)												
5. CASH PAID OUT (a) Purchases (Merchandise)												
(b) Gross Wages (Excludes withdrawals)												
(c) Payroll Expenses (Taxes, etc.)												
(d) Outside Services												
(e) Supplies (Office and operating)												
(f) Repairs and Maintenance												
(g) Advertising												
(h) Car, Delivery, and Travel												
(i) Accounting and Legal												
(j) Rent												
(k) Telephone												
(l) Utilities												
(m) Insurance												
(n) Taxes (Real estate, etc.)												
(o) Interest												
(p) Other Expenses (Specify each)												
(q) Miscellaneous (Unspecified)												
(r) Subtotal												
(s) Loan Principal Payment												
(t) Capital Purchases (Specify)												
(u) Other Start-up Costs												
(v) Reserve and/or Escrow (Specify)												
(w) Owner's Withdrawal												
6. TOTAL CASH PAID OUT (Total 5a thru 5w)												
7. CASH POSITION (End of month) (4 minus 6)												
ESSENTIAL OPERATING DATA (Non-cash flow information) A. Sales Volume (Dollars)												
B. Accounts Receivable (End of month)												
C. Bad Debt (End of month)												
D. Inventory on Hand (End of month)												
E. Accounts Payable (End of month)												
F. Depreciation												

SBA FORM 1100 (1–83) REF: SOP 60 10 Previous Editions Are Obsolete

SBA Cash Flow Projection Form

FLOW PROJECTION

Form Approval:
OMB No. 3245–0019
Expires: 8–31–91

	TYPE OF BUSINESS				PREPARED BY				DATE		

6		7		8		9		10		11		12		**TOTAL**		
														Columns 1—12		
Estimate	Actual	Estimate	Actual	Estimate	Actual	Estimate	Actual	Estimate	Actual	Estimate	Actual	Estimate	Actual	Estimate	Actual	
																1.
																2. (a)
																(b)
																(c)
																3.
																4.
																5. (a)
																(b)
																(c)
																(d)
																(e)
																(f)
																(g)
																(h)
																(i)
																(j)
																(k)
																(l)
																(m)
																(n)
																(o)
																(p)
																(q)
																(r)
																(s)
																(t)
																(u)
																(v)
																(w)
																6.
																7.
																A.
																B.
																C.
																D.
																E.
																F.

Form SS-4
(Rev. April 1991)
Department of the Treasury
Internal Revenue Service

Application for Employer Identification Number

(For use by employers and others. Please read the attached instructions before completing this form.)

EIN

OMB No. 1545-0003
Expires 4-30-94

Please type or print clearly.

1 Name of applicant (True legal name) (See instructions.)

2 Trade name of business, if different from name in line 1

3 Executor, trustee, "care of" name

4a Mailing address (street address) (room, apt., or suite no.)

5a Address of business (See instructions.)

4b City, state, and ZIP code

5b City, state, and ZIP code

6 County and state where principal business is located

7 Name of principal officer, grantor, or general partner (See instructions.) ▶

8a Type of entity (Check only one box.) (See instructions.)
- ☐ Individual SSN _____
- ☐ REMIC
- ☐ State/local government ☐ National guard
- ☐ Personal service corp.
- ☐ Estate
- ☐ Plan administrator SSN _____
- ☐ Other corporation (specify) _____
- ☐ Federal government/military ☐ Church or church controlled organization
- ☐ Trust
- ☐ Partnership
- ☐ Farmers' cooperative
- ☐ Other nonprofit organization (specify) _____ If nonprofit organization enter GEN (if applicable) _____
- ☐ Other (specify) ▶ _____

8b If a corporation, give name of foreign country (if applicable) or state in the U.S. where incorporated ▶

Foreign country

State

9 Reason for applying (Check only one box.)
- ☐ Started new business
- ☐ Hired employees
- ☐ Created a pension plan (specify type) ▶ _____
- ☐ Banking purpose (specify) ▶ _____
- ☐ Changed type of organization (specify) ▶ _____
- ☐ Purchased going business
- ☐ Created a trust (specify) ▶ _____
- ☐ Other (specify) ▶ _____

10 Date business started or acquired (Mo., day, year) (See instructions.)

11 Enter closing month of accounting year. (See instructions.)

12 First date wages or annuities were paid or will be paid (Mo., day, year). **Note:** *If applicant is a withholding agent, enter date income will first be paid to nonresident alien. (Mo., day, year)* . . . . ▶

13 Enter highest number of employees expected in the next 12 months. **Note:** *If the applicant does not expect to have any employees during the period, enter "0."* . . . . ▶

Nonagricultural	Agricultural	Household

14 Principal activity (See instructions.) ▶

15 Is the principal business activity manufacturing? . . . . ☐ Yes ☐ No
If "Yes," principal product and raw material used ▶

16 To whom are most of the products or services sold? Please check the appropriate box. ☐ Business (wholesale)
☐ Public (retail) ☐ Other (specify) ▶ ☐ N/A

17a Has the applicant ever applied for an identification number for this or any other business? . . . . ☐ Yes ☐ No
Note: *If "Yes," please complete lines 17b and 17c.*

17b If you checked the "Yes" box in line 17a, give applicant's true name and trade name, if different than name shown on prior application.

True name ▶ Trade name ▶

17c Enter approximate date, city, and state where the application was filed and the previous employer identification number if known.

Approximate date when filed (Mo., day, year) | City and state where filed | Previous EIN

Under penalties of perjury, I declare that I have examined this application, and to the best of my knowledge and belief, it is true, correct, and complete | Telephone number (include area code)

Name and title (Please type or print clearly.) ▶

Signature ▶

Date ▶

Note: *Do not write below this line. For official use only.*

Please leave blank ▶	Geo.	Ind.	Class	Size	Reason for applying

For Paperwork Reduction Act Notice, see attached instructions. Cat. No. 16055N Form **SS-4** (Rev. 4-91)

Application for Employer Identification Number (IRS Form SS-4)

List of
Action Steps

Index

Study Guide

CONTENTS

1

Doorways to Small Business

Matching

Match each numbered item with the lettered statement that best describes it.

1. target customer
2. mind workers
3. gap
4. megashifts

5. privatization
6. Business Plan
7. high-growth industry

8. primary research
9. segment
10. buying an ongoing business

_____ A. when government services are taken over by a commercial firm
_____ B. the enterprise gathering information in the field on its own
_____ C. the customer with the highest probability of buying your product or service
_____ D. doorway one
_____ E. a slice of the total market
_____ F. from a national economy to a world economy
_____ G. a blueprint for your business
_____ H. denizens of the Information Society
_____ I. an area in which emerging market demand exceeds supply
_____ J. where market needs are not being met

True/False

Determine whether each statement is true or false and enter a T (True) or F (False) in the space.

_____ 1. During the 1980s, almost half the *Fortune* 500 companies fell from the list.
_____ 2. One reason you can succeed in small business is because you can move faster than the giants of big business.
_____ 3. Because big business takes a long time to get into position, "cracks" of opportunity open in the market floor.
_____ 4. If you learn to see with new eyes, you should be able to deduce a life-style from the contents of a shopping cart in the supermarket.
_____ 5. Psychographics means a study of population data.
_____ 6. According to job expert Tom Jackson, you'll change jobs only once during your lifetime.
_____ 7. Most new jobs in the private sector of our economy are created by firms with less than 200 employees.
_____ 8. The term *smokestack society* refers to businesses located in California's Silicon Valley.
_____ 9. Secondary research means you're gathering predigested information that's been printed or otherwise assembled for you.

_____ 10. The service sector of the U.S. economy will continue to shrink as we approach 2000.

_____ 11. One reason for focusing on an achievement-oriented skills picture is to boost your confidence so that you can excel in your great adventure.

_____ 12. For the purposes of this book, a small business is any venture with spirit.

_____ 13. Brainstorming is an exacting analytical task, bolstered by logic, which is carefully based on numerical data gathered from stock quotations and demographics.

_____ 14. The father of brainstorming was Attila the Hun.

_____ 15. *Megatrends 2000* was written from data assembled by information engineer Derek Campbell.

_____ 16. There are four doorways to small business ownership.

_____ 17. No matter which doorway you choose, you should develop a Business Plan.

_____ 18. If you buy a franchise, you'll be buying a Business Plan from the franchisor.

_____ 19. Labor unions are growing, both in size and in power.

_____ 20. According to Naisbitt, we are moving from an industrial society to an information society.

_____ 21. In the eighties, big business again began to grow. The business media called it "upsizing."

_____ 22. Elder care is a growth industry.

_____ 23. The "enchanted fortress" is where an imaginary family of the future lives, works, and plays.

Multiple-Choice

Select the best response for each item and enter the corresponding letter in the space.

_____ 1. To do new-eyes research, you:
   a. research books and periodicals about information processing.
   b. see an optician.
   c. use your intuition to play marketplace detective.
   d. watch videotapes instead of reading texts.

_____ 2. Which one of the following job titles is not considered an "information" job title?
   a. teacher.
   b. bureaucrat.
   c. insurance broker.
   d. coal miner.

_____ 3. The book that will give entrepreneurs a quick overview of the movement of society in the next 10 to 15 years is:
   a. *Up the Organization!*
   b. *The One-Minute Manager.*
   c. *Thriving on Chaos.*
   d. *Megatrends 2000.*

_____ 4. Which one of the following entrepreneurs from the case studies in Chapter 1 is the least enmeshed in the Information Society?
   a. Joseph Talmadge—liqueur expert.
   b. Derek Campbell—engineer.
   c. Judd O'Herlihy—branch manager.
   d. Marci Reid—travel agent.

_____ 5. Interviewing small business owners in the field is an example of:
   a. secondary research.
   b. your definition of success.
   c. how you remember the Industrial Age.
   d. primary research.

_____ 6. The document that stands between you and small business failure is your:
   a. SBA management leaflet 6602.03.
   b. first year's ROI.
   c. Business Plan.
   d. skills dossier.

_____ 7. You can generate a secret profit profile of a business if you know only certain key figures because:
  a. you can estimate some expenses with reasonable accuracy.
  b. net profit always equals about 10 percent of cost of goods sold.
  c. the IRS makes all business income tax returns available for public scrutiny.
  d. all small businesses have about the same return on investment.

_____ 8. Most people enter small business:
  a. by starting from scratch.
  b. by inheritance.
  c. because they have disdain for cash management.
  d. by purchasing an existing business or franchise.

_____ 9. Businesses are classified by a coding system known as the:
  a. American Business Code.
  b. Standard Industrial Classification.
  c. Business Classification Standard.
  d. Retail/Service/Manufacture Code.

_____ 10. There are three types of research:
  a. main, secondary, and private.
  b. retail, service, manufacturing.
  c. primary, secondary, and private.
  d. primary, secondary, and new eyes.

_____ 11. Faith Popcorn:
  a. popularized the concept of cocooning.
  b. is noted for her "New Age" forecast.
  c. demonstrated the potential of microwave cooking.
  d. is consumed in great quantities by certain religious groups.

Short-Answer

1. What are your career plans? What industry do you want to be working in 5 years from now?

_____

  Why? _____

  10 years from now? _____

2. What would you do if you had one year off, with no money worries?

  1st priority _____

  2nd priority _____

  3rd priority _____

3. Name three small businesses in your immediate area that you think meet your criteria for success.

  a. _____

  b. _____

  c. _____

4. List four criteria for success in small business.

  a. _____

  b. _____

  c. _____

  d. _____

5. What skills do you have that will help you succeed in small business? (see Action Step 8)

    a. _____   d. _____

    b. _____   e. _____

    c. _____   f. _____

6. What do you need to learn to supplement the skills that you already have?

    a. _____

    b. _____

    c. _____

7. Review your field interviews from Action Step 9 and summarize what you learned about the most outstanding of the businesses interviewed.

Name of business _____

Type of business _____

Industry _____

Location _____

Owner's name _____

Owner's personality _____

_____

Target market:

    Sex _____

    Age _____

    Income _____

    Education _____

    Residence _____

    Occupation _____

    Life-style summary _____

    _____

Owner's promotional strategy _____

_____

Gross sales (if available) _____

Profits (if available) _____

Marketing budget _____

Rent _____

Salaries _____

Anything that could be improved _____

_____

Mistakes owner will admit to _____

_____

Any recommendations on banker, attorney, accountant, other?

_____

Capsule summary (In what way is this a helpful model for your business?):

_____

_____

8. Profit profile. After you have interviewed three or four business owners, use your numbers to develop a profit profile. List what you know. Then try to figure out what each business was making.

a. Gross sales _____

   Cost of goods sold _____

   Rent _____

   Salaries _____

   Marketing _____

   FICA/benefits (est. 20%–30% of salaries) _____

   Other expenses (est. 8%–12% of gross sales) _____

b. Gross sales _____

   Cost of goods sold _____

   Rent _____

   Salaries _____

   Marketing _____

   FICA/benefits (est. 20%–30% of salaries) _____

   Other expenses (est. 8%–12% of gross sales) _____

c. Gross sales _____

   Cost of goods sold _____

   Rent _____

   Salaries _____

   Marketing _____

   FICA/benefits (est. 20%–30% of salaries) _____

   Other expenses (est. 8%–12% of gross sales) _____

d. Gross sales _____

   Cost of goods sold _____

   Rent _____

   Salaries _____

   Marketing _____

   FICA/benefits (est. 20%–30% of salaries) _____

   Other expenses (est. 8%–12% of gross sales) _____

2

The Big Picture: Charting Trends for Your Small Business

Matching

Match each numbered item with the lettered statement that best describes it. (Statements P–T on page 8.)

1. trend
2. life cycle
3. one-color stationery
4. shelf velocity
5. new-eyes research
6. deep discount
7. market signal
8. high touch
9. the railroads
10. workaholic
11. heavy user
12. target customer
13. fad
14. information
15. *Wall Street Journal*
16. trade journal
17. bank
18. gap analysis
19. Faith Popcorn
20. *Sales and Marketing Management* magazine

_____ A. forgot what business they were in
_____ B. a person whose chief joy in life comes from achievements at work
_____ C. a trend that doesn't last
_____ D. reading this gives you a big picture update
_____ E. a publication written and distributed for the members of a particular industry or business
_____ F. a procedure for identifying unmet needs in the marketplace
_____ G. an institution that rents money
_____ H. as you consume it, it grows
_____ I. a large moving tendency that can be intuited and used to advantage by the entrepreneur who can see the handwriting on the wall
_____ J. a smart purchasing move that helps save entrepreneurs money at start-up time
_____ K. speed at which merchandise sells
_____ L. a creative view of the marketplace that can be correlated with secondary sources
_____ M. when the marketplace is flooded, this is what products sell at
_____ N. society's attempt at balancing the electronic technology of the Information Age with human softness
_____ O. they are everywhere, and they tell you where a product is on the life cycle
_____ P. a four-stage pathway of inevitability for virtually all industries, products, and services
_____ Q. a target customers who buys the lion's share of a particular product or service
_____ R. the person most likely to buy your goods and/or services
_____ S. "mom foods"
_____ T. *Survey of Buying Power*

True/False

Determine whether each statement is true or false and enter a T (True) or F (False) in the space.

_____ 1. The life-cycle yardstick is important because it will give you a quick sense of what's happening in the world of business.

_____ 2. Because of the positioning of designer jeans in the marketplace and also because of the HMUF (high mark-up factor), manufacturing designer jeans would be a lucrative venture for the creative entrepreneur.

_____ 3. You really don't need to decide what business you're really in until the doors of your business have been open for at least a year.

_____ 4. Mary Clarke was really in the business of stabling horses.

_____ 5. The automobile industry has been in a high-growth phase since the early 1980s.

_____ 6. One reason the railroads went into decline was because they forgot what business they were really in.

_____ 7. Hula hoops, designer jeans, Rubik's cube, and spidery wall-walker toys are all examples of marketplace fads.

_____ 8. *Megatrends 2000* was based on research from 6,000 local papers over a period of a dozen years.

_____ 9. Once you succeed in defining your business, you can sit tight and watch those dollars roll in, because a definition is the final word.

_____ 10. If you think you're in one kind of business, and your target customers think you're in something else, the obvious strategy is to show those customers the door, fast.

_____ 11. Letterhead stationery is helpful to your information-gathering activities because it tells the world you're serious about going into business.

_____ 12. Another way of talking about being in software sales is by saying you're in the problem-solving business.

_____ 13. When you play marketplace detective, you can learn more about trends in small business by studying the national chains than by wasting time studying locally owned or regionally owned businesses.

_____ 14. Market signals can be helpful indicators for workers in large industries as well as for small business owners.

_____ 15. One reason a business like Private Screenings can exist is because certain segments of the marketplace are adopting a more relaxed attitude about sex.

_____ 16. There is no need to "walk the neighborhood" and spy on strangers when you can find out everything you need to know by writing the appropriate U.S. government agency for the needed data.

_____ 17. If you see a shopping cart loaded with baby food, disposable diapers, dog food, boxed cereal, and large cartons of milk, you can assume that the shopper has a senior citizen life-style, loves fishing, hunting, knitting, billiards, bingo, and dry martinis on the weekend.

_____ 18. A full parking lot is absolute proof of a booming shopping center.

_____ 19. If you're eager to try your wings in small business, there's no need to waste time taking a lot of personality tests.

_____ 20. If you're in the baby bedding business, a child's nursery can be your marketplace.

_____ 21. Changing ethnic diversity brings about abundant niche opportunities.

_____ 22. Laredo, Texas, has a median household effective buying income that is higher than that of Nassau–Suffolk, New York.

Multiple-Choice

Select the best response for each item and enter the corresponding letter in the space.

_____ 1. The life-cycle yardstick is an important tool because:
   a. it is an absolute mathematical instrument.
   b. it always correlates with the Dow–Jones averages.
   c. it can help you target a growth segment of a growth industry.
   d. it will prevent you from making foolish mistakes with your time and money.

_____ 2. A good example of a hot growth industry would be:
   a. sedan-sized autos.
   b. robotics.
   c. tobacco.
   d. railroads.

_____ 3. If you get into a business like toy retailing, your survival will depend on how well you can:
   a. keep one eye on the future.
   b. handle a 30-hour work week.
   c. forget you used to be a kid and concentrate on accounting controls.
   d. understand computer programming language.

_____ 4. Gap analysis and segmentation:
   a. depend for their success on how close you are to getting your MBA in marketing.
   b. are deeply mathematical in nature.
   c. are fun because they allow you to be imaginative.
   d. always correlate precisely with high-level entrepreneurial theory from the major universities.

_____ 5. Knowing what business you're in is important because:
   a. it will guarantee you an income of six figures in your first year.
   b. it means you'll never have to waste time redefining your business goals.
   c. it cuts down customer confusion.
   d. it can be ascertained by amassing statistics from the files of the U.S. Census Bureau.

_____ 6. Railroads in the United States went into a decline for all the reasons below except which of the following?
   a. The RRs forgot what business they were in.
   b. The new plastic tracks became portable and flexible.
   c. Jumbo jets carried people and goods faster.
   d. The interstate highway system connected the country and made travel and shipping more flexible.

_____ 7. Which of the trends below was not much of a consideration in the intimate apparel business?
   a. Specialized consumer tastes.
   b. A geographic shift from Frost Belt to Sunbelt.
   c. High-tech/high-touch.
   d. Relaxing attitudes about sex.

_____ 8. You are out walking in your target neighborhood. You see baby strollers, people walking dogs, four-year-old station wagons, bikes, newly planted lawns. The trees are small and supported with sticks. Some of the streets are still being put in. You can make the following marketplace assumption:
   a. adult condo complex, restricted to retirees over 60.
   b. singles condo complex catering to people of both sexes between 22 and 33 years old.
   c. family residential area, perhaps for first-time buyers.
   d. old established residential area, heart of town.

_____ 9. One of the newest hot-growth industries may well be:
   a. automobile manufacturing.
   b. book publishing.
   c. steel mills.
   d. bio-genetics.

_____ 10. One of the many signals that a giant industry is in trouble would be:
   a. layoffs, shrinking back orders, slow payment of bills, deferred maintenance.
   b. sponsorship of rock concerts in the desert.
   c. bringing in consultants on creativity, right hemisphere problem-solving, and the arts of Japanese management.
   d. deciding what business they're in.

Short-Answer

1. Where is your industry on the four-stage life-cycle yardstick? If you're in the decline stage, can you think of a related business that's in a different stage? Do any of your skills qualify you to move to a business venture in another stage?

_____

_____

_____

_____

2. Write down what business you're really in.

_____

Now write down what *other* business you're in. (For example, if you want to open a camera shop where your major activity will be the memory business, you'll have several minibusinesses to be aware of: processing, camera rental, your photographer's school, retailing. List all your possible minibusinesses here.) _____

_____

3. How old is your industry? How old is your particular segment? Below, list five to seven turning points in your industry. (For example, if you're thinking of going in the printing business, you should know that one major breakthrough came with Gutenberg, back in the 1400s. If you're in the computer service business, you know that your industry was born in the summer of 1969, when IBM let go of its profitable computer packages.)

Date   Turning Point/Trend

1.

2.

3.

4.

5.

4. **Model for a Shopping Cart Survey. Part 1.** Your venture will be more fun if you train your mind to look for marketplace data. The following is a composite study, drawn from the marketplace. To prepare for Action Step 15, use this case as a model. Imagine you observe the following:

A. Contents of cart:
   1. Imported beer, 2 cases
   2. Mixed nuts, 4 cans
   3. 16 steaks, porterhouse
   4. Greens, tomatoes, imported olives

   5. French bread
   6. 17 Idaho potatoes, carefully selected
   7. Cheese, imported Camembert
   8. Cognac, 2 bottles

B. Shopper description:
   Clothes—Bermuda shorts, expensive shirt
   Shoes—tennis, no socks
   Jewelry—gold I.D. bracelet, gold watch, wedding band
   Hair style—razor cut, medium
   Eyeglasses—dark, prescription
   General appearance—neat, careful dresser, excellent tan

The next step is to briefly summarize your observations. You should emerge with a pretty solid profile, as follows:

Marketplace Observations: This upscale TC was observed on a Sunday afternoon at a food store located in an upper-middle-class residential area. Census data for the area suggested a median household income of $65,000. The total bill came to $129.97, and was paid with cash from a large sheaf of bills. The TC was preparing for a party. Based on observation only, the following demographic profile can be assumed:

Sex: male
Age: early 50s
Education: high probability for college degree
Occupation: executive
Income: $50,000+
Residence: $170,000+

Part 2. When you move out into the arena to do your shopping cart survey, use the case as a guide. First, list the contents of the cart. Second, describe the shopper. Third, summarize your observations.

A. Contents of cart:

1.

2.

3.

4.

5.

6.

7.

8

B. Shopper description
Clothes—
Shoes—
Jewelry—
Hair-style—
General appearance—
　　Marketplace Observations:

Part 3. To develop your marketplace probe further, consider these questions:
Where is the location of the life-cycle yardstick?
Leaving the food store, how far would you have to drive to feel you're in a different economic customer base?
Did you make your study at rush hour? Lazy weekend afternoon? Early morning?
If you saw our upscale TC buying the same $129 worth of groceries at 2:30 P.M. on a weekday, what would you conclude about his occupation?
If a store is open 24 hours, what does it suggest about the target customers?
Is there any way you can sell your goods or services to any of the customers profiled?

5. Write down five business names that would tell your TC what business you're in. When you get your list, check with friends and fellow students. What do they think the names mean? (*Hint:* Quick Copy, Hamburger Hamlet, One-Hour Foto, $1 Cleaners.)

1.

2.

3.

4.

5.

6. List your three most important information sources; on a separate sheet of paper write a brief paragraph about what you learned from each that will help you shape your Business Plan.

1. _____

2. _____

3. _____

3

Power Marketing

Matching

Match each numbered item with the lettered statement that best describes it.

1. power marketing
2. business objectives
3. psychological rewards
4. no competition
5. life cycle
6. positioning
7. industry breakthrough
8. component parts
9. forecasting
10. segment
11. demographics
12. psychographics
13. problems
14. support services
15. brainstorm
16. matrix grid
17. software
18. product
19. power pricing
20. clone

_____ A. one of the four P's
_____ B. screen or filter through which ideas are passed in order to form solutions
_____ C. a new development in a particular product that changes the arena of competition
_____ D. a four-stage yardstick that helps you look more carefully at business opportunities
_____ E. the program that runs the computer
_____ F. a free-for-all idea session that calls on creativity and flights of imagination for help in coping with problems
_____ G. an activity that is usually trimmed with a product's price
_____ H. a study of life-style—buying habits, dreams, attitudes, ambitions, and so on
_____ I. a slice of the marketplace pie
_____ J. a procedure practiced by market researchers that attempts to predict the future
_____ K. a tool that helps you exploit gaps in the marketplace and connect your skills to your research
_____ L. a feeling of satisfaction, hard to express, but quite real and powerful
_____ M. an organized set of dreams that you are trying to translate into reality through hard work, tenacity, and information
_____ N. means you're alone in your segment, like the first hunter arriving at the still and silent pond
_____ O. one example of an industry breakthrough in the microcomputer industry
_____ P. a strategy for establishing yourself on a ladder in the mind of the prospect
_____ Q. can be turned into opportunities by the streetwise entrepreneur
_____ R. a study of population involving measurable observables like sex, age, income, and education
_____ S. is determined by the value to the customer
_____ T. "copycat" computer with a lower price

True/False

Determine whether each statement is true or false and enter a T (True) or F (False) in the space.

_____ 1. Power marketing is a tool that helps you aim your mind at a particular segment of the marketplace.
_____ 2. All five members of the Info Team case study had technical or engineering backgrounds.

_____ 3. Listing business objectives helps you focus and plan.

_____ 4. The father of brainstorming was Alexander the Great of Persia.

_____ 5. People get together in teams to balance their strengths and weaknesses.

_____ 6. The average small business can get up and running in 7 days.

_____ 7. If you can locate an industry that really has magnetic pull for you, you'll be more interested and have more fun.

_____ 8. When researching, you can do a much better job if you forget organization and just dive in.

_____ 9. In the computer industry, the life cycle of a piece of hardware can be as short as 18 months.

_____ 10. Cutting prices is always the best way to build a business.

_____ 11. Listen carefully to your clients' needs in order to learn how to sell them.

_____ 12. A matrix grid will match the objectives of the business with possible solutions.

_____ 13. The Info Team in the case study finally decided the best business to be in was retailing hot computer hardware.

_____ 14. Once you begin to profile your target customer, you're on your way to finding your segment.

_____ 15. An eager entrepreneur can transform a problem into a business opportunity.

_____ 16. In the early micro days, when manufacturers were trying to market software, one of the obvious problems was user frustration.

_____ 17. In marketing circles, "support" means there are services to backstop and expand the value of the sale.

_____ 18. The obvious target customer for a school that teaches computer software techniques is an unhappy micro user who cannot understand the complicated documentation.

_____ 19. Armonk is GHQ for IBM.

_____ 20. One of the key moves in power marketing occurs when you use a little entrepreneurial alchemy to translate problems into solutions.

Multiple-Choice

Select the best response for each item and enter the corresponding letter in the space.

_____ 1. Power marketing convinced the Info Team to go into which of the following segments:
   a. hardware repair.
   b. software production.
   c. computer education.
   d. none of the above.

_____ 2. Which of the following are reasonable business objectives?
   a. safety of investment.
   b. psychological rewards.
   c. fun and adventure.
   d. all of the above.

_____ 3. The name of the grid used to sift data and correlate objectives is:
   a. Bernoulli's Sieve.
   b. matrix.
   c. Alchemist's Urn.
   d. Iacocca's Ladle.

_____ 4. Which of the following was not a problem that could be transformed into an opportunity by the Info Team?
   a. unhappy, frustrated users.
   b. IBM had declared bankruptcy.
   c. minimal support from manufacturers.
   d. confusion in the marketplace.

_____ 5. Which of the following best describes the primary target customer discovered by the Info Team?
   a. female, 45–57, college degree plus, income $55,000, suburban/rural, owns stable, rides six days a week.
   b. female, 18–34, some college, metro residence, $17,500, clerical/supervisory, reads _Cosmo, Glamour._
   c. male, 18–34, some college, rural residence, $19,500, construction/crafts/artist/artisan.
   d. male, 18–35, some college, might own PC, access to computer at work, urban/suburban, $35,000, lives near computer store.

_____ 6. Power pricing means:
   a. Selling below cost to kill off competition.
   b. The value the target places upon it.
   c. bait and switch.
   d. forcing the customer to buy through intimidation.

_____ 7. The phrase that best describes what was happening in the computer hardware marketplace in the early 1980s is:
   a. gentlemen's agreement not to compete.
   b. Bernoulli Effect.
   c. hot competition.
   d. Apple took over IBM HQ at Armonk.

_____ 8. In 1983, the life cycle of a piece of computer hardware could be as short as:
   a. 9 months.
   b. 36 months.
   c. 3 months.
   d. 18 months.

_____ 9. Which of the following is not an accurate description of power marketing?
   a. a tool that helps you exploit gaps in the marketplace.
   b. a highly quantified system, firmly based in statistics.
   c. a technique that aims the power of your mind at a particular segment of the marketplace.
   d. a way to connect skills to a body of research.

_____ 10. One reason you need to be alert to industry breakthroughs:
   a. they give you the ammunition to jeer at your competitors.
   b. they prevent your key employees from selling company secrets.
   c. they give you the chance to change the competitive arena.
   d. they guarantee you a nonturbulent, debt-free start-up.

Short-Answer

1. Briefly describe your total market. (This is easier than it sounds. *Example:* The total market for the computer school would be everyone who owns, uses, or plans to own a micro.)

_____

_____

_____

2. Segment your market, using logic combined with associative leaps. For help in starting segmentation, think of a large industry that's highly visible, like the auto industry. You can segment according to *size* (Pinto, Cadillac limo), *price* (Mercedes, Chevette), *age* (Model T, Stutz Bearcat), *rarity* (Royale—there were only six) *versus mass-market* (Toyota), *country of origin* (Japan, Sweden, Germany, France, United States), *geographic distribution* (front-wheel drive Saabs in New England, Pacific Northwest; four-wheel drive Subarus in New Mexico; large sedans in the Midwest). Sometimes, it helps to create your own mind map. Use this space for your map.

3. Profile your target customer.

Person	Business
Sex:	Size:
Age:	Industry:
Income:	Number of employees:
Occupation:	Type of employees:
Residence:	Branch offices:
Education:	Location:
Marital status:	Product/Service:
Geographic region:	SIC code:
Cultural origin:	Public/Private:
Religion:	
Leap into psychographics:	
Buying habits:	
Dreams:	
Ambitions:	
Attitudes:	

For help on your psychographic leap, see Box 4.3.

4. List major problems faced by the segments you discovered.

1. _____

2. _____

3. _____

4. _____

5. Brainstorm mad solutions for each major problem in the space. Use a mind map, a list, or whatever else is useful to you.

6. Use this matrix grid to squeeze some conclusions out of your data. Along the left hand side, list your business objectives. Along the top, list your solutions. In the boxes, place a +, 0, or − each time an objective clicks with a solution. Key: + = 3, 0 = 2, − = 1. Then find your total and see where you stand in your adventure.

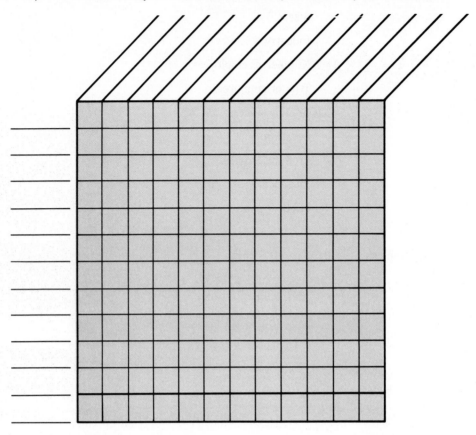

7. What has been the most fun so far in your adventure? _____

   Why was it fun? _____

   _____

4

Profiling the Target Customer

Matching

Match each numbered item with the lettered statement that best describes it.

1. target market magazines
2. heavy user
3. Hugh Hefner
4. *Playboy* empire
5. demographic data
6. newspaper
7. *McCall's* reader
8. magazine rack
9. display ad department
10. competition
11. baby boom
12. primary target customer
13. invisible target customer
14. interview
15. psychographics
16. profiling
17. Business Plan
18. SIC codes
19. VALS onion
20. segmenting

_____ A. a sudden increase in the number of births during a given period that results in a marketing phenomenon some 20 years later
_____ B. what develops when two or more hungry combatants decide they want the same slice of the marketplace pie
_____ C. drawing a magic circle around your customer
_____ D. a study of life-styles
_____ E. a customer who emerges, like magic, after you have been in business for a while
_____ F. the most visible segment of your target market
_____ G. *McCall's, Cosmo, Playboy, Time*
_____ H. a blueprint for your business
_____ I. a target customer who accounts for a high percentage of sales of a certain product or service
_____ J. an entrepreneur with a clear picture of his target customer
_____ K. the place you write to when asking for demographic information from magazines and newspapers
_____ L. a kingdom built on images and information
_____ M. an often overlooked guide to interest areas in a specific community
_____ N. female, 19–55, $27,000, metro-suburban, a high percentage are married, with children under 18; a high percentage are employed
_____ O. facts and numbers relating to the study of population
_____ P. one good local source of marketing data
_____ Q. an excellent technique for getting to know your target customer face-to-face
_____ R. federally sponsored standardized classification system of major industries and elements
_____ S. includes purchasing habits of survivors and sustainers
_____ T. is like slicing a pie

True/False

Determine whether each statement is true or false and enter a T (True) or F (False) in the space.

_____ 1. It is impossible for an entrepreneur to acquire new skills.

_____ 2. *Psychographics* refers to crazy people who write on walls with spray paint.

_____ 3. One of the best sources of customer profiles is the display ad departments of magazines.

_____ 4. If you can find out what your TC reads, watches, or listens to, you'll make your promotion task simpler.

_____ 5. When you go out for interviews, there's no real advantage to making up questions in advance if you just hit the street and wing it.

_____ 6. Interviewing target customers is a very useful technique when you're gathering information about the marketplace.

_____ 7. Once they heard about Fred's soccer shop, invisible customers began to appear.

_____ 8. If you've been in business before, there's no real need to waste time profiling your customers again and again. Just get to work and tell them how sharp you are.

_____ 9. A car driven by your target customer can be an indicator of income, self-image, and life-style.

_____ 10. Sarah Routledge is an example of a cagey entrepreneur because she learned how to survive by studying the needs and wants of the marketplace.

_____ 11. A habitual reader of romance fiction is one example of a heavy user.

_____ 12. The target market for *Cosmopolitan* magazine is predominantly male, 35–45, Master's degree or higher, $42,000 income, living in three metro areas: Los Angeles/San Diego; Seattle/Tacoma; Dallas/Fort Worth.

_____ 13. In the 1990s, we are surrounded by special-interest magazines advertising a host of special-interest products.

_____ 14. If a magazine goes under, one cause might be that, like the railroads, it forgot what business it was in.

_____ 15. *McCall's* is *Playboy's* biggest competition for readers.

_____ 16. One reason to observe people at magazine racks is so you can begin to correlate life-style with reading behavior.

_____ 17. Advertising revenue is important for a magazine because it pays the bills.

_____ 18. A magazine cover is an important sales tool.

_____ 19. The use of a file on competitive intelligence is illegal and of little value.

_____ 20. One way to begin market research is to start with what you read, listen to, watch, or buy—and then contrast your habits with habits of people from another life-style.

Multiple-Choice

Select the best response for each item and enter the corresponding letter in the space.

_____ 1. The visionary entrepreneur who built the Playboy Empire from a small business that started at a kitchen table in Chicago was:
   a. Mayor Richard Daley.
   b. Lee Iacocca.
   c. Hugh Hefner.
   d. Ray Kroc.

_____ 2. Which of the following data doesn't fit the *Playboy* reader profile?
   a. male, 18–34.
   b. urban/suburban residence.
   c. housewife, five children, heavy user of romances.
   d. consumer of alcoholic spirits.

_____ 3. Which of the following magazines is probably not vying for the same reader as *McCall's?*
   a. *Redbook.*
   b. *EasyRider.*
   c. *Ladies' Home Journal.*
   d. *Good Housekeeping.*

_____ 4. A terrific book that profiles target customers is:
   a. *Subliminal Seduction.*
   b. *The Great Gatsby.*
   c. *Writing the Natural Way.*
   d. *Guerilla Tactics in the Job Market.*

_____ 5. Which of the following magazines is more special-interest than general-interest?
   a. *Colliers.*   c. *Coronet.*
   b. *Look.*   d. *Runner's World.*

_____ 6. The letter from the romance publisher to Sarah Routledge:
   a. was a pink rejection slip.
   b. described a possible target reader.
   c. was an agreement to write a dictionary for gourmet cooks.
   d. contained several grammatical errors and misspelled words.

_____ 7. Competition in business can be defined as a situation that arises:
   a. when the world was young and green.
   b. in the Garden of Eden.
   c. when two hungry contestants go after the same slice of marketplace pie.
   d. when everyone leaves the arena.

_____ 8. Which of the following places should you avoid for help in launching a new business?
   a. the SBA.   c. banks.
   b. SCORE.   d. get-rich-quick magazine ads.

_____ 9. Which of the following was not a factor in the success of Fred Bowers's soccer shop?
   a. Investors liked his Business Plan.
   b. He knew soccer, had coached it.
   c. After he'd been open awhile, invisible customers began to appear.
   d. The tennis-boom bubble burst, and a lot of people became overnight soccer players.

_____ 10. Which of the following questions would give you the least help when you interview potential target customers?
   a. How did you like the store?
   b. When I open up a similar (and far superior) place next door, can I count on you to switch your business?
   c. Do you shop here often?
   d. How far did you drive to get here?

Short-Answer

1. List five magazines or periodicals that you read regularly.

   1.   4.

   2.   5.

   3.

2. Ask two friends what magazines they read regularly.

                     Friend 1   Friend 2

   1.

   2.

   3.

   4.

   5.

How can you correlate what your friends read with their life-styles and consumption patterns?

_____

_____

_____

3. Select one magazine from your list for a quick market analysis.
   a. The cover is a sales tool. Describe the photo/art/layout and the words:

   What dominates?
   What attracts?

   To what market does the cover or front page appeal? _____

   _____

   b. Ads pay for the magazine. Using Chapter 4 of your text as a guide, analyze the ads.
      Age-range of models:
      Dress/clothing:
      Major activity:

   c. Editorial content usually supports or extends the message of the advertisers. Describe the editorial content. Range of topics covered:

      1.

      2.

      3.

      4.

      How does the copy relate to the ads? _____

      _____

      _____

      _____

4. In a list or brief paragraph, describe the life-style of your primary target customer. (Questions to get you started: What are your TC's ambitions? Attitudes? Activities? Dreams? Buying habits?) Remember you are trying to get under the skin of your TC.

   _____

   _____

   _____

   _____

   _____

5. List five publications probably read by your target customer. (Use one of the directories available in your library like *Ulrich's, Gale's Directory, Standard Rate and Data*.)

   1.

   2.

   3.

   4.

   5.

6. Pay a visit to the market research department of your local newspaper. Tell them you're starting a new business and you're developing your promotion mix. Describe the target market you're trying to reach, then ask their market researchers for assistance and advice. Summarize what you learn here.

_____

_____

_____

_____

7. Census Bureau Data. Visit the nearest Federal Depository to locate the following information: List 10 items you purchased in the last 6 months, and list the SIC Codes of at least five of them.

	Product	SIC Code
1.		
2.		
3.		
4.		
5.		
6.		
7.		
8.		
9.		
10.		

8. Using the latest _Survey of Buying Power_ (published by _Sales and Marketing Management_ magazine), select an area that would be most likely to contain the target customers for your product or service.

Area: _____

9. Develop 10–15 questions to use when you interview target customers. For a start, see the questions from the Julia Gonzales case study in Chapter 4.

1. _____
2. _____
3. _____
4. _____
5. _____
6. _____
7. _____
8. _____
9. _____
10. _____
11. _____
12. _____
13. _____

14. _____

15. _____

10. List the names of 3–5 target customers you interviewed, and in a brief sentence state your conclusions from each interview.

1. _____   _____

2. _____   _____

3. _____   _____

4. _____   _____

5. _____   _____

5

Reading the Competition

Matching

Match each numbered item with the lettered statement that best describes it.

1. embryo
2. competition
3. target customer
4. arena
5. competition is weakest
6. stealing customers
7. profit

8. product innovation
9. blind competition
10. decline stage
11. ladder
12. gasoline service station
13. mystery shopper
14. maintaining a presence

15. competing with yourself
16. competitor test matrix
17. changing the arena
18. product differentiation
19. core market
20. positioning

_____ A. a focus of design that attempts to set a product off from its competitors by price, service, or repairs
_____ B. a metaphor for how a target customer ranks similar businesses; it also represents your step-by-step journey to the top
_____ C. a tool which allows you to rank your competitors in a number of areas, including image, location, innovation, and flexibility
_____ D. establishing a ladder inside the mind of the prospect, or target customer
_____ E. when transforming a product or service by adding a simple benefit also transforms the nature of competition
_____ F. first stage of a business life cycle
_____ G. a heated contest in which the combatants have lost their ability to see clearly while they seek to destroy the other
_____ H. an effective way to demonstrate that you've kept your image in the mind of the customer
_____ I. involves two steps: 1) you develop a first-class quality product; 2) when competitors smell money and try to penetrate your market with a cheapie, you've got one ready to ship
_____ J. an example of a service business in the mature stage of the life cycle
_____ K. a disguise adopted by cagey entrepreneurs as they study their competitors
_____ L. a form of technical breakthrough
_____ M. time to leave the arena
_____ N. one of your main reasons for being in business
_____ O. the person most likely to buy your product or service
_____ P. what ensues when two or more hungry combatants go after the same narrow slice of the marketplace pie
_____ Q. consumers whose perceived needs best fit the characteristics of a product
_____ R. in the early stage of the market cycle
_____ S. a strategy for surviving in the mature stage of the life cycle
_____ T. a metaphorical battleground where business contests occur

True/False

Determine whether each statement is true or false and enter a T (True) or F (False) in the space.

_____   1. Competition is not affected in any way by the four-stage life cycle.
_____   2. Product innovation is not important enough for top management to worry about.
_____   3. If you choose a business in the mature stage, you're going to have to steal more customers than you would have to steal in the growth stage.
_____   4. There is more competition in the embryonic stage than in all of the other stages put together.
_____   5. There has never been a business venture started over alcoholic beverages at lunchtime.
_____   6. The team which developed skates for ducks was unbalanced by having too many technical people and engineers.
_____   7. Pricing is very easy to establish in the embryonic stage.
_____   8. The reason production runs get longer in the mature stage is because business owners want to take full advantage of capital equipment and experienced management.
_____   9. If you spend dollars on advertising in the growth stage, and then can't follow up with distribution (getting the product to the consumer), you're going to lose sales and credibility.
_____   10. In the embryonic stage, resellers and distributors clamor for your products.
_____   11. One good way to promote is through contests.
_____   12. Smaller firms rarely win price wars.
_____   13. One signal that a product is in the mature stage occurs when manufacturers bring out several variations.
_____   14. A faddish product can reach the decline stage in 90 days.
_____   15. When a product such as rocking chairs enters the decline stage, there still might be opportunities for small entrepreneurs who sell to the core market.
_____   16. A helpful definition for positioning is "establishing a ladder in the mind of the customer."
_____   17. One good way of dealing with your competitors is to study their operations while you probe for strengths you can neutralize and weaknesses you can exploit.
_____   18. If you're going into an industry in which you don't have much experience, your best strategy for disarming the competition is to dive in and scare them with the force of your splash.
_____   19. When researching your competition, helpful tools include a camera and a map of the area.
_____   20. Competing with your own products by developing cheap product B is dishonest.

Multiple-Choice

Select the best response for each item and enter the corresponding letter in the space.

_____   1. The book that goes into detail about ladders in the mind of the customer or prospect is:
        a. *Guerilla Tactics in the Job Market.*
        b. *Nine American Lifestyles.*
        c. *Positioning: The Battle for Your Mind.*
        d. *The Third Wave.*
_____   2. Which of the following is not a smart competitive strategy?
        a. packing expensive lenses in popcorn.
        b. being ready with cheap product B to follow quality product A.
        c. changing the arena by product innovation.
        d. fighting to the bitter end, to the final gasp of the decline stage.
_____   3. A competitor test-matrix will help you to get a fix on:
        a. image.
        b. location.
        c. flexibility.
        d. all of the above.
_____   4. Which of the following is not a sound strategy for disarming the competition?
        a. Do it better.

b. Treat your TCs like people.

c. Do it faster.

d. Start a price war the day you throw open your doors.

_____ 5. The arena that shifts a huge market can be the size of a:

a. quarter.

b. TV screen.

c. microchip.

d. all of the above.

_____ 6. Competing with yourself in business means:

a. you've got cheap product B ready to throw into the arena.

b. you wait for the decline stage before you advertise.

c. you argue with yourself about the 4 P's.

d. you enjoy playing both sides of the chessboard at once.

_____ 7. If you're planning on opening a gasoline service station, you'll be in which stage of the life cycle?

a. embryo.

b. growth.

c. maturity.

d. decline.

_____ 8. Which of the following is not likely to occur in the embryo stage?

a. not much competition.

b. complete product acceptance.

c. limited distribution.

d. experimental pricing.

_____ 9. If you advertise your product, and get the TCs panting for it, and your distribution channels are not ready, what's likely to happen?

a. The competition will hold off shipping until you're ready.

b. Potential customers will keep clippings and videotapes of your ads and keep calling the retailers to check on availability.

c. You're going to lose sales and credibility.

d. Chase Manhattan will offer you an interest-free line of credit until you get your machinery rolling.

_____ 10. In what stages of the market life cycle is your competition the weakest?

a. growth.

b. growth, maturity.

c. embryo.

d. maturity, decline.

Short-Answer

1. Now you've got a good idea where your business will be on the life-cycle chart. Some segments of your business may be in different stages. For example, if you were to open a record store, you'd have LPs in decline, cassettes in late maturity, CDs in high growth, and video holograms on floating laser-driven bubble chips in the embryo stage. Use the life-cycle chart here. Segment the various phases of your business, and position each in its proper slot.

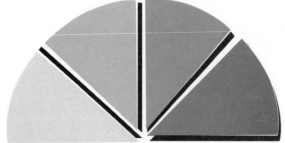

2. List three competitors you think will be tough for you to handle.

   1. _____

   2. _____

   3. _____

3. Develop an analytical stance on each competitor. View them first from the outside and then move inside. (In the next step, these notes will be transferred to a competitor test matrix.)

Competitor A—from the outside
   Name:
   Location:
   Geographic proximity to market:
   Parking:
   Image
      perceived by you:
      perceived by TC:
      perceived by neighbors:
   Advertising:

If this were your business and you had unlimited funds, what changes would you make? _____

_____

_____

_____

From the inside
   Layout:
   Service:
   Atmosphere:
   Quality of merchandise:
   Cleanliness:
   Perceived sales volume:
   Pricing:

What changes would you make? _____

_____

_____

Competitor B—from the outside
   Name:
   Location:
   Geographic proximity to market:
   Parking:
   Image
      perceived by you:
      perceived by TC:
      perceived by neighbors:
   Advertising:

If this were your business and you had unlimited funds, what changes would you make? _____

_____

_____

From the inside
  Layout:
  Service:
  Atmosphere:
  Quality of merchandise:
  Cleanliness:
  Perceived sales volume:
  Pricing:

What changes would you make? _____

_____

_____

Competitor C—from the outside
  Name:
  Location:
  Geographic proximity to market:
  Parking:
  Image
    perceived by you:
    perceived by TC:
    perceived by neighbors:
  Advertising:

If this were your business and you had unlimited funds, what changes would you make? _____

_____

_____

From the inside
  Layout:
  Atmosphere:
  Quality of merchandise:
  Cleanliness:
  Perceived sales volume:
  Pricing:

What changes would you make? _____

_____

_____

4. Use this competitor test matrix to compare the data you gathered in question 3.

Name of Competitor	Location	Proximity to market	Parking	Image (you)	Image (TC)	Image (neighbors)	Advertising	Layout	Service	Atmosphere	Quality of merchandise	Cleanliness	Perceived sales volume	Pricing
A														
B														
C														
D														
E														
F														

5. Networking your way in. Who do you know who knows someone who can give you inside information on your competition? Banker? Stock-broker? Librarian? Vendor salesperson? List possibilities here.

1.

2.

3.

6. Changing the arena. Once you study your competitors, you may have to make only one improvement to change the arena, thereby disarming your competition. *Example 1:* A manufacturer of baby bedding discovered that his competitors were slow on deliveries. By speeding up his own deliveries, he won the admiration of his customers. *Example 2:* An entrepreneur saw an increase in the number of two-wage-earner households so he developed a door-to-door cleaning service. Again, delivery was the key. How will you change your arena? _____

_____

_____

7. Pretend you had unlimited funds. What's the wildest idea you can think of for disarming your competition? Mind map your thought processes here.

6

Promotion: Connecting with the Customer

Matching

Match each numbered item with the lettered statement that best describes it.

1. P-O-P display
2. trade show
3. personal selling
4. promotional mix
5. freebies

6. piggy back
7. co-op advertising
8. direct mail
9. free ink
10. news conference

11. grand opening
12. mailing list broker
13. big spender list
14. leads club
15. Chamber of Commerce

_____ A. all the elements that you blend to maximize the most effective communication to your TC
_____ B. they can grab your customer's attention, create interest in a new product, or allow you to gather market research
_____ C. should act as a silent sales clerk
_____ D. ties local promotional activities to national or regional advertising efforts
_____ E. can be a very expensive way of selling
_____ F. a place where denizens of the same industry gather to present their products and services to one another
_____ G. advertising costs are subsidized by participating vendors
_____ H. promotes local businesses and statewide and national business legislation
_____ I. a group of business and professional people who meet regularly to exchange sales clues
_____ J. a good way to keep track of those few customers that give you a big share of your business
_____ K. using the mail to attract individual customers
_____ L. print media attention—usually in response to effective news releases and personal cultivation
_____ M. firms who will sell you names of potential customers who fit your target market profile
_____ N. the big bang event to herald your arrival in the marketplace
_____ O. calling in members of the media to communicate a newsworthy event

True/False

Determine whether each statement is true or false and enter a T (True) or F (False) in the space.

_____ 1. A contest drawing is a really easy way to build your mailing list.

_____ 2. Magazines will often rent you their subscriber lists.

_____ 3. Trade shows display your product or service in a high-intensity way.

_____ 4. The owner of a small firm is often its most effective salesperson.

_____ 5. If you listen, your target customers will tell you what it takes to induce them to buy.

_____ 6. The first step to gaining free ink (free publicity) is to probe your business and find something newsworthy.

_____ 7. Success in direct mail depends upon how well you have defined your target market.

_____ 8. P-O-P displays are usually very expensive.

_____ 9. Promotion is a pure science, and may be handled with numbers and rules.

_____ 10. A good ad will gain both the attention and interest of the target customer.

_____ 11. A smaller ad is likely to get lost on a page.

_____ 12. Newspapers often offer special supplements at reduced cost. The offer often includes free editorial copy.

_____ 13. A highly visible owner is often the best form of promotion.

_____ 14. Effective advertising is expensive, but you always get what you pay for.

_____ 15. Vendors often furnish tear sheets free of charge.

_____ 16. Leads clubs are made up of people from the same profession, business, or industry.

Multiple-Choice

Select the best response for each item and enter the corresponding letter in the space.

_____ 1. Market research is:
   a. asking your customers what they think.
   b. analyzing census data in the library.
   c. reviewing and analyzing appropriate secondary information.
   d. all of the above.

_____ 2. Promotion is:
   a. clawing your way up the corporate ladder.
   b. advancing one idea over another.
   c. all the things that you do to communicate your business message to your potential customers.
   d. limited to personal selling and paid advertising.

_____ 3. Display advertising is easy to spot because it is:
   a. usually sold by the column inch or fraction of a page.
   b. something that is put in your shop window.
   c. less graphic than classified advertising.
   d. most effective for products that require that they be in motion for demonstration purposes.

_____ 4. Point-of-purchase displays:
   a. always match your merchandising scheme.
   b. are silent salespeople.
   c. are never free.
   d. are primarily available to customers in the industrial and government markets.

_____ 5. Cooperative advertising:
   a. is usually more expensive than other forms of advertising.
   b. is always based on the national ad rate.
   c. rarely is subsidized by the vendor.
   d. none of the above.

_____ 6. A winning promotional mix:
   a. is the most effective blend of all elements to reach the target customer.
   b. consists of product development, distribution channels, and the four P's.
   c. is the same as the product mix, only with more flair.
   d. should be blended carefully to nullify the impact of random consumer perception.

_____ 7. A press kit should:
   a. include photographs of principals, the facility, and the product or service in use.
   b. relate newsworthy facts about the firm.

    c. be presented in an attractive folder to influential representatives of the media.

    d. all of the above.

_____ 8. Coupons:

    a. give you positive feedback on your promotion.

    b. should have an expiration date and multiple-use disclaimers.

    c. should be coded to identify the source and tested in small quantities before major use.

    d. all of the above.

_____ 9. Direct mail:

    a. is most effective when the potential customers are few in number and can be accurately located.

    b. must have twelve-digit zip code addresses.

    c. needs a response of at least 50 percent to justify its use.

    d. is the least sophisticated form of communication with your customers.

_____ 10. Commission sales representatives:

    a. are a fixed business cost.

    b. require no training or field assistance.

    c. should always be avoided because they lack motivation.

    d. none of the above.

Short-Answer

1. Study the list in Chapter 6 on "The Right Promotional Mix," and then list three to six components of your promotional strategy.

    _____   _____

    _____   _____

    _____   _____

2. Clip or copy three to five examples of free ink for a small business in your area. Describe them.

    1.

    2.

    3.

    4.

    5.

3. Free ink/free air (publicity) can save you a lot of advertising dollars. On a separate sheet of paper, use a mind map or list to brainstorm ways you can get free ink for your business.

4. A trade show can be important to your business. List the upcoming trade shows in your area. (*Hint:* you can get information from trade associations and local convention centers; from *Exhibit Schedule,* published by Successful Meetings, 1422 Chestnut Street, Philadelphia, PA 19102; and from *Trade Show Convention Guide,* Budd Publications, Box 7, New York, NY 10004.) _____

    _____

    _____

5. **At the Show.** What devices are people using to gather primary data on their potential customers?

    _____

    _____

6. **At the Show.** Look around. What surprised you?

    _____

    _____

7. **At the Show.** On a separate sheet of paper, draw a rough diagram of the main floor. Enter the names of exhibitors. Label eating areas, restrooms, entrances, exits. Then use arrows to indicate traffic flow. Where is the most traffic?

8. List three trade associations that deal with firms in your industry and in your market area that might be helpful to you:

_____

_____

_____

9. Develop two techniques for building a mailing list for your business:

1. _____

_____

2. _____

_____

10. List three sources that will help you do secondary market research:

1. _____

_____

2. _____

_____

3. _____

11. Finish this sentence: Proprietors of small firms are usually effective in the selling function because

_____

_____

12. List three actions you can take to enhance your personal profile and call attention to your business:

1. _____

2. _____

3. _____

13. List three media kit sources that contain information on at least one segment of your market:

1. _____

2. _____

3. _____

14. What three ways can a map help you conduct market research?

1. _____

2. _____

3. _____

15. List three government agencies and/or public utilities that might have information on the projected growth of an area:

1. _____

2. _____

3. _____

16. Describe how a sales leads club works: _____

_____

_____

17. Brainstorm a novel promotion that would be appropriate for your business:

_____

_____

18. Rough out a promotional budget. Try to list your promotional tools (advertising, free ink, contest, direct mail, and so on) in priority order and then estimate what each would cost.

Tool	Cost
1.	
2.	
3.	
4.	
5.	

19. After you rough out your promotional budget, write down the first step you need to take to get things rolling:

_____

_____

7

Location

Matching

Match each numbered item with the lettered statement that best describes it.

1. anchor tenant
2. food store
3. gross lease
4. 100 percent location
5. master plan
6. security factors

7. triple net lease
8. signage
9. census tracts
10. lease with option to purchase
11. cost per square foot
12. zoning

13. CC & Rs
14. traffic counts
15. labor pool
16. footprint
17. local newspapers
18. retail lease

_____ A. one type of destination location
_____ B. major foot traffic draw for customers
_____ C. usually provided by police departments and insurance companies
_____ D. sign requirements and where sign may be placed
_____ E. useful to ensure rights of occupancy at the discretion of the tenant
_____ F. how monthly rent is often quoted on commercial or industrial buildings
_____ G. U.S. government data on demographics of a specific area
_____ H. a projected plan for growth or redevelopment of specific land use
_____ I. fixed rent without additional assessments
_____ J. mythical perfect site—a useful benchmark
_____ K. tenant can be charged for taxes, insurance, and common area maintenance in addition to base rental
_____ L. often a source of recent market data in specific areas
_____ M. covers conditions and restrictions that are a part of the deed
_____ N. how much space a building takes up on the lot
_____ O. provided by the department of highways or independent research firms
_____ P. regulation for use, policed by city or county government
_____ Q. available workers often listed by occupation
_____ R. a lease that may be long and have many restrictions

True/False

Determine whether each statement is true or false and enter a T (True) or F (False) in the space.

_____ 1. A 100 percent location is mythical and probably doesn't exist.
_____ 2. A good location is more important for a brand new business than for an existing one.
_____ 3. A plumbing service business does not require a high traffic location.
_____ 4. A manufacturing business might play it smarter to locate near raw materials and a labor pool than near its customers.
_____ 5. A small retail merchant does not need to worry about drawing traffic generated by nearby stores.

_____ 6. Part of your location consideration should be to check on the level of municipal services.

_____ 7. If you have a great business, your customers will always find you.

_____ 8. High visibility can save you some advertising dollars.

_____ 9. Business locations have life cycles.

_____ 10. Real estate leasing agents are expensive, and you should do your best to avoid them.

_____ 11. An anchor tenant is found most commonly in boatyards.

_____ 12. Highway departments frequently do traffic-flow studies.

_____ 13. Most local planning agencies will let you view their master plan for an area.

_____ 14. Public utility companies have no need to do long-range planning activities on population growth and energy needs.

_____ 15. Once you settle on your location, there is no need for you to double-check with municipal authorities on restrictions and land use.

_____ 16. Leases are drawn by landlords and their lawyers and there is little in a lease to protect the tenant.

_____ 17. The smartest way to break a lease is to throw a gigantic and obnoxious lease-breaking party.

_____ 18. Net and gross leases are exactly the same except that a gross lease is much less expensive.

_____ 19. A good lease, like a good contract, is fair to both parties and tells each what to expect from the other.

_____ 20. Newspapers and chambers of commerce have useful information on local markets.

Multiple-Choice

Select the best response for each item and enter the corresponding letter in the space.

_____ 1. A good example of a destination location is:
   a. a food store or doctor's office.
   b. a gift shop specializing in china.
   c. a flower shop.
   d. usually marked in red on your city map.

_____ 2. Gross leases are:
   a. usually based on cost per square yard.
   b. agreements that include everything in the monthly rate.
   c. less common today than in the 1970s.
   d. intended to make rent a variable cost for the tenant.

_____ 3. Generally speaking, a 100 percent location:
   a. has no competition within a 10-mile radius.
   b. costs twice as much as a 50 percent location.
   c. is the perfect place for your business.
   d. must be visible from the street.

_____ 4. A mall location:
   a. has more foot traffic.
   b. has the most restrictions.
   c. usually comes with a fixed plus percentage of sales rate.
   d. all of the above.

_____ 5. The best location:
   a. is away from all competition.
   b. is always the least expensive place for your business.
   c. makes you accessible to customers, suppliers, workers, transportation, and so on.
   d. demands a sharp building, expensively maintained and well-lighted for security reasons.

_____ 6. A gift shop, to be successful:
   a. needs to be close to high-traffic anchor retailers.
   b. is a destination location.
   c. will do well near hardware stores.
   d. will usually be leased on an industrial net basis.

_____ 7. A labor pool:
    a. is a place for workers to relax during inclement weather.
    b. is termed illegal under the Taft–Hartley Act.
    c. will affect the location of a manufacturing firm more than a service firm.
    d. is seldom a concern in a high-income area.

_____ 8. A cost of living cap or ceiling on the rent:
    a. will be of little help if hyperinflation occurs.
    b. will limit your annual rent increase.
    c. is standard on most commercial leases.
    d. tends to favor the landlord.

_____ 9. Restrictive covenants:
    a. are discriminatory and illegal.
    b. dictate what you cannot do to a tenant.
    c. should be read and understood before you sign your lease.
    d. both a and b.

_____ 10. The commercial lease:
    a. is a standard legal form and, by statute, cannot be modified.
    b. is designed by the building owner to protect the owner's interest.
    c. need not be shown to a prospective tenant's legal counsel because it has already been drawn up by a competent attorney and all lawyers are members of the same bar.
    d. is usually no more binding than the lease signed by apartment dwellers.

Short-Answer

1. List the elements of a 100 percent location for your business:

_____

_____

_____

_____

2. List five kinds of businesses that are destination locations. Then list five that are not:

Destination Locations	Not Destination Locations
1. _____	1. _____
2. _____	2. _____
3. _____	3. _____
4. _____	4. _____
5. _____	5. _____

3. On a separate sheet of paper, make a rough drawing of your ideal site location in a commercial or industrial center. In your drawing, label the anchor tenant, your potential neighbors if there's a vacant building you're looking at, competitors (if any), parking (count the slots available to you), access, traffic, peak hours. If you're looking at a specific building, focus on suitability. For example, would you want a hearing aid store next to a record store? A book shop next to an auto body shop? Will your customers need a map to find you?

4. Develop a ranking of commercial or industrial centers in your area and arrange in order of priority (which is best for your firm?).

1. _____

2. _____

3. _____

4. _____

5. Information on local crime rates can be obtained from:

   _____

6. Information on local labor pools can be obtained from:

   _____

7. List variables that need to be weighed when you're considering certain types of leases:

   _____   _____   _____

   _____   _____   _____

8. A high-visibility location could save you money that would normally be spent on:

   _____

9. List three ways you can determine the going market rate of a square foot of space in your area:

   1. _____

   2. _____

   3. _____

10. How much parking space will you need? _____ At what times of day can you antici-

    pate peak parking needs? _____

11. Locations, like people and products and industries, go through life cycles. Where is your location on the life-cycle yardstick?

12. In what ways does the location affect a firm's image?

    _____

    _____

    _____

13. For your type of business, list some advantages of being

    1. close to competitors: _____

       _____

       _____

    2. away from competitors: _____

       _____

       _____

14. A mature business might have less need for a 100 percent location. Explain.

_____

_____

15. A lease that allows the landlord to charge tenants for taxes, insurance, and improvements is called a _____ lease.

16. A lease that calls for a fixed rate of rent per month is called a _____ lease.

17. An anchor tenant adds value to your location because:

_____

_____

18. A CPI cap in a lease accomplishes the following:

_____

_____

19. Only the following will legally release you from the obligations of a lease:

_____

_____

_____

8

Surprises You Can't Afford

Matching

Match each numbered item with the lettered statement that best describes it.

1. fringe benefits
2. partnerships
3. CC & Rs
4. workers' disability insurance
5. opportunity cost
6. specific business experience

7. energy audit
8. fidelity bond
9. licenses, police permit
10. building inspector
11. flood, fire, earthquake, and so on
12. misuse of product

13. shrinkage
14. huge increases in the prime rate
15. major supplier going out of business
16. penalty clause
17. owner only can sign checks

_____ A. have a high dissolution rate
_____ B. other payroll costs, like health plans, vacations, sick days, FICA
_____ C. covenants, conditions, and restrictions contained in the deed that limit the use of real estate
_____ D. additional business cost, required in most states
_____ E. specific investment costs in terms of time and capital
_____ F. what creditors look for first in an entrepreneur
_____ G. insurance to protect you from dishonest employees
_____ H. supplied by most power companies
_____ I. although a nuisance, are there to protect you and the community
_____ J. may be required by city, county, and state agencies before you open your doors
_____ K. will force contractors to finish the job on schedule
_____ L. is a strong argument for secondary sources of supply
_____ M. should be factored into costs
_____ N. can become the problem of the manufacturer
_____ O. can eat your profit with high debt cost
_____ P. can be insured against
_____ Q. will give you more control over the firm's cash

True/False

Determine whether each statement is true or false and enter a T (True) or F (False) in the space.

_____ 1. It is better not to seek permission from building inspectors, because they'll just get in your hair and cause you tons of grief.
_____ 2. State and local controls are always in the best interests of small business.
_____ 3. Start-up costs for most small businesses usually run 47 percent below owner estimates.
_____ 4. A personal financial statement is a balance sheet.

_____ 5. Assets minus liabilities equal net worth.

_____ 6. People who keep a personal budget usually have less trouble understanding cash management.

_____ 7. Timing is a key planning ingredient.

_____ 8. Good planning includes a long list of what-ifs and optional strategies for dealing with changing circumstances.

_____ 9. An entrepreneur is as likely to underestimate the amount of time required to set up a small business as he is the amount of capital required.

_____ 10. Most entrepreneurs fail to calculate the true value of the time they invest in their firms.

_____ 11. Job benefits for employees rarely exceed 10 percent of salary.

_____ 12. Any new business is automatically exempted from Social Security (FICA) payments during its first 12 months of operation.

_____ 13. Small businesses are more likely to be embezzled by dishonest employees than larger firms.

_____ 14. It is much safer to have one giant customer than it is to nickel and dime yourself to death with a lot of smaller customers.

_____ 15. Planning is a day-to-day matter because even the near term is impossible to anticipate.

_____ 16. Every business should provide the owner with two sources of financial return.

_____ 17. Fidelity bonding is often considered to be a form of sexual harassment.

_____ 18. Risk management and insurance are exactly the same.

_____ 19. The less the deductible amount, the more the insurance cost.

_____ 20. Insurance companies often put together packages for particular types of businesses.

Multiple-Choice

Select the best response for each item and enter the corresponding letter in the space.

_____ 1. A personal financial statement:
   a. is a balance sheet.
   b. is totally unlike the financial statement of a business.
   c. often includes goodwill.
   d. is seldom required if the owner is guaranteeing the debts of the firm.

_____ 2. Public utility companies:
   a. usually request advance deposits.
   b. can help you estimate your bills.
   c. will tell you how to save energy.
   d. all of the above.

_____ 3. City hall:
   a. has no enforcement power if you violate city codes.
   b. will tell you what special permits are required for your business.
   c. is full of fools who have an interest only in stopping you from making a living.
   d. will never be influenced by other established businesses who don't want to see you open.

_____ 4. Your first estimate of monthly expenses:
   a. will probably be lower than the real amount spent.
   b. will not be necessary, because estimating is a foolish waste of time. (Future profits are guaranteed to protect any overspending that occurs.)
   c. will probably be higher than the real amount spent.
   d. need not include minor details like office equipment and supplies.

_____ 5. Advertising expenses:
   a. will be most needed in your early months of operation.
   b. should be divided equally among all available media.
   c. should be placed under the firm control of a major advertising agency.
   d. should be adjusted downward if sales lag.

_____ 6. An insurance agent can provide you with the following types of protection:
   a. employee fidelity bond.
   b. partnership insurance.

       c. fire, theft, and liability.

       d. all of the above.

_____ 7. Your competitors:

       a. will always treat you fairly.

       b. will do all they can to keep you from getting their customers.

       c. will shop you for weaknesses.

       d. b and c.

_____ 8. The best way to minimize surprises is to:

       a. have lots of business experience.

       b. stay on top of your accounting reports.

       c. read trade journals, newspapers; attend trade shows.

       d. all of the above.

_____ 9. Which of the following will help you identify missing inventory?

       a. color coding.

       b. weekly lie detector test for employees.

       c. regular body search; regular inspection of employee homes.

       d. frequent and random counting of inventory.

_____ 10. Most inventory shrinkage is caused by:

       a. sophisticated embezzlers.

       b. employees.

       c. organized crime figures.

       d. customers who pilfer.

Short-Answer

1. List the agencies (if any) that will need to inspect or approve your business facility.

   1. _____   4. _____

   2. _____   5. _____

   3. _____   6. _____

2. Contact your local planning and zoning departments to learn what ordinances you will have to follow. Briefly note what you learn here: _____

_____

_____

_____

3. What unforeseen surprises did the small business owners you interviewed (in Action Step 9) encounter? _____

_____

4. Contact your local public utility for a forecast of increased energy costs for the next 5 to 10 years. Request energy-saving guidelines for your small business. Summarize the guidelines here.

_____

_____

_____

5. List other investment options you could pursue with your money if you did not begin your own business. _____

_____

6. Since you're thinking about starting your own business, devise an audit of your time for a realistic idea of how much time and energy you have to invest. Here's how. Use a 2-week period. In a separate notebook, divide each day into 15-minute slots. For 2 weeks, write down what you did every 15 minutes. Start with the past 2 hours. What did you do?

| Hour One | Hour Two |

1st quarter:
2nd quarter:
3rd quarter:
4th quarter:
When you finish your time audit, sit down and study it. Ask yourself what percentage of your time you had to rest? Do you have the tenacity to do sustained work? Where were you most excited? Where did insights occur?

7. If you're thinking about forming a partnership, list special provisions you need to include in your partnership agreement. (See Chapter 12.)

_____

_____

_____

_____

8. List in priority the possible circumstances that could adversely affect your business.

1. _____

2. _____

3. _____

4. _____

9. List at least two reasons you should think about bonding your employees. (What circumstances could arise that would make you wish you *had* bonded them?)

1. _____

_____

2. _____

_____

10. Contact a security alarm company to discuss your security needs. List the systems they recommend for small businesses like yours. _____

_____

_____

11. Identify a backup banker or capital source: _____

12. What techniques can be employed to evaluate the character and resources of a potential partner? (Helpful hint: to find out if you and your partner are really meshing, see Chapter 13.) _____

13. Contact an insurance agent who specializes in small business. On a separate sheet of paper, list the types of coverage you'll need, along with prices for premiums.

14. Contact some vendors and find out what percentage of your sales will be offset by returns of defective goods. Write the percentage down:
   Vendor 1:
   Vendor 2:
   Vendor 3:

15. List areas in which your business might be liable: _____

_____

_____

_____

9

Numbers and Shoebox Accounting

Matching

Match each numbered item with the lettered statement that best describes it.

1. turnover
2. projected profit and loss
3. cash-flow projection
4. projected sales forecast

5. return on investment
6. break-even point
7. cost of goods sold
8. fixed expenses

9. extended dating
10. net profit
11. gross profit

_____ A. sales minus cost of goods sold
_____ B. payment terms usually beyond 30 days
_____ C. that point where you make no profit and have no loss
_____ D. gross profit minus expenses
_____ E. anticipated sales for future time periods
_____ F. annual sales divided by average inventory investment
_____ G. how much profit you estimate you will earn
_____ H. the percentage rate of return on the capital invested in the business
_____ I. a projected analysis of working capital needs
_____ J. cost of inventory, including freight
_____ K. type of expenses required just to look like you're in business

True/False

Determine whether each statement is true or false and enter a T (True) or F (False) in the space.

_____ 1. High markup is usually needed for high-fashion items and items with a slow stock turn rate.
_____ 2. For the small business owner, most seasonal purchasing is done 6–11 months ahead.
_____ 3. Many seasonal vendors will extend credit well into the season.
_____ 4. In the travel and printing businesses, it's common practice to collect money before the product or service is delivered.
_____ 5. Because of slow receivables, the bed and breakfast business has slow cash flow problems.
_____ 6. The quicker you can resupply inventory, the more stock you need to carry.
_____ 7. Every business that extends credit should set aside a reserve for bad debt.

_____ 8. The manufacturing business has much less need for working capital than a service business of the same magnitude.

_____ 9. Writing checks on your business checking account will help you track expenses.

_____ 10. Most trade associations publish information on monthly sales percentages for their members.

_____ 11. Cash management means knowing where your cash is, and making sure you use it for maximum efficiency.

_____ 12. An accurate sales forecast is one key to developing a winning Business Plan.

_____ 13. A projected profit and loss statement will tell you when you're going to start making a profit.

_____ 14. When you do project profit and loss, you may also find out what legal form you should choose for your business.

_____ 15. One year of sales divided by the average inventory gives you the stock turnover rate.

_____ 16. As a general rule, the higher the stock turn, the higher your anticipated mark-up.

_____ 17. Gross profit minus expenses equals net profit.

_____ 18. No problems in a business are so serious that they can't be solved by giant increases in sales.

_____ 19. If a corporation anticipates a first-year loss, then the founders should consider starting out as a Subchapter S corporation.

_____ 20. Extended dating means a long courtship with your main vendor.

Multiple-Choice

Select the best response for each item and enter the corresponding letter in the space.

_____ 1. The term _break-even point_ signifies:
   a. piercing the corporate veil.
   b. that period in business which is prior to making a hefty profit.
   c. a theoretical point between profit and loss.
   d. a time when cash flow is equalized.

_____ 2. Extended dating means:
   a. a long courtship between the entrepreneur and one of the target customers.
   b. extended payment terms.
   c. a process used to develop plums for the fresh fruit industry.
   d. none of the above.

_____ 3. Return on investment means:
   a. the percentage of earnings based on amount of investment.
   b. finding lost capital.
   c. dividends paid by a _Fortune_ 500 corporation.
   d. retained earnings.

_____ 4. an income statement projected over months:
   a. traces the flow of cash through the business cycle.
   b. is a snapshot taken at an exact time in a business.
   c. requires an attorney to process it through the court system.
   d. is a moving picture of your business.

_____ 5. A balance sheet:
   a. consists of assets and liabilities.
   b. is very much unlike a personal financial statement.
   c. is no longer required by bankers when you apply for a loan.
   d. develops a finely tuned balance between profit and loss.

_____ 6. Turnover rate refers to:
   a. the timely rotation of dated stock.
   b. a figure you get when you divide annual sales by average inventory.
   c. rolling over bank assets worth more than $50,000.
   d. a ratio that, if reduced, will increase profitability by a specified percentage over the term specified.

_____ 7. Cost of goods sold:
   a. will yield gross profit when deducted from sales.

      b. shows cost less allowances of goods and materials.

      c. minus total expenses equals net profit before taxes.

      d. all of the above.

_____ 8. A cash flow statement:

      a. may include bank loans.

      b. shows total cash available for each month.

      c. allows you to identify cash needs.

      d. all of the above.

_____ 9. The income statement:

      a. tells you when you will make a profit.

      b. is a financial snapshot.

      c. gives you the net profit before taxes.

      d. both B and C.

_____ 10. A manufacturing business:

      a. is not capital intensive.

      b. will probably need cash for a long period of time.

      c. will have fewer cash flow problems than a bed and breakfast operation.

      d. none of the above.

Short-Answer

1. Project your sales percentages by the month for a 12-month period for a model business in your industry. For example, if the model business does 3% in January, you write 3% in the box. What's the percentage in February? In March?

   Jan. _____ %   Apr. _____ %   July _____ %   Oct. _____ %

   Feb. _____ %   May _____ %   Aug. _____ %   Nov. _____ %

   Mar. _____ %   June _____ %   Sept. _____ %   Dec. _____ %

2. Which financial projection is the most important and becomes the basis for all other financial projections? _____

   _____

3. When do you expect to become profitable? _____

   When would you change the legal form of your business? _____

4. What is your industry standard for a stock-turn ratio? _____

   What is your source? _____

5. What will your average mark-up cost be? _____

6. Depending on the business, customers pay *before* delivery, *at time of* delivery, or *after* delivery. Learn the payment standards, lags, and so on in your business. When are your customers most likely to pay for services? _____

   _____

7. If you offer credit, what percentage might be uncollectible? _____

8. List the reasons for using written, numbered purchase orders:

   _____

   _____

   _____

9. Describe accounts receivable. _____

   _____

10. Describe accounts payable. _____

_____

11. Briefly discuss the reasons for using a cash-flow projection. _____

_____

_____

12. What is a break-even point? How do you determine it? Let's follow one example.
    Your fixed expenses are $120,000.
    Your variable expenses are $1.07 per unit.
    You're selling the gizmo at $3.98 per unit.

$$\text{Break-even point (units)} = \frac{\$120,000}{\$2.91} = 41,237 \text{ (rounded)}$$

To figure break-even sales volume, multiply break-even units needed by selling price per unit.

$$41,237 \times \$3.98 = \$\rule{2cm}{0.4pt}$$

13. List three to six ways you can use your income statement.

_____   _____

_____   _____

_____   _____

14. What is an electronic spreadsheet? _____

_____

15. How are Subchapter S corporations taxed? _____

_____

10

Buying a Business

Matching

Match each numbered item with the lettered statement that best describes it.

1. income stream
2. the deal
3. magic threshold
4. business brokers
5. escape hatch
6. covenant not to compete

7. financial records
8. accounts receivable
9. tangible assets
10. goodwill
11. ill will

12. sacrificed goods
13. earnout
14. decision to buy a business
15. apparently honest seller
16. bulk sales escrow

_____ A. a must when buying a business; among other things, it helps you make sure inventory is not tied up by creditors
_____ B. seller must do something else for a while
_____ C. intangible asset that seller will use to raise asking price
_____ D. point for tough negotiation because they keep losing value
_____ E. everything you can touch
_____ F. picture of an income stream
_____ G. means unhappy customers
_____ H. paying off the seller with future earnings
_____ I. distressed goods, usually sold at any price
_____ J. should be handled with logic, not emotion
_____ K. a signal for you to be suspicious; check out motives anyway
_____ L. one good reason for buying an ongoing business
_____ M. a shorthand way of talking about negotiating terms
_____ N. what you cross to get inside a business
_____ O. agents who sell businesses
_____ P. a device that allows you to back out of the purchase of a business painlessly

True/False

Determine whether each statement is true or false and enter a T (True) or F (False) in the space.

_____ 1. The overwhelming reason for buying a business that's already going instead of building one with your own hands is money.
_____ 2. The smart buyer will plunge into a business because of a sudden surge of raw emotion.
_____ 3. Every business in the country is for sale some time.

_____ 4. Deals are like buses. If you miss one, another one will be along soon.

_____ 5. The investigative and information-gathering tactics for buying a business or for buying a franchise are very different.

_____ 6. Your best bet for finding a business to buy is to search the classified section of your local paper under Business Opportunities.

_____ 7. An earnest money deposit is to show the seller you are an interested buyer and not a "lookie-loo."

_____ 8. The main function of an offer with an escape hatch is to cheat the IRS.

_____ 9. Goodwill is an example of a tangible asset.

_____ 10. The covenant not to compete is to keep the seller from opening a similar business in your market area.

_____ 11. A buyer should study the financial records for at least 5 years back if they are available.

_____ 12. Examples of tangible assets include real estate, equipment, fixtures, goodwill, and inventory.

_____ 13. In small business, success can rest on the shoulders of one or two key employees.

_____ 14. If you get it in writing, the IRS will allow you to deduct the cost of a covenant not to compete over the life of the covenant.

_____ 15. A smart seller is going to ask you to pay him for building up an invisible wealth of goodwill.

_____ 16. Franchise means you're buying a license.

_____ 17. When you're evaluating a franchise, you go through most of the same steps you would use to evaluate a business for sale.

_____ 18. In the overall business-buying strategy, the terms for the deal are more important than the purchase price.

_____ 19. Fraud is sometimes practiced by sellers of businesses.

_____ 20. Bankruptcy can be a great opportunity to buy a business if you are careful.

Multiple-Choice

Select the best response for each item and enter the corresponding letter in the space.

_____ 1. The overwhelming reason for buying a business that's already going instead of building one with your own hands is:
   a. attractive inventory.
   b. goodwill.
   c. income stream.
   d. employees who need the work.

_____ 2. An advantage of buying an ongoing business is:
   a. less cash up front.
   b. a good deal on fixtures and equipment.
   c. a possible bargain in hidden inventory.
   d. all of the above.

_____ 3. The last place to look for a business to buy is:
   a. your own network of associates.
   b. classified ads in the newspaper.
   c. local bankers.
   d. business brokers.

_____ 4. If you are asked to make an "earnest-money" deposit, you should handle it with:
   a. a cashier's check, made out to seller.
   b. an offer with an escape hatch.
   c. a lawyer.
   d. a CPA.

_____ 5. When you explore the inner intricacies of a business, check the following:
   a. financial history.
   b. your suppliers.
   c. the seller's motives.
   d. all of the above.

SHORT-ANSWER **SG-49**

6. Accounts receivable that are 6 months old are worth approximately:
   a. 90 cents on the dollar.
   b. 70 cents on the dollar.
   c. 50 cents on the dollar.
   d. 30 cents on the dollar.
7. When checking out all the tangible assets, your job is to evaluate all of the following except:
   a. real estate.
   b. goodwill.
   c. equipment/fixtures.
   d. inventory.
8. All of the following contribute to ill will except:
   a. delivery.
   b. cash.
   c. advertising.
   d. service.
9. When evaluating a franchisor, check out all the following except:
   a. blood types of franchisors.
   b. how long this franchise has been in business.
   c. who are the officers.
   d. number of franchised operations like this one in existence.
10. All of the questions below except for one are good to ask franchisors:
    a. What's included in the franchise fee?
    b. What's the duration of the agreement?
    c. What level of training and service can you offer?
    d. Say I get tired of this business—can I relocate any time I wish?

Short-Answer

1. Identify a business that you think is a real money machine.

   Type of business: _____

   Name: _____

   Address: _____

2. Where is it on the life cycle? _____

3. Once you've found the business and checked its position on the life cycle, gather more data about it. Visit your city or county planning office. What are the plans for the area for the next 5–10 years?

   Five years: _____

   _____

   Ten years: _____

   _____

4. Go to the site. On a separate sheet of paper, diagram everything you can.

   Traffic flow
   Major arterials
   Access
   Parking (Is parking lot a drop-off point for car-poolers?)
   Is building in good repair? (If not, what will it need before you move in?)

5. Take a good look at the customers. Describe what they're wearing: _____

Describe what they're driving: _____

_____

What can you deduce about their life-style? _____

_____

How far do they travel to get here?

    Longest distance: _____

    Shortest distance: _____

    Average distance: _____

Interview some customers. What do they say about the business? _____

_____

_____

_____

About the trading area? _____

_____

_____

Is there mostly goodwill? _____

Is there mostly ill will? _____

6. Investigate your neighbors. Which neighbors will help you draw customers?

_____

_____

_____

Which neighbors won't help?

_____

_____

Where is your major competition? How strong is the competition? Can competitors move into this trading area?

Location of competitors: _____

Strength: _____

Assault probabilities: _____

7. Move inside the business. Either contact the owner directly or get the assistance of a business opportunity broker. Study the sales figures. Check profit percentages. Evaluate the tangible assets. Of special importance are:

   a. Sales. List the percentage of change for the past 5 years.

      1.

      2.

      3.

      4.

      5.

   b. Profit. List the profit figures for the past 5 years.

      1.

      2.

      3.

4.

5.

c. Tangible assets. Using the format that follows, list all assets. Look at the books and write down the accounting value. Then go out into the marketplace and get the current value.

Asset	Accounting Value	Current Value
1. _____	_____	_____
2. _____	_____	_____
3. _____	_____	_____
4. _____	_____	_____

d. Terms. What kind of terms can you negotiate with the seller? (Try to get the seller to let you pay for the business out of profits you make after you take possession.)

_____

_____

8. You'll want to know if the vendors who have been supplying the seller will continue to supply you, as the new owner. Interview them. Will vendors continue to supply you?

_____

_____

_____

_____

What suggestions do they have for improving the business?

_____

_____

_____

Can you get credit terms? (What are they?)

_____

_____

_____

9. Rethink your moves. Does it look as if you could do better by starting your own business from scratch instead of buying this business?

_____

_____

_____

_____

11

Shaking the Money Tree

Matching

Match each numbered item with the lettered statement that best describes it.

1. capital
2. banker
3. bank
4. guaranteed loan
5. money guru
6. possible source of money
7. accounts receivable financing

8. BDCs
9. character
10. plastic
11. capacity
12. collateral
13. SBICs
14. Business Plan

15. vendor form
16. unsecured credit
17. venture capital firms
18. limited partner
19. private placement
20. going public

_____ A. shows you pay your bills on time
_____ B. one gateway to the world of money
_____ C. showcase for displaying all the ideas and information you've gathered in your venture adventure
_____ D. detailed information on each supplier
_____ E. life insurance
_____ F. provided by some banks and factoring firms
_____ G. knows more about money than you do
_____ H. goal is to increase employment within their specific state
_____ I. licensed by the SBA to provide money to small firms
_____ J. one type of SBA loan
_____ K. lenders who want equity participation
_____ L. regarded by some people as a formidable fortress or great modern cathedral
_____ M. tangible assets that can secure a loan
_____ N. your liquid cash
_____ O. earning power; ability to repay a loan
_____ P. street name for credit cards
_____ Q. guaranteeing loans and payments with your signature
_____ R. selling your securities in the open financial market
_____ S. investors who are not stockholders, have no liability
_____ T. capital stock sale to a limited group of investors

True/False

Determine whether each statement is true or false and enter a T (True) or F (False) in the space.

_____ 1. Money creates its own world, with its own customs, rules, myths.
_____ 2. "Collateral" indicates that you have a visible money stream for lenders to dip into.

_____ 3. Banks are conservative, and they probably won't want to lend you start-up money unless you sign over your house.

_____ 4. People lend money to people.

_____ 5. One good way to conserve cash is to persuade your customers to give you cash deposits when they place orders.

_____ 6. When goods are moving slowly, the best strategy is to shelve them in the back room or warehouse and hold until next season.

_____ 7. It is best to avoid collateralizing your loans, unless you have no choice.

_____ 8. When you have to borrow money, you should shop around.

_____ 9. Buying smart is not nearly as important as raising money or selling.

_____ 10. When negotiating, you should use a lot of open-ended questions like: "what else can you do for me?"

_____ 11. When you're ready, it's a good idea to shake the money trees close to home first.

_____ 12. Borrowing on your life insurance can be a good source of money for your new business.

_____ 13. An unsecured personal line of credit from your bank is not a good source of money for a brand-new business.

_____ 14. Credit unions are considered nonbank lending sources.

_____ 15. The SBA has only one kind of loan program: "guaranteed."

_____ 16. The SBA makes fewer guaranteed loans than any other type.

_____ 17. SBICs (Small Business Investment Corporations) are privately operated companies that are licensed by the state within which they operate.

_____ 18. Venture capitalists come in lots of shapes—family firms (Rockefeller), industrial arms (GE), bank arms (B of A), and other arms (private groups of investors).

_____ 19. Venture capitalists will usually let you run the show if you give them a healthy ROI.

_____ 20. How well you buy is not nearly as important as how well you sell.

Multiple-Choice

Select the best response for each item and enter the corresponding letter in the space.

_____ 1. Before hunting the great money tree, you should:
   a. sit at the feet of a money guru.
   b. sketch out your Business Plan.
   c. befriend a banker, and befriend a backup banker.
   d. all of the above.

_____ 2. All of the following questions are good to ask your prospective banker except:
   a. What do you think of my Business Plan?
   b. Do you lend money to large businesses?
   c. Do you make SBA-guaranteed loans?
   d. What are your criteria for loans?

_____ 3. Which of the following is not a good strategy for dealing with bankers?
   a. asking for money before you ask for advice and information.
   b. luring a banker to your own turf.
   c. negotiating for your line of credit or your loan while you're still working.
   d. getting yourself a backup bank while you're negotiating with another bank.

_____ 4. Which of the following is not a good tip on saving?
   a. work out of your home.
   b. lease your equipment.
   c. borrow money on goods (inventory) that aren't selling.
   d. get your landlord to make onsite improvements and finance the cost over the term of the lease.

_____ 5. Which of the following items do you want to ask for on your Vendor Form?
   a. amount of minimum purchase.
   b. terms of dating or extended payment.

      c. nearest competitor handling the same line.

      d. all of the above.

_____ 6. All of the following are reasons why lenders would want to lend you money for your business except:

      a. no competition.

      b. good marketing strategy.

      c. good profit picture.

      d. good ROI (return on investment).

_____ 7. Which of the following is not a good tip on saving?

      a. use as little commercial space as you can.

      b. keep your liquid cash in a safe place (like a lock box).

      c. shop nonbank lenders.

      d. look into R & D partnerships for product development funds.

_____ 8. The following are good sources of money for your new business, except:

      a. refinancing your car, boat, camper, or airplane.

      b. researching your assets (coin collections, old baseball cards, and so on).

      c. selling that crummy stock you've been holding.

      d. finding a competitor that's doing a good deal of business and borrowing from him.

_____ 9. Which of the following is not a good source of money for your small business?

      a. venture capital firm.

      b. stock brokerage house.

      c. Goodwill Industries.

      d. credit union.

_____ 10. It's best to line up personal credit:

      a. after you begin your new venture.

      b. when you are in a cash bind.

      c. before you leave your salaried job.

      d. Personal credit is useless for a business.

Short-Answer

1. Visit your local bank. Find out the following:

  A. Name of chief officer:

_____

  B. Do they lend money to small businesses? _____

  C. Do they make SBA-guaranteed loans? _____

    1. If yes, do they lend money to start-ups? _____

    2. If yes, do they have a minimum and maximum loan amount? _____

    3. If yes, what are the time-periods for repayment?

_____

    4. If yes, what's the percentage rate? _____

  D. What are their criteria for loan approval?

_____

  E. Ask them to describe the loan approval process.

  F. Do they offer lines of credit? If so, under what conditions and what terms?

_____

_____

G. Ask this question: "Would you review my Business Plan?"

    Answer: _____

2. When you have found one bank that makes small business loans, phone some more until you locate two or three that make loans to start-ups.

Backup Bank 1

A. Name of bank: _____

B. Lending rate: _____

C. SBA-guaranteed loans: _____

D. Contact person: _____

Backup Bank 2

A. Name of bank: _____

B. Lending rate: _____

C. SBA-guaranteed loans: _____

D. Contact person: _____

Backup Bank 3

A. Name of bank: _____

B. Lending rate: _____

C. SBA-guaranteed loans: _____

D. Contact person: _____

3. When talking to bankers, try to get insight into how they evaluate small business loans. Try these questions for probes:

A. What types of businesses are they most interested in?

_____

_____

B. Are there any they won't lend money to?

_____

_____

C. Ask your banker to rate each of the items below in relation to the loan-decision process. What's important? What's not important? Try to get your banker to use a 1–10 scale.
   1. target customer
   2. amount and type of competition
   3. industry trends
   4. product or service
   5. marketing strategy
   6. method of selling
   7. profit picture, both gross and net
   8. return on investment
   9. founders' team
   10. personal assets or net worth

4. List friends or relatives who might be willing to invest in your business (or lend you money for the business):

_____

_____

_____

5. Explore your list in Question 4, above. Select two or three people from that list to talk to. Let them see your Business Plan. Talk over the possibilities of getting them on board as investors.

A. On a separate sheet of paper, list all their objections.

B. Then list their positive comments.

C. For each objection, come up with a solution. There's a good chance you'll get the same objections from bankers and venture capital people. On your sheet of paper, summarize your findings as shown:

Objection	Solution
1.	1.
2.	2.
3.	3.
etc.	etc.

6. If you're in a class, form several teams. If you're not in a class, get together some friends and relatives. Develop two lists. The first list contains the areas you believe the federal government should get out of. The second list contains areas where you think the government could be of more help. Compile your findings, vote on the major suggestions, and compose a letter to your congressman, state senator, legislator, assemblyman, alderman, senator, or other representative.

A. Areas where the government could be more helpful:

1. _____

2. _____

3. _____

4. _____

5. _____

6. _____

7. _____

8. _____

B. Areas the government should get out of:

1. _____

2. _____

3. _____

4. _____

5. _____

6. _____

7. _____

8. _____

12

Legal Concerns

Matching

Match each numbered item with the lettered statement that best describes it.

1. corporate shield
2. partnership agreement
3. lawyer
4. partnerships
5. corporation
6. limited partnership

7. sole proprietor
8. general partner
9. personal guarantee
10. corporate reports
11. form a subchapter S corporation
12. corporate president

13. shareholders
14. offshore corporations
15. a corporate charter
16. minute book
17. do-it-yourself corporation

_____ A. unlimited liability
_____ B. a legal form that gives the owner absolute control
_____ C. limits liability of noncorporate investors
_____ D. a way of organizing your business so that you can have tax flexibility
_____ E. taxed as an individual
_____ F. member of the taxi squad; not needed to form sole proprietorship
_____ G. a written contract between two or more people that describes duties, sharing of profits, and dissolution
_____ H. stands between you and your creditors
_____ I. are tricky and may not save you money
_____ J. another name for corporate owners
_____ K. must be an employee of the business
_____ L. if you are losing money
_____ M. a good source of secondary research material when you are studying legal forms of business
_____ N. often required by bankers to secure a corporate loan
_____ O. must be kept current
_____ P. may not provide the benefits you need
_____ Q. tells the state what your corporation will be doing

True/False

Determine whether each statement is true or false and enter a T (True) or F (False) in the space.

_____ 1. A company which is incorporated in Delaware can only do business in California as a foreign corporation.
_____ 2. Most growth businesses do not need outside infusions of cash.
_____ 3. A Sub S corporation is limited to seventy-five owners.
_____ 4. Sub S corporate owners have unlimited liability.
_____ 5. A sole proprietor is limited to setting aside only $500 per year for retirement.
_____ 6. All corporate fiscal tax years must end on December 31.
_____ 7. The president, and major corporate stockholder, is technically an employee.

_____ 8. A partnership agreement, drawn up by a lawyer, is required in order to establish a general partnership.

_____ 9. When setting up a corporation, you should secure the services of a "hot" trial attorney.

_____ 10. A corporation usually has more money-raising ability than other legal forms of business ownership.

_____ 11. In a limited partnership, one of the partners must be a general partner.

_____ 12. A corporation is said to have snob appeal.

_____ 13. To the consumer, the legal form of business ownership is often invisible.

_____ 14. You can form a partnership with a handshake.

_____ 15. A Sub S corporation is taxed at the regular corporate rate.

_____ 16. Once you are incorporated, lenders are less likely to seek a personal guarantee.

_____ 17. D.B.A. means "doing business as" and is the same as a fictitious name.

_____ 18. The corporate legal entity requires registration with the U.S. Department of Commerce.

_____ 19. Each stockholder of a Sub S corporation is responsible for debts of officers.

_____ 20. Once you begin as a sole proprietorship you can't incorporate.

Multiple-Choice

Select the best response for each item and enter the corresponding letter in the space.

_____ 1. A partnership:
   a. is a shield between you and trouble.
   b. will make you immortal.
   c. is taxed at the same rate as an individual.
   d. is very difficult to establish.

_____ 2. A sole proprietor has:
   a. absolute control; no need for written agreements; lots of money-raising ability; limited liability.
   b. divided control; no need for written agreements; limited money-raising ability; limited liability.
   c. absolute control; need for written agreements; limited money-raising ability; unlimited liability.
   d. absolute control; no need for written agreements; limited money-raising ability; unlimited liability.

_____ 3. A corporation has:
   a. shared control; a need for a lawyer to form; snob appeal; cancellation by death.
   b. shared control; lots of good reasons for a lawyer to form; snob appeal; an adjustable tax year.
   c. divided control; no need for written agreements; unlimited liability; adjustable tax year.
   d. absolute control; limited liability; adjustable tax year; no need for written agreements.

_____ 4. A limited partnership has:
   a. at least two partners; an overwhelming need for written agreements; moderate capital-raising ability.
   b. absolute control; no need for written agreements; a tax tier divided into four stages.
   c. shared control with limited partner; no need for written agreements; personal tax rate.
   d. control by general partner; no need for written agreements; a four-stage tax tier, graduated by increments of $25,000.

_____ 5. Which of the following questions is not helpful when you're dealing with a prospective lawyer?
   a. What kind of signals suggest that I should designate my company stock as IRS Section 1244?
   b. Can you give me a concrete example of how IRS Section 368 (a) (b) works?
   c. How does my corporation handle the "depreciation recapture" rule?
   d. Can you give me a concrete example of how the Bernoulli effect relates to cash flow?

_____ 6. Whom would be least helpful when using your network to search for a good lawyer?
   a. your friends.
   b. local business associations.
   c. local bar association.
   d. local bankers.

_____ 7. All of the following are true about programmer/entrepreneur Paul Webber except:
   a. Paul was a computer programmer.
   b. Paul sold out to Jerry.
   c. Mildred became Paul's new partner.
   d. Mildred didn't know the business.

_____ 8. You limit your personal liability when you:
   a. form a corporation.
   b. form a sole proprietorship.
   c. become a general partner.
   d. sign a personal guarantee.

_____ 9. As a sole proprietor, you:
   a. upgrade your image.
   b. control your fiscal year.
   c. guarantee continuity.
   d. none of the above.

_____ 10. What a corporation won't do:
   a. limit your liability.
   b. eliminate taxes altogether.
   c. let you upgrade your image.
   d. let you set aside more dollars for retirement.

Short-Answer

Note: Items 1 to 4 can be completed as either an individual or class project.

1. Find a lawyer who has worked with several small businesses. Ask small business owners whom they have worked with and who they would recommend to help you with your start-up.
   a. Find the owners through:
      1. Chamber of commerce (See if you can attend a meeting as a guest.)
      2. Local bankers
      3. Local accountants
      4. Leads clubs
      5. Local shopping centers or business parks (entrepreneurs love to talk about business)
   b. On a separate sheet of paper, list the names you come up with. Use the following headings:

Name of Lawyer	Source	Recommend?

   c. Continue the list until at least one lawyer has been recommended three or four times.
2. Select a name from C, above. Give the lawyer a call. Say you're starting a new business and you're in the process of selecting an attorney and that he or she has been recommended by several owners. You'd like to arrange a get-acquainted meeting. If there is no charge, set up a meeting. If there is a charge, go to the next name on the list.
3. Once you get a meeting set up, ask the following questions:
   a. Does working with small businesses provide the bulk of revenue for your practice?
   b. Can you give me the names of small businesses you've worked with? Preferably one sole proprietor, one partnership, and one corporation?
   c. Could you give me a breakdown of different types of fees? What fee basis do you suggest for working with a new start-up like mine?
   d. What's the extent of your experience with real estate leases? What's a normal charge for reviewing a lease?
   e. Are there other small business professionals you would recommend who might help me?

      1. Accountant: _____

      2. Banker: _____

      3. Insurance agent: _____

      4. Tax person: _____
   f. Have you ever worked with a client who bought or sold a business?

      Name: _____

      Name: _____

g. If yes, what are the major items to watch for in a buy-out? In a sale?

_____

_____

_____

4. Immediately after your meeting, write down your reactions.

    a. Comfort-level—Did you feel comfortable with this person?

    b. Confusion quotient—Could you understand what he or she was saying?

    c. Expertise—Did you feel he or she knew the ins and outs of the world of small business?

    d. Other—Write your reactions here.

5. Team Project. If possible, divide your group into three teams—sole proprietors, partners, and corporate types. Each team will then do in-depth research on the pros and cons of one type of legal form of business ownership. Select a spokesperson from each team to present findings. Develop a matrix grid (see Chapter 3 for a model), and rate all three forms.

    a. Suggested sources:

      1. Books

        Inc. Yourself, McQuown

        How to Form Your Own Corporation without a Lawyer for Under $50, Nicholas

        Incorporating Your Business, Kirk

      2. Recent articles

        Inc. magazine

        Venture magazine

        Wall Street Journal

      3. Interviews with local business owners (Ask them the pros and cons of their type of ownership.)

      4. Attorneys, accountants, and other professionals

    b. Categories for organizing your research:

      1. Ease of starting

      2. Ability to raise capital

      3. Liability

      4. Costs

      5. Lifespan

      6. Government regulation or control

      7. Personal interest

      8. Decision-making process

      9. Power to attract key employees

     10. Strengths and weaknesses of management team

     11. Taxes

     12. Divided authority

     13. Possible disagreements

     14. General partnership

     15. Limited partnership

     16. General corporation

     17. Sub S corporation

13

Building a Winning Team

Matching

Match each numbered item with the lettered statement that best describes it.

1. entrepreneur
2. enterprise
3. DISC
4. D
5. I

6. S
7. C
8. top-heavy team
9. brainstorming
10. Harry R. Marquez

11. successful team building
12. Janet Ames
13. balance
14. one-to-one interviews
15. secret ballot

_____ A. the last step in a large team-building process, when team members select teammates
_____ B. diplomatic, accurate, understands need for control, gets job done, can establish standard operating procedures
_____ C. a French word that means master architect, master builder
_____ D. industry, money, initiative
_____ E. the secret is to analyze yourself first
_____ F. DISC scale—stands for Influencing
_____ G. everybody interviews everybody else
_____ H. Dominance and Influence types all over the shop, competing like crazy, not answering the phones
_____ I. personality profile, useful for team-building
_____ J. DISC scale—stands for Dominance
_____ K. DISC scale—stands for Steadiness
_____ L. case study entrepreneur who was bright, quick, impatient, a dreamer
_____ M. one way to utilize your precious people-resources
_____ N. DISC scale—stands for Compliant
_____ O. the essential ingredient of a successful team

True/False

Determine whether each statement is true or false and enter a T (True) or F (False) in the space.

_____ 1. The word *entrepreneur* comes from the Latin *il miglior fabbro*, which means "the little craftsman."
_____ 2. Harry R. Marquez was a poor student.
_____ 3. A company is no better than its people.
_____ 4. A small business management team doesn't need balance so much as it needs salespeople to clear out the inventory.
_____ 5. The DISC system was developed in the late seventies by Jacob Bernoulli, a psychologist working in a lab with rats. The copyright is owned by Bernoulli Effect, Inc.

_____ 6. The beauty of the DISC grid is that it shows at a glance where you are and what DISC types will help you get a balanced team together.

_____ 7. On the DISC grid, Harry R. Marquez is an I, or Influencing type of person.

_____ 8. Frederick R. Winslow, on the other hand, is a definite S, which stands for Steadiness.

_____ 9. Janet Ames, the woman who came to work at Marquez Robotics as manager, was a C.

_____ 10. The smaller the organization, the more important the team.

_____ 11. Networking your competitors and vendors is a good way to build a winning team with people who know the business.

_____ 12. If you're first-rate, you'll hire first-rate people.

_____ 13. If you're second-rate, you'll also hire first-rate people because you'll realize you need them.

_____ 14. Happiness is knowing who you are—and being able to exploit it.

_____ 15. Given the chance, people will hire themselves.

_____ 16. Your business can't grow until it has the right people.

_____ 17. Charlene Webb built a team of part-time workers who did more to help the store than full-time employees.

_____ 18. A DISC grid can show at a glance where you are.

_____ 19. It's possible to include part-time employees as key team members.

_____ 20. If you have strong team members, a mission statement will be redundant.

Multiple-Choice

Select the best response for each item and enter the corresponding letter in the space.

_____ 1. The work _entrepreneur_ comes from the Latin verb:
a. _bigetan._
b. _pre-hendere._
c. _prise._
d. _Star Trek._

_____ 2. Mind movies include:
a. slides of your trip.
b. sights.
c. fun people you met along the way.
d. all of the above.

_____ 3. Harry R. Marquez started a company that built:
a. hot sports cars.
b. computers.
c. robots.
d. lasers.

_____ 4. Frederick S. Winslow was a good member of the Marquez Team because he had a solid background in:
a. sales.
b. inventing.
c. designing.
d. finance.

_____ 5. In team building it is important to:
a. build your team before it's too late.
b. test them out before it starts costing you money.
c. hire good people, then listen to them.
d. all of the above.

_____ 6. The Harry R. Marquez personality analysis concluded that Harry:
a. understands need for procedures and controls.
b. is a dreamer.
c. is diplomatic with everyone.
d. all of the above.

_____ 7. Which of the following personality styles does _not_ form part of the DISC acronym?
a. Dominance.

    b. Sado-masochism.
    c. Influencing of others.
    d. Compliance.

_____ 8. Rudy Bowman, a classic S, is no slouch as a team member. Steadies are important to the team because they:
    a. are extremely creative.
    b. make good managers.
    c. love to control a very small turf.
    d. hog the spotlight and are good at entertaining the clients.

_____ 9. Richard White developed a step-by-step method of teambuilding, which involved all of these except:
    a. Carl Rogers encounter groups.
    b. ice-breaker.
    c. one-to-one interviews.
    d. secret balloting.

_____ 10. E. G. Bogard turned out to be a Developer. Which does not fit Mr. Bogard?
    a. prefers innovative solutions.
    b. displays lots of self-reliance.
    c. loves to operate the telephone switchboard.
    d. fears boredom.

Short-Answer

1. Take a breather and think about your trip so far.
    a. What have you learned?

    _____
    _____
    _____

    b. Has it been fun?

    _____
    _____

    c. Who have you met that you found interesting, exciting, or especially helpful?

Name	Personality Type
1.	
2.	
3.	

2. Brainstorm your ideal team.
    a. Sit down with a few friends, relatives, or classmates who have a good feel for the type of business you plan to start. Ask everyone to list your strengths and weaknesses. (You can tell them briefly about the DISC scale and ask them whether you're a D, I, S, or C.) Compile their analyses here. Then thank them and go on to part B alone.

Strengths	Weaknesses	DISC Type

b. Once you discover how people perceive you, it's time to brainstorm the other members of your ideal team—people who will balance your strengths and weaknesses. What kind of people do you need for balance? Use the spaces provided to list your ideal team members.

Job Strengths	Personal Qualities	DISC Type
1. _____	_____	_____
2. _____	_____	_____
3. _____	_____	_____
4. _____	_____	_____
5. _____	_____	_____

Do any of the people who are helping you fit the ideal team? Who? _____

_____

Why? _____

_____

What would it take to get them on your team? _____

_____

3. Now that you have an idea what kind of team you need, take your thoughts out into the business arena and see how many players you can find.

Name	Team Position	Now Employed	DISC Type
a. _____	_____	_____	_____
b. _____	_____	_____	_____
c. _____	_____	_____	_____
d. _____	_____	_____	_____
e. _____	_____	_____	_____

4. Bring your new team together (or form a team with your classmates) and learn what they think of your organization. What should it look like? What image should it project? How can they help? Brainstorm some company objectives and organizational ideas. Keep track of your team's ideas on a separate sheet of paper.

14

The Entrepreneur's Toolkit

Matching

Match each numbered item with the lettered statement that best describes it.

1. defining problems and tasks
2. applications software
3. micro
4. fax machine

5. electronic spreadsheet
6. word processing
7. computer hardware
8. memory

9. operating system
10. modem

_____ A. will fit on a desk; often called a personal computer
_____ B. will allow a document to be transferred over telephone lines
_____ C. the portion of the computer that you can see and touch
_____ D. the program that drives the computer
_____ E. capacity to store information
_____ F. program designed to perform a specific function
_____ G. a generic term for computerized accounting software
_____ H. the first step toward considering the purchase of a computer
_____ I. required in order to have a telephone connection between computers
_____ J. a highly efficient and flexible capacity for creating letters, documents, and so on.

True/False

Determine whether each statement is true or false and enter a T (True) or F (False) in the space.

_____ 1. It is a violation of copyright law to copy and sell proprietary software.
_____ 2. Computer hardware is the program that drives the computer.
_____ 3. A computer system is both hardware and software.
_____ 4. A modem will let your computer talk to another computer.
_____ 5. The most important consideration in buying your first computer system is dealing until you squeeze the price down to a respectable level.
_____ 6. A hard disk or Winchester drive is far less expensive than a floppy disk drive.
_____ 7. A floppy disk is a defective hard disk.
_____ 8. When a disk becomes "floppier" through exposure to humidity, and also through extended use, it is now in the "mature stage" and will allow hardware to interface with programs from any operating system whatsoever.
_____ 9. A new microcomputer should go through its burn-in period in a very warm office situation.

_____ 10. Fifty percent or more of your computer budget should be allocated to software.

_____ 11. Computerphobia is a disease that occurs when a user-friendly program is debugged and the result is electric shock and information sickness.

_____ 12. The first step before purchasing a computer should be to define the problems that need solving in your business.

_____ 13. More and more, you need to understand programming languages (BASIC, Pascal, FORTRAN, COBOL) before purchasing a computer for business use.

_____ 14. Computers are useful in the performance of repetitive tasks.

_____ 15. There are good reasons for purchasing a small home computer before you need one in your business.

_____ 16. The experts say that when you're buying a computer, you should select the hardware on the basis of a well-known logo, then find software to fit, then begin developing applications to your particular type of business.

_____ 17. Microcomputers are of small value in spreadsheet analysis.

_____ 18. It can take 30–90 days to switch from a manual accounting system to a computerized system.

_____ 19. Smart phones, fax machines, and pagers are just a few of the tools that will allow you speed up commuications in the 1990s.

_____ 20. There is a strong chance that word-processing software will make business use of the typewriter obsolete.

Multiple-Choice

Select the best response for each item and enter the corresponding letter in the space.

_____ 1. The first step in purchasing a computer should be:
   a. evaluating your physical space availability.
   b. learning a programming language.
   c. looking for a well-known company logo so you'll be assured of service and support.
   d. evaluating your needs.

_____ 2. Computers are most useful:
   a. in performing repetitive tasks.
   b. in digesting the inertial flow produced by AT&T's UNIX.
   c. in performing one-time functions.
   d. in developing antidotes to the Bernoulli Effect as it relates to corporate time management.

_____ 3. Powerful word processing programs can:
   a. speed up letter composition.
   b. personalize form letters.
   c. merge names and addresses from a mailing list.
   d. all of the above.

_____ 4. Some word processors have the capacity to:
   a. correct spelling.
   b. sign your name to letters.
   c. work without electrical power.
   d. both A and B.

_____ 5. A floppy disk:
   a. is warm and soft.
   b. contains instructions for the hardware.
   c. can be played at different rpms.
   d. is not subject to copyright laws.

_____ 6. Software:
   a. is open copyrighted.
   b. gives instructions to the hardware.
   c. is often for sale in retail stores.
   d. all of the above.

_____ 7. A microcomputer:
   a. is different from a personal computer.

   b. usually weighs over 200 pounds.
   c. costs more than a minicomputer.
   d. none of the above.

_____ 8. A good way to learn about the micro for small business is to:
   a. read computer magazines.
   b. talk to people in similar businesses who are using computers.
   c. enroll in a course in microcomputer fundamentals.
   d. all of the above.

_____ 9. A computer system:
   a. consists of software and hardware.
   b. is software alone.
   c. requires a CPU and a hard disk drive before it will operate.
   d. is required by the IRS for all retail firms incorporated after 1979, as result of the Berkman-Sterns Act.

_____ 10. A video display terminal:
   a. can be almost any color.
   b. is like a TV screen.
   c. can cause eye fatigue.
   d. all of the above.

Short-Answer

1. What's the first step when you're thinking about buying a computer?

   _____

2. The second step? _____

3. The third? _____

4. Describe the routine functions of your business that might be handled by a computer. (Hint: invoicing, accounting, mailing list, form letters, and so on.)

   _____

   _____

   _____

   _____

   _____

5. List new office accessories that will help in your business. _____

   _____

6. What three computer magazines would be most helpful for your type of business?

   1. _____

   2. _____

   3. _____

7. Name two more ways to keep up with computer developments:

   1. _____

   2. _____

8. Visit a computer store. Tell the salesperson what your business problems are. Ask for suggestions about solutions. What advice are you given?

   _____

   _____

_____

_____

9. Network your way to several computer consultants. What do they suggest in the way of a system? What is the value of using a consultant? Can they save you money on your system? Summarize their advice. _____

_____

_____

_____

_____

10. List your purchase options.

	Software	Hardware
Costs: Outright Purchase	_____	_____
Lease	_____	_____

11. On a separate sheet of paper, develop a time-line chart for installation or conversion to a micro system that will handle your business tasks. Events might include:
    Education
    Purchase evaluation/shopping
    Testing
    Consulting
    Info/file conversion
    Operator training
    Decision day

12. For comparative purposes, contact two accounting services in your area and find out what they would charge to handle some of your routine tasks. (If you check the _Wall Street Journal,_ you'll see ads for free seminars for small business owners, placed by large computerized companies like ADP.)

    Firm 1: _____

    Firm 2: _____

13. List sources in your area for computer education. Start with the yellow pages, under "Computer." You'll find courses at public schools, private colleges, specialized computer training centers, dealer-operated schools, weekend seminars, and so on.

    _____

    _____

    _____

    _____

14. Using your 5-year growth plan, describe four or five functions that you would like a computer to perform after you've been in business awhile.

    1. _____
    2. _____
    3. _____
    4. _____
    5. _____

15

Buying a Franchise

Matching

Match each numbered item with the lettered statement that best describes it.

1. franchisee
2. franchise exposition
3. franchisor
4. corporate franchise
5. operating manual
6. franchise fee
7. brand name recognition

8. advertising fee
9. license agreement
10. economies of scale
11. uniform quality standard
12. voluntary chain
13. lease and location assistance
14. equipment and tenant improvements

15. lender's preference
16. right of first refusal
17. Hallmark
18. Century 21
19. Dale Carnegie

_____ A. owned by franchisor
_____ B. percentage of sales to cover administrative costs and franchisor's profits
_____ C. similar to a Business Plan
_____ D. presold customers
_____ E. percentage of sales to cover promotions
_____ F. the owner of a franchise
_____ G. an international real estate franchise
_____ H. generally less restrictive than a state-approved franchise
_____ I. the organization that is selling franchises
_____ J. a show organized to present franchisors to the public
_____ K. mass purchasing power—sometimes passed on to franchisee
_____ L. a personal development service franchise
_____ M. not a franchise, but a distribution plan
_____ N. usually required of all franchisees
_____ O. Ace Hardware
_____ P. usually supplied to retail franchisees by franchisor
_____ Q. often offered to existing franchise owner on new locations
_____ R. an extra expense usually not included in franchise fee
_____ S. bankers often view franchisee more favorably than they do independent business owners

True/False

Determine whether each statement is true or false and enter a T (True) or F (False) in the space.

_____ 1. Franchisors are independent owners of franchise operations.
_____ 2. Ground-floor opportunities are always ideal for the prospective franchise owner.

_____ 3. Most lenders prefer to lend money to a franchise operator than to a new start-up.

_____ 4. Coca-Cola bottlers own franchises.

_____ 5. Service-sector franchises are enjoying a lot of growth.

_____ 6. Auto dealerships are seldom franchises.

_____ 7. Despite their high visibility, franchises play only a minor role in the U.S. economy.

_____ 8. A franchise fee is the same as a royalty fee.

_____ 9. Voluntary chains and franchise operations are identical.

_____ 10. A franchise contract cannot be canceled except in case of fraud.

_____ 11. The franchisor is more of an entrepreneur than the franchisee.

_____ 12. A franchise generally is a safer venture for a person with few business skills.

_____ 13. Most states have strict laws governing franchises.

_____ 14. Existing franchise owners often have an inside track for purchasing a new franchise near their area.

_____ 15. Franchise owners often feel that they are employees more than independent owners.

_____ 16. All franchise offerings are approved by the Federal Trade Commission before they are offered to the public.

_____ 17. Big firms as well as small independent firms can be franchisees.

_____ 18. It's illegal for the franchisor to buy back a failing franchise.

_____ 19. It's always wise to investigate the track record of the principles behind the franchisor.

_____ 20. A franchise agreement will protect your territory from other franchise owners, as well as from owners of similar franchises.

Multiple-Choice

Select the best response for each item and enter the corresponding letter in the space.

_____ 1. The right of first refusal for a new location:
   a. is usually offered to existing franchisees.
   b. is illegal under antitrust laws.
   c. is discouraged because the franchisor usually wants the operators to focus all their time on just one single location.
   d. gives potential new operators an equal opportunity to purchase a new franchise.

_____ 2. Many franchisors:
   a. own some of their outlets themselves.
   b. are true entrepreneurs.
   c. expand with little capital by selling franchises.
   d. all of the above.

_____ 3. A good reason for purchasing a franchise is that:
   a. they have a lower failure rate than most new start-up firms.
   b. they have a recognized name and have cloned their tested ideas.
   c. they offer ongoing supervision and advice to franchisees.
   d. all of the above.

_____ 4. Most franchisees:
   a. have few restrictions on their operations.
   b. do not have to pay a royalty fee.
   c. pay both a royalty fee and an advertising fee.
   d. pay a percentage of net profits to the franchisor.

_____ 5. A franchise and a distributorship differ in that:
   a. a distributor does not pay a royalty fee.
   b. a distributor agreement is usually more complex.
   c. it's more difficult for a distributor to terminate the agreement.
   d. in most states, there is no difference.

_____ 6. An example of a voluntary chain is:
   a. Avis Rent A Car.
   b. Holiday Inn.

    c. True Value Hardware.

    d. Volunteers of America.

_____ 7. In the 1980s, the franchise industry demonstrated growth in:

    a. bowling establishments.

    b. fast-food, printing, and service industries.

    c. Mrs. Field's Cookies.

    d. nuclear energy.

_____ 8. A reason for electing not to buy a franchise is that:

    a. a franchise is not a truly independent business.

    b. you might be as successful as an independent and avoid the franchise fee and the royalty payment.

    c. the franchisor guarantees the franchisee profitability.

    d. both a and b.

_____ 9. A successful franchise owner:

    a. is likely to be offered opportunities to purchase additional locations before others are.

    b. can substitute his name in place of the franchisor.

    c. need not heed the instructions of the franchisor.

    d. is exempt from state and federal regulations.

_____ 10. When considering the purchase of a franchise you should:

    a. interview other franchise owners.

    b. review the financial strength of the franchisor.

    c. consult an attorney to examine the contract.

    d. all of the above.

Short-Answer

1. Identify a franchise that you believe is earning a high income on investment:

Type of business _____

Name _____ Address _____

What percentage of maximum capacity do you estimate they are realizing? _____

Estimate of total sales _____

Franchise fee _____

Your estimate of all expenses _____

Your estimate of profits _____
A. List the advantages of owning the franchise.

_____

_____

_____

B. List the disadvantages of owning the franchise.

_____

_____

_____

2. List 5–10 service franchises that are operating in your area.

_____   _____

_____   _____

_____   _____

_____   _____
_____   _____

3. Contrast a franchise, a distributorship, and a voluntary chain.

_____
_____

4. Identify a franchise that has failed and list the reasons it failed.

_____
_____

5. List franchises that you believe are well suited to absentee ownership.

_____   _____
_____   _____
_____   _____

6. Identify an independently owned business that operates near, and competes against, a franchise.

Business _____ Address _____

How well is it doing? _____

How could it do better? _____

7. Examine the annual report (10-K) of a franchisor whose stock is publicly traded. What observations can you make?

_____
_____

8. List some types of business that you believe are well suited for franchising.

_____   _____
_____   _____
_____   _____

16
Pulling the Plan Together

Matching

Match each numbered item with the lettered statement that best describes it.

1. Business Plan
2. executive summary
3. "magic numbers"
4. appendixes
5. cover letter
6. excitement

7. net profit
8. cash-flow section
9. entrepreneur
10. demand
11. selling seats
12. industry overview

13. competitors
14. information business
15. projected balance sheet
16. bad management
17. leasing equipment

_____ A. the reason cited by experts for the failure of most small businesses
_____ B. a fast-growing industry that offers many opportunities for eager entrepreneurs
_____ C. a numerical tool that shows what your business will be worth after a certain period of time if your fore-casts are accurate.
_____ D. hungry combatants who are eyeing the same slice of the marketplace pie
_____ E. a smart way to save money at start-up time
_____ F. a long look at an industry, compiled from important dates, breakthroughs, failures, and opportunities
_____ G. a portable blueprint of your business
_____ H. a way of talking about how many units will be sold
_____ I. a brief introduction to your Business Plan that summarizes what your business is and why it will succeed
_____ J. a major source of revenue for airlines, movie theatres, and industrial schools
_____ K. income, cash flow, balance sheet
_____ L. a person who has lots of ideas
_____ M. where you put resumes, photographs, location diagrams, product descriptions, or articles from industry journals
_____ N. allows you to aim the Plan at a specific reader
_____ O. what's left in the kitty after you subtract expenses
_____ P. your banker will probably look here first
_____ Q. your reader's response to your Business Plan

True/False

Determine whether each statement is true or false and enter a T (True) or F (False) in the space.

_____ 1. A Business Plan is your roadmap to riches.
_____ 2. Your Business Plan could be the most important document you've ever prepared.

_____ 3. A Business Plan has nothing to do with keeping your entrepreneurial creativity on track.

_____ 4. The Business Plan is portable.

_____ 5. Good business planning is not hard work.

_____ 6. Section I of the business plan is the numbers section.

_____ 7. The numbers section includes the income statement, cash flow projections, and projected balance sheet.

_____ 8. Sections I and II of the Plan are followed by various appendixes.

_____ 9. To aim the Plan to a specific reader, you write a special cover letter.

_____ 10. Each time you send the plan to a different reader, all you need to do is pull out your old cover letter and address it to the new reader.

_____ 11. The cover letter should be 5,000 words long, minimum.

_____ 12. The purpose of writing the cover letter is to open the door gently, to make way for future discussion.

_____ 13. The cover letter should not offend the reader by explaining how the money will be repaid. Save money talk for the appendixes.

_____ 14. Investors love hot ideas.

_____ 15. Percentages and dollar amounts speak more loudly than words; mention numbers whenever you can.

_____ 16. You should briefly profile the businesses that compete directly with you.

_____ 17. Save your ideas on how you're going to ace the competition for the appendixes.

_____ 18. Since a lot of consideration should be given to pricing, you might start with what your TC sees as a good value.

_____ 19. The great thing about a location is that it's so tangible.

_____ 20. Almost every study you read on small business failure puts the blame on bad management.

_____ 21. Job descriptions will help you control the people who work for you.

_____ 22. With the income statement, the main figure you are seeking is gross sales.

_____ 23. Doing a cash flow projection once a year, with a casual 6-month update, is all that's required for most small firms.

_____ 24. With a projected balance sheet, you're trying to predict, on paper, what your business will be worth at the end of a certain period of time.

_____ 25. Section I gets readers interested in the Plan; Section II is where you hook them.

Multiple-Choice

Select the best response for each item and enter the corresponding letter in the space.

_____ 1. When you are in business, a Business Plan can:
   a. keep your creativity on track.
   b. keep your power grooved.
   c. both a and b.
   d. none of the above.

_____ 2. When doing your Plan, you will probably:
   a. work hard.
   b. stay up late and lose some sleep.
   c. save time in the end.
   d. all of the above.

_____ 3. Section I includes all but which of the following?
   a. assessments of the competition.
   b. bids from contractors.
   c. profiles of target customers.
   d. a look at your team.

_____ 4. Section II should include all but which of the following?
   a. management resumes.
   b. balance sheet.
   c. cash flow projection.
   d. income statements.

_____ 5. Appendixes to your Plan could include all but which of the following?
   a. detailed resumes.
   b. personal financial statements.
   c. a design of your marketing plan.
   d. bids from contractors.

_____ 6. The cover letter should:
   a. glorify your management team.
   b. tell your reader why you're sending the Plan.
   c. describe your TC with demographics and psychographics.
   d. explain, in a minimum of 5,000 words, how you're going to disarm the competition.

_____ 7. In describing your business, you:
   a. need to excite your reader about the business.
   b. could include photographs of equipment and location in an appendix.
   c. could refer to another appendix providing diagrams that show traffic flow, parking, access, transportation lines, and so on.
   d. all of the above.

_____ 8. The target market for the Software School was:
   a. the world.
   b. bounded on the south by San Clemente, on the north by Long Beach, La Habra, and Brea.
   c. too soft to profile.
   d. diagrammed in detail by several movie studios who paid the school $2 million for rights to film a $40 million Compu-Kids movie in late 1983.

_____ 9. The primary target customer for the Software School was:
   a. female, age 13–17, subscriber to _Seventeen_ magazine.
   b. male, 55–67, poker player, resident of Leisure World.
   c. female, 22–54, $27,000 income, metro-suburban residence, married, two children under 18 living at home, subscriber to _McCall's_ magazine.
   d. small business, 1–30 employees, sales from $250,000 to $5 million, with a major output of paper.

_____ 10. When assessing your competition, you should look into all but which of the following?
   a. strengths.
   b. weaknesses.
   c. key employees.
   d. their private company books.

Short-Answer

1. Write two cover letters for your Business Plan. Letter A should be addressed to your banker or another prospective lender. Letter B should be addressed to a person you'd like to have on your team—one of your key members. Use the following to prepare your letters.

   Letter A

   Name: _____

   Position: _____

   Address: _____

   Goal for writing: _____

   Some items you must include: 1. _____

   2. _____

   3. _____

Letter B

Name: _____

Position: _____

Address: _____

Goal for writing: _____

Some items you must include: 1. _____

2. _____

3. _____

2. Now turn loose your creativity. In this space, develop an outline or mind map that you can turn into a paragraph or two describing your business. You want to excite your reader. Cover the following: What business you're in; description of product/service; what's unique about your business; what industry you're in. Whenever you can, use dollars or percentages to base your dream on reality.

3. Now put your marketing data into a free-flow description of your market and your target customer. Use the following categories to organize your thoughts.

Industry Overview. _____

_____

_____

_____

Target Market. _____

_____

Target Customer (Primary). _____

_____

Target Customer (Secondary). _____

_____

4. List your major competitors and describe their strengths and weaknesses.

Competitor A

   Strengths: _____

   Weaknesses: _____

Competitor B

   Strengths: _____

   Weaknesses: _____

Competitor C

   Strengths: _____

   Weaknesses: _____

Competitor D

   Strengths: _____

   Weaknesses: _____

Competitor E

   Strengths: _____

   Weaknesses: _____

5. Develop your "attack plan" here. What techniques will you use to get the best, most cost-effective response from your market? How do you plan to disarm your competitors?

_____

_____

_____

_____

_____

_____

_____

6. Write a brief summary of why you picked your location. In your reader's mind, build the picture of the perfect location, the site that cannot fail.

_____

_____

_____

_____

_____

Now list all the benefits of this location to target customers.

_____

_____

_____

7. Let's hear it for your management team! List the members in order of their importance to the business. For each member, note experience, accomplishments, education, training, flexibility, imagination, tenacity, and finally, what they can do to help make your business a winner.

Team Member A: _____

_____

_____

Team Member B: _____

_____

_____

Team Member C: _____

_____

_____

Team Member D: _____

_____

_____

8. Now that your management team is in place, list the other types of personnel you'll need. Cover the topics listed here.

Skills: _____

_____

_____

Pay: _____

_____

_____

Training

    Kind: _____

    Length: _____

Fringe Benefits: _____

_____

_____

_____

Overtime: _____

_____

_____

17

Fast-Start Mini-Business Plan

Matching

Match each numbered item with the lettered statement that best describes it.

1. the complete plan
2. new eyes research
3. to profile your customers
4. business cards
5. a business dream

6. even the most successful business
7. on equipment items
8. what business are you really in
9. in order to stay in business
10. Fast-Start Mini-Business Plan

11. practice trains the eye
12. sales goals
13. leasing
14. rolling projection
15. school parent's group

_____ A. gives you a blueprint to follow month by month through the first year
_____ B. you're using the business as a probe into the marketplace
_____ C. separates your business from all the other businesses out there
_____ D. to figure this out, look at your business from the point of view of the customer
_____ E. a creative view of the marketplace that can be correlated with secondary sources
_____ F. a business must communicate with potential customers
_____ G. overlooks something
_____ H. become a marketplace detective
_____ I. to consider the person as a prospect
_____ J. inexpensive, handy reminders
_____ K. a nonbusiness organization that might act as a sales group
_____ L. you can save money by buying used
_____ M. costs more in the long run
_____ N. provide information you need to forecast your variable expenses
_____ O. after you complete your first month in business, make a projection for your fourth month

True/False

Determine whether each statement is true or false and enter a T (True) or F (False) in the space.

_____ 1. If you're going it alone, with money you can afford to lose ($500, $1,000, even $5,000), and if the loss of that money won't jeopardize your loved ones and bring the wolves howling at your door, use the Fast-Start Mini-Business Plan.
_____ 2. The complete plan gives you a blueprint to follow year by year through the first decade.

_____ 3. With the Fast-Start Mini-Business Plan, you're using the business as a probe into the marketplace.

_____ 4. Starting part-time is harder and riskier.

_____ 5. Sam Walton, the founder of Wal-Mart, could have used the Fast-Start Mini-Business Plan for a business start-up costing $50,000 to $100,000.

_____ 6. To figure out what business you're in, look at your business from the point of view of the customer.

_____ 7. To find home-based businesses, tune in your entrepreneurial radar.

_____ 8. Even the most successful businesses overlook something.

_____ 9. It is a good idea to chat with customers of your competitors.

_____ 10. It is usually easy to attract customers away from established competitors by charging less for the same thing.

_____ 11. Being a marketplace detective can help you profile your customers.

_____ 12. Use a logo that offers an insight into your business.

_____ 13. Always carry lots of business cards.

_____ 14. Once your business cards are done, research ways of reaching customers.

_____ 15. On equipment items, you can save money by buying imports.

_____ 16. You can find good deals from an owner who's going out of business.

_____ 17. Leasing provides you a lot of flexibility up front.

_____ 18. Sales goals provide the driving force for you and your team.

_____ 19. Around the ninth month of business, develop a full 12-month plan for your second year.

_____ 20. As you gain experience in the big world of small business, start setting your sights further out.

Multiple-Choice

Select the best response for each item and enter the corresponding letter in the space.

_____ 1. If you're going it alone, with money you can afford to lose _____, and if the loss of that money won't jeopardize your loved ones and make wolves howl at your door, use the Fast-Start Mini-Business Plan:
   a. $50, $100, even $500.
   b. $500, $1,000, even $5,000.
   c. $5,000, $10,000, even $50,000.
   d. $5,000, $10,000, even $20,000.

_____ 2. The complete plan gives you a blueprint to follow month by month through the first _____ of your business.
   a. 6 months.
   b. 12 months.
   c. 18 months.
   d. 60 months.

_____ 3. Starting a business on a part-time basis lessens your:
   a. profits.
   b. cash flow.
   c. risk.
   d. advertising.

_____ 4. A business dream can help separate your business from everyone else who's out there trying to:
   a. make a profit.
   b. increase cash flow.
   c. advertise.
   d. compete with you.

_____ 5. In pricing, learn to see the value of your product or service:
   a. in the marketplace.
   b. to your competitors.
   c. to your suppliers.
   d. through the eyes of your customers.

_____ 6. Use a logo that offers:
    a. A 10 percent discount.
    b. a message.
    c. an insight into your business.
    d. a picture.

_____ 7. On equipment items, you can save money by:
    a. buying used.
    b. leasing.
    c. both a and b.
    d. none of the above.

_____ 8. After you complete your first month in business:
    a. revise months two and three.
    b. project your fourth month.
    c. project your second month.
    d. none of the above.

_____ 9. With long-range planning, you can line up money:
    a. when you need it.
    b. before you need it.
    c. after you need it.
    d. none of the above.

_____ 10. When your plan is complete, you need to act. Your first step is to:
    a. get your business license.
    b. order your checks.
    c. make your first sale.
    d. make lists of things that need doing.

Short-Answer

1. Write a paragraph or two describing the risk(s) you are taking in starting this business. What are the rewards? Are they worth the risk? Can you recover from these risks without a great deal of discomfort? Finally, are the risks minimal enough so that you can write a Fast-Start Mini-Business Plan or would you be safer and smarter to take a little more time and write a complete business plan?

_____

_____

2. Turn your creativity loose. In this space, develop an _outline_ or _mind map_ that you can turn into a _paragraph or two_ describing your business. Cover the following: what business you're in; description of the product or service; what's unique about your business; what industry you're in. Whenever you can, use dollars or percentages to give a foundation to your dream.

3. Now put your marketing data into a free-flow description of your market and your target customer. Use the following categories to organize your thoughts:

Industry overview _____

_____

Target Market _____

_____

Target Customer (primary) _____

_____

Target Customer (secondary) _____

_____

4. List your major competitors and describe their strengths and weaknesses.

Competitor A

Strengths _____

Weaknesses _____

Competitor B

Strengths _____

Weaknesses _____

Competitor C

Strengths _____

Weaknesses _____

Competitor D

Strengths _____

Weaknesses _____

Competitor E

Strengths _____

Weaknesses _____

5. Develop your "attack plan" here. What techniques will you use to get the best, most cost-effective response from your market? How do you plan to disarm your competitors?

_____

_____

_____

_____

_____

6. Write a brief description of your business image. When your customers look at your business, what do they perceive? What pricing position do you plan to establish? Compare yourself to your competitors.

_____

_____

_____

_____

_____

_____

_____

_____

_____

_____

7. Again, turn your creativity loose. In the space below, do a rough sketch of your company logo and business card. Then sketch what you would like your first ad to look like. Be sure to include benefits: how does this format benefit the customer?

_____

_____

_____

_____

_____

_____

_____

_____

_____

_____

_____

_____

_____

_____

8. Start a list of prospective customers in the space below. Be as specific as you can. Once you run out of names, start listing organizations or other ways you will be able to meet prospective customers. Should you start your own leads club? What other direct sales techniques will you use?

_____

_____

_____

_____

_____

_____

_____

_____

_____

_____

_____

_____

_____

Answers

1 Doorways to Small Business

Matching

A. 5	D. 10	G. 6	J. 3
B. 8	E. 9	H. 2	
C. 1	F. 4	I. 7	

True/False

1. F	7. T	13. F	19. F
2. T	8. F	14. F	20. T
3. T	9. T	15. F	21. F
4. T	10. T	16. F	22. T
5. F	11. T	17. T	23. T
6. F	12. F	18. T	

Multiple-Choice

1. C	4. A	7. A	10. D
2. D	5. D	8. D	11. A
3. D	6. C	9. B	

2 The Big Picture: Charting Trends for Your Small Business

Matching

A. 9	F. 18	K. 4	P. 2
B. 10	G. 17	L. 5	Q. 11
C. 13	H. 14	M. 6	R. 12
D. 15	I. 1	N. 8	S. 19
E. 16	J. 3	O. 7	T. 20

True/False

1. T	7. T	13. F	19. F
2. F	8. T	14. T	20. T
3. F	9. F	15. T	21. T
4. F	10. F	16. F	22. F
5. F	11. T	17. F	
6. T	12. T	18. F	

Multiple-Choice

1. C	4. C	7. B	9. D
2. B	5. C	8. C	10. A
3. A	6. B		

3 Power Marketing

Matching

A. 18	F. 15	K. 1	P. 6
B. 16	G. 14	L. 3	Q. 13
C. 7	H. 12	M. 2	R. 11
D. 5	I. 10	N. 4	S. 19
E. 17	J. 9	O. 8	T. 20

True/False

1. T	6. F	11. T	16. T
2. F	7. T	12. T	17. T
3. T	8. F	13. F	18. T
4. F	9. T	14. T	19. T
5. T	10. F	15. T	20. T

Multiple-Choice

1. C	4. B	7. C	9. B
2. D	5. D	8. D	10. C
3. B	6. B		

4 Profiling the Target Customer

Matching

A. 11	F. 12	K. 9	P. 8
B. 10	G. 1	L. 4	Q. 14
C. 16	H. 17	M. 6	R. 18
D. 15	I. 2	N. 7	S. 19
E. 13	J. 3	O. 5	T. 20

True/False

1. F	6. T	11. T	16. T
2. F	7. T	12. F	17. T
3. T	8. F	13. T	18. T
4. T	9. T	14. T	19. F
5. F	10. T	15. F	20. T

Multiple-Choice

1. C	4. A	7. C	9. D
2. C	5. D	8. D	10. B
3. B	6. B		

6 Promotion: Connecting with the Customer

Matching

A. 4	E. 3	I. 14	M. 12
B. 5	F. 2	J. 13	N. 11
C. 1	G. 7	K. 8	O. 10
D. 6	H. 15	L. 9	

True/False

1. T	5. T	9. F	13. T
2. T	6. T	10. T	14. F
3. T	7. T	11. T	15. T
4. T	8. F	12. T	16. F

Multiple-Choice

1. D	4. B	7. D	9. A
2. C	5. D	8. D	10. D
3. A	6. A		

5 Reading the Competition

Matching

A. 18	F. 1	K. 13	P. 2
B. 11	G. 9	L. 8	Q. 19
C. 16	H. 14	M. 10	R. 5
D. 20	I. 15	N. 7	S. 6
E. 17	J. 12	O. 3	T. 4

True/False

1. F	6. F	11. T	16. T
2. F	7. F	12. T	17. T
3. T	8. T	13. T	18. F
4. F	9. T	14. T	19. T
5. F	10. F	15. T	20. F

Multiple-Choice

1. C	4. D	7. C	9. C
2. D	5. D	8. B	10. C
3. D	6. A		

7 Location

Matching

A. 2	F. 11	K. 7	O. 14
B. 1	G. 9	L. 17	P. 12
C. 6	H. 5	M. 13	Q. 15
D. 8	I. 3	N. 16	R. 18
E. 10	J. 4		

True/False

1. T	6. T	11. F	16. T
2. T	7. F	12. T	17. F
3. T	8. T	13. T	18. F
4. T	9. T	14. F	19. T
5. F	10. F	15. F	20. T

Multiple-Choice

1. A	4. D	7. C	9. C
2. B	5. C	8. B	10. B
3. C	6. A		

8 Surprises You Can't Afford

Matching

A. 2	F. 6	J. 9	N. 12
B. 1	G. 8	K. 16	O. 14
C. 3	H. 7	L. 15	P. 11
D. 4	I. 10	M. 13	Q. 17
E. 5			

True/False

1. F	6. T	11. F	16. T
2. F	7. T	12. F	17. F
3. F	8. T	13. T	18. F
4. T	9. T	14. F	19. T
5. T	10. T	15. F	20. T

Multiple-Choice

1. A	4. C	7. D	9. D
2. D	5. A	8. D	10. B
3. B	6. D		

9 Numbers and Shoebox Accounting

Matching

A. 11	D. 10	G. 2	J. 7
B. 9	E. 4	H. 5	K. 8
C. 6	F. 1	I. 3	

True/False

1. T	6. F	11. T	16. F
2. T	7. T	12. T	17. T
3. T	8. F	13. T	18. F
4. T	9. T	14. T	19. T
5. F	10. T	15. T	20. F

Multiple-Choice

1. C	4. D	7. A	9. D
2. B	5. A	8. D	10. B
3. A	6. B		

10 Buying a Business

Matching

A. 16	E. 9	I. 12	M. 2
B. 6	F. 7	J. 14	N. 3
C. 10	G. 11	K. 15	O. 4
D. 8	H. 13	L. 1	P. 5

True/False

1. T	6. F	11. T	16. T
2. F	7. T	12. F	17. T
3. T	8. F	13. T	18. T
4. T	9. F	14. T	19. T
5. F	10. T	15. T	20. T

Multiple-Choice

1. C	4. B	7. B	9. A
2. D	5. D	8. B	10. D
3. B	6. C		

11 Shaking the Money Tree

Matching

A. 9	F. 7	K. 17	P. 10
B. 2	G. 5	L. 3	Q. 16
C. 14	H. 8	M. 12	R. 20
D. 15	I. 13	N. 1	S. 18
E. 6	J. 4	O. 11	T. 19

True/False

1. T	6. F	11. T	16. F
2. F	7. T	12. T	17. T
3. T	8. T	13. F	18. T
4. T	9. F	14. T	19. T
5. T	10. T	15. F	20. F

Multiple-Choice

1. D	4. C	7. B	9. C
2. B	5. D	8. D	10. C
3. A	6. A		

12 Legal Concerns

Matching

A. 8	F. 3	J. 13	N. 9
B. 7	G. 2	K. 12	O. 16
C. 6	H. 1	L. 11	P. 17
D. 5	I. 14	M. 10	Q. 15
E. 4			

True/False

1. T	6. F	11. T	16. F
2. F	7. T	12. T	17. T
3. F	8. F	13. T	18. F
4. F	9. F	14. T	19. F
5. F	10. T	15. F	20. F

Multiple-Choice

1. C	4. A	7. B	9. D
2. D	5. D	8. A	10. B
3. B	6. C		

13 Building a Winning Team

Matching

A. 15	E. 11	I. 3	M. 9
B. 12	F. 5	J. 4	N. 7
C. 1	G. 14	K. 6	O. 13
D. 2	H. 8	L. 10	

True/False

1. F	6. T	11. T	16. T
2. T	7. F	12. T	17. T
3. T	8. F	13. F	18. T
4. F	9. T	14. T	19. T
5. F	10. T	15. T	20. F

Multiple-Choice

1. B	4. A	7. B	9. A
2. D	5. D	8. C	10. C
3. C	6. B		

14 The Entrepreneur's Toolkit

Matching

A. 3	D. 9	G. 5	I. 10
B. 4	E. 8	H. 1	J. 6
C. 7	F. 2		

True/False

1. T	6. F	11. F	16. F
2. F	7. F	12. T	17. F
3. T	8. F	13. F	18. T
4. T	9. F	14. T	19. T
5. F	10. T	15. T	20. T

Multiple-Choice

1. D	4. A	7. D	9. A
2. A	5. B	8. D	10. D
3. D	6. D		

15 Buying a Franchise

Matching

A. 4	F. 1	K. 10	P. 13
B. 6	G. 18	L. 19	Q. 16
C. 5	H. 9	M. 17	R. 14
D. 7	I. 3	N. 11	S. 15
E. 8	J. 2	O. 12	

True/False

1. F	6. F	11. T	16. F
2. F	7. F	12. T	17. T
3. T	8. F	13. T	18. F
4. T	9. F	14. T	19. T
5. T	10. F	15. T	20. F

Multiple-Choice

1. A	4. C	7. B	9. A
2. D	5. A	8. D	10. D
3. D	6. C		

16 Pulling the Plan Together

Matching

A. 16	F. 12	K. 3	P. 8
B. 14	G. 1	L. 9	Q. 6
C. 15	H. 10	M. 4	
D. 13	I. 2	N. 5	
E. 17	J. 11	O. 7	

True/False

1. T	8. T	15. T	22. F
2. T	9. T	16. T	23. F
3. T	10. F	17. F	24. T
4. T	11. F	18. T	25. T
5. F	12. T	19. T	
6. F	13. F	20. T	
7. T	14. T	21. T	

Multiple-Choice

1. C	4. A	7. D	9. D
2. D	5. C	8. B	10. D
3. B	6. B		

17 Fast-Start Mini-Business Plan

Matching

A. 1	E. 2	I. 11	M. 13
B. 10	F. 9	J. 4	N. 12
C. 5	G. 6	K. 15	O. 14
D. 8	H. 3	L. 7	

True/False

1. T	6. F	11. T	16. T
2. F	7. T	12. T	17. T
3. T	8. T	13. T	18. T
4. F	9. T	14. T	19. T
5. T	10. F	15. F	20. T

Multiple-Choice

1. B	4. D	7. C	10. D
2. B	5. D	8. B	
3. C	6. C	9. B	